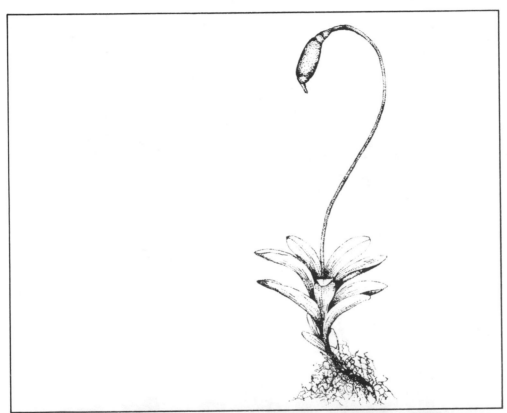

mosses:

Utah and the West

Seville Flowers, 1900-1968

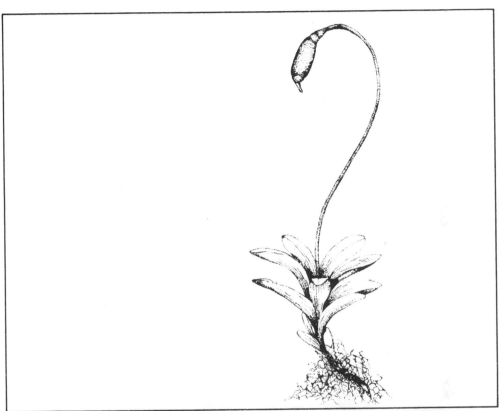

mosses:

Utah and the West

by Seville Flowers   Edited by Arthur Holmgren

Brigham Young University Press

Library of Congress Cataloging in Publication Data

Flowers, Seville, 1900-1968.
    Mosses: Utah and the West.
    1. Mosses—Utah. 2. Mosses—The West. I. Title.
QK541.5.U8F58   588.2'09792   72-96422
ISBN 0-8425-1524-0

Brigham Young University Press, Provo, Utah 84602
© 1973 by Brigham Young University Press. All rights reserved
Printed in the United States of America
1973 2.5M 10793

Contents

	Species	Page
FOREWORD		xvii
PREFACE		xix
INTRODUCTION		1
Morphology		3
Ecology and Distribution		57
Collecting and Preparing an Herbarium		68
Methods of Study		70
DESCRIPTIVE CATALOG		75
Key to Families and Genera: Class Musci		75
Sphagnales		84
Sphagnaceae		84
Sphagnum	5	84
Bryales		92
Fissidentaceae		92
Fissidens	3	92
Dicranaceae		96
1. Distichium	2	98
2. Ceratodon	2	101
3. Seligeria	1	104
4. Dichodontium	1	105
5. Oncophorus	1	107
6. Dicranoweisia	1	108
7. Dicranella	1	111
8. Dicranum	3	112
9. Paraleucobryum	1	118
Pottiaceae		119
1. Astomum	1	121
2. Weissia	4	122
3. Gymnostomum	2	128
4. Eucladium	1	131
5. Trichostomum	1	132
6. Hyophila	1	136
7. Tortella	3	137

8. Didymodon	3	140
9. Bryoerythrophyllum	1	146
10. Barbula	9	149
11. Phascum	1	162
12. Pottia	4	165
13. Pterygoneurum	3	171
14. Aloina	1	176
15. Crossidium	3	177
16. Desmatodon	6	184
17. Tortula	11	196
18. Scopelophila	1	216
Encalyptaceae		217
1. Encalypta	3	219
Grimmiaceae		226
1. Grimmia	19	226
2. Racomitrium	1	263
3. Scouleria	1	266
Orthotrichaceae		267
1. Orthotrichum	14	268
2. Amphidium	1	297
Funariaceae		300
1. Funaria	2	300
2. Entosthodon	2	304
3. Physcomitrium	4	309
Splachnaceae		314
1. Tayloria	1	315
Aulacomniaceae		316
1. Aulacomnium	2	316
Timmiaceae		319
1. Timmia	2	320
Bartramiaceae		323
1. Anacolia	1	323
2. Bartramia	1	326
3. Philonotis	2	327
Bryaceae		336
1. Mielichhoferia	1	337
2. Leptobryum	1	338
3. Pohlia	10	341
4. Bryum	19	356
5. Mnium	8	383
Leskeaceae		398
1. Helodium	1	398
2. Thuidium	1	399
3. Lescuraea	4	401
4. Leskeella	2	408
Hypnaceae		413
1. Climacium	1	416

2. Eurhynchium	2	417
3. Brachythecium	15	420
4. Scleropodium	2	450
5. Homalothecium	1	454
6. Tomenthypnum	1	455
7. Amblystegium	8	457
8. Platydictya	1	472
9. Campylium	4	473
10. Calliergon	3	480
11. Hygrohypnum	5	482
12. Drepanocladus	4	494
13. Cratoneuron	4	504
14. Hypnum	6	510
15. Plagiothecium	3	520
16. Platygyrium	1	524
17. Orthothecium	1	526
Neckeraceae		528
1. Neckera	2	529
Fontinalaceae		530
1. Fontinalis	4	532
2. Dichelyma	1	538
Polytrichales		540
Polytrichaceae		540
1. Atrichum	1	541
2. Pogonatum	1	541
3. Polytrichadelphus	1	544
4. Polytrichum	4	546
MAP		554
GLOSSARY		555
INDEX		563

ERRATA

P. xi: Vickery—not Vickers

P. 290, caption: alpestre—not alpestra

Pp. 496–511: 7 plates are out of place, as follows:

Plate on p. 496 is *Cratoneuron filicinum*—should be on p. 507.

Plate on p. 499 is *Cratoneuron commutatum* and *C. decipens*—should be on p. 509.

Plate on p. 501 is *Cratoneuron falcatum*—should be on p. 511.

Plate on p. 503 is *Drepanocladus uncinatus*—should be on p. 496.

Plate on p. 507 is *Drepanocladus aduncus*—should be on p. 499.

Plate on p. 509 is *Drepanocladus fluitans*—should be on p. 501.

Plate on p. 511 is *Drepanocladus exannulatus*—should be on p. 503.

Foreword

Mosses: Utah and the West makes a very substantial and original contribution to our knowledge of the mosses of the western United States, based, as it is, on the long professional career of an outstanding resident bryologist. Before Seville Flowers began his extensive bryological research, Utah was considered to have a relatively small and uninteresting moss flora because of its generally low rainfall; this book, however, treats 256 species in 77 genera and 18 families, a large proportion of which were discovered in Utah for the first time by its author.

In a letter to me dated January 7, 1965, Dr. Flowers said "My Moss Flora of Utah is nearly complete, except for a few tag ends," tag ends about which he was writing for information in order to tie them up. For nearly a decade, then, the manuscript for this book has lain fallow, and the bryological community owes an enormous debt of gratitude to Professor Arthur H. Holmgren, a close friend of Seville Flowers, for his attention in seeing it through the press.

Except for his graduate work at the University of Chicago, where he received his doctorate in 1931, Seville Flowers spent his whole professional career in Utah, and was a member of the faculty of the University of Utah from 1936 until his death; before that he taught at the Carbon County High School in Price. This long residence in and familiarity with his native state gave him a deep awareness, in the field, of the ecological niches in which bryophytes occur.

Dr. Flowers' interest in bryophytes must have begun very early in his botanical career. In the preface to his publication, "The Hepaticae of Utah," published by the University of Utah in 1961, he says, "The present paper presents the results of the slow accumulation of specimens and data covering thirty-five years," which (including the time lapse between writing the manuscript and its publication) would take us back to approximately 1925, when he graduated from the University of Utah. What seems to be his first bryological paper appeared in 1929, "A preliminary list of Utah mosses" (*Bryologist*), which had been "identified through the courtesy of Mr. A. T. Beals." He adds further in this same paper, "Mr. A. O. Garrett of Salt Lake City has done considerable to stimulate interest in bryological study in Utah and it is largely through his influence that this work has been undertaken." In 1934, Dr. Flowers issued an up-dated version of his 1929 paper, "Mosses of

Utah," a mimeographed publication that ran to 88 pages. His thoughtful paper, "The Bryophytes of Utah" (*Bryologist*), published in 1936, gives a general ecological description that coordinates the geographical distribution of the bryophytes with the vegetational zones and higher-plant communities of Utah, and is obviously a by-product of his doctoral dissertation, "Vegetation of the Great Salt Lake Region," published in 1934 (*Botanical Gazette*).

The beautifully executed and original illustrations form one of the finest features of this book; Seville Flowers became an extraordinarily accurate and skillful bryological artist through the years. Other examples of his excellent bryological illustrations appear in "The Hepaticae of Utah" already cited, in his monographs of *Philonotis* (1935) and *Encalypta* (1938) in Grout's *Moss Flora of North America North of Mexico,* in his world monograph of the genus *Anacolia* (*Bull. Torrey Bot. Club.* 79:161–185. 1952), and in his shorter papers, which are too numerous to list here.

William Campbell Steere

Preface

My appreciation and respect for Dr. Seville Flowers began in 1935 when I was a student in the first class on Mosses of Utah offered at the University of Utah. I had already begun my life's work on taxonomy of flowering plants, otherwise I might have found my way into bryology. The enthusiasm of Seville Flowers will always be remembered by all who had even a casual acquaintance with this dedicated man.

I have been honored to edit what seems like a work of a lifetime, but a list of publications by Dr. Flowers includes major works on algae, hepatics, and ferns; and I personally know that he was an agrostologist very much at home with grasses in the West. My biggest hope is that I have done nothing to detract from a work that many others have helped to bring to light of day.

It is at this point that the work of Dr. Howard Crum, University of Michigan, should be mentioned. His many hours of painstaking work were evident on every page and Dr. Flowers may have even wanted his name listed as an author. Dr. Crum's critical readings resulted in numerous changes that will enhance this manual for all who will use it.

Four people at the University of Utah should be acknowledged early in this preface—Doctors Kimball Harper, I. Bill McNulty, Robert K. Vickers, Jr., and Dell Wiens. It is entirely possible that they are the ones who rescued the manuscript from oblivion as they sought the help of Dr. Howard Crum and also obtained a grant from the University of Utah Research Committee.

Dr. Stanley L. Welsh of the Botany Department of Brigham Young University was consulted and has helped many times with numerous details. The careful work of Marilyn Miller of the Editorial Department of the Brigham Young University Press is appreciated, and I want to congratulate all those staff members of the Brigham Young University Press who have made this a beautiful book by the excellence of their work.

We were asked to reduce the manuscript by nearly one-third and this was done largely by eliminating long lists of citations of collections by Dr. Flowers. The professional bryologist may want or need to consult the original manuscript for this information. Cosmopolitan mosses known in about every county of Utah have been recorded as to their ubiquitous occurrence, whereas a rare species known from only one or two collections will have been cited in more detail. Keys to species that also included varieties were often shortened by eliminating varietal separations when the varieties were described in considerable detail. The many important comments on ecology were left intact as written by Dr. Flowers, as it is here that the work of many years in the field shines through the text and illustrations.

Many items ordinarily included in a preface are to be found in the Introduction by Seville Flowers. I added numbers to all key couplets so that contrasting statements could be found more readily, especially in the lengthy key to families and genera.

Mosses: Utah and the West is a monumental work on mosses of Utah and contiguous areas, providing keys, illustrations, descriptions and information on geographical distribution and habitats, and detailed observations by Seville Flowers. The flora will be useful to bryologists, range men, foresters, ecologists, and other botanists. This manual will serve as a guide to the moss flora of most of the intermountain region.

Arthur H. Holmgren

Introduction

1.1 The first collection of mosses from Utah was made by Sereno Watson, botanist with the United States geological exploration of the fortieth parallel headed by Clarence King. The specimens were identified by Thomas P. James and most of them are included in an annotated list published in the report of the expedition in volume 5, pages 389-411 (1871). They total 49 species and 3 varieties, with 3 species new to science. Eight additional species collected by Watson are cited from Utah in Lesquereux and James' *Manual of North American Mosses* (1884).

1.2 In this same manual, Increase A. Lapham, a geologist and botanist of Milwaukee, is credited with collecting 1 species. Marcus E. Jones botanized in Utah for several years before becoming librarian and curator of the Museum of the University of Deseret in 1889. During that year he collected 14 species of mosses in the Brighton-Alta district of the Wasatch Mountains. The specimens are now in the Cryptogamic Herbarium of the University of Utah. Mosses which he gathered in other parts of Utah were sent to museums elsewhere. In 1911 Marius P. Henderson, a student at the University of Utah, wrote an undergraduate thesis *The Mosses of the Vicinity of Salt Lake City,* which lists, with notes and comments, 25 species and 1 variety. All except 4 of his specimens are preserved in the herbarium of the University of Utah. A. O. Garrett, instructor of botany at East High School in Salt Lake City, collected a few mosses in the vicinity of Salt Lake City and sent them to E. B. Bartram for identification; the specimens are now in Bartram's herbarium at Harvard University. In 1925, Mr. Garrett gave a course in bryology at the Brigham Young University summer school at Aspen Grove on the east slope of Mt. Timpanogos in the Wasatch Mountains. His class of 6 students gathered specimens which were put up in duplicate sets, one of which was sent to Bartram for identification. About 500 specimens yielded 85 species, and the collection later came into my custody and formed the nucleus of the moss herbarium at the University of Utah. After taking that course, I pursued bryology as a hobby in much of my free time. Since 1935 I have offered courses in bryology at the University of Utah. Many students and colleagues have contributed to the herbarium, notably LeRoy Behling who gathered about 875 specimens in northern Utah. A mimeographed manual, *Mosses of Utah* (1934), which describes and illustrates 185 species, served as a

1

reference for class use. Five hundred copies were issued, and copies were placed in various libraries in the state.

1.3   The present work is based on a study of about 12,000 specimens gathered over a period of 47 years in almost every section of Utah and bordering parts of neighboring states. A conservative view of classification and speciation has been adopted. The treatments of *Orthotrichum, Philonotis, Bryum, Amblystegium,* and *Drepanocladus* defy precise delineation, inasmuch as there are some intergrading variations. Citations of synonyms have been restricted to those showing the source of specific names, beginning with Hedwig's *Species Muscorum,* 1801, and to those having had wide usage within recent times. The recent *Index Muscorum* by Van der Wijk and Margadant and "A List of the Mosses of North America by Crum, Steere, and Anderson, in *The Bryologist* 68(1965):377–432 have aided greatly in bringing many names and the authorities up to date. For valued opinions on critical specimens for the loan or exchange of specimens, I am indebted to William C. Steere, Winona H. Welch, Elva Lawton, H. S. Conard, G. N. Jones, Gary L. Smith, and the late E. B. Bartram, A. J. Grout, A. LeRoy Andrews, T. C. Frye, R. S. Williams, Fay A MacFadden, A. C. Weatherby, and William R. Maxon.

CLASSIFICATION

1.4   The classification adopted in this treatment is that presented in H. N. Dixon's *Student's Handbook of British Mosses,* 3d ed. (1924), except for some modifications made to suit the limited number of families, genera, and species found in Utah. The outline given below is a conspectus of orders and subdivisions and includes some groups not known in Utah in order to permit comparisons in the following discussion of morphology; such groups are indicated by an asterisk.

1.5   I.   Order SPHAGNALES. Stems erect with regularly whorled branches; leaves ecostate, with dimorphic cells; capsules ovoid, dehiscent by a lid, sessile on a massive foot embedded in the apex of a pseudopodium; capsule wall without air chambers; spores arising from the inner layer of the amphithecium and continuous over a dome-shaped columella; peristome lacking. One family, Sphagnaceae.

1.6   II.   Order *ANDREAEALES. Saxicolous; stems erect; leaves ecostate, with cells of one kind; capsule oblong, dehiscent by 4 longitudinal slits, sessile on a massive foot embedded in the apex of a pseudopodium; capsule wall without air chambers; spores arising from the outer layer of the endothecium and continuous over the summit of the slender columella; peristome lacking. One family, Andreaeaceae.

1.7   III.   Order BRYALES. Gametophyte various; leaves mostly unistratose; capsules various, borne on a seta with the foot embedded in the apex of a normal stem, dehiscent by a lid; capsule wall often with air chambers; spores arising from the outer layer of the endothe-

2

cium, surrounding the columella which is continuous with the lid; peristome, when present, of 16 jointed teeth and often an endostome of cilia and/or segments.

A. Suborder Haplolepideae. Peristome teeth in 1 row, often cleft to deeply divided into 32 slender divisions. Families: Fissidentaceae, Dicranaceae, Pottiaceae, Encalyptaceae, and Grimmiaceae.

B. Suborder Diplolepideae. Peristome of 2 rows of processes, an outer row of teeth and an inner row of segments and/or cilia.

1. Acrocarpae. Mostly erect mosses with the archegonia and later sporophytes borne at the apex of the main stem or a well-developed branch; basal joints of the peristome teeth without fine transverse lines. Families: Orthotrichaceae, Funariaceae, Splachnaceae, Timmiaceae, Aulacomniaceae, Bartramiaceae, and Bryaceae.

2. Pleurocarpae. Mostly creeping mosses, freely to pinnately branched, with archegonia and later sporophytes borne on a very short budlike branch on the sides of the stem or of secondary stems; basal joints of the peristome teeth mostly with fine transverse lines. Families: Leskeaceae, Hypnaceae, Neckeraceae, and Fontinalaceae.

1.8 IV. Order *TETRAPHIDALES. Gametophyte essentially like that of the *Bryales;* capsules on long setae, ovoid to oblong, dehiscent by a lid, the walls without air chambers; peristome of 4 solid, triangular teeth composed of both endothecium and inner layers of the amphithecium. Family, Tetraphidaceae.

1.9 V. Order *BUXBAUMIALES. Gametophyte similar to that of the *Bryales* but sometimes much reduced; the sporophyte sometimes ± saprophytic; capsules large, dorsiventrally asymmetric, and usually oblique to the seta, with large air chambers; outer peristome lacking or of 1–4 rows of linear, jointed teeth of varying lengths; endostome a tall, pleated, conical, membranous tube exceeding the teeth. Families: Buxbaumiaceae and Diphysciaceae.

1.10 VI. Order POLYTRICHALES. Stems stout, with leaf traces traversing the cortex and a large central strand of heterogeneous cells; leaves bearing few to many longitudinal lamellae; capsule walls with air chambers; peristome of 32-64 short, ligulate, solid teeth attached by their tips to a membranelike expansion of the tip of the columella (called an epiphragm). Family, Polytrichaceae.

MORPHOLOGY

GAMETOPHYTE

2.1 Mosses are small plants which grow in a wide variety of terrestrial and aquatic situations on dry, damp, or wet soil; dry, damp, or wet rocks

3

and rotten wood; on the roots or trunks of trees; or submerged in springs, swamps, brooks, rivers, ponds, or lakes. They consist of little stems that bear small leaves and branched hairlike rhizoids which serve to anchor the plants to the substratum. The 2 main groups of mosses differ in their particular manner of growth: those which grow erect in loose or compact tufts, often forming sods; and those which grow more or less prostrate, either creeping over the substratum in mats or more or less ascending in interwoven masses.

2.2   Some species are very small, as in *Phascum* and *Pterygoneurum,* which are erect forms only a few mm high, whereas most species range in size from 1–10 cm. Some species of *Polytrichum* may reach as much as 40 cm and some species of *Dawsonia* (found in southeastern Asia and Australia) may grow to a height of 50 cm. The submerged stems of *Fontinalis antipyretica* reach as much as 70 cm in length.

2.3   In the erect mosses the rhizoids usually occur at the bases of stems, but in a few kinds they may occur high up on the stems and form dense tufts among the leaves, as in some of the Bartramiaceae. In prostrate mosses the rhizoids are usually confined to the lower sides of the stems, next to the substratum, and may be present mainly on the older parts, but in some kinds they are often in tufts well toward the ends.

2.4   When moist, mosses are usually bright or dark green; less commonly yellowish green, straw colored, golden yellow, yellowish brown, dull olivaceous; and rarely pale whitish green or dark purplish. When dry the leaves of some species are not much changed in form, but those of other species may become infolded, shriveled, or variously twisted and contorted in a characteristic manner. Some do not change color very much, whereas others assume darker shades of green, dull olivaceous, brownish, or blackish. In many species the dry shriveled plants are drab and unlovely; but when moistened by rain or dew they quickly absorb water and spread in beautiful hues, sometimes accented with bright red.

PROTONEMA AND SHOOT

2.5   When a spore falls on a suitable substratum, under favorable conditions of moisture and temperature, it swells, splits the outer spore coat, and emits a protuberance which quickly becomes green and grows into a long cylindrical cell. This cell divides by a transverse wall while the terminal cell continues to elongate; the division is repeated many times, until a filament of cylindrical cells forms end to end (figs. 1–2). Only the terminal cell of the series divides, but after several cells have been formed, some of the older ones bulge laterally near the anterior end and form branches which develop by successive divisions of their own terminal cells (figs. 3–4), which begin to elongate in the same manner as the main axis. The branches rebranch several times to form the protonema (plural, protonemata). The cells behind each terminal cell continue to elongate in such a way that the cross walls become diagonal.

4

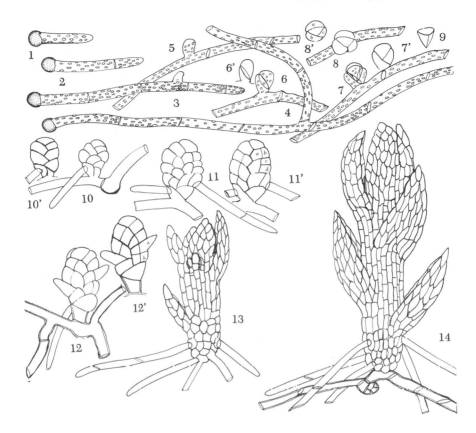

Figs. 1–14. Spore germination, growth of the protonema and development of the young shoot of **Bryum creberrimum.** 1–2. Spore germination. 3. Branch papilla. 4. Position of a branch. 5. Bud papilla. 6, 6'. First division of the bud papilla. 7, 7'. Second and third divisions of the young bud. 8, 8'. The same view from above, successive divisions, **a, b,** and **c.** 9. Diagram of the pyramidal apical cell. 10, 10'. Eleven-celled stage of a young shoot showing the first rhizoid. 11, 11'. Showing the periclinal division of a segment, forming an inner cell, **a,** and an outer cell, **b,** and the anticlinal division of the outer cell, forming an upper cell, **c,** and a lower cell, **d.** 12, 12'. Showing the origin of a leaf primordium from an upper cell, **a,** and a lower cell giving rise to stem tissue, **b.** 13–14. Further growth of the young shoot, ×100.

2.6 As the protonema grows, some of the cells send out a protuberance resembling the early stage of a branch filament, but instead of becoming a long cylinder, the apex swells to form a pear-shaped bud primordium (fig. 5). The primordium divides by three successive vertically diagonal walls (figs. 6–8)* and results in a tetrahedral apical cell which resembles an inverted pyramid (fig. 9) with 1 free curved wall on the upper surface and 3 inner walls. Since the upper surface wall takes no part in subsequent divisions, it is customary to think in terms of the 3 inner walls and to speak of this kind of apical cell as 3-sided, having 3 cutting faces. As the apical cell divides to form new cells parallel

---

*Figures marked prime (') are optical sections of the corresponding surface views.

along each cutting face, several segments are cut off, and the bud enlarges. At about this stage 1 of the first-formed segments becomes papillose and grows out as the first rhizoid (figs. 10, 10'). It elongates, divides, and forms branches in a manner precisely like the protonema, but lacks chloroplasts, is smaller in diameter, and has thicker, brownish or reddish cell walls. As growth proceeds other rhizoids develop.

LEAF AND BRANCH DEVELOPMENT

2.7 After 9–12 segments have been cut off from the apical cell, the last ones formed divide periclinally, i.e., parallel with the outer surface, forming inner (figs. 11, 11'a) and outer cells (fig. 11'b). The outer cell then divides anticlinally, i.e., perpendicular to the surface, forming an upper cell toward the apex (fig. 11'c) and a lower cell toward the base (fig. 11'd). The upper cell grows outward and by 2 diagonal cell divisions forms a 2-sided apical cell of a leaf primordium (figs. 12, 12'a). The lower cell usually gives rise to several outer cortical cells in the stem, but it may enlarge and divide by 3 vertically diagonal intersecting walls to form the apical cell of a branch bud. During these events further periclinal and anticlinal divisions of the segments give rise to the inner and outer tissue of the stem. While this is the basic pattern of cell division in the stems of most mosses, there are variations. For example, in *Sphagnum, Andreaea,* and *Fontinalis* a segment divides periclinally into an outer and inner cell. Then the outer cell divides periclinally to produce a secondary outer cell which gives rise to a leaf

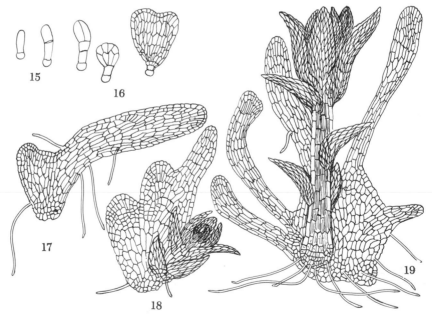

Figs. 15–19. Sphagnum squarrosum. 15. Spore germination. 16–17. Growth of the protonema. 18–19. Growth of the young gametophyte shoots, × 25.

primordium and a second inner cell. The 2 inner cells give rise to internal tissue of the stem. Young shoots of a typical moss with primordial leaves are shown in figs. 13–14.

2.8   In some mosses other types of apical cells occur. The apical cells of *Distichium* and *Fissidens* are more or less wedge shaped with 2 cutting faces, (although in *Fissidens* the stem begins with a 3-sided apical cell which soon changes). In both genera the leaves are in 2 opposite rows, which makes the shoots conspicuously flat. Some other genera are known to have 2-sided apical cells. In certain species of *Mnium* and *Thuidium* the apical cells seem to vary from 2- to 5-sided according to the age of the stems.

2.9   In *Sphagnum* the spore germinates and grows into a filament of several short cells (fig. 15); then the terminal cell divides vertically instead of transversely to form 2 cells side by side (fig. 16). After several divisions of these 2 cells, a 2-sided apical cell forms, cuts off segments right and left and gives rise to a flat protonema 1 cell thick. The protonema is more or less wedge shaped but later becomes heart shaped. Eventually it becomes irregularly branched and 1–4 mm across with rhizoids on the underside and at the margins (figs. 17–19).

2.10   The spore of *Andreaea* divides into 3 or 4 cells before the spore coat is ruptured. When they break out, the cells form a small mass from which short filaments grow and expand into a ribbonlike protonema 1 cell thick and 2 to several cells wide. As the protonema elongates, it becomes branched, with uniseriate filaments of short cells at the apex and sides. Occasionally the protonema and its filaments become 2 to several cells thick here and there.

2.11   In most mosses the protonema withers away or becomes transformed into rhizoids as soon as the stem becomes well anchored to the substrate. However, in a few species of minute mosses, it proliferates considerably and persists throughout the growing season. Examples are seen in *Ephemerum, Nanomitrium, Buxbaumia,* and *Diphyscium,* which have exceedingly short stems with only a few small leaves; these species continue to draw nourishment from the protonemata.

STEMS

2.12   In the vocabulary of bryology, the term stem has two meanings: (1) the central axis alone—in this sense it is used in dealing with the length, diameter, epidermal cells, and internal structures; and (2) the shoot or axis, including the leaves—in this latter sense it is used to describe the appearance of the moss as a whole, such as a slender, stout, thick, or swollen shoot, with the tips blunt, pointed, or hooked—features largely owing to the mantle of leaves.

2.13   A stolon is a creeping stem, more or less anchored to the substratum by tufts of rhizoids on the underside. In some cases the leaves of a stolon become progressively smaller toward the end, as in certain species of *Mnium* and *Brachythecium* (fig. 20).

2.14 Rhizomes are horizontal, underground stems—usually dark brown and more or less denuded of leaves—from which erect leafy stems arise. They occur in a number of mosses, such as in some species of *Polytrichum* or as in *Climacium* (fig. 21 and 32). (The so-called rhizome in *Polytrichum* is not a separate stem but the basal portion of the procumbent stem.) Flagella are exceedingly slender stems bearing much reduced leaves; they are gradually or abruptly tapered from the ends of normal shoots. Flagellate, flagelliferous, and flagelliform are terms frequently used to describe the plants which bear them (fig. 22).

2.15 A few mosses have simple stems, as in *Distichium* and *Leptobryum* (fig. 23), but the great majority are branched. Branches may arise at various points on the circumference of the stem just above a leaf; however, they are not strictly axillary because they originate from the lower of 2 cells cut off from the same segment, and it is the upper cell which produces the leaf.

2.16 In some erect mosses the branches assume a spreading or ascending habit (fig. 24); others are fastigiate with several branches more or less

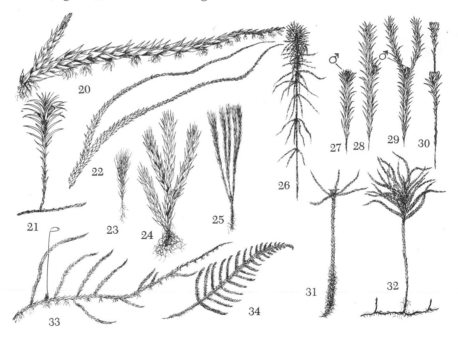

Figs. 20–34. Habits of stems, ×.64. 20. Stolon of **Brachythecium salebrosum.** 21. Rhizome of **Polytrichum commune.** 22. Flagellate shoot of **Leskeella tectorum.** 23. Simple stem of **Leptobryum pyriforme.** 24. Branched stem of **Bryum pseudotriquetrum.** 25. Fastigiate stem of **Grimmia calyptrata.** 26. Verticillate or whorled branching of **Sphagnum capillaceum.** 27–28. Subfloral innovations of **Orthotrichum affine.** 29. False dichotomy by two subfloral innovations. 30. Innovations from old perigonial bud of **Polytrichum juniperinum.** 31. Whorled subfloral innovations of **Philonotis fontana.** 32. Dendroid branching of **Climacium dendroides.** 33. Irregularly pinnate branching of **Brachythecium salebrosum,** a pleurocarpous moss. 32. Regularly pinnate branching of **Hypnum revolutum.**

erect and of approximately the same height, as in many densely tufted species (fig. 25). In *Sphagnum,* branches are borne at intervals along the axis in whorls, that is, in clusters of 3 or more at about the same level around the circumference. At the summit of the axis, the young branches are short, densely crowded, and spread out in all directions in a compact head. Below the summit, the axis elongates so that the branches become more widely spaced and, as they lengthen, assume a drooping habit (fig. 26).

2.17 In the erect mosses the archegonia (the female reproductive organs) and often the antheridia (the male organs) arise from the apical cell and recently formed segments and thus terminate the growth of the stem. In many instances this induces the formation of one or more lateral stem buds immediately below the reproductive buds—the new branches growing from them are commonly called subfloral innovations. In a number of mosses only 1 subfloral innovation is formed; it may grow upward and push the old archegonial or antheridial bud to 1 side and appear to continue the main stem (figs. 27, 28). When this is repeated, the axis becomes a sympodium of successive branches. In some instances 2 subfloral innovations grow up equally on either side of the old floral bud and make it appear as if the stem were forked or dichotomously branched (fig. 29). True dichotomy is not known in mosses because the apical cell does not divide equally into 2 apical cells which might then develop into 2 equal branches, although some authors describe these stems as dichotomously branched, using the term in a sense that is apparent but not real. In *Polytrichum* a new stem grows out of the middle of the male inflorescence in the same direction as the old stem and thus appears terminal in origin, but it is no different from the situation described above—the new bud is still morphologically lateral to the original apical cell (fig. 30). In *Philonotis,* 3 or more subfloral innovations form a characteristic whorl of branches just below the summit of the main axis (fig. 31). According to the species, innovations may arise from the base, middle, or apex of older stems independent of the male or female buds. Often some condition in the environment induces their development: extreme cold or wet, warm humid air, prolonged exposure to the high light intensity at high altitudes or latitudes, extreme crowding, breakage by various vicissitudes in nature, or damage by insects.

2.18 In *Climacium* an underground rhizome gives rise to erect secondary stems which bear a dense cluster of stout tapering branches at the summit; these spread in all directions like the crown of a tree (fig. 32).

2.19 In most prostrate mosses lateral buds originate from the main stem more or less alternately in 2 opposite rows and give rise to a pinnately branched shoot. In many species the branches are irregularly spaced and often of different lengths, thus irregularly pinnate (fig. 33). In some species, however, the branches are closely spaced and equal in length or they gradually diminish toward the apex of the axis. They are then regularly pinnate, as in some species of *Eurhynchium* and

9

Hypnum (fig. 34). As growth continues for several seasons, certain branches assume dominance by elongating and becoming rebranched. These are designated as secondary stems to distinguish them from the original or primary stem.

STRUCTURE OF STEMS

2.20 Stems range from about 0.1 mm in diameter to more than 1 mm. Stems may be round in cross section or more or less compressed in some creeping forms; they are triangular in *Plagiopus* and five-angled in *Bryum, Mnium* and *Polytrichum.*

2.21 The simplest stems are more or less homogeneous in structure, and consisting of 4- to 6-angled, thin-walled cells, with the largest cells in the center and progressively smaller ones toward the outside (fig. 35). The outer 2–4 layers may be thin walled in the younger part of the stem, but in many mosses they become variously thick walled and usually darker yellowish, orange, or reddish. As the stem becomes older the wall thickening increases and extends progressively inward to the inner cortical cells. Sometimes the cells of the entire cortex become thick walled and colored, as in *Orthotrichum* (fig. 39). The outermost layer is generally called the epidermis, although the terms exodermis and outer cortical cells are sometimes used. Externally the epidermal cells are oblong to the linear with transverse end walls. The outer surface is usually smooth, but in a few species the cells are beset with small, protruding, cuticular thickenings called papillae. In *Hygrohypnum ochraceum, Plagiothecium muellerianum,* several genera of Bartramiaceae, and some species of *Hypnum,* the epidermal cells are enlarged, thin walled, and hyaline, a strong contrast to the small thick-walled cortical cells internal to them (fig. 36). In some species of *Sphagnum,* such as S. *squarrosum* and S. *capillaceum,* the stems have 1–5 layers of large, thin-walled, outer cortical cells overlying a zone of small thick-walled cells (plate 1, fig. 3). The epidermis of the branches of *Sphagnum* is of two types: (1) some species have uniform cells, each with 1 or more large pores; (2) others have nonporous cells and larger cells with a short protruding neck at the upper end with a pore at its tip, the so-called retort cells (plate 2, fig. 3). Stems of many mosses have a central strand of small, angular, thin-walled cells which resembles a primitive vascular bundle but is of a doubtful conductive function. In some species it is small and often indistinct, but in others, especially those with a strong costa in the leaves, the strand is strong and ranges up to as much as ⅓ the diameter of the stem (figs. 36, 37, 38).

2.22 In *Bryum* and *Mnium,* leaf traces, consisting of groups of small thin-walled cells with a dorsal arch of steroids, extend into the outer cortex of the stem where they end blindly (fig. 38). In *Timmia* a branch arises just below the apex of the stem and, as the 2 axes elongate, the large central strand divides just below the point where a branch diverges. In most mosses, however, there is no connection between the central strand of the main stem and its branches.

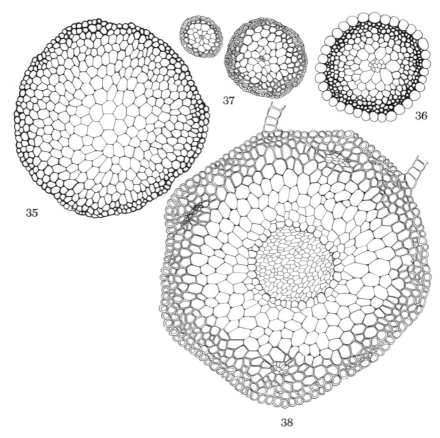

Figs. 35–38. Cross sections of moss stems, ×100. 35. Stem without a central strand. **Merceya latifolia.** 36. **Amblystegium serpens** with a small central strand. 37. **Hygrohypnum ochraceum** with central strand and epidermis of enlarged, thin-walled, hyaline cells. 38. **Mnium medium** with a large central strand.

2.23   The Polytrichaceae have the most highly developed stem. For example, *Polytrichum commune* has a large central strand composed of greatly elongated cells with tapered overlapping ends. In cross section, cells in the center are disposed in rows of 2–4 cells separated by thin walls, but the walls between the rows are thickened and reddish orange. These cells are empty (except for globules of protoplasmic residues here and there) and have the appearance of tracheids; however, they lack pits in the walls and have more slenderly tapered ends. The whole central strand suggests a primitive protostele. The cells of the inner cortex, external to the thin-walled "tracheids," are rather abruptly larger and shorter with slightly thickened lateral walls and thin transverse end walls. The lumina contain abundant proteinaceous material and at times starch and oil droplets, best seen in longitudinal section. In cross section this zone appears denser, accentuating the central strand. The cells of the middle cortex are large with less dense contents and thick, yellowish walls; they grade into smaller, thicker-walled, and

11

more highly colored cells toward the outside. The epidermis and 1 or 2 underlying rows of cells form a dense rind in which the cells have very small lumina and dark red walls (fig. 40).

2.24 Guide cells of the costa extend from the leaf base downward at a steep angle through the cortex to join the central strand as a leaf trace (fig. 41). The lateral and more or less transverse end walls are thin and have little or no contents. In the outer cortex the girdle cells are disposed in 1 or 2 tangential rows 6–8 cells wide (fig. 42), but as they extend farther down into the cortex they diminish in size and lateral extent, and

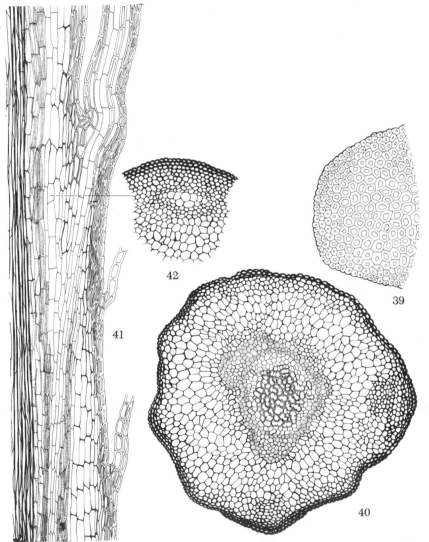

Figs. 39–42. Moss stems, ×100. 39. **Orthotrichum affine,** older stem with uniformly thick-walled cells throughout. 40–42. Cross and longitudinal sections of the stem of **Polytrichum commune,** explanation in text.

the faces then consist of irregular clusters of 6–12 thin-walled cells—contrasting with the thick-walled, colored cortical cells around them. In cross section a number of traces may be seen. Those which join the central strand become almost completely encircled with the denser, inner cortical cells which arch outward around them (fig. 40).

LEAVES

2.25   In most mosses the leaves are simple structures which consist of a lamina of a single layer of cells and a costa or midrib 2 to several cells thick in various widths and lengths. The blade is sessile and broadly inserted on the stem in most species, but in others it is variously tapered to the base with a correspondingly narrower insertion. The ventral surface of the leaf is the upper, or inner, side—facing the stem and the dorsal surface is the back of the leaf—away from the stem. Very small mosses have minute leaves 0.5 mm long or less; in larger species the leaves may be up to 10 or more mm long.

2.26   Comal leaves are crowded in a cluster or rosette at the ends of stems and are so designated to distinguish them from the stem leaves immediately below. In some mosses the comal leaves are scarcely different from the stem leaves; in others the outer ones are larger, sometimes with greater spread and, in certain species, longer points. In some prostrate mosses the stem leaves are proportionately larger and broader than those of the branches.

2.27   The leaves of nearly all mosses are spirally arranged on the stem. Since the apical cell is 3-sided, it might be expected that the leaves would be in 3 vertical rows, but in most mosses the segments cut off from the apical cell are asymmetric, the right side much thicker than the left side, so that as growth proceeds the apical cell gradually turns counterclockwise. In some genera it turns more strongly than in others. Since the leaves are already arranged in ⅓ spirals, this tortion growth shifts them further into a distorted spiral.   Arrangement in rows is evident, for example, in *Conostomum* with the leaves in 5 vertical rows and in some species of *Philonotis* in 5 spiral rows. In a few genera the arrangement is obvious. In most genera, the exact arrangement is obscured by the closeness and stance of the leaves. Various investigators have found phyllotaxy of 2/5 and 3/8 in a number of genera, 5/13 in *Polytrichum*, and 8/21 in *Leskea*. In *Fissidens* and *Distichium* the leaves are disposed alternately in 2 opposite rows; in *Fontinalis* the leaves are often in 3 conspicuous rows.

2.28   The position of the leaves on the stem and the manner in which they diverge give mosses a characteristic appearance. The habit of the leaves, both moist and dry, offers some characteristic features which aid in identification. Erect leaves stand more or less vertically at a very steep angle so as to give the shoot a slender appearance (fig. 43). When the leaves are closely overlapping, like shingles on a roof, the terms appressed or imbricated are applied. When the stance of the leaves gives the shoot a smooth, cylindrical appearance, it is described as julaceous

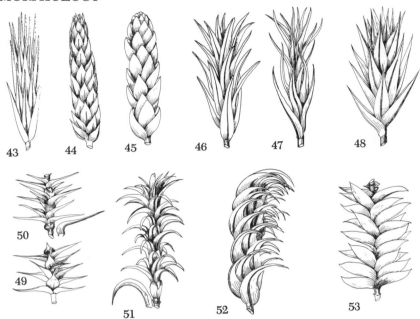

Figs. 43–53. Stance of moss leaves, ×4. 43. Erect, appressed or imbricated. 44. Julaceous, imbricated. 45. Tumid or turgid. 46–47. Erect-patent. 48. Patent or open. 49. Spreading. 50. Squarrose-spreading. 51. Squarrose-recurved. 52. Falcate. 53. Complanate.

(fig. 44); when concave leaves are loosely imbricated so that the shoot seems swollen, the terms tumid or turgid may be applied (fig. 45). Erect-patent leaves diverge at angles of about 25° or less; or they may diverge at a wider angle and curve upward shortly above the base in an erect position (figs. 46, 47). Patent leaves diverge more or less stiffly at angles of 30° to 60° (fig. 48). Spreading leaves diverge from the stem at angles greater than 60°, sometimes even to 90° (fig. 49). Squarrose leaves have the base more or less erect, often partially clasping the stem, while the upper part abruptly curves outward in a spreading manner (fig. 50). Recurved leaves clasp the stem in a similar manner, but the blade gradually curves backward and away from the stem (fig. 51). Secund, or homomallous leaves are all turned to one side of the stem (fig. 52). Complanate leaves are flattened in the same plane in 2 apparent rows and give the shoot a flat appearance (fig. 53).

2.29   In some species the leaves are not much changed on drying; at most only slightly shrunken and sometimes longitudinally wrinkled. In others the leaves may become closely appressed to the stem or folded lengthwise; others may be straight or spirally twisted around the stem. In some species the dry leaves arch from the base and curve inward at the tips; in others the blades may be undulate at the margins or variously crisped and contorted (figs. 54–57).

2.30   The shapes of leaves differ widely among different kinds of mosses but

14

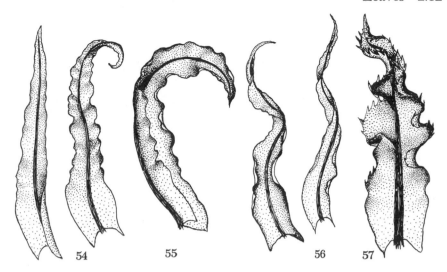

Figs. 54–57. Dry habit of leaves. 54–55. Undulate. 56–57. Crisped, ×10.

are of more or less the same form in any given species. Fully developed leaves usually occur on the middle section of stems in most mosses, but in some, especially short-stemmed mosses, the largest leaves are found toward the tips. In identification the leaves from the middle section are taken as the standard of size and shape. In many mosses the leaves of the branches are smaller and narrower than those of the stems.

2.31 The following terms describe the shapes of leaves: *Orbicular*: round or nearly so (fig. 58). *Ovate*: broader toward the base (fig. 59). *Obovate*: broader toward the apex (fig. 60). *Oval*: broader in the middle and more or less equally rounded at each end (fig. 61). *Oblong*: with the margins somewhat parallel (fig. 62). *Ligulate*: the base truncate with the margins more or less parallel, and either broadly rounded or variably narrowed to an obtuse or pointed tonguelike apex (figs. 63, 64). *Spatulate*: the base narrower, gradually broadened upward to a rounded or abruptly narrowed apex, like an old-fashioned spatula (fig. 65). *Linear*: long and narrow, gradually tapering upward, or with the margins somewhat parallel (fig. 66). *Lanceolate*: broader near the more or less narrowed base and gradually tapering to a pointed apex (figs. 67, 68). *Elongated-triangular*: more or less truncated at the base, gradually and evenly tapering to the apex, like an isosceles triangle (fig. 69). *Deltoid*: like an equilateral triangle, broader at the base (fig. 70). *Subulate*: long and narrow, gradually or abruptly narrowed from a broader base and tapering to a slender rigid apex (figs. 71–72).

2.32 Besides these basic forms, many leaves have other modifying features which lend individuality to the plants as a whole. Thus, the leaves of some mosses are curved to one side rather than straight. When the curvature is less than a semicircle they are falcate (fig. 72) and when it is greater they are circinate (fig. 73); sometimes the tips approach the

15

base of the leaf, almost in a circle. Secund leaves are all directed to one side of the stem and may be straight, falcate, or circinate.

2.33   The blade may be flat or variously concave, sometimes only at the base (figs. 70 and 80); in some species it may be keeled and boat-shaped or more rounded like the bowl of a spoon (fig. 58). In a few species the apex arches inward, like a hood; then it is described as cucullate (fig. 74). When a leaf has the margins widely incurved along its length, it is described as channelled or canaliculate (fig. 76), and tubulose when the margins meet (fig. 77). When the back of a leaf is sharply angled, it is keeled (fig. 78). In some extreme forms the 2 halves of the blade are folded together lengthwise, in which case the leaf is conduplicate, as in some species of *Fontinalis* (fig. 79). In many mosses the leaf is plicate with 1 or more longitudinal folds (fig. 73), and in a few it is transversely wavy or undulate (fig. 75).

2.34   Acute leaves terminate in a sharp angular point, either narrow or broad,

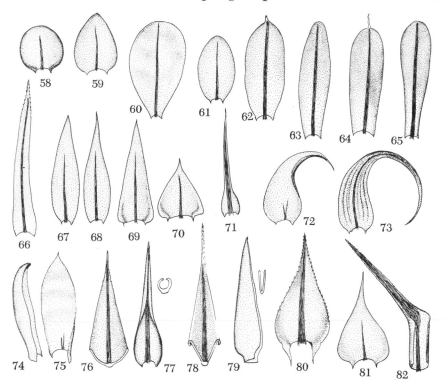

Figs. 58–82.   Forms of leaves, ×5. 58. Orbicular, concave. 59. Ovate-acute. 60. Obovate. 61. Oval. 62. Oblong, mucronate. 63. Ligulate. 64. Lingulate-apiculate. 65. Spatulate. 66. Linear. 67. Lanceolate, narrowly acute. 68. Lanceolate-acuminate. 69. Elongate-triangular. 70. Deltoid, base excavate. 71. Subulate from an ovate base. 72. Falcate. 73. Circinate-plicate. 74. Cucullate, concave. 75. Surface undulate. 76. Canaliculate. 77. Tubulose. 78. Keeled, margin revolute. 79. Conduplicate, clasping at the base. 80. Ovate-lanceolate with decurrent auricles at the base, margin serrate. 81. Ovate-acuminate, base cordate. 82. Abruptly subulate and divergent from an oblong, clasping base.

but less than a right angle (figs. 59, 67, and 69). Obtuse leaves terminate in a broadly angular or narrowly to broadly rounded apex (figs. 60–65). Truncate is the term occasionally used to describe an abruptly cutoff obtuse apex. Retuse and emarginate leaves are narrowly or broadly notched at the apex, respectively. Acuminate has two meanings: evenly tapering to a very narrow tip (fig. 67) or abruptly narrowed to a long slender tip (fig. 68). The latter sense, which is more precise, is used in this work. Subulate apices are slender, stiff, and awl-like. A cuspidate apex is gradually or rather abruptly narrowed to a slender point not distinctly set off from the main body of the blade (fig. 84). Mucronate is a more abrupt short point (fig. 62), and apiculate is a very abrupt, soft, slender tip (fig. 64). Awned leaves terminate in a slender or coarse, usually white, hair point, sometimes as long or longer than the blade, smooth or toothed (figs. 85–86).

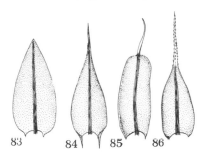

Figs. 83–86.   The leaf costa, ×5. 83. Costa percurrent. 84. Costa shortly excurrent to a mucronate tip. 85. Costa excurrent to a smooth slender awn (piliferous or aristate). 86. Costa excurrent to a spinulose awn.

2.35   The leaves may be scarcely narrowed at the base and inserted along their entire width (figs 64 and 69), but more commonly the leaves are gradually to abruptly narrowed to the insertion. When the base is broadly rounded and arched inward to the insertion, it is cordate (fig. 81). Leaves may clasp the stem only at the insertion (fig. 79) or by enlarged and strongly differentiated bases (fig. 82). Auricles are dilations at the basal angles of leaves, like little ears; decurrent leaves have the basal margin prolonged downward on the stem (figs. 80 and 84). In *Distichium* and *Polytrichum*, as well as some species of *Timmia* and *Bartramia*, the bases are abruptly enlarged and clasp the stems, while the upper parts, sometimes long and slender, are sharply divergent or even recurved.

2.36   The leaf margins may be plane, reflexed, or rolled backward—revolute (fig. 78). In *Weissia* the margins are rolled inward, or involute. In some species of *Polytrichum* the upper laminae on each side are sharply inflexed, roofing over the broad costa. The margins may be entire or toothed throughout, or toothed only in the upper part (and sometimes only at the apex), more rarely only at the base. When the teeth are blunt and project outward, the margin is dentate (denticulate, diminutive), but when they are sharp and project forward, they are serrate

17

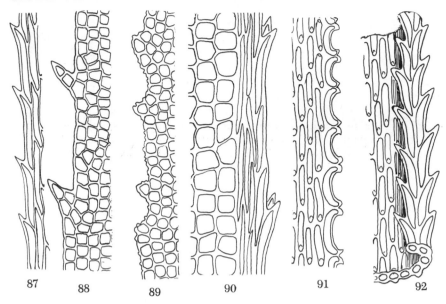

Figs. 87–92. Leaf margins, ×120. 87. Serrate by the projection of the upper ends of the marginal cells, **Brachythecium lamprochryseum.** 88. Serrate, the teeth formed by 1–3 cells, **Timmia bavarica.** 89. Margin irregularly notched, **Trichostomum tenuirostre.** 90. Margins bordered with narrow cells and doubly serrate **Mnium marginatum.** 91. Margin doubly serrate, **Philonotis fontana.** 92. Margins doubly serrate by the projection of the upper ends of the marginal and submarginal cells, **Philonotis fontana.**

(serrulate, diminutive). The teeth may be formed by the outward projection of the upper ends of marginal cells (fig. 87), or they may be composed of one or more cells (fig. 88). In a few mosses the margins are irregularly notched (fig. 89). In certain species of *Anacolia, Bartramia,* and *Mnium,* the teeth are paired, and the margins are said to be doubly serrate (fig. 90). In some species of *Philonotis* the leaves are doubly serrate because both ends of adjoining marginal cells project outward (fig 91). In some mosses in which the serrate leaf margins are recurved or revolute, the submarginal cells may form apparent teeth by the projection of the ends of the cells (fig. 92). This circumstance may give a singly serrate leaf margin a doubly serrate appearance but not in the same sense as described above.

CELL STRUCTURE

2.37   In the leaves of most mosses the lamina is unistratose throughout, but in certain ones the marginal cells may be 2 cells thick (bistratose) and in a few species as much as 5 cells thick. In many mosses, such as some species of *Bryum* and *Mnium,* the leaves are bordered by long, narrow cells which often become thick walled and sometimes more highly colored (fig. 90). In some species the upper ½ or ⅔ of the blade is bistratose, but in others only the upper part and also lines extending

18

toward the base are bistratose, as in certain species of *Grimmia, Orthotrichum,* and *Tortula.* Among these mosses it is not unusual to observe isolated cells or small groups of a double thickness. Usually the bistratose areas appear more densely chlorophyllose and opaque than the adjacent unistratose areas in surface view. Occasionally the bistratose areas are transparent enough so that the lower layer of cells can be distinguished.

2.38　The cells of the lamina may be of considerable diagnostic value. The pattern formed by the network of cell walls is called the areolation, which may be lax in some leaves with very thin walls or firm to rigid when the walls are thicker. In some mosses the areolation is nearly uniform throughout the leaf, but more often the basal, apical, or marginal cells differ from the medial ones. In the majority of the acrocarpous mosses the upper leaf cells are short and the basal cells are longer and usually wider. The reverse situation exists in most pleurocarpous mosses, with the upper cells longer and the basal ones proportionately shorter and wider.

2.39　The cell cavity, or lumen (lumina, plural), decreases as the cell walls become thicker. The contents of the cells may differ in density in different parts of the same leaf and in the leaves of various kinds of mosses. In some the chloroplasts are relatively few, distinct and bright green, but in others they are more numerous, often darker green, and sometimes so dense as to render the leaf quite opaque. In the leaves of some species the cells are chlorophyllose to the base, but more often the chloroplasts become progressively fewer toward the base and are very often lacking. In some cases the upper chlorophyllose cells give way abruptly to hyaline basal cells, as in *Tortella* and some species of *Tortula* and *Encalypta.*

2.40　The shape and size of the upper medial cells of the lamina are generally taken as the basis for comparison with those of the base, margins, and apex. The size may be mentioned in general terms as small, medium, or large, but more precisely the length and width of the cells are measured in microns with the use of an ocular micrometer in a compound microscope. Quadrate cells are square or nearly so, but often become more or less rounded when the walls become thickened (fig. 93). Frequently some cells are transversely elongated. Rectangular and oblong forms are longer than they are wide, the former with parallel sides and square ends (fig. 94), the latter with more or less parallel sides and more or less rounded ends (fig. 95). Fusiform cells are broadest in the middle and taper to pointed ends which overlap (fig. 96). Rhomboidal cells have the dimensions of the rectangle but with the end walls oblique in the same direction (fig. 97). Hexagonal figures may be isodiametric or elongated (fig. 98). Intergrading shapes are cited by compound terms, such as oblong-linear, oblong-hexagonal, or irregularly rhomboidal-hexagonal. Linear cells have proportions of 6–15:1, or longer, the sides more or less parallel, the ends rounded or tapering to points and usually overlapping. In addition, they may be straight or flexuous, i.e., loosely wavy, sometimes described as vermicular (figs. 99–100).

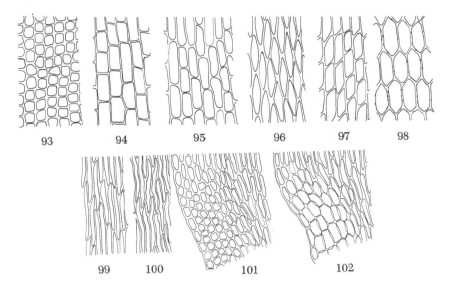

Figs. 93–102. Shapes of leaf cells, ×100. 93. Quadrate. 94. Rectangular. 95. Oblong 96. Fusiform. 97. Rhomboidal. 98. Hexagonal, walls pitted. 99. Linear. 100. Linear, flexuous or vermicular. 101. Quadrate alar cells of **Brachythecium collinum.** 102. Enlarged, inflated alar cells of **Brachythecium rivulare.**

2.41 The cell walls remain thin in some mosses, but in others they become progressively thicker with age—either in the upper part of the lamina, as in many acrocarpous species, or mainly in the basal cells of many pleurocarps. Ordinarily as walls become thicker they also become more intensely colored—yellowish, reddish brown, orange, or red. In some species the thick walls become pitted, a condition often described as porose. Some species of *Mnium* have moderately thick yellowish walls with rather obscure pits revealed as shadowy spots (fig. 98). The upper cells in some species of *Dicranum* and the basal cells in some pleuro-carpous species have strongly thickened walls with conspicuous pits.

2.42 Alar cells are those at the basal angles of the leaves. In some mosses they are much like other basal cells, but in many others they are ob-viously differentiated. For example, the inner basal cells may be elongated, whereas the alar cells are rather abruptly shorter and quad-rate to shortly rectangular (fig. 101), or they may be larger, wider, and sometimes thinner walled and inflated (fig. 102). In some instances they are thicker walled and often more highly colored.

2.43 The surfaces of the lumina may be flat or bulging. When strongly con-vex the cells are said to be mammillose. The cuticle over each cell may be smooth or beset with one or more papillae, which are small, nipple-like protuberances formed by a localized thickening of cuticular sub-stance. When present, the leaves, stems, rhizoids, or setae are said to be papillose. They may range from being low and convex to high and pointed (figs. 103–5). In some species of *Orthotrichum* they are bifurcate, i.e., tall and forked (fig. 106). In many of the Pottiaceae and *Encalypta* they are C-shaped with as many as 6–8 over each cell (fig. 107). In *Tortula papillosissima* a single very tall papilla over each cell is hollow and terminates in a branched antlerlike crown (fig. 108). In *Philonotis* a single papilla occurs over the somewhat projecting end walls of the elongated cells (fig. 109). In *Dicranoweisia crispula* longitudinal ridges of cuticular substance extend over the surface of the leaf independently of the individual cells (fig. 110). In most papillose leaves the papillae are fewer and weaker toward the base of the leaf and are usually completely absent from the basal cells.

COSTA

2.44   According to the genus and species, the costa varies in length, width, and thickness. Generally, it tapers from the base upward and may disappear ½–¾ the distance toward the apex in some species; it may extend farther in others. In a number of species it terminates in a tooth projecting from the back of the leaf. When it extends to the apex, it is said to be percurrent (fig. 83); when it extends beyond the apex, it is excurrent (fig. 84). In the latter instance, it may form a short point of a variable nature described as cuspidate, mucronate, or apiculate. A striking feature of some species of *Grimmia, Tortula,* and several other

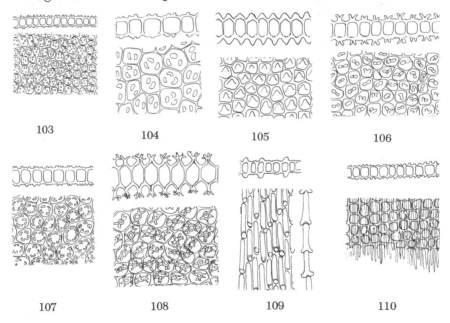

103   104   105   106

107   108   109   110

Figs. 103–110.   Papillae or cuticular outgrowths of the upper medial cells, × 100. 103. **Trichostomum tenuirostre.** 104. **Desmatodon cernuus.** 105. **Dichodontium pellucidum.** 106. Bifurcate papillae of **Orthotrichum alpestre.** 107. C-shaped papillae of **Tortula ruralis.** 108. Tall hollow papillae with branched, antlerlike tips of **Tortula papillosissima.** 109. Papillose by the projection of the lower ends of the cells of **Philonotis fontana.** 110. Longitudinal cuticular ridges extending over the surface of the leaf of **Dicranoweisia crispula.**

genera are excurrent white hair points, either smooth or toothed, short or long—some occasionally as long as or longer than the blade in a few species (figs. 85–86). Hair points of this sort are often called awns. Well-developed costae may be quite flat, (only 2–4 cells thick but 6–10 cells wide), or convex to cylindrical, (often standing out conspicuously at the back of the blade), and 8–12 cells thick.

2.45   A costa is entirely lacking in *Sphagnum, Fontinalis,* and some species of *Campylium, Calliergon,* and *Neckera.* In *Hypnum, Plagiothecium,* and a few other genera and species, the costa is very weak, short, and double; in these it is usually less than ¼ the length of the blade (figs. 72 and 75). Some species of *Hygrohypnum* have stout forked costae reaching ¼–½ the length of the blade. In certain species of *Dicranum* the base of the costa often occupies as much as a third of the width of the leaf, while exceedingly wide costae occupy almost the entire width of the leaf above the thin sheathing base in *Polytrichum, Pogonatum, Distichium* and some species of *Bartramia* (fig. 82).

2.46   In *Crossidium* and *Aloina* (figs. 111, 112) the upper ventral side of the costa bears green filaments, 2–7 cells long, which range from few to numerous, are often very crowded, and appear as a dark green opaque mass. Lamellae are flat sheets of cells in 1–9 layers, attached by one edge lengthwise on the costa, especially in the Polytrichaceae. In most genera they occur only on the ventral side but in *Oligotrichum* they occur on the dorsal side as well. There may be as few as 2–4 in *Atrichum* and as many as 70 on the very wide costae of *Polytrichum*

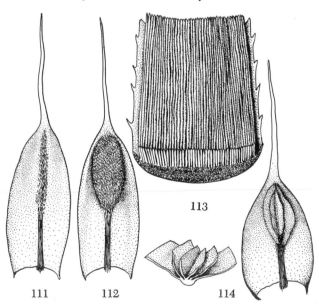

Figs. 111–114. Costal outgrowths. 111. Costal filaments of **Crossidium aberrans.** 112. Dense costal filaments of **Aloina pilifera.** 113. Costal lamellae of **Polytrichum commune.** 114. Costal lamellae of **Pterigoneurum ovatum,** ×10.

(fig. 113) and *Pogonatum*. Lamellae also occur in a few other genera; in *Pterygoneurum* 2–4 of them are borne on the upper side of the costa (fig. 114); in addition these sometimes bear masses of short chlorophyllose filaments on the inner faces.

2.47   The leaves of *Fissidens* are unique in that the 2 sides of the blade are folded together and clasp the stém as a pair of vaginant laminae, with 1 side prolonged to form a ventral terminal lamella; a dorsal lamella also extends down the back of the costa from the apex to the base or nearly so (fig. 115). Although these leaves appear to be inserted edgewise on the stem, they are actually no different in basic morphology from other moss leaves—as shown by the structure of the costa in the lower part of the leaf, where ventral guide cells are oriented transversely in the direction of the vaginant laminae which thus make up the true leaf. It is also revealing that the dorsal and ventral lamellae are lacking from the perigonial leaves and from some of the first formed leaves at the base of the stem (fig. 116).

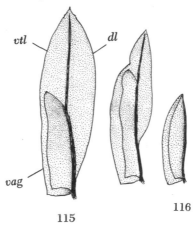

115   116

Figs. 115–116. Leaves of **Fissidens limbatus,** × 10. 115. Stem leaf, **vag,** vaginant lamina, **v t l,** ventral terminal lamina ,and **d l,** dorsal lamina. 116. Outer and inner perichaetial leaves, × 10.

2.48   The cells of the costa are generally longer and narrower than those of the lamina and range from 2 to many cells thick. In different genera and species the costae show considerable variation in anatomy, as revealed in cross and longitudinal sections. The highest development of the costa occurs in its broader, thicker, lower portion.

2.49   The costae of many mosses are composed of more or less homogeneous cells although cells in the central region are usually the largest and become gradually smaller, and sometimes thicker walled, toward the periphery. This condition occurs in some species with a fairly thick costa but more frequently in those with slender or weak costae (fig. 117).

2.50   Strong well-developed costae usually have a heterogeneous structure which shows in cross section a differentiation in cell size and wall thickness or in longitudinal section differences in linear dimensions. (The latter features are shown even better when the costae are mascerated to isolate the cells. This is done by trimming off the laminae and gently boiling the costae in concentrated nitric acid on a slide for a few moments; then the cells are carefully washed repeatedly with water. The cells may be teased apart with micro needles or gently rubbed apart with the finger pressing on a cover glass.) Some of the many structural forms of heterogeneous costae are described below:

2.51   1. Costae with medial guides. In a considerable number of mosses 1 or 2 rows of large, moderately thick-walled guide cells (the Deuter cells of the Germans) extend transversely through the costa in a line continuous with the cells of the laminae. Lengthwise they are mostly oblong to sublinear with the longitudinal walls thicker than the more or less transverse end walls; they bear some similarity to tracheids of higher plants (fig. 129). Standing next to them, dorsally and ventrally, are 1 to several irregular rows of small, thick-walled, more highly colored cells with very narrow lumina called stereids. Longitudinally they are mostly linear with slenderly tapering and strongly overlapping ends; they resemble libriform fibers of higher plants (figs. 130–131). They are commonly referred to as dorsal and ventral stereid bands, the former often being 1 to several cell layers thicker than the latter (figs. 118–19). The dorsal superficial cells may resemble the adjacent stereids or they may be slightly larger with wider luminae (fig. 122). In a few species, large thick-walled cells are interspersed singly among them. They may be smooth on the outer surface, papillose, or in some instances toothed from the upper ends. In a few mosses they bear dorsal ridges, as in *Dicranum scoparium*. The ventral superficial cells vary in different species. They may resemble the adjacent stereids or they may be much larger; in a few instances they are vertically elongated and often chlorophyllose (fig. 127). They may be smooth or papillose or bear costal filaments or lamellae.

2.52   2. Costae with subventral guides. Many mosses have only a dorsal stereid band with the subventral guides overlain with ventral superficial cells (figs. 120–21).

2.53   3. Costae with ventral guides. In a few mosses 1 or 2 rows of guide cells form the ventral surface of the costa with a dorsal stereid band or larger thinner-walled cells (figs. 122–23).

2.54   4. Costae with Begleiter cells. The costae of *Mnium* and the Polytrichaceae show a high degree of development, with groups of thinner-walled accessory cells dorsal to the guides; (figs. 124-25). In position and form they suggest a primitive phloem. The guide cells and Begleiter together resemble a primitive vascular bundle.

2.55   In *Mnium*, the costa is convex on both sides with a medial row of large, thin-walled, more or less angular guides subtended in the center by a small oval or round group of very small Begleiter cells; beneath

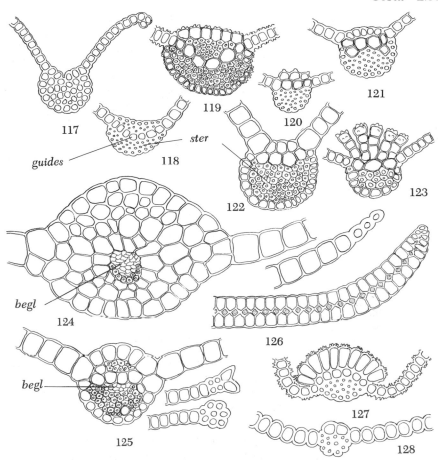

Figs. 117–128. Costal structures, × 100. 117. Homogeneous costa of **Grimmia.** 118–128. Heterogeneous costae. 118. **Eucladium verticillatum,** costa with medial guides and dorsal and ventral stereid bands. 119. **Tortella tenuirostre,** costa with medial guides, dorsal and ventral stereid bands and large ventral cells. 120–121. **Phascum cuspidatum** with subventral guides and large ventral cells. 122. **Merceya latifolia,** with two rows of ventral guides. 123. **Crossidium aberrans,** with ventral superficial guides bearing costal filaments. 124. **Mnium medium,** with medial guides in several irregular rows and **begl,** Begleiter cells and a small arc of stereids. 125. **Mnium marginatum,** with medial guides and **begl,** Begleiter cells and small thick-walled marginal cells, 2- to 3 stratose. 126. **Paraleucobryum enerve.** 127. **Desmatodon convolutus** with ventral cells vertically elongated. 128. **Pottia latifolia** with two ventral guides and small dorsal stereid band.

them are 2 rows of very small stereids. In *Mnium medium* 2–4 rows of large, chlorophyllose cells stand above and below, their walls becoming thicker and more highly colored as they approach maturity (fig. 124); in related species, isolated stereids are scattered among these green cells. In *Mnium serratum* there are ventral and dorsal stereid bands (fig. 125). The Begleiter cells often become crushed by the enlargement of the surrounding cells as the leaves become older; very often only a small, irregular, discolored spot marks their location.

25

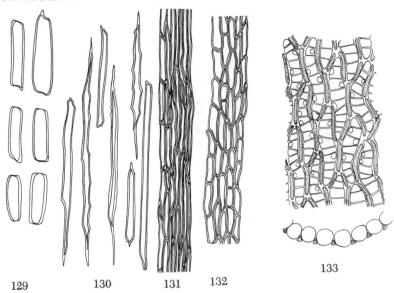

Figs. 129–133. Costal cells of **Merceya latifolia,** × 100. 129. Isolated guide cells. 130. Isolated stereids. 131. Stereids intact. 132. Dorsal epidermal cells intact. 133. Cells of a branch leaf of **Sphagnum squarrosum,** × 100.

2.56 In *Paraleucobryum* the costa occupies practically the entire width of the leaf, at least in the upper part, and is composed of large hyaline cells mixed with, or enclosing, small, angular chlorophyllose cells (fig. 126). In *Leucobryum* there are 2 or more layers of large hyaline cells with large internal pores and a submedial layer of small green cells.

2.57 In *Desmatodon convolutus* the costa is broadly convex on the ventral side and in cross section shows a cushionlike layer of large ventral cells above a single row of guides (fig. 127). *Pottia latifolia* has a slender costa with 2 ventral superficial guides and a small, dorsal stereid band (fig. 128).

2.58 The central part of the broad costa in various genera of the Polytrichaceae shows a similar arrangement of cells; however, the Begleiter cells are much larger and strung out in an irregular zone 2–3 layers thick, while the dorsal and ventral stereid bands often have larger cells interspersed among them. The dorsal epidermal cells are fairly large with moderately thick walls and a very thick cuticle on the outside. The ventral cells are large, thin walled and bear lamellae (plate 144, fig. 3, plates 145–48, fig. 5).

2.59 The leaves of *Sphagnum* consist of green linear cells which form a network of large, empty, rhomboidal, hyaline cells whose walls are reinforced on the inside with ringlike, or spiral, fibril bands; the leaves are usually perforated with large round or elliptical pores. According to the species, the chlorophyllose cells may have one face exposed on the ventral or the dorsal side of the leaf or on both sides; or they may be completely enclosed by the adjacent hyaline cells (fig. 133).

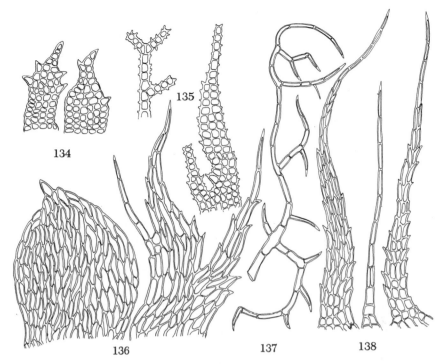

Figs. 134–138. Paraphyllia. 134. **Leskeella tectorum.** 135. **Thuidium abietinum.** 136. **Hypnum haldanianum.** 137. **Climacium dendroides.** 138. **Cratoneuron falcatum.**

PARAPHYLLIA

2.60 Paraphyllia are filamentous or small, leaflike outgrowths from the cells of the stems and are characteristic of certain genera and species of pleurocarpous mosses. They may be composed of cells arranged end to end in simple or branched filaments, as in *Climacium dendroides* (fig. 137), or they may develop a broader base, 2 to several cells wide, and taper to a slender apex as in *Thuidium abietinum* (fig. 135) and *Cratoneuron falcatum* (fig. 138). Small leaflike scales occur in many genera and may be sporadic in some species, as in *Leskeella tectorum* (fig. 134), and constant in others. In a number of genera they occur only at the bases or in the axils of branches. They become quite large and leaflike in a few species, as in *Hypnum haldanianum* (fig. 136), in which they are polymorphous, narrow to broad, and entire to palmately divided. In *Helodium* the paraphyllia are extremely crowded and cover also the base of the costa and margins of the leaves.

VEGETATIVE REPRODUCTION

2.61 Every living cell of the leafy moss plant is an independent unit, and under certain conditions each cell is capable of producing rhizoids and secondary protonemata which may give rise to buds and eventually new shoots. Thus, a single moss plant can produce numerous new shoots, which accounts for the propensity of these plants to form dense tufts and mats. Dry stems and leaves are more or less brittle and easily broken by the vicissitudes of nature. Such fragments transported by wind, water, and animals to favorable habitats may regenerate and establish new colonies. Many species, like *Tortula ruralis* and *Barbula vinealis,* seldom produce spores but become widely and abundantly distributed by vegetative means in dry regions of the western states.

2.62 Certain cells of the stems and leaves may produce specialized outgrowths called brood bodies, propagula, or gemmae, which become easily detached and propagate the plants. Large numbers of mosses are known to produce them, some rarely, others freely. Many of these struc-

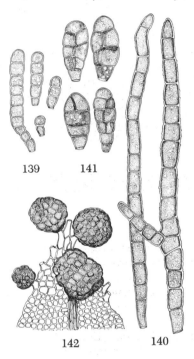

Figs. 139–142. Propagula, × 100. 139. **Orthotrichum pumilum.** 140. **Bryum capillare.** 141. **Dicranoweisia cirrata.** 142. **Grimmia hartmanii** var. **anomala.**

tures are somewhat rhizoidal in nature, usually lack chlorophyll, and consist of short cells with dense contents. As a rule, the walls are thick, yellowish brown, reddish, or sometimes nearly black, smooth or papillose. In some mosses they are unicellular; more often they are multicellular and shortly cylindrical, as in some species of *Orthotrichum* in which they are borne on both sides of the leaves (fig. 139), or in clusters at the ends of the costae. Sterile plants of *Bryum capillare* often produce dense clusters of simple or branched filamentous brood bodies in the axils of leaves (fig. 140). In many mosses the propagula assume a variety of definite forms—elliptical, obovoid, fusiform, or globose, as in *Dicranoweisia cirrata* (fig. 141). *Grimmia hartmanii* var. *anomala* produces multicellular globose brood bodies in clusters at the tips of the upper leaves (fig. 142). A considerable number of mosses sporadically produce similar bodies on the rhizoids.

2.63 Propagula of a different sort are produced by a few mosses; for example, the main stem of *Aulacomnium androgynum* is prolonged beyond the apical leaves into a naked green "pseudopodium" on which minute fusiform propagula are borne in a globose head at the summit (fig. 143). On a favorable substratum, these bodies give rise to secondary protonemata and rhizoids. *Aulacomnium palustre* produces similar pseudopodia but with some propagula scattered below and others clustered toward the summit (fig. 144).

2.64 Bulbils—propagula which are essentially buds with incipient stems and leaves—grow into new plants after falling on a favorable substratum. Sterile plants of *Leptobryum pyriforme,* especially when grown in greenhouses, occasionally produce dark, purplish, globose bulbils singly on the stems; these are easily visible to the naked eye. Sterile plants of

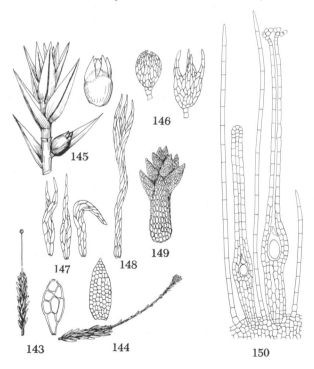

Figs. 143–150. Propagulae, gemmae, archegonia. 143. **Aulacomnium androgynum** and 144. **A. palustre** showing pseudopodia bearing propagulae, × .25 and × 35. 145–149. Gemmae. 145. **Pohlia rothii,** × 2.5 and × 5. 146. **Pohlia bulbifera,** × 20. 147. **Pohlia proligera,** × 25. 148. **Pohlia annotina** var. **decipiens,** × 25. 149. **Philonotis marchica,** brood branch, × 25. 150. Young and mature archegonia of **Bryum caespiticium,** × 100.

some species of *Pohlia* commonly produce brood bodies of characteristic and recognizable forms. In *Pohlia rothii,* red ovoid brood bodies
with several leaf points are borne in the axils of leaves, either singly
(fig. 145) or occasionally in groups of 2–4. Sometimes they elongate
and acquire more leaves before they are shed. The gemmae of *Pohlia
bulbifera* are much smaller, yellowish, obovoid bodies with several
clasping or erect leaf points (fig. 146). They are usually abundant and
occur 2 or 3 together in each leaf axil on stalks of 2 or 3 cells. In
Pohlia proligera the brood bodies are small, yellowish green, slender
bodies with 1 or 2 leaf points and occur in groups of 4 or more in each
leaf axil. They range from elliptical to linear and are straight or variously contorted, sometimes hooked (fig. 147). *Pohlia annotina* var. *loeskei*
bears 2–5 yellowish green brood bodies in each leaf axil, which often
give the upper part of the sterile stems a fuzzy appearance. Each has a
tiny, elongated, twisted stem with 2–4 erect, acute leaf points (fig. 148).
Several species of *Philonotis* occasionally develop slender brood
branches with small leaves. They form a basal abscission zone of enlarged inflated cells which causes the branch to separate from the
stem (fig. 149). The main stem of *Pohlia wahlenbergii* may develop a
reddish abscission zone of thin-walled cells causing the terminal portion
of the current season's growth to fall.

SEXUAL REPRODUCTION

2.65   The female sex organ, the archegonium, is a small cylindrical structure
consisting of a slender neck at the base of which is a slightly dilated
venter mounted on a rather stout stalk. At maturity the neck is tubular
and is made up of a single layer of cells disposed in superimposed
circular tiers of 6 cells that surround an axial row of neck canal cells.
The venter, (and often the adjoining base of the neck), may become
2–4 cells thick, according to the species, and contains the ventral cell
and egg (fig. 150). The neck may range from as few as 12 to as many
as 40 cells in length. The basal stalk is solid and several cells thick.
The archegonia are borne at the tips of the stems or branches, or in
lateral buds in clusters ranging from a few to as many as 60, according
to the species.

2.66   Paraphyses are erect, sterile, hairlike organs which surround or are
scattered among the archegonia. They consist of cylindrical or barrel-
shaped cells arranged end to end forming filaments of uniform diameter
in most species, but in others they are clavate, or club shaped, the upper
cells becoming wider toward the summit (and in a few mosses 2–4
cells wide). They are longer than the archegonia and serve as an extra
means of protection. The cells contain a few chloroplasts which disappear with age, while the walls may remain colorless or become
tinted—yellowish, brownish, or red—especially at the tips. Paraphyses
are numerous in most species but few or even lacking in others. Clusters
of archegonia and paraphyses are surrounded by a number of protective leaves forming a female bud, the perichaetium. Such leaves are
called perichaetial leaves.

2.67 Acrocarpous mosses bear the archegonia and later the sporophyte at the apex of the main stem or a well-developed branch, and since one of the archegonia originates from the apical cell, the forward growth of the axis is terminated. This is the basic feature of this group of mosses, nearly all of which grow erect and are more or less tufted. In many acrocarpous mosses the female buds are scarcely distinguishable from the comal buds of sterile stems. However in some genera and species of this group, the female buds are quite evident because of larger or longer perichaetial leaves.

2.68 Pleurocarpous mosses bear the archegonia in small slender buds at the sides of the main stems and therefore do not terminate the forward growth of the main axis. The perichaetial leaves are much longer and narrower than stem leaves.

2.69 The male sex organ is an antheridium which is made up of a short basal stalk that supports a sac, 1 cell layer thick, in which sperm cells develop (fig. 155 l, m). According to the species, the sacs range from shortly ovoid to cylindrical. When young, they are green—the jacket cells containing chloroplasts—but as they mature, the chloroplasts disappear and the cell walls of old empty sacs usually become brown or reddish. Paraphyses are also associated with antheridia and are commonly of the same sort as those in the female buds of the corresponding species. They range from few in *Grimmia* to very abundant in *Philonotis*.

2.70 The perigonium is the male bud and consists of a cluster of antheridia and paraphyses surrounded by more or less specialized perigonial leaves (figs. 151–52). The number of antheridia in a single perigonium ranges from a few in some species to as many as 100 in others. In most acrocarpous mosses the antheridia terminate the growth on the main stems and branches.

2.71 Superficially, the terminal perigonia may not be readily distinguishable from the tips of sterile stems because the perigonial leaves are some-

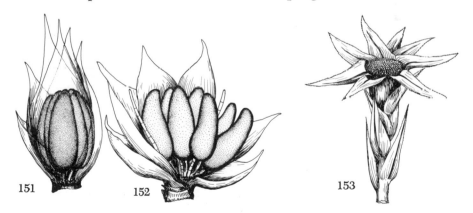

Figs. 151–153. Perigonia. 151. Budlike perigonium of **Grimmia dupretii,** × 20. 152. The same dissected to show the antheridia, × 20. 153. Discoid perigonium of **Philonotis fontana** showing the specialized perigonial leaves, × 5.

times scarcely differentiated and it may be necessary to dissect the stem tips in order to demonstrate the presence of the antheridia, especially when there are only a few of them. In a few species, however, the terminal perigonia are more or less swollen and budlike, or they may be discoid with large numbers of antheridia and paraphyses clearly exposed and often brightly colored. Also, in such cases, the perigonial leaves are usually larger and of different shape than the subtending stem leaves. For example, in some dioicous species of *Pohlia* the perigonium is budlike with the bases of the perigonial leaves broadly dilated and clasping one another, while the upper portions are abruptly narrowed to slender limbs (plate 72, fig. 12). Among species with discoid perigonia, dioicous species of *Mnium* have broad perigonial leaves which form a cup around the central disc; *Polytrichum* has perigonial leaves with broadly clasping bases, abruptly narrowing to short erect tips forming a cup, and those of *Philonotis fontana* have similar clasping leaf bases but with longer and narrower limbs which spread radially, like a little calyx surrounding a bright reddish disc (fig. 153).

2.72 Lateral perigonia are borne in the axils of stem leaves in all pleurocarpous mosses and some autoicous acrocarpous mosses. They are usually small and ± ovoid, with the perigonial leaves much smaller than the stem leaves, usually broadly ovate to shortly ovate-lanceolate and closely imbricated. In acrocarpous mosses they commonly occur immediately below the perichaetium, as in autoicous species of *Grimmia* and *Orthotrichum*. In many mosses the antheridia are quite small, often few in number and with infrequent or no paraphyses.

2.73 Some mosses have the male and female organs segregated on male and female plants, a condition described as dioicous or unisexual. Both sex organs occur on the same plants in monoicous (bisexual) species. Monoicous plants may be synoicous (with archegonia and antheridia in the same inflorescences), paroicous (with antheridia just below the terminal group of archegonia, but in or very near the same inflorescence), or autoicous (with separate male and female inflorescences on the same plants).

2.74 Certain other mosses give evidence that the disposition of the sexes is not always constant. For example, some stems of *Atrichum undulatum* and *A. papillosum* produce antheridia the first year and archegonia the following years. Certain species of *Bryum* and *Mnium* may have both dioicous and synoicous plants growing in the same tuft. Again, synoicous plants and strictly archegonial plants are often found mixed together with no strictly antheridial plants in evidence. More rarely one may find 1 or 2 antheridia in a female bud of an otherwise autoicous species, especially among pleurocarpous mosses.

DEVELOPMENT OF THE ARCHEGONIUM AND ANTHERIDIUM

2.75 The ontogeny of the archegonia of mosses is essentially uniform. In *Bryum pseudotriquetrum,* the archegonium originates as a papilla at the stem tip (fig. 154a). It divides by 2 vertically diagonal walls (fig. 154b, c) which result in a 2-sided apical cell (fig. 154d) that divides again by similarly diagonal walls until 4–8 segments are formed (fig. 154e); these become the basal stalk. The apical cell then becomes 3-sided (fig. 154f) and each face cuts off a single segment (fig. 154g). The apical cell then divides more or less transversely and forms a cover cell (fig. 154h) and a central cell (fig. 154i). Next, the 3 segments which surround the central cell divide vertically to form a tier of 6 cells (fig. 154j); these in turn divide transversely several times to form the lower part of the neck (fig. 154k). Anticlinal divisions of the cover cell form the upper part of the neck (fig. 154l), while transverse divisions of the central cell (fig. 154m) give rise to an axial row of neck canal cells (fig. 154n), the lowest member of which is the primary ventral canal cell (fig. 154o) that finally divides into a ventral canal cell (fig. 154p) and larger egg (fig. 154q).

2.76   The antheridium originates at the tip of the stem as a papilla that divides transversely 2 or 3 times (fig. 155a, b). The terminal cell then divides by a vertically diagonal wall (fig. 155c), followed by a similar division at an angle with the first wall (fig. 155d). This forms a 2-sided apical cell that divides repeatedly in a similar manner, cutting off 5–10 segments right and left. At this stage the young antheridium is round in cross section and shows 2 segments, one usually larger than the other (fig. 155e). The larger cell divides more or less vertically (fig.

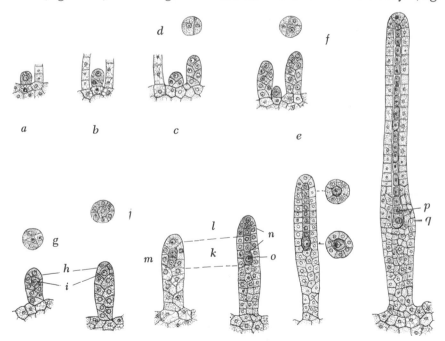

Fig. 154. Ontogeny of the archegonium of **Bryum pseudotriquetrum,** × 100. Explanation in text.

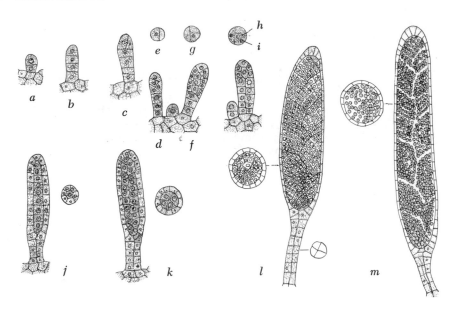

Fig. 155. Ontogeny of the antheridium of **Bryum creberrimum**, × 100. Explanation in text.

155f) from the outer wall of the larger cell to the inner wall of the smaller one (fig. 155g) and results in 2 unequal cells. The larger of the cells appears somewhat triangular in cross section and divides by a vertical periclinal wall to cut off an inner primary spermatogenous cell (fig. 155h) and an outer jacket cell (fig. 155i). The 3 jacket cells which result from these divisions divide further by anticlinal and transverse divisions as the antheridium increases in size. Simultaneously the primary spermatogenous cells divide—at first by transverse walls—and form a single row (fig. 155j). Later they divide in 3 directions, giving rise to numerous small sperm mother cells (fig. 155k, l, m).

2.77   A succession of antheridia comes to maturity over a period of 1 to several weeks according to the species. When fully ripe and moistened with dew, rain, or melting snow, the jacket cells and the mucilaginous sperm mass absorb water, which creates internal pressure. Finally the larger cells at the tip of the antheridium split apart and the viscid substance containing the sperm quickly oozes out. The cytoplasmic residue around the individual sperm rapidly dissolves. The sperm become active and swim about freely while movement of the surrounding water aids in transporting them to the archegonia.

2.78   When the archegonia reach maturity, the walls of the neck-canal cells break down and the protoplasts form a mucilaginous substance which absorbs water at those times which would also be favorable to the discharge of sperms. The neck cells also become swollen; the internal pressure causes the cells at the tip of the neck to spread apart, like a little funnel, and the mucilage oozes out. It obviously has a chemotropic attraction for the sperms since they swim around the orifice and make their way down the neck canal, often in great numbers. Eventually one of the sperms penetrates the egg membrane at a receptive spot, thus effecting fertilization. The fertilized egg, the zygote, is the first cell of the sporophyte generation.

THE SPOROPHYTE

2.79   The first division of the zygote is transverse and cuts off a lower cell that gives rise to a shortly cylindrical foot and an upper cell which in turn gives rise to a cylindrical "spear" which differentiates later into a stalk (seta) and a capsule (sporogonium). The extent to which the spear elongates varies, according to the species, from shorter than the capsule to several cm long. The foot, seta, and capsule constitute the sporophyte which remains attached to the gametophyte.

2.80   The first division of the foot initial is diagonal to the original transverse wall. This is followed by a second wall diagonal to the first. The resultant 2-sided apical cell divides further with similar diagonal walls cutting to the right and left. Shortly after the segments are cut off they divide again by periclinal walls; the inner and outer cells thus formed then divide by anticlinal walls (fig. 156). As the cells become elongated, further divisions are more irregular and the identity of the apical cell becomes more or less obscured. The foot as an absorbing organ probably draws nourishment from the mother plant. At the same time, it exerts a stimulating effect, probably hormonal in nature, upon the tissue of the stem tip which causes the cells to proliferate and grow into a short, fleshy, cylindrical sheath called a vaginula. Unfertilized archegonia are commonly scattered over the surface of this structure.

2.81   The upper segment of the zygote divides in a similar manner to form a 2-sided apical cell which cuts off cells by diagonal walls, alternately right and left (fig. 156, 1–1). The segments are irregular but tend to become more regular as they grow; the outer portions of the primary walls tend to become horizontal (fig. 156, 2–2) and the inner portions somewhat vertical in a zigzag fashion (fig. 156, 3–3). During this reorientation, second vertical walls form at right angles to the zigzag walls so that in cross section there are 4 triangular cells, like pie sections (fig. 158a, b). Each of the latter divides by an anticlinal wall from the original outer wall to one of the inner walls, forming 2 cells, 1 triangular and the other 4-sided (fig. 158b, 1, 2). Next, the 4-sided cells divide by periclinal walls so that the outer daughter cells, together with the 4 triangular cells of the previous division, form 8 amphithecial cells which surround the 4 inner endothecial cells (fig. 158e, f, g). The endothecial cells then divide by periclinal walls to form 4 central cells and 4 surrounding cells which quickly divide again by anticlinal walls (fig. 158h). These divisions are again repeated and result in about 16 rather large central cells and about 24 to 30 somewhat smaller cells in a single layer with denser contents (fig. 158i). Meanwhile the amphithecial cells divide repeatedly, first by periclinal walls, later by anticlinal walls; the resultant cells are disposed in more or less regularly radiating rows (fig. 158i and j).

2.82 Apical growth repeats these events as the cells elongate proximally; the amphithecial cells give rise to the cortex of the seta while those of the endothecium form the central strand. As the embryo grows, the cells of the surrounding archegonium divide repeatedly and give rise to a sheath, the calyptra, which encloses the spearlike sporophyte (fig. 157 cal). Accelerated growth of the spear tears away the calyptra from the vaginula. It is carried upward on the elongating tip, and serves as a protective hood over the tender growing point; the cell walls early become very thick (fig. 158a, cal). In a few mosses, particularly in the Orthotrichaceae, the base of the calyptra is left at the summit of the

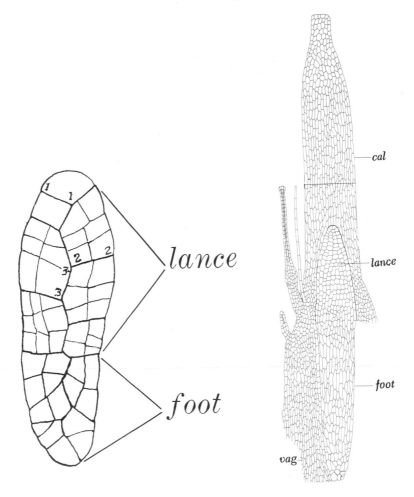

Figs. 156–157. Embryo. 156. Young embryo of **Bryum creberrimum** showing early stages of the foot and sporophyte lance, ×300. 157. Young embryo of **Bryum caespiticium** with associated sporophyte tissues, ×100.

36

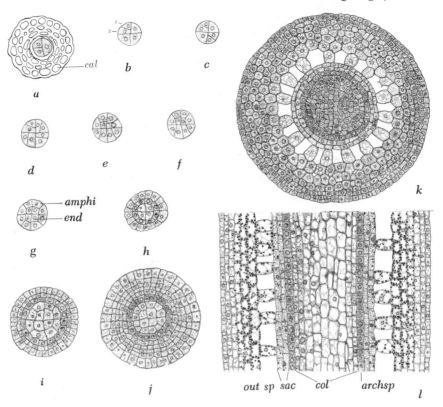

Fig. 158. Ontogeny of the sporophyte, **Bryum caespiticium,** ×75. Explanation in text.

vaginula and forms a short, collarlike sheath around the base of the seta called an ocrea (plate 53, fig. 5). Further details of the calyptra will be discussed later.

2.83   The seta matures from the base upward, the lower part often reaching maturity before the terminal capsular part is fully differentiated. In most species the structure of the seta resembles that of the stem. A central strand of small, more or less thin-walled, angular cells with transverse end walls, merges with an outer rind of small, thick-walled colored cells. In *Grimmia calyptrata* the slender seta has a small central strand (fig. 159); in *Mnium medium* the stouter seta has a proportionately larger central strand (fig. 160). In *Timmia bavarica* the central strand is fairly large and surrounded by a sheath of large, thick-walled cells which resembles an endodermis (fig. 161). In the seta of *Polytrichum juniperinum* the cells of the central strand are proportionately larger and thicker-walled than those of other mosses and also have a thicker-walled endodermal sheath. The inner cortex consists of large, thin-walled, loosely connected cylindrical cells with large intercellular air spaces which abruptly give way to a broad outer rind of small, very thick-walled cells of the outer cortex (figs. 162–63).

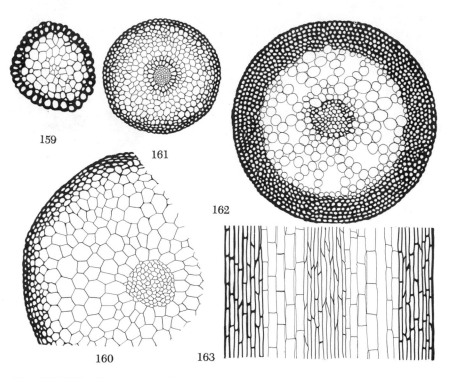

Figs. 159–163. Structure of the setae, ×75. 159. **Grimmia calyptra.** 160. **Mnium medium.** 161. **Timmia bavarica.** 162–163. **Polytrichum juniperinum.** Explanation in text.

2.84 As the seta approaches maximum length, the capsule begins to differentiate. Cell division becomes less regular; the outer layer of denser endothecial cells gives rise to a single layer of archesporial cells; and the central cells give rise to a rather large columella. The innermost cells of the amphithecium, next to the archesporium, become periclinally elongated and form the first layer of the outer part of the spore sac. Differences in the rate of division among the distal cells cause certain adjacent cells to separate—creating air spaces (fig. 158k). The same tissues are shown in medial longitudinal section at a slightly later stage (fig. 158l). At this stage the neck of the young capsule is much distended by air spaces and the sporangial region is much narrower (fig. 164). From this stage onward the single layer of archesporial cells divides periclinally into 2 layers and shortly afterward the cells begin to separate into spore mother cells which are suspended in a mucilaginous liquid. The spore mother cells assume a rounded shape and draw nourishment from this liquid during reduction division and formation of spore tetrads. During these events the sporangial region becomes distended and the capsule assumes the mature form shown in fig. 165. From an early stage of the embryo, the cells of the amphithecium and their derivatives are chlorophyllose and photosynthetically active; it is only during the maturation of the spores that

38

the chlorophyll disappears from the sporophyte. In most mosses the sporogenous cells cease at the point where the cells of columella and amphithecium together constitute the neck. The sporogenous cells also cease slightly below the mouth where the columella and amphithecial cells continue into the lid (fig. 165). At maturity, 2 or 3 layers of narrower cells derived from both the amphithecium and endothecium make up the tubular wall which surrounds the columella (fig. 165, sp.). The cells of the epidermis (the exothecial cells in bryological terminology) become variously thicker walled and colored; and in many species true stomata may be formed either in the neck or sporangial region, or both (fig. 165 st). Usually a stomata mother cell assumes a somewhat oval shape and then divides through the long axis. The middle lamella between the resultant guard cells partially dissolves and gives rise to a slitlike pore. In a few mosses, as in *Funaria*, the middle

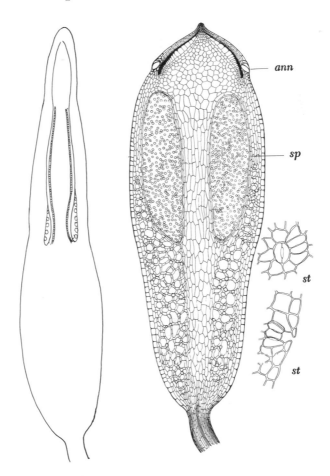

Figs. 164–165.   Bryum caespiticium. 164. Longitudinal section of a young capsule, ×75. 165. Longitudinal section of a mature capsule, **ann**, annulus, **sp**, sporangium wall, ×50. **st**, stomata, ×100.

lamella and subsequent stomatal pore form only in the middle of the mother cell which becomes a single guard cell with a central pore.

THE PERISTOME

2.85 The distal end of the capsule is closed by an operculum or lid which is usually separable from the sporangial part when mature and dry, because of a ring of specialized cells, the annulus (fig. 165 ann). The lid is commonly 2 to several cell layers thick. Within the opercular region, there arises a circle of rigid elongated teeth which collectively constitute a peristome. The lower families of the *Bryales* have a single peristome of 16 teeth (figs. 166–67), whereas the more advanced families have a second inner circle of thinner processes which make up the endostome. In addition, slender hairlike processes may be present;

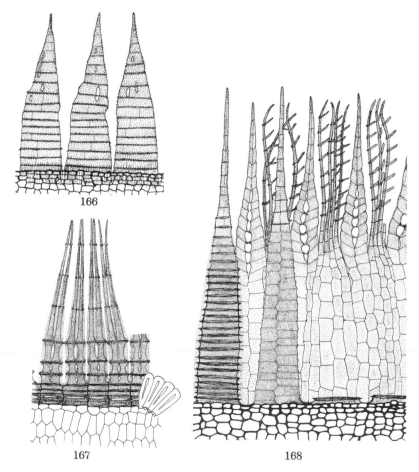

166

167   168

Figs. 166–168. Peristome teeth, ×50. 166. Single teeth of **Grimmia dupretii.** 167. Single teeth of **Ceratodon purpureus,** each tooth divided into two divisions. 168. Double peristome of **Bryum caespiticium** showing endostome of segments and cilia arising from a high basal membrane.

they are called cilia, to distinguish them from the broader segments of the endostome (figs. 168–69).

2.86   Different groups of mosses show much variation in the ontogeny of the peristome. Cross sections near the base of the lid and medial longitudinal sections of submature capsules show the manner in which the peristome develops. Figs. 172 and 173 show such sections of *Bryum caespiticium,* which exemplifies the formation of the peristomes in Bryaceae, Bartramiaceae, and most pleurocarpous mosses. The annulus of *Bryum* consists of a row of small cells and 2 rows of much enlarged cells with very thick walls when fully mature. The epidermal cells of the lid become thick walled (figs. 172 and 173a) and are subtended by 2 layers of thin-walled cells (fig. 173b). Beneath the latter

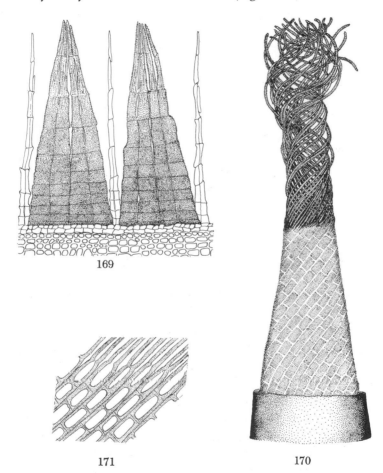

Figs. 169–171. Peristome teeth. 169. Double peristome of **Orthotrichum alpestre,** teeth in pairs, endostome of eight cilia. 170. Single peristome of **Tortula norvegica,** basically of 16 teeth united into a high basal tube and divided above into 32 hairlike, spirally twisted divisions. 171. Junction of the basal tube and the separation of the teeth into hairlike divisions, × 100.

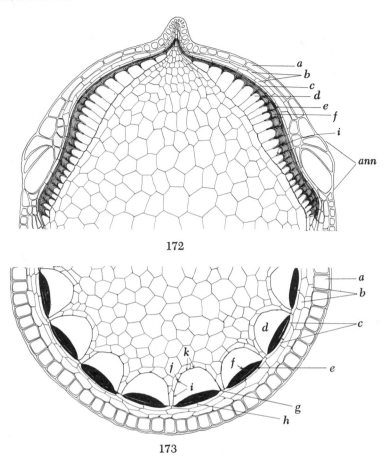

Figs. 172–173. Bryum caespiticium. 172. Medial longitudinal section through the lid and mouth of the capsule, ×100. 173. Cross section through the base of the lid, ×100. Explanation in text.

are 2 concentric rows of cells, an outer row of 32 small flat cells (fig. 173c) and an inner row of 16 greatly enlarged cells (fig. 173d). These are disposed so that 2 small outer cells are opposite a single large inner cell. The teeth are formed by the deposition of successive layers of wall substance on the inner periclinal walls of the outer row of 32 small cells (figs. 172 and 173e) and by very thick layers on the outer periclinal and horizontal walls of the inner row of 16 large cells (fig. 173f). The thickenings do not quite reach the vertical anticlinal walls (fig. 173g) which remain thin and break apart at maturity, thus separating the teeth. When the vertical anticlinal walls of the smaller outer cells which stand opposite the center of the large cells (fig. 173h) dry out and break up at maturity, they leave a divisural zigzag line extending down the outer face of each tooth. The thick horizontal walls form the ventral lamellae (fig. 173i).

2.87 The endostome is formed by much lighter thickenings on the inner periclinal walls of the 16 large cells (figs. 172 and 173i) and the outer adjacent walls of the numerous small internal cells (fig. 173j). The lower part of the endostome remains intact as a basal membrane, but the upper part becomes split into 16 keeled segments, which alternate with the teeth, and 1–3 cilia opposite each tooth (fig. 173k).

2.88 In *Timmia bavarica* the events in the origin of the peristome are much the same as in *Bryum*. The 16 wide cells of the inner row are radially enlarged and do not form ventral lamellae. Also, the thickening on the inner faces of the joints is uniform and moderate on the lower half of each tooth; but the upper part is laid down in the form of thick vertical bars or ridges making it appear strongly striated. The basal membrane comprises the lower third of the endostome and arises in a manner similar to that in *Bryum,* but the cells are more strongly thickened (fig. 174c). However, at the upper limit of the basal membrane the thickening changes abruptly. At this point, 4 vertical rows of cells opposite each tooth form 4 stout cilia by the deposition of a thick vertical bar of wall substance on the outer periclinal wall of each cell so that it projects into the lumen (fig. 175b). There are 64 cilia at their points of origin; further up adjacent pairs unite to form 32 bars opposite each tooth, and pairs of these in turn unite still higher up to form 16 cilia at the summit (plate 66, fig. 5).

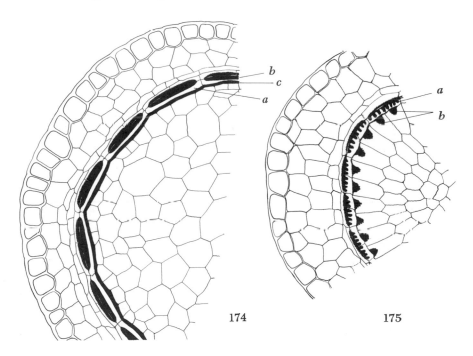

Figs. 174–175. Cross section through the base of the lid of **Timmia bavarica.** 175. Cross section through the upper part of the lid, ×100. Explanation in text.

2.89   In *Funaria hygrometrica* cross sections through the lower part of the lid show 16 large cells between adjacent rows of 32 cells each. In this case, the outer teeth form in a manner similar to those of *Bryum* but only the inner walls of the same large cells become lightly thickened and form 16 shorter segments opposite the teeth. Eventually the 2 rows become separated when the anticlinal walls of the original 16 cells dry out and break apart at maturity (plate 62, fig. 7).

2.90   *Tortula norvegica* has a peristome of 32 very long, spirally twisted, hairlike teeth arising from a high basal tube in which the cells are disposed in 16 spiral rows (fig. 170). At the summit of the basal tube, heavy thickenings develop close to the longitudinal anticlinal walls of each spiral row of cells and separate into 2 hairlike teeth (fig. 171). Cross sections of submature capsules near the base of the tall, beaklike lid show a single layer of thin-walled cells beneath the thick-walled epidermis, and internal to these thin-walled cells is a circle of 16 wide cells which (fig. 177a) abuts 16 to 32 internal cells (fig. 177b), the number varying at different levels. The peristome tube is formed by the thickening of the inner periclinal walls of the 16 outer cells and the outer periclinal walls of the inner circle of cells (figs. 176 and 177c). This is the reverse of the situation in *Bryum* where there are 32 outer cells and 16 inner ones. At the summit of the tube, the thickening of the periclinal walls becomes abruptly restricted to thick, papillose, longitudinal strands, which become the hairlike teeth and are adjacent to the thin anticlinal walls (figs. 176, 178 and 179d).

2.91   In most other genera and familes with a single peristome, the situation at the base of the developing peristome is much the same as that shown in fig. 177 except that the basal tube may be very much shorter or lacking. The 16 vertical rows of wide cells split to the base at maturity into separate entire teeth (fig. 166), or the teeth may be variously cleft or divided into 2 or more narrow divisions (fig. 167). Among some genera and species, the peristome may be poorly developed or entirely lacking because of the failure of the cell walls to become thickened in the usual manner.

CAPSULES

2.92   The form of the capsule and the mode of origin of the archesporial cells and of the peristome are major criteria upon which the orders of mosses are based. In the various families and genera of the *Bryales* the peristomes all originate in the same general manner although they may differ in form and smaller details. Brief descriptions of the orders follow, so that the differing characteristics may be distinguished.

2.93   TETRAPHIDALES. *Tetraphis pellucida* has a cylindrical capsule with a tall, conical lid beneath which 4 large, solid teeth occupy the entire inner part (fig. 180). The lid separates from the urn along the middle lamellae between the thick-walled marginal cells of the lid and the thinner-walled marginal cells of the mouth (fig. 181). Cross sections through the base of the lid of the young capsules show a single layer of large

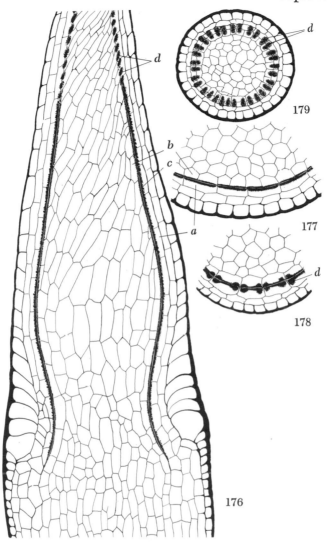

Figs. 176–179. Tortula norvegica. 176. Medial longitudinal section through the lid and mouth of the capsule. 177. Cross section through the base of the lid. 178. Cross section through the middle of the lid. 179. Cross section through the upper part of the lid, ×100. Explanation in text.

epidermal cells subtended by 3 concentric circles of small, thick-walled cells and a central core of large thin-walled cells (fig. 182). At maturity the single layer of lid cells separates from the outer circle of small thick-walled cells while the latter, together with all of the inner cells, splits into 4 large divisions (fig. 183). Fig. 184 shows the dorsal aspect of a single unjointed tooth composed of oblong to linear cells with overlapping ends. When dry, the capsule contracts below the mouth and the teeth gape open allowing the spores to escape (fig. 180b). When moistened, the capsule swells and the teeth clamp tightly together (fig. 180c).

45

2.94 **BUXBAUMIALES.** This is a small order of mosses which includes 4 genera with greatly reduced gametophytes and rather large, dorsoventrally asymmetric capsules with thin walls and a very large, continuous air chamber traversed by filamentous trabeculae of cylindrical cells arranged end to end (fig. 186).

2.95 In *Buxbaumia* the gametophyte consists mainly of a densely branched protonema upon which a very short stem arises and bears minute, scalelike, deeply dentate or laciniate leaves which wither away after fertilization. The stem and sporophyte subsequently become partially saprophytic on humus, in soil, or on rotten wood by the development of abundant rhizoids emanating from the thickened, somewhat tuberous vaginule. The seta is stout, 1.5–2 cm tall, dark reddish, and beset with warty protuberances which are composed of 1–3(4) cells. Internally

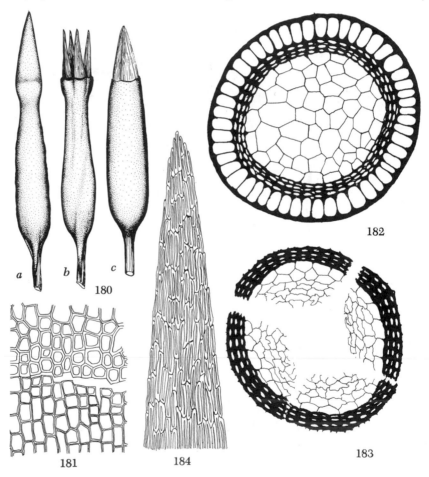

Figs. 180–184. Tetraphis pellucida. 180. Capsules, ×10. 181.. Thick-walled cells of the lid separating from the thinner-walled cells of the mouth, ×100. 182. Cross section through the base of the lid. 183. Cross section through the four teeth, ×50. Explanation in text. 184. Dorsal surface of a tooth, ×50.

there is a well-defined central strand surrounded by an inner cortex of vertically cylindrical cells with large intercellular spaces, similar to those in the setae of *Polytrichum,* and an outer cortex of very thick-walled reddish cells. The spore sac portion of the capsule is ovate, 2–4 mm long, and oblique to the small, short neck (figs. 186, 187). The dorsal surface is flattish and the ventral surface broadly ventricose with a shiny reddish ring of small thick-walled cells around the periphery at the junction of the two surfaces (fig. 185). The small neck joins the ventral posterior portion; internally it has an air chamber which surrounds the columella. The small mouth and conical lid protrude from the anterior tip on the dorsal side and are generally upturned like a little beak. The lid separates from the urn by a false annulus composed of several layers of irregular, thick-walled, reddish brown cells within its base. After the lid falls this structure is revealed as a conspicuous, low, tubelike crown around the mouth of the capsule (fig. 188a). Sometimes it becomes cleft into triangular divisions. The annulus of most mosses is made up of 2 to several rows of differentiated epidermal cells, but the annulus in *Buxbaumiales* arises from several layers of differentiated subepidermal

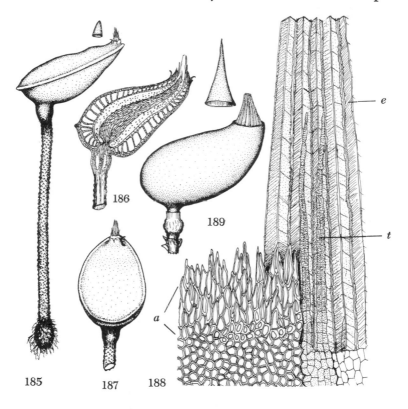

Figs. 185–189. Capsules. 185–188. **Buxbaumia aphylla.** 185. Sporophyte, side view. 186. Longitudinal section of capsule. 187. Dorsal view of capsule, ×10. 188. Portion of the peristome: **a,** false annulus, **t,** peristome tooth, **e,** pleated endostome, ×50. 189. **Diphyscium foliosum.** Side view of sporophyte, ×10.

cells. The peristome is variable and may consist of from 1–4 rings of papillose, linear to filiform teeth of various lengths (fig. 188t). Each tooth originates from 3 vertical rows of cells with greatly thickened adjacent walls in a manner similar to the formation of the teeth of *Bryum*. The high, truncated, conical endostome is pale whitish, 16- to 32-keeled, and pleated to the summit with no divisions into segments or cilia (fig. 188e). The angles of the pleats are thickened and rather strongly papillose, while the intervening plates are thin and smooth or very finely papillose. The origin of the endostome is much like that of the basal membrane of *Bryum*.

2.96   In *Diphyscium foliosum* the stem is very short and bears oblong to linear leaves with percurrent costae and small, isodiametric, papillose cells, much like those of *Didymodon* or *Tortella* among the Pottiaceae. The perichaetial leaves, however, are very different—much larger and ovate-lanceolate with a stout, long, excurrent costa and laciniate apex. The plump, elongate-ovoid capsules are immersed and nearly sessile, broadly ventricose on the ventral side, with the mouth and tall conical lid directed upward (fig. 189). They sit obliquely on a very short seta and are nestled within the perichaetial leaves like chubby little birds sitting on nests with their beaks facing the strongest incidence of light. A distinct annulus derived from the epidermal cells is present. The high, truncated, pale endostome is exactly like that of *Buxbaumia*, except that it is constantly 16-keeled. The outer peristome is lacking or has only 16 very short teeth which alternate with the outer papillose keels of the endostome.

2.97   POLYTRICHALES.   The capsules in this order differ from those described above in several respects. The spore sac extends to the base of the capsule and has air chambers between it and the columella and also between it and the exothecial cells; the neck may be very short or suppressed while the summit of the seta in most species is dilated and forms a spongy swelling with numerous stomata called an hypophysis. The latter is often separated from the capsule by a constriction. The peristome is made up of 32–64 short, solid, ligulate teeth (fig. 190). A medial ridge, 4–6 cells high, extends upward from the base of each tooth on the inside; it decreases in height toward the summit. Thus, the teeth are somewhat triangular in cross section near the base (fig. 191). The cells of the columella, at the level of the inward arched teeth, form a thin membrane, an epiphragm of small angular cells in a single layer which stretches across the mouth. The tips of the teeth are attached to it in little depressions around the perimeter. The teeth are composed of linear, thick-walled, fiberlike cells which extend vertically up the sides and meet at the apex of each tooth. At the base they arch sideways and meet similar cells of the adjacent teeth (fig. 190). At the base, the teeth join a broad zone of thick-walled cells arranged in more or less regular rows. In very young capsules before the teeth are formed, all the cells in this area are transversely oblong and disposed in more or less vertical rows. In forming the teeth, these cells begin to elongate laterally and to exert pressure on each other around the cir-

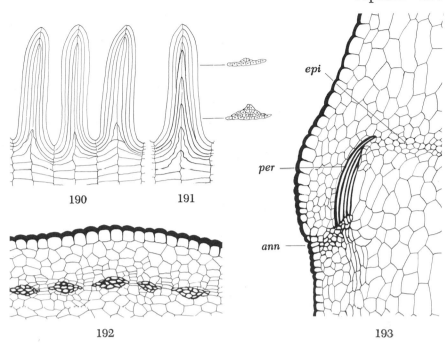

Figs. 190 193. Polytrichum junipcrinum. 190. Dorsal view of three peristome teeth. 191. Ventral view of a single tooth with three cross sections. 192. Cross section through the base of the lid showing the developing teeth, ×50. 193. Medial longitudinal section through the lid and mouth of a submature capsule showing the **ann**, annulus, **per**, peristome tooth, and **epi**, the developing epiphragm, ×50.

cumference of the capsule. Since the cell walls are thin and plastic, adjacent vertical rows become arched upward (fig. 190). Eventually the cells become very long, the walls heavily thickened, and the lumina very narrow or nearly closed.

2.98   Cross sections of submature capsules, slightly above the level of the annulus, show rather large epidermal cells with thick walls on the outer surface; these cells are subtended by 4 or 5 layers of irregularly polyhedral, thin-walled cells. Just within the latter, cross sections of the peristome teeth appear as groups of small thick-walled cells, mostly 6–8 cells wide and 3 or 4 cells thick in the middle (fig. 192.) In medial longitudinal sections these cells are linear and slightly incurved, the outer ones the longest, the inner ones progressively shorter (fig. 193). The cells of the columella are large and irregular but become abruptly smaller and isodiametric across the horizontal plane opposite the tips of the teeth where they constitute the epiphragm.

2.99   ANDREAEALES is a small order of very dark to blackish mosses found on rocks. After fertilization the embryo stimulates rapid growth of the vaginula and of the apical part of the stem tissue which jointly elongate into a naked green axis, a pseudopodium, which thrusts the sporophyte beyond the perichaetial leaves. It resembles a seta, but the elliptical to oblong cylindric capsule is sessile on a globose to shortly cylindrical foot embedded in the slightly dilated summit of the pseudopodium (figs. 194–196).

2.100 In the development of the capsule, the archesporium arises like a hood from the outer layer of the endothecium and covers the apex of the columnar columella; it extends to the bottom of the urn. There is a short zone of sterile tissue between the base of the spore sac and the foot which could be regarded as a neck or hypophysis, although it has no air chambers or stomata. The capsular wall consists of oblong, very thick-walled, reddish brown epidermal cells and 3–5 irregular layers of thin-walled amphithecial cells without intercellular spaces (fig. 196). In the absence of lid and annulus the capsule opens by four vertical slits which extend from just below the tip nearly to the base. These slits correspond to rows of small, bistratose epidermal cells which split apart when the dry walls of the larger epidermal cells shrink and the capsule contracts, resulting in four outward-arched bands or valves with widely gaping spaces between them (fig. 195).

2.101 SPHAGNALES is a small order of one family and one genus totally unlike other mosses. It is restricted to wet boggy situations. Like *Andreaea*, the fertile stems of *Sphagnum* grow into a naked pseudopodium at the summit of which the vaginula encloses a bulbous foot. A seta is lacking; the capsules are globose to ovoid. A major difference is shown in the ontogeny of the capsule. The archesporial cells arise

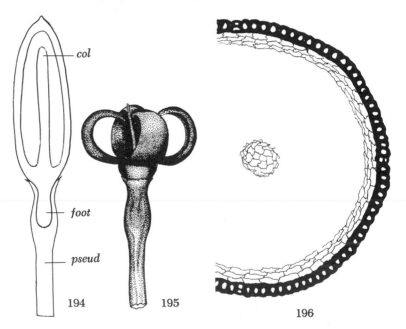

col

foot

pseud

194   195

196

Figs. 194–196. Andreaea rothii. 194. Diagram of a longitudinal section of a capsule, showing the **pseud,** pseudopodium, foot, and **col,** columella. 195. Dry capsule, ×10. 196. Cross section of a capsule, ×50.

from the inner layer of the amphithecium and arch in a domelike fashion over the apex of the columella which becomes massive in the mature capsule (fig. 197). The capsule wall consists of oval to oblong epidermal cells with thick reddish walls (these form trigones in the angles between cells), numerous primitive stomata (two guard cells but no pore), and several layers of thin-walled amphithecial cells without air chambers. The capsule dehisces by a low-convex lid, like an inverted saucer, which splits along a circle of small thin-walled cells around the upper part of the capsule. A peristome is not formed.

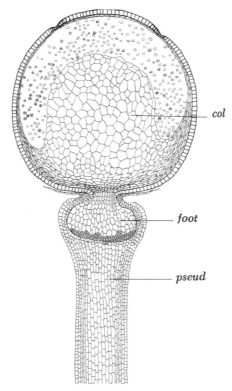

Fig. 197. Medial longitudinal section through the capsule and upper part of the **pseud,** pseudopodium of **Sphagnum; col,** columella, ×50.

2.102 BRYALES is the largest order and is composed of numerous families whose capsules differ greatly. A typical capsule of this order consists of a sporangium, the spore-sac region, with a lid or operculum at the distal end and a more or less narrowed neck joining the seta. The capsules of some mosses do not have an externally evident neck although in most cases there actually is a sterile base region, however short or obscure. The neck may vary from very short to half the length of the capsule and in a few instances even longer. Capsules range in length from less than 1 mm to as much as 8 mm, according to the species. The following terms are used in describing shapes of capsules:

globose, ovoid, obovate, ellipsoidal, oblong, cylindric, pyriform, and turbinate. They may be erect, inclined, cernuous, or pendent; they are further characterized by being symmetric or asymmetric or curved. The mouth may be straight or slightly oblique to the long axis of the capsule. Capsules with a swelling on the upper side are described as gibbous; when the swelling is at the base they are ventricose. A small goiterlike swelling at one side of the base is a struma. A swelling or dilation around the base of the sporangium is an apophysis (also called an hypophysis), as in *Polytrichum* and *Splachnum*.

2.103 Mature capsules may be light yellowish, yellowish brown, reddish brown, or distinctly reddish. In many species the mouth is darker or more highly colored; the operculum is sometimes shiny. Old empty capsules frequently become darker.

2.104 Dry mature capsules usually assume a characteristic form. Some become slightly shrunken; others become finely to coarsely wrinkled, often with the neck very shrunken. Often capsules are slightly to strongly constricted below the mouth. In some species the capsules are longitudinally ribbed. Most curved capsules become more strongly curved or arcuate when dry.

2.105 The new section also varies according to the species. The most common shapes are convex and conical and range from low, like an inverted saucer, to narrowly conical or almost subulate. The apex may be obtuse to broadly rounded or terminate in a point. When the lid is hemispherical with a short point, it is often described as mammillate. When the point is abruptly long and slender, the lid is said to be rostrate or beaked; it may be straight or bent.

ANNULUS

2.106 The lid becomes detached from the urn by a separation of cells at the annulus. This occurs in several ways. The following examples will illustrate some of the ways by which the lid is shed.

2.107 In *Bryum* and *Mnium* the marginal cells of the lid and 2 rows of large thick-walled cells which make up the annulus overlap like shingles on a roof. The annulus cells are firmly attached to a circle of small, thick-walled quadrate cells which are attached to the mouth of the urn. When mature and dry, the cells of the annulus are shrunken and appear oblong in surface view, but when wetted the walls swell greatly and cause the upper ends to tear away from beneath the overlapping cells of the lid and coil backward, an action described as revoluble. This action also tears the small quadrate cells away from the marginal cells of the urn and the annulus falls free (fig. 198). A demonstration of this process may be made by cutting off the upper fourth of a dry operculate capsule of *Bryum* with a razor blade and carefully boiling it in 70% ethyl alcohol to remove the spores. The lid with the annulus attached is then separated from the mouth of the urn with small needles; then with the inner surface uppermost the lid may be cut in

2 halves. The halves are mounted in this position in alcohol and covered with a cover glass. A drop of dilute Hoyer's solution is introduced at the edge of the cover slip and the preparation immediately placed under the microscope whereupon the swelling of the walls of the annulus and their separation from the overlapping cells of the lid can be clearly observed.

2.108   Using the same general method, one may observe other means of separation on the outer surface. In *Tortula ruralis* the annulus is simple and consists of 1–3 rows of small, quadrate to oblong, thick-walled cells between the thinner-walled cells of the lid and mouth of the urn (fig. 199). When wetted (as above), the annular cells swell and separate from the lid but usually are more or less persistent on the mouth. In *Orthotrichum alpestre* the reverse situation prevails: the annulus consists of 2 or 3 rows of very thin-walled cells which connect the lid and urn—both of these have small thick-walled marginal cells, which swell and rupture the thin-walled annular cells when wetted (fig. 200).

2.109   Among mosses without a definite annulus, the junction of the lid and urn is marked by several rows of smaller and usually thicker-walled cells. In some species the marginal cells of the lid are the thickest and swell more strongly, as in *Tetraphis* (fig. 181), while in others there is

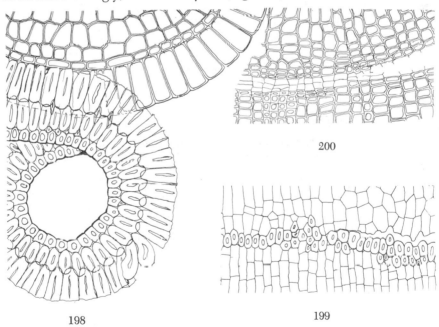

200

198

199

Figs. 198–200. 198. **Bryum creberrimum,** an inner portion of the lid showing the separation of the revoluble annulus. 199. **Tortula ruralis,** showing the separation of the thin-walled cells of the lid, above, from the thick-walled cells of the annulus which remains on the mouth of the urn. 200. **Orthotrichum alpestre,** showing the rupture of the thin-walled cells joining the lid with the mouth of the urn, × 100.

not so much a difference in the thickness of the walls as that the separation is brought about by differences in degrees of swelling.

2.110   The separation of the lid does not always coincide with the swelling caused by moist conditions; rather, the separation takes place during the shrinkage of the saturated cell walls as they dry out. In *Sphagnum,* shrinkage of the drying capsule causes the lid to pop off along a line of weakness at the mouth—usually audibly and sometimes with a noticeable puff of spores.

2.111   In a few mosses a lid is not differentiated from the urn; there is no special device which opens the capsule at maturity. In these cleistocarpous forms the exothecial cells are about the same size and shape, except at the extreme base and apex, as in *Phascum.* Eventually the capsule wall ruptures irregularly by the fracture of the individual cells.

2.112   The exothecial cells vary widely. They may be more or less isodiametric, oblong, hexagonal, or irregular, with walls straight or variously curved to sinuous and thin or thick. Usually the 2 to several rows of cells immediately below the mouth of the urn are smaller, often thicker walled, and more highly colored. Sometimes those of the neck are shorter, of a different shape, and often thinner walled. Capsules which become ribbed and furrowed when dry usually have alternate longitudinal rows of thick- and thin-walled exothecial cells. The stomata may be restricted to the neck, to the region of the spore sac, or they may occur in both areas. Most mosses have superficial stomata (phaneropore) flush with the surface of the surrounding exothecial cells (fig. 201); however, in some species of *Orthotrichum* and *Pohlia* the stomata are immersed (cryptopore) below the adjacent exothecial cells which partially overhang them and have walls facing the orifice (figs. 202, 203).

TEETH

2.113   Most of the *Bryales* have 16 elongated-triangular or lanceolate, yellowish, yellowish brown, or reddish peristome teeth, which are more or

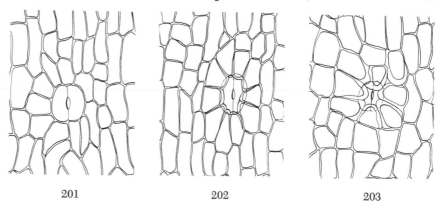

201   202   203

Figs. 201–203. Position of the stomata in **Orthotrichum.** 201. Superficial in **O. affine.** 202. Immersed but widely exposed in **O. pallens** var. **parvum.** 203. Deeply immersed in **O. alpestre,** ×100.

less prominently jointed by darker thickenings of the transverse walls. In some species the thickenings, called lamellae, project from the inner faces of the teeth. (The term joint is used with two meanings in the description of the teeth: it is applied to the darker and often thickened transverse cell walls, including the lamellae, and also to the plates or sections between the transverse walls. These structures are not truly jointed since they are not articulated.) In most species the teeth show a nearly straight or zigzag medial divisural line. The outer surface of the teeth may be smooth or variously roughened with papillae, which may lie in straight or sinuous lines forming characteristic patterns in some species. The term striate has been used to describe the latter type of markings, but it is also applied to straight or branched ridges, as in *Orthotrichum cupulatum* and its relatives. In *Timmia* the inner face of the upper joints of the teeth have strong vertical barlike striations which are also papillose, while the outer face of the lower joints has fine horizontal striations and fine scattered papillae. In *Philonotis* the teeth have a single large, globose or ovoid thickening between the upper joints on the inner face. Most pleurocarpous mosses have very fine striations on the lower joints.

2.114   Some authors segregate 2 suborders based on the differences in the peristome: (1) the Haplolepideae is characterized by a single peristome of 16 teeth. The teeth may be entire, perforated with thin spots or holes, or variously cleft into 2–4 slender divisions, as in some species of *Grimmia* (fig. 166). In *Fissidens, Ceratodon,* and many of the Dicranaceae, each tooth is divided nearly to the base into 2 pronglike divisions, often strongly jointed (fig. 167). In many of the *Pottiaceae* the teeth are more or less united below and form a basal membrane; the upper extremities are variously divided into sometimes more or less spirally twisted slender divisions (fig. 170). (2) The Diplolepideae includes the families with a double peristome. The exostome is the outer circle of teeth; the endostome is the inner circle of segments and may often include cilia as well. The peristome of *Funaria* has 2 rows of teeth each, the inner ones opposite the outer ones. The outer teeth are joined at their tips to a small perforated membrane (plate 62, fig. 7). In *Orthotrichum* the outer peristome is composed of 16 elongate-triangular teeth, separate but more often in pairs; the endostome is represented by 8, or sometimes 16, cilia 1–2 cells wide, which alternate with the teeth (fig. 169). In a few species of *Orthotrichum* a preperistome stands opposite and outside the teeth. This is composed of short processes which vary from 1 to several joints in height but rarely exceed half the length of the teeth. These are free, and partially, or completely attached to the teeth. The preperistome arises as a thickening of the outer periclinal walls and the transverse anticlinal walls of the cells which give rise to the teeth. The preperistomal projections are frequently fragmentary, discontinuous, and often attached to the teeth by narrow stalks like tiny mushrooms. They often appear as extra thickenings on the outside of the teeth.

2.115   The endostome of *Timmia* was described earlier (see #2.113). Briefly

2.116   it consists of a high basal membrane abruptly divided into 64 cilia. The groups of 4 cilia, which stand opposite the teeth, become united into pairs and finally into 16 terminal tips. The joints are nodose and sometimes appendiculate (plate 66, fig. 5).

2.116   In *Fontinalis,* the endostome consists of 16 cilia which are joined side by side by transverse appendages to form a conical trellis (plate 140, fig. 9).

2.117   The Bartramiaceae, Bryaceae, and pleurocarpous mosses show the highest development of the peristome. The outer teeth are strong; the endostome has a more or less high basal membrane which bears lanceolate, keeled, and often longitudinally perforated segments. These segments alternate with the teeth and usually the 1–4 cilia which are opposite the teeth. The cilia may or may not bear peglike appendages on 1 side. In some species the cilia are rudimentary or lacking, especially in those species with erect capsules.

2.118   A number of genera and species scattered among several families have no peristome and are designated as gymnostomous. This condition is interpreted as a result of evolutionary reduction.

CALYPTRA

2.119   At maturity, the calyptra of most mosses is a thin, membranous, conical to campanulate hood which is shed early in the development of the sporophyte. It may taper evenly to a point, but in many species it is dilated at the base and bears a short or long beak. The base may be entire, ragged, or fringed; the body may be split on one side (cucullate), or split at two or more points (mitrate). *Encalypta* has a large, thickish, yellowish, cylindrical calyptra which covers the capsule to the base, or nearly so, and often persists even after the spores are shed. In some species it is roughly papillose on the outside. In the Orthotrichaceae the calyptra is moderately thick, light yellowish, widely conical or campanulate, and covers the capsule halfway or more; the surface is mostly plicate and usually bears a few erect hairs, but in a few species the surface is flat and may be smooth or papillose and naked. The calyptra of *Polytrichum* is cucullate, covers the capsule to the base or nearly so, and bears a dense coating of yellowish, downward directed hairs.

SPORES

2.120   Spores may be globose, ovoid, reniform, or tetrahedral; they may range from 6–8 μ in diameter in some species of *Grimmia* to as much as 250 μ in some species of *Archidium.* They may be pale yellowish, yellowish brown, brown, reddish brown, and in a few instances red or purplish. The spore wall is double—it consists of an outer thicker layer (the exine) and a thin inner membrane (the intine). The exine may be smooth, wrinkled, or finely to coarsely papillose, sometimes spinulose, and in some genera reticulate. The contents of the spore are rich in oil and usually contain fine granules of starch. According to the species, spores may remain viable for relatively short periods of 2–4 months, as long as 5 years, or (rarely) even more.

ECOLOGY AND DISTRIBUTION

THE LAND

3.1   A small area in Washington County, in southwestern Utah, lies below a 3,000 foot elevation and represents the northern limit of the Lower Sonoran Zone. About 60 percent of the land area of the state is composed of (1) lowlands or flat desert country which ranges from 4,300 feet, near Great Salt Lake,   to nearly 6,000 feet at the upper limit of the Escalante Desert in southwestern Utah and (2) some high desert plains in the eastern and southeastern part of the state. In the latter areas, the Canyonlands Province is an intricately dissected high desert plain with many deep box canyons surmounted by massive and much eroded buttes and pinnacles of red shale and sandstone, often finely sculptured by wind and frost.

3.2   A chain of mountains, about 10,000 to 13,000 feet in elevation, extends across Utah from the northeastern Wasatch and Uinta Mountains to the southwestern Aquarius Plateau and the Pine Valley Mountains. The Wasatch and Fish Lake plateaus and the Canyon, Pavant and Tushar mountains are the principal links in the midsection of this chain. West of these mountains lies the Great Basin, in which minor basin ranges extend in a north-south direction and are separated by broad valleys which are interconnected by diagonal passes. None of these smaller mountain ranges have sufficient altitude or extent to maintain permanent streams. The high Deep Creek Mountains extend along the Utah-Nevada state line. The Grouse Creek and Raft River Mountains are isolated in the northwestern corner of the state. Eastward from the main mountain axis, in the north-central region, the west and east Tavaputs Plateaus extend into Colorado, flanked by the Uinta Basin on the north and Castle Valley and Grand River Valley on the south. From the southern part of the main mountainous axis the Kaiparowitz Plateau extends eastward to the Colorado River. The high La Sal, Abajo, and Henry mountains are isolated islandlike groups of volcanic peaks which rise from the high desert plains of the Canyonlands Province. Throughout the state, igneous, sedimentary, and metamorphic rocks of great variety range from Precambrian to Recent, representing nearly every geologic period and providing a wide variety of mineral conditions.

CLIMATE

3.3   The average annual precipitation in the lowlands is 10 inches or less; some areas receive as little as 6 inches. The average temperature ranges from 59.7° F in southern Utah at elevations of about 3,000 feet to about 50° in northern Utah at about 4,400 feet. At these elevations, the average precipitation increases about 6 inches and the average temperature decreases about 3° F for every 1,000 foot rise in elevation.

PLANT COMMUNITIES AND ASSOCIATED MOSSES

3.4 The lowlands and upland plains, at about 4,300 to 6,000 feet, are predominantly saline deserts which receive an average annual precipitation of 10 inches or less. The vegetation is mainly salt desert shrub with some shortgrass. *Atriplex confertifolia,* commonly called shadscale, is the most widely distributed shrub in the western deserts and commonly extends in continuous communities from the lower elevations to the gently rising alluvial slopes. It is a round-topped, silvery gray shrub, 1–2 feet tall, with thorny branches which bear thickish, broadly ovate leaves covered with dense scales. It has widely spreading shallow roots and depends mainly on moisture from precipitation. *Kochia americana* var. *vestita* (gray molly) and *Eurotia lanata* (winter fat) are smaller gray shrubs frequently associated with shadscale; each by itself dominates local communities. *Atriplex canescens* (four-winged salt bush) is a larger, silvery gray shrub with narrower leaves, confined mainly to gullies, ravines, and terraces of the larger rivers.

3.5 Communities of *Sarcobatus vermiculatus* (greasewood) are locally dominant in bottom lands, along drainage ways and terraces bordering rivers. Greasewood is an erect, dark or yellowish green shrub, usually 2–3 feet tall but it may reach as much as 15 feet, with pale, thorny branches bearing fleshy linear leaves. It has a deeply penetrating tap root and is noted as a groundwater indicator. The inkweeds, *Suaeda torreyana* and *S. occidentalis,* are often associated with it.

3.6 Other prominent shrubs scattered in these communities are *Yucca angustissima, Y. harrimaniae, Ephedra viridis, E. torreyana, E. nevadensis, Coleogyne ramosissima* (the blackbush), *Opuntia hystricina* and *O. rhodantha* (prickly pear cacti), *Gutierrezia sarothrae* (matchweed), and *Artemisia filifolia* (the sand sagebrush). *Tetradymia glabrata, T. spinosa* and *T. nuttallii* (the horsebushes), and *Grayia spinosa* (hop sage) are locally abundant on some dry, rising slopes.

3.7 *Bouteloua gracilis* (blue grama) and *Hilaria jamesii* (galleta grass) form shortgrass communities of lesser extent.

DESERT MOSSES

3.8 The moss flora of the deserts is sporadic. One may traverse these regions for miles without seeing a trace of moss and then suddenly encounter communities of one or more species which range from small scattered colonies to well-populated areas 2 or 3 acres in extent. A conspectus of typical desert mosses of this region includes 16 species of the Pottiaceae, 6 species of *Bryum,* 3 of *Grimmia,* 2 of *Funaria,* and 1 of *Encalypta.* These do not include the occasional occurrence of other upland mosses along the upland borders of deserts or in certain mesophytic niches in the midst of dry plains and some sandy areas.

3.9 *Tortula ruralis* is the most common moss in deserts and one of the most common species in other communities extending to the high mountain peaks. It occurs locally in scattered or concentrated tufts around the bases of shrubs, among beds of cacti, and occasionally in dense communities on open soil. *Tortula brevipes, T. bistratosa,* and *T. intermedia* are essentially desert species which extend to the bases of mountains, while *T. inermis* occurs most often on dry ledges and at the bases of cliffs in more broken country, such as dry canyon sides. *Tortula mucronifolia* is much more local on soil around bushes and the bases of rocks. *Pterygoneurum ovatum* is frequent or locally abundant and occasionally occupies the open spaces between shrubs continuously over wide areas—in some instances so densely that one can scarcely avoid treading on it. It especially favors disturbed soil. *Pterygoneurum subsessile* is less frequent and *P. lamellatum* rare. *Crossidium aberrans, C. desertorum, C. griseum, Aloina pilifera,* and *Pottia nevadensis* are infrequent or rare species largely confined to deserts. *Barbula vinealis* and *B. bescherellei* occur locally and occasionally in abundance on dry sandy slopes and small dunes in the Canyonlands region. Neither is particularly limited to deserts, yet the large populations in some desert areas are impressive. The latter is a Mexican species reaching its northern limit in southern and eastern Utah.

3.10 Several species of *Bryum* are frequent and often abundant on some low-lying level places. They are usually sterile and indeterminable but from a few fruited plants encountered, *B. caespiticium* and *B. creberrimum* appear to be the most common species, with *B. angustirete, B. inclinatum* and *B. bicolor* less frequent to rare (in that order). In similar situations *Funaria hygrometrica* and *F. muehlenbergii* are found, although the latter is more frequent on the soil of dry slopes and at the bases of cliffs along the larger rivers in desert areas.

3.11 Large rocks, rocky outcrops and cliffs commonly skirt the bases of mesas and upland slopes where *Grimmia anodon, G. plagiopodia, G. rauii,* and varieties of *G. apocarpa* occur.

RIVER COMMUNITIES

3.12 The Colorado and Green Rivers are the main water courses which cross the desert areas and support hydrophytic communities of mosses, particularly in deep gorges and box canyons. Along the channels where sandstone cliffs and masses of broken rock are washed by the rivers, a dense coating of mosses commonly develops, especially where shade prevails for a considerable part of the day. These plants are usually small and underdeveloped, because most of them are submerged and scoured by flood waters until late June or early July, when the rivers subside. With this late start they are seldom able to reach even a moderate degree of growth—and they rarely fruit. *Didymodon tophaceus,* by far the most abundant, is frequently mingled with *Marchantia polymorpha.* Less abundant are *Didymodon trifarius, Eucladium verticillatum, Gymnostomum recurvirostrum, G. aeruginosum,* and a species of *Bryum* in a sterile and indeterminable state. Locally *Fissidens obtusifolius* var. *marginatus* forms very thin coatings on damp rocks, mainly along the high water levels, and is distinctively light yellowish green.

Barbula cruegeri, of a similar habitat, reaches its northern limit in the Canyonlands region; it is essentially a Coastal Plains species of tropical and subtropical America.

MOIST HABITATS

3.13 Mosses often flourish on dripping cliffs and around springs. Here *Gymnostomum aeruginosum, G. recurvirostre,* and *Eucladium verticillatum* are the dominant species, usually well fruited and frequently in deep tufts along wet or damp seams of horizontal bedding planes of sandstone and shale. They may form continuous green velvety cushions several meters across. The two species of *Didymodon* mentioned above are also quite abundant. Less frequent and more widely dispersed are *Fissidens grandifrons, Barbula fallax, Desmatodon obtusifolius, Pottia heimii, Tortula mucronifolia, Funaria hygrometrica, F. microstoma, Bryum capillare, B. gemmiparum, B. angustirete, B. pseudotriquetrum, Philonotis marchica, Amblystegium varium, A. juratzkanum, A. americanum, A. tenax,* and its forma *marianapolitana.*

3.14 Hydrophytic situations in saline deserts are notably poor in mosses. *Funaria hygrometrica* and various species of *Bryum, Amblystegium,* and *Brachythecium* sometimes eke out an existence under such inhospitable conditions. Mosses flourish mainly in salt-free areas, freshwater lakes, ponds, swamps, and wet meadows. Areas that are mainly man-made often harbor abundant growths of 1 to several species. Lakes and ponds in parks and on private grounds frequently invite *Fontinalis duriaei, F. antipyretica, F. hypnoides, Drepanocladus fluitans,* and *D. exannulatus.* Swamps and wet meadows, notably in Cache Valley and around Bear and Utah Lakes, provide habitats for abundant *Drepanocladus aduncus* and its protean forms, while some large springs near the bases of mountains, rocks, and cement installations in streams, open conduits, and fish hatcheries favor *Amblystegium tenax, A. fluviatile, A. riparium,* and *Hygrohypnum luridum, Barbula vinealis, B. cylindrica, Didymodon tophaceus, D. trifarius, Merceya latifolia,* and various species of *Bryum.*

3.15 *Amblystegium serpens, A. kochii,* and *Brachythecium collinum* often grow in shaded lawns, around dwellings, and in parks; *Funaria hygrometrica, Barbula unguiculata,* and species of *Bryum* are frequent along the edges of shrubbery or in footpaths and cracks of sidewalks. Wet ditch banks and, infrequently, old masonry walls harbor the same species, as well as several rarities such as *Tortula muralis, Physcomitrium hookeri,* and *P. pyriforme.*

SALINE SITUATIONS

3.16 Saline soil inhabited by mosses may contain as much as 0.8% salt with sodium chloride the dominant constituent and considerably higher amounts when sulphates predominate. Due to leaching by rain and snow, the surface on which the mosses lie usually contains less salt than the soil immediately beneath, but the salt is often drawn to the surface by evaporation of water. The actual concentration of the soil solution in contact with living parts of mosses is difficult to estimate, but experiments have shown that the spores of certain mosses do not germinate in solutions higher than 0.2% and give the best germination in water from natural springs in salt-free areas. It appears that in saline soils spores germinate during the winter when the salts are leached out by rain and snow. Once the protonemata and leafy shoots are established, they adapt to a gradual increase in the concentration of the soil solution as water evaporates. Very often mosses become established on small crests of soil where the salt content is low. Here, above the general level of soil, they build up little islands of sod which become accentuated by wind erosion. Fresh water from rain or snow mediates fertilization and spores are matured in most of the mosses observed, although in many instances the capsules may fail to form spores (particularly in *Bryum*). This effect is caused by either the absence of moisture before the sporophytes mature or by the toxic affects of a high concentration of salt when moisture is present.

3.17   In soil around Great Salt Lake and the adjacent Salt Lake desert, sodium chloride commonly exceeds 90% of the total soluble salts. Samples of surface soil supporting the growth of mosses was analyzed for hydrogen-ion concentration, principal cations, and total salts. In every instance the chlorides far exceeded the sulfates, while sodium bicarbonate was very low, and normal carbonates lacking. The following table shows the hydrogen-ion concentration and total salts:

Species	pH	Percentage of total salts in dry weight of soil
Tortula ruralis	8.6	0.86
Tortula brevipes	8.6	0.86
Pterygoneurum ovatum	8.6	0.53
Pottia nevadensis	8.6	0.25
Funaria hygrometrica	8.6	0.60
Bryum caespiticium	8.6	0.62
Bryum creberrimum	8.6	0.60
Bryum angustirete	8.6	0.20

3.18   These were the highest values obtained. In this same region are localized areas in which the soils run high in normal carbonates, but mosses were never observed growing on them.

3.19   At elevations ranging from 4,500 to 6,000 feet, the benchlands and foothills arise abruptly or gradually from the desert plains. Broad mesalike terraces skirting the bases of the mountains in eastern Utah are a constant feature of the landscape, while in the western part of the State the mountains arise abruptly from the valley floor or from the upper limits of long, gradual alluvial slopes. The soils are mostly free of salt, except on some lower slopes where the residual rocks carry soluble salts.

3.20   In areas receiving 10 to 14 inches of average annual precipitation *Juniperus osteosperma* and *Pinus edulis* or *P. monophylla* form the familiar juniper-pinyon forests characteristic of the intermontane region of the west, especially in mesas, high terraces, and rising foothills. The undergrowth is mostly sparse, and much bare soil is exposed. In other areas where there is a precipitation of 14–20 inches, *Agropyron spicatum* is the dominant species in bunchgrass communities which often alternate with scrub oak communities of *Quercus gambelii*, the two types of vegetation often forming variegated patterns on the lower slopes of the mountains and extending into the mouths of canyons. Less commonly, *Artemisia tridentata* (the big sagebrush) occurs in certain areas. Also, in this climatic zone, and extending into the montane belt, *Pinus ponderosa* (yellow or ponderosa pine) occurs in local groves and small forests across southern Utah and in the Colorado-Green River Basin. The best display of such a forest is the Kaibab Forest on the north side of Grand Canyon in northern Arizona. The upper limits of the basal zone vary widely with latitude and topography but usually terminate at elevations of 6,000 to 7,500 feet in southern Utah and about 1,000 feet lower in the northern part of the state.

3.21   *Phascum cuspidatum* var. *americanum* and var. *schreberianum* are about the only mosses restricted to open terraces, hillsides, and upland valleys. They are commonly associated with *Pterygoneurum ovatum* and *P. subsessile,* and together they form small tufts on open soil, among grasses or at the bases of shrubs. None of them extend upward on the mountain slopes to any extent. The ever-present *Tortula ruralis* occurs in many habitats ranging from dry sandy soil under junipers and pinyon pines to shaded rocky outcrops in the mouths of canyons and upward on mountain slopes where it often forms deep, thick sods, sometimes well fruited. *Homalothecium nevadense* is commonly associated with it, while other species of general distribution include *Tortula papillosissima, T. inermis, T. mucronifolia, T. intermedia, Encalypta vulgaris* and var. *mutica, Funaria hygrometrica, Timmia austriaca, Bryum caespiticium, B. creberrimum, B. capillare, Brachythecium collinum* and its var. *idahense,* and *Eurhynchium pulchellum,* all frequent in damp or rather dry banks, bases of trees, rocks and under crevices of cliffs. On dry sunny rocks *Grimmia apocarpa, G. anodon, G. plagiopodia, G. calyptrata, G. montana, G. alpestris,* and *G. pulvinata* are widely distributed; *Orthotrichum cupulatum, O. hallii,* and *O. alpestre* occur on shaded rocks, mainly in canyon bottoms and ravines.

3.22   In the Canyonlands and upper Colorado-Green River Basin *Fissidens limbatus, Weissia controversa, W. ligulaefolia, W. perligulata, W. tortilis, Pottia heimii, Tortella fragilis,* and *T. tortuosa* occur on sandstone ledges or at the bases of cliffs where precipitation water drains, and the sandy soil is least disturbed by wind. On shaded slopes, and at the bases of shrubs and large rocks, open tufts of *Encalypta vulgaris* var. *mutica, Barbula vinealis, B. bescherellei,* and *Bryum angustirete* and thick mats of *Hypnum vaucheri, H. revolutum,* and occasionally *Brachythecium fendleri* are generally greatly infiltrated with sand. Extending across southern Utah and northward into this region, small hoary cushions of *Grimmia pulvinata* and *G. rauii* dot shaded rocks, while large, convex, blackish cushions of *G. orbicularis* often form patterns against the reddish background of sandstone cliffs and large rocks. *Anacolia menziesii,* a moss frequently found on shaded rocks in the Pacific coastal states, occurs sparingly in Zion Canyon. Extending from the northern and eastern states into the borders of this region. *Ditrichum flexicaule* fo. *brevifolium* and loose brittle masses of *Thuidium abietinum* grow on shaded, north-facing slopes in Yampa Canyon, Moffat County, Colorado, about five miles east of the Utah state line.

3.23   Within the basal zone, the ecological conditions in the bottoms of deep canyons which dissect the higher mountains are much more mesophytic than on the open front of ranges, high terraces, and benchlands. Here, surface water and cool air currents descend from higher elevations. *Populus angustifolia* (the narrowleaf cottonwoods), *Betula occidentalis* (river birch), *Acer negundo* (box elder), and *A. grandidentatum* (bigtooth maple) are the dominant streamside trees which, together with numerous mesophytic shrubs and herbs, provide cooler and more humid conditions favorable to a moss flora of enriched montane species which descend into the canyons. Among prominent species in damp or wet places along the brooks and springs of the canyons are *Bryoerythrophyllum recurvirostre, Desmatodon obtusifolius, Funaria hygrometrica, Timmia bavarica, T. austriaca, Philonotis fontana,* several species of *Bryum, Mnium serrulum, Amblystegium serpens, A. juratzkanum, A. compactum, Hygrohypnum ochraceum, H. bestii, Brachythecium rivulare,* and *B. lamprochryseum.* Upward on shaded banks and among rocks, *Tortula mucronifolia, Brachythecium collinum* and its var. *idahense, B. suberythrorrhizon,* and *B. delicatulum* appear in fine, well-fruited colonies. Bark-inhabiting species of *Orthotrichum* occur sporadically in this zone, sometimes in abundance, particularly on the bark of narrowleaf cottonwood, boxelder, and bigtooth maple. *Orthotrichum affine* and *O. alpestre* are the most common species, while *O. pumilum* is more local and *O. pallens* var. *parvum* rare. *Orthotrichum alpestre* is also abundant on dry, shaded rocks, and *O. macounii* is widely distributed in canyon bottoms of the higher mountains. *Orthotrichum anomalum, O. strangulatum,* and *O. texanum* occur more frequently in northern Utah; *O. jamesianum* is locally abundant and *O. laevigatum* rare in the Raft River Mountains in the northwestern corner of the state.

3.24   Among the rarities of this basal zone, *Grimmia alpicola* var. *latifolia* occurs in quantity submerged on granite rocks in the swift brook of Bells Canyon near Salt Lake City, and in the same locality *Tayloria acuminata* was gathered on wet, decaying vegetable matter. *Aulacomnium adrogynum,* so abundant in the northwestern states, occurs sparingly on decaying wood in Lambs and Mill Creek canyons east of Salt Lake City, and in a most unusual habitat deep in the recesses of frothy volcanic cinder in the Craters of the Moon National Monument in south-central Idaho at about 6,000 feet elevation, where the surrounding terrain is very dry desert. Two species of *Neckera* occur sparingly in our range: *N. menziesii* appears to be confined to a small area in City Creek Canyon near Salt Lake City where it forms loose mats on dry, shaded, limestone cliffs; and a small amount of var. *limnobioides* was gathered from a similar habitat in American Fork Canyon in Utah County. *Neckera pennata* var. *oligocarpa* occurs in small patches at widely scattered stations, chiefly on well-shaded overhanging rocks. Specimens were found on Elk Ridge in San Juan County, Utah; in Black Canyon in Gunnison County, Colorado; and at Toroweep, Mohave County, Arizona.

3.25   Montane vegetation, more or less continuous in the higher mountains, occurs in discontinuous stands on lower plateaus and minor basin ranges, the altitudinal range depending largely on topography, but varying from 6,000–9,000 feet. The average annual precipitation is between 20 and 40 inches. Snow pack and groundwater maintain many springs, permanent brooks, and a few ponds and small lakes.

MONTANE ZONE

3.26   Throughout the state *Populus tremuloides* (aspen), *Pseudotsuga menziesii* (Douglas fir), and *Abies concolor* (white fir) are the dominant trees in the Montane Zone, while *Picea pungens* (blue spruce) is locally abundant in the Wasatch and Uinta mountains. These trees form forests on north- and some east-facing slopes, with *Quercus gambelii* (Gambel oak), *Prunus virginiana* (chokecherry), *Cercocarpus ledifolius* (mountain mahogany), *Amelanchier alnifolia* and *A. utahensis* (serviceberry), and mixed shrubs on the south- and west-facing slopes. Narrow-leaf cottonwood and river birch persist as the dominant brookside trees at the lower limits of the zone but are replaced upward by *Alnus tenuifolia* (alder), several species of willows, especially *Salix lutea, S. lasiandra,* and *S. scouleriana,* and *Cornus stolonifera* (red osier dogwood). Many brookside situations where mosses grow are shaded by current bushes, *Ribes petiolare, R. viscosissimum, R. wolfii,* and *R. inerme* and by the black twinberry, *Lonicera involucrata.* Except for rocky promontories, cliffs and talus slopes, most of the terrain is covered by forests and shrubby communities with a few grassy meadows and thickets in wider canyon bottoms and mountain valleys.

3.27   The mosses of this zone show the widest variety and the largest populations, many of them having broad altitudinal ranges. The canyon bottoms and various slope exposures together with rocky outcrops, springs, seepage areas, wet cliffs, rivulets, and rapid mountain brooks offer great diversity of microclimatic conditions.

3.28   On moist to rather dry soil and rocks, or under overhanging roots of trees, in crevices and on ledges, *Tortula ruralis, Brachythecium collinum,* and *Eurhynchium pulchellum* are common throughout the mountains and may be associated with one to several other frequent species including *Tortula norvegica, T. papillosissima, T. mucronifolia, Desmatodon cernuus, D. plinthobius, Barbula eustegia, B. unguiculata, Tortella tortuosa, Fissidens limbatus, Ceratodon purpureus, C. conicus, Timmia bavarica, Bryum argenteum, B. creberrimum, B. caespiticium, B. cirr-*

hatum, Atrichum selwynii, Brachythecium collinum, var. *idahense, B. fendleri, B. starkei, B. suberythrorrhizon, B. erythrorrhizon,* and *Homalothecium nevadense.* Rare are *Bryum sandbergii* and *B. uliginosum,* each thus far known from a single collection.

3.29   Other dominant species growing primarily on dry rocks, decaying logs, or at the bases of trees are *Dicranoweisia crispula* and *Hypnum revolutum.* Mosses restricted to dry rocks, mainly in woods and open thickets, include *Grimmia apocarpa* and var. *conferta* and var. *ambigua, G. dupretii, G. alpicola, G. atricha, G. donniana, Orthotrichum alpestre, O. macounii, O. hallii, O. texanum, O. laevigatum, Lescuraea radicosa, L. incurvata, L. patens,* and *L. saxicola* (the species of each genus in descending order of frequency). *Desmatodon obtusifolius* is frequent or locally abundant on damp rocks, especially sandstone and quartzite, often along intermittent drainage ways. *Platydictya jungermannoides* and *Homomallium adnatum* are rather uncommon minute pleurocarps on dry shaded limestone. *Encalypta vulgaris,* with its var. *mutica* and *apiculata,* are everywhere in shaded crevices, although *E. ciliata* is exceedingly rare in Utah. *Dicranum viride,* on decaying logs, is also very rare.

3.30   With increasing moisture, mosses become more abundant and more varied, often crowding together on more or less permanently moist soil, rocks and decaying logs, sometimes forming thick green or yellowish tufts, expanded sods or spreading mats frequently accented with reddish tints of capsules or old leaves. Conspicuous are *Distichium capillaceum* and *Leptobryum pyriforme,* small light green plants with slender leaves which often give the tufts a velvetlike appearance. *Bryoerythrophyllum recurvirostrum, Funaria hygrometrica, Pohlia cruda, P. nutans, P. wahlenbergii, Bryum creberrimum, B. pseudotriquetrum, Amblystegium serpens, A. juratzkanum,* and *A. kochii* are common and widely distributed in many moist situations. Less frequent, occasional, or sometimes locally abundant are *Dichodontium pellucidum, Barbula vinealis, B. cylindrica, B. muralis, B. fallax, Didymodon tophaceus, D. rigidulus, Hyophila involuta. Weissia controversa, Bryum capillare, Brachythecium salebrosum, B. oxycladon, B. albicans, Campylium chrysophyllum, C. stellatum, C. hispidulum,* and *Drepanocladus uncinatus.* Some of these mosses occur also in wet places around springs, saturated brook banks, or on areas sometimes splashed with water, and in seepage areas and slopes where water trickles among them. Here they mingle with aquatic and semi-aquatic species peculiar to these situations. In boggy areas and along quiet brooklets in shady recesses of small side canyons, there are splendid sprays of large *Mniums,* including *M. affine, M. medium,* and *M. punctatum,* ample sods of *Philonotis fontana* (or one of its several varieties), or lush mats of *Drepanocladus uncinatus, Brachythecium lamprochryseum,* and *B. rivulare.* Wet soil and loose rocks are particularly favorable to *Pohlia wahlenbergii, P. cruda, P. longicolla, Bryum turbinatum, B. miniatum, B. weigelii, B. creberrimum, B. pseudotriquetrum,* and *Mnium serratum.* Some vigorous growths of *Bryum turbinatum, B. miniatum, Mnium serratum,* and species of *Philonotis* often acquire strong reddish tints when growing in wet sunny places.

3.31   The dominant aquatic mosses of the Montane Zone are *Cratoneuron filicinum, C. falcatum, Hygrohypnum luridum* (in its many forms), and *H. ochraceum.* Frequent or locally abundant are *Scleropodium obtusifolium, Cratoneuron williamsii, Hygrohypnum molle,* and *H. bestii,* while *H. smithii* is found only occasionally. These plants may be attached to rocks, wood, or mud; they may be submerged or emergent in situations ranging from standing water to dashing cataracts. They may also hang in festoons on wet cliffs and around waterfalls. They commonly form dense mats but sometimes become long and stringy, or they may crowd together in deep erect tufts, especially in quiet or standing water. In many places they become infiltrated with sediments or become fossilized in a tuft deposit. Diatoms commonly become attached to the leaves, and small gelatinous colonies of blue green algae frequently lodge among the shoots and leaves.

3.32   Here and there in slow meandering brooks traversing mountain valleys or in wet meadows, loose straggling growths of *Amblystegium riparium, Brachythecium rivulare, Drepanocladus uncinatus, D. aduncus, D. exannulatus, D. fluitans, Fontinalis duriaei, F. hypnoides, F. neomexicana* are occasionally encountered.

3.33   Subalpine and alpine environments occur in the higher mountains above 10,500 feet, although the subalpine region may descend as low as 8,700 feet in the canyons of larger mountain masses. An east-west anticlinal uplift extends about 100 miles in northeastern Utah and forms the Uinta Mountains, the crest of which is composed of Pre-Cambrian quartzite; it is the largest continuous area above 10,000 feet in the state. The peaks of the main axis range upward to 13,400 feet in elevation and are characterized by numerous large cirques and extensive moraines which extend down into broad valleys. Several hundred ponds and small lakes in catchment basins, meadows, and rock fields are fed by numerous rivulets. Siliceous rocks maintain acid soils, and small bogs are common in wet meadows, thickets, and borders of ponds.

3.34   The dominant forest trees of general distribution are *Picea engelmannii* (Engelmann spruce), *Abies lasiocarpa* (black or subalpine fir), and aspen; *Pinus contorta* (lodgepole pine) is especially abundant in the Uinta Mountains. Conspicuous shrubs and small trees are *Prunus virginiana* (chokecherry), *Physocarpus malvaceus* (western ninebark), *Ceanothus velutinus* (snow brush), *Pachistima myrsinites* (mountain lover), *Arctostaphylos platyphylla* (manzanita), *A. uva-ursi* (bearberry), and, in regions of acid soil, *Vaccinium scoparium, V. occidentale,* and *V. membranaceum* (blueberries). At higher elevations *Juniperus communis* var. *depressa* (common juniper) is prevalent in open woods and extends beyond to open rocky ridges, often skirting low growths of wind timber. Along brooks and in seepage areas, willows are conspicuous and include *Salix bebbiana, S. geyeriana, S. glaucops,* and *S. sub-*

coerulea. Dwarfed alders and the black twinberry *Lonicera involucrata* often persist along brooks in high alpine meadows and rock fields.

3.35   In the crest of the Uinta Mountains, the Aquarius Plateau and the high peaks of the Wasatch, LaSal, Tushar, and Deep Creek mountains—the principal areas above timberline—are rock fields, sedge meadows, and scattered stands of low shrubs and dwarfed trees which lie against a background of bold cliffs and barren summits subtended by long talus slopes. The vernal aspect may appear as late as the first of July and autumn snows may come as early as the first of October. Freezing temperatures, occurring every month, together with high light intensity, induce a red pigmentation in many mosses of exposed situations.

3.36   In the following discussion of habitats, subalpine and alpine species are designated with an asterisk(*).

3.37   Aquatic species submerged in ponds and lakes are dominated by *Drepanocladus exannulatus* and *Fontinalis antipyretica*, while *F. hypnoides*, *F. neomexicana*, *Dichelyma falcata*, *Drepanocladus fluitans*, and several forms of *D. aduncus* are less frequent or locally abundant. Some of these mosses also occur on rocks or wood in cold brooks where *Hygrohypnum luridum* and *H. ochraceum* and its var. *flaccidum* are generally dominant. Other associated species include *Grimmia alpicola* var. *rivularis*, *G. agassizii*, *Cratoneuron falcatum*, and *C. williamsii*. *Scouleria aquatica* is known, thus far, only on granite rocks in Lake Mary above Brighton in the Wasatch Mountains.

3.38   Acid bogs occur mostly in the Uinta Mountains where *Sphagnum capillaceum*, *S. warnstorfii*, and *S. recurvum* var. *tenue* frequently form deep spongy masses on the banks of ponds and brooklets and often also in wet meadows. *Sphagnum squarrosum* is less common and often mixed with other species. *Aulacomnium palustre* is conspicuous in many wet places and becomes the dominant moss in some wet meadows where it forms large tufts on hummocks and banks. *Helodium blandowii* often forms deep colonies here and there in similar places while *Climacium dendroides* is more scattered.

3.39   On damp or wet soil and rocks bordering cold brooks and springs, *Philonotis fontana* and its varieties *pumila, americana,* and *caespitosa, Pohlia wahlenbergii, Bryum turbinatum, Drepanocladus uncinatus, Cratoneuron falcatum,* and *C. williamsii* grow in extensive tufts or mats; and in some broad seepage areas these same plants form deep emergent masses. On open soil along brooks and in damp rocky meadows *Polytrichum juniperinum*, *P. piliferum, Polytrichadelphus lyellii, Desmatodon latifolius* (and its more frequent var. *muticus*), *Ceratodon purpureus, Funaria hygrometrica, Bryum creberrimum, B. pseudotriquetrum,* and *B. pallescens* are scattered everywhere. Other species frequently mingled with them are *Pogonatum alpinum*, with varieties *brevifolium* and *arcticum. Atrichum selwynii*, *Oncophorus virens*, *Bartramia ithyphylla, Pohlia cruda, P. longicolla, *P. drummondii*, *P. bulbifera, *P. acuminata*, *P. rothii*, *P. annotina* var. *loeskei, Bryum torti-

*folium, B. weigelii, B. argenteum, Mnium serratum, *M. blyttii, M. or-thorhynchum, M. punctatum, Campylium stellatum, *Calliergon stramineum, *C. cordifolium, Tomenthypnum nitens, *Hypnum lindbergii, H. pratense, *Plagiothecium denticulatum,* and *P. muellerianum.* Among occasional or rare mosses, the following have been found only in the Uinta Mountains. *Dicranum scoparium* (so abundant elsewhere in the United States) occurs mainly in damp meadows and along the edges of thickets where it forms rather low sterile tufts. *Racomitrium canescens* grows mainly on flattish rocks in meadows forming thin mats along the edges against the soil. *Dicranum neglectum, *Paraleucobryum enerve, *Distichium inclinatum, *Dicranella schreberianum, *Pottia latifolia* var. *pilifera, *Desmatodon laureri, *Tortella nitida, *Orthothecium diminutivum,* and *Plagiothecium pulchellum* grow on damp soil.

3.40 In shady woods or at edges of thickets *Brachythecium starkei, B. nelsonii, B. erythrorrhizon, B. campestre, Drepanocladus uncinatus, Pohlia nutans,* and several species of *Bryum* are often abundant on damp soil at the bases of rocks and on decaying logs. *Dicranoweisia crispula* and *Hypnum revolutum* are especially common in the same areas on rocks and rotten wood, while *Pseudoleskea radicosa,* and *P. incurvata* are confined to rocks. The ubiquitous *Tortula ruralis, T. norvegica, Brachythecium collinum,* and *Eurhynchium pulchellum* are also abundant in many habitats and range upward to the highest peaks. On shaded ledges, in crevices of cliffs, and among loose talus, mosses nestle in solitary tufts or characteristic communities of *Polytrichum piliferum, Tortella tortuosa, Barbula cylindrica, Encalypta vulgaris* var. *mutica, Bryum capillare,* and *Mnium arizonicum.*

3.41 *Grimmia alpestris* is exceedingly common on rocks everywhere, forming small hoary cushions with a characteristic bluish cast. *Grimmia montana, G. anodon,* and *G. donniana* are less frequent, and *G. agassizii, *G. hartmanii* var. *anomala, Orthotrichum alpestre, O. macounii, O. laevigatum,* and *Amphidium lapponicum* are comparatively rare.

COLLECTING AND PREPARING
AN HERBARIUM

4.1 Recommended for field use are: (1) a canvas side sack or vasculum, (2) a supply of newspapers cut to suitable size or small paper sacks measuring about 2½ x 5 inches (also a few larger ones), (3) a pencil, (4) pocket knife, and (5) a hand lens of 10x or 12x secured on a stout cord.

4.2 Mosses may be collected at any time of the year but certain small ones, such as *Grimmia, Pterygoneurum, Phascum,* and *Acaulon,* should be gathered in the spring while the lids and calyptrae are on the capsules. A specimen is simply lifted from the substratum by hand. The excess soil, leaf litter, conifer needles, or twigs can be removed by a knife. Some tufted mosses like *Grimmia* are held together by fine soil, so they should be loosened from the rock with caution and handled so as not to lose the calyptrae which may still be on the capsules or lodged among the leaves. The specimen is placed in a sack or envelope previously labeled with the exact time and place of the collection. Such data may include any of the following: moisture, substrate, exposure, vegetation, and altitude. All the specimens from the same locality may be placed in a larger paper bag and labeled as follows: state, county, mountains or valley, canyon, distance and direction from the nearest town or landmark, or longitude and latitude, date, and elevation.

4.3   At home the specimens may be further cleaned and trimmed to convenient size, with any fallen calyptrae or sporophytes recovered and placed in small envelopes. Damp or wet specimens are spread out to dry; thick cushions or sods may be cut vertically into thin slices to be placed in envelopes. Some thick mats may be flattened between several thicknesses of newspapers or herbarium felts under light pressure for several hours, then removed and dried in the air in a shaded place. It is essential that each specimen be kept with the original sack or envelope upon which the data are recorded.

4.4   Permanent collection envelopes should be folded from a good quality of paper (preferably 100% cotton stock of 20- or 24-pound substance). A standard size of about 4 x 5½ inches can be made from 8½ x 11 inch sheets as follows. Bring the lower edge upward about ¾ the length of the sheet and crease. Next, fold about 1½ inches of each side inward and crease. Finally, fold the upper flap downward. Small envelopes made similarly for very small specimens or loose pieces should be made of thinner paper and placed in those of standard size.

4.5   As each specimen is identified, it should be numbered and the name and data recorded opposite the corresponding number in a catalog. Labels may be written on the outside of the flap before the envelope is folded or on special printed forms to be pasted on the flap. As the number of specimens in a private herbarium increases, the catalog numbers on the envelopes become increasingly important. Therefore, I find that the best position for them is on the same line preceding the name at the upper left-hand corner. A sample label:

8710.   *Mnium medium* B.S.G.

Utah: Salt Lake County, Wasatch Mountains,
   Big Cottonwood Canyon at Brighton. On
   wet soil by rivulet in deep shade.   8,800 feet.

S. Flowers, coll. & det.   August 5, 1947.

4.6   For beginners shoe boxes are ideal for storage and can usually be obtained free. Boxes 6 x 18 inches and 4½ inches deep with tight lids will accommodate 50 or 60 specimens filed in a card catalog fashion. Beginners often file specimens according to families, but as a collection increases in size and variety, it becomes more convenient to file them alphabetically by genus. There is less chance of misplacing specimens, and expansion is easier.

METHODS OF STUDY

5.1 A compound microscope is the first and most expensive necessity for a serious study of mosses. This should include 10x and 43x objectives, a 10x ocular provided with an ocular micrometer and a substage condenser with an iris diaphragm. Recent models include a built-in base illuminator. Other tools include (1) a 10x or 15x hand lens (2) two pairs of forceps with fine curved points filed smooth and flat on the inner faces (3) microscope slides (4) cover glasses (5) slide labels (6) alcohol lamp (7) 1 or 2 ounce bottles for liquids (8) medicine droppers (9) scissors (10) single-edged safety razor blades (11) a millimeter ruler and (12) a towel or absorbent tissues. Minute insect pins can, with the aid of pliers, be pushed by the blunt ends into wooden match sticks or handles cut from soft wood. Two of these make excellent dissecting needles for especially fine work. A hand lens mounted on an adjustable holder will serve as a dissecting microscope. (Although a binocular microscope is a luxury, many workers consider it a virtual necessity.) A sheet of glass with white paper under it makes an excellent surface upon which to work.

5.2 Bryologists have an advantage over other botanists in that bryophytes are practically indestructible with the roughest handling, and it is possible to have seemingly fresh material for study at any time. Dried mosses, however old, will return to a fresh natural appearance when soaked in cold water for a few minutes or immediately plunged into hot water.

5.3 At the beginning of study of a specimen, the dry habit, the color, nature of the leaves, and characteristics of the capsules should be checked under the hand lens. Depending on the size of the moss, one or more shoots should be removed from the tuft or mat and freshened in water. Some workers lay out several small dishes for specimens and pour boiling water over them; others dip each plant separately in a pan of hot water; while many others place the shoots in a few drops of water on one end of a slide heated over an alcohol lamp—taking care to tilt the glass from side to side to distribute the heat. Finely divided plant debris and soil particles lodged among leaves should be washed out by placing the shoots under the faucet in a finely-meshed, round-bottomed sieve.

5.4 Leaves can be pulled from a shoot in a drop of water by using two pairs of forceps or by scraping with a single-edged razor blade. Perigonial and perichaetial leaves should be pulled apart with forceps and mounted separately. In some pleurocarpous mosses the stem and branch leaves are different and should be mounted separately, preferably under 2 cover glasses on the same slide. Leaves from the middle third of the stem are generally fully developed and the ones to which descriptions

70

apply. It is well to include 1 or 2 defoliated stems to see if decurrent leaf bases have been left in place and if the stem bears paraphyllia.

5.5   The peristome and exothecial cells are prepared by first removing troublesome spores through repeated boiling and rinsing. Tapping or stroking the urn toward the mouth hastens their removal. If not too large, capsules may be mounted whole, but to provide a clearer view of the parts, a capsule with a good peristome can be cut crosswise just below the mouth with a razor blade. Then the mouth can be cut vertically on opposite sides and the 2 halves carefully drawn apart. One half should be mounted with the teeth up and the other half with endostome up. The endostome can be separated from the teeth with micro dissecting needles and mounted separately. The lower part of the capsule can be cut off crosswise near the base and the remainder cut vertically into 2 halves. With micro needles the remains of the spore sac should be scraped out and the preparation mounted with exothecial cells up. All these may be arranged under 1 cover glass, but I find it easier to mount very small structures under separate cover glasses on the same slide.

5.6   Cross sections of stems, leaves, and setae are cut freehand as follows: (1) obtain a cutting block of smooth soft pine about 1 x 1 x 5 inches; (2) cut white cardboard and thin, hard-surfaced tracing paper into strips about ¼ x 1 inch; (3) place a strip of cardboard near one end of the cutting block on the proximal edge; (4) relax the moss in boiling water, select one or more good clean shoots and gently press them between absorbent tissue paper or blotters; (5) roll a strip of the tracing paper longitudinally into a tight scroll; then open it and place the shoots longitudinally in the first coil of the scroll using fine forceps; (6) using the thumbs and index fingers of both hands, carefully roll the shoots up in the strip. At first this may be a little difficult, as too much water left in the moss tends to soften the paper; (7) hold the scroll to the light and, locating the upper ends of the shoots, grasp the scroll with forceps just beyond them; (8) lay the preparation longitudinally on the cardboard strip near the proximal edge, holding it down with the nail of the left index finger placed at the apices of the shoots; (9) with a new safety razor blade held between the thumb and index finger of the right hand, cut off the anterior tip of the paper scroll and discard; (10) cut sections of the stems and leaves through the tracing paper, using the fingernail as a guide. The razor blade must be held vertically and at right angles to the preparation. As the sections are cut, the fingernail is gradually drawn backward to expose a very small portion of the tip. The advantage of using tracing paper is that the fingernail can be drawn backward over the smooth surface without disturbing the moss within. Each person will need to develop his own technique in cutting. Some use a chopping motion; others rock the razor back and forth, heel-and-toe fashion; and still others use a slicing action.

5.7   Once cutting is accomplished, have available a clean slide with a few drops of water and from time to time remove the sections with the tips

·of forceps previously dipped in water. Sections tend to cling to the razor blade which may be dipped in the water. After the whole length of the shoot has been cut and removed to the slide, tease the pieces of paper apart, freeing the sections of stems and leaves. Then add a drop or two of water to facilitate the removal of the larger sections of the tracing paper. The excess water can be evaporated by holding the slide over an alcohol lamp until a thin layer is left. A drop of 10% glycerin will keep the sections from drying while the better ones are drawn off to one side and the rest of the debris wiped from the slide. Some large stems can be sectioned better after the leaves have been stripped off. Large leaves may be removed and sectioned in a single fold of tracing paper. Once a blade has been used, it must be examined under low power of the microscope for nicks or ragged edges before a second use.

5.8 Routine examinations are generally made of material mounted in water. Thick and obscure or densely chlorophyllose leaves in lactophenol and gently heated become clear and often show the cells, cell markings, or bistratose areas to better advantage. Lactophenol is prepared by mixing equal parts of lactic acid, phenol, glycerin, and distilled water.

5.9 To make permanent slides of various parts of a specimen (or even whole shoots and capsules, if small enough): (1) prepare 1 or 2 ounces of about 10% glycerin in distilled water and add 2–3 drops of melted phenol; (2) apply a drop or two to the material on a slide and allow to concentrate to the consistency of pure glycerin; (3) blot away the excess and add glycerin jelly or Hoyer's medium and cover with a warmed cover glass, avoiding bubbles.

5.10 Glycerin jelly is prepared as follows: (1) soak 1 g of gelatin in 6 cc of distilled water until the water is imbibed; (2) melt in a hot water bath and stir in 7 cc of glycerin and 2 or 3 drops of liquid phenol. When thoroughly mixed, allow bubbles to rise and disappear in a steam bath. When cool the mixture becomes firm. For use, cut out small portions, melt on a slide, arrange objects in it, and carefully lower a warmed cover glass over them. Label immediately. Some people prefer to warm a small jar of the jelly over a source of gentle heat, such as a light bulb, warming table, or radiator, and apply the melted jelly with a medicine dropper. In many respects this is easiest, but with repeated melting the jelly becomes too thick and excess heating causes it to deteriorate.

5.11 To prepare Hoyer's solution: (1) soak 30 g of gum arabic in 50 cc of distilled water at room temperature in a covered 400 or 500 cc beaker until dissolved—this may take as long as 48 hours; (2) add 200 g U.S.P. chloral hydrate, stir in well, and allow to stand until clear; (3) pour in 20 cc of glycerin and stir well at frequent intervals until thoroughly blended; (4) store in a narrow-mouthed bottle with a tightly fitting cap and dispense into a 1- or 2-oz. bottle for use; (5) keep tightly covered and apply to moist preparations directly with a medicine dropper. Some moss leaves shrink if placed directly in the medium. These should be brought up through concentrated glycerin water first. It is advisable to label the slides directly as they are made, taking care to include the name of the moss, location and number of the specimen. Allow the slides to lie on an open tray for about a week to permit the mounting medium to harden.

5.12   Slides may be stored in slide boxes or wrapped singly in a fold of paper and placed in the envelope containing the specimen.

5.13   In the descriptions and keys in this work, measurements of the stems, leaves, and other parts are given as averages, and one may expect occasional measurements to be smaller or larger than the average. Notable exceptions are indicated by numbers in parentheses after the usual range of size, thus, 4–8(10) mm long means the part is usually 4–8 mm but sometimes as much as 10 mm long. The length and particularly the width of cells of various parts are measured from the middle lamella on one side to the middle lamella on the opposite side. Since some cell walls become considerably thickened on the inside, often obscuring the middle lamellae, one may measure the width between the left-hand limit of the lumen of one cell and the left-hand limit of the lumen of the adjacent cell. Ten or 12 measurements of cells in a given area should be made and the average determined.

5.14   The illustrations of the various parts of mosses are usually drawn to a standard scale: habit of growth, x 1 or 2; portions of the shoots, x 5 or 10, according to the size of the plants; leaves and capsules, x 20; cells x 300 or sometimes 150; peristome teeth, x 150.

Descriptive Catalog

KEY TO FAMILIES AND GENERA:
CLASS MUSCI

PLANTS WITHOUT TRUE ROOTS, STEMS OR LEAVES

6.1 Gametophytes green and conspicuous, consisting of a simple or branched multicellular axis or stem which bear lateral appendages (or leaves) in 2 to many rows, and branched, filamentous, septate rhizoids. Leaves mostly 1 cell thick and with a midrib or costa 2 to several cells thick. Sex organs in terminal or lateral buds on the same or different plants; male sex organ an antheridium which consists of a short basal stalk and an oval or club-shaped sac, 1 cell thick, in which numerous sperms develop; female sex organ and archegonium which consists of a tubular neck, 1 cell layer thick with a central neck canal when mature, a slightly swollen base, containing one egg, and a basal stalk. At maturity the sperms loosen in the presence of water, swim to the archegonium and down the neck canal to fertilize the egg and form a zygote, which is the first cell of the diploid sporophyte generation. It gives rise to a multicellular, lance-shaped embryo consisting of a foot or absorbing organ thrust into the stem of the mother plant from which nourishment is drawn, and a slenderly cylindrical stalk or seta at the summit of which a capsule, or sporogonium, develops. Within the young capsule, spore mother cells undergo reduction division to produce spores and thus give rise to a new haploid gametophyte generation. On a favorably moist substrate a spore germinates to form a green, filamentous (or sometimes flat) protonema on which buds develop and grow into leafy plants.

6.2 1. Plants whitish to whitish green

2. Plants whitish green, often tinged with red, pink, or brown; soft and spongy; stems long and erect; branches whorled, distant below, crowded into a compact head at the summit; in dense masses on banks of brooks and lakes and in bogs in high Uinta mountains .... *Sphagnum* 7.2

2. Plants whitish, small, very short, and growing close to the soil in dry places; leaves ovate, the upper half lacking chlorophyll ....

6.3 KEY TO FAMILIES AND GENERA

.... *Bryum argenteum* 19.136

6.3   1. Plants green or yellowish to dark green or blackish; branches not whorled

6.4   3. Shoots flat; the leaves arranged in 2 opposite rows (or appearing to be)

       4. Leaves appear to be arranged on edge to the stem and split at the base, clasping the stem and the next higher leaf .... *Fissidens* 8.7

       4. Leaves not on edge to the stem or split at base

          5. Leaves linear-subulate, abruptly divergent from an oblong clasping base, in 2 opposite rows, plumose and delicate; capsules long-exserted, oblong to subcylindric, yellowish brown .... *Distichium* 9.5

          5. Leaves obovate to oblong or ovate-lanceolate, not clasping at the base, in several rows but twisted at the base so as to appear to be in 2 opposite rows; shoots creeping and prostrate

             6. Prostrate shoots not branched; leaves distant, becoming gradually smaller toward the ends of the stems (which are often stoloniform); margins of the leaves mostly bordered with linear, thick-walled cells; plants medium sized to very large, on damp or wet soil, rotten logs or rocks .... *Mnium* 19.145

             6. Prostrate shoots variously branched; leaves not bordered

                7. Costa short and double or lacking; leaves mostly ovate-lanceolate; leaf cells mostly linear; capsules on long setae, cylindric and curved; on damp or wet soil and rocks .... *Plagiothecium* 21.351

                7. Costa short and double or long and single; leaves oblong, cells rhomboidal to hexagonal; capsules on short setae, oblong to cylindric, erect and straight; on dry or damp rocks and bark of trees .... *Neckera* 22.2

6.5   3. Shoots not flat; leaves in more than 2 rows

       8. Plants dark to blackish green, submerged or floating; stems often denuded toward the base

          9. Leaves in 3 rows; stems often stringy at the base

             10. Leaves ovate-lanceolate to lanceolate; costa lacking .... *Fontinalis* 23.4

             10. Leaves narrowly lanceolate to lanceolate-subulate, secund; costa slender, percurrent to excurrent .... *Dichelyma* 23.26

9. Leaves in more than 3 rows; costa percurrent to excurrent

   11. Shoots regularly to irregularly pinnately branched; leaves lanceolate, costa stout, percurrent to excurrent; capsules inclined and asymmetric .... *Amblystegium* 21.124

   11. Shoots not pinnately branched, in loose or dense tufts; leaves broadly ovate to ovate-lanceolate or ligulate, acute to broadly obtuse; capsules erect and symmetric or nearly so, globose to ovoid on a very short seta, immersed to emergent .... Grimmiaceae 12.1

8. Plants variously green but not blackish when submerged; if blackish, then growing on dry rocks and tree trunks

   12. Mosses large, treelike, with erect secondary stems which arise from underground stolons and bear a dense cluster of branches at the summit; on damp or wet soil and humus at high elevations .... *Climacium* 21.5

   12. Mosses not treelike

      13. Stems regularly to irregularly branched, creeping and anchored by rhizoids from the underside, or ascending to erect, especially when growing in water or very wet places; sporophytes from budlike lateral branches; pleurocarpous

      14. Leaf cells short, smooth or often papillose on 1 or both sides; peristome teeth without fine transverse lines on the lower joints; dull or yellowish green plants .... Leskeaceae 20.1

      14. Leaf cells mostly longer and smooth, oblong-rhomboidal to long linear, if short, then plants bright green; peristome teeth with fine transverse lines on the lower joints .... Hypnaceae 21.1

      13. Stems erect to ascending, branches mostly erect, anchored at the base; sporophytes terminal on the main stem or well-developed branches; acrocarpous

      15. Plants large, dark green; leaves crisped or erect, stiff and wiry when dry, oblong-lanceolate to lanceolate-ligulate

         16. Costa bearing longitudinal lamellae on the upper side; peristome teeth 32–64, very short, ligulate, unjointed, attached to an epiphragm .... Polytrichaceae 24.1

            17. Leaves ligulate, base not dilated, lamellae 6 or less in our species, blade undulate with transverse rows of teeth on the back; capsules cylindric, teeth 32 .... *Atrichum* 24.4

            17. Leaves oblong- to linear-lanceolate from a dilated

77

clasping base, costa occupying nearly the width of the blade, lamellae numerous, 30 or more

18. Capsules ovoid-oblong to cylindric, smooth, erect to inclined when dry; teeth about 32 .... *Pogonatum* 24.9

18. Capsules angular with 4 longitudinal ridges; teeth about 64

19. Capsules nearly square to oblong, boxlike, erect to horizontal when dry, ridges equidistant .... *Polytrichum* 24.27

19. Capsules slightly swollen below, narrowed to the mouth, inclined to horizontal when dry, the 2 upper ridges stronger and closer together than the weaker lower ridges .... *Polytrichadelphus* 24.21

16. Costa not bearing lamellae, slender and distinct; capsules never angled, shortly ovoid to ovoid-oblong, inclined; teeth 16, jointed with an inner peristome of numerous cilia; under rocks, on soil and on tree roots and in mountain crevices .... *Timmia* 17.2

15. Plants small to medium sized with leaves various, or if large, the leaves broad and obovate to ligulate

6.6 20. Upper medial leaf cells isodiametric to shortly oblong

21. Leaf cells smooth

22. Plants dark to blackish green, often hoary on the surface, in dense cushions or tufts on dry rocks; seta short, straight or arcuate; capsules immersed to shortly exserted .... *Grimmia* 12.4

22. Plants of various shades of green but rarely blackish green, if so, growing on soil or in crevices

23. Leaves narrowly lanceolate with slender apices; alar cells enlarged and inflated, at least in some leaves; peristome teeth deeply cleft into two jointed divisions

24. Leaves strongly crisped when dry, the base broadly dilated; capsules frequent, cylindric, curved and asymmetric, strumose .... *Oncophorus* 9.39

24. Leaves, in our species, not crisped when dry, straight and imbricated, often falcate-secund, the tips sometimes broken off; capsules rare .... *Dicranum* 9.57

23. Leaves various, without enlarged or inflated alar cells

25. Leaves ovate-lanceolate to slenderly lanceolate

78

26. Capsules frequently present; leaves strongly crisped when dry

   27. Capsules cylindric, strumose, erect when moist, inclined at right angles and longitudinally sulcate when dry, chestnut brown; teeth cleft into 2 strongly jointed prongs; on dry or moist soil .... *Ceratodon* 9.17

   27. Capsules shortly oblong to cylindric, not strumose, erect and smooth when dry; teeth entire to irregularly cleft into weakly-jointed linear divisions; on dry rocks and fallen tree trunks .... *Dicranoweisia* 9.44

26. Capsules rare in our species; leaves may or may not be moderately crisped when dry; mainly on dry or wet soil and rocks .... *Didymodon* 10.82

25. Leaves broadest near the middle or above, ± narrowed at the base

  28. Plants medium sized to large, mostly in dry or wet, shaded places of foothills and mountains

   29. Leaves spatulate to oblong-lanceolate, acute to shortly acuminate, entire, not bordered; costa excurrent as a long sharp yellowish point; capsules cylindric, erect; teeth divided into 32 spirally twisted hairlike divisions from a high tessellated basal membrane .... *Tortula mucronifolia* 10.260

   29. Leaves elliptical, obovate, oblong or oblong-lanceolate acute to broadly rounded, ± strongly narrowed at the base; margins entire to strongly toothed, mostly bordered with narrow thick-walled cells; capsules oblong to pyriform, pendent or horizontal; teeth lanceolate, not divided .... *Mnium* 19.145

  28. Plants small; on dry soil, in foothills and valleys

   30. Leaves with white hair points; lamina flat or concave but margins not involute

    31. Costa bearing simple or branched chlorophyllose filaments on the upper side, short and few or long and dense, often spreading laterally over the blade; capsules cylindric, long exserted, erect; peristome of 32 spirally twisted hairlike divisions .... *Crossidium* 10.203

    31. Costa bearing 2–4 lamellae on the upper side; these sometimes bear chlorophyllose filaments on the sur-

faces and appear as a dense, opaque granular mass; seta short; capsules immersed to well exserted, globose to ovoid or cylindric; peristome lacking or very fragile and difficult to demonstrate .... *Pterygoneurum*   10.181

30. Leaves without hair points; costa very broad and occupying most of the width of the leaf, thick and bearing a dense mass of chlorophyllose filaments; narrow margins of the blade strongly involute .... *Aloina*   10.197

6.7   21. Leaf cells papillose

   32. Margins of the leaves involute, plants small

      33. Capsules with a lid; peristome present or lacking .... *Weissia*   10.12

      33. Capsules splitting open irregularly .... *Astomum*   10.6

   32. Margins of leaves flat or revolute

      34. Leaves broadest at the base, ovate to narrowly lanceolate

         35. Margins of leaves toothed at the base .... *Eucladium*   10.48

         35. Margins of leaves toothed above the base or entire

            36. Stems often prolonged as green pseudopodia bearing green gemmae on the sides or in a globose cluster; leaves serrate to nearly entire .... *Aulacomnium*   16.2

         36. Stems not forming pseudopodia

            37. Hyaline basal cells extending up the margins of the leaves in a V-shaped fashion; leaves strongly crisped when dry .... *Tortella*   10.66

            37. Hyaline basal cells not extending up the leaf margins

               38. Plants reddish except at the green tips; capsules frequent, oblong to cylindric, erect and symmetric; leaves obscurely to coarsely toothed at the extreme apex .... *Bryoerythrophyllum*   10.101

               38. Plants yellowish, brown or blackish below, rarely reddish

                  39. Capsule long exserted; teeth usually divided into slender divisions

                     40. Plants short or tall and slender, forming dense cushions or expanded sods on wet, limey cliffs

or rocks, light or bluish green on the surface; leaves oblong to linear-lanceolate, acute or blunt, not crisped when dry; margins plane or revolute below; capsules oblong, erect; peristome lacking .... *Gymnostomum* 10.33

40. Plants mostly medium sized, bright to dark green

    41. Leaves linear-lanceolate to narrowly ligulate from an oblong base, gradually or abruptly acute, strongly crisped when dry; margins plane, entire to irregularly notched above; mostly on shaded soil or rocks and in crevices .... *Trichostomum* 10.54

    41. Leaves ovate-lanceolate to lanceolate; slenderly acute or broader above and obtuse; margins revolute; capsules oblong to cylindric, erect; on wet or dry soil, rocks or cliffs

        42. Peristome teeth short and straight, variously cleft to divided .... *Didymodon* 10.82

        42. Peristome teeth divided into 32 long spirally twisted hairlike divisions from a very short basal membrane .... *Barbula* 10.110

39. Capsules immersed to shortly exserted, globose to cylindric, smooth or longitudinally furrowed when dry; teeth 16, triangular-lanceolate, usually in 8 pairs; plants dark green, olivaceous or blackish; leaves mostly oblong-lanceolate to lanceolate; on dry rocks or bark of trees .... *Orthotrichum* 13.5

34. Leaves broadest near the middle or above, narrowed at the insertion

    43. Leaves finely to coarsely serrate above; cells bearing a single large conical papilla in the middle; leaves shortly oblong ligulate to lanceolate and widely acute to broadly rounded; capsules rare .... *Dichodontium* 9.33

    43. Leaves entire; papillae smaller, usually 2 or more on each cell, sometimes weak or lacking, frequently C-shaped or O-shaped

        44. Margins of the leaves bordered by larger, often orange cells; leaves broadly ligulate-spatulate, rounded at the apex, acute to bluntly mucronate; submerged or on wet rocks of limestone regions; capsules rare .... *Scopelophila* 10.306

44. Margins of leaves not bordered with larger cells; capsules frequent

45. Plants small, less than 1 cm tall; leaves ovate to obovate or oblong-lanceolate to ligulate, acute to shortly acuminate in our species; mostly on soil

46. Plants yellowish green; capsules ovoid, immersed or projecting horizontally between perichaetial leaves; lid not differentiated .... *Phascum* 10.152

46. Plants green; capsules on a long seta, erect, shortly oblong to cylindric; peristome lacking in our species .... *Pottia* 10.162

45. Plants small to large; leaves mostly oblong to ligulate, acute to broadly rounded, often with hyaline hair points

47. Calyptra large and persistent, yellowish, covering half or all of the capsule; capsules erect, cylindric, emergent to shortly exserted, smooth or longitudinally furrowed when dry .... *Encalypta* 11.3

47. Calyptra small, thin and falling early (seldom seen)

48. Peristome teeth 16, divided into 2–3 slender prongs, sometimes irregularly so, straight or slightly twisted from a low basal membrane; capsules oblong to cylindric (ovoid, asymmetric and cernuous in *D. cernuus*); seta erect (curved and capsule pendent in *D. laureri*) .... *Desmatodon* 10.221

48. Peristome teeth 16, divided into 32 long hairlike divisions, strongly spirally twisted from a high tessellated basal membrane (except in *T. muralis*); capsules erect, cylindric, straight or slightly curved .... *Tortula* 10.252

6.8 20. Upper leaf cells oblong to linear

49. Leaf cells papillose because of projecting end walls; leaf margins mostly serrate; capsules globose to shortly ovate, inclined, furrowed when dry

50. Leaves subulate, abruptly divergent from an oblong clasping base; costa occupying nearly the entire width of the upper part of the blade .... *Bartramia* 18.10

50. Leaves ovate-lanceolate to triangular-lanceolate, base not differentiated but often plicate, straight or falcate-secund; costa slender, percurrent to long excurrent; shoots often with whorled subfloral innovations, often with a tomentum of ferruginous rhizoids extending high up .... *Philonotis* 18.16

49. Leaf cells smooth

    51. Shoots usually clothed with a tomentum of ferruginous rhizoids well toward the summit; leaves narrowly lanceolate to subulate from a broad base with a single strong fold on each side; capsules rare, globose to shortly oblong, thin walled, finely wrinkled when dry; peristome lacking .... *Anacolia*   18.4

    51. Shoots not tomentose with ferruginous rhizoids often dense, brown to reddish, mostly confined to the base of the shoots

      52. Leaves usually broadest above the base, broadly elliptical, obovate to ligulate, usually acute; cells mostly rhomboidal to hexagonal

        53. Leaves strongly bordered with linear, thick-walled cells .... *Bryum*   19.63

        53. Leaves not bordered with linear cells

          54. Capsules ovoid to ovoid-cylindric, unchanged when dry, abruptly narrowed to a very long necklike hypophysis which tapers very gradually into the seta, wrinkled when dry; exothecial cells transversely elongated, very thick walled; peristome teeth divided to the base into 32 long linear divisions, often tangled or broken .... *Tayloria*   15.3

          54. Capsules pyriform, without a hypophysis; exothecial cells vertically elongated; teeth not divided or peristome lacking

            55. Capsules asymmetric, gibbous, inclined on an erect seta or pendent on a widely curved seta when moist, furrowed to irregularly wrinkled when dry .... *Funaria*   14.4

            55. Capsules symmetric, erect to slightly inclined, smooth when dry, only the neck wrinkled

              56. Seta long; capsules elongate-pyriform, neck rather long; peristome present .... *Funaria*   14.4

              56. Seta short; capsules shortly pyriform or ovoid-pyriform, neck short; peristome lacking .... *Physcomitrium*   14.36

      52. Leaves broadest at the base

        57. Leaves linear-subulate from a broader base; costa occupying nearly the entire width of the blade; capsules small,

horizontal, slenderly pyriform, slightly gibbous, neck long and slender; annual .... *Leptobryum* 19.10

57. Leaves ovate-lanceolate or oblong; costa slender

58. Leaf cells mostly narrowly hexagonal to linear, or shorter in a few species, the marginal ones not distinctly narrower or forming a distinct border

59. Capsules erect, elongate-pyriform, neck slender; outer peristome teeth lacking; endostome of linear-subulate segments from broadened bases; rare plants on wet limestone rocks and cliffs .... *Mielichhoferia* 19.4

59. Capsules inclined to pendent, short to long pyriform; peristome double, teeth lanceolate; sterile stems of some species bearing deciduous gemmae in the axils of upper leaves ....*Pohlia* 19.16

58. Leaf cells mostly rhomboidal to hexagonal, the marginal ones much longer, narrower and thicker walled, forming a ± distinct border; capsules inclined to pendent, shortly to longly pyriform or clavate, straight to slightly incurved .... *Bryum* 19.63

SPHAGNALES

SPHAGNACEAE

7.1 Protonema a thin, flat, lobed thallus, the leafy stem arising from the margin. Stems erect, bearing spirally disposed fascicles of 3–10 branches, the fascicles distant below, crowded at the apex. Stem and branch leaves different; leaf cells dimorphous. Male branches with leaves ± imbricated, forming a sort of catkin; antheridia arising singly at the sides of the leaves, on very slender stalks, globose to ovoid. Female branches short, with large perichaetial leaves; archegonia 1–5, terminal, paraphyses lacking. After fertilization the stem becomes elongated and exserted from the perichaetium as a naked green pseudopodium, the sporophyte developing at its apex; foot massive and bulbous, dilating the apex of the pseudopodium; seta lacking; urn subglobose, ovoid or elliptical, at maturity irregularly splitting the membranous calyptra; columella arising from the endothecium, massive, not connected with the operculum and completely overarched by the amphithecium from which the spores arise; annulus and peristome lacking; operculum low, saucer-shaped and deciduous. Spores tetrahedral. One family and one genus.

SPHAGNUM L.

7.2 Plants on wet soil, humus, or rocks, sometimes in water, soft and spongy, pale or whitish green, often tinged with red, yellow or brown. Stems mostly simple, occasionally with 1–2 secondary axes; 1–3 branches in each fascicle, shorter, thicker, and ± spreading, the others long, slender, and hanging parallel with the main stem. Fascicles distant below and densely crowded at the summit in a compact head. The main stem in cross section showing a medulla of thin-walled cells surrounded by a cortex of thick-walled cells, and, in most species, an outer cortex of ± enlarged thin-walled cells in 1–5 layers. Stem leaves spirally inserted, distant, pale and flaccid, erect above, reflexed against the stem below, obovate, ligulate or triangular, ecostate. Branch leaves erect, imbricated to spreading or squarrose, broadly ovate-acuminate to narrowly lanceolate, ecostate, often toothed at the apex; cells of two kinds: (1) large, sinuously rhomboidal, empty, hyaline cells, reinforced internally with spiral or ringlike fibrils, the free walls perforated with pores, these often large, 1–10 or more per cell; (2) linear chlorophyll cells bordering the hyaline cells on all sides and situated in one of three positions (as seen in cross section): (a) with broader exposure on the ventral side of the leaf, (b) with broader exposure on the dorsal side, or (c) equally exposed or central and not at all exposed. The cells of stem leaves similar but the narrow cells also hyaline, the large ones generally without fibrils or only weak fibrils, pores few or lacking.

7.3 *Sphagnum* is an old Greek name, originally applied to tree-inhabiting lichens and possibly derived from *sphoggos*, a sponge, because of its spongy texture. In historical documents the name appears first in Pliny's *Naturalis Historia* as *Sphagnos* and *Sphacos*. These words may have been derived from *Phascos* which Theophrastus used for tree lichens in his *On the History of Plants*. Lobel was the first to apply the name to a moss, in 1581, and Dillenius established the genus in modern sense in 1741.

7.4 Other structures of importance are as follows. The outer layer of enlarged thin-walled cells of the stem has no special structures in most species, but in a few the cells may have one or more pores or internal fibrils, or both. The outer layer of cells of the branches may be of one kind and uniformly inflated, but in most species there are also larger retort cells, the upper ends of which are slightly narrowed, curved outward, and perforated by a pore at the tip. The dorsal walls of the upper cells of the stem leaves, and frequently the ventral walls as well, are resorbed so that the vertical walls form an erose or lacerate fringe at the apex.

7.5 In studying branch leaves, only the thicker spreading branches are used, and only leaves from the lower ⅔ of the branch. The denuded branch is mounted whole for the study of the outer cortical cells. To section branch leaves, three or four branches may be placed parallel on a strip of cardboard and sections cut through the lower ⅔, thus yielding a great number of leaf and branch sections. The position of the chlorophyll cells can usually be determined without cutting sections by examining both the ventral and dorsal views of branch leaves.

7.6 SPHAGNACEAE

When the broader exposure of these cells is toward the dorsal surface, the dorsal view, in perfect focus, will show the spiral fibrils of adjacent hyaline cells which appear to arise from the lateral walls, well apart and separated by chlorophyll cells, (plates 1 and 2, figs. 15–19, 26, 133). The ventral view, when brought into focus, will show the fibrils apparently arising from a single narrower line just above the chlorophyll cells. When the chlorophyll cells have the broader exposure ventral, the reverse positions of the fibrils may be observed. None of our species have the chlorophyll cells in a medial position; in such plants both dorsal and ventral views show the fibrils apparently arising from a single dividing line. The pores in the upper hyaline cells of the branch leaves of some species are thickened around the periphery, which gives them a ringed appearance.

7.6 The colors of the upper foliage and the woody cylinder of the main stem are used as taxonomic features. Some species do not contrast in color with the basic pale green and are ± uniform throughout, although many tend to become straw colored or brownish in the older parts. Others develop red, yellow, or brown tints. Not all shoots show this coloration, so that a generous quantity of the plant should be collected. If the characteristic color is present, particularly in the woody cylinder, some of the better-developed stems will show it, even in dried specimens viewed with the naked eye, although some specimens may require hand lens examination, or even cross sections of the stem.

7.7 1. Plants rather stout; branch leaves squarrose from a broadly ovate clasping base; in cross section chlorophyll cells triangular to trapezoidal, with broader exposure on the dorsal side of the leaf; stem leaves oblong-ligulate, slightly lacerate at the somewhat truncate apex .... 1. *S. squarrosum* 7.9

7.8 1. Plants rather slender; branch leaves ovate-acuminate to lanceolate, erect and imbricated, or with the upper part divergent when dry; stem leaves shortly ligulate to triangular-ligulate, toothed or only slightly erose at the rather narrow apex

2. Chlorophyll cells of branch leaves in cross section isosceles-triangular, with broader exposure on the dorsal surface; outer cortical cells not much differentiated. 2. *S. recurvum* var. *tenue* 7.11

Plate 1. 1–9. Sphagnum squarrosum. 1. Habit sketch, X.4. 2. Portion of the main stem showing a fascicle of branches, X1.2. 3. Cross section of portion of main stem, X40. 4. Outer cortical cells of the branch showing retort cells, X40. 5. Stem leaf, X8. 6. Cells of stem leaf, X80. 7. Branch leaf, X8. 8. Cells of stem leaf, X80. 9. Cross section of branch leaf, X80.

10–18. Sphagnum recurvum var. **tenue.** 10. Habit sketch, X.4. 11. Portion of the main stem showing a fascicle of branches, X1.2. 12. Cross section of portion of main stem, X40. 13. Outer cortical cells of branch showing retort cells, X40. 14. Stem leaf, X4. 15. Cells of stem leaf, X80. 16. Branch leaves, X8. 17. Cells of branch leaf, dorsal view, X80. 18. Cross section of branch leaf, X80.

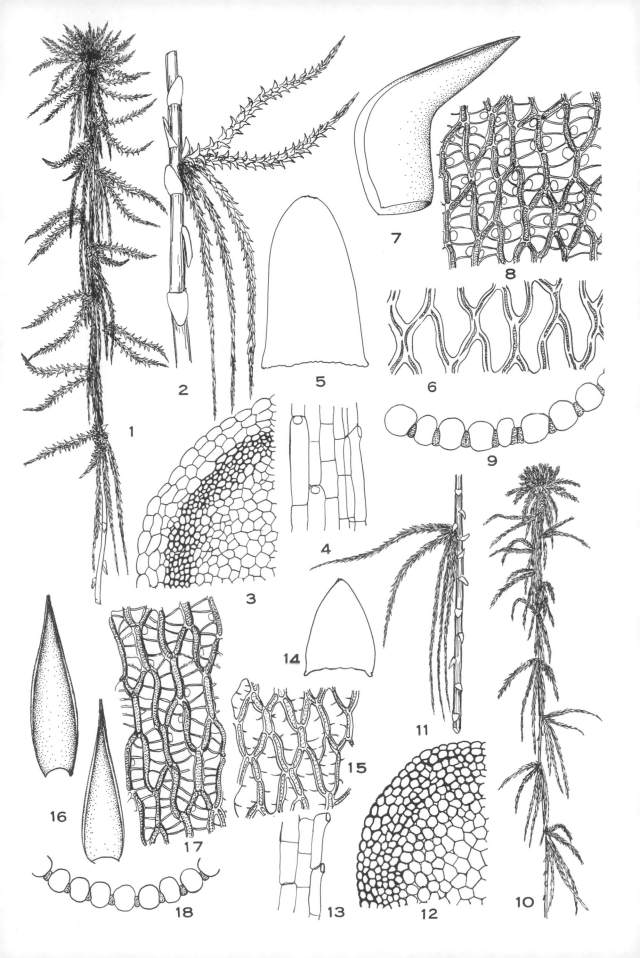

2. Chlorophyll cells of branch leaves with broader exposure on the ventral surface; outer cortical cells of the main stem enlarged and thin-walled, in 1–4 layers

3. Plants clear green or red to red tinged; woody cylinder of the stem often conspicuously red

4. Stem leaves rather gradually tapering to a narrow apex; dorsal surface of the branch leaves in the upper ½–⅔ with rather large elliptical pores adjacent to the lateral walls of hyaline cells .... 3. *S. capillaceum* 7.14

4. Stem leaves more broadly ligulate, rather suddenly narrowed to a broadly obtuse or somewhat truncate apex; dorsal surface of branch leaves in the upper ½–⅔ with very small oval or rounded pores with conspicuous rings .... 4. *S. warnstorfii* 7.17

3. Plants conspicuously brownish in the upper parts; woody cylinder of the stem yellowish brown to reddish brown .... 5. *S. fuscum* 7.19

7.9 **1. Sphagnum squarrosum** Crom. Plants stout, in loose or dense deep tufts, bright green, sometimes slightly glaucous or yellowish. Outer cortical cells of the main stem enlarged, thin walled, in 2–3 layers, without fibrils or pores; woody cylinder green to reddish brown. Stem leaves spreading to reflexed, 2–3 mm long, rather large, ovate to ovate-ligulate, concave and broadly rounded, the apex somewhat erose; hyaline cells without fibrils or pores, short above, narrower and becoming elongated at the base, narrower toward the margins of the leaves and forming an indistinct border which widens at the base. Branches long and slenderly tapering, in fascicles of 5, 2 of them spreading; cortical cells in 1–2 layers, without fibrils or pores, the retort cells only slightly differentiated. Branch leaves with a broadly ovate clasping base, abruptly narrowed and squarrose at the middle to an ovate-triangular upper part, 2–3 mm long, concave, the margins involute above, the apex blunt, 2- to 3-toothed; hyaline cells proportioned 1:4–8 in the middle, shorter toward the apex, and narrowly rhomboidal, strongly fibrillose throughout; 1–10 medium sized pores in the dorsal walls. The marginal cells linear, forming a border 2–3 cells wide; chlorophyll cells triangular to trapezoidal with the broader exposure dorsal, in some leaves oblong and almost medial with nearly equal exposure on both surfaces. Monoicous. Capsules numerous when produced, large and globose; spore yellow. Type locality, European. Plate 1, figs. 1–9.

7.10 Europe, Greenland to Alaska, southward to Pennsylvania and California.

7.11 **2. Sphagnum recurvum** P. Beauv. var. **tenue** Klinggr. Plants small and slender, in dense, often deep, tufts, light green, often tinged with yellow or brown. Woody cylinder of the stem green or yellowish, often not strongly developed, the walls only moderately thickened, without an outer cortex of large thin-walled cells, the surface layer without fibrils or pores. Stem leaves small, 0.5–0.8 mm long, triangular-ligulate to ovate-triangular, narrowly obtuse to rounded, often slightly erose, margins involute above, with a border of narrow cells often spreading across the base; hyaline cells mostly short, without fibrils or pores. Branches 5 per fascicle, 2 spreading; retort cells of the cortex with inconspicuous necks. Branch leaves erect at the base, the upper part recurved when dry, lanceolate, small, 1–1.2 mm long, apex slender, narrowly obtuse, somewhat obtuse, 2- to 3-toothed; margins strongly involute above. Dorsal walls of hyaline cells with 0–6 small pores; chlorophyll cells triangular with the broader exposure dorsal. Dioicous, rarely fruiting. Plate 1, figs. 10–18.

7.12   The typical form of S. *recurvum* is larger, of a medium size, with longer leaves undulate at the margins. The var. *tenue* is recognized by the absence of a well-differentiated, thin-walled cortex on the stem, small stem leaves, chlorophyll cells exposed dorsally, and the dorsal walls of the hyaline cells of branch leaves with only a few small pores (sometimes entirely lacking).

7.13   Europe and Asia. Greenland to Alaska, southward to Pennsylvania, Michigan, Nebraska, Utah and Washington.

7.14   **3. Sphagnum capillaceum** (Weiss) Schrank. Plants slender to moderately robust, usually in short compact tufts but often tall and slender, light green, frequently tinged with red. Woody cylinder of the stem usually reddish, the cortical cells in 2–4 layers, thin walled, without fibrils or pores, rectangular. Stem leaves rather large, triangular-ovate, concave, the apex ± involute, bluntly pointed and toothed; border of narrow cells strong, widened at the base, the cell walls often pitted; hyaline cells rhomboidal above, longer and narrower toward the margins and the base, the upper ones with traces of fibrils, usually without pores, occasionally divided by partitions; some stem leaves often approaching the form and structure of the branch leaves, these intermediate in character, having rather strong fibrils and, frequently, pores. Branches in fascicles of 3–5; cortical cells in 1 layer, without fibrils, retort cells with conspicuous necks. Branch leaves ovate-lanceolate to lanceolate reaching 2 mm long, imbricated, the apex slightly spreading when dry, involute above, the apex narrow and toothed; margins entire, bordered with 2–3 rows of narrow cells; hyaline cells rhomboidal above, becoming longer toward the base, strongly fibrillose throughout; pores along the lateral walls on the dorsal side variable, 3–6 or as many as 12 per cell, rather large, elliptical, 6–10 μ wide, not ringed or weakly ringed; chlorophyll cells triangular to trapezoidal in cross section with the broader exposure on the ventral side. Monoicous or dioicous; rarely fruiting in our region. Plate 2, figs. 1–9.

7.15   Europe, Asia, and South America. Greenland to Alaska, southward to Virginia, Wisconsin, Colorado, Utah and Washington. Summit County: Uinta Mountains, Stillwater Fork, on stream banks, 9,600 ft.

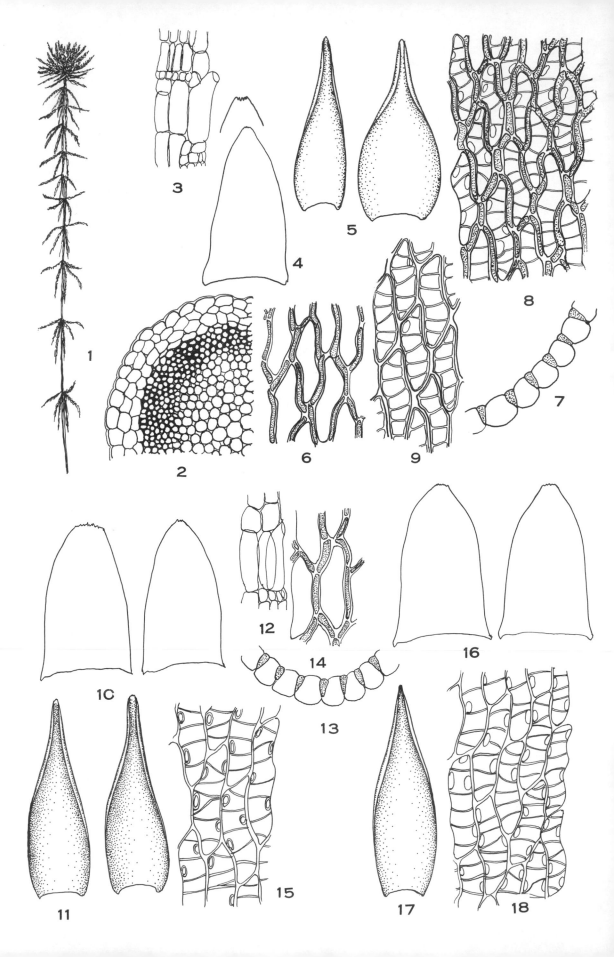

7.16 An extremely variable species. The following 2 species closely resemble it and have been treated as varieties by some authors. The present plants have branch leaves rather broadly ovate-lanceolate in contrast with the following species in which the branch leaves are more nearly lanceolate and have pores in the dorsal walls of the hyaline cells, just above midleaf, only about half as wide, or less.

7.17 **4. Sphagnum warnstorfii** Roell, Russ. Similar to the last in size, light green, the upper foliage and woody cylinder of the stem frequently red or red tinged. Stem leaves rather more broadly ligulate, more abruptly narrowed to a bluntly erose apex, with or without very weak fibrils; pores usually lacking. Branch leaves lanceolate, imbricated with the upper part slightly divergent when dry, involute above and toothed at the apex; dorsal walls of the hyaline cells in the upper $\frac{1}{2}$–$\frac{2}{3}$ with very small, mostly rounded, strongly ringed pores, 3–5 μ wide; chlorophyll cells mostly triangular with the broader exposure ventral. Dioicous, rarely fruiting. Plate 2, figs. 10–15.

7.18 Greenland to Alaska, southward to Connecticut, Michigan, Minnesota, and across the continent to Washington, Colorado and Uinta Mountains in Utah.

7.19 **5. Sphagnum fuscum** (Schimp.) Klinggr. Plants similar in stature to the last species but very slender and weak, in dense and often deep tufts, pale green and usually tinged with brown above, straw colored below; woody cylinder of the stem yellowish to brown. Stem leaves ligulate, broadly rounded at the apex, slightly erose; hyaline cells with very weak or no fibrils, pores lacking. Branch leaves ovate-lanceolate to lanceolate, involute above, toothed at the narrow apex; dorsal walls of the hyaline cells in the upper $\frac{1}{2}$–$\frac{2}{3}$ with small to medium sized oval to elliptical pores, 4–7 μ wide, with or without rings; chlorophyll cells triangular to trapezoidal in cross section, the broader exposure ventral. Dioicous; fruit rare. Plate 2, figs. 16–18.

7.20 Our most common species, abundant on wet banks of brooks and lakes or in boggy meadows in the Uinta Mountains.

7.21 Europe, Greenland to Alaska, southward to Connecticut, Michigan,

---

Plate 2. 1–9. **Sphagnum capillaceum.** 1. Habit sketch, X.4. Cross section of portion of main stem, X40. 3. Outer cortical cells of branch showing retort cell, X40. 4. Stem leaf, X8. 5. Two branch leaves, X8. 6. Upper cells of stem leaf, X200. 7. Cross section of branch leaf, X80. 8. Cells of branch leaf, ventral view, X80. 9. Same, dorsal view, X80.

10–15. **Sphagnum warnstorfii.** 10. Two stem leaves, X8. 11. Two branch leaves, X8. 12. Outer cortical cells of branch, X80. 13. Cross section of branch leaf, X80. 14. Cells of stem leaf, ventral view, X80. 15. Cells of branch leaf, dorsal view, X80.

16–18. **Sphagnum fuscum.** 16. Two stem leaves, X8. 17. Branch leaf, X8. 18. Cells of branch leaf, dorsal view, X80. **Note:** The size and habit of our plants of **S. warnstorfii** and **S. fuscum** are so much like that of **S. capillaceum** that sketches would scarcely show any difference.

Colorado, Utah and Washington. Duchesne County: Uinta Mountains, near Mirror Lake, 10,300 ft.

7.22 The brownish color is the most conspicuous feature. The pores in the dorsal walls of the hyaline cells of the branch leaves vary considerably in size, in some plants being nearly as small as those in *S. warnstorfii*.

BRYALES

FISSIDENTACEAE

8.1 Plants small or medium sized, leaves in 2 rows, alternate, appearing to be inserted edgewise giving the shoot a very flat appearance, the upper or inner lamina appearing split in the lower ⅓–⅔ of the leaf, the two halves clasping the stem and the base of the leaf above. Leaf cells ± isodiametric, angular, often irregularly so, smooth, mammillose or papillose, sometimes elongated at the base. Costa well developed, ending below the apex or shortly excurrent. Sporophyte lateral or terminal; capsules mostly small, exserted, obovate to shortly cylindrical, erect and symmetric or inclined and ± asymmetric; lid conic, short to long rostrate; peristome single, teeth 16, deeply bifid into slender divisions, mostly strongly jointed, usually bright reddish, usually strongly incurved when dry.

8.2 The curious structure of the leaf has been explained in several ways, but the following appears to be the best. The two clasping basal halves represent the leaf proper and are called the vaginant lamina. This is evident in the lowermost leaves of many stems where the smaller leaves are like the usual type of moss leaf in structure. The lower or outer lamina represents a dorsal outgrowth of costa (the dorsal lamina), while the upper (inner or ventral) lamina represents a ventral outgrowth of the costa. In addition to this evidence, the orientation of the cells of the costa as seen in cross section strongly supports this interpretation.

FISSIDENS Hedw.

8.3 With characters of the family. A very large genus of which we have only three species.

8.4 The name, from the Latin, means split tooth, alluding to the form of the peristome teeth.

8.5 1. Plants small and delicate; not aquatic; leaves oval, oblong or ligulate, up to 2 mm long; unistratose; costa ending 3–7 cells below the apex

    2. Leaves narrowly acute, shortly acuminate, or abruptly apiculate, margins bordered to near the ± denticulate apex .... 1. *F. limbatus* 8.7

    2. Leaves broadly rounded, obtuse .... 2. *F. obtusifolius* 8.13

8.6 1. Plants large and coarse; aquatic; leaves linear-lanceolate, 2–4 mm

long; several cells thick toward the costa; costa ending just below
the apex .... 3. *F. grandifrons*   8.21

8.7   **1. Fissidens limbatus** Sull.[*] Plants small, in loose to rather dense tufts,
often solitary or scattered on bare soil, commonly among other mosses,
dark green. Stems erect, 3–10(20) mm high, mostly simple but sometimes branched from near the base, green throughout, becoming reddish
at the base; rhizoids confined to the base. Leaves oblong or ligulate,
narrowly acute to shortly acuminate or abruptly apiculate, one shape
usually predominating in a given plant, the perichaetial leaves narrower
at the apex, 1–1.2(2) mm long; vaginant lamina extending ½–⅔ the
length of the upper leaves; dorsal lamina usually reaching the stem
in upper leaves, but often ending well above the base of lower leaves
or even in most leaves of some plants; margins ± serrulate at the apex,
bordered with 1–3 rows of hyaline, thin-walled, linear cells from near
the base to near the apex, border of the vaginant lamina becoming ±
widened toward the base and edged there by oblong cells in 1–3 rows;
costa ending 3–8 cells below the apex; upper medial leaf cells irregularly 5- to 6-sided, isodiametric to slightly elongated in various directions,
often tending to be in regular rows in most plants, 8-10(13) μ wide
(or long), smooth, chlorophyllose, the walls clear and distinct; basal
cells scarcely different, a few oblong along the costa, slightly wider, a
few more elongated at the extreme base. Autoicous. Seta 2.5–7 mm
long; capsules obovate to shortly oblong, urn 0.5–1.1 mm long, contracted below the mouth when dry, yellowish brown to reddish brown;
exothecial cells regularly oblong, the lateral walls thicker than the
transverse walls; annulus lacking; divisions of the peristome teeth
nodulose to spirally thickened and finely papillose above, the lower
joints transversely striated with fine papillae. Spores 12–14 μ, finely
papillose. Plate 3, figs. 1–8.

8.8   On damp or wet soil and rocks, usually in shade. Throughout Utah,
but local in distribution, often abundant.

8.9   British Columbia and Alberta southward to New Mexico and California.

8.10   Our plants differ from the typical form in that most of the capsules are
erect or very slightly inclined. Only rarely are they inclined as much
as 45° and somewhat asymmetric. The oblong cells edging basal linear
marginal cells are sometimes quite short, and this fact together with
the erect capsules suggests *Fissidens sublimbatus* Grout. The latter
occurs in southern Arizona and New Mexico. Our plants are somewhat
intermediate.

8.11   In two specimens collected in Niotche Canyon, Sevier County, the
leaves have no edging of shorter wider cells along the border of hyaline linear cells. Both answer well *Fissidens viridulus*, except that they
are autoicous, like *F. limbatus*, and not dioicous. The capsules are small,
erect, and symmetric or nearly so.

---

[*]This species is treated as *F. bryoides* Hedw. by Elva Lawton in *Moss Flora of
the Pacific Northwest.*

8.12   The differences usually cited in *Fissidens bryoides, F. limbatus,* and *F. sublimbatus* are so slight and intergrade so freely that it is difficult to admit them as full species. They are all autoicous, some are said to have the capsules erect and symmetric, or mainly so, others inclined and asymmetric, or mainly so. In *F. bryoides* the costa and border of the leaf margin converge at the apex, but in the other two species the costa and border cease 2–3 or as much as 7 cells below the tip.

8.13   **2. Fissidens obtusifolius** Wils. var. **obtusifolius.** Plants small, scattered or in loose tufts, dark to bright green. Stems short, mostly 1–2 mm tall but occasionally reaching 10 mm. Lower leaves small and distant, the upper ones oval to oblong-ligulate, 0.5–0.8 mm long, broadly rounded at the apex; margins entire throughout, without a border of narrow cells except in the perichaetial leaves in which the vaginant lamina may be indistinctly bordered by elongated cells; vaginant lamina ½–¾ the length of the leaf; dorsal lamina reaching the stem in the upper leaves; costa moderately slender, ending 3–7 cells below the tip; upper medial cells irregularly 2- to 6-sided, angular to slightly rounded, shortly oblong to hexagonal, the long axes extending in various directions, 7–10(12) μ wide, rarely in regular rows, those in the vaginant lamina somewhat larger and more regularly quadrate to oblong at the base. Dioicous, Seta terminal, comparatively stout, 2–3 mm long; capsules erect and symmetric, the urn 0.5 mm long or less, obovate to oblong; divisions of the peristome teeth rather vaguely spirally thickened, finely papillose below; operculum conic, apiculate to shortly rostrate. Spores 18–25 μ.

8.14   On damp or wet rocks, often inundated.

8.15   New England States to West Virginia and Alabama, westward to Minnesota, Utah and Texas.

8.16   2a. Var. **kansanus** Ren. & Card. Vaginant laminae of mature stem leaves and perichaetial leaves bordered with oblong to linear cells, usually becoming thick walled and hyaline, the dorsal lamina sometimes with a narrow, less distinct border. Plate 3, figs. 9–12.

8.17   San Juan County, Devil Canyon, near Verdure, 6,300 ft. The border on the dorsal lamina of our specimen is lacking.

8.18   2b. Var. **marginatus** Flow. Plants mostly 1.5–3 mm tall, simple to sparingly branched. Upper leaves oval-oblong to shortly oblong-lingulate, about 0.6 mm long, rounded-obtuse, some of them mucronate because of a single projecting cell; vaginant laminae of all but the lowest leaves

---

Plate 3.   1–8. Fissidens limbatus. 1. Habit sketches, X.4. 2. Single shoot, X6. 3. Five lower leaves, X8. 4. Four upper leaves, any of these forms may predominate in a plant, X8. 5. Two leaf apices, X80. 6. Basal and marginal leaf cells, X80. 7. Five capsules, X8. 8. Portion of peristome teeth, X60.

9–12. Fissidens obtusifolius var. **kansanus.** 9. Single shoot, X6. 10. Two upper leaves, X8. 11. Leaf apex, X80. 12. Basal and marginal leaf cells of the inner perichaetial leaves, X120.

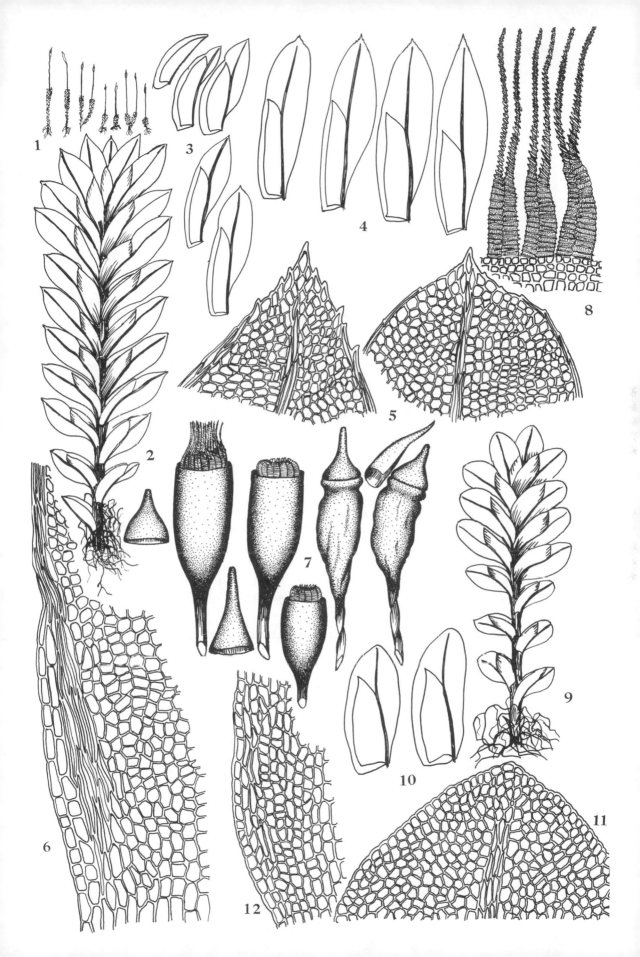

8.19   bordered to the base with elongated, narrower cells which become thick walled and hyaline when mature, in the lower half edged with 1–2 rows of quadrate to oblong chlorophyllose cells; margins of the dorsal and ventral laminae variable, without a border or with an indistinct partial border on upper leaves and a distinct border sometimes extending nearly to the apex of perichaetial leaves which may be as much as 1 mm long and sometimes slightly dentate at the tip. Capsules erect and symmetric, obovate to broadly oval, urn mostly 0.5 mm long or less, occasionally reaching 0.8 mm. Spores 18–22 μ. Plate 149, figs. 7–8.

8.19   Kane County: Colorado River, Glen Canyon, on damp sandstone walls above the edge of the river, 3,200 ft.

8.20   Differs from var. *kansanus* in having the border of narrow hyaline cells on the vaginant laminae edged with quadrate to oblong chlorophyllose cells.

8.21   **3. Fissidens grandifrons** Brid. Plants large, stiff, loosely tufted, dark green becoming olivaceous with age, often encrusted with lime, the lower parts eroded. Stems 3–15 cm tall, erect to ascending, simple or with numerous branches, suberect and rigid. Leaves crowded and imbricated, dark green and opaque, often yellowish, 2–3 mm long, lanceolate to linear-lanceolate; margins entire to finely crenulate-denticulate all around, without a border, narrowly obtuse, often acute in the uppermost leaves; vaginant lamina exceeding half the length of the leaf; costa disappearing just below the apex; leaf cells in several layers toward the costa, unistratose at the margins, irregularly 4- to 6-sided, isodiametric to elongated in various directions, strongly incrassate, 7–12 μ wide. Dioicous. Sporophytes exceedingly rare, in axils of upper leaves; seta 1–1.5 cm long; capsule erect and symmetric or nearly so, urn oblong, 1.2 mm long; lid conic-rostrate; peristome deeply inserted, the divisions rough. Spores 15–24 μ. Plate 4, figs. 1–4.

8.22   On wet rocks, aerial or submerged in rivulets and brooks, often around waterfalls and dripping cliffs in limestone regions. Not common but usually abundant locally.

8.23   Southern Canada, Washington to California, eastward to New York and south to Tennessee.

8.24   This large, coarse, rigid moss contrasts strongly with our other species, and the several layers of cells in the laminae immediately distinguishes it from all other North American species of *Fissidens*.

DICRANACEAE

9.1   Plants small to large, mostly tufted, often in expanded sods, in some genera gregarious. Stems erect, branched; central strand mostly present. Leaves various, shortly ovate-lanceolate to lanceolate or subulate, often with a clasping base; upper leaf cells quadrate to linear, smooth or variously papillose; basal cells usually $\pm$ enlarged; costa slender to very stout, ending in the apex, percurrent to long and often spinulose-excurrent. Setae in our genera long and erect; capsules ellipsoid to cylindric, erect and symmetric to inclined or cernuous, smooth or conspicuously furrowed when dry; in some genera and species strumose; operculum present in our genera ± long beaked; peristome teeth 16, usually cleft or divided 1/2–4/5 down into 2 or occasionally 3 slender divisions, sometimes variously perforated, irregularly divided or entire (*Dicranoweisia*), mostly vertically or obliquely striate and sometimes papillose. Calyptra cucullate or mitrate.

9.2   A difficult family to distinguish from the Ditrichaceae and Seligeriaceae and for that reason the three families have been combined here. Dicranoid refers to the predominating two divisions or prongs of the split teeth which in most genera, are vertically or obliquely striate. In spite of the inadequacy of a collective description, most of the genera of the family are easily recognized. *Dicranoweisia* is an intermediate genus which could be almost equally well accommodated to the Pottiaceae.

9.3   1.   Shoots very flat; leaves in 2 rows, abruptly and stiffly divergent from a long, whitish, clasping base; upper leaf cells papillose on both ends .... 1. *Distichium*   9.5

9.4   1.   Shoots not flattened; leaves in several rows, ovate to lanceolate or subulate.

2.   Plants minute, shoots less than 5 mm tall; capsules less than 1 mm long, obovate to pyriform, teeth shortly triangular-lanceolate, entire or sometimes cleft, smooth; exclusively on damp or wet rocks .... 3. *Seligeria*   9.28

2.   Plants usually larger; capsules larger, mostly oblong to cylindric, teeth usually longer and commonly divided into 2 or more slender divisions, striated or papillose

3.   Leaves crisped when dry

4.   Leaves shortly ovate-lanceolate to lanceolate-ligulate, acute to broadly obtuse; margins closely serrate, often with a few coarse teeth toward the apex; leaf cells short, each with a large conical papilla in the center .... 4. *Dichodontium*   9.33

4.   Leaves ovate-lanceolate to lanceolate, slenderly acute to blunt; upper leaf cells smooth or with small papillae

5.   Upper leaf cells quadrate to rounded or irregular

6.   Capsules erect and smooth when dry; teeth entire, perforated or irregularly cleft to divided, fragile; leaves 2-stratose on the upper margin and sometimes in the upper lamina; on dry rocks, fallen logs and tree trunks ....
.... 6. *Dicranoweisia*   9.44

6.   Capsules inclined, curved or cernuous when dry, often strumose at the base; on soil and rocks

97

7. Capsules cylindric, strumose, cernuous and strongly furrowed when dry, teeth divided 4/5, strongly barred .... 2. *Ceratodon* 9.17

7. Capsules curved when dry, strumose but not furrowed, yellowish brown; teeth cleft ½ way down; alpine .... 5. *Oncophorus* 9.39

5. Upper leaf cells oblong to linear; plants small; leaves mostly spreading from an ovate half-clasping base .... 7. *Dicranella* 9.52

3. Leaves straight or widely curved or twisted but not crisped when dry, straight or secund when moist, strongly channeled or subtubulose, tips often broken; alar cells enlarged, inflated, and often colored

8. Costa convex at back, not occupying the entire width of the blade showing guides and stereids in cross section .... 8. *Dicranum* 9.57

8. Costa flat, occupying the entire width of the blade above, consisting of large empty cells on both sides with small, angular, chlorophyllose cells between them .... 9. *Paraleucobryum* 9.73

1. DISTICHIUM B.S.G.

9.5 Plants in dense tufts. Stems slender, simple or occasionally forked by innovation; central strand large, the outer cortical cells smaller, thick walled and colored. Leaves spreading in 2 opposite rows, rendering the shoot flat, base elongated and ± clasping, the upper portion abruptly divergent and narrowed to a linear-subulate or awnlike apex; costa broad and occupying most of the upper portion, excurrent, forming a very rough or occasionally entire awn, in cross section showing a row of guides and both dorsal and ventral stereids and thick-walled dorsal superficial cells; lamina forming narrow wings; upper cells oblong to sublinear, mostly with a single papilla at each end (sometimes nearly smooth); basal cells elongated, wider, thin walled and hyaline, smooth. Seta elongated; capsules ovate to cylindric, erect and symmetric or inclined and ± asymmetric, neck short; annulus large; operculum conic or slightly rostrate; peristome teeth 16, cleft or divided into 2 or partially

---

Plate 4. 1–4. Fissidens grandifrons. 1. Habit sketches, X.4. 2. Leaves, one eroded, X8. 3. Cross section of leaf, X120. 4. Leaf apex and upper cells, X120.

5–11. Distichium capillaceum. 5. Habit sketches, X.4. 6. Leaves, X8. 7. Leaf apices and upper leaf cells, X120. 9. Three capsules, X8. 10. Spores, X120. 11. Peristome teeth, X60.

12. Distichium capillaceum var. **curvatum.** Capsules, X8.

13–15. Distichium inclinatum. 13. Three capsules, X8. 14. Spores, X120. 15. Peristome teeth, X60.

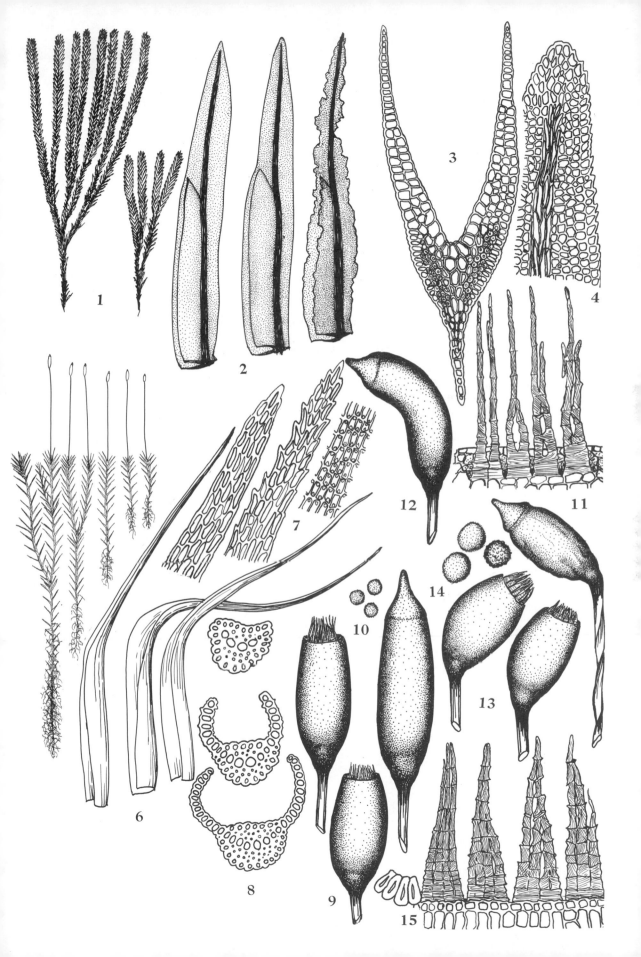

1 2 3 4

6 7 10 11 12 14 13

8 9 15

3 slender divisions, often very irregular, frequently broken, the joints with fine oblique or nearly vertical striations, and sometimes finely papillose besides. Spores smooth to finely papillose. Calyptra cucullate.

9.6   Name from the Greek, meaning two series and referring to the 2-ranked leaves.

9.7   1. Capsules ovoid-oblong to oblong-cylindric, erect and symmetric or nearly so .... 1. *D. capillaceum* 9.9

9.8   1. Capsules distinctly inclined or curved, ± asymmetric .... 2. *D. inclinatum* 9.14

9.9   **1. Distichium capillaceum** (Hedw.) B.S.G. var. **capillaceum.** Plants light green. Stems 1–5(10) cm tall, slender, densely interwoven below with reddish brown rhizoids. Leaves 2–4 mm long, the oblong sheathing base about 1 mm long, the upper part linear-subulate and spreading at about 45°; costa short to long excurrent, the awn entire to serrate; lamina narrow, the margins plane and entire; upper cells shortly oblong to irregularly elongate-hexagonal, mostly with a papilla at each end, sometimes nearly smooth; basal cells hyaline, linear, often flexuous, about 3–5 μ wide. Seta 0.5–2 cm long, slender; capsule ovoid to oblong-cylindric, 1–2 mm long or occasionally cylindric and reaching 2.6 mm long without the lid, erect and symmetric or nearly so, light or yellowish brown, becoming darker with age, smooth or minutely longitudinally wrinkled when dry; teeth irregularly cleft to divided, often imperfect or broken, reddish at maturity, finely striated and often finely and densely papillose in addition; lid conic to conic-rostrate. Spores very finely papillose, 17–23 μ. Plate 4, figs. 5–11.

9.10   On wet or damp substrata, stream banks, rotten logs, rocks, seepage areas, dripping cliffs, often in crevices. Common in the mountains throughout Utah.

9.11   Greenland to Alaska, southward to New York, Great Lakes Region, and in the Rocky Mountains to Arizona. Nearly world wide in mountains.

9.12   1a. Var. **curvatum** Flow. Capsule cylindric and strongly curved. Spores 20–23. This is probably a hybrid between the species and *D. inclinatum.* Plate 4, fig. 12.

9.13   Summit County, Uinta Mountains.

9.14   **2. Distichium inclinatum** (Hedw.) B.S.G. Differs from the last species in being shorter, darker, duller green, the leaves closer together, less spreading and the distichous arrangement less conspicuous, the clasping base shorter, the upper cells thicker walled, the subula shorter. Seta shorter, 0.5–1.5 cm long; capsules ovoid, inclined and asymmetric, usually darker colored; peristome teeth shorter, triangular-lanceolate, 2–3 cleft and perforated, often irregularly so, the joints with fine oblique or transverse striations. Spores large, 30-45 μ, finely to coarsely papillose. Plate 4, figs. 13–15.

9.15 In habitats like those of the last species but much less common.

9.16 Greenland and Labrador, southward along the St. Lawrence River, Minnesota, Montana, northern Utah and California.

2. CERATODON Brid.

9.17 Mostly small plants in dense tufts or sods, green above, brownish below, often tinged with red when old. Stems erect, forked by innovations; central strand present. Leaves usually crowded, imbricated and erect-patent to somewhat crisped and twisted when dry, ± patent when moist, ovate- to linear-lanceolate; margins recurved; costa strong, ending below the tip or long excurrent; upper leaf cells quadrate to shortly rectangular, smooth. Mostly dioicous. Sporophyte terminal, often becoming lateral by innovation; perichaetial leaves long and convolute sheathing. Seta long; capsules oblong-ovate to cylindrical, with a small struma at the base, erect when young, usually slightly asymmetric, when young nearly erect to cernuous, longitudinally furrowed; operculum high conic to rostrate; peristome teeth 16, from a short basal membrane, cleft nearly to the base into 32 slender divisions joined by crossbars, strongly trabeculate at the base, nodulose upward and finely papillose throughout, often bright reddish. Calyptra cucullate.

9.18 Name from the Greek meaning horn tooth, from the resemblance of the peristome teeth to horns of the goat.

9.19 1. Costa ending slightly below the leaf apex, percurrent or shortly excurrent, not forming a hair point; upper margins of leaves usually ± dentate .... 1. *C. purpureus* 9.21

9.20 1. Costa excurrent to a short or long yellowish hair point; upper margins of leaves entire or nearly so .... 2. *C. conicus* 9.24

9.21 **1. Ceratodon purpureus** (Hedw.) Brid. Plants green when young, tinged with red or brown when old. Shoots variable according to habitat: short in open dry situations, leaves short and crowded; in moist shaded places longer, more slender, the leaves generally longer and less crowded. Stems mostly 5–15 mm tall (up to 5 cm or more in damp or wet situations), usually branched by innovations, occasionally with long, slender innovations bearing reduced leaves. Leaves ± crisped or twisted when dry; erect-patent to patent when moist, ovate-acuminate, ovate-lanceolate, triangular-lanceolate or linear-lanceolate, one shape generally predominating in a given specimen, the upper and comal ones 1–2.7 mm long, the lower ones shorter; margins entire to dentate above, widely recurved nearly to the apex; costa strong, in some leaves occupying as much as $\frac{1}{4}$–$\frac{1}{3}$ the width of the leaf base; percurrent to shortly excurrent, at most mucronate, not forming a hair point; upper leaf cells quadrate to shortly rectangular, often irregularly so, 7–10 μ wide, rather thick walled and smooth; basal cells becoming slightly larger and oblong, generally chlorophyllose. Dioicous. Seta yellow to dark reddish, 1–2.5 cm long; capsules oblong-ovoid to shortly

101

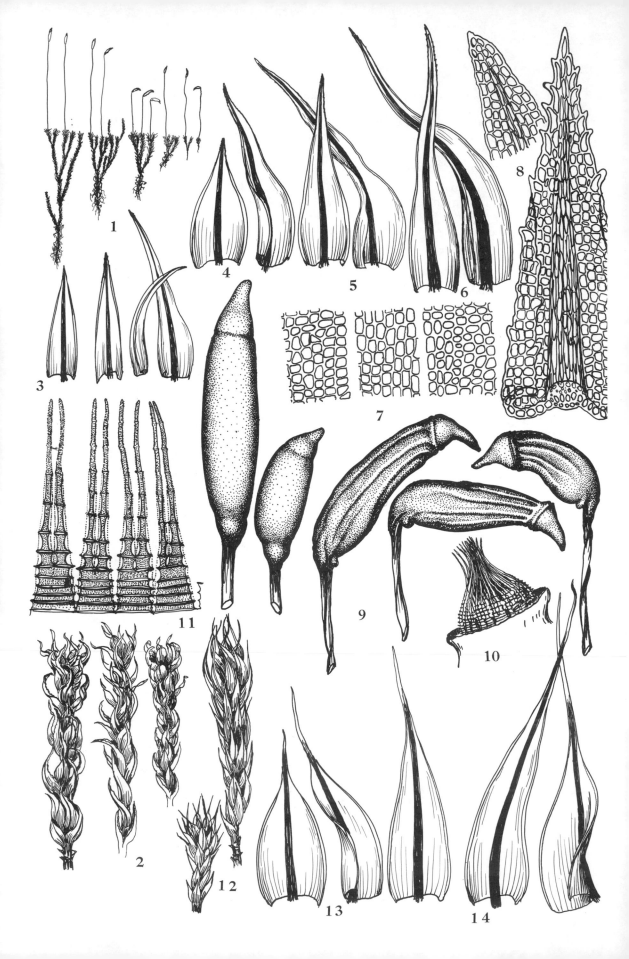

1

3

4

5

6

8

7

11

9

10

2

12

13

14

cylindrical, usually asymmetric, the mouth often slightly oblique, the neck short, with a small struma on 1 side; erect or inclined when moist, strongly inclined to cernuous and strongly longitudinally furrowed when dry, light reddish to dark reddish chestnut; operculum high conic to short rostrate, bent downward; peristome teeth varying considerably in slenderness of the divisions, strongly arched inward, the tips converging. Spores 10–15 μ, smooth, mature in spring or early summer. Plate 5, figs. 1–11.

9.22 On exposed soil, soon drying out, in open places in shady woods, or in damp or wet places, along streams or in seepage areas. Common on plains and hillsides, open places in thickets or woods. Cosmopolitan.

9.23 I do not regard var. *xanthopus* Sull. as worthy of systematic rank. As originally characterized, the costa is percurrent, the seta yellow, and the lid often beaked. I find these traits intimately associated in different combinations with those of the species proper. The yellowish seta appears to be a developmental condition as the color in different plants or even in the same tuft may range through intergrading tints from pale yellowish to dark chestnut. The variation in the shape and length of the leaves is remarkable.

9.24 2. **Ceratodon conicus** (Hamp.) Lindb.* Plants generally more yellowish green, the leaves not crisped when dry, but erect and $\pm$ appressed, often closely imbricated or slightly twisted together at the tips of the stems, patent when moist; shapes variable as in the last, but costa excurrent to a short or long hair point, this sometimes becoming nearly as long as the blade. Inner perichaetial leaves widely acute, obtuse or truncate, the costa ending below the apex. Capsules often nearly erect when dry. Plate 5, figs. 12–14.

9.25 Growing mainly on dry soil in open places, foothills and mountains. Said to be rare but not uncommon in our region.

9.26 Alaska, Washington, British Columbia, Idaho, Utah and Minnesota. Europe.

9.27 I find the fruiting specimens usually small and agreeing well with the original description, but more often I find larger sterile shoots mixed in tufts of normal *C. purpureus*. In such mixtures the plants of *C. conicus* stand out quite distinctly among the more compact, yellowish green shoots, owing to the leaves appressed and imbricated, the upper and comal ones terminating in yellowish brown hair points, these spreading

---

*Treated as *C. purpureus* (Hedw.) Brid by Lawton.

Plate 5. 1–11. Ceratodon purpureus. 1. Habit sketches, X.4. 2. Portions of shoot showing dry habit of leaves, X2.8. 3–6. Upper and comal leaves of four different plants showing variations in size and shape, X8. 7. Three areas of upper medial leaf cells from different plants, X120. 8. Two leaf apices, X120. 9. Capsules, X8. 10. Peristome, X24. 11. Peristome teeth, X60. See also fig. 167.

12–14. Ceratodon conicus. 12. Portions of two shoots showing dry habits of the leaves, X2.8. 13–14. Upper and comal leaves of two different plants, X8.

or sometimes slightly twisted together at the tips of the stems. (They often resemble small plants of *Bryum caespiticium* when dry.) While the contrast between the two plants is marked in many specimens, especially those growing mixed together, I also find considerable intergradation.

3. SELIGERIA B.S.G.

9.28 Plants very small, less than 5 mm tall. Stems simple or branched from the base; central strand present. Upper leaves the largest, oblong to lanceolate or subulate; costa wide, percurrent to excurrent into a long subula. Seta fairly long; capsules well exserted, shortly ovoid to pyriform, often with a short neck, less than 1 mm long; annulus lacking; peristome present or lacking. Calyptra cucullate. Named in honor of Ignaz Seliger, a pastor and botanist of Silesia. Growing on rocks, usually damp limestone.

9.29 **Seligeria campylopoda** Kindb. in Macoun. Plants usually scattered in patches among kepatics or other mosses; stems less than 1 mm tall, simple or branched from the base. Leaves narrowly oblong to lanceolate, erect-patent to patent or recurved when moist, incurved to erect when dry, the comal ones the largest, 1–1.3 mm long, the lower ones smaller, acute to obtuse; margins plane throughout or narrowly recurved below, entire to vaguely serrulate above; costa percurrent or ending below the apex; upper cells of various or mixed shapes, quadrate to shortly oblong, sometimes rounded or oval, 6–9 μ wide, moderately thick walled, smooth; basal cells larger, clearer, oblong, often with some sublinear, 8–12 μ wide, thin walled. Autoicous or sometimes dioicous. Seta 1–2(3) mm long, curved or somewhat flexuous; capsules small, reddish brown, shortly obovate to pyriform, the urn less than 1 mm long, becoming cuplike or more strongly pyriform, the neck shrunken when dry, the mouth typically slightly narrowed but sometimes wide and slightly flaring, especially in smaller capsules; exothecial cells mostly oblong, thin walled, 1–2 rows at the mouth strongly compressed and thick walled, a few rather large imperfectly formed stomata in the neck; peristome teeth shortly triangular-lanceolate, dark reddish brown, entire or sometimes cleft or sparingly perforated, joints 7–9(12), the upper part often broken off and appearing truncate, erect to recurved when dry; lid long rostrate; annulus lacking. Spores globose, 8–11 μ, smooth or finely punctate, light yellowish brown. Plate 9, figs. 9–15.

9.30 On damp or wet shaded rocks.

9.31 Montana to Newfoundland, Utah, Iowa, Ohio and New York. Rare. Utah County: Wasatch Mountains, Mt. Timpanogos above Aspen Grove at Columbine Falls, 9,000 ft.

9.32 Our single collection consists of five fruited shoots scattered in a mat of *Pseudoleskea incurvata*. In comparison with a specimen from the type locality, Owen Sound, Ontario, it differs only slightly: the leaves are less slender in the upper part, the upper cells on the whole slightly

104

longer and thinner walled with fewer quadrate cells scattered among them, and the mouth of the capsules wider or somewhat spreading when dry.

4. DICHODONTIUM Schimp.

9.33 Plants medium sized, densely tufted, green to yellowish above. Stems slender, central strand present, often indistinct in younger parts; rhizoids smooth. Leaves ± crisped when dry, patent to recurved when moist, ovate-lanceolate to elongated-ligulate; margins plane above, finely to coarsely serrate, sometimes nearly entire; costa stout, ending shortly below the tip; upper leaf cells isodiametric, quadrate to rounded, conical-mammillose on both sides; basal medial cells wider, oblong, smooth and clear. Dioicous. Seta long, erect; capsule ovoid to oblong, nearly erect to inclined, smooth when dry; annulus lacking; peristome teeth reddish, cleft halfway down into 2 slender divisions, vertically striate and sometimes papillose. Calyptra cucullate.

9.34 Name from the Greek, meaning divided tooth, referring to the split peristome teeth.

9.35 **Dichodontium pellucidum** (Hedw.) Schimp. Plants densely tufted or gregarious, green to yellowish green above, brownish below. Stems slender, 1–3(10) cm tall, simple or sparingly branched, often with slender innovations, moderately radiculose below and often at the bases of the innovations. Leaves ± incurved, crisped and often twisted when dry, spreading to squarrose when moist, rather open, variable, ovate-lanceolate to elongated-ligulate, 1–5 mm long, one shape and size usually predominating; base ± clasping; apex narrowly acute to broadly obtuse; margin flat above, recurved near the base, nearly entire, finely serrulate-denticulate or coarsely and often irregularly serrate above; costa stout, ending below the apex, in cross section showing 2–5 guides, these mainly subventral with 1–2 rows of dorsal stereids and occasionally with 1–3 ventral stereids at midleaf, superficial cells strongly mammillose-papillose; upper leaf cells ± isodiametric, quadrate to irregularly angular or rounded, 8–12 μ wide, clear to obscure, each cell with a single conic-mammillose projection on each side; basal medial cells wider, oblong, smooth and hyaline; basal marginal cells quadrate, forming a border 1–3 cells wide. Dioicous. Seta yellowish to light reddish brown, 1–2 cm high; capsules ovoid to oblong, mostly inclined, sometimes nearly erect, yellowish brown, becoming darker with age, neck not differentiated, 1–1.5 mm long without lid, contracted under the mouth when dry, otherwise smooth; lid rather high convex, short to long rostrate, rather large; peristome teeth dark red, finely vertically striate and papillose. Spores smooth to finely papillose, 15–18 μ. (Sporophytes rare, described from Grout's *North American Musci Perfecti* 110). Plate 6, figs. 1–9.

9.36 On damp or wet soil and rocks, along streams, in wet meadows and around rocky seepage areas, at high altitudes in our region.

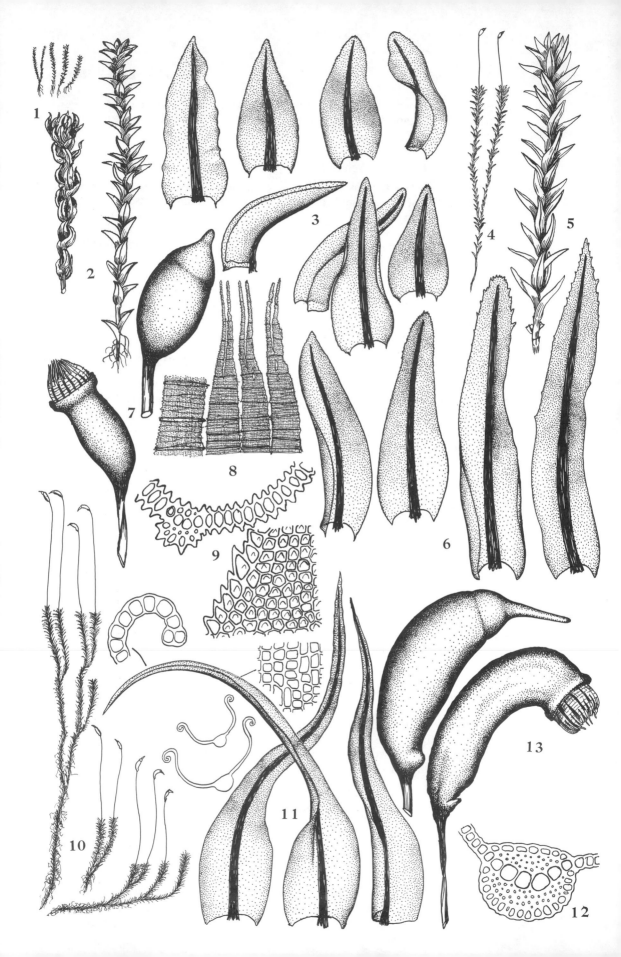

9.37 Europe. New Jersey and Pennsylvania across the Great Lakes region, to Utah and California, and northward.

9.38 Exceedingly variable but easily recognized by the mammillose papillae on the upper leaf cells and by the finely serrulate-denticulate leaf margin.

5. ONCOPHORUS (Brid.) Brid.

9.39 Plants medium sized, in dense tufts, bright to yellowish green. Stems erect or ascending, branched; central strand present. Leaves ± crisped when dry, erect-patent to widely spreading or squarrose when moist, broadly to narrowly lanceolate or subulate, often from an ovate or oblong ± clasping base; margins ± recurved, entire to coarsely serrate or irregular above; costa stout, ending just below the tip or shortly excurrent, in cross section showing a row of guides and both dorsal and ventral stereid bands, the latter someimes weak; upper cells small, quadrate, rounded or shortly rectangular, smooth to strongly papillose or mammillose, the marginal rows bistratose in some species; basal cells becoming wider and more elongated, oblong, smooth and hyaline; alar cells sometimes differentiated. Autoicous. Seta long, erect or curved; capsules oblong to oblong-cylindric, erect and symmetric or curved and asymmetric, often strumose at the base; lid conic, usually with a long bent beak; annulus poorly developed or lacking; peristome teeth usually red, cleft ½–⅔ down into slender divisions, sometimes merely perforated, longitudinally striated throughout, often coarsely papillose above. Spores mostly papillose. Calyptra cucullate.

9.40 The name is Greek for bearing a goiter, and alludes to the swelling at the base of the capsule on one side.

9.41 **Oncophorus virens** (Hedw.) Brid. Sods usually yellowish green, often quite deep. Stems erect or ascending, moderately to freely branched, 1–4(10) cm long or high; central strand large; outer cortical cells small, thick walled and colored; rhizoids commonly dense at the base. Leaves crisped, quite open, the upper portion usually widely spreading when dry, patent to spreading or squarrose when moist, narrowly lanceolate from an ovate or oblong ± clasping base, gradually recurved or sharply divergent from the base, 2.5–4.5 mm long, canaliculate or keeled; apex slenderly pointed or blunt; margins mostly recurved except at the apex and base, sometimes 1 side plane entire to irregularly notched or serrate above; costa stout, percurrent to shortly excurrent, in cross section showing 3–9 guides with strong dorsal and ventral stereid bands; upper

---

Plate 6. 1–9. Dichodontium pellucidum. 1. Habit sketch of small short-leaved form, X.4. 2. Dry and moist habit of same, X2. 3. Leaves of same, X8. 4. Habit of larger long-leaved form, X.4. 5. Portion of a shoot of same, X2. 6. Leaves of same, X8. 7. Capsules, X8. 8. Peristome teeth, X60. 9. Upper leaf cells and cross section, X120.

10–12. Oncophorus virens. 10. Habit sketches, X4. 11. Leaves, X8. 12. Cross section of costa, X120. 13. Capsules, X8.

cells mostly quadrate to shortly rectangular, 6–9 μ wide, the marginal row bistratose, at least above and often nearly to the base, smooth and usually quite clear; basal cells oblong to sublinear, wider, hyaline, the walls quite firm; alar cells ± differentiated, ranging from a group of gradually enlarged, thin-walled cells to abruptly enlarged cells, sometimes forming conspicuous auricles. Seta 1–3.4 cm high, yellowish at maturity, becoming reddish brown with age; capsules oblong to elliptic-oblong, curved and asymmetric, strumose at base; urn 1.5–2.2 mm long, reddish brown, smooth to slightly wrinkled when dry; lid high conic, the beak long and bent; peristome teeth dark red, the joints vertically striate with rows of small papillae on the outer surface, finely papillose on the inner face and at the extreme tips of the divisions. Spores 18–24 μ, roughened with the low papillae. Plate 6, figs. 10–12.

9.42   On moist or wet soil, rocks or rotten wood, in meadows, on shaded banks, along brooks and around seepage areas, frequent at high altitudes in our region.

9.43   Alaska to California and through the Rocky Mountains to New Mexico; less common eastward through the Great Lakes Region to Quebec and Greenland.

6.   DICRANOWEISIA Lindb. ex Mild.

9.44   Plants rather small to medium sized, in dense tufts or sods, mainly on bases of trees, dry rocks, in crevices of decorticated logs or old wood, bright to yellowish green above, brownish below. Stems erect, branched; central strand present. Leaves strongly crisped when dry, erect-patent to spreading when moist, lanceolate to linear or subulate from an ovate to oblong subclasping base; apex slenderly acute to blunt; costa ending just below the apex or subpercurrent; upper leaf cells small, quadrate to rounded; basal cells slightly wider, shortly oblong to linear, hyaline and smooth. Autoicous. Perichaetial leaves variable, the inner usually convolute-clasping, abruptly obtuse or acute or narrowed to an acuminate, elongated upper portion. Seta long, erect; capsule ovoid to cylindric, erect and symmetric or slightly curved, smooth to minutely longitudinally wrinkled when dry, mouth rather small; lid conic-rostrate; annulus lacking or indistinctly differentiated; peristome teeth 16, triangular-lanceolate, quite short, inserted well below the mouth, entire to cleft 1/3–1/2 down into slender divisions, nearly smooth to densely and finely papillose, often striate on the middle joints, very fragile and soon broken. Calyptra cucullate.

9.45   The name is a combination of *Dicranum* and *Weissia*. A genus difficult to distinguish since most of the traits are common to both Dicranaceae and Pottiaceae.

9.46   **Dicranoweisia crispula** (Hedw.) Mild. Tufts yellowish green, sometimes dark green. Stems 1–2(3) cm tall. Leaves linear-lanceolate or subulate, canaliculate above, from a ± oblong base, gradually narrowed upward, 2–3.4 mm long, slenderly acute to obtuse; margins plane and erect, in a

108

few leaves sometimes slightly recurved at midleaf, entire to irregularly notched or dentate above; costa stout, percurrent or vaguely disappearing just below the tip, in cross section showing 1 row of medial guides with dorsal and ventral stereid bands in the middle portion of the leaf, the latter lacking high up and toward the base; upper cells quadrate to rounded or shortly rectangular, 7–10 μ wide, frequently in longitudinal rows, in a marginal row bistratose well toward the base, the upper half of the lamina unistratose, bistratose in spots or lines, or bistratose throughout, sometimes only on 1 side of the leaf, smooth or longitudinally ridged-striate, the ridges extending over as many as 10–18 cells, in cross section appearing as papillae on the cells and over their vertical longitudinal walls; basal cells slightly wider, hyaline, the walls usually firm, oblong to sublinear, the alar cells not differentiated or in a few leaves gradually enlarged, sometimes those at the extreme angles inflated. Inner perichaetial leaves convolute-clasping their whole length, broadly obtuse to acute or shortly acuminate, the outer rather abruptly narrowed to a lanceolate upper portion shorter than the clasping base. Seta 5–10 mm long, yellowish, becoming reddish brown with age; capsule elliptic-oblong to oblong-cylindric, usually erect and symmetric but occasionally slightly curved, yellowish brown, becoming darker with age, narrowed to a rather small, darker colored mouth, urn 1.3–2 mm long, smooth to minutely longitudinally wrinkled when dry; lid conic, long-rostrate; annulus lacking or poorly developed; teeth short, yellowish to reddish brown, darker at the base, triangular-lanceolate, entire or sometimes cleft above, smooth to finely and densely papillose, often striate on the middle joints, the midline faint or lacking, fragile and soon broken. Spores globose, 13–17 μ, smooth, maturing in spring. Plate 7, figs. 1–12.

9.47   On trees, fallen trunks, especially in the cracks of decorticated logs, on dry or damp rocks, especially in narrow crevices. Common throughout Utah in the higher mountains.

9.48   Greenland and Labrador. British Columbia to California, eastward to Montana, Colorado and New Mexico; sporadically in northeastern United States, Maine, New York, and Michigan.

9.49   Common and often abundant in the mountains of Utah and surrounding states. In gross aspect the plants are remarkably uniform, but a number of variations occur in the finer details of several organs, these appearing in various combinations according to the particular plant. The stem leaves, commonly entire, may also be coarsely and irregularly dentate in the upper part. The leaf cells are commonly described as smooth, mammillose, or moderately papillose. The presence of papillae is practically impossible to demonstrate in surface view, and in most of our plants papillae as such do not occur. Cross sections of leaves show what appear to be papillae but in reality are longitudinal ridges of particularly clear cuticular material extending like little strings over the surfaces of as many as 10–18 cells. With careful focusing and adjustment of the light, these structures appear as faint longitudinal striations in surface view.

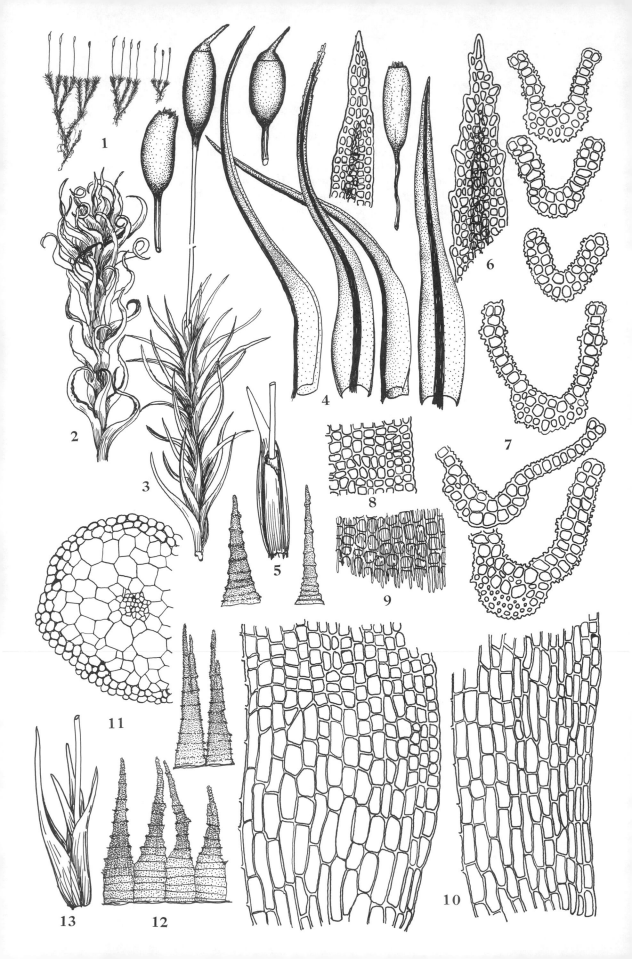

9.50 The present species has often been confused with *Dicranoweisia cirrata* (Hedw.) Lindb. in Mild. In European specimens the two plants were originally contrasted as follows: *D. crispula*: leaf margins plane and erect or incurved; alar cells of some leaves enlarged and often inflated. *D. cirrata*: leaf margins strongly revolute in some leaves; alar cells not differentiated. Many leaves of *D. crispula* may be deceiving since the bistratose margins often give the appearance of being narrowly recurved, while in a few leaves they are actually slightly recurved in the middle. In contrast, many leaves of *D. cirrata* have strongly recurved margins, some to the extent of one and a half turns, although a good many are plane on one or both sides.

9.51 In the majority of North American plants, the alar cells of *D. crispula* are not at all differentiated or only gradually and slightly enlarged, rarely becoming sufficiently enlarged or inflated in some leaves to be noticeable. The var. *contermina* (Ren. & Card.) Grout was erected to accommodate plants with undifferentiated alar cells and abruptly acuminate inner perichaetial leaves. Since most of our plants have undifferentiated alar cells associated with acute to broadly obtuse convolute-clasping inner perichaetial leaves, var. *contermina* loses much of its supposed individuality and rests only on the clasping but scarcely convolute inner perichaetial leaves with rather long acuminate upper portions. Plate 7, fig. 13.

7. DICRANELLA (C.Muell.) Schimp.

9.52 Mostly small yellowish green to bright green plants, scattered or in dense tufts on damp soil. Stems simple or branched, erect to ascending with a small central strand and dense rhizoids at the base. Leaves gradually lanceolate to abruptly lanceolate-subulate from an ovate or oblong, clasping base, erect to squarrose-spreading or secund, straight or crisped when dry; margins entire or serrate in the upper part; costa broad, ending several cells below the apex, percurrent or excurrent, sometimes toothed at back above; upper cells shortly oblong to linear, rather thick walled, smooth; basal cells longer and clear. Dioicous or rarely monoicous. Seta long, usually erect and straight, yellowish at maturity, becoming reddish brown with age; capsules subglobose to oblong-cylindric, erect and symmetric or curved and asymmetric, inclined to cernuous, strumose in some species, smooth or slightly ribbed when dry; annulus present or absent; teeth usually erect, cleft to about

---

Plate 7. 1–12. **Dicranoweisia crispula.** 1. Habit sketches, X.4. 2. Portion of shoot showing dry habit, X.4. 3. Moist habit with capsules, X4. 4. Typical leaves, X8. 5. Inner perichaetial leaves and base of seta, X6. 6. Two leaf apices. 7. Cross sections of the upper laminae of different leaves showing variations in the bistratose condition. 8. Upper medial leaf cells. 9. Section of the upper lamina cut almost parallel with the surface showing the longitudinal cuticular ridges, X120. 10. Basal and alar cells from leaves of different plants showing the usual range of variation, X120. 11. Cross section of the stem, X70. 12. Peristome teeth showing variations in shape and basal connection, X60.

13. Var. contermina. Inner perichaetial leaves, X6.

.the middle into 2(3) slenderly tapering divisions, papillose above and longitudinally striate below with fine papillae in rows.

9.53 The name is the dimunitive of *Dicranum*.

9.54 **Dicranella schreberiana** (Hedw.) Dix. Plants in dense tufts, bright green. Stems 1–3 cm tall, with rhizoids confined to the base. Leaves small and distant below, becoming larger and more crowded above, 1.5–2.5 mm long, squarrose from an ovate or oblong half-clasping base, gradually or abruptly narrowed to a lanceolate-subulate upper portion, crisped or twisted when dry; apex gradually and narrowly acute or somewhat broader and more suddenly acute; margins bluntly serrate in the upper half or near the tip; costa ending shortly below the apex, percurrent or slightly excurrent, rather broad at the base, upwards to 60 μ wide, often toothed at the back above; upper cells oblong to sublinear, 6–12 μ wide, mostly about 10 μ wide, becoming shorter in the shoulders and longer in the sheathing base, elongate oblong to linear. Dioicous. Seta 1–1.5 cm long; capsules small, 0.8–1.5 mm long, ovoid to oblong, not strumose, curved and inclined to cernuous, contracted below the mouth when dry; lid often as long as the urn, conic with a long curved or inclined beak; annulus lacking; peristome teeth red, cleft ⅓–½ down, long in proportion to the urn, vertically striate and united at the base. Spores 15–17 μ, yellowish brown.

9.55 On damp soil, on banks of brooks and ditches, around seepage areas, and in meadows. Rare in Utah.

9.56 British Columbia to Oregon, Idaho and Utah, eastward across southern Canada and northern United States to Quebec and Pennsylvania, Europe, Caucasus Mountains, Siberia, New Zealand, and Tasmania. Summit County: Uinta Mountains, Stillwater Fork of Bear River at Christmas Meadows, 8,800 ft.

8. DICRANUM Hedw.

9.57 Plants medium sized to large, loosely to densely tufted, often forming expanded sods. Stems mostly erect, sometimes ascending, usually branched. Leaves broadly to narrowly lanceolate, straight to strongly secund, often falcate, canaliculate to subtubulose; margins plane, entire to strongly serrate above; costa narrow to very wide, flattish to semi-terete, ending below the apex to long excurrent; upper cells quadrate to rectangular or rhomboidal to fusiform, smooth or slightly papillose, unistratose or bistratose; basal leaf cells shortly rectangular to oblong to linear, often enlarged; alar cells not particularly differentiated to greatly enlarged, often thin walled, inflated and colored, sometimes forming distinct auricles. Dioicous. Male plants minute or equaling the female plant (sometimes dwarfed and resting on leaves or tomentum of female plants). Seta erect, single or occasionally 2–3 from one perichaetium, long; capsules oblong to cylindric, erect and symmetric to inclined or arcuate; operculum usually long rostrate; peristome single, teeth 16, ± cleft ½ down to 2 or occasionally 3 divisions, mostly vertically pitted-striate, often papillose above, usually reddish or reddish brown. Calyptra cucullate.

9.58   The name is from the Greek, meaning 2-pronged fork, in reference to the 2-pronged peristome teeth.

9.59   1. Plants medium sized; leaves straight with most of the tips broken off; costa without stereids; cell walls thin, rarely becoming pitted; on trees or wood .... 1. *D. tauricum*   9.61

9.60   1. Plants mostly large; leaves not broken off; costa with medial guides and a few stereids on 1 or both sides; on soil or rocks, in the high mountains.

   2. Leaves straight when moist; costa without dorsal ridges, smooth or roughened with low papillae on back above .... 2. *D. spadiceum*   9.65

   2. Leaves falcate-secund (or straight in fo. *orthophyllum*); costa bearing 2–4 dorsal, serrated ridges 1–2 cells high .... 3. *D. scoparium*   9.69

9.61   **1. Dicranum tauricum** Sapehin. Plants in dense tufts on rotten logs or bases of tree trunks, rarely on soil or rocks, rather dark green to bright yellowish green above, brownish to olivaceous below. Stems branched, 0.5–2.5(5) cm tall; central strand present, the outer layer of cortical cells small and moderately thick walled, sometimes densely clothed with reddish rhizoids. Leaves quite dense, erect to somewhat patent, and mostly straight when dry, erect-patent and strict to slightly secund at the stem tips when moist, all but the comal leaves broken off, normally narrowly lanceolate, very slenderly tapering to a nearly filiform apex, tubulose to strongly channeled, 3–5(6) mm long when intact; margins flat, entire or the apex slightly serrulate; costa flat and wide, mostly occupying 1/5 or less of the width of the leaf at the base, indistinctly long excurrent, in cross section showing 1 row of guides without stereid bands but often with 1 or partially 2 rows of rather large dorsal cells; upper leaf cells shortly rectangular, commonly becoming longer below the broken point, 6.9 μ wide, moderately thick walled, unistratose and smooth; basal cells oblong to linear, wider and pellucid, quite firm, often somewhat pitted; alar cells usually greatly enlarged, oblong, frequently strongly inflated, commonly reddish in color and forming distinct auricles, usually not extending to the costa, there being 2–4 rows of narrow cells intervening, these often thick walled and reddish. Dioicous. Seta yellowish to yellowish brown, becoming darker with age, 1–2 cm long; capsules cylindric, erect and symmetric, yellowish brown, becoming darker with age, urn 2–3 mm long, the neck region very short, smooth to minutely longitudinally wrinkled when dry; operculum long rostrate, often inclined; annulus lacking; teeth reddish brown, irregularly cleft 1/2 or more, usually smooth below, irregularly obliquely striate and often papillose above, sometimes nearly smooth throughout. Spores 12–16 μ, yellowish and smooth. Plate 8, figs. 1–4.

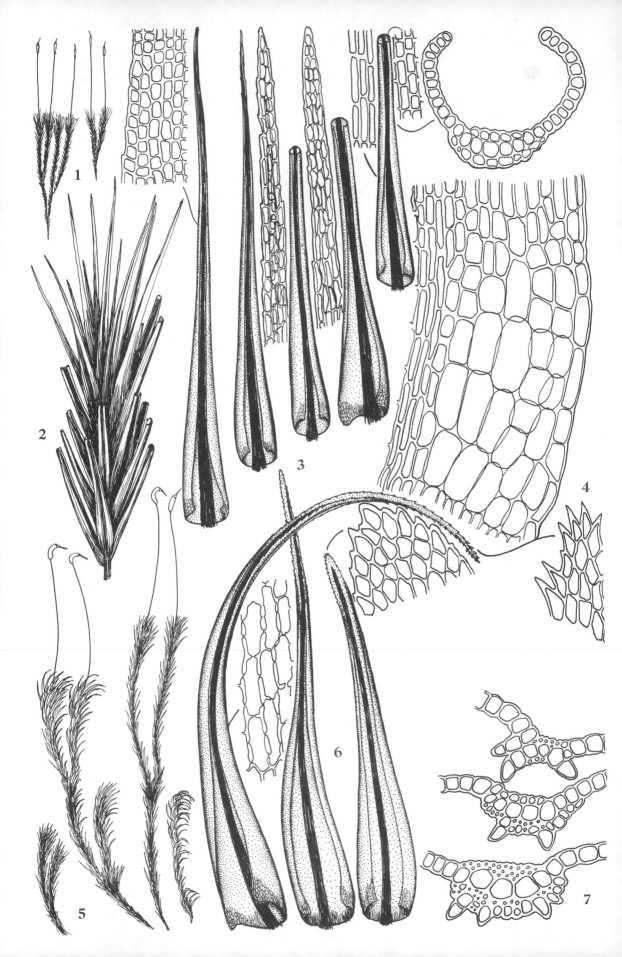

9.62   Rare in Utah; mostly on rotten logs and stumps or the lower trunks of trees, usually in shady woods; more rarely on soil or rocks.

9.63   Europe. Alaska to California, Idaho, Wyoming and Utah. Utah County: Mt. Timpanogos, Stewart's Fork, 6,100 ft.

9.64   The erect strict leaves with a flattened costa lacking stereid bands, the upper half broken off and the enlarged and often inflated alar cells not extending to the costa are characteristics that readily identify sterile plants. The costa may appear wider if the leaf base is not flattened out. Other distinctive features are the unistratose lamina of shortly rectangular smooth cells. The erect and symmetric capsules are frequently present. The teeth vary quite widely in the degree of splitting, some being almost entire, others cleft nearly to the base. The divisions vary in thickness, some being rather thickish to the apex, others very slender and tapering, sometimes quite nodulose. The oblique striations may be fine or coarse, dense to few and widely spaced, and often irregularly disposed.

9.65   **2. Dicranum spadiceum** Zett. Plants medium sized, in dense tufts or sods, dark green, becoming brownish green or blackish below. Stems 1–4(5) cm tall, sparingly branched, sparingly or not at all tomentose below. Leaves straight, broadly lanceolate, evenly tapered to a slender, channeled or subtubulose upper part, 3–4(5) mm long, as much as 1.2 mm wide, narrowly auricled at the base, patent to loosely erect when moist, widely curved or twisted when dry; margins entire to strongly serrate in the upper part; costa narrow, about 1/9 the width of the blade at the base, percurrent or vaguely excurrent, often rough on the back above, flattish with 5–6(7) medial guides and a few small stereids on either surface; medial cells smooth, oblong to sublinear, often irregular, ± pitted, mostly 12–14 μ wide, becoming thick walled early, especially dorsally; apical cells irregularly quadrate and shortly rectangular; basal cells near costa linear, thick walled and colored; alar cells rather abruptly enlarged, thin walled and inflated, quadrate to rectangular, nearly extending to the costa. Setae up to 2 cm long, yellowish becoming yellowish brown with age; capsules cylindric-arcuate, 2–2.5 mm long, not strumose, furrowed when dry; annulus distinct; peristome teeth vertically striate. Spores up to 20 μ, mature in late summer (sporophyte description taken from Limpricht, as *D. neglectum*). Plate 9.

9.66   Rare in Utah. On wet or damp alpine rocks and soil.

9.67   Europe and Northern Asia. Alaska to Oregon, Montana, Wyoming and Utah. Duchesne County: Uinta Mountains, Ottoson Basin, 11,200 ft.

9.68   Closely related to *Dicranum muehlenbeckii* from which it differs mainly in the much narrower costa and somewhat smaller size. It is treated

---

Plate 8.   1–4. Dicranum tauricum. 1. Habit sketches, X.4. 2. Portion of a shoot, X4. 3. Leaves, X8, detail, X120. 4. Typical alar cells, X120.

5–7. Dicranum scoparium. 5. Habit sketches, X.4. 6. Leaves, X8, detail, X120. 7. Three cross sections of costa at different levels, X120.

as a variety of the latter by many authors. I have gathered *D. muehlen-beckii* in the high mountains of Colorado but have not found it in Utah. It is a variable moss with several varieties attached to it and is said to intergrade with *D. fuscescens*.

9.69   **3. Dicranum scoparium** Hedw. Plants large, in deep, loose or dense tufts on soil, rocks and rotten wood, often forming expanded sods, mostly bright glossy yellowish green above, brownish below. Stems 2–12 cm tall; colored, densely white tomentose within, well toward the apex, becoming ferruginous below; central strand small; 2–3 layers of outer cortical cells small, thick walled. Leaves in the typical form lanceolate-subulate, strongly secund or sometimes straight, subtubulose or strongly channeled, 4–9 mm long, when dry erect or secund, sometimes erect-patent to irregularly spreading; apex typically slenderly tapering to an acute or blunt tip, but often shorter and broader with a widely acute or obtuse tip; margins normally strongly serrate above, but often nearly entire; costa rather narrow and flattish, ending in the apex, or shortly excurrent, at the back above bearing 2–4 longitudinal ridges or lamellae 1 cell high, these often toothed, sometimes weak or lacking, in cross section showing a single row of guides, usually with irregularly disposed dorsal and ventral stereids and large dorsal cells; upper cells oblong, rhomboidal or fusiform, shorter on the margins and often at the extreme apex, rather thick walled, ± pitted, frequently becoming strongly incrassate, colored, and porose with age, smooth, toward the base little changed or gradually more elongated and usually more strongly porose; basal cells shortly oblong to linear, often wider, several rows near the costa and at the margins smaller and narrower; alar cells quadrate to oblong, moderately to strongly differentiated, in some leaves abruptly enlarged, usually colored and strongly inflated, not reaching the costa. Dioicous. Male plants very small, often attached to the female stems by rhizoids. Seta 2–3 cm long, yellowish brown, becoming reddish with age; capsules cylindric, strongly arcuate, slightly contracted under the mouth and smooth to weakly furrowed when dry, nearly erect to inclined or curved and slightly asymmetric when moist, urn 3–4 mm long, neck well defined; operculum hemispheric with a long straight rostrum ½ as long as the urn or equal to it, bent or spirally twisted when dry; annulus lacking; peristome teeth bright to dark reddish, cleft ½ down into 2 or occasionally 3 divisions, these generally acuminate and tapering to slender apices, vertically striate below and usually papillose above. Spores globose, yellowish brown, slightly papillose, 16–24 μ. Calyptra rather larger and often quite persistent, cucullate, long beaked. Plate 8, figs. 5–7.

Plate 9.   1–8. Dicranum spadiceum. 1–2. Habit sketches moist and dry, X.4. 3. Leaves, X8. 4. Leaf apices. 5. Upper medial cells. 6. Lower medial cells. 7. Basal and alar cells, X120. 8. Cross sections at two levels, X120.

9–15. Seligeria campylopoda. 9. Habit sketches, X.4. 10. Same, X2. 11. Upper and lower leaves, X8. 12. Leaf apices, X120. 13. Upper medial cells, X120. 14. Capsules, X8. 15. Peristome teeth, X60.

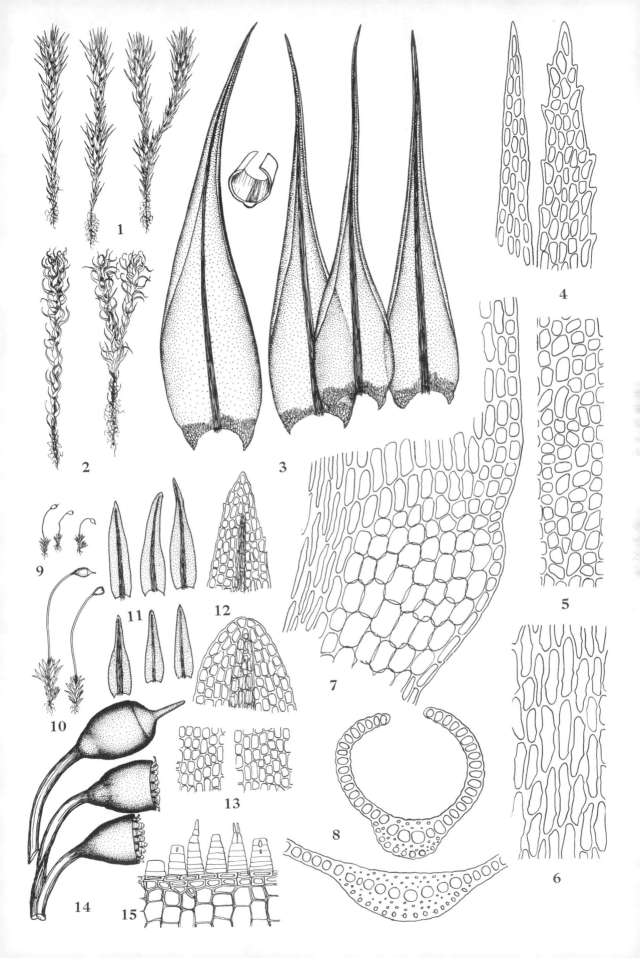

9.70 DICRANACEAE

9.70 On soil, humus, rotten wood and rocks, usually in shady places. Circumboreal in the temperate zone. Very common in the more humid regions, rare or lacking in arid climates, occasional in high mountains southward into Mexico.

9.71 Duchesne County: Uinta Mountains, near Mirror Lake, 10,000–10,300 ft.

9.72 Rare in Utah. Thus far only sterile plants have been observed near Mirror Lake. They are fairly typical but rather small and variable in different habitats and different parts of the same tufts. The leaves are generally shorter than usual, moderately secund to nearly straight, the apices somewhat shorter than in typical forms.

9. PARALEUCOBRYUM (Limpr.) Loesk.

9.73 Plants resembling *Dicranum*, medium sized to rather large, in dense tufts. Leaves elongate-lanceolate, tapering to a subulate apex; costa very broad and flat, occupying the upper part of the leaf, consisting of large empty cells on both sides with a row of small angular, chlorophyllose cells between them or variously interspersed with them, stereids and guides lacking; unistratose cells of the lamina confined to the base; alar cells much enlarged, often inflated and becoming reddish. Dioicous. Capsules erect, cylindric; peristome as in *Dicranum*.

9.74 The name comes from Greek and means *beside Leucobryum*, that is, resembling *Leucobryum* which has a similar costal structure.

9.75 **Paraleucobryum enerve** (Thed). Loesk. Plants becoming rather stout, in dense erect tufts, light green above, brown below, 2–5 cm tall, branches erect, rhizoids few at the base. Leaves long and narrowly lanceolate, tapering to a subulate tip, straight or slightly falcate, 4–7 mm long; margins incurved, ± tubulose above, entire or sometimes toothed at the apex; costa occupying about 9/10 of the leaf base with a narrow strip of unistratose lamina 3–6 cells wide extending upward and finally giving way to the broad costa in the upper part of the blade; surface cells of the costa oblong-linear; alar cells much enlarged, usually inflated and forming auricles, becoming reddish in older leaves, extending about halfway toward the middle of the base. Seta 1–2 cm long; capsules oblong to oblong-cylindric, straight or slightly curved, 2–2.5 mm long; neck short; lid long and slender, as long as the capsule or nearly so, straight or curved.

9.76 A rare alpine moss, on soil or rocks.

9.77 Europe. Alaska to British Columbia, in high mountains of Colorado, New Mexico and Utah. Duchesne County: Uinta Mountains, Lake Fork Basin, 11,000 ft.

9.78 Superficially this plant resembles a small pale *D. scoparium*. The leaves appear to be without a costa, as the specific name suggests, but actually the costa occupies nearly the entire width of the upper blade, except for a narrow unistratose margin of 1 or 2 cells.

118

POTTIACEAE

10.1 Plants minute to large, usually ± densely tufted or in expanded sods. Stems erect or sometimes ascending, simple or variously branched, central strand mostly present, but sometimes lacking; rhizoids mostly restricted to the base. Leaves variable in shape and stance, usually dense and in several ranks; costa mostly stout, ending shortly below the apex or excurrent, often prolonged into a hair point; upper cells short, isodiametric to shortly rectangular, often irregular, relatively thick walled and mostly papillose, the papillae various, simple, forked, C-shaped or O-shaped, weak to very coarse, frequently densely chlorophyllose and obscure; basal cells usually enlarged, firm or thin walled, clear.

10.2 Capsules sessile and immersed to long exserted, globose to cylindric, erect and symmetric or nearly so, cleistocarpous, gymnostomous, or with 16 peristome teeth, these short to very long, nearly entire to perforated, cleft, or divided into 32 slender divisions, straight and erect to strongly spirally twisted, sometimes from a tubular basal membrane; operculum conic and usually long rostrate. Calyptra cucullate, falling early.

10.3 A large family difficult to describe adequately. Related to the Dicranaceae through *Dicranoweisia*, and to Encalyptaceae.

10.4   1. Leaves oblong to lanceolate or linear-lanceolate, mostly broadest at or near the base, ± gradually narrowed upward; costa with medial guides and both dorsal and ventral stereid bands, the latter often weak (subfamily Trichostomoideae)

    2. Leaf margins strongly involute or incurved, at least at the apex; plants small

      3. Capsules without a dehiscent lid, cleistocarpous .... 1. *Astomum* 10.6

      3. Capsules with a dehiscent lid, teeth present or lacking .... 2. *Weissia* 10.12

    2. Leaf margins flat or revolute

      4. Hyaline basal leaf cells extending from the costa diagonally upward along the margins in V-like fashion .... 7. *Tortella* 10.66

      4. Hyaline basal leaf cells not extending diagonally upward

        5. Plants small, mostly yellowish or brownish below, without noticeable red color; upper margins of leaves entire; usually growing on wet limestone or calcareous sandstone cliffs or rocks; dioicous

          6. Peristome lacking; basal margins of leaves entire or finely dentate by projecting papillae, usually fruiting freely .... 3. *Gymnostomum* 10.33

          6. Peristome teeth erect, variously divided; lower margins of leaves conspicuously serrulate-denticulate by projecting up-

119

per angles of the cells, just above the area of enlarged basal cells, otherwise entire .... 4. *Eucladium* 10.48

5. Plants larger, or if small, with conspicuous red coloration

    7. Peristome teeth 32, from a very low basal membrane, spirally twisted; dioicous .... 10. *Barbula* 10.110

    7. Peristome teeth erect, or rarely slightly twisted

        8. Plants strongly tinged with brick red; clear green, at the tips; leaves often with a few coarse teeth at the extreme apex; margins narrowly revolute to near the apex; capsules usually abundant; monoicous .... 9. *Bryoerythrophyllum* 10.101

        8. Plants yellowish or brown below, or if bright reddish, not as above in all particulars; fruit rare

            9. Leaves brittle, ligulate to linear-lanceolate, undulate, rather abruptly acute; margins minutely crenulate and often irregularly notched, plane throughout or recurved only in the lower half .... 5. *Trichostomum* 10.54

            9. Leaves usually soft, mostly broader, acute to broadly obtuse or rounded

                10. Leaves broadly ligulate, base not dilated but strongly incurved, clasping and ± decurrent, mostly acute; margins coarsely serrate above; cells mammillose on the upper surface, smooth below .... 6. *Hyophila* 10.60

                10. Leaves ovate to ovate-lanceolate from a dilated base, not particularly clasping; acute to broadly rounded; entire throughout; cells papillose or sometimes nearly smooth .... 8. *Didymodon* 10.82

10.5   1. Leaves ovate, oblong, ligulate or spatulate, usually broadest near the middle or above; costa with 1–3 rows of ventral or subventral guides and only a dorsal stereid band (subfamily Pottioideae)

    11. Costae bearing ± erect filaments or lamellae on the ventral side (often appearing as an opaque green mass on the upper half), mostly small xerophytic mosses, in lowlands

        12. Costa with 2–4(6) lamellae, which sometimes bear green filaments and appear as an opaque, green, granular mass .... 13. *Pterygoneurum* 10.181

        12. Costa bearing filaments only, dense and spreading over most of the upper surface of the leaf or reduced to short chains of cells or only strong bulging cells

            13. Leaves with strongly incurved margins; stem without a central strand .... 14. *Aloina* 10.197

13. Leaves with erect or flat margins; stem with a central strand .... 15. *Crossidium*   10.203

11. Costae without ventral outgrowths

14. Plants very small, yellowish green, growing on dry soil, in low-lands and foothills; capsules immersed to emergent, subglobose to ovoid, apiculate, indehiscent .... 11. *Phascum*   10.152

14. Plants small to large; capsules emergent to long exserted, de-hiscing by an operculum

15. Leaves bordered with narrowly elongated or thick-walled smoother cells (frequently more highly colored)

16. Leaves ovate to oblong-ligulate; plants small to medium sized

17. Upper leaf margins with a few coarse teeth; peristome lacking; lid persistent on the columella .... 12. *Pottia*   10.162

17. Upper leaf margins entire; lower margins 2- to 3-stratose; peristome present; lid (in our species) entirely dehis-cent .... 16. *Desmatodon*   10.221

16. Leaves bordered with several rows of enlarged, thick-walled cells often tinged with orange; ligulate-spatulate, margins of the lamina clavate in cross section; plants large, sub-mcrgcd in streams or on wet calcareous rocks and cement installations .... 18. *Scopelophila*   10.306

15. Leaves not bordered, or if so, peristome teeth long and strong-ly spirally twisted

18. Peristome teeth relatively short, erect or slightly twisted, arising from a very short basal membrane

19. Teeth short, often much reduced, not divided, but usually irregularly perforated .... 12. *Pottia*   10.162

19. Teeth short to moderately long, mostly cleft to irregular-ly divided to the base into slender divisions, sometimes slightly twisted .... 16. *Desmatodon*   10.221

18. Pcristomc tccth unitcd in a high tubular basal mombrano, (except in *T. muralis*), divided above into 32 long hairlike divisions and spirally twisted in 1–3 complete turns .... 17. *Tortula*   10.252

1. ASTOMUM Hamp.

10.6   Plants small. Stems simple or sparingly branched. Leaves crisped when dry, patent to recurved when moist, mostly lanceolate or linear-lan-ceolate, the comal ones the largest, usually 2–3 mm long, the lower ones small, strongly keeled, the upper margins strongly involute; costa strong, disappearing below the tip to shortly excurrent; upper leaf cells small, quadrate to rounded-hexagonal; ± strongly papillose. Autoicous. Capsules immersed to shortly exserted, subglobose to oblong-ovoid, apiculate to rostrate; operculum none; only slightly differentiated but not dehiscent; peristome lacking. Calyptra cucullate or rarely mitrate, smooth.

10.7 A small genus which in a sterile condition can scarcely be distinguished from *Weissia*

10.8 The name, from the Greek, alludes to the differentiated lid (no mouth).

10.9 **Astomum occidentale** Flow. Plants small, low and densely tufted, green to yellowish green above. Shoots mostly 3–4 mm tall, usually with very short, dense branches near the apex. Leaves incurved and crisped when dry, mostly erect or erect-patent when moist, a few lower ones recurved, the upper ones linear-lanceolate to lanceolate-ligulate, 1.3–2 mm long, the lower ones shorter and proportionately wider; apex tapering, acute to abruptly rounded-obtuse, often shortly mucronate; margins strongly involute above, plane below; costa as much as 75 μ wide near the base, only slightly tapered, ending below the apex or percurrent to a short mucro often formed by the lamina and composed of a few larger thick-walled cells; upper cells quadrate to transversely elongated, 6–9 μ wide, bearing 1 to several low papillae; basal cells wider, oblong, thin walled and hyaline. Autoicous or sometimes paroicous. Seta 1–2 mm long, yellowish brown; capsules emergent to long exserted, small ovoid-elliptical, the upper portion gradually narrowed and prolonged into an erect or inclined beak, 0.7–1 mm long; annulus lacking and lid not separating; beak 0.3–0.6 mm long; exothecial cells thin walled, ± quadrate at the point where the mouth would normally occur, oblong-hexagonal above and below. Spores globose, yellowish brown, finely and densely papillose, 15–20 μ. Calyptra cucullate. Plate 12, figs. 1–6.

10.10 Utah, Millard County: House Mountains, Swasey Gulch, on wet or damp limestone cliff, 6,000 ft.

10.11 Closely related to *Astomum phascoides*, but that species has ovate-lanceolate to linear leaves more gradually tapering to acute apices, costa more regularly percurrent, seta shorter, capsules broadly ovoid and emergent, and spores larger (27–30 μ).

2. WEISSIA Hedw.

10.12 Plants small to medium sized, densely tufted, often in expanded sods, sometimes scattered. Stems simple or branched; central strand present, often indistinct. Leaves ± crisped or incurved when dry, erect-patent to spreading or recurved when moist, mostly narrow, the upper portion canaliculate to subtubulose with margins erect to inrolled; costa usually stout, mostly percurrent or shortly excurrent, in cross section showing a medial row of guides with dorsal and ventral stereid bands; upper cells quadrate to shortly rectangular, angular or with the corners rounded, moderately to strongly papillose with simple or forked papillae; basal cells usually becoming elongated, hyaline and smooth. Seta erect, fairly long; capsules erect and symmetric or nearly so, ovate to subcylindric, smooth to sulcate when dry; peristome lacking, rudimentary, or well developed; operculum mostly long rostrate. Spores spherical, smooth to very finely papillose, usually lightly colored. Calyptra cucullate.

10.13   Named in honor of Friedrich Wilhelm Weiss, a botanist of Goettingen.

10.14   Our plants are an intergrading series of four species in which the outlines of the leaves and degree of incurving of the laminae vary. The disposition of sex organs is variable, most species being paroicous and autoicous in the same tuft, or even on the same stem. Many paroicous plants are close to being synoicous.

10.15   1. Peristome of 2–3 rudimentary joints to fairly well developed and consisting of 5–10 joints; leaves linear-lanceolate from an oblong base, strongly involute at the margins, acute to mucronate; costa 20–50 μ wide near the base .... 1. *W. controversa*   10.17

10.16   1. Peristome lacking; mouth of the capsule usually partially closed by a fugaceous membrane; costa 60–80 μ wide
   2. Leaves ± patent; margins strongly involute
      3. Leaves narrowly ligulate-lanceolate; costa 40–65 μ wide near the base; synoicous, paroicous and autoicous in the same tuft .... 2. *W. ligulaefolia*   10.21
      3. Leaves ovate to ligulate, the costa 50–80(100) μ wide near the base .... 3. *W. tortilis*   10.25
   2. Leaves spatulate, ligulate or linear, widely incurved to subtubulose; margins flat and erect, not involute except at the extreme apices of a few leaves; costa 50–70(80) μ wide .... 4. *W. perligulata*   10.29

10.17   1. **Weissia controversa** Hedw. Plants green to yellowish green above, brownish below. Stems moderately branched, 3–5 mm high, occasionally reaching 10 mm; rhizoids few to rather dense. Leaves crisped and curled when dry, erect-patent to patent when moist, the lower ones small, becoming larger upward, 1–2.5 mm long, mostly linear-lanceolate or linear-subulate, gradually tapering from an oblong base; apex narrowly acute or briefly acuminate, margins above the base strongly incurved or involute, entire; costa 35–50 μ wide near the base, percurrent to shortly excurrent to a short stout mucro; upper cells 7–10 μ wide, moderately papillose, clear or opaque; basal cells wider, oblong to rhomboidal, clear and smooth, firm, but often thin walled and inflated at the insertion. Polygamous, autoicous or paroicous. Seta 3–7 mm long, yellowish; capsules 0.8–1.5 mm long, ovoid, elliptic or oblong-cylindric, dark yellowish brown to reddish brown, firm, minutely wrinkled to strongly plicate when dry; lid long rostrate, 0.6–0.7 mm long, usually remaining in and falling with the calyptra; peristome variable, often rudimentary, each tooth consisting of 2–3 joints almost completely concealed within the mouth of the capsule, or as many as 5–10 joints, more regular and ± lanceolate in shape, pale yellowish to reddish brown, finely and densely papillose; annulus of 2 rows of thick-walled cells. Spores 17–20(23) μ, finely papillose, Plate 10, figs. 1–10.

10.18 On damp soil and rock, in shady places. Widely distributed and more or less cosmopolitan but comparatively rare in Utah.

10.19 Salt Lake County: Brighton, Wasatch Mountains, on talus slope between Lake Mary and Twin Lakes, 9,700 ft.; Parry's Hollow north of Salt Lake City, 5,000 ft.

10.20 The presence of the peristome and absence of a membrane over the mouth of the capsule are the main features of distinction; the leaves often vary considerably in shape and degree of incurving of margins and are often so much like the leaves of the following species that distinguishing sterile plants becomes tricky.

10.21 **2. Weissia ligulaefolia** (Bartr.) Grout. Plants light to dark green, sometimes slightly glaucous above, olivaceous or brownish below, simple or branched; rhizoids few and often coarse. Leaves crisped when dry, erect-patent when moist, lanceolate-ligulate, with the base evenly passing into the upper part or slightly dilated and oblong, mostly 1.5 mm long, the lower leaves shorter and broader; apex narrowly acute or blunt, often mucronate; margins involute above, plane below; costa 40–65 μ wide near the base, disappearing in the apex or shortly excurrent to a mucro; areolation similar to that of other species. Synoicous or paroicous and often autoicous. Seta yellowish, 2–3 mm long; capsules ovoid to elliptic, 0.8–1.3 mm long, thin walled, usually $\pm$ sulcate when dry; peristome lacking, mouth bordered internally by pale membrane. Spores 14–18 μ, brown, finely papillose. Plate 10, figs. 11–17.

10.22 On dry soil or rocks, often under overhanging rocks.

10.23 Arizona and Southern Utah.

10.24 The synoicous inflorescence appears here and there in some tufts that are otherwise paroicous or monoicous, and in one specimen, every young perichaetium opened proved to be synoicous. On the average, the leaves are intermediate in form between W. *controversa* and W. *tortilis*, although the latter has a much stouter costa in its larger phases.

10.25 **3. Weissia tortilis** (Schwaegr.) C. Muell. Plants bright green to brownish green above, brownish to reddish brown below; variable in size according to the habitat. Stem reaching 2 cm tall but usually only 2–5 mm tall.

Plate 10. **1–10. Weissia controversa.** 1. Habit sketches, X.4. 2–3. Moist and dry habits, X4. 4. Lower leaves. 5. Upper leaves, X8. 6. Cross section of a leaf. 7. Two apices of typical leaves. 8. Upper medial and basal cells, X120. 9. Capsules, X8. 10. Peristome teeth from three different capsules showing variations in development, X60.

11–17. Weissia ligulaefolia. 11. Habit sketches, X.4. 12. Lower leaves. 13. Upper leaves. 14. Perichaetial leaf, X8. 15. Cross section of leaf, X120. 16. Stem tips dissected to show the various disposition of the antheridia and archegonia, X60. 17. Capsules, X8.

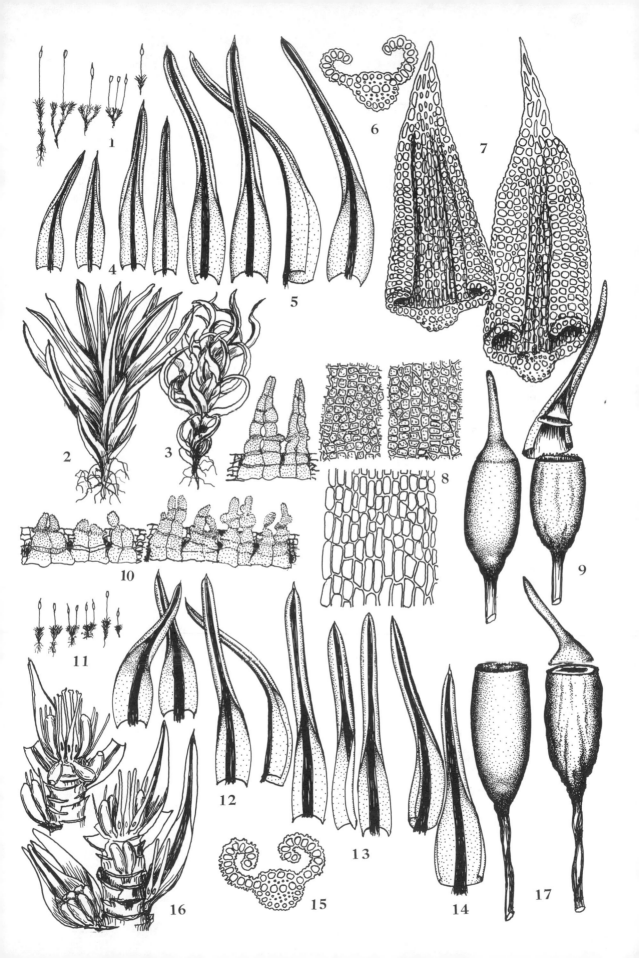

Leaves oblong-lanceolate, usually with a broad base, mostly 1–2 mm long, the lower leaves and those of depauperate plants ovate to shortly oblong from a wide base and proportionately broader; apex obtuse, blunt or widely acute, often mucronate; margins strongly involute; costa of larger leaves very stout, commonly 60–80 μ wide near the base and reaching over 100 μ in the largest leaves, becoming dark reddish brown with stereid bands more conspicuous when old; upper cells quadrate to shortly rectangular, 7–10 μ, low papillose; area of oblong basal cells smaller than in other species or scarcely differentiated. Monoicous. Seta yellowish, 2–6 mm long; capsules 0.8–1.7 mm long, ovoid-elliptic to oblong-cylindric, the mouth narrowed; exothecial cells thin walled; peristome lacking, the mouth with a pale fugaceous membrane. Spores 14–18 μ. Plate 11, figs. 9–14.

10.26   On dry or damp soil, often under overhanging rocks or in protected crevices.

10.27   Arizona and southern Utah to Texas; Europe.

10.28   Much like W. *ligulaefolia* but only autoicous and the fruit rare, the leaves broader and less strongly involute and the costa stouter.

10.29   **4. Weissia perligulata** Flow. Plants small to medium sized, bright green to yellowish or brownish green above. Stems 0.5–2 cm tall. Leaves fairly dense, incurved or sometimes crisped when dry, widely spreading to squarrose-recurved when moist, oblong-ligulate to linear-ligulate, the upper 2–3 mm long, the lower shorter and often proportionately broader, margins erect or in a few leaves very narrowly involute at the apex; apex widely acute to rounded, often mucronate; costa not prominent at the back, 50–90 μ wide near the base, percurrent or ending below the apex in many obtuse leaves; cells moderately incrassate, quadrate to short-rectangular, 6–10(12) μ, sometimes irregular, moderately to strongly papillose; basal cells oblong, firm, smooth, hyaline. Autoicous and paroicous. Seta 2.5–8 mm long, yellowish to light reddish brown; capsules shortly ovoid to ellipsoidal, the urn 0.8–1.3 mm long, usually sulcate when dry, light yellowish brown, darker at the mouth; lid long rostrate, ½–⅔ the length of the urn; mouth naked or with a very thin, short, fugaceous membrane. Spores 15–18 μ, nearly smooth to finely papillose. Plate 11, figs. 1–8.

10.30   Usually on dry or damp soil in shade, often under overhanging rocks, at the bases of cliffs, or in crevices, endemic.

10.31   Millard County: House Mountains, Swazey Gulch, 6,150 ft. San Juan

---

Plate 11.   1–8. **Weissia perligulata.** 1. Habit sketches, X.4. 2. Dry habit. 3. Moist habit, X4. 4. Lower leaves. 5. Upper leaves. 6. Two leaves of unusually large form, X8. 7. Leaf apices. 8. Cross section of leaf, X120.

9–14. **Weissia tortilis.** 9. Habit sketches, X.4. 10. Moist habit, X4. 11. Lower leaves. 12. Upper leaves. 13. Leaves of dwarfed form, often associated with the typical form, X8. 14. Leaf apices, X120.

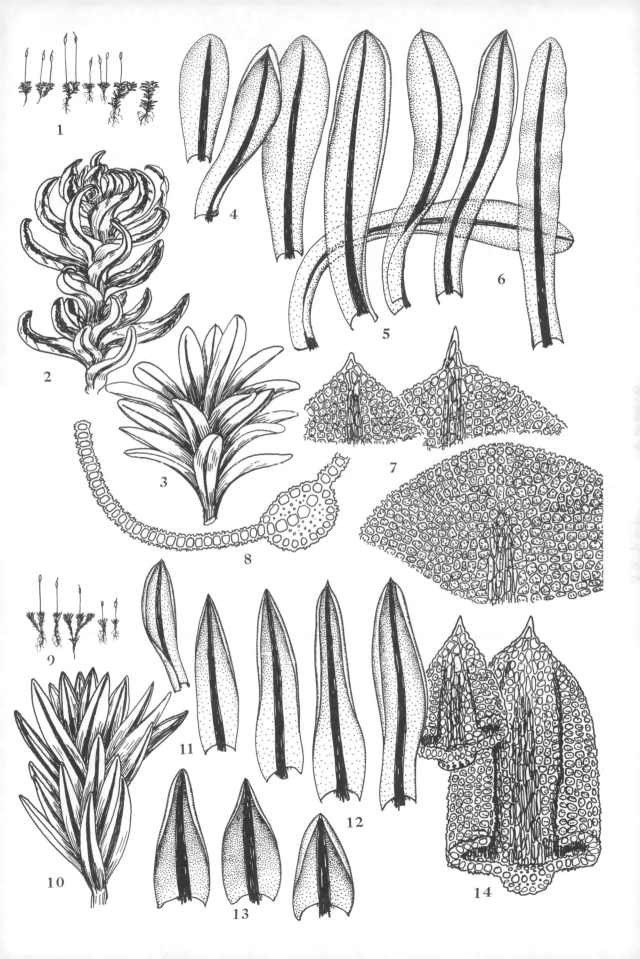

County: Hatch Rock, 5,700 ft.; Indian Canyon, near Kelley's Ranch, 5,500 ft.

10.32   The tufts are generally small, the plants frequently scattered. In the series from Indian Canyon I found the species associated with *Fissidens limbatus, Weissia ligulaefolia, Desmatodon obtusifolius, Tortella fragilis,* and *Brachythecium fendleri.* For autoicous plants they produce relatively few capsules, but every specimen thus far collected has at least 10 fruiting stems. Two specimens from Indian Canyon were mixed with *W. ligulaefolia,* which I was able to verify by the synoicous sexual condition and the leaves. This situation suggested that *W. perligulata* might be only an extreme variation of *W. ligulaefolia,* but since there was no intergradation in the form of the leaves and none of the plants showed the synoicous condition, I concluded that they were sufficiently distinct. The specimen from Hatch Rock is the largest of the series with leaves reaching three millimeters in length and forming rosettes. The plants from the House Mountains grew in wet crevices and have much narrower leaves than plants in the other collections.

3. GYMNOSTOMUM Nees & Hornsch.

10.33   Plants small, in dense cushions or expanded sods, usually growing on wet cliffs or rocks, dark green to yellowish green above, yellowish to pale brownish below. Stems slender and fragile; central strand small, often indistinct. Leaves generally incurved to erect, not crisped when dry, erect to recurved-spreading when moist, ligulate to narrowly lanceolate, acute or obtuse, rarely exceeding 1.5 mm in length; margins entire or nearly so; costa ending in or shortly below the apex; upper cells quadrate, rounded or shortly rectangular, lightly to densely papillose, sometimes nearly smooth; basal cells mostly wider and longer, hyaline and smooth or occasionally lightly or distantly papillose. Dioicous. Seta erect, yellowish to yellowish brown; capsule long exserted, ovoid to oblong-ovoid, erect and symmetric, the urn smooth or lightly wrinkled when dry, 0.5–1.3 mm long; neck short, with a few stomata; peristome lacking, annulus usually lacking; operculum conic-long rostrate, the beak usually sharply inclined. Calyptra cucullate.

10.34   The name from the Greek means naked mouth and refers to the absence of peristome teeth.

10.35   1. Leaves rather opaque; upper cells somewhat obscure; margins plane; capsules usually yellowish brown at maturity; columella not attached to the lid; spores 10–14 μ .... 1. *G. aeruginosum* 10.37

10.36   1. Leaves more transparent, the upper cells clear; margins mostly recurved on 1 side; capsules usually reddish brown at maturity; columella remaining attached to the lid and falling with it; spores 17–22 μ .... 2. *G. recurvirostrum* 10.41

10.37   1. **Gymnostomum aeruginosum** Sm. Plants in small cushions to widely expanded sods, usually on wet limestone cliffs, dull dark green to yellowish green. Stems erect and slender, freely branched and fragile, often interrupted nodulose, 1–8 cm high; leaves erect and appressed when dry, erect-patent to spreading-recurved when moist, rather dense, oblong-lanceolate to linear-lanceolate, the upper ones the largest, 0.7–1.5 mm long, ± carinate, the apex acute or blunt, rarely obtuse in a few leaves; costa 50–75 µ wide near the base, with medial guides and dorsal and ventral stereid bands (in the latter position often few or weak, lacking in the upper half of the leaf); upper cells mostly quadrate to rounded, a few shortly rectangular, 7–10 µ wide, rather densely chlorophyllose, papillose on both sides, somewhat obscure; basal cells gradually becoming larger, shortly rectangular to oblong, often quite chlorophyllose well toward the insertion, the lowest ones clear and smooth, the walls usually firm; marginal cells generally smaller, often slightly dentate by the projecting papillae. Seta 2–4 mm long, yellowish to brownish; capsule ovoid to shortly oblong, yellowish brown at maturity, becoming darker with age, reddish at the mouth, rather thin walled; operculum completely dehiscent. Spores 10–14 µ, finely papillose. Plate 12, figs. 7–14.

10.38   On wet calcareous cliffs and rocks.

10.39   North America, Europe, Asia, and North Africa. Utah, Sevier, Garfield and San Juan counties in Utah.

10.40   The appearance of this plant is much like that of G. recurvirostrum, but the contrasting characters are constant. The obscure areolation of the leaves may be difficult to judge without direct comparisons. The difference in size of the capsules seems to be remarkably constant. In spite of the dioicous habit, the plants are usually richly fruited, the cushions often bristling with capsules.

10.41   2. Gymnostomum recurvirostrum Hedw. var. recurvirostrum. Plants in small cushions or widely expanded sods, often deep green to yellowish green, sometimes tinged with brown above. Stems 1–8 cm tall, freely branched and fragile, yellowish, becoming brownish with age, rarely reddish; rhizoids few to dense, ferruginous. Leaves variable in shape and stance, incurved or infolded, erect to spreading but not particularly twisted when dry, erect-patent to squarrose-recurved when moist, oblong-lanceolate to narrowly lanceolate, keeled, sharply to bluntly acute, often with a few leaves obtuse, usually recurved on 1 side, entire or denticulate at base by projecting papillae; costa stout, ending shortly below the apex; upper cells rounded quadrate or rectangular, 8–12 µ wide, papillae strong and dense to low and wide, sometimes nearly lacking in some leaves; basal cells firm, rectangular to oblong or rhomboidal-hexagonal, about 12 µ wide, clear and smooth or with a few widely spaced papillae. Seta yellowish at maturity, becoming light reddish brown with age, 4–8 mm long; capsule light reddish brown at maturity, becoming darker with age, reddish at the mouth, smooth to minutely wrinkled when dry, subglobose to ovoid; annulus lacking; operculum with a long slender beak, usually sharply bent, remaining attached to the columella after dehiscence. Spores 17-22 µ, finely papillose. Plate 12, figs. 15–20.

129

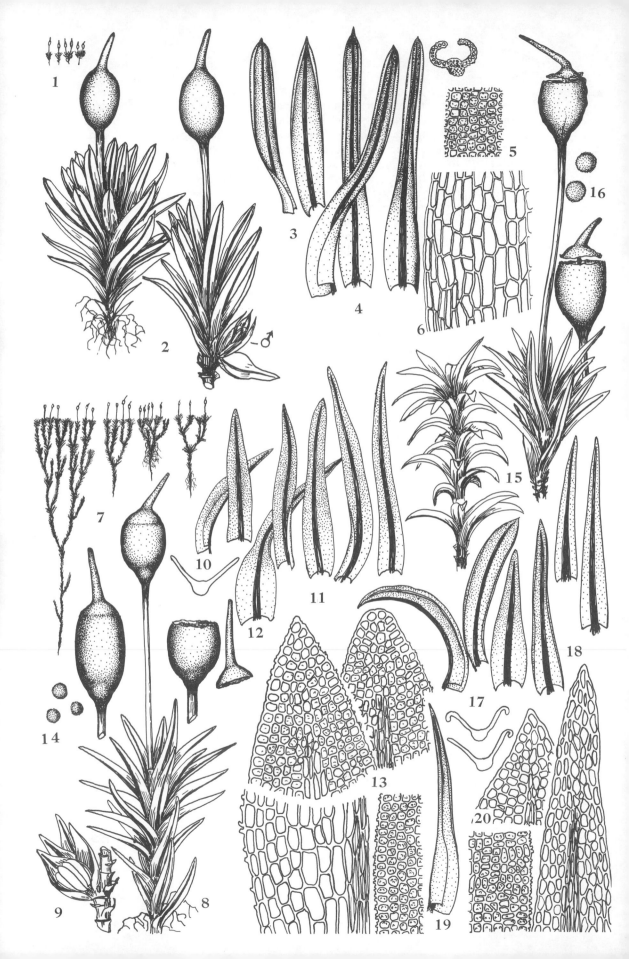

10.42 On wet, calcareous cliffs or rocks, sometimes on sandstone containing very little calcium.

10.43 Europe, Asia, North Africa, Mexico, Central America, West Indies, southern Andes, Labrador to South Carolina, west to Alaska and southern California, Utah: Grand and Kane counties.

10.44 The difference in size of spores seems to be the most constant contrast between this plant and *G. aeruginosum.* The leaves are more pellucid, but this is often difficult to evaluate without direct comparisons. Some leaves are plane on the margins, but usually a few can be found with the margins recurved on one side. The leaf cells tend to be longer and slightly wider, and the capsules darker, with the lid more or less persistent on the columella.

10.45 Plants from wet sandstone cliffs in the Colorado River Basin show considerable contrast in leaf characters with those from wet limestone cliffs in the Wasatch Mountains. The former have squarrose-recurved leaves, wider in the upper part and rather suddenly narrowed to the apex. In contrast, the plants from the Wasatch Mountains are more like the typical form with erect-patent to patent, lanceolate leaves, sometimes quite narrow and gradually tapering to a slender apex, as shown in the illustrations. The sandstones of the eastern and southern parts of the state often contain considerable calcium so that a number of calciphilous plants are found in these regions.

10.46 2a. Var. **latifolium** (Zett.) Flow. ex Crum. Differs from the species in papillose stems and more strongly papillose leaves.

10.47 Kane County: Colorado River, Hidden Passage, 3,336 ft. San Juan County: Colorado River, Aztec Canyon near Rainbow Natural Bridge, 3,470 ft.

4. EUCLADIUM B.S.G.

10.48 Plants freely branched, in deep tufts or cushions, often encrusted or infiltrated with a calcium deposit, yellowish green to bluish green above, pale yellowish brown below. Stems slender; central strand lacking. Leaves appressed, only slightly twisted above when dry, erect-patent to spreading when moist, mostly linear-lanceolate, the base sometimes dilated, oblong, margins flat, entire above, toothed just above the base;

Plate 12. **1–6. Astomum occidentale.** 1. Habit sketches, X.4. 2. Two plants, X4. 3. Two lower leaves. 4. Three upper leaves, X4. 5. Upper leaf cells, × 100. 6. Basal leaf cells, X120.

7–14. Gymnostomum aeruginosum. 7. Habit sketches, X.4. 8. Portion of plant and capsules, X4. 9. Dissection of perigonial bud. 10. Two lower leaves. 11. Four upper leaves. 12. A perichaetial leaf, X8. 13. Two leaf apices and the lower and upper leaf cells, X120. 14. Spores, X8.

15–20. Gymnostomum recurvirostum. 15. Portions of two plants showing variation in stance of leaves, X4. 16. Spores, X80. 17. Two leaves of the broader recurved type. 18. Four leaves of the narrow erect type. 19. A perichaetial leaf, X8. 20. Two leaf apices with rather smooth cells, and upper leaf cells with papillae, X120.

costa very stout, percurrent or shortly excurrent, with medial guides and dorsal and ventral stereids; upper cells quadrate to shortly rectangular, with low rounded papillae; basal cells suddenly enlarged, perfectly smooth and hyaline, oblong, becoming linear on the basal margins. Dioicous. Seta long, straight; capsule erect and ± symmetric, elliptic-oblong to cylindrical; peristome teeth 16, flat, 2–3 cleft or perforated finely papillose, erect; operculum conic with a long slender beak. Calyptra cucullate.

10.49   The name, of Greek origin, means well branched.

10.50   **Eucladium verticillatum** (Brid.) B.S.G. Stems 1–8 cm tall, repeatedly forked, usually appearing verticillate because of densely clustered comal leaves at successive innovations; rhizoids usually few. Leaves 0.8–2.5 mm long, linear-lanceolate to linear-subulate. Narrowly acute or shortly mucronate by the slightly excurrent costa; margins plane, abruptly toothed above the base; costa stout, green or yellowish to the base, disappearing in the apex to excurrent as a stout mucro; upper cells 7–12 μ wide, quite clear and green. Rarely fruiting. Female plants predominant, archegonia few, the perichaetial leaves scarcely differentiated from the lower stem leaves, the bases somewhat more dilated, Plate 13, figs. 10–16.

10.51   Growing on wet rocks, soil or wood, particularly around springs, dripping cliffs and brooklets in calcareous regions.

10.52   Widely distributed in the North Temperate Zone (including North Africa).

10.53   Superficially the plants resemble *Gymnostomum* and some species of *Didymodon*. The narrow leaves with wide costae and marginal teeth above the base are distinctive features.

5. TRICHOSTOMUM Bruch.

10.54   Plants in dense or loose tufts, erect, yellowish green to dark green above, brown to dusky below. Stems simple or branched; central strand present, often weak or sometimes lacking. Leaves narrow and lanceolate to sublinear, usually from an oblong or ovate base, crisped and twisted when dry, variously spreading or recurved when moist, concave-canaliculate, usually chlorophyllose and brittle; margins plane throughout or ±involute above; costa percurrent to shortly excurrent, in section

Plate 13.   1–9. Didymodon rigidulus. 1. Habit sketches, X.4. 2. Portion of shoot, X4. 3. Two lower leaves, X8. 4. Two upper leaves, X8. 5. Three cross sections of the upper part of leaf, showing the bistratose margins. 6. Cross section of leaf at the middle. 7. Three leaf apices showing upper cells. 8. Basal leaf cells from different leaves, X120. 9. Cross sections of stems showing well-defined central strand, X20, detail, X80.

10–16. Eucladium verticillatum. 10. Habit sketches, X.4. 11. Cross section of stem, X60. 12. Three lower leaves. 13. Four upper leaves, X8. 14. Three cross sections of leaf at apex, middle, and base. 15. Upper leaf cells. 16. Basal leaf cells showing toothed margin, X120.

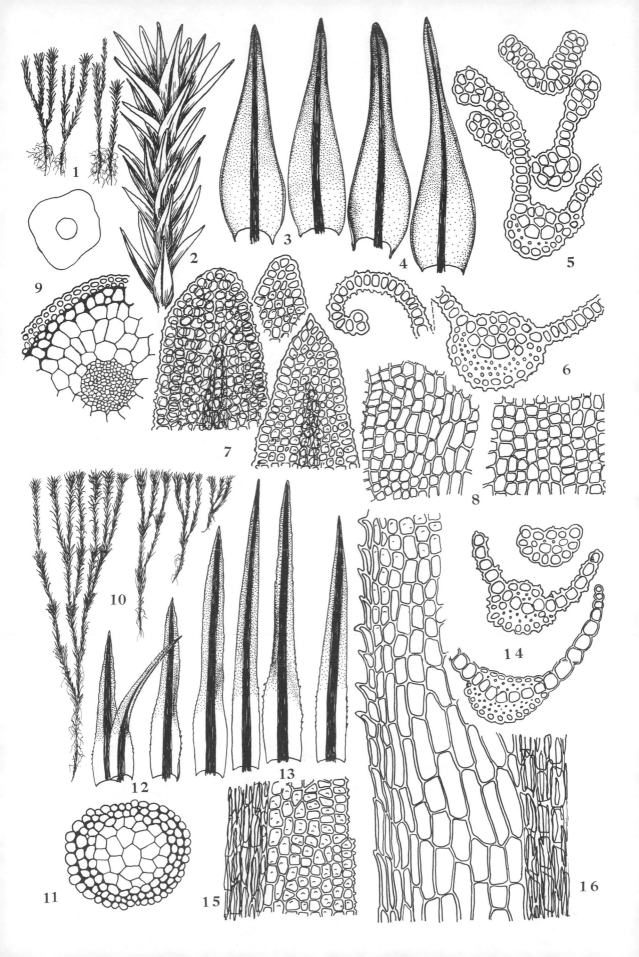

showing a strong dorsal and a smaller ventral stereid band; upper cells small, rarely over 10 μ wide, isodiametric to irregular, densely papillose; basal cells rather abruptly enlarged, rectangular, hyaline and often thin walled. Dioicous or autoicous. Seta long and erect; capsule oblong to cylindric, erect and symmetric or nearly so; lid conic, long rostrate, straight; teeth rather short, straight and erect, not twisted, divided into 32 slender divisions or irregularly split and perforated along the midline, or occasionally entire, finely papillose.

10.55 Name from the Greek for hairy mouth, alluding to the fine teeth of the peristome.

10.56 **Trichostomum tenuirostre** (Hook. & Tayl.) Lindb. Quite variable in habit and form of the leaves, ranging from short dense tufts or sods to loose soft tufts, the latter especially in crevices of cliffs. Leaves loosely to strongly twisted when dry, in some plants patent to spreading from the erect base when moist, usually crowded, variable in size and narrowness of the upper part, 2.5–4 mm long, gradually oblong-lanceolate to narrowly linear-lanceolate from an oblong erect base, suddenly narrowing to the apex or tapering gradually from a broader base to a very slender apex, sharply to bluntly acute, terminating in several larger, thick-walled, clear cells, often with 1–3 coarse teeth, canaliculate to keeled, often strongly undulate or flexuous, densely chlorophyllose, opaque, brittle and easily broken; costa ending in or below the apex, or shortly excurrent (rare in our plants), ventral superficial cells oblong in surface view; margins plane and entire or, more typically, irregularly notched and finely crenulate by the constriction of the marginal cells at their cross walls; upper cells 7–10 μ wide, quadrate to irregularly isodiametric, rather thick walled, each cell bearing 3–8 small papillae, these often connected in pairs, $\pm$ opaque; basal cells rather suddenly enlarged, wider, shortly rectangular to elongate-oblong, hyaline to reddish, smooth, walls thick and firm but often becoming thin and inflated at the extreme base. Dioicous. Fruit rarely formed. Spores 10–14 μ, maturing in autumn. Plate 14, figs. 7–11.

10.57 On damp or wet soil and rocks, open meadows, along brook banks, or in crevices.

10.58 Europe, Greenland to Manitoba, southward to North Carolina and the Great Lakes region; mountains of Utah and Arizona.

10.59 Sterile plants resemble *Barbula cylindrica*. The main difference lies in the short, erect, untwisted teeth and plane leaf margins of *Trichostomum*. The texture of the leaves is characteristic, appearing to be soft

---

Plate 14. **1–6. Aloina pilifera.** 1. Habit sketches, X.4. 2. Two lower leaves. 3. Three upper leaves, X8. 4. Cross section of leaf. 5. Upper leaf cells, X120. 6. Capsules, X8.

7–11. Trichostomum tenuirostre. 7. Habit sketches, X.4. 8. Leaves, X8. 9. Basal leaf cells. 10. Apex and upper leaf cells, X120. 11. Capsules and peristome teeth, X8 and X60.

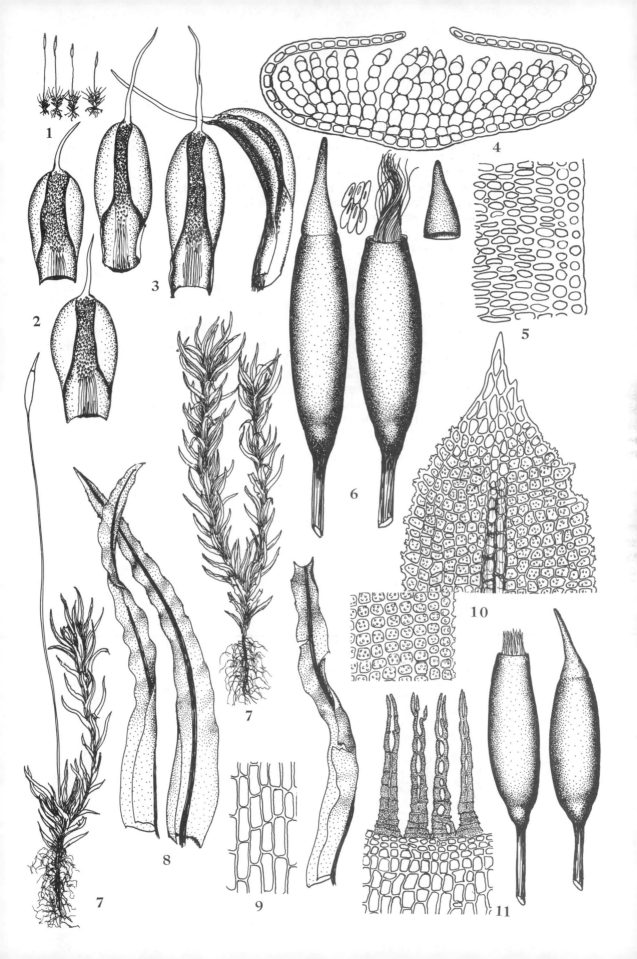

and tender but actually brittle and easily broken in handling, forming angular fractures. The lamina is ± undulate or flexuous, opaque and densely chlorophyllose. The minutely crenulate margins with coarser, irregular notches are characteristic, although *B. cylindrica* often shows the latter irregularities. The texture of the leaves resembles that of *B. unguiculata*, whereas *B. cylindrica* has firmer leaves, more flexible and not brittle, the margins not minutely crenulate, the general color usually brighter, less dull and opaque, the cells either nearly smooth or coarsely papillose, sometimes warty.

6. HYOPHILA Brid.

10.60 Plants mostly less than 3 cm tall, variously tufted. Stems with a central strand; leaves linear-lanceolate to broadly oblong-ligulate, usually crowded, crisped when dry, open to spreading when moist, ± clasping at base, acute to broadly rounded at the apex, entire to coarsely serrate and flat at the margins; costa ending below the apex, percurrent, or forming a short mucro, in cross section showing a row of medial guides and dorsal and ventral stereid bands; upper cells small (less than 14 μ wide), smooth to papillose, isodiametric, angular to rounded; basal cells usually rectangular, thinner walled and hyaline. Dioicous. Seta erect, long and slender; capsules ovoid to cylindrical; annulus present, falling early; lid conic to long rostrate, the cells in straight rows; peristome mostly lacking. Calyptra cucullate.

10.61 The name is taken from the Greek, meaning rain, and rain or water loving.

10.62 **Hyophila involuta** (Hook.) Jaeg. Plants bright to dull or dark green, rather loosely tufted. Stems forked, 1–3 cm tall, with central strand, cortex of large thin-walled cells, and a rind of smaller, very thick-walled reddish cells. Leaves rather crowded, incurved or crisped when dry, open to spreading-recurved when moist, oblong-lanceolate to ligulate, concave and canaliculate, 1.5–3.5 mm long, the base clasping and ± decurrent; apex rather narrowly acute to broadly obtuse (sometimes rounded), often apiculate; margins plane when moist (inrolled when dry), usually incurved at the base, entire to coarsely and often irregularly serrate in the upper half; costa prominent at the back; upper cells ± quadrate, 6–14 μ wide, mammillose and often slightly papillose on the upper or ventral side, smooth on the dorsal side, toward the base becoming gradually oblong and hyaline, but only slightly wider. Seta 6–10 mm long; capsules cylindric, about 2 mm long, becoming reddish brown at full maturity; peristome lacking; lid with a long straight beak. Plate 40, figs. 6–10.

10.63 On wet or damp rocks in shady places.

10.64 West Indies, Mexico to South America, Europe, Asia, Pacific Islands. New York, Ontario and Michigan, south to Florida; Arizona and Utah. Salt Lake County: Wasatch Mountains, Little Cottonwood Canyon, Tanner's Flat, 7,000 ft.

10.65   Fertile plants are known in the United States only from New Jersey and Tennessee. In the present collections the leaves vary from 1.5–3.5 mm long, but they are quite uniformly oblong-ligulate and the margins curve inward from the upper ⅓–¼ to acute or blunt apices. Only a few leaves are actually obtuse. The margins are mostly coarsely and irregularly serrate above, only occasionally nearly entire. In addition, the central strand and rind of small, thick-walled, reddish cells in the stem, the medial guides in cross sections of the costa, and the ventrally bulging and dorsally plane leaf cells serve to identify sterile plants.

7. TORTELLA (Lindb.) Limpr.

10.66   Plants erect, in loose or dense tufts or expanded in compact sods, mostly yellowish green above, yellowish to brown below, soft to brittle. Stems erect, less than 1 cm to 7 cm tall, slender to rather stout, simple or branched; central strand lacking or present in some species; rhizoids few at the base or dense, reddish and smooth. Leaves ± crowded, mostly crisped and twisted when dry, erect-patent to spreading or recurved when moist, oblong to linear-lanceolate from a hyaline base, widest at or slightly above the base, gradually tapering upward or ± abruptly narrowed above to sharply acute or mucronate point, in some species obtuse, mucronate, and often cucullate, concave, canaliculate, laminae sometimes undulate at the margins; margins plane, entire to crenulate or with a few teeth at the extreme apex; costa percurrent to shortly excurrent, in cross section showing a single row of guides and dorsal and ventral stereid bands; upper leaf cells isodiametric, mostly quadrate to rounded, chlorophyllose, and densely papillose with C-shaped papillae; basal cells abruptly enlarged, hyaline, thin walled, and smooth, extending obliquely from the costa up the margins in V-shaped fashion. Seta terminal, long and erect; capsules erect or slightly curved, elliptic to cylindric, symmetric or nearly so, smooth when dry; operculum conic shortly to longly rostrate, straight or inclined; annulus none; peristome teeth arising from a very low basal membrane, divided into 32 divisions which are mostly filiform and ± spirally twisted (in some species rather short and nearly erect), often ± united at the joints below, reddish and finely papillose.

10.67   The name is a Latin diminutive meaning twisted and refers to the peristome.

10.68   1. Leaves rarely broken off at the apex, strongly crisped and twisted when dry, spreading to recurved and ± flexuous when moist; margins undulate .... 1. *T. tortuosa*   10.70

10.69   1. Leaves brittle, all but the apical ones broken off, the upper ones often much curved but not crisped or twisted when dry, strict, erect or divergent when moist

2. Costa percurrent, often ending in larger clear cells, the point short; the upper lamina rather broad, with somewhat undulate margins .... 2. *T. nitida*   10.74

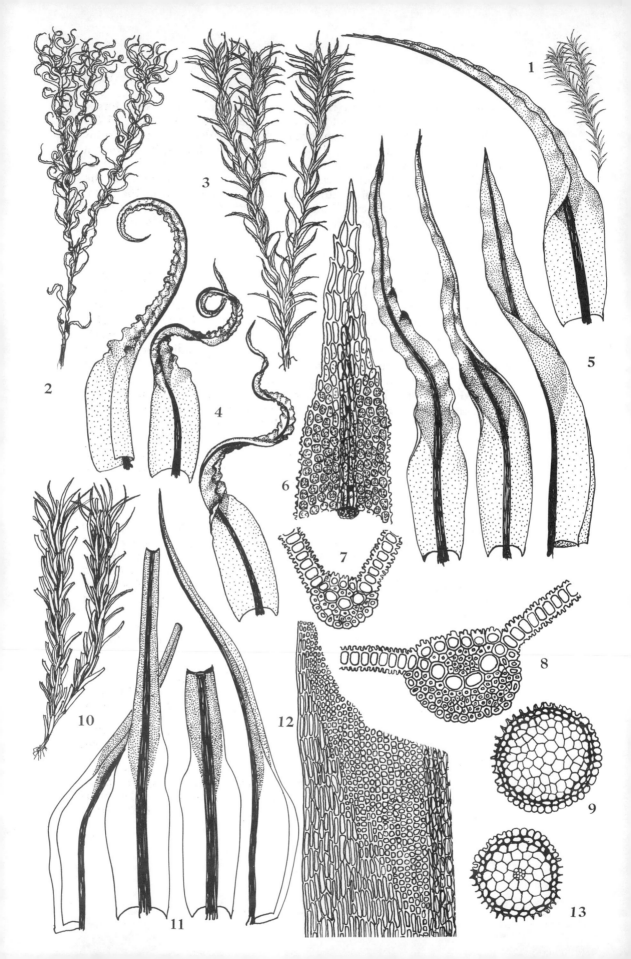

2. Costa indistinctly long-excurrent to a thickish hair point; the upper lamina narrow, not undulate .... 3. *T. fragilis*   10.78

10.70   1. **Tortella tortuosa** (Hedw.) Limpr. Plants in dense tufts, often forming deep and extensive sods, yellowish green, glaucous green or dark green above, yellowish brown to brown below. Stems stout, 1–7 cm tall, usually with several short branches near the apex; central strand lacking; rhizoids sparse to dense at the base, reddish brown. Leaves strongly crisped and twisted when dry, when moist spreading to recurved and flexuous, narrowly lanceolate to linear-lanceolate from a pale, erect, oblong base, 2–6.5 mm long, gradually tapering to a narrowly acute apex, upper lamina usually canaliculate and ± undulate; margins entire or sometimes with a few sharp teeth at the extreme apex; costa stout, percurrent to shortly excurrent to a sharp tip; upper cells isodiametric, quadrate or irregularly 4- to 6-sided, moderately thick walled, 9–12 μ wide, chlorophyllose and densely papillose with stout, rounded papillae; basal cells oblong to linear, abruptly elongated, smooth and hyaline, extending obliquely from the costa to the margins in V-shaped fashion, about as wide as the upper cells. Dioicous. Seta 1.5–3 cm long, reddish to reddish brown, often paler above, twisted to the left when dry; capsule oblong-cylindric to cylindric, straight or slightly curved, 2–3.5 mm long, yellowish, becoming reddish brown at maturity; operculum conic-rostrate, 1.5–2.5 mm long; peristome teeth twisted in 2–3 turns, reddish, densely and finely papillose. Spores yellowish, finely papillose, 8–12 μ. Plate 15, figs. 1–9.

10.71   Mostly in the crevices of rocks or on soil under overhanging rocks, usually in canyons or on shaded mountain slopes in our region.

10.72   Widely distributed in North America, and almost worldwide.

10.73   Infrequent in Utah but sometimes locally abundant in large tufts. Distinguished from the following species by the larger size, thicker stems without a central strand, leaves larger and wider in the lower part, the undulate lamina, and crisped and twisted dry habit.

10.74   2. **Tortella nitida** (Lindb.) Broth. Plants in dense tufts, dark to light or yellowish green, brown below. Stems simple or slightly branched, 1–3 cm high, central strand present; rhizoids moderately abundant at the base. Leaves linear-lanceolate, 2–3(7) mm long, brittle, the tips often broken off, acute to shortly acuminate, undulate, entire but finely crenulate by the bulging marginal cells, erect-patent when moist, the upper part curved in circles from an erect base when dry, not crisped or twisted, the lower leaves not much curved, costa stout, pale and often

---

Plate 15.   1–9 Tortella tortuosa. 1. Habit sketch, X.4. 2–3. Dry and moist habit, X2. 4. Dry leaves. 5. Moist leaves, X8. 6. Typical leaf apex and upper cells, X100. 7–8. Cross sections of the costa at two levels, X120. 9. Cross section of the stem, X100.

10–13. Tortella fragilis. 10. Habit sketch, moist, X4. 11. Typical leaves, X8. 12. Lower and basal leaf cells, X60. 13. Cross section of the stem, X100.

shiny at back, especially when dry, percurrent or nearly so; upper cells quadrate, hexagonal, transversely elongated or shortly oblong, 8–11(12) μ wide, firm and rather thick walled, chlorophyllose, with moderately dense small papillae, a few apical cells of some leaves with unbroken tips abruptly enlarged, hexagonal and clear; basal cells abruptly larger, hyaline, and oblong, extending up the margins. Dioicous. Fruit rare. Seta less than 1 cm long; capsules oblong-cylindric, pale brown, erect, 1–1.5 mm long, somewhat furrowed when dry; lid conic, with an oblique beak about ⅓ as long as the urn; teeth short, imperfect, very slightly twisted, yellowish, and papillose. Plate 16, figs. 1–10.

10.75 On damp or dry soil and rocks, and in crevices. Rare.

10.76 Europe, Algiers. Southern Canada and northern United States. Duchesne and Wayne counties.

10.77 Our specimens are scanty, sterile, and of minimum size but appear to agree with the basic traits of the gametophyte as described by several authors. They seem to be intermediate between *T. tortuosa* and *T. fragilis*.

10.78 **3. Tortella fragilis** (Hook. & Wils.) Limpr. Plants medium sized in dense compact tufts or sods, green above, yellowish to brownish below. Stems slender, usually branched, 1–6 cm tall; mostly short, with a small distinct or indistinct central strand; rhizoids few to dense at the base, reddish. Leaves mostly erect, straight or incurved to slightly twisted when dry, erect to erect-patent when moist, narrowly lanceolate to linear from a pale oblong base, concave-canaliculate; the apex very slenderly acute, brittle, nearly all the leaves except those at the extreme apex broken, the broken ones commonly 2–3.5 mm long, unbroken ones 3–6.5 mm long; margins entire, flat, rarely slightly undulate; costa and areolation like those of the last species. Dioicous. Capsule much as in the last species but rare. Plate 15, figs. 10–13.

10.79 On dry or moist soil and in crevices of rocks.

10.80 Europe and Asia. Across Northern United States and Canada, south to New Jersey, Missouri and Utah.

10.81 This differs from the last species in that leaves are more nearly erect when moist, strict, much more narrowly tapering to an indistinctly excurrent costa which is thickish, green, and very brittle. In our region the plants are smaller than *T. tortuosa*, but about the same size as *T. nitida*, with which it seems to intergrade, the latter having the leaves less narrowly pointed, with margins undulate and costa percurrent.

8. DIDYMODON Hedw.

10.82 Plants in loose or dense tufts, dull dark green, often yellowish, to olivaceous or brownish green, frequently tinged with red, often infiltrated with silt or calcareous deposit. Stems erect, usually sparingly branched, rather slender; central strand lacking, indistinct or well defined, outer cells of the cortex thin walled to variably thickened and colored; rhizoids relatively few, mainly basal, sometimes bearing 1- to 5-

celled globose or ovoid, reddish brown gemmae. Leaves broadly ovate-lanceolate to slenderly lanceolate or ligulate, moderately concave, acute to broadly rounded; margins entire, mostly revolute in the lower half; costa percurrent or ending shortly below the apex, in cross section showing 1–2 rows of large subventral cells or stereids, a single row of guides, and a definite dorsal stereid band of 2–3(4) rows of cells, the ventral superficial cells usually large, the dorsal superficial cells usually only slightly larger than adjacent stereids; upper cells quadrate, shortly rectangular or irregular, usually rounded at the angles, smooth to moderately papillose. Dioicous. Seta elongate, straight; capsules elliptical to long-cylindric, erect, straight or slightly inclined, smooth when dry; annulus lacking; operculum conic-rostrate; peristome teeth 16, straight or slightly oblique, short, entire and flat to variably cleft, perforated or divided to the base into slender divisions, the basal membrane very short. Calyptra cucullate.

10.83   The name, derived from the Greek, means double or twin tooth and refers to the split teeth of the peristome.

10.84   1. Leaf margins and apex of laminae 2- to 3-stratose; comal leaves mostly slenderly lanceolate from an ovate base, bluntly acute to narrowly obtuse .... 1. *D. rigidulus* 10.86

10.85   1. Leaf margins and laminae 1-stratose throughout

   2. Plants rather dark green, olivaceous or brownish green, often tinged with red above and becoming reddish below; leaves oblong-lanceolate to ligulate, the comal ones broadly rounded or bluntly acute, the lower ones acute to obtuse; costa ending 3–10 cells below the tip, reddish below or throughout; basal cells mostly oblong, clear .... 2. *D. tophaceus* 10.91

   2. Plants dull yellow green above, becoming light brownish below; leaves broadly ovate-lanceolate, the comal ones narrowly to broadly acute, sometimes obtuse; costa green or yellowish, disappearing in the apex; basal cells short, quadrate to shortly oblong, chlorophyllose .... 3. *D. trifarius* 10.97

10.86   **1. Didymodon rigidulus** Hedw. Plants in small to medium sized, dense tufts, dull yellowish green to brownish green above, reddish brown below. Stems 1–2 cm high; central strand large and well defined, 52–70 μ across, composed of numerous small, thin-walled cells, 15–20 cells across the diameter; cortical cells large, thin walled and angular, the outer 2–3 layers abruptly smaller, usually very thick walled and reddish; rhizoids rather few, reddish, smooth and mainly basal. Small, subspherical, stalked gemmae often produced in axils of upper leaves. Leaves ± crisped when dry, spreading rigidly from a divergent or somewhat erect base, the upper part lanceolate to linear-lanceolate from an ovate base, rather evenly tapered to an acute, blunt or sometimes rounded-obtuse apex, the comal ones larger and usually more narrowly lanceolate, 2–2.5 mm long, moderately concave below, channeled above;

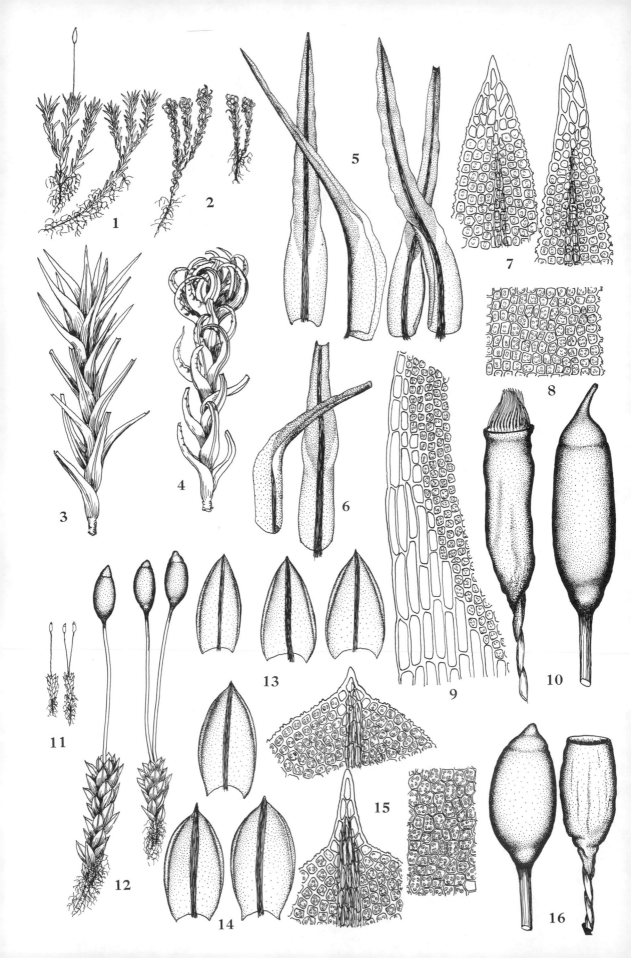

margins strongly revolute in the low ¾–½, 2- to 3-stratose in the upper half as well as in the apex of the lamina; costa conspicuous at the back, disappearing in the thickened apex of the leaf, dull greenish in younger leaves, reddish brown in older ones; upper cells quadrate, rounded or transversely elongated, 7–12 μ in longest diameter, thick walled, smooth or moderately papillose, 1–4 rows on the upper margins 2- to 3-stratose; basal cells becoming wider, 12–18 μ, either predominantly quadrate or shortly rectangular, usually clear, the walls thick and smooth. Seta 5–10 mm long, reddish; capsule erect, straight, shortly cylindrical, reddish and smooth when dry; operculum conic-rostrate; peristome teeth comparatively short, cleft or divided to the base into slender divisions, erect or very slightly twisted, light reddish brown and finely papillose. Plate 13, figs. 1–9.

10.87   On damp or wet rocks and soil in calcareous regions.

10.88   Europe. Widely distributed in the West, British Columbia to California, throughout the Rocky Mountains to western Texas, rare in the East, Minnesota, Ontario and Newfoundland. Cache and Weber counties.

10.89   The well-developed central strand of the stems and 2- to 3-stratose upper margins and extreme apices of the leaves are the most distinctive features of this plant. Small subglobose, stalked gemmae in the axils of the upper leaves are said to be a constant feature, but our specimens did not reveal them.

10.90   This moss may be mistaken for *D. tophaceus* inasmuch as a few of the comal leaves of some stems have broadly rounded apices, but in *D. tophaceus* the leaves are unistratose throughout, and the central strand of the stem is lacking or very indistinct. Also *D. tophaceus* has decurrent leaves.

10.91   **2. Didymodon tophaceus** (Brid.) Lisa. Plants in loose or dense tufts, dark green, olivaceous or reddish green above, yellowish brown to reddish brown below, often infiltrated with silt or calcareous deposit. Stems 1–5 cm, sometimes 10 cm, tall; central strand lacking or indistinct; rhizoids few, mostly confined to the base, often bearing 1–5 celled globose or ovoid gemmae. Leaves loosely to closely appressed, decurrent, often incurved, but not much crisped when dry, stiff and strict, erect-patent, not or slightly recurved when moist, lanceolate, oblong-lanceolate to ligulate, some or all of the comal ones broadly rounded to obtuse at the apex, the others broadly acute or blunt; margins revolute well toward the apex, unistratose; costa prominent at the back, usually

---

Plate 16. 1–10. **Tortella nitida.** 1–2. Moist and dry habit sketches, X.4. 3–4. Upper portions of moist and dry shoots, X4. 5–6. Upper and lower leaves, X8. 7. Leaf apices. 8. Upper medial cells. 9. Basal cells, X120. 10. Capsules, X8.

11–16. **Pottia arizonica** var. **mucronulata.** 11. Habit sketches, X.4. 12. Habit, X4. 13. Lower leaves. 14. Upper leaves, X8. 15. Leaf apices and upper medial cells, X120. 16. Capsules, X8.

tinged with red at the base or reddish throughout, ending 3–10 cells below the tip; areolation mostly bright and clear, often reddish throughout in older leaves; upper cells quadrate to oblong, rounded or oval, the walls thick, mostly 10–14 μ wide, usually clear, the younger ones often chlorophyllose and somewhat opaque, smooth or with rather wide low papillae (most abundant on the dorsal surface); basal cells wider and longer, mostly oblong, thick walled, smooth, clear and usually reddish, the basal marginal cells shorter, smaller and thicker walled. Seta 6–15 mm long, reddish; capsules elliptic to cylindric, erect and straight or slightly inclined, 1.3–2.5 mm long without the lid, smooth and dark reddish when dry, bright reddish when moist, neck short and distinct with 2 rows of large stomata; lid conic-rostrate; peristome teeth erect, simple, slender and flat or variously cleft and perforated to divided near the base into filiform divisions, basal membrane very short or lacking, pale yellowish to yellowish brown, finely papillose. Spores light yellowish brown, 10–13 μ, smooth. Plate 17, figs. 1–9.

10.92 Growing on wet calcareous rocks and soil, frequently on concrete installations, around springs and dripping cliffs.

10.93 Widely distributed in North America and Europe.

10.94 Rarely fruiting. Much like *D. trifarius* and easily confused with it. The differences between the two species cited in keys are sometimes difficult to demonstrate. In nearly all the present plants I find *D. tophaceus* more strict in habit, with narrower leaves standing stiffly at angles of about 30° to 45°, giving the shoots a more slender appearance. Also, they are consistently tinged with reddish brown below (and red throughout in some older plants). The costae are proportionately narrower and more distinct, consistently reddish in the lower part or throughout; the basal leaf cells are oblong and clear, and the areolation throughout the entire leaf is usually bright and clear. In some plants the leaves are mostly lanceolate.

10.95 In contrast, *D. trifarius* is predominantly laxer, with broader leaves usually more or less wide-spreading and sometimes almost squarrose, giving the shoots a stouter appearance. The plant as a whole is a dull green or yellowish green color, rarely tinged with red, the lower parts pale yellowish brown to brownish, the costae broad and often somewhat indistinct at the margins, greenish or yellowish throughout, rarely reddish tinged at the base, the basal cells usually chlorophyllose, mostly shorter, quadrate to shortly oblong, but sometimes irregularly oblong

---

Plate 17. 1–9. **Didymodon tophaceus.** 1. Habit sketches, X.4. 2. Portion of shoot, X4. 3. Three lower leaves. 4. Two comal leaves, X8. 5. Apex of lower leaf, X200. 6. Apex of comal leaf. 6. Basal leaf cells, X120. 7. Two perigonial leaves. 8. Two capsules, X8. 9. Portion of the peristome, viewed from the inside, X50.

10–16. D. trifarius. 10. Habit sketches, X.4. 11. Portion of shoot, X4. 12. Three lower leaves. 13. Two comal leaves, X8. 14. Apex of lower leaf. 15. Apex of comal leaf. 16. Basal leaf cells, X120.

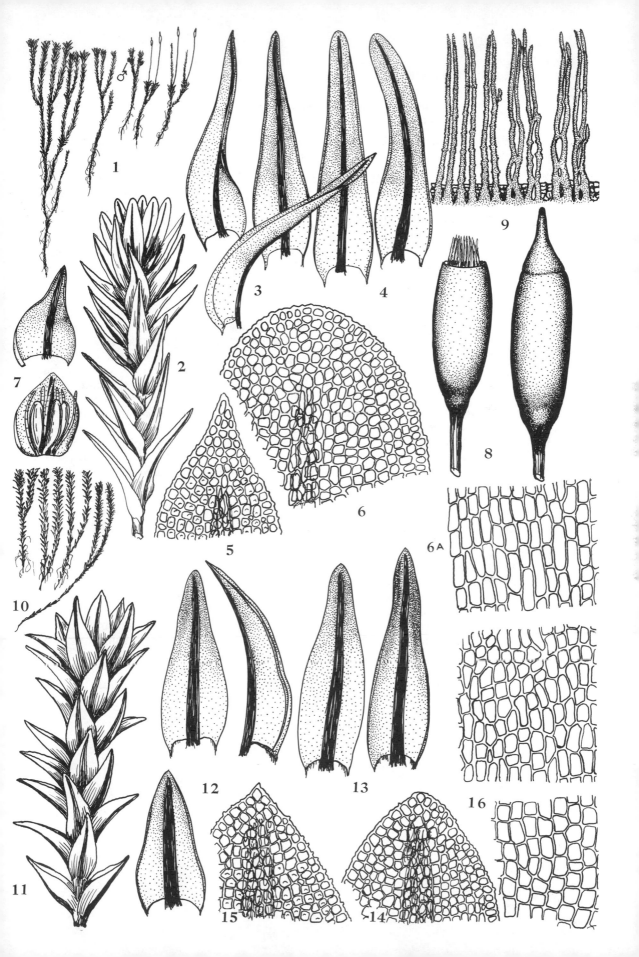

to rhomboidal; the areolation of the leaf is dull greenish and often somewhat opaque.

10.96 *D. tophaceus* is noted for its accumulation of calcareous deposits as characteristic tufaceous rocks, which have been called didymodontoliths.

10.97 **3. Didymodon trifarius** (Hedw.) Roehl. Plants in loose or dense tufts, often infiltrated with sedimentary material or encrusted with a calcareous deposit, dull green, yellowish green or brownish green above, pale yellowish brown to brownish below, never becoming rusty reddish. Stems 1–2 cm high, sparingly branched; central strand lacking or indistinct; cells of the outer cortex rather abruptly smaller, often thin walled and greenish, sometimes thick walled and colored in older parts. Leaves erect or closely imbricated, scarcely crisped when dry, erect-patent to recurved when moist, rather stiff, ovate-lanceolate, often broadly so, 1.3–1.5 mm long, channeled, the comal ones mostly widely acute or blunt, sometimes a few broadly rounded, the lower ones shorter, often narrowly obtuse to rounded, often decurrent at the base; margins unistratose, plane throughout or revolute well toward the apex, variable in the same plant; costa stout and wide, often indistinct at the margins, greenish to yellowish, rarely tinted with red at the base, ending vaguely in the apex; upper cells quadrate to shortly rectangular, angular or with the angles rounded, 10–14 μ wide, smooth or moderately papillose, lightly chlorophyllose throughout, moderately thick walled; basal cells mostly short, quadrate to oblong, $\pm$ chlorophyllose, seldom clear and rarely tinted. Rarely fruiting; seta about 1 cm long; capsule and peristome much like those of *D. tophaceus*. Plate 17, figs. 10–16.

10.98 On wet soil, rocks and wood in springs, and along streams, in calcareous regions.

10.99 Europe. Widely distributed from Canada to Mexico, rather rare in the southeastern states.

10.100 Nearly always sterile, this dull and often dirty greenish or yellowish moss is often overlooked. For comparison with *D. tophaceus*, see notes under that species. It may be confused with *Barbula fallax* since the ventral costal cells in the upper half of the leaves are oblong to linear. However, the present plants rarely become rusty red at the base of the stems, and the costa is usually green, yellowish or brownish, but not a distinct reddish color. The leaf cells are much less regular, often varying from quadrate to oblong or oval and various shapes mixed together. Also, the cells are usually larger, 10–14 μ wide but in this respect may vary widely, some plants having cells only 8–12 μ wide.

9. BRYOERYTHROPHYLLUM Chen.

10.101 Plants in dense tufts, green to yellowish green above, rusty reddish below. Stems with a central strand. Leaves mostly lanceolate from an often reddish base; margins revolute; costa strong, percurrent or nearly so; upper cells small, quadrate to rounded, papillose; basal cells elongated, thin walled, usually hyaline or pale brownish. Capsules shortly

146

oblong to cylindric, erect to very slightly curved in our species; peristome of 16 slender erect teeth from a very low basal membrane, not divided.

10.102 The name, from the Greek, means red-leaved moss.

10.103 **Bryoerythrophyllum recurvirostre** (Hedw.) Chen. var. **recurvirostrum.** Plants small to medium sized, in dense tufts or cushions, sometimes in expanded sods, bright green to yellowish green above, the lower portion a bright rusty red. Stems erect, usually much branched, 0.5–6 cm tall; central strand fairly large to medium sized, composed of small thin-walled cells, these often collapsing early; cortical cells large, thin walled and angular, the 2 outermost layers much smaller, thick walled and reddish; rhizoids usually dense below, reddish and smooth. Leaves rather dense, flexuous to crisped and curled when dry, erect-patent to spreading-recurved from an erect base when moist, lanceolate to linear-lanceolate (almost ligulate in some xerophytic forms), usually from an ovate or oblong, somewhat clasping base, 2–3 mm long, the lower ones smaller and shorter; apex gradually or rather suddenly acute, sometimes blunt; margins revolute nearly to the apex, entire or with a few coarse yellowish teeth at the extreme tip; costa stout, ending in the apex or percurrent to a single stout cell forming a mucro, in cross section showing a single row of medial guides and a large dorsal stereid band and a smaller ventral band (the latter often lacking high up in the leaf) and ventral superficial cells rather large and papillose; upper cells ± isodiametric, 4- to 6-angled, often irregular, 7–11 μ wide, rather thick walled, densely papillose with simple or C- or O-shaped papillae, ± obscure; marginal cells unistratose; basal cells becoming larger and longer, oblong to sublinear, smooth, up to 14 ± wide, usually hyaline but thin walled, often reddish, the walls firm but sometimes thin and more or less inflated. Synoicous or paroicous. Seta erect, straight or flexuous, 7–9 mm long, bright reddish brown when mature; capsules erect and symmetric or slightly curved with the mouth somewhat oblique, bright reddish at maturity, urn 1–2 mm long, little changed when dry, smooth or minutely striate or rugulose; exothecial cells mostly oblong, 4- to 6-sided, 2–3 rows below the mouth, small, short and thick walled; annulus of 2–3 rows of oval or shortly oblong cells with exceedingly thick walls; neck region short with a few large stomata; lid conic with a rather short oblique rostrum; teeth rather short, erect, linear, with a strong medial line and often becoming perforated upward, the upper 1–2 joints frequently cleft, pale yellowish to yellowish brown, often reddish at the joints, smooth to minutely roughened with fine papillae, fragile and usually soon broken off. Spores 13–20 μ, yellowish, finely punctate, maturing in late June to August. Calyptra cucullate. Plate 18, figs. 1–10.

10.104 On wet or damp soil and rocks, particularly along streams and around seepage areas, but not uncommon on soil under overhanging rocks sometimes where it is quite dry. It is said to be favored by calcareous rocks and soil, but it is nearly as frequent in regions of siliceous and ferromagnesian rocks.

147

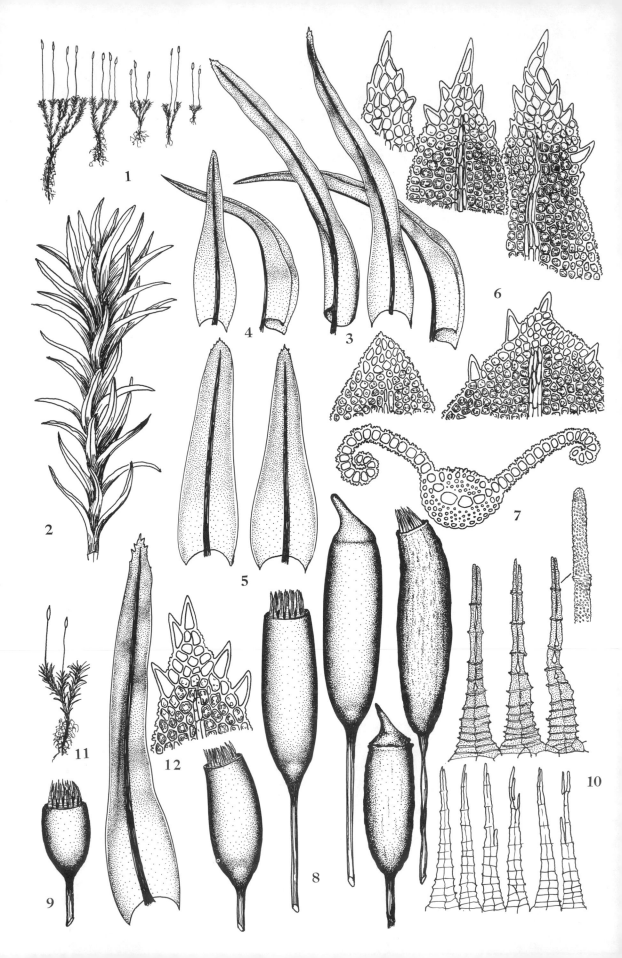

10.105   Eurasia, North Africa, and Tasmania. Greenland to Alaska, southward to New Jersey, the Great Lakes region and Iowa, and in the mountains of the West through Utah, New Mexico, Arizona and California.

10.106   Common in the mountains throughout the state. (This moss had long been known as *Didymodon rubellus* and more recently as *D. recurvirostris.*) The rather small size, the rusty red color of the lower portions of the plant, the narrowly lanceolate to linear leaves, frequently with a few coarse teeth on the margin at the extreme apex, and the reddish brown, oblong to cylindric capsules are the outstanding characteristics. The principal variations are as follows: some small forms have the upper leaves shorter than usual, more lanceolate in outline, the lower ones even smaller, as shown in fig. 4 of the plate. Certain xerophytic forms may have proportionately broader leaves, some of them almost ligulate, as shown in fig. 5. I have one specimen with unusually small oval to obovate capsules borne on otherwise typical leafy plants. One is shown in fig. 9.

10.107   9a. Var. **dentatum** (Schimp.) Flow. Plants larger and more robust, less densely tufted. Leaves larger, 3–4.8 mm long, with the margin less revolute in the upper part, usually with much coarser marginal teeth at the apex; the seta 10–18 mm long and the capsules 1.5–2.8 mm long. In the same habitat, but much less frequent. Plate 18, figs. 11–12.

10.108   Utah County: Stewart's Creek and North Fork of Provo River, 5,800 ft. Both specimens were found growing with *Tortula mucronifolia.*

10.109   The variety is said to intergrade with the species, but the two specimens cited above contrast strongly with all my specimens of the species, especially in size.

   10. BARBULA Hedw.

10.110   Plants small to medium sized, densely to loosely tufted, often scattered among other mosses, usually favored by calcareous conditions, dark green to yellowish green, often dull and tinged with red above, brownish to reddish brown below. Stems erect or ascending, simple or forked, the branches often slender and with juvenile leaves of a different character from those of the main stem; central strand usually present but often indistinct or lacking, even in the same plants; rhizoids few to moderately dense, reddish and smooth. Vegetative buds or gemmae may appear sporadically on the rhizoids or in leaf axils of some species.

Plate 18.   1–10. Bryoerythrophyllum recurvirostrum. 1. Habits of growth, X.4. 2. Portion of stem, X4. 3. Three typical leaves. 4. Two leaves of a small form. 5. Two upper leaves of a xerophytic form, X8. 6. Five leaf apices showing variations. 7. Cross section from middle of leaf showing structure of costa, X120. 8. Five capsules showing variations. 9. Unusually small, short capsule, X8. 10. Portions of the peristome teeth from capsule of different specimens, showing variations, X60.

11–12. Var. dentatum. 11. Habit sketch, X.4. 12. Leaf with apical cells in detail, X8 and X120.

Leaves widest at the base, ovate-lanceolate to ligulate-lanceolate or linear-lanceolate, often from a differentiated basal portion, the lower leaves shorter, the upper longer and usually narrower in the upper part, erect and appressed to strongly contorted when dry, erect-patent to spreading or recurved when moist, narrowly acute to blunt or broadly obtuse; margins entire, mostly recurved to revolute, at least in the lower third of the leaf, weakly so or plane in some species; costa usually stout, ending a few cells below the apex to long-excurrent, often disappearing in the upper part of the leaf, in section showing 2–6 medial guides (at least in the lower half of the leaf, usually subventral elsewhere), the ventral stereids 1–3 cells thick, the dorsal stereid band larger, 2–6 cells thick; lamina unistratose (in our species); upper cells small, mostly 7–10(15) μ wide, quadrate to shortly oblong, often becoming rounded or irregular, usually thick walled, normally chlorophyllose, opaque and densely papillose, but very often becoming moderately clear, the papillae low and rounded and in some plants smooth; basal cells either little different, slightly wider and smoother, or elongated thin walled and clear but rarely noticeably wider. Dioicous. Seta erect, rather long and straight, yellowish to red, twisted when dry; capsule shortly ovate to long-cylindric, straight to slightly curved, erect to slightly inclined, mostly reddish to dark brown, smooth to minutely longitudinally wrinkled when dry; operculum long-rostrate, mostly ½ to ¾ the length of the urn; annulus scarcely differentiated in some species, in others strongly marked, revoluble and deciduous; peristome teeth divided into 32 hairlike divisions arising from a narrow basal membrane, spirally twisted in 1–3 turns, in some species often becoming ± erect and spreading after the lid has fallen, reddish and finely papillose, sometimes becoming pale with age. Spores 6–11 μ, smooth. Calyptra cucullate.

10.111   The name is a Latin diminutive for beard and refers to the long hairs of the peristome.

10.112   1. Leaves oblong to lanceolate-ligulate or sublinear, obtuse to broadly acute; costa stout, ending below the apex or shortly excurrent to a mucro

2. Leaf cells strongly papillose with small papillae, usually ± chlorophyllose and opaque; leaves oblong-ligulate to sublinear, brittle and easily broken when dry; apex broadly rounded, often mucronate, sometimes suddenly narrowed to a broadly acute point; margins essentially entire but sometimes minutely crenulate, revolute to the middle

3. Plants small

4. Gemmae obovate, stalked, greenish to reddish brown, always present in axils of upper leaves .... 1. *B. cruegeri* 10.114

4. Gemmae lacking; perichaetial leaves the largest, strongly convolute and sheathing the base of the seta; seta yellow, twisted to the left; costa ending 3–5 cells below the apex ....
.... 2. *B. eustegia* 10.118

3. Plants medium sized; perichaetial leaves not convolute or sheathing the base of the seta; seta reddish, twisted to the right; costa mostly excurrent to a short mucro .... 3. *B. unguiculata*   10.122

2. Leaf cells smooth or with low rounded papillae, usually pale and quite clear; leaves oblong-lanceolate to lanceolate-ligulate, widest at the base, gradually tapering to a rounded-obtuse to bluntly acute apex; margins entire, plane or weakly revolute below .... 4. *B. ehrenbergii*   10.126

10.113   1. Leaves lanceolate to subulate from a distinctly broader ovate to oblong base, usually gradually tapering upward to a slenderly acute or blunt apex; costa disappearing vaguely in the apex or excurrent; margins recurved to strongly revolute, at least in the lower half

5. Costa vaguely long-excurrent as a fleshy tip in the upper leaves, the tips rather brittle when dry

6. Leaf margins revolute only at the base or in the lower half .... 6. *B. acuta*   10.134

6. Leaf margins revolute to the apex or nearly so; plants usually larger than the last .... 7. *B. bescherellei*   10.138

5. Costa ending below the apex or disappearing in it

7. Ventral costal cells oblong to linear in the upper half of the leaf; plants dull yellowish to brownish green .... 5. *B. fallax*   10.130

7. Ventral costal cells mostly quadrate, similar to the adjacent cells of the lamina

8. Leaves ovate-lanceolate to lanceolate, 1.5–2.5 mm long, not flexuous; margins recurved to revolute to well above the middle .... 8. *B. vinealis*   10.142

8. Leaves narrowly lanceolate from a broadly ovate base to linear-lanceolate, 2.5–5 mm long, ± flexuous, the margins recurved only in the lower third or less .... 9 *B. cylindrica*   10.147

10.114   **1. Barbula cruegeri** Sond. ex C. Muell. Plants small, loosely caespitose or scattered, light green, frequently becoming yellowish to glaucescent above, brown below. Stems 3–8(20) mm tall, reddish when mature. Gemmae obovate, multicellular, stalked, reddish brown, constantly present on the stems among the upper leaves. Leaves distant, variously inrolled and curled, or imbricated, when dry, spreading to recurved when moist, mostly oblong or oblong-lanceolate, 1–1.5 mm long, the lower ones shorter, mostly rounded obtuse with a short point; margins revolute in the lower half or frequently plane throughout; costa green or yellowish, mostly excurrent to a very short mucro; upper cells quadrate, or a few shortly rectangular to 5- to 6-sided, 6–9 μ wide, thin walled, chlorophyllose, opaque, each bearing 2–6 small papillae; basal cells quadrate to oblong, becoming wider, 9–14 μ, chlorophyllose to clear,

151

smooth and frequently thicker walled. Seta red, variable in length; capsule erect, oblong to shortly cylindric, pale, thin walled; lid long rostrate, sometimes as long as the capsule; annulus lacking; peristome teeth deep red, closely twisted, often somewhat cancellate or trabeculate at the base and appendiculate above, fragile and soon disappearing from deoperculate capsules. Spores very small and smooth. (Description of the sporophyte taken from Steere in Grout's *Moss Flora of North America*.) Plate 19, figs. 1–7.

10.115   On dry or moist calcareous rocks and soil, usually in shady places.

10.116   Northern South America, Central America, the Antilles, Mexico, and the southeastern United States; New Jersey to Florida and west to Texas, Missouri, Arizona and Utah. Kane County.

10.117   This plant resembles a small form of *B. unguiculata* but is readily distinguished by the obovate reddish brown gemmae in the upper leaves (so abundant on some plants as to give a reddish color to the apices of the stems).

10.118   **2. Barbula eustegia** Card. & Thér. Plants small, in loose or dense yellowish green tufts or sods. Stems very short, 1–3, rarely 10, mm high. Leaves incurved and infolded, ± strongly twisted and contorted, brittle and easily broken when dry, spreading to recurved when moist, soft and tender, 0.7–1.5 mm long, oblong-ligulate to linear or sometimes linear-lanceolate, canaliculate, broadly obtuse to abruptly acute and often shortly recurved at the tip; margins finely crenulate, plane to slightly revolute; costa ending 3–10 cells below the apex, usually pale, papillose on the back; upper cells subquadrate to shortly oblong or irregular, chlorophyllose and rather obscure, moderately thick walled, each bearing 2–7 small but rather high C- or O-shaped papillae, 7–10 μ wide; basal cells gradually becoming longer and wider, oblong, smooth, and clear. Perichaetial leaves large and convolute-clasping, the inner ones ecostate and terminating in an abrupt apiculus, the outer leaves costate with less abruptly narrowed, but longer, upper portions. Seta yellowish, twisted to the left when dry, 7–20 mm long; capsule erect, ovate-oblong, urn 0.7–1.3 mm long, narrowed at the mouth, operculum long rostrate, nearly as long as the urn, smooth to minutely longitudinally ridged when dry; annulus of 2 rows of larger cells, revoluble; teeth often nearly as long as the urn, dark reddish, twisted in 2–3 turns, finely papillose. Spores smooth, 7–8 μ. Plate 20, figs. 1–9.

Plate 19.   1–7. Barbula cruegeri. 1. Habit sketches, X.4. 2. Habit sketches, moist and dry, X2. 3. Upper portion of stem dissected to show gemmae among upper leaves, X4. 4. Several gemmae. 5. Six leaves, X8. 6. Upper leaf cells, X120. 7. Basal cells, X120.

8–12. Barbula bescherellei. 8. Habit sketches, X.4. 9. Four stem leaves. 10. Two perichaetial leaves, X8. 11. Two leaf apices showing the vaguely excurrent costae. 12. Upper leaf cells and basal cells, X120.

13–19. Pottia arizonica var. **mucronulata.** 13. Habit sketches, X.4. 14. Habit sketches moist and dry, X2.8. 15. Four leaves, X8. 16. Upper leaf cells, X80. 17. Calyptra, X8. 18. Two dry capsules, X8. 19. Spores, X120.

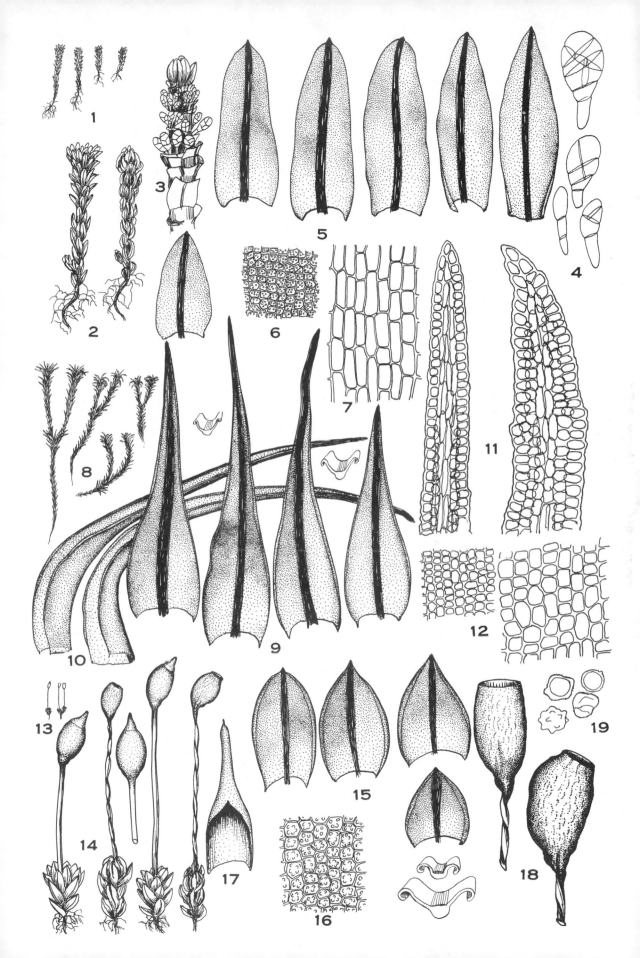

10.119 On damp or rather dry soil, mostly in shady woods in the mountains.

10.120 Western Canada, Washington, Montana, Idaho and Utah.

10.121 This, the smallest member of the genus in our range, resembles *B. convoluta*, which has not yet been collected in Utah, although I gathered some if it on Mink Creek, south of Pocatello, Idaho. The perichaetial leaves of *B. convoluta* are truncate to abruptly and bluntly acute, with the costa often excurrent as a mucro, while in our plants these leaves are acute to acuminate (the inner ones more or less apiculate and ecostate, the outer ones subulate and costate).

10.122 **3. Barbula unguiculata** Hedw. Plants medium sized, usually in short tufts or sods, about 0.5 cm high, but sometimes reaching as high as 2 cm, usually dark or dull green with a ± glaucous caste above, brown or dusky below. Leaves erect and appressed, ± contorted or spirally twisted when dry; erect-patent to spreading or somewhat squarrose-recurved when moist, oblong to ligulate, concave-canaliculate, often from a differentiated ovate base, 1.2–2.5 mm long, soft and tender when moist but brittle when dry, broad above, rapidly narrowed to a rounded-obtuse or bluntly acute apex, shortly mucronate to widely acute; margins revolute in the lower ½ or ⅔; costa usually green or yellowish brown, strongly papillose on the back, percurrent to shortly excurrent, terminating in larger, thick-walled, yellowish cells forming the mucro; upper cells quadrate to shortly oblong, 6–8(10) μ wide, thin to thick walled, densely papillose with small papillae, chlorophyllose and quite obscure; basal cells wider and longer, thin walled, smooth, and clear. Perichaetial leaves slightly longer and narrower from a ± dilated sheathing base, but not convolute. Seta erect and reddish, variable in length, 1.3–2.5 cm long; capsule erect, symmetric or slightly curved, oblong to rather long cylindric, the urn 1–2.5 mm long, smooth or minutely striate when dry; operculum tall conic-rostrate, straight or inclined, about half the length of the urn; annulus not differentiated; teeth dark reddish, spirally twisted in 2–3 turns. Spores yellowish brown, 8–10 μ, smooth, maturing in early spring. Plate 20, figs. 10–14.

10.123 On soil and rocks in both dry and moist situations, fields, lawns, gardens, roadsides and banks, in valleys and mountains, often on disturbed soil.

10.124 Europe. Common in the eastern states from Newfoundland to North Carolina, westward to Montana, Utah and New Mexico where it becomes rare.

Plate 20. 1–9. **Barbula eustegia.** 1. Habit sketches, X.4. 2. Same, X.8. 3. Stem leaves. 4. Perichaetial leaves, X8. 5. Two leaf apices, showing upper cells. 6. Basal leaf cells, X120. 7. Capsules, X8. 8. Portion of annulus, X80. 9. Antheridial cluster with perigonial leaves, X8.

10–14. **Barbula unguiculata.** 10. Habit sketches, X.4. 11. Same, X2. 12. Five stem leaves, X8. 13. Two leaf apices showing upper cells, X120. 14. Perichaetial leaves, X6.

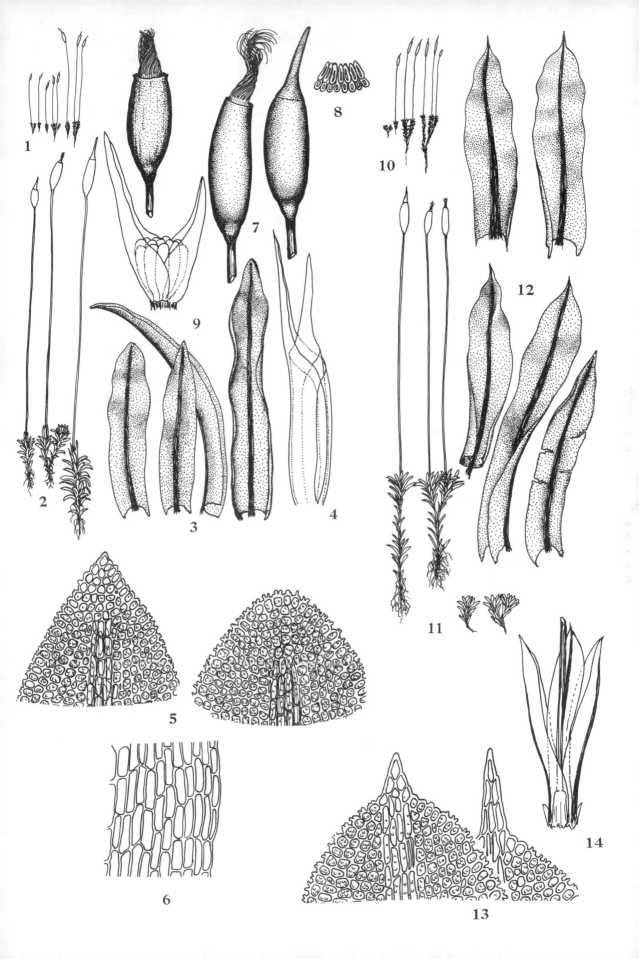

10.125   The outstanding features of this plant are the blunt, abruptly apiculate leaves, the tender texture with a tendency to break when dry, the obscure green color, often somewhat glaucous, and the finely crenulate margins. *Trichostomum cylindricum* has similar leaves, but they are usually larger and linear-lanceolate. Sterile plants are distinguished from *Desmatodon obtusifolius* by the distinctly excurrent costa.

10.126   **4. Barbula ehrenbergii** (Lor.) Fleisch. Plants in dense or loose tufts, dull green to yellowish green, often brownish and frequently encrusted with a calcareous deposit. Stems slender and often weak, 1.5–5 cm tall; central strand small, often lacking in young parts. Leaves rather distant, often appearing 3-ranked, ± erect with the upper part crisped or contorted when dry, erect-patent to squarrose-divergent or recurved when moist, ligulate to oblong-lanceolate, 1.5–3 mm long, broadest at the base, mostly widely tapering and rather suddenly narrowed to an obtuse or acute apex; margins plane or slightly recurved below on 1 or both sides; costa wide and stout, ending several cells below the leaf tip, ventral superficial cells oblong in surface view, in cross section showing a ventral stereid band 1–3 cells thick and medial guides; upper cells quadrate to shortly oblong or irregular, 10–12 μ wide, usually thick walled, smooth or with low rounded papillae, chlorophyllose in younger leaves but becoming clear with age; basal cells slightly wider, becoming elongate-oblong, pellucid. Sterile in our region. Plate 21, figs. 12–15.

10.127   On wet soil and rocks around springs and streams rich in calcium, often submerged and frequently encrusted with calcium carbonate.

10.128   Infrequent and of wide distribution. Europe and Asia. Missouri, Oklahoma, Texas, Utah, Mexico.

10.129   The flaccid texture of the stems and leaves is characteristic, as are the oblong-lanceolate leaves, broad above and suddenly acute to rounded-obtuse, the essentially plane margins, and the large pellucid leaf cells, smooth or with low rounded papillae. The ventral superficial cells of the costa are elongated, like those of *B. fallax*, and the younger, more evenly tapered leaves with predominantly acute apices, could easily pass for the latter if the innovations were not growing from older typical stems.

10.130   **5. Barbula fallax** Hedw. Plants forming dense cushions or wide sods of dull yellowish green or darker green, often tinged with red or brown above, brown to somewhat reddish brown below. Stems 1–3 cm high; central strand weak or indistinct. Leaves usually quite distant throughout, not forming a very dense comal cluster, erect to appressed and ± twisted when dry, patent to widely spreading or recurved when moist, lanceolate from an ovate base, 1.5–2.5 mm long, canaliculate and often recurved backward, gradually tapered upward to a slender acute or bluntly acute apex, the base often plicate on each side; margins revolute or recurved in the lower ½ or ⅔, plane above; costa broad and stout, gradually narrowed upward, disappearing in the apex or ending a few cells below the tip; the ventral cells of the costa elongated in the

156

upper half of the leaf; upper cells variable in size and shape, isodiametric to shortly oblong, quadrate, rounded or irregular, usually thick walled, 7–11(16) μ wide, smooth to densely papillose, the papillae usually low and rounded, 3–8 per cell; basal cells often scarcely differentiated and chlorophyllose to the base but usually slightly larger and longer, mostly shortly rectangular, but with many quadrate ones, the latter toward the margins, clear, smooth and fairly thick walled. Seta red, 1–1.5 cm long; capsule elongate-ovoid to shortly cylindric, erect and symmetric or near-ly so, urn 1–2 mm long; operculum narrowly rostrate, often nearly as long as the urn; peristome teeth dark, clear red, twisted in 2–3 turns before dehiscence of capsule, arising from a narrow basal membrane, usually becoming untwisted after the operculum falls, sometimes ir-regularly spreading to nearly erect. Spores smooth, 10–14 μ, yellowish green to yellowish; maturing in late autumn to early spring. Plate 21, figs. 1–5.

10.131   On damp or wet soil, on banks, rocks, around springs and brooks, often in open places.

10.132   Common and widely spread in the eastern states, Nova Scotia to Vir-ginia, westward to Minnesota and Iowa, further west becoming infre-quent or rare, Montana, Idaho and Utah.

10.133   The plants vary with the habitat, the leaves ranging from broadly ovate-lanceolate, the whole range often appearing in the same tuft. Some plants are firm, the cells regular in shape; others are flaccid, the cells rather lax and tending to be irregular, often widely variable in size and ranging upward to 17 μ wide. The folds on either side of the costa at the base are supposed to be a good diagnostic feature, but in our western forms they appear only in a few leaves. In some specimens the margins of the leaves are plane throughout with a few markedly revolute margins—the contrast even on the same stems is often remark-able. Firm plants usually have well-developed papillae on the leaf cells, but in most pale or lax forms the papillae are low and rounded, diffi-cult to demonstrate, or virtually lacking in some leaves. The strongest feature is the elongated ventral costal cells as observed in surface view. This distinguishes the plant from *B. vinealis,* which has ventral costal cells similar to the cells of the lamina. Species of *Didymodon* (such as *D. trifarius* and *D. tophaceus*) in the sterile state may be difficult to distinguish from the present species. They have elongated ventral costal cells and otherwise resemble *B. fallax. Barbula ehrenbergii* is similar to the present species, differing in that the leaves are wider in the upper part and oblong-lanceolate, with margins more constantly plane and cells larger and more pellucid.

10.134   **6. Barbula acuta** (Brid.) Brid. Plants medium sized, usually in dense tufts or sods, dark green to olivaceous, often strongly tinged with red or brown above, brown to reddish below. Stems slender, less than 1 cm tall or sometimes reaching 3 cm; central strand present, often indistinct. Leaves moderately dense, erect to closely appressed, little or not at all contorted when dry, stiffly spreading, often $\pm$ squarrose or even re-

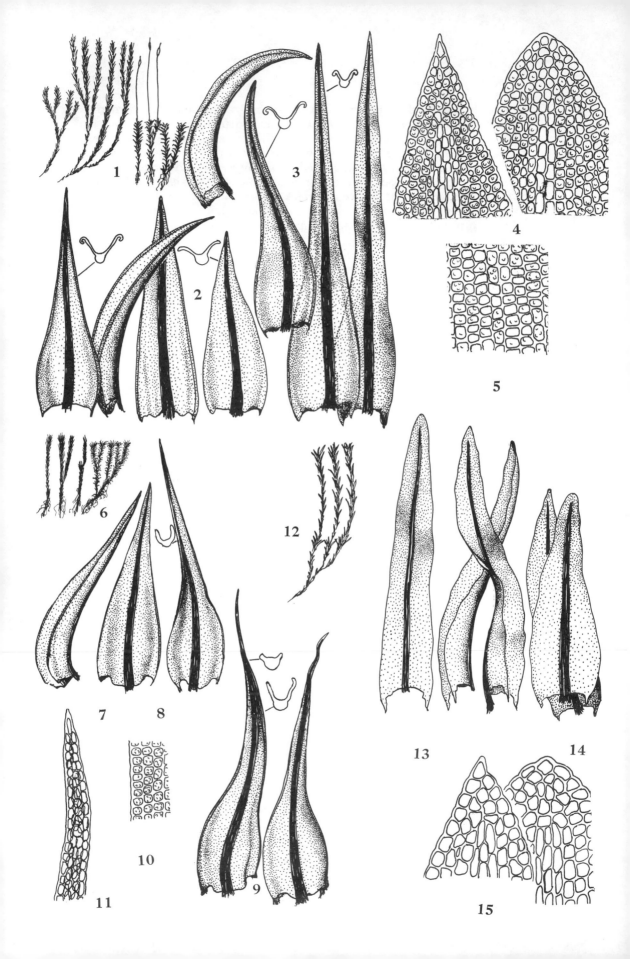

curved when moist, brittle, the apices often broken off, 1–2 mm long, keeled-canaliculate, ovate-lanceolate to lanceolate or subulate from an ovate base, the lower ones notably smaller with the stout costa ending in the apex or percurrent, the upper ones larger, ± abruptly narrowed from the broad base, the costa disappearing in the slender apex to long excurrent, usually dark green and often irregularly flexuous; margins revolute in the lower midportion, forming a border 1 cell wide along the upper part of the costa; upper cells 7–10 μ wide, quadrate to short-ly rectangular, often rounded and irregular, usually clear, moderately thick walled, smooth or with low, rounded papillae; basal cells slightly wider and more regularly quadrate to shortly oblong, some of them transversely elongated, in some leaves quadrate to the base, clear and smooth. Seta 5–12 mm long, reddish; capsule mostly shortly ovoid-elliptic to oblong-cylindric, the urn 1–1.5 mm long; lid narrowly conic, about half the length of the urn; peristome teeth rather short for the genus, twisted in about 1 turn (often nearly erect in old deoperculate capsules), arising from a very narrow basal membrane. Spores 8–10 μ, smooth, usually maturing in winter or early spring. Plate 21, figs. 6–11.

10.135 On dry or damp soil, in crevices or under overhanging rocks, usually in the presence of calcium salts.

10.136 Europe. Widely scattered in the western states but rather rare. British Columbia to southern California, eastward to Montana to New Mexico. San Juan County.

10.137 Much like *Barbula vinealis* in general appearance and also in the form of the lower leaves, but the upper leaves have the costa filling the subulate apex and are thus excurrent. The cells are chlorophyllose, variably thick walled in the apex and apparently merging with similar cells of the costa. The excurrent part is usually green, straight or irregularly flexuous, often with a single row of cells of the lamina forming a wing-like flange extending upward, essentially entire but more or less irregularly crenulate. The shorter peristome teeth are distinctive (although the plants rarely fruit). The sandstones of southeastern Utah bear considerable calcium carbonate which favors this moss.

10.138 **7. Barbula bescherellei** Sauerb. in Jaeg. Plants ± densely tufted, usually reddish brown to olivaceous, but sometimes dark green above, brown to reddish below. Stems rather rigid, mostly 0.5–2 cm tall (reaching 4 cm elsewhere); central strand indistinct. Leaves rather dense, erect and loosely appressed, little or not at all crisped when dry, stiffly erect-patent

---

Plate 21. 1–5. Barbula fallax. 1. Habit sketches, X.4. 2. Five leaves of short-leaved form. 3. Three leaves of long-leaved form, X8. 4. Two leaf apices showing upper cells. 5. Basal leaf cells, X120.

6–11. Barbula acuta. 6. Habit sketches, X.4. 7–8. Lower stem leaves. 9. Two upper leaves, X8. 10. Upper leaf cells. 11. Tip of the excurrent costa, X120.

12–15. Barbula ehrenbergii. 12. Habit sketch X.4. 13. Three leaves of long-leaved form. 14. Two leaves of short-leaved form, X8. 15. Two leaf apices showing upper cells, X120.

to ± squarrose-spreading when moist, 1–2.3 mm long, the comal ones reaching 2.4–3 mm, ovate-lanceolate to ovate-subulate, the apex narrowly acute; costa strong and long-excurrent in some of the comal leaves, strongly percurrent in most other leaves, often colored like the lamina; margins revolute nearly or quite to the apex in most leaves, often forming a narrow border along the gradually excurrent costa; upper cells mostly 7–10 ± wide, quadrate to rounded or shortly rectangular, often irregular, nearly smooth to low rounded papillose, fairly thick walled, usually clear; basal cells only slightly wider, quadrate to shortly rectangular or some of them transversely elongated, smooth, ± chlorophyllose to the base. Seta red, 1–2 cm long; capsule dark red, long and cylindrical, gradually narrowed toward the mouth; lid long rostrate, reaching half the length of the urn; peristome long and twisted in about 2 turns, the short basal membrane inserted below the mouth. (Sporophyte description from Steere in Grout's *Moss Flora of North America*.) Plate 19, figs. 8–12.

10.139 On dry or damp soil, open slopes or at bases of rocks.

10.140 Abundant on sandy soil in Glen Canyon of the Colorado River and adjacent regions; Arizona and Mexico.

10.141 This moss is abundant in the canyons and tributaries of the Colorado River on dry sandy soil where it assumes a reddish brown to greenish red color. At the bases of shaded rocks it may be dark green. All the material observed was sterile. The plant resembles *B. acuta* and *B. vinealis* in habit and appearance. In the sterile state it is difficult to distinguish from *B. acuta*, but *B. acuta* has leaves with the margins revolute to widely recurved only in the lower half or less, while in the *B. bescherellei* most of the leaf margins are revolute nearly to the apex. The degree to which the costa is excurrent in the upper leaves is about the same in both plants. *Barbula bescherellei* has a longer and more cylindric capsule than *B. acuta*. *Barbula vinealis* is abundant in the same region and varies widely in shape of leaves, but it has the costa ending below the apex of the leaf.

10.142 **8. Barbula vinealis** Brid. Plants loosely to densely tufted, often scattered, growing in water, damp places, or on dry desert hillsides, dark green to olivaceous or brownish, often tinged with red. Stems very short to elongated, up to 3 cm tall; central strand present but indistinct. Leaves distant to crowded, incurved-imbricated to contorted when dry, erect-patent to widely recurved when moist, broadly to narrowly ovate-lanceolate, often with a differentiated ovate base, sometimes short and oblong-ovate, 0.7–2 mm long, acute, often bluntly so; margins usually revolute ⅔–¾ the length of the blade, sometimes plane on 1 or both sides; costa disappearing below the apex, ventral superficial cells short and similar to the cells of the lamina; upper cells quadrate to rounded or irregular, 7–10 μ wide, often thick walled and chlorophyllose, rather opaque to quite clear, typically densely papillose but variable, sometimes nearly smooth; basal cells quadrate to shortly oblong, sometimes a few cells longer, only slightly wider than the upper cells, usually clear and smooth. Seta reddish, 1–1.8 cm long; capsules oblong to short-ly cylindric, the urn 1–1.7 mm long, dark reddish and smooth when dry; lid slenderly rostrate, about half the length of the urn; peristome teeth somewhat short for the genus, frosty reddish, becoming paler with age, twisted in 1 or nearly 2 turns at dehiscence, often becoming nearly straight in deoperculate capsules, fragile. Spores yellowish brown, 8–10 μ, smooth, maturing in early spring or summer.

10.143   On damp or dry soil and rocks, sometimes in water, usually in regions of limestone or calcareous sandstone.

10.144   Central America, Eurasia and North Africa. Widely distributed in the western states, Alaska to Mexico, eastward to Montana, Colorado, and New Mexico.

10.145   This moss is extremely variable. The description has been broadened somewhat, and even so one must be liberal in its interpretation. The basic features are the habit of growth, ovate-lanceolate leaves with nar-rowly acute or bluntly acute apices, the margins usually revolute for ⅔ or more the length of the blade, the short basal cells scarcely different from the upper ones but more regularly quadrate to shortly oblong, the variable papillae and the upper ventral costal cells more or less quadrate and similar to those of the adjacent lamina.

10.146   In desert regions the plant commonly grows in crevices and on dry ledges of sandstone rocks, under overhanging rocks where rain water drips and in similar places. Here the stems may be very short and the sods dense or spread open by the infiltration of windblown sand, often strongly tinged with red or brown, the leaves rather short and strongly imbricated when dry, the tips incurved, often in a spiral. Some forms have unusually short leaves less than 1 mm long, broadly ovate-lanceolate, the apices acute to exceedingly blunt, the leaf cells thick walled and practically smooth. In the same habitats, especially in dry sandstone areas of southeastern Utah, *B. acuta* is frequently found. It resembles the present species but differs mainly in the very long excurrent costa of the upper leaves. At the other extreme, *B. cylindrica* resembles larger forms of the present plant, the two somewhat intergrading. The latter plant has much longer and narrower leaves, more strongly crisped when dry, the margins revolute only in the lower half or third.

10.147   9. **Barbula cylindrica** (Tayl.) Schimp. in Boul. Plants densely tufted or scattered among other mosses, dark green and usually tinged with red or brown above, brownish to reddish below, soft. Stems 1–6 cm tall; central strand usually present but often weak or lacking. Leaves small and distant below, becoming larger and forming a dense comal tuft above, incurved and contorted when dry, spreading to recurved when moist, narrowly to rather broadly lanceolate from an ovate or oblong base, tapering to a slenderly acute or subacute apex, ± flexu-ous, concave-canaliculate to keeled, 2–5 mm long; margins recurved to closely revolute in the lower half; costa ending in the apex, ventral superficial cells similar to those of the adjacent lamina, in section showing a row of subventral guides and a strong dorsal stereid band with a single row of ventral cells or with a weak ventral stereid band of 1–4 cells; upper cells mostly quadrate to irregular (some transversely elongated), 6–10 μ, rather thick walled, usually densely papillose, but sometimes with low weak papillae, or occasionally with large warty papillae; basal cells little different from the upper ones, slightly wider, quadrate to shortly oblong, the extreme basal ones usually chlorophyllose and smooth, but sometimes becoming clear and reddish. Seta erect, 1.5–3 mm long, $\pm$ flexuous, reddish brown at maturity; capsule oblong-cylindric, 1.5–2.4 mm long, the lid slenderly rostrate, about half the length of the urn; peristome teeth twisted in 1–3 turns, very long and slender, dusty reddish or apricot color, becoming paler with age. Spores 8–10 μ, smooth, maturing in May.

10.148   On dry or damp soil and rocks, occasionally in wet places, usually in shade.

10.149   Europe. Pacific Coast region from Alaska to Mexico, eastward to Montana, Idaho, and Utah.

10.150   Fairly common locally but rarely fruiting. I have only one well-fruited specimen. The moss, is distinguished from *B. vinealis* by the larger size, the larger leaves (2.5–5 mm long), usually more strongly recurved from the stem, and the margin plane in the upper ½ or ⅔ and the upper part more or less flexuous.

10.151   Some forms of *Trichostomum tenuirostre* resemble the present plant but have more brittle leaves which are irregularly notched on the margins and have elongate-oblong basal cells occupying the entire leaf base and oblong ventral cells covering the costa. Also the leaf margins are not recurved in *T. tenuirostre*.

11. PHASCUM L. ex Hedw.

10.152   Plants small, in tufts or cushions, often gregarious. Stems short, 1–10 mm high, simple or sparingly branched; central strand lacking; rhizoids few to moderately dense, reddish, smooth, often bearing large multicellular gemmae. Leaves ovate to oblong-lanceolate, acute or acuminate; margins entire or nearly so, mostly revolute in the middle part; costa slender to moderately stout, excurrent to a sharp mucro or long, smooth hairlike awn, in cross section showing 1 row of large, thin-walled ventral cells, a single row of guides, a rather strong dorsal stereid band and dorsal superficial cells with rather large lumina; upper cells quadrate,

---

Plate 22.   1–4. **Phascum cuspidatum.** 1. Habit sketches, X.4. 2. Five plants showing variations in position and stance of sporophyte, X3.2. 3. Two leaves, X8. 4. Cross sections of costa, X120.

5–7. Var. **henrici.** 5. Habit sketch, X3.2. 6. Two leaves, X8. 7. Cross sections of costa, X120.

8–13. Var. **schreberianum.** 8. Habit, X3.2. 9. Two leaves, X8. 10. Cross section of costa, X120. 11. Apical cells. 12. Medial cells, X100. 13. Five capsules, X8.

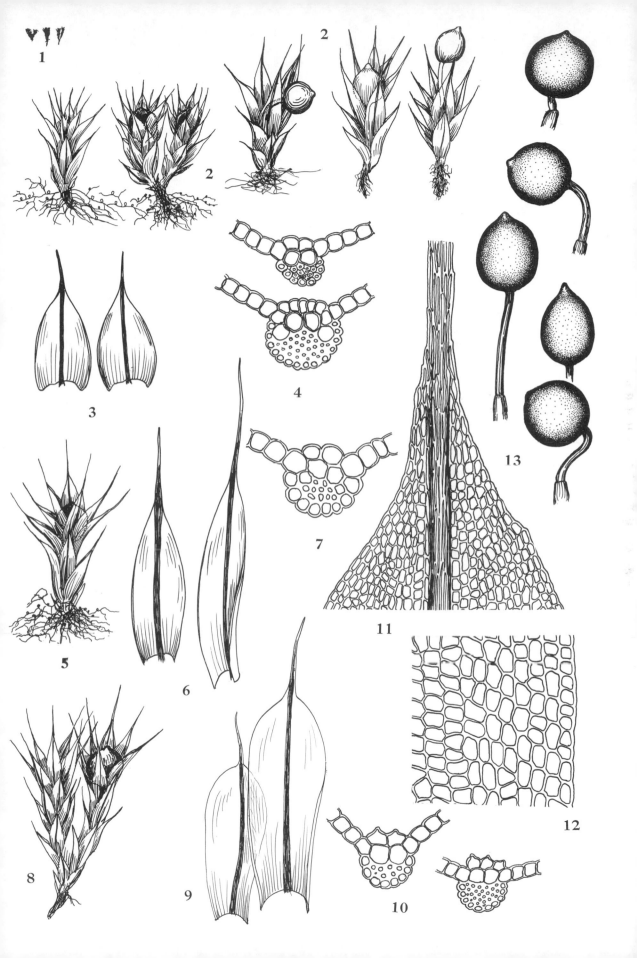

oblong, or hexagonal, thin walled, mostly convex, ± papillose but sometimes smooth; basal cells larger, rectangular, hyaline and mostly smooth. Paroicous or synoicous. Seta short, straight or curved; capsules without a lid, immersed to slightly emergent, sometimes protruding laterally from between the perichaetial leaves, subglobose to elliptic-ovoid, bluntly apiculate, dehiscent by irregular splitting or decay of the capsule wall. Spores rather large. Calyptra cucullate, sometimes becoming mitrate.

10.153 The name *phascon* was first used by Theophrastus for the lichen *Usnea barbata* but seems to have been a term applied to various cryptogams.

10.154 **Phascum cuspidatum** Hedw. var. **cuspidatum.** Plants in dense tufts or cushions of a characteristic yellowish green color when dry. Stems 1–2 mm high. Upper leaves closely imbricated, infolded or ± twisted when dry, patent when moist, ovate to oblong-lanceolate, acuminate, concave, 1–2 mm long; costa rather slender, excurrent to a short or rather long, yellowish, smooth mucro; upper cells usually clear, 15–25 μ wide, and up to 38 μ long, papillose on both sides above or on the dorsal side only with 2–several simple, C- or O-shaped papillae per cell; basal cells wider and larger. Paroicous or autoicous. Seta ranging from about ¼ to twice the length of the capsule, straight or curved; capsule subglobose to ovoid, bluntly pointed at the apex, 0.8–1.2 mm long, immersed to emergent, sometimes protruding laterally from between the perichaetial leaves. Spores 24–35 μ, globose. Plate 22, figs. 1–4.

10.155 On dry soil, often among grasses or shrubs or in open places. Rare in our region and mostly represented by the varieties described below.

10.156 Davis, Salt Lake, Sevier and Millard counties.

10.157 Var. **henrici** (Ren. & Card.) Wijk & Marg. Leaves longer, oblong-lanceolate, 1.5–2.2 mm long with long, yellowish piliferous points, often as long as the blade. Plate 22, figs. 5–7.

10.158 Washington County: Pine Valley Mountains, Santa Clara Creek Canyon, 7,000 ft.

10.159 Var. **schreberianum** (Dicks.) Brid. Much like var. *henrici* but having elongated stems with lower leaves smaller and distantly disposed, upper cells smooth or less commonly with each cell bearing a single large low papilla, this condition appearing more commonly on the ventral cells of the costa. Seta shorter than the capsule, straight or commonly slightly curved. Known in America only from Utah. Plate 22, figs. 8–13.

10.160 Cache and Salt Lake counties.

10.161 The species and its varieties occur in the same sort of habitats and commonly grow together, the latter variety being the most common. The spores mature in early spring from February to May. In our region the plants occur commonly along the bases of the higher mountains and foothills at elevations between 4,400 and 5,600 ft., usually on rich loamy soil among grasses and sagebrush or in open places between clumps of scrub oak.

12. POTTIA (Reichenb.) Ehrh. ex Fuernr.

10.162 Plants small to medium sized, loosely to densely tufted, mostly growing on soil and in crevices of rocks. Stems simple or branched, mostly short, with or without a central strand; rhizoids relatively few to moderate at the base. Leaves spreading, erect or closely imbricated, the plants sometimes bulbiform, the upper and comal ones often much larger than the lower stem leaves, broadly ovate, ligulate, spatulate or lanceolate, obtuse, acute or acuminate, concave and keeled; margins plane or revolute, entire to serrulate; costa subpercurrent to long excurrent, in cross section showing 1–2 rows of ventral guides, these often convex, a small dorsal stereid band and rather large dorsal superficial cells; upper cells quadrate to hexagonal, often becoming rhomboidal, smooth or papillose, thin walled but often becoming thick walled with age; upper marginal cells sometimes differentiated and forming a border; basal cells larger and longer, thin walled, smooth and hyaline. Multicellular globular or ovoid gemmae occasional in some species. Paroicous, synoicous or autoicous. Seta mostly long, erect, straight or flexuous, twisted when dry; capsules obovate, ovate to cylindric, erect, symmetric to slightly curved, base rounded or with a differentiated neck with superficial stomata; mouth narrow to wide; peristome lacking or when present, the teeth ranging from short stubs to linear-lanceolate, entire, 2-cleft or irregular, finely papillose; annulus present or lacking, persistent or deciduous; operculum mostly deciduous, persistent in a few species and free or attached to the columella, convex to conic with a short to long beak, ± inclined. Spores mostly large, usually dark reddish brown, papillose or tuberculate. Calyptra cucullate, smooth to rough.

10.163 Named in honor of John F. Pott, an English botanist.

10.164 1. Plants bulbiform; leaves hyaline at the tips and with long hyaline hair points; capsules with a peristome; lid free, not attached to the columella .... 4. *P. latifolia* 10.177

10.165 1. Plants not bulbiform; leaves not hyaline at the apex; peristome lacking

    2. Plants small; lid free; some of the spores coarsely tuberculate or irregularly wrinkled, all of them finely papillose .... 3. *P. arizonica* 10.174

    2. Plants medium sized; lid persistent on the columella; none of the spores tuberculate or wrinkled

        3. Leaves mostly densely chlorophyllose; upper cells papillose; margins bordered with smooth, yellowish, slightly elongated, thick-walled cells; costa subpercurrent to shortly excurrent .... 1. *P. heimii* 10.166

        3. Leaves sparingly chlorophyllose; upper cells smooth; margins

without a distinct border; costa excurrent to a stout mucro or hair point .... 2. *P. nevadensis* 10.170

10.166 **1. Pottia heimii** (Hedw.) Hamp. Plants small, in dense tufts or expanded turflike mats, green to yellowish green above, yellowish to reddish brown below. Stems 4–10 mm high, up to 0.6 mm in diameter, in cross section showing a central strand of small cells, the cortical cells large, thin walled, and angular, 1–2 rows of outermost cells smaller and slightly thicker walled, usually darker in color. Leaves ± infolded or incurved, and sometimes twisted when dry, spreading to erect and imbricated when moist, shortly ovate to longly lanceolate, the upper ones largest, 2–3.5 mm long, abruptly acute to gradually long-acuminate, concave, straight or sometimes recurved with the base subclasping; margins plane, some leaves slightly to coarsely serrate at the apex, others entire throughout; costa subpercurrent to shortly excurrent; upper cells 10–20 μ wide, moderately thick walled, smooth to densely papillose with numerous C-shaped papillae, hence clear to opaque, usually bordered by 2–5 rows of slightly more elongated, smoother, thicker-walled, yellowish to reddish cells, forming a border; basal cells becoming larger, oblong, thin walled, hyaline and smooth, often lax, bordered by several rows of narrow thick-walled reddish cells. Polygamous, mostly autoicous or dioicous. Seta 4–18 mm long, yellowish to brown, twisted to the left when dry; capsule ovate-elliptic to cylindrical, 1–3 mm long without lid, yellowish when young, becoming reddish brown, neck short, smooth to finely longitudinally wrinkled when dry; peristome lacking; lid attached to the columella and persistent, convex to conic, long beaked, straight or bent; annulus of 1–2 rows of small, rounded, exceedingly thick-walled cells, persistent on margins of mouth or lid. Spores ovoid to subreniform, yellowish brown to reddish brown, rather coarsely papillose, 20–40 μ in longest diameter, maturing in late spring or early summer. Plate 23, figs. 1–7.

10.167 On damp or wet soil and rocks, mainly in limestone regions but frequently in regions of sandstone and igneous rocks. Abundant locally, usually at elevations from 4,000 to 8,500 ft.

10.168 Across Canada: British Columbia, Alberta, Saskatchewan, Manitoba, Quebec, New Brunswick. From Washington through Idaho, Montana, Wyoming, Alaska, California, Nevada, Utah, and New Mexico.

10.169 Numerous varieties of this species have been proposed, based mainly on differences in the size and shape of leaves, papillae on leaf cells, and dimensions of capsules. However, there are no clear-cut limits to any of these features, and they intergrade in different combinations. The

---

Plate 23. **1–7. Pottia heimii.** 1. Habit sketch, X.4. 2. Five leaves, X8. 3. Leaf apex. 4. Medial leaf cells, X120. 5. Dissection of fertile stem tip showing position of antheridia and archegonia, X4. 6–7. Capsules, X8.

8–12. Pottia nevadensis. 8. Habit, X.4. 9. Five leaves, X8. 10. Leaf apex, X120. 11–12. Capsules, X8.

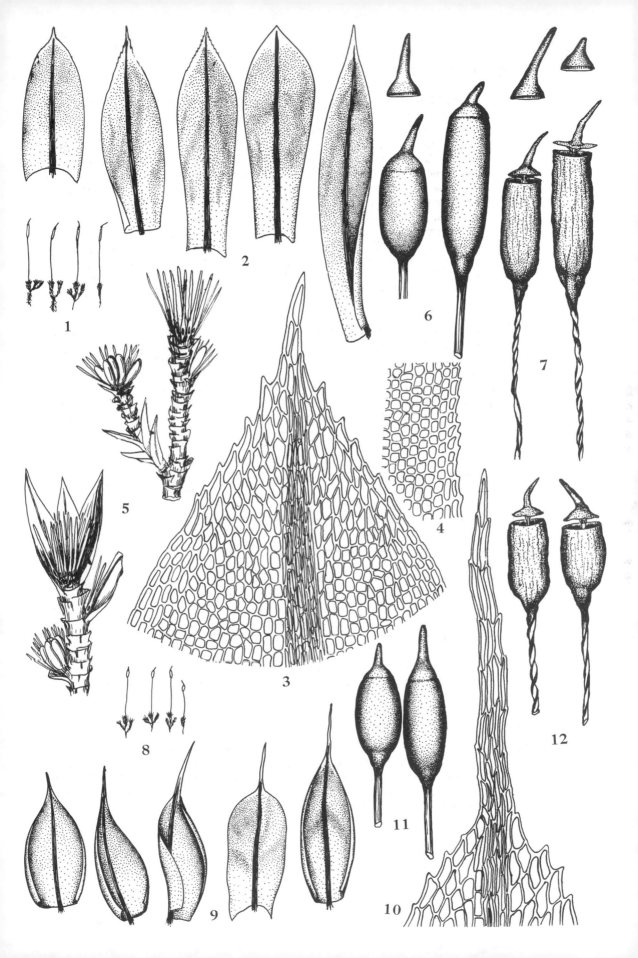

disposition of sex organs varies even in the same tuft. The usual condition is autoicous, the antheridia being borne at the apex of a small basal branch, while the archegonia are apical on the main stem. The paroicous condition is also frequent, the antheridia forming a small, axillary cluster below the perichaetial leaves. The following less frequent dispositions of the sex organs were observed: a single axillary archegonium on a small male branch; a cluster of archegonia with 1–2 antheridia (synoicous); solitary antheridia in the axils of the upper leaves of the main stem with few or no paraphyses; small male buds in the axils of upper leaves of main stems, and axillary paraphyses without sex organs. The small male branches often disarticulate from the main stem easily, the bases having an abscission zone of large thin-walled inflated cells. Occasionally one encounters plants with unusually short setae, only about 4 mm long, and others with unusually long setae, as much as 2 cm long.

10.170 **2. Pottia nevadensis** Card. & Thér. Plants small, loosely to densely tufted, often forming sods. Stems 1–3 mm high, in section showing a central strand, large, thin-walled cortical cells becoming smaller outwardly, the epidermal layer of smaller cells, only slightly thicker walled and brownish. Occasionally globose to ovoid, multicellular, reddish brown, gemmae form on the lower portion of the stems or rhizoids close to the stem. Leaves infolded and often twisted when dry, imbricated when moist, the upper ones large and forming a cluster, the lower smaller, broadly ovate to obovate, concave, 2–2.5 mm long, the hair point excluded; apex blunt, acute or briefly acuminate, margins entire throughout or some leaves with a few coarse teeth at the apex, plane to incurved; costa usually yellowish brown, mostly excurrent to a smooth mucro or a hair point, in some leaves subpercurrent; upper cells thin walled, 10–17 μ wide, sparingly chlorophyllose, smooth or lightly papillose, papillae, if present, few, low, rounded; upper marginal cells mostly diagonally rhombic, somewhat thicker walled but not forming a distinct border; basal cells larger, wider and hyaline with a border of smaller narrower cells. Autoicous. Seta 5–10 mm long, yellowish to reddish brown; capsule ovoid-elliptic to shortly ovate-cylindric, 1–2 mm long, not including the lid, becoming rather dark reddish brown; neck distinct, short, with several stomata; peristome lacking; lid attached to the columella and long-persistent, convex to conic, tapering to a rather thick inclined beak about 1 mm long; annulus of 1–2 rows of very thick-walled, rounded, yellowish cells, usually persisting on the margins of the mouth and base of lids. Spores ovoid to subreniform, finely papillose, 18–30 μ in longest diameter. Calyptra smooth. Plate 23, figs. 8–12.

10.171 On damp or wet soil, sometimes where it dries out in summer.

10.172 A rather rare moss known only from Nevada, Utah, northern Arizona, British Columbia and either Saskatchewan or Alberta. Salt Lake County: shore of Great Salt Lake, north of Saltair, 4,240 ft. Box Elder County: below Pilot Peak near Nevada state line, ca. 20 mi. north of Wendover, 4,400 ft. Arizona. Mohave County: Pipe Spring, ca. 4,700 ft.

10.173   Distinct from *P. heimii* in the shorter smooth leaves with a stout mucro or hair point and the consistently shorter capsules.

10.174   **3. Pottia arizonica** Wareh. in Grout. var. **arizonica.** Plants small, loosely caespitose or scattered. Stems 1–3 mm tall; central strand present. Leaves loosely imbricated and incurved when dry, ± spreading when moist, ovate to oblong-ovate, concave, the margins widely revolute well toward the apex, the upper ones 1–1.3 mm long, acute to short-acuminate, the lower ones shorter; the costa percurrent to long excurrent as a hair point; upper cells 7–13 μ wide, thin to thick walled, ± chlorophyllose, with 3–6 C- or O-shaped papillae per cell; basal cells larger, thin walled, less papillose or smooth, oblong, the marginal ones shorter. Autoicous, paroicous or partly synoicous. Sporophytes single or in pairs. Seta 3–5 mm long, yellowish to reddish brown; capsule golden brown, ovate to elliptical, slightly asymmetric, the mouth often slightly oblique; neck short, slightly contracted below the mouth and minutely to moderately shrunken when dry; exothecial cells mostly rectangular, some tending to be 6-sided, rather thin walled, 2–4 rows below the mouth quadrate to transversely elongated, smaller and thicker walled; stomata in the neck, large and numerous; lid conic, straight or slightly inclined; annulus not differentiated; peristome of 16 irregular, ± truncated teeth arising from a low basal membrane, yellowish brown and densely papillose. Spores 18–25 μ, some of them coarsely tuberculate or irregularly wrinkled, smooth to finely papillose. Calyptra papillose at the tip. Represented in Utah by the following variety.

10.175   3a. Var. **mucronulata** Wareh. Costa percurrent or at most excurrent to a short mucro, not a hair; peristome lacking but sometimes a low basal membrane is present. Plate 16, figs. 11–16 and plate 19, figs. 13–19.

10.176   On dry sandy soil, southern California, Arizona, and southern Utah. San Juan County: Colorado River at mouth of Lake Canyon, 3,360 ft.; Colorado River at mouth of Aztec Canyon, 3,340 ft.

10.177   **4. Pottia latifolia** (Schwaegr.) C. Muell. var. **latifolia.** Plants small, often bulbiform, in loose clusters or sometimes closely disposed, pale green to silvery. Stems 1–2 mm long; central strand present. Upper leaves are the largest, and usually imbricate both dry and moist, often forming little bulblike buds, broadly ovate to obovate, the base usually narrowed and somewhat sheathing, apex broadly obtuse-rounded to apiculate, 1–2 mm long, the lower leaves shorter, often broader than long; margins plane or sometimes narrowly recurved, entire throughout or serrulate at the apex; costa yellowish, thin and weak, ending below the apex, in cross section showing 2 large thin-walled ventral cells and a small dorsal stereid band; upper cells 9–15 μ wide, walls variable, thin to thick, smooth, sparsely chlorophyllose, often hyaline, at the apex walls of the ventral side of the lamina thin and mammillose-bulging, those on the dorsal side thick, sometimes becoming very thick, plane and yellowish; apical cells hyaline and very thick walled; basal cells usually abruptly oblong, larger and broader, 12–30 μ wide, thin walled,

169

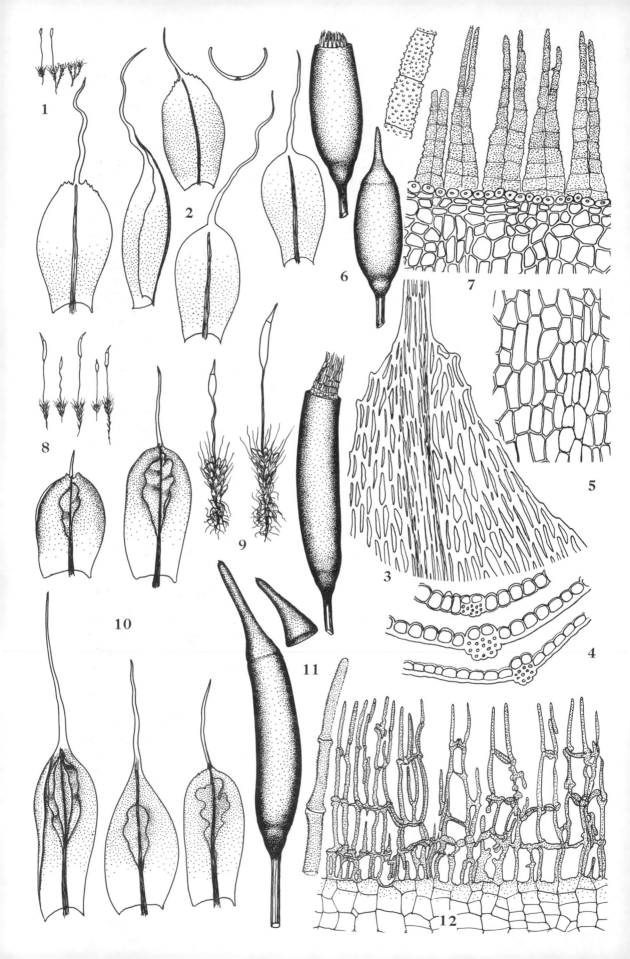

hyaline or sparsely chlorophyllose. Autoicous. Seta erect, yellowish to reddish brown, 4–10 mm long; capsules ovoid to elongate-elliptic, narrowed at the mouth, 1–1.8 mm long (the lid excluded); neck short, with stomata; exothecial cells irregularly oblong, thick walled; annulus of 1–3 rows of very thick-walled, paler yellowish cells; lid convex with a short or rather long, thick beak, inclined or bent; peristome of 16 slender teeth, cleft above and ± perforated below, sometimes short, reddish brown and rather coarsely papillose, arising from a narrow basal membrane concealed below the margin of the mouth. Spores globose to subreniform, coarsely papillose, 33–48 μ, maturing in spring. Represented in Utah by the following variety.

10.178   4a. Var. **pilifera** (Brid.) C. Muell. Costa excurrent to a long hyaline hair point, 1–1.5 mm long, often exceeding the length of the blade; some leaves ± acute, or slightly acuminate, somewhat tapering to the base of the hair point; apical cells often exceedingly thick walled, the lumina rhomboidal to linear, cells of the upper 1/5–2/3 hyaline, the lower ones often weakly chlorophyllose. Plate 24, figs. 1–7.

10.179   Alaska and Canadian Rocky Mountains. Summit County: Henry's Fork, Uinta Mountains, 9,200 ft.

10.180   A rare plant. The species and variety may occur mixed together in the same sod or they may be entirely separate. Some leaves of the variety may lack the hair points. In Lesquereux and James, *Manual of North American Mosses,* either the species or variety is credited to the Uinta Mountains (neither specifically designated).

13. PTERYGONEURUM Jur.

10.181   Plants small in dense convex tufts or expanded sods, usually grayish green and hoary. Stems erect, short, simple or branched; central strand lacking, in cross section the outer 2 rows of cortical cells slightly smaller and usually reddish brown, but the walls not thickened; rhizoids confined to the base. Leaves ovate, obovate or spatulate, erect or imbricated when dry, patent when moist, strongly concave, obtuse, acute or sometimes acuminate, terminating in a short to very long hyaline smooth hair point often much longer than the leaf blade; margins plane or somewhat revolute, entire throughout or more often toothed or even lobed at the apex; costa broad and strong, widest in the upper part of the leaf and bearing 2–4(6) chlorophyllose lamellae on the ventral surface, these highest toward the apex and tapering toward the base of the leaf; margins entire or toothed, the surfaces often bearing chlorophyllose filaments which may form a dense green granular mass, cells

---

Plate 24. 1–7. Pottia latifolia var. pilifera. 1. Habit sketches, X.4. 2. Five typical leaves, X8. 3. Areolation of the leaf apex, X60. 4. Cross sections of lamina and costa at three levels of the leaf, X60. 5. Medial leaf cells, X120. 6. Two capsules, X8. 7. Portion of the peristome, X60, with detail, X200.

8–12. Pterygoneurum lamellatum. 8. Habit sketches, X.4. 9. Same, X1.2. 10. Five typical leaves. 11. Two capsules, X8. 13. Portion of the delicate peristome, X240.

of the lamellae and filaments mostly swollen and papillose; upper cells quadrate to shortly oblong or transversely elongated, often irregular and becoming rounded to rhomboidal at the apex, thin to fairly thick walled, smooth or papillose on the dorsal surface, walls of the dorsal surface usually thicker than those of the ventral surface; basal cells larger and broader, quadrate to oblong, thin walled, and hyaline. Autoicous or paroicous. Seta very short to moderately long, the capsules erect, immersed to well exserted, subglobose to cylindric; exothecial cells rather large, irregularly rectangular; neck with superficial stomata; peristome lacking or very fragile; annulus lacking; operculum convex with a short or long beak, straight or bent. Spores globose, smooth to coarsely papillose. Calyptra cucullate or mitrate, smooth. Small branches of the current season's growth are frequently deciduous and they separate from the main stem by developing large, more or less inflated and colored basal cells at the point of junction, which serve as abscission devices and readily form rhizoids. The capsules mature in early spring. Fertilization commonly occurs in the fall, and young green capsules may appear as early as October.

10.182   The name from the Greek means winged nerve.

10.183   1. Capsules immersed to emergent calyptra mitrate ....
.... 1. *P. subsessile*   10.185

10.184   1. Capsules emergent to long exserted; calyptra cucullate

2. Capsules shortly ovoid to ellipsoidal, emergent to shortly exserted; peristome lacking; cells of the operculum vertical; leaves smooth on the back .... 2. *P. ovatum*   10.189

2. Capsules oblong to cylindric, straight or curved, long exserted; peristome very thin and fragile, usually remaining in the lid; cells of the operculum in oblique rows; leaves papillose on the back ....
.... 3. *P. lamellatum*   10.193

10.185   **1. Pterygoneurum subsessile** (Brid.) Jur. Plant grayish green. Stems 2–3(5) mm high. Leaves erect and appressed, imbricated, often in a terminal budlike cluster, mostly obovate, obtuse to briefly acuminate, strongly concave, the margin incurved, often cucullate at the apex, entire or bluntly dentate above, often lobed at the apex, 0.8–1.7 mm long; costa long excurrent to a hyaline, smooth or bluntly toothed awn often longer than the blade; costal lamellae mostly 4, about half as wide as the lamina; margins entire or bluntly dentate; surface smooth, mammillose or papillose, sometimes bearing short chlorophyllose filaments; upper cells quadrate to rounded or transversely elongated, often oblong to rhomboidal at the apex, 12–17 μ wide, thin to thick walled, often sparingly chlorophyllose, smooth or sometimes papillose on the dorsal surface; enlarged hyaline basal cells often extending high up in the blade. Autoicous or paroicous. Seta short; capsules immersed to emergent, sometimes slightly exserted, globose to subglobose, 0.4–0.8 mm long without the lid, ± shrunken and wrinkled with the mouth dilated when dry, usually dark reddish brown; peristome lacking; lid convex with a short to long, rather stout, straight, or inclined beak. Spores globose or subglobose, densely and finely papillose, 30–55 μ. Calyptra mitrate. Plate 25, figs. 9–17.

10.186   On soil or occasionally rocks, mainly on desert plains and foothills in our region, common and doubtless present in every county in the state.

10.187   Western North America from Canada to Mexico, eastward to Illinois, Europe.

10.188   Common in dry desert regions, often abundant locally, especially on shoulders of drainage ways, washes and ditches, along roadways and on disturbed soil. It often grows mixed with *P. ovatum,* and wherever the one grows the other may be expected. The mitrate calyptra is the general rule although it may be cucullate in some plants.

10.189   **2. Pterygoneurum ovatum** (Hedw.) Dix. Plants gray green to bright green. Shoots often bulblike, 2–3(5) mm high. Leaves concave and closely imbricated, erect, ovate, obovate or shortly oblong, mostly acuminate but sometimes acute or broadly obtuse, 0.8–1.5 mm long; margins widely incurved, plane or slightly revolute, entire; costa excurrent to a short and slender or very long and stout, hyaline, smooth or slightly dentate awn; costal lamellae 2–4(6), at most about half as wide as the lamina, highest near the apex, smooth, mammillose or papillose, often bearing chlorophyllose filaments on the faces; margins entire to bluntly dentate; upper marginal cells variable, quadrate to strongly rhomboidal, the medial cells quadrate to rounded, shortly oblong or hexagonal, 10–14 μ wide, thin to very thick walled, smooth on the back; basal cells larger and wider, thin walled, hyaline, rectangular, often extending high up the blade. Autoicous or paroicous. Seta short to fairly long; capsules emergent to well exserted, ovoid to oblong-cylindric, 0.6–1.8 mm long without lid, dark reddish brown, finely to irregularly wrinkled when dry; peristome lacking; lid convex conic with a short to long inclined beak. Spores finely to rather coarsely papillose, 20–36 μ, ripening in early spring. Calyptra cucullate. Plate 25, figs. 1–8.

10.190   Mostly on soil or in the crevices of rocks, commonly in foothills, plains, or saline deserts.

10.191   Europe. Western North America from Canada to Mexico, eastward to the Great Plains States. Very common and doubtless in every county of Utah.

10.192   One of the commonest mosses in the state. Its neat little cushionlike tufts crown the tops of clods of dry, weather-roughened, loose soil, especially where there has been disturbance, as along natural drainage courses, ditches, roadsides, or abandoned farmlands. In open saline deserts it serves as a stabilizer of soil; the little tufts form protective caps on the crests of fine soil clods curved around the bases by wind erosion. Often tufts or mats become so infiltrated with fine soil that only the fuzzy surface created by the long white awns of the leaves reveals that plants are there. The fruit is usually abundant, the tufts

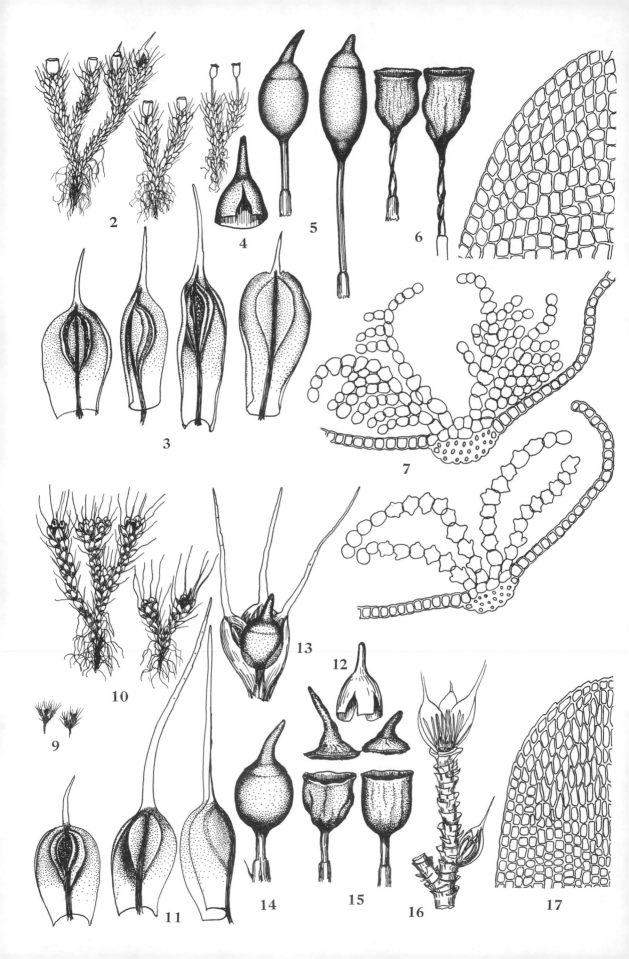

fairly bristling with dark reddish brown capsules. The length of the seta is variable; sometimes the capsules are barely exserted; then again they may be well elevated. The calyptra is nearly always cucullate, but in some plants with short setae it may be mitrate.

10.193 **3. Pterygoneurum lamellatum** (Lindb.) Jur. Plants gray green or frequently bright green. Stems 4–8(12) mm high. Shoots often bulbiform, especially when growing scattered. Leaves concave, appressed and imbricated, crisped and incurved when dry, obovate, ligulate or spatulate, 0.8–2 mm long, shortly acuminate to broadly rounded obtuse, or occasionally emarginate at the apex; margins entire to serrulate at the apex, plane slightly recurved above; costa excurrent to a short or long, hyaline, smooth or bluntly dentate awn; costal lamellae variable, 2–4(0), often irregular, highest near the apex, tapering toward the base, commonly ± undulate, often 1 or both lamellae on 1 side of the costa smaller and more irregular than those on the opposite side; margins entire to lobed; lamella cells quadrate, shortly oblong to irregularly rhomboidal, smooth to low papillose, often bearing chlorophyllose filaments; upper cells quadrate, oblong or transversely elongated, becoming ± rhomboidal at the apex, usually rather thick walled, 13–18 μ wide, usually clear green, moderately chlorophyllose, ± mammillose and typically with low papillae on the dorsal surface, but in many leaves practically smooth; basal cells larger, usually hyaline, but frequently green nearly to the insertion. Autoicous. Seta erect, 3–12 mm long, twisted to the right when dry; capsule well exserted, oblong to cylindrical, erect, straight or slightly curved, urn 1–3.8 mm long, dark reddish brown, minutely longitudinally ribbed, or reticulately wrinkled when dry, sometimes almost smooth; mouth narrow; neck short; exothecial cells relatively thin walled, mostly elongate-rectangular to linear, some of them irregularly rhomboidal; annulus poorly differentiated, composed of 1–3 rows of quadrate to rounded, ± overlapping cells with exceedingly thick walls, these remaining as a border around the mouth or falling separately; peristome short, thin, pale reddish brown or yellowish, exceedingly fragile and usually remaining in the operculum, basal membrane short and hyaline, teeth abruptly cleft into 32 or more filamentous divisions united by cross bars at the base, forming a fenestrated net, the upper joints nodulose, and free, equal or unequal, straight to slightly twisted to the right, finely papillose, generally about ¼ the length of the operculum, but sometimes much longer, the upper joints often fragmentary and remaining in the beak of the operculum; operculum

---

Plate 25. 1–8. **Pterygoneurum ovatum.** 1. Habit sketch, X.4. 2. Habit sketches, X3.2. 3. Four typical leaves. 4. Calyptra. 5. Two moist capsules. 6. Two dry capsules, X8. 7. Two cross sections of leaf and costa showing variations in development of costal laminae. 8. Upper leaf cells, X120.

9–17. Pterygoneurum subsessile. 9. Habit sketches, X.4. 10. Habit sketches, X3.2. 11. Three typical leaves. 12. Calyptra, X8. 13. Capsule and perichaetial leaves, X6. 14. Moist capsule. 15. Two dry capsules with calyptra, X8. 16. Defoliated stem showing terminal perichaetium and lateral budlike perigonium, X4.8. 17. Upper medial and marginal leaf cells, X120.

long conic-rostrate, usually inclined, the cells disposed in oblique rows, 0.7–1.5 mm long. Spores globose to shortly ovoid, very finely papillose, 20–25(28) μ. Calyptra cucullate. Plate 24, figs. 8–12.

10.194 On dry and often saline soil in desert regions; rare but locally abundant.

10.195 Europe. Utah and Arizona.

10.196 This is a rare moss known in North America only from Utah and southern Arizona. It is larger than the other two species of the genus and is at once recognized by oblong to cylindrical capsules; the lids have obliquely disposed cells as opposed to the vertical arrangement in the other species. The peristome is very fragile and nearly always falls with the lid. After carefully soaking, one can sometimes ease the lid off and still leave at least part of the peristome on the mouth of the capsule. The leaves are usually greener than in the other species. The costal lamellae are often very irregular in size and shape, lobed, or even entirely lacking.

14. ALOINA (C. Muell.) Kindb.

10.197 Plants small, scattered or in short dense tufts on dry or damp calcareous soils, usually dull and tinged with red or brown. Stems short, rarely exceeding 0.5 mm tall, mostly simple, central strand lacking. Leaves thick and rigid, incurved and imbricated when dry, erect-patent to recurved when moist, ovate to oblong-ligulate, mostly broadly rounded or blunt at the apex, lamina broadly incurved or infolded, ± subtubulose in the upper ½ or ⅔, the base concave and ± hyaline; margins entire; costa very broad, occupying about half the width of the blade, in cross section 2–5 cell layers thick, the dorsal cells continuous with and smaller than the cells of the lamina, very thick walled on the outer surface, medial cells generally large and thin walled, the ventral cells often chlorophyllose and bearing chlorophyllose filaments 2–5 cells long, the latter forming a dense mass over the entire ventral surface of the costa in the upper portion of the leaf; upper cells of the lamina quadrate to transversely elongated, incrassate and smooth, the dorsal wall often very thick, becoming reddish with age; basal cells larger, thinner walled, hyaline, sometimes oblong. Dioicous or synoicous. Male plants minute and budlike. Seta elongate; capsule well exserted, elliptic-oblong to subcylindrical, erect and symmetric or nearly so; neck short; operculum tall conic or thick rostrate; annulus double or triple, ± persistent; peristome teeth 32, long, filamentous, arising from a very low basal membrane, spirally twisted in 1–2 turns, finely and densely papillose. Calyptra cucullate, rostrate.

10.198 Name derived from *Aloë*, a genus of succulent liliaceous plants.

10.199 **Aloina pilifera** (De Not.) Crum & Steere. Plants scattered or in short dense tufts or sods, dull olivaceous to reddish brown. Stems mostly simple, usually less than 0.5 mm high, rhizoids coarse, confined to the base, sometimes bearing brown, multicellular, ovoid gemmae. Leaves appressed and incurved when dry, erect-patent to recurved from an erect base when moist, upper ones oblong-ligulate, 1.5–2.3 mm long, the lower ones ovate-oblong or shorter, apex broadly rounded, ± abruptly hyaline hair-pointed, the hair point varying up to 1.4 mm long, smooth; margins strongly infolded, ± cucullate at the apex and subtubulose in the upper part; margins entire; costal filaments simple or branched, the cells swollen, oval to barrel shaped, the terminal cell pyriform with the distal wall very thick and yellowish orange; upper medial leaf cells oval to transversely elongated, mostly 18–22(28) μ wide, 10–20 μ long, incrassate, the dorsal wall the thickest and often strongly tinged with red, smooth; basal cells oblong, quadrate or transversely elongated, angular and hyaline, up to 28 μ wide and 90 μ long, mostly thin walled but often with the transverse walls and angles thickened. Dioicous. Seta variable in length, mostly 7–10 mm long (as short as 4 mm in our plants, up to 15 mm elsewhere), reddish; capsule elliptic to subcylindric, erect and ± symmetric, urn 1.5–3 mm long, wrinkled when dry, mouth somewhat narrowed; exothecial cells mostly oblong, rather firm, not strongly differentiated at the mouth, only 1 or 2 rows of cells shorter and somewhat thicker walled; neck short, with 1–2 rows of large, superficial stomata; annulus conspicuous; peristome teeth long, spirally twisted at dehiscence but tending to straighten out; operculum tall conic to conic-rostrate, straight or bent. Spores 10–17 μ, smooth. Plate 14, figs. 1–6.

10.200   On dry, often saline soils.

10.201   Europe. Guadalupe Island. Arizona. Southern Utah and Arizona to California.

10.202   The strongly infolded lamina of the leaves distinguishes this plant from species of *Crossidium*. The basal membrane of the peristome of the present plants is shorter than usual, often barely visible above the mouth of the capsule.

15. CROSSIDIUM Jur.

10.203   Plants small, in dense hoary tufts, rarely exceeding 6 mm in height. Stems erect, simple or sparingly branched, central strand present, of smaller thin-walled cells, cortex of large thin-walled cells, the outer 1–3 layers smaller, slightly thicker walled and darker in color; rhizoids moderately abundant, smooth, reddish. Leaves shortly ovate to spatulate, acuminate to obtuse or retuse, mostly with a terminal awn, in some plants exceeding the length of the leaf blade; margins entire or toothed at the apex, mostly narrowly recurved in the upper part; costa stout, with a narrow dorsal stereid band, guides ventral in single row, usually large, with a single layer of enlarged, thin-walled, ventral, superficial cells which proliferate in some plants to form a convex parenchymatous mass, from which arise ventral costal filaments 1–5 cells in length, either scattered and short, or densely crowded and forming a dark green, opaque mass on the upper half of the leaf; upper leaf cells short, quadrate to rounded or shortly rectangular, often transversely elongated,

177

moderately thin to thick walled, mostly becoming wider and more elongated toward the base. Dioicous or autoicous. Seta erect, of moderate length; capsule oblong-cylindric or oblong-elliptic, erect, straight or slightly curved; operculum tall conic or deeply thimble shaped, cells spirally arranged; peristome of 32 deeply cleft hairlike divisions arising from a short basal membrane, short and nearly erect or long and spirally twisted, finely and densely papillose, mostly orange red. Calyptra large, cucullate.

10.204 The name, from the Greek, meaning a pitcher or jar, refers to the capsule.

10.205 1. Upper margins of leaves hyaline, often toothed; cells very thick walled, oval, oblique; costal filaments very abundant, in a dense convex mass spreading over half the width of the leaf ....
.... 1. *C. griseum* 10.207

10.206 1. Leaves not bordered with hyaline cells

2. Leaf cells strongly papillose to nearly smooth, or sometimes only mammillose; costal filaments, mostly short and fewer, only spreading slightly beyond the width of the costa, often reduced to single bulging cells or entirely lacking in some or most leaves; the terminal cells mostly blunt and bearing 3–8 low rounded papillae ....
.... 2. *C. aberrans* 10.210

2. Leaf cells smooth; costal filaments longer and more abundant, spreading over half the width of the lamina, the terminal cells mostly bearing 2 long teeth .... 3. *C. desertorum* 10.217

10.207 **1. Crossidium griseum** (Jur.) Jur. Plants in low, dense, grayish green, hoary tufts. Stems simple or sparingly branched, 4–6 mm tall. Leaves erect, incurved on the margins and at the apex when dry, patent to spreading when moist, broadly ovate to ovate-oblong, broadest at the base, 1–2 mm long, deeply concave in the upper central part, incurved with spreading hyaline wings, often appearing sigmoid on either side in cross section; apex obtuse or acuminate and tapering into the long, smooth or slightly toothed hair point which may be nearly as long as the blade or even exceed it in length; costa broad above and bearing on the ventral surface a dense opaque mass of green filaments, occupying ⅔ of the width of the leaf in the upper half, the filaments 3–5(7) cells long, simple or forked, with the terminal cell usually elongated with the distal wall very thick, often colored, bearing 1–4 prominent (often hornlike) papillae, the proximal cells ovoid and bulging or barrel shaped, thin walled and chlorophyllose, arising from a convex mass of thin-walled parenchymatous tissue proliferating from the costa; guides dorsal, stereid band rather narrow; upper cells smooth, obliquely elongated, very thick walled and hyaline, forming a broad border, becoming oval and chlorophyllose toward the costa; medial cells transversely elongated and at length becoming wider, quadrate to oblong and thin walled in the base. Autoicous. Seta 7–10 mm long, orange red or yellowish brown; capsule erect or nearly so, oblong-cylindric, straight or very slightly curved, 1.7–2.2 mm long, reddish brown, smooth or faintly striate when dry; operculum tall, widely conic, or conic-rostrate, up to 0.25 mm high, teeth cleft into 32 hairlike divisions, erect or weakly spiral, finely and densely papillose, distinct or irregularly joined or perforated here and there, united at the base and forming a very narrow basal membrane, bright orange red; annulus double. Spores globose, 10–12 μ. Calyptra very narrowly conic, cucullate, 2–2.5 mm long. Plate 26, figs. 1–7.

10.208   On dry soil and in crevices.

10.209   Central Europe, Caucasus Mountains, Syria and Central Asia. Northern Arizona, California, southern Utah.

10.210   **2. Crossidium aberrans** Holz. & Bartr. Plants small reaching 10 mm tall but usually only 2–5 mm high, in loose or compact tufts, often interwoven at the base with rhizoids, dark green and somewhat hoary when dry, bright, clear green when moist. Stems simple or branched, often with innovations from axils of leaves, 0.2–0.33 mm in diameter; central strand not strongly differentiated, usually of smaller cells sometimes scarcely distinguishable from the larger, thin-walled cells of the central region, the outer 1–3 rows smaller, slightly thicker walled and usually darker colored. Leaves erect, incurved or spirally twisted when dry, spreading, soft and tender when moist, up to 1.5 mm long but often only 0.6 mm long when growing in very dry places, shortly ovate to oblong-ligulate, broadest at the base, $\pm$ concave; margins recurved above or throughout; apex obtuse or occasionally acute or retuse; costa slender below, dilated above, excurrent to a smooth hyaline hair point, nearly equalling or exceeding the length of the blade but often much shorter (entirely lacking in fo. *epilosum*); ventral costal filaments variable, usually represented by a single, strongly mammillose cell crowned with 1–8 papillae, scattered or crowded, scarcely projecting laterally beyond the costa, in some plants scarcely different from adjacent cells of the lamina, the papillae lacking; at the other extreme the filaments are composed of 2–4 thin-walled, rounded or barrel-shaped cells, the terminal one bearing papillae, spreading laterally slightly beyond the margin of the costa or covering about $\frac{1}{4}(\frac{1}{2})$ the width of the leaf blade; upper cells rounded hexagonal, toward the middle becoming quadrate, oblong or irregularly 4- to 6-sided, many of them transversely elongated, variable in size, in some plants 10–15 μ wide, in others 12–21 μ wide, in cross section bulging, mammillose to barrel shaped, the apical cells bearing single papillae, mostly on the dorsal side; basal cells wider, mostly oblong, the area occupied by them varying in different leaves and different plants, in some short leaves scarcely differentiated, in some long leaves extending upward $\frac{1}{2}$ the length of the blade. Usually paroicous but sometimes partly dioicous with an antheridia terminal. Seta 11–15 mm long, reddish brown; capsule oblong-cylindric, about 2 mm long without the lid, erect to slightly inclined, straight or slightly curved; neck short with a few large stomata; lid tall-conic, rather thick, 0.8–1 mm tall, its cells spirally arranged; annulus of 1–2 rows of very thick-

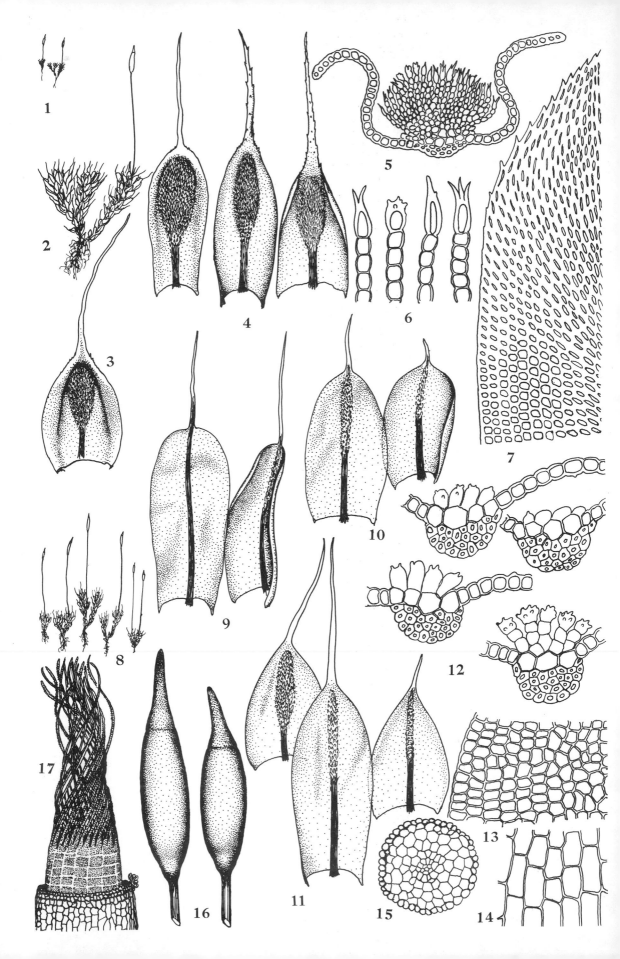

walled cells; peristome of 32 slender hairlike, strongly papillose, bright orange or ferruginous teeth arising from a short basal membrane and spirally twisted in 1–1.5 complete turns (with the lid off sometimes becoming quite straight), 0.7–0.8 mm long. Spores globose to shortly ovoid, about 10 μ, smooth. Calyptra cucullate, about 3 mm long. Plate 26, figs. 8–17.

10.211   On dry, often saline, soil of deserts and hillsides, often on ledges and under overhanging rocks.

10.212   Eastern Washington, California, Utah and Arizona.

10.213   Locally abundant and quite variable in size and leaf characteristics according to habitat. The ventral costal filaments may be conspicuous, 2–4 cells high, thin walled, densely packed together and spreading laterally so as to cover about half the width of the blade. At the other extreme, and of common occurrence, many plants have most of the leaves devoid of costal filaments, while in a few well-developed leaves they are reduced to singly depressed, or strongly bulging mammillose cells usually bearing 1–8 weakly to strongly developed papillae. In plants of the latter kind, the costal outgrowths may escape casual observation, but in most instances they can be detected in surface view, especially along the margins of the costa where the bulging papillae-tipped cells often give a good view in optical section. Cross sections of the upper half of the leaves clearly show their presence.

10.214   *Desmatodon convolutus* has a very prominent transverse row of enlarged, green ventral costal cells which may lead one to mistake this plant for *Crossidium aberrans*. However, in the former, the costa is rather flat and weak at the base and becomes conspicuously broader and thicker in the upper part, ending just below the apex or forming an apiculus.

10.215   The key to the species of Crossidium in Grout's *Moss Flora of North America* calls for "leaf cells strongly papillose." I find that some leaves may show weak papillae on some of the apical cells, often evident on the marginal cells and on cells here and there in the lamina. Although an occasional leaf may show them plainly, they are usually demonstrated with difficulty, even in cross sections. With persistence, however, they can be recognized in at least a few leaves of most plants.

10.216   Occasional specimens with leaves lacking hair points. Uintah County, Green River, 1 mi. below Split Mountain, on dry soil bank, 4,820 ft.

Plate 26. 1–7. **Crossidium griseum.** 1. Habit sketches, X.4. 2. Same, X2. 3–4. Four leaves, X8. 5. Cross section of leaf showing typical development of costal filaments, X40. 6. Distal portions of four costal filaments showing characteristics of terminal cells, X120. 7. Upper medial and marginal leaf cells, X120.

8–17. **Crossidium aberrans.** 8. Habit sketches, X.4. 9–11. Leaves from three different plants showing variations in development of costal filaments, X8. 12. Four cross sections of upper costa from different plants showing variations in costal outgrowths, X80. **Note:** Costal outgrowths may be lacking in some leaves. 13. Upper medial and marginal leaf cells. 14. Basal leaf cells, X120. 15. Cross section of stem, X40. 16. Two average capsules, X8. 17. Peristome, X40.

10.217 **3. Crossidium desertorum** Holz. & Bartr. Plants very short and densely tufted, yellowish green, olivaceous or reddish brown, ± hoary on the surface, but usually sparingly so. Stems erect, 3 mm high or less. Leaves erect, incurved at the tips and closely imbricated when dry, erect-patent to spreading when moist, oblong-ligulate and broadly obtuse but some often acute, mostly 1–1.5 mm long, the comal ones reaching 2.2 mm but in less developed plants as small as 0.5 mm long, concave; margins entire, narrowly revolute in the upper half, but sometimes plane throughout in some leaves; costa weak at the base, stronger above, in the upper and comal leaves excurrent to a smooth hyaline hair point of variable length, reaching as much as 1.4 mm long but in lower leaves percurrent to shortly mucronate, in the upper half bearing a dense mass of branched filaments on the ventral surface which spread laterally over the lamina more than ½ its width; terminal cells of the branches mostly conical and smooth, but often blunt and bearing 2–3 papillae, upper cells mostly quadrate to shortly oblong, often with some of them rhomboidal to irregular, especially in the apex, smooth, rather thin walled and clear, 12–15 μ wide; basal cells becoming oblong, wider, up to 24 μ, thin walled and hyaline, the marginal ones often much smaller and shorter. Dioicous. Seta reddish, 1–2 cm long, as short as 0.5 mm in depauperate plants; capsules 1.5–2 mm long without lids, cylindric but gradually tapering to a narrower mouth, erect to slightly inclined, straight or slightly curved; basal membrane of the peristome very short and concealed below the mouth or extending as much as 70 μ above the mouth; teeth long and twisted in 2 full turns at dehiscence, but often shorter and less twisted in less developed plants, reddish brown, paler at the base, densely and finely papillose with tall papillae; lid tall conic. Plate 27, figs. 1–7.

10.218 On dry soil and rocky ledges.

10.219 Arizona to southern California and southern Utah. San Juan County: Colorado River at mouth of Lake Canyon, 3,400 ft.

10.220 In the *Moss Flora of North America*, Grout compares the type specimen from Pima County, Arizona with the European *Crossidium chloronotos* (Brid.) Limpr., stating that the peristome teeth of *C. desertorum* are shorter and less twisted but have a wider basal membrane. This is true of less well-developed plants in my collections, but in the same tuft I find that most of the plants have larger capsules with longer teeth twisted in 2 turns. The basal membrane varies from practically lacking, as in European plants, to well developed. Since the type speci-

---

Plate 27. 1–7. Crossidium desertorum. 1. Habit sketches, X.4. 2. Four leaves of well-developed plants, X8. 3. Two leaves of a short, extremely xerophytic plant, X8. 4. Upper leaf cells, X120. 5. Terminal cells of costal filaments, X120. 6. Five capsules, X8. 7. Two peristomes showing variations in height of the basal membrane and length of the teeth, X20.

8–12. Tayloria acuminata. 8. Habit sketches, X.4. 9. Three typical leaves, X8. 10. Two leaf apices with upper cells, X120. 11. Three capsules of average shape, X8. **Note:** Urn may range from subglobose to cylindrical. 12. Exothecial cells, X80.

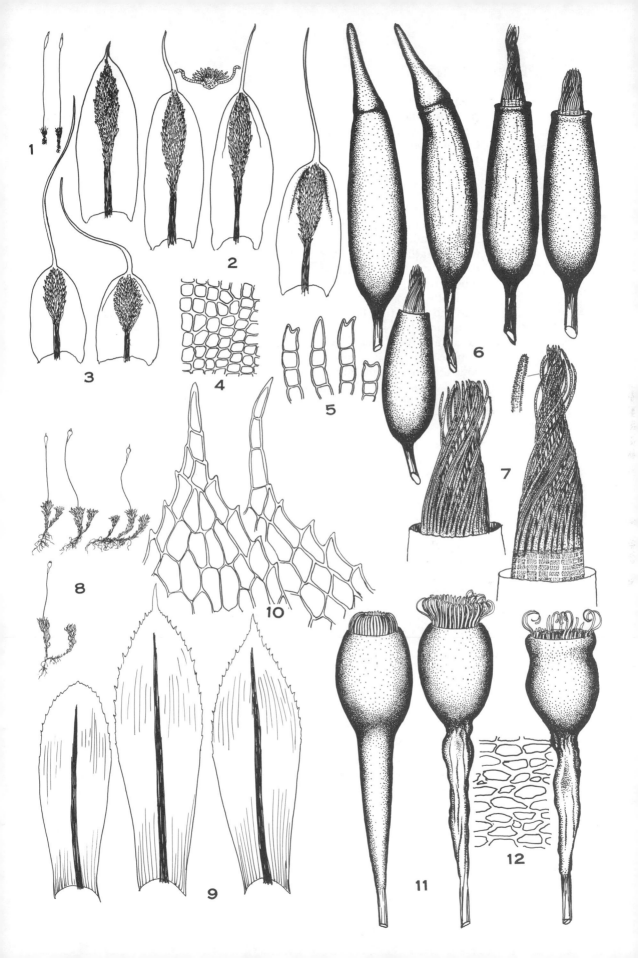

men and others which I have seen are less developed or depauperate, the present collections, which are well developed and richly fruited, probably represent the plant better. In the latter condition it approaches *C. chloronotos* even more closely and may ultimately prove to be only a form of it.

16. DESMATODON Brid.

10.221   Plants small to medium sized, loosely to densely tufted, frequently forming compact cushions. Stems erect, simple or branched, in cross section showing a central strand which is often weak or lacking. Leaves usually rather dense, erect and appressed or incurved to twisted when dry, mostly erect-patent to patent, rarely recurved to widely spreading when moist, ovate, oblong, oblong-lanceolate, ligulate or sometimes spatulate, broadly acute to shortly acuminate or rounded-obtuse; margins mostly entire, toothed near the apex in some species, revolute, plane, or incurved; costa usually stout, ceasing below the apex or excurrent to a mucro or awn, in cross section showing a single (occasionally double) row of 2–4 subventral guides with a single, or partially double, row of ventral cells above and strongly dorsal stereid band below, the dorsal superficial cells usually larger; upper medial leaf cells quadrate, hexagonal or shortly rectangular, often irregular; upper marginal cells undifferentiated or somewhat smaller, thicker walled and clearer, in some species forming a distinct border; upper cells mammillose to papillose; basal cells usually becoming larger, smooth, more elongated, hyaline, and thin walled, the marginal ones mostly narrower, sometimes as a pale border. Perichaetial leaves not much differentiated. Seta long, twisted, erect (curved in *D. laureri*); capsules erect and symmetric (asymmetric and cernuous in *D. cernuus* and *D. laureri*, ovoid, oblong or cylindric, smooth to finely wrinkled when dry; stomata few in the neck region; operculum conic to rostrate, straight or inclined; annulus ± conspicuous, often persistent; peristome teeth divided into 2–3 long slender divisions, these sometimes short, erect or slightly twisted, often irregular, densely and finely papillose, from a low basal membrane. Calyptra cucullate.

10.222   The name, from the Greek, means band tooth and refers to the basal membrane of the peristome.

10.223   1. Upper marginal leaf cells oblong to linear and thick walled, forming a distinct border; capsules inclined to pendulous

      2. Plants rather small; the leaves up to 2.5 mm long; upper cells smooth to slightly papillose; capsule short, ovoid, asymmetric, curved, and cernuous; cells of the lid in straight rows; peristome teeth erect, not twisted .... 5. *D. cernuus* 10.244

      2. Plants rather large; comal leaves up to 5 mm long; cells strongly papillose; capsules cylindric, nearly symmetric, erect to inclined or widely pendulous; cells of the lid in oblique rows; teeth twisted in 1 turn .... 4. *D. laureri* 10.240

10.224 1. Upper marginal leaf cells undifferentiated or shortly elongated (rarely a few oblong-linear), thick walled, smooth, and more pellucid; capsules erect and symmetric, shortly oblong to clyindric

    3. Upper leaves obtuse with long, smooth, hyaline hair points, ½ as long as the blade or longer, the lower leaves ± muticous and often acute .... 2. *D. plinthobius* 10.232

    3. Upper leaves muticous or at most mucronate to apiculate

        4. Costa of the upper leaves excurrent to a sharp mucro or to a short but distinct hair point; leaf cells mostly 12–16 μ wide; mostly subalpine or alpine .... 1. *D. latifolius* 10.225

        4. Costa of the upper leaves usually ceasing below the apex, rarely percurrent; leaf apex often mucronate because of the prolongation of cells of the lamina

            5. Leaves oblong to ligulate, broadly obtuse, mostly mucronate or apiculate; costa stout, tapering upward

                6. Plants small to minute, leaf cells mostly 8–12 μ wide, rather thick walled, and opaque; upper marginal cells often thicker walled, smoother, and clearer; mostly montane .... 3. *D. obtusifolius* 10.236

                6. Plants larger; leaf cells regularly 14–18(22) μ wide, thin walled and clear, without a border; mostly subalpine or alpine .... 1a. var. *muticus* 10.228

            5. Leaves ovate, ovate-oblong or ligulate, widely acute; costa very stout, increasing in width upward, widest above; plants of dry lowland plains and hillsides .... 6. *D. convolutus* 10.248

10.225 **1. Desmatodon latifolius** (Hedw.) Brid. var. **latifolius.** Plants in dense tufts, usually bright green above, brownish below. Stems 2–20 mm high, in cross section showing a central strand of rather small cells, a cortex of larger angular cells becoming smaller outward, 1–2 rows of the outermost cells rounded, darker, but slightly, if at all, thicker walled. Leaves ± erect and appressed, infolded and incurved to twisted when dry, ± spreading when moist, crowded above, distant and smaller below, oblong to spatulate, 2–3 mm long, acute or obtuse; margins entire, narrowly to widely revolute from the base to near the apex on 1 or both sides; costa weak at base, fairly stout at midleaf, tapering to the apex, in the upper leaves excurrent as a mucro or short hair point, in the lower leaves often ceasing below the apex, the mucro then formed by the cells of the lamina; upper cells often quite irregular, 10–18(22) μ wide, the walls moderately thick to thick, usually quite clear, each cell bearing 2–6 moderately high C- or O-shaped papillae; upper marginal cells not differentiated; basal cells rather abruptly longer and wider, oblong to rectangular, smooth, hyaline, and thin walled, the marginal ones much narrower and forming a border. Autoicous. Seta straight or flexuous, yellowish at maturity, becoming dark reddish with age, 1–2

185

cm long, twisted to the left below, to the right above; capsule oblong to cylindric, erect and symmetric or nearly so, 1–2 mm long without the lid, slightly shrunken or minutely striate when dry, brown, becoming reddish brown with age; exothecial cells irregularly oblong, 4- to 6-sided, rather thin walled; neck short, with a few large, superficial stomata; annulus of 2(3) rows of small cells with exceedingly thick walls, usually persistent; peristome teeth 2(3)-cleft into slender division, often irregularly split, the bases united at the joints, commonly incurved when dry with the old columella extending beyond them, densely papillose throughout; lid conic and obliquely rostrate, 0.6–1.2 mm long, the cells in vertical rows. Spores globose to ovoid, papillose, 17–25(30) μ, maturing in summer. Plate 28, figs. 1–8.

10.226 On dry or damp rocks, soil, humus, or rotten wood, usually in shaded places, often near streams where the atmosphere is humid. Subalpine or alpine.

10.227 Greenland to Unalaska. California, Arizona, and New Mexico, common in Rocky Mountains.

10.228 1a. Var. **muticus** (Brid.) Brid. Plants somewhat taller and more branched, the tufts often looser, the costa of the upper leaves ceasing below the apex which may be obtuse, acute, or apiculate. Plate 28, figs. 9–10.

10.229 Colorado and Utah.

10.230 The species is not likely to be mistaken for anything else. The variety might be taken for a large form of *D. obtusifolius*, but in that species the leaf cells are much smaller and more opaque.

10.231 A specimen from the Fish Lake Plateau in Sevier County has unusually broad, strongly incurved leaves, leaf cells 17–24 μ wide, and some capsules curved throughout or abruptly bent below the mouth.

10.232 **2. Desmatodon plinthobius** Sull. & Lesq. Plants 1–4 mm high (in our region smaller than usual), in dense or rather loose, dark olivaceous or brownish tufts. Stems 0.4–0.8 mm long; central strand small. Leaves appressed or incurved, often somewhat spirally twisted when dry, erect-patent to patent when moist, the upper the largest, 0.1–1.5 mm long, oblong-ligulate rounded-obtuse and obtuse-apiculate, many comal leaves ending in a smooth hyaline awn up to 1.5 mm long; margins entire, revolute well toward the apex; costa terete, excurrent or percurrent or

---

Plate 28. 1–8. **Desmatodon latifolius**. 1. Habit sketches, X.4. 2. Same, X2. 3. Typical leaves, X8. 4. Cross section of costa at midleaf, X120. 5. Leaf apex, X8. 6. Dissected stem tip showing autoicous male bud, X4. 7. Capsules, X8. 8. Portion of peristome, X60.

9–10. Var. **muticus**. 9. Typical leaves, X8. 10. Upper leaf cells, X120.

11–15. **Desmatodon plinthobius**. 11. Habit sketches, X.4. 12. Three upper leaves. 13. Two lower leaves. 14. Capsules, X8. 15. Cross section of costa and leaf margins, X120.

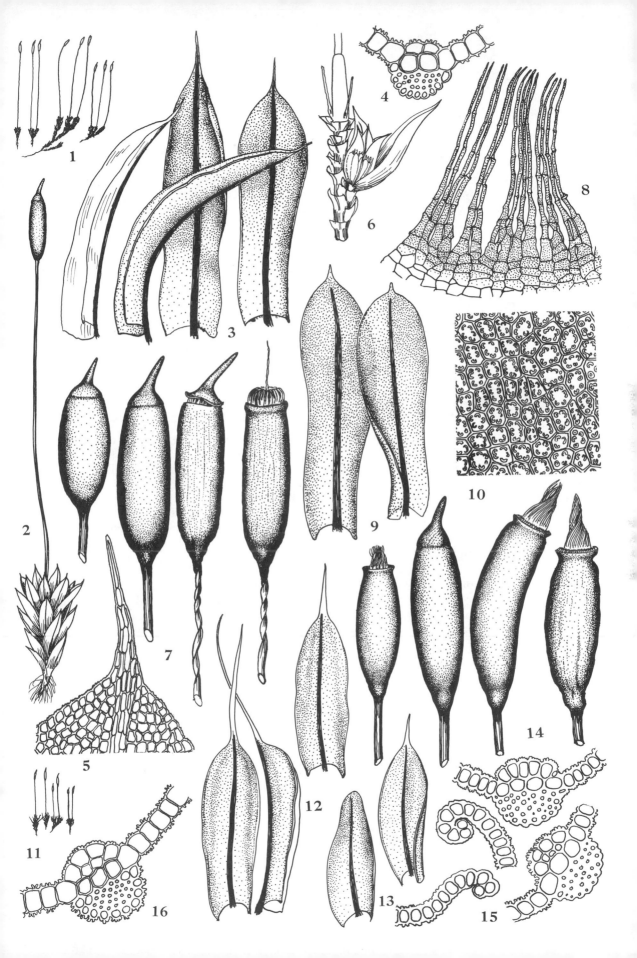

ending below the tip in some leaves; upper cells variable in size, 8–10(14) μ, each bearing 2–6 coarse, C-shaped papillae; marginal cells sometimes thicker walled and less densely papillose, sometimes nearly smooth; basal cells large, hyaline, and thin walled, occupying ¼–⅓ the leaf base. Usually dioicous, but often autoicous. Seta reddish brown at maturity, straight, 6–12 mm long; capsule reddish brown, oblong to cylindrical, erect and symmetric or nearly so, little changed when dry, usually with minute longitudinal wrinkles, ± contracted below the mouth, urn 1.5–3 mm long, mostly small in our plants; exothecial cells oblong, 4- to 6-sided, mostly thin walled, here and there with adjacent longitudinal walls heavily thickened forming lines; neck short, with a few large stomata; annulus of 2 rows of cells with exceedingly thick walls, the upper row elongated, the lower ± isodiametric, usually persistent; peristome of 16 teeth cleft into 2(3) hairlike divisions, yellowish brown and densely papillose with fine, tall, slender, pale papillae, often irregularly perforated, slightly to rather strongly spirally twisted, often nearly 1 full turn, varying from 0.1–0.6 mm long; operculum conic-rostrate, 0.5–1.5 mm long, with cells in oblique rows. Spores smooth, 8–11 μ. Plate 28, figs. 11–15.

10.233   On soil, rocks, and walls.

10.234   Pennsylvania to Georgia, west to Iowa, Texas, Arizona, and Utah.

10.235   In typical form this moss is easy to identify, but it resembles *Tortula muralis* so much that some plants may be difficult to recognize. *D. plinthobius* usually has smaller, more opaque, upper leaf cells (8–10 μ wide), without a border of thick-walled, smoother, marginal cells; some of the leaves are muticous; the basal membrane of the peristome is short but projecting 2–3(4) joints above the mouth of the capsule; the teeth are only slightly spiral and comparatively shorter. *Tortula muralis*, in typical form, has leaves with cells 10–14 μ wide and less opaque, the upper margins bordered with elongated, smoother, thick-walled, pale cells, the basal membrane of the peristome lacking, the teeth long and spirally twisted in 2–3 turns. Many forms of the latter do not have the upper marginal cells elongated, although they are usually thick walled and less papillose. Judging from the relatively few specimens from Utah, both species are uncommon although perhaps locally abundant. Our forms are small, ± atypical and difficult to separate. About the only reliable character is the shorter, less twisted peristome teeth of *D. plinthobius*.

10.236   **3. Desmatodon obtusifolius** (Schwaegr.) Schimp. Plants in dense or loose tufts, dark green above, sometimes tinged with red or brown, yellowish to dark brownish below. Stems 1–12 mm high; central strand present, often indistinct, the small central cells not sharply set off from the larger

---

Plate 29.   **Desmatodon laureri.** 1. Habit sketches, X.4.   2. Same, X2.   3. Typical leaves, X8. 4. Leaf apices. 5. Upper medial leaf cells. 6. Basal medial cells. 7. Cross sections of leaf margin at different levels, X120. **Note:** Cross section of costa on Plate 28, fig. 16. 9. A portion of the peristome, X60.

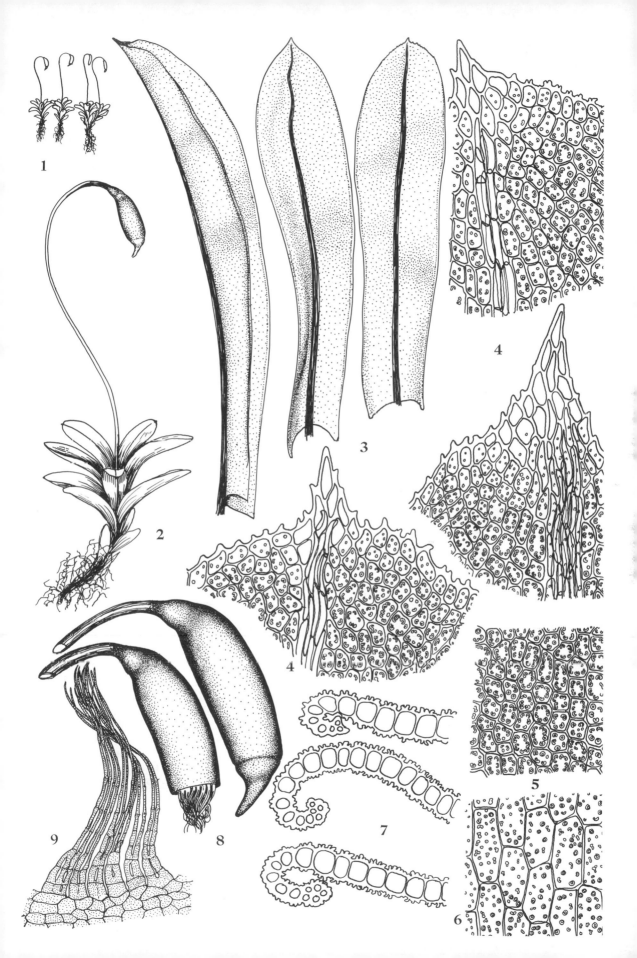

cells of the cortex. Leaves ± erect, infolded and incurved, loose or appressed, crispate, often spirally so when dry, erect to recurved when moist, mostly 1–2 mm long, in some plants up to 3 mm, shortly to longly ligulate or spatulate, concave, bluntly acute to broadly rounded, usually shortly mucronate and occasionally apiculate in some leaves, the projecting tips usually formed by the apical portion of the lamina, less commonly by the percurrent costa, in some plants a few leaves acute; margins entire, plane to revolute, often to the apex; costa mostly ceasing just below the tip, occasionally percurrent or shortly excurrent into the mucro, ± terete above, flatter in the base, smooth to papillose on the back above; upper cells 4- to 6-sided, often irregular, sometimes in rows, 8–12(17) μ wide, chlorophyllose and obscure or occasionally quite clear, densely papillose with C-shaped papillae; upper marginal cells often thicker walled, clear, yellowish and smoother, some of them often elongated in a ± distinct border; basal cells becoming gradually larger and longer, up to 22 μ wide, rectangular to hexagonal, thinner walled, smooth, and clear, the marginal ones narrower. Monoicous but the male branches soon separating from the female and then apparently dioicous. Seta erect and straight, 5–10 mm long, twisted to the right when dry; yellowish to reddish brown; capsule erect or nearly so, shortly oblong to cylindric, urn 2–4 mm long, brown to chestnut colored, smooth to minutely longitudinally wrinkled when dry, neck short, with a few large stomata, exothecial cells 4- to 6-sided, oblong to rhomboidal or irregular, rather thin walled, 1–3 rows below the mouth shorter but not notably thicker walled; annulus of 2 rows of small, thick-walled, usually persistent cells, lid short and thimble-like to tall and conic-rostrate, usually ± inclined, the cells obliquely arranged; peristome teeth variable, short to rather long, up to 0.4 mm long including the basal membrane, often much reduced, nearly straight to spirally twisted 1 turn, mostly irregularly divided nearly to the base into 2(3) filiform divisions, these entirely separate, perforate at the base or somewhat anastomosing, densely and finely papillose, reddish brown. Spores smooth, 8–14 μ. Plate 30, figs. 1–8.

10.237   On wet or dry soil and rocks, usually in shaded places, under overhanging rocks, frequent around streams, springs, or waterfalls.

10.238   Widely distributed from New Brunswick to Vancouver Island, south to Pennsylvania, Missouri, Arizona and California.

10.239   A well marked species though variable in most of its characteristics. The leaves range from shortly oblong to rather longly ligulate, often somewhat spatulate, usually broadly obtuse with a short bluntish mucro, but sometimes obtuse or rather long apiculate. In some plants some leaves may be acute. The upper leaf cells are typically 10–12 μ wide, but forms with cells as small as 8 μ or as large as 12–16 μ occur. The upper margins of the leaves may or may not be bordered with 1–4 rows of thick-walled cells, usually smoother and more pellucid than the adjacent cells; sometimes a few, or even most of them, are elongated and oblong to sublinear. A careful study of Grout's type of *Desmatodon coloradensis* reveals that it is only a small form of *D. obtusifolius*.

Several similar forms have been found, and these intergrade with typical plants. After a search through many specimens, unquestionable cases were found in which male branches were connected with female branches, proving the monoicous condition, and ample evidence was found to show that the male branches separate from the females by an abscission zone consisting of large inflated cells at the point of divergence. The peristome teeth vary in length, some being quite short and others unusually long, and often twisted nearly 1 turn when the operculum is still in place, but tending to straighten out after it falls.

10.240 **4. Desmatodon laureri** (Schultz) B.S.G. Plants in compact sods or large loose tufts, green above, pale yellowish to dark brown below. Stems 2–10(25) mm high, in cross section showing a central strand, outer cortical cells only slightly differentiated if at all, usually thin walled and bulging when young. Upper leaves 2.5–5.5 mm long, strongly crisped and variously twisted when dry, the lower ones less so, comal leaves of sterile plants often recurved-spreading from an erect base, forming a rosette when moist, those of fertile stems erect-patent to spreading, the lower leaves ± erect, oblong-ligulate, narrowed at the insertion, wide near the apex, rather suddenly narrowed to an acute or shortly acuminate or apiculate tip, sometimes obtuse-apiculate, broadly rounded concave throughout, often becoming flattish with age; margins recurved to the shoulders, becoming flat at the apex, and often at the base, entire throughout or with a few fine to coarse teeth at the apex; costa ending just below the apex, the apiculate tip formed by the lamina, but in some leaves percurrent and forming the apiculus, yellowish green, becoming reddish with age in the lower half, terete in the middle; upper cells 10–17(21) μ wide, thin walled, densely papillose, the papillae rather low, C- or O-shaped, often slightly bifurcate, 4–12 per cell, clear and distinct; marginal cells below the shoulders of the leaf much narrower, forming a distinct border 2–8 cells wide, the extreme marginal ones very small and bistratose; basal cells becoming gradually wider and longer, oblong, the intermediate ones with as many as 20–30 papillae per cell, the extreme basal ones smooth, clear, usually reddish and often thick walled; basal marginal cells narrow, forming a distinct border. Autoicous. Seta erect below, curved or widely arched above, 1–1.8 cm long, yellowish at maturity, becoming reddish brown with age, when dry twisted to the left, or to the left below and the right above, often straight but becoming curved when moistened; capsule erect, inclined, or pendent and longitudinally wrinkled when dry, strongly inclined to pendent when moist, 1.5–2.5 mm long, subcylindric, nearly symmetric or slightly curved; operculum conic with an oblique rostrum, the cells spirally arranged; annulus of 2–3 rows of small thick-walled cells; peristome teeth rather suddenly narrowed upward and divided into 2–3 linear-filiform divisions, often slightly perforated at the base, yellowish brown to reddish brown below, paler above, finely and densely papillose, about 0.5 mm long, twisted 1 full turn at dehiscence of the operculum, often becoming less twisted with age. Spores 30–50 μ, rather coarsely papillose. Plate 28, fig. 16, and Plate 29.

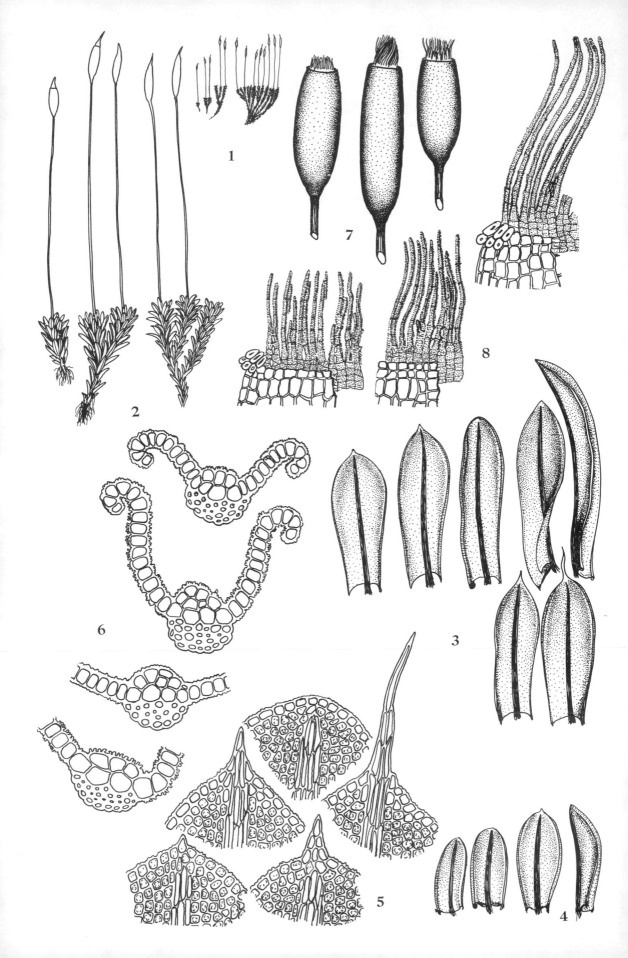

10.241   On damp soil or in crevices of rocks, usually in woods or shaded ravines, subalpine to alpine.

10.242   Greenland. Arctic America, Europe, and Asia. Vancouver Island and British Columbia, southward through the Rocky Mountains to Utah and Colorado. Summit County: Uinta Mountains, Henry's Fork, 9,300 ft. (mixed with *D. latifolius*).

10.243   It is the largest species of the genus, frequently compared with *D. cernuus*, both having inclined and ± asymmetric capsules. The present species is generally larger, with longer leaves wider at the apex, and the costa ending mostly below the apex; the capsules are longer, more pendent, and nearly symmetric with twisted teeth.

10.244   **5. Desmatodon cernuus** (Hueb.) B.S.G. Plants in dense or loose sods or cushions, 2–20 mm high, green to yellowish green, often tinged with brown. Seta with central strand lacking; outer cortical cells colored, but only slightly thicker walled than the inner ones. Leaves erect, variously incurved and infolded, ± contorted, but not strongly crisped when dry, erect-patent to patent when moist, 2–2.5 mm long, oblong to oblong-spatulate, acute or sometimes blunt and apiculate or mucronate by the excurrent costa; upper margins plane, ± denticulate by the projecting blunt angles of the cells; lower margins revolute, bordered with narrower cells and often colored; costa often colored at the back, excurrent to a short apiculus; upper cells irregular, 14–21 μ wide and 14–45 μ long, thin walled, bulging or mammillose, smooth to weakly papillose; upper marginal cells smaller, gradually becoming long and narrow toward the base; basal cells larger, lax and oblong; basal marginal cells linear, often colored, forming a border 1–4 cells wide and often 2-layered. Autoicous. Seta 1–2 cm long, reddish brown, twisted to the left below and to the right above, straight or sometimes curved to contorted; capsule short, ovoid, and asymmetric, inclined to cernuous, 1.3–1.8 mm long without the lid, neck short, dark reddish brown at maturity, smooth or lightly striate and contracted under the mouth when dry; exothecial cells isodiametric to rectangular, 4- to 6-sided, shorter in the neck and with a few large stomata, shorter below the mouth; annulus of 2 rows of thick-walled cells; peristome teeth about 0.24 mm long, slightly spiralled at dehiscence, becoming straight, deeply cleft into 2 narrow divisions often united at the joints above and perforated below, often irregular, yellowish brown and densely and finely papillose; operculum shortly conic-rostrate, the thick beak inclined downward, about ⅓ the length of the urn, cells short, in ± vertical rows. Spores 30–50 μ, coarsely papillose. Plate 31, figs. 10–15.

10.245   On damp or dry soil, apparently favored by limestone, tolerating mildly saline soils.

Plate 30. Desmatodon obtusifolius. 1. Habit sketches, X.4. 2. Same, X2. 3. Upper leaves of typical form showing variations. 4. Leaves of small form growing in dry places, X8. 5. Leaf apices showing variations in the upper marginal cells, X60. 6. Cross sections of costa at different levels, X120. 7. Capsules, X8. 8. Portions of peristome teeth from three different capsules, X60.

10.246   Alaska to Quebec, Ohio, Wisconsin, North Dakota, Wyoming, Colorado, Utah and Nevada.

10.247   The short, cernuous capsule and the delicate texture of the leaves are distinctive features.

10.248   **6. Desmatodon convolutus** (Brid.) Grout. Plant 2–10 mm high, usually short, loosely to densely tufted, the stems often spaced by infiltrated soil, dark green, often tinged with red, when dry appearing dark olivaceous to blackish. Stems simple or sparingly branched; central strand distinct or often indistinct in very short stems; cortex of large, thin-walled, angular cells, 1–2 layers smaller at the periphery, these usually thick walled and reddish in plants of dry deserts; rhizoids rather few, reddish brown, smooth. Leaves infolded, incurved and imbricated or spirally crowded, ovate-acuminate to oblong-ovate, sometimes subspatulate, twisted when dry, spreading to somewhat recurved when moist, rather broadly acute to shortly acuminate, some blunt or obtuse, sometimes hyaline-tipped, deeply concave, sometimes nearly cucullate; margins entire, revolute; costa stout, increasing in width upward, strongly convex ventrally, often appearing granulose ventrally, the ventral cells often vertically elongated, forming a high arch; upper cells opaque to clear, often reddish on either side of the costa, quadrate to shortly oblong, some transversely elongated or 5- to 6-sided, 10–13(18) μ wide, those near the costa usually the largest, thin walled when young, becoming thick walled and reddish with age, those near the costa often with the dorsal wall considerably thickened, usually papillose with thick, low, simple or C-shaped papillae, these occasionally stout; 3–8 marginal rows smooth or nearly so (in some plants the leaves are practically smooth throughout); lower cells often in regular rows; basal cells variable in different leaves, oblong, quadrate or transversely elongated, 16–20 μ wide, walls fairly thick to thin, the transverse walls commonly thicker, or the angles thickened. Autoicous. Seta 5–12 mm long, erect, reddish; capsule ovoid to shortly oblong-cylindric, erect and symmetric, urn 1–2 mm long, smooth to finely striate when dry, reddish to reddish brown when mature, neck short, with a few large stomata, mouth ± narrowed, sometimes slightly oblique; operculum conic, obliquely rostrate, ¼–½ the length of the urn; annulus indistinct, of 1–2 rows of thick-walled cells; peristome teeth divided into 2 equal or unequal linear divisions, finely and densely papillose, straight or in long forms slightly twisted, commonly poorly developed with short irregular divisions. Spores ovoid

---

Plate 31. **1–9. Desmatodon convolutus.** 1. Habit sketches, X.4. 2. Same, X2. 3. Typical leaves. 4. Two leaves of small forms, X8. 5. Upper medial leaf cells showing variations, papillae omitted. 6. **Juxtacostal cells.** 7. Cross sections of leaf and costa at three levels, X120. 8. Dissection of stem tip showing autoicous condition, X4. 9. Portions of peristomes from different capsules, X60.

10–15. Desmatodon cernuus. 10. Habit sketches, X.4. 11. Typical leaves, X8. 12. Cross sections of costa at two levels. 13. Leaf apex and   upper medial cells, X120. 14. Capsules, X8. 15. Portion of peristome. X60.

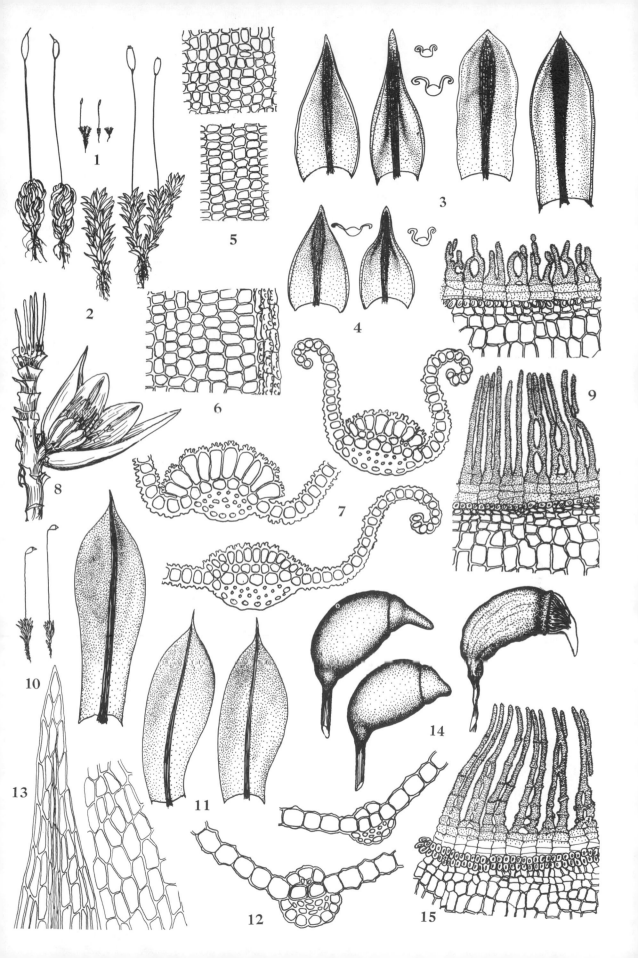

to subglobose, smooth to finely punctate, 18–28 μ, maturing in the spring. Plate 31, figs. 1–9.

10.249 On soil and in crevices of rocks, usually in dry places of deserts, valleys and hillsides, tolerating mildly saline conditions.

10.250 Europe, Asia, Africa and Australia. Southern Utah and Arizona to Southern California and Mexico.

10.251 The stout costa, broadest in the upper part of the leaf, is the most distinctive feature of this moss. The upper part of the lamina is often deeply concave, being longitudinally incurved-outcurved, so as to obscure the exact shape of the leaf which may appear to be more or less ovate-lanceolate when in reality it is broader. Variability in the shape of the upper leaf cells and their papillosity is also marked.

17. TORTULA Hedw.

10.252 Plants small to large, usually in dense or loose tufts, mostly dark olivaceous to blackish, often hoary, dark to bright green, and often tinged with red above, when dry, brown to yellowish or reddish below when moist, mostly on soil or among rocks, some species peculiar to tree trunks. Stems erect to ascending, simple or branched; central strand present or lacking: Leaves mostly oblong to ligulate or spatulate, often obovate to oblanceolate, broadest at the middle or above, usually $\pm$ narrowed at the base, little changed or variously infolded, crisped or twisted when dry, the lower ones usually erect, the upper commonly spreading, sometimes recurved, often forming a rosette; lamina mostly concave-canaliculate, nearly flat in some species; margins plane or variously recurved to revolute; costa usually strong, ending below the tip to excurrent, often prolonged as a hyaline or reddish hair point, in cross section showing 1–2, or partially 3 rows of medial guides, 1–2 rows of ventral cells often much like the adjacent cells of the lamina, rarely overarching the costa, and a dorsal stereid band; upper leaf cells mostly isodiametric, rounded, quadrate to 6-sided, frequently densely papillose with simple, bifurcate, stellate, C- or O-shaped papillae, often very rough; basal cells becoming wider and longer. Perichaetial leaves not much differentiated. Seta erect, short to long; capsules mostly cylindric, sometimes oblong-cylindric, erect, straight or slightly curved, mostly reddish brown when mature, neck short with 1–2 rows of large, superficial stomata; operculum variably conic, short and thimble-shaped to long rostrate, straight or slightly bent, the cells obliquely or spirally disposed; annulus of 1–4 rows of short thick walled cells; peristome inserted below the mouth and arising from a basal membrane of variable height, from very short and inconspicuous to a prominent, obliquely tessellated tube up to ⅔ the total length of the peristome; teeth 32, hairlike, finely papillose and spirally twisted in 1–2 complete turns. Spores relatively small, smooth or finely punctate. Calyptra cucullate.

10.253 The name is a Latin diminutive meaning twisted, in reference to the peristome.

10.254 1. Margins of leaves ± conspicuously bordered with 1–6 rows of thicker-walled, less papillose, colored or paler cells; awn smooth; plants small, monoicous; peristome tube lacking or very short .... 1. *T. muralis* 10.256

10.255 1. Margins of the leaves not conspicuously bordered

    2. Peristome tube lacking or very short; plants small, monoicous; awn smooth --- 1. *T. muralis* 10.256

    2. Peristome tube evident, often very high, tessellated

        3. Upper leaf cells smooth, rarely low papillose, large and clear, 18–28 μ; costa excurrent to a short mucro or spine ----------------- .... 2. *T. mucronifolia* 10.260

        3. Upper leaf cells papillose, often densely so

            4. Costa percurrent or excurrent to a short mucro or spine, never an awn; leaves obtuse to nearly acute; monoicous ---------------- .... 3. *T. inermis* 10.264

            4. Costa excurrent to a long awn

                5. Awn smooth; capsules usually long-cylindrical, slightly curved, chocolate brown at maturity; peristome tube 1/6– 1/2 the length of the teeth .... 4. *T. brevipes* 10.268

                5. Awn slightly to strongly toothed, often spinulose

                    6. Leaves erect-patent to spreading but not squarrose-recurved when moist

                        7. Leaf margins plane in the upper ¼–½; lamina unistratose above

                            8. Plants in dense, dark, often hoary tufts or cushions; leaf cells usually 8–10 μ; peristome tube pale yellowish to white, teeth loosely twisted in 1 turn or less .... 5. *T. intermedia* 10.273

                            8. Plants in loose tufts, not particularly hoary; leaf cells 12–16 μ; basal membrane of peristome frosty reddish; teeth twisted 1.5–2 turns; synoicous ---------------------- .... 6. *T. princeps* 10.277

                      7. Leaf margins revolute to near the apex; lamina bistratose in the upper part .... 7. *T. bistratosa* 10.281

                  6. Leaves ± squarrose-recurved when moist; leaf cells mostly 10–16 μ, up to 24 μ in some forms of *T. norvegica*, especially those with narrowly acuminate leaves 10.285

                    9. Leaf margins plane in the upper ¼–⅓; apex broadly obtuse, acute or narrowly acuminate; awn distinctly reddish in the lower half or throughout; lower stem

leaves usually ferruginous throughout; mostly growing at altitudes above 5,500 ft. .... 8. *T. norvegica* 10.285

9. Leaf margins revolute to near the apex; awn mostly hyaline throughout, occasionally reddish at the base; lower stem leaves mostly yellowish to brownish; growing at all elevations

   10. Leaf apex broadly rounded to somewhat narrowed, obtuse or truncate, often emarginate, abruptly awned

      11. Free surfaces of the leaf cells attenuated to protuberances equalling the thickness of the main body of the cell in height and crowned with a 2- to 4-furcate papilla, O-shaped (or less frequently, C-shaped) in surface view; robust plants .... 9. *T. papillosissima* 10.293

      11. Free surfaces of cells flattish, convex or low conical, each bearing 4–8 simple, bifurcate, or stellately branched papillae, mostly C- or O-shaped in surface view; usually stout plants; common .... 10. *T. ruralis* 10.297

   10. Leaf apex ± narrowed to an acute or acuminate, hyaline, toothed tip, continuous with broadly decurrent base of the awn, the latter often reddish in the lower half or throughout .... 11. *T. ruraliformis* 10.301

10.256   **1. Tortula muralis** Hedw. Plants small, in loose or dense tufts, green, bluish green, or brownish, often hoary. Stems 0.4–1.5 mm tall; central strand present. Leaves erect, infolded to incurved, often twisted at the stem tips when dry, erect to erect-patent or somewhat spreading when moist, the comal leaves oblong- to oblong-ligulate or spatulate. 1.5–3 mm long, the lower ones shorter, ± concave, broadly rounded obtuse, truncate or retuse; margins usually revolute to the apex; costa terete, usually roughly papillose at back above, abruptly excurrent to a long, smooth, excurrent, hyaline hair point, often nearly as long as the blade; upper cells 8–14(17) μ wide, chlorophyllose and often obscure, each cell bearing 2–8 irregularly C-shaped papillae varying from weak to coarse, simple or bifurcate, 1–4 rows at the margins often slightly larger, thicker walled, and less strongly papillose and chlorophyllose, sometimes becoming yellowish and clear, but extremely variable, often scarcely differentiated; basal cells quadrate to oblong, thin walled and hyaline, gradually larger toward the base. Monoicous or partly dioicous. Seta yellowish when young, becoming reddish brown and finally dark chocolate brown when old, 1–2 cm long; capsules 1–2.7 mm long, oblong-cylindric to cylindric, reddish brown, becoming darker when old, smooth or finely striate when dry; operculum tall, thimble shaped and bluntly rounded at the apex or conic with a thick rostrum, the cells spirally disposed, about ⅓ the length of the urn; annulus or 2 rows of thick-walled cells; peristome teeth twisted in 1–3 turns, arising from a short basal membrane 2–4 cells high and barely extending above the mouth. Spores smooth or finely punctate, 7–11 μ, maturing in the spring or early summer. Plate 32, figs. 1–7.

10.257   On dry or moist calcium-bearing rocks or soil, especially on cement installations and the mortar of stone walls.

10.258   Worldwide in distribution.

10.259   Uncommon in Utah and other arid regions but very abundant in the Pacific Northwest. The border of thick-walled smoother cells is poorly or not at all differentiated, and some sterile plants might be referred to *T. brevipes* or *Desmatodon plinthobius*.

10.260   **2. Tortula mucronifolia** Schwaegr. Plants in dense tufts, dark green, often with a bluish cast. Stems rarely exceeding 1 cm in height; central strand about ⅓ of total diameter of the stem. Leaves moderately to strongly crisped, often infolded and incurved, sometimes spirally twisted when dry, erect-patent to patent when moist, usually dense, often forming little more than a comal tuft, oblong-lanceolate to spatulate, gradually narrowed to an acute or acuminate apex, widely concave, 2–3.5 mm long; margins flat above, narrowly revolute near the base, entire; the basal margin often colored; costa tapering, gradually, excurrent to a short or long mucro; upper cells usually clear and light green, usually thin walled, 16–28 μ wide, smaller and often thicker walled toward the margin, smooth or sometimes with low papillae; basal cells gradually becoming elongate, oblong, thin walled, hyaline, and sometimes inflated; basal marginal cells smaller, quadrate to shortly oblong, thick walled in a revolute border. Autoicous. Seta 1–2.3 mm long, yellowish to reddish brown; capsules long-cylindric, 2–2.5 mm long without the lid, reddish brown, becoming dark brown with age; neck region with 1 row of stomata; peristome tube high, tessellated, pale at the base, pink or peach colored above; teeth very slender, reddish, strongly twisted; operculum tall conic, 1–2.2 mm long, the cells spirally disposed. Spores globose, 14–18 μ, finely punctate-echinulate. Calyptra cucullate. Plate 32, figs. 8–12.

10.261   On damp soil, usually in shaded places, often under overhanging rocks or tree roots, in crevices or in the open.

10.262   Widely distributed in the Northern Hemisphere. In North America, from the Arctic southward to New York, Illinois, Iowa, New Mexico and Arizona. It is abundant in the Rocky Mountains and eastward but less common on the Pacific Coast where *T. subulata* seems to replace it. In Utah it is very common in canyons and on shaded mountain slopes and doubtless occurs in every county.

10.263   The clear, green, smooth leaves with a stout sharp mucro or short awn formed by the shortly excurrent costa make this plant easily identifiable. Occasionally one sees forms with low weak papillae, which, together with the smaller thick-walled cells forming the leaf border, would lead one to place them in *T. subulata* Hedw. However, *T. subulata* has much

199

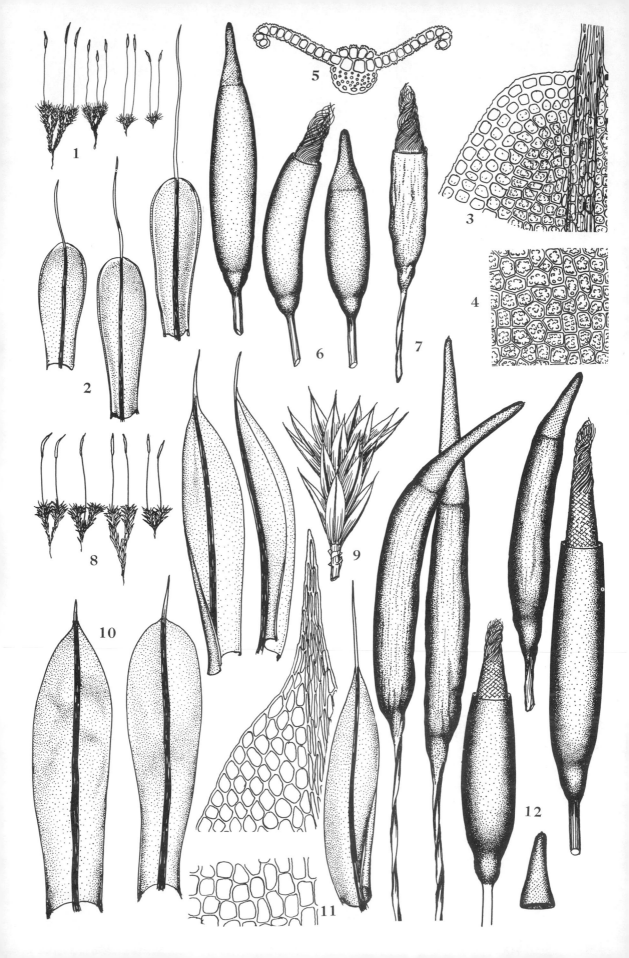

stronger papillae, usually C-shaped, with marginal cells oblong, and rarely has the clear areolation of *T. mucronifolia*. In the western states, *T. mucronifolia* is typically montane and approaches the lowland only on foothills and in the mouths of canyons and ravines. It is very common and nearly always richly fruited. Occasionally it becomes large. I have one specimen with capsules 5.2 mm long and the peristome 1.8 mm long.

10.264   **3. Tortula inermis** (Brid.) Mont. Plants densely tufted, often gregarious, dark green to somewhat glaucous, often tinged with red, the lower parts reddish to brown. Stems reaching about 2 cm tall, but often much shorter; central strand often large and well developed, reaching about one half the total diameter of the stem. Leaves infolded and incurved, usually spirally twisted at the stem apex when dry, erect to erect-patent or somewhat spreading when moist, usually forming a conspicuous comal tuft, commonly 2–3 mm long and sometimes up to 5 mm long in well-developed plants, oblong to long ligulate, concave, narrowly obtuse to shortly acute, sometimes ending in a short point; margins revolute to the apex, entire, without a border of differentiated cells; costa stout, conspicuous at the back, reddish and roughly papillose, ending shortly below the leaf apex, percurrent or shortly excurrent to an apiculus (although the apiculus may be formed by the cells of the lamina); areolation usually quite clear, the upper cells usually thin walled, 10–16 μ wide, densely papillose on both sides with C- and O-shaped papillae; basal cells wider, oblong, thin walled and hyaline, smooth, smaller on the borders. Autoicous. Seta 1.2–2(2.5) cm long, reddish brown; capsule usually long-cylindric but often short, 2–4.5 mm long (excluding lid), reddish brown becoming very dark brownish black with age; operculum very long and narrowly conic, almost awl-shaped in some capsules up to 2 mm long, the cells spirally arranged; annulus double or triple; peristome tube pale, frosty reddish pink, about ¼–⅔ the length of the peristome which is twisted in 1–2 full turns, light reddish, densely and finely papillose, and up to 2 mm long. Spores globose, 10–12 μ, minutely punctate or granular, ripening in spring. Plate 33, figs. 5–7.

10.265   On soil and rocks.

10.266   Throughout the southwestern part of the United States; Wyoming, Colorado and New Mexico, westward to California.

10.267   A distinctive moss not likely to be confused with any other species. Common and undoubtedly in every county of the state. It is especially common in the dry Colorado River Basin and southern Utah, usually at the bases of cliffs and large rocks.

Plate 32. 1–7. **Tortula muralis.** 1. Habit sketches, X.4. 2. Leaves, X8. 3. Portion of typical leaf apex. 4. Upper medial leaf cells. 5. Cross section of leaf, X120. 6. Capsules, X8.

8–12. **Tortula mucronifolia.** 8. Habit sketches, X.4. 9. Portion of shoot, X2.8. 10. Leaves, X8. 11. Leaf apex and upper medial cells, X120. **Note:** Some forms have lightly papillose cells. 12. Capsules, X8.

10.268   **4. Tortula brevipes** (Lesq.) Broth. Plants loosely to densely tufted, often infiltrated with fine soil, green to grayish green, often hoary on the surface. Stems 1–4 mm tall. Leaves dark brownish, reddish, or olivaceous, erect and ± appressed, infolded, often crisped and spirally twisted at the apex when   dry, erect-patent to spreading when moist but not squarrose-recurved, 1–3 mm long, oblong to ligulate varying to spatulate or oblong-lanceolate, concave in the upper part, mostly obtuse, often broadly rounded or truncate but frequently acute to briefly acuminate; margins broadly recurved to revolute above, nearly plane at the base; costa stout, prominent at the back, reddish and often roughly papillose, convex above; excurrent as a smooth awn up to 2 mm long or only an apiculus, often percurrent or ceasing below the apex in some lower leaves (or even in some plants); upper cells 10–17 μ wide, usually thin walled, mostly densely papillose and opaque; enlarged basal cells mostly oblong, up to 26 μ wide, thin walled and hyaline, mostly smooth, often extending high up in the leaf to about half its length. Dioicous or autoicous. Seta 8-24 mm long, bright reddish brown when young, very dark with age; capsule mostly long cylindric, 3–3.5 mm long, without the lid, and with the long narrowly conic lid appearing even narrower, reddish brown becoming very dark chestnut or chocolate brown at maturity; lid about 1.5 mm long, its cells spirally disposed; peristome tube generally high, the teeth tightly coiled 1.5–2 turns, finely papillose, pale yellowish to a frosty peach color; annulus of 2–3 rows of cells. Spores globose to oval, 12–17 μ, smooth or very finely punctate. Plate 33, figs. 1–4.

10.269   On dry calcareous soils throughout the state, usually in desert regions but also in canyons and on mountain sides.

10.270   Washington to California, Idaho to Colorado.

10.271   Related to *T. muralis* but differing in the much longer and darker capsules with a higher basal peristome tube. Also the upper marginal leaf cells are not noticeably thicker walled than those internal to them.

10.272   Local variations show plants in which the leaves are shortly oblong, often with a very short hair point, scarcely more than apiculate or even muticous; other plants show oblong-ovate leaves with a narrow apex ranging from acute with percurrent costa to narrowly obtuse, with the costa ending below the apex. These forms are difficult to locate in the usual descriptions and keys. Very often the larger part of a tuft may have nonpiliferous leaves and a small part typically developed. The capsules are occasionally much shorter and straighter. I have seen them oblong-cylindric and only 2 mm long. The length of the peristome tube varies from about 1/6–1/2 the length of the teeth. Many of our plants

---

Plate 33.   1–4. Tortula brevipes. 1. Habit sketches, X.4. 2. Three lower leaves. 3. Four upper leaves. 4. Capsules showing variations, X8.

5–7. Tortula inermis. 5. Habit sketches, X.4. 6. Typical leaves. 7. Capsules showing variations, X8.

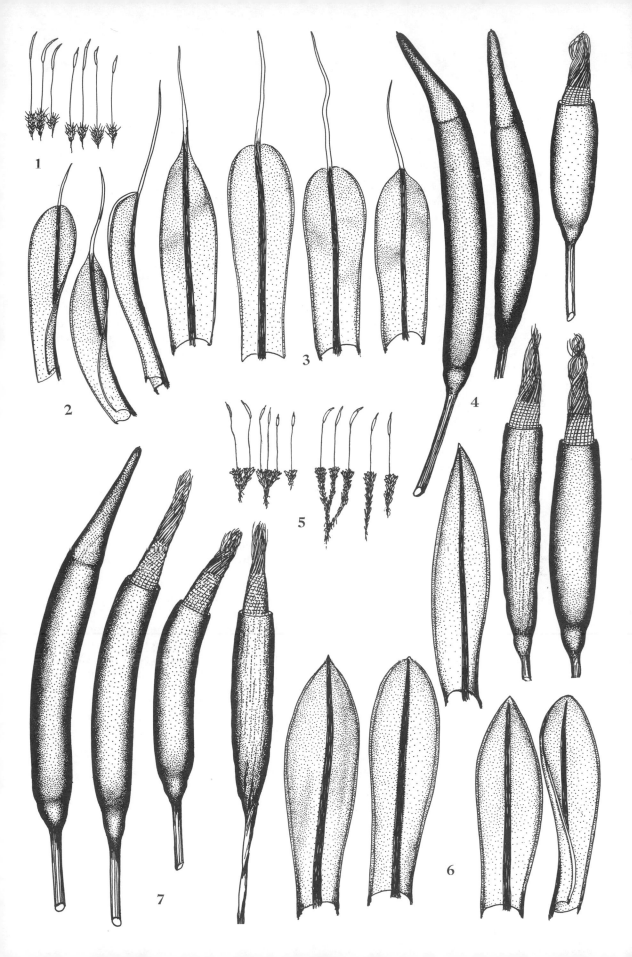

have leaves acute or acuminate, often imperceptibly merging with the base of the excurrent costa. While most plants are dioicous, about ⅓ of the specimens show some autoicous stems, and to judge by the frequency with which capsules are produced, it is likely that this condition is even more frequent.

10.273 **5. Tortula intermedia** (Brid.) De Not. Plants of medium size, in loose or compact tufts, dark olivaceous to blackish green and often hoary when dry. Stems up to 4 cm high but usually shorter; central strand lacking. Leaves erect-patent to spreading but not squarrose when moist; infolded and appressed when dry, only slightly twisted, 2–4 mm long, oblong to ligulate, obtuse to slightly emarginate, canaliculate; margins plane in the upper ¼–½, revolute below; costa stout, reddish, ± roughened on the back, especially above, abruptly excurrent to a long, hyaline, variably toothed awn, 0.7–2.5 mm long, the teeth distant or dense; upper cells typically small, 7–10 μ wide but variable in western plants, up to 14–17 μ wide, chlorophyllose and often opaque but sometimes quite clear, with 2–10 small C-shaped (rarely O-shaped) papillae, these usually low and dense; short green cells usually extending down the lower margins; basal cells oblong, wider in center, hyaline and smooth, narrow at the margins. Dioicous. Seta yellowish brown to reddish brown, 1–1.5 cm long; capsule shortly cylindrical or occasionally fairly long, 2–3 mm long without the lid, reddish brown to dark chocolate brown; annulus of 2–3 rows of persistent cells; lid tall conic ⅓–½ the length of the urn, the cells spirally disposed; peristome pale yellowish or whitish, rarely becoming reddish, the tube variable ⅓–¾, teeth loosely twisted at a steep angle, usually making only 1 turn or less. Spores finely papillose, 10–15 μ. Plate 34, figs. 1–4.

10.274 On soil.

10.275 Widely distributed across northern United States, extending southward to California, Arizona, and adjacent states.

10.276 In our region many smaller *Tortula* resemble undersized forms of *T. ruralis*. These plants show a wide diversity of characters many of which cannot be definitely related to the traditional limits of established species. It would be ill advised to give even varietal names to these plants as it is becoming increasingly evident that they represent genetical or ecological variants of a single species. The plants from Zion Canyon approach *T. intermedia*, while those from northern Utah show leaf cells larger than the typical form. The small size, darker color, erect-spreading leaves, and pale whitish peristome, with teeth twisted only 1 turn or less, are common to all. I have some specimens with traits of *T. intermedia* but with strongly squarrose-recurved leaves, others with erect leaves

---

Plate 34. **1–4. Tortula intermedia.** 1. Habit sketches, X.4. 2. Two lower leaves. 3. Three upper leaves. 4. Capsules, X8.

5–8. Tortula princeps. 5. Habit sketches, X.4. 6. Dissected perichaetium showing synoicous condition, X4. 7. Two upper leaves. 8. Three lower leaves, X8.

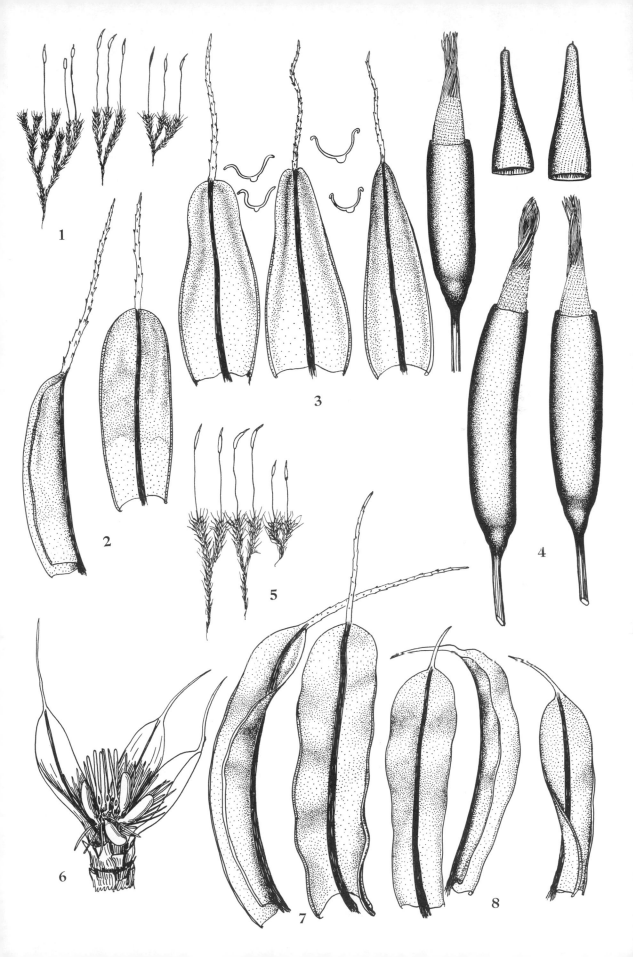

revolute to the apex. Some approach *T. bistratosa* in having a few cells in two layers in the upper part of some leaves. Others have characters of *T. intermedia* except that the peristome is well colored and the teeth strongly twisted. Prolonged study of these forms consumes time and rarely gives any satisfaction.

10.277   **6. Tortula princeps** De Not. Plants in dense tufts or mats, dark green to blackish when dry, green to olivaceous, often tinged with red when moist. Stems 2–10 cm tall; central strand lacking. Leaves crowded in rosettes at the apices of innovations, often forming interrupted verticil; upper leaves the largest, usually broadly ligulate or spatulate, 2–5 mm long, canaliculate, the apex bluntly acute to broadly rounded; margins revolute in the lower ½–⅔, plane above; costa stout, rough, red and conspicuous at back, abruptly excurrent as a long, hyaline, spinulose hair point, sometimes reddish at the base, variable, sometimes short; upper cells mostly 10–14(17) μ, each cell with 4-6 coarse but usually low C-shaped papillae; basal cells larger, oblong, abruptly hyaline and smooth, the marginal cells smaller, forming a border. Synoicous or sometimes polygamous. Seta 1–3 cm long, reddish; capsules short to long cylindric, 2–5 mm long without the lid, reddish brown, becoming dark brown with age; lid 1.3–1.7 mm long, tall-conic with cells spirally disposed; basal membrane of the peristome light reddish yellow, becoming paler or white with age, teeth about as long as the tube, twisted in 1–2 turns. Spores 10–16 μ, globose, smooth. Plate 34, figs. 5–8.

10.278   On dry soil and rocks in shady woods or in exposed situations.

10.279   Alaska to California, northern Idaho, and southern Utah. Europe, Asia, Africa, South America, and Australia. Washington County: near St. George, 3,600 ft.

10.280   The two specimens cited above are not typical, although they have most of the basic characteristics of *T. princeps*. Both are undersized, rather densely tufted, with leaves erect-patent when moist and the inflorescences definitely synoicous. The leaf margin may revolute in the lower half or nearly to the apex, and the areolation may appear lax and delicate. The known range is the Pacific coastal region and eastward to northern Idaho. Many coastal species appear also in southwestern Utah and this fact supports the conclusion that the present plant is an underdeveloped form resulting from dry climate.

10.281   **7. Tortula bistratosa** Flow. Plants small to medium sized, dark green to brownish green, often tinged with red or becoming reddish throughout with age. Stems 0.5–2.5 cm tall, densely to loosely tufted or gregarious. Leaves mostly 1.5–2 mm long, imbricated, infolded and incurved at the apex when dry, patent to recurved when moist, not squarrose, ovate-ligulate to oblong-ligulate, broadly to rather narrowly obtuse, strongly canaliculate, the upper ½ or ⅓ longitudinally incurved-recurved so as to appear narrowed, sigmoid on either side in cross section; margins narrowly revolute nearly or quite to the apex; costa stout, prominent at the back, nearly smooth to strongly roughened at the back above with simple or forked papillae, these often exceedingly large at the apex where some of them may be very tall and toothed on the sides, excurrent to a hyaline hair point, shorter than to slightly exceeding the length of the lamina, moderately serrate-toothed to nearly smooth; lamina bistratose in the upper third and in lines toward the base (in some leaves 3-stratose here and there), often with a unistratose border above, 1–6 cells wide, the base unistratose; upper cells mostly 9–12 μ wide, moderately thick walled, densely papillose with low to moderately high, simple or bifurcate papillae, chlorophyllose and often obscure; basal cells becoming elongated and wider, thin walled, smooth, and hyaline, the hyaline area often extending high up in the leaf and abruptly delimited. Dioicous. Seta 7–14 mm long, reddish to dark reddish brown; capsules cylindric, 2–2.5 mm long, yellowish brown, becoming dark reddish; exothecial cells oblong-linear, thick walled; stomata large, superficial, few, in 1 row in the lower neck region; annulus double or triple; peristome tube pale yellowish, obliquely tessellated, teeth strongly twisted, orange to reddish, densely papillose; operculum narrowly elongated-conic, often slightly bent, usually quite thick, apex blunt. 1.5–2 mm long. Spores 10–13.5 μ, $\pm$ globose, light brown to yellowish, smooth. Calyptra cucullate, covering the whole capsule or only the upper half. Plate 35.

10.282   On dry, often saline soil, in lowland regions, common deserts.

10.283   Washington, Oregon, southern Idaho, Wyoming, Colorado, Nevada, Arizona, and New Mexico.

10.284   This plant has the appearance of an undersized *T. ruralis* with leaves more erect to spreading and in the dry state longitudinally infolded and incurved at the apex and not crisped or twisted. When flattened out the leaves are ovate-ligulate to oblong-ligulate, but in the natural state the upper half appears variably narrowed owing to a strong longitudinal reverse curve on either side (appearing sigmoid on either side of the costa in cross section). Usually the lamina is bistratose to the margin in the upper third of the leaf, although it may sometimes include half the length of the leaf. Nearly all leaves have a unistratose border variable in extent from a rather wide triangular wedge extending diagonally upward from the costa to the margin, to a gradually narrowing border extending well up toward the apex. It is not uncommon to find leaf sections showing a partially 3-stratose condition. (In one case a section taken from a point high up toward the apex of the leaf was 3-stratose practically throughout and even 4-stratose here and there.)

10.285   **8. Tortula norvegica** (Web.) Wahlenb. Plants typically montane to alpine, in deep loose tufts, dark green, tinged with red above, usually reddish throughout below. Stems 1–10 cm tall; central strand lacking. Leaves erect, $\pm$ appressed and infolded, and often twisted when dry, squarrose-recurved when moist, concave, the lower leaves often erect; oblong-spatulate to oblong-ligulate (in some forms ovate-lanceolate to lanceolate), obtuse to narrowly acute; margins revolute below, plane in upper $\frac{1}{3}$; costa stout, red, excurrent to a moderately spinulose to nearly

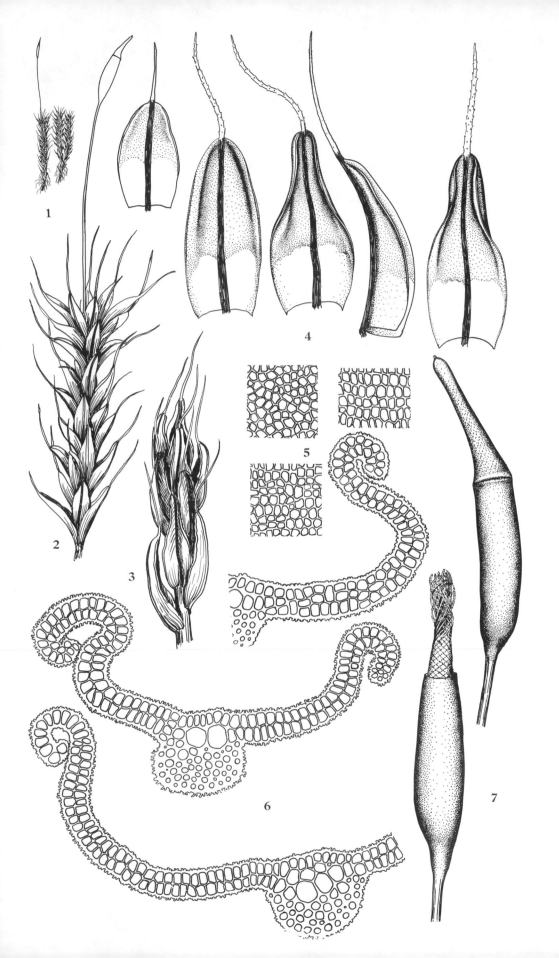

smooth, red hair point, often broad and decurrent at the base; upper cells often thin walled and angular, 10–14 μ (or sometimes 17–28 μ), dark green, often opaque, coarsely verrucose-papillose, sometimes stellate-papillose; basal cells oblong hyaline, smooth and wider, with green or reddish short marginal cells. Dioicous. Seta 1–2 cm long; capsule 1–3 mm long; lid very narrowly conic; annulus of 1–3 rows of cells; peristome tube high, pale yellowish to dusty orange-red, tessellate, the teeth twisted in 1.5 turns or more. Spores 10–15 μ, smooth or very finely punctate. Plate 36, figs. 1–7.

10.286   Montane and alpine, on soil or in crevices of rocks.

10.287   Greenland to Alaska southward in the Rocky Mountains to New Mexico and Arizona. Europe, North Africa.

10.288   This is typically a montane to alpine moss intergrading somewhat with *T. ruralis.* It has been suggested that *T. norvegica* is merely an alpine form of *T. ruralis,* but I commonly find them growing close together under similar habitat conditions, even on the same rock, each one maintaining its typical characteristics. Ordinarily *T. ruralis* prefers the open, more sunny places and while primarily a lowland plant common on deserts, it extends upward to high peaks of 11,000 ft. elevation or more. *Tortula norvegica* appears in shaded canyons as low as 4,000 ft. in our region and is extremely common in woods and on shaded rocks between 5,000 and 10,000 ft. It is exceedingly variable and intergrades with *T. ruraliformis* with which it shares the same type of habitat and altitudinal range.

10.289   There are several forms worthy of comment since they deviate widely from the typical form. Notable among these are forms having unusually large thin-walled upper leaf cells, the sizes ranging from 14–18 μ up to 21-27 μ in longest diameter. In most instances, plants of this sort are pale to dark green and tend to shrivel more strongly when dry. Many of them grow in tufts and mats of other mosses like *Eurhynchium pulchellum, Brachythecium collinum,* and *Homalothecium nevadense.* The range of leaf shape is also wide. Some plants have very short oblong-ovoid leaves, quite flat and suddenly long piliferous. Similar forms have very short hair points, often nearly smooth, with some leaves muticous, the costa ceasing far below the apex. At the other extreme are forms with leaves ranging from ovate-lanceolate to lanceolate, the apex often narrowly acute and merging with the wide basal wings of the excurrent costa. Such forms are scarcely to be distinguished from *T. ruraliformis* except for the red hair points. Among these variable forms is a curious condition where the costa is interrupted near the leaf apex by a mass of thin-walled chlorophyllous tissue, three to eight cells thick, beyond which the costa resumes its form at the apex and continues as

Plate 35. 1–4 **Tortula bistratosa.** 1. Habit sketches, X.4. 2. Moist habit. 3. Dry habit, X2. 4. Typical leaves, X8. 5. Upper medial leaf cells from three different leaves (papillae omitted). 6. Cross sections from upper portions of leaves showing variations in the bistratose condition, X80.

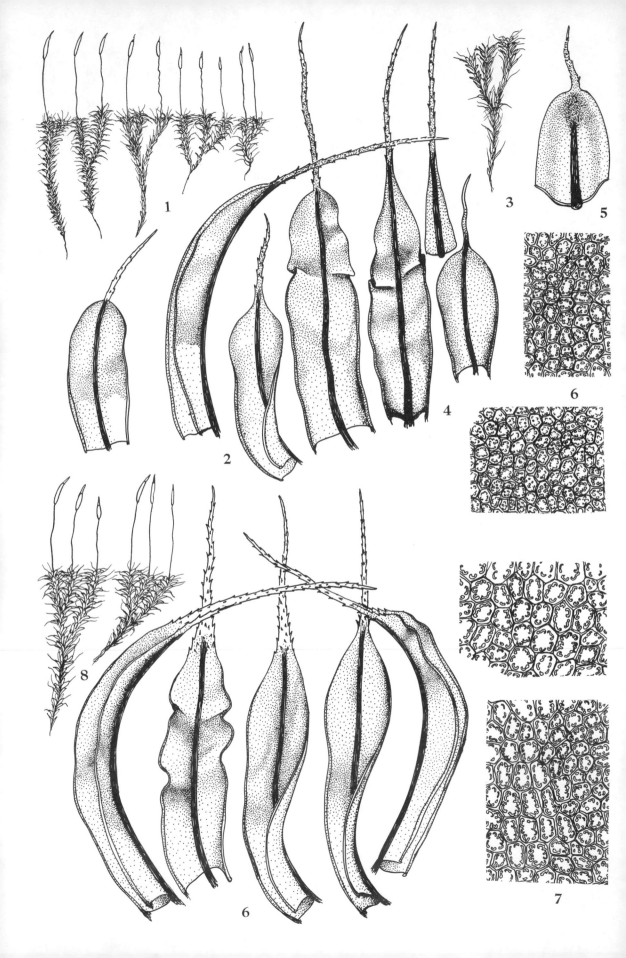

1 2 3 4 5 6 7 8 6

a long or short hair point. In some plants this circumstance predominates; in others it is less common.

10.290   I have gathered a curious form from shaded crevices under a sandstone ledge in Red Canyon of the Green River in Daggett County at 5,600 ft. The costa terminates in a thick, blunt, green point, sometimes forming a rather long, green, smooth hair. Many of the leaves are muticous or merely bluntly pointed.

10.291   In addition to these variations we may find tufts having all of the leaves standing more or less erect or evenly spreading, not at all squarrose-recurved as in the typical form. This feature might be attributed to habitat conditions, but I have one tuft of moss with both types of habit: half the tuft is typical in form with strongly recurved leaves, small firm leaf cells and a continuous costa, while the other half has erect leaves, thin-walled cells and an interrupted costa. In the former the leaves were infolded and appressed when dry, and in the latter they were strongly twisted and often spirally contorted. In a number of these forms the moist leaves are only slightly concave and lie almost perfectly flat on a slide.

10.292   Attempts to erect varietal names for these forms would prove futile since they are linked together by a maze of intergrading characters. The above description has been broadened to include some of these variations, but the remainder will have to be found by referring to these notes.

10.293   **9. Tortula papillosissima** (Copp.) Broth. Plants with the facies of a large *T. ruralis*, densely to loosely tufted, gray green above, yellowish brown below when dry, up to 6 cm tall. Stems lacking a central strand. Leaves loosely to closely appressed, infolded and imbricated or somewhat spirally twisted when dry, strongly squarrose-recurved when moist, 5–6 mm long, the hair points excluded, canaliculate, $\pm$ narrowed toward the apex, widely obtuse to slightly retuse, occasionally with the hair point slightly decurrent; margins revolute from the base to near the apex; costa very stout, prominent and reddish at the back, beset with high cylindrical or apically branched papillae, excurrent to a strongly spinulose hyaline hair point, 3–4 mm long; upper cells with walls moderately thick, 14–17(22) μ, with 1 (rarely 2) large, hollow, conical or cylindrical salients on each side, these equalling the thickness of the main body of the cells in height, each crowned at the apex with a compound, 2- to 4-furcate papilla, usually with each branch again bifurcate, the whole structure resembling pedicellate antlers, becoming shorter on

Plate 36. 1–7. **Tortula norvegica.** 1. Habit sketches, X.4. 2. Typical leaves, X8. 3. Habit sketch of slender lax form, X.4. 4. Two leaves from an extreme form having narrow apices. 5. Apex of leaf of unusual form with costa ending below the apex and with a mass of laminar cells, 2–4 cells thick, occupying the medial apical region, X8. 6. Upper medial leaf cells from two different plants showing average variations in size, shape, and papillation. 7. Upper medial leaf cells of larger dimensions from two unusual forms, X120. **Note:** Intergrades are common.

8–9. Tortula ruraliformis. 8. Habit sketches, X.4. 9. Typical leaves, X8.

the marginal cells and toward the leaf base, mostly O-shaped, but sometimes C-shaped in surface view; basal cells ± abruptly larger and longer, smooth, hyaline, and thin walled. Dioicous. Seta 1.4–2.2 cm long; capsule 3.5–5.5 mm long without the lid, becoming dark reddish brown to chocolate brown with age; lid narrowly conic, 1.4–2.2 mm long; calyptra about 5 mm long. Spores yellowish green to yellowish brown, 12–15 μ, finely granular. Plate 38.

10.294   In crevices of limestone rocks, on soil, and occasionally on the bases and exposed roots of trees, usually in mountainous regions at elevations of 3,600 to 7,600 ft.

10.295   Washington to Nevada, southern Idaho, Montana, Colorado, New Mexico, Arizona. Europe.

10.296   The most distinctive feature of this moss is the single, large, high, O-shaped papilla located centrally over each cell and crowned with antler-like branches at the summit. The stems of the papillae are hollow and in cross sections of the leaves the papillae are often as tall as the width of the main body of the cells.

10.297   **10. Tortula ruralis** (Hedw.) Gaertn., Meyer & Scherb. Plants densely to loosely tufted, sometimes forming wide loose mats, typically green, tinged with red when moist, dark olivaceous, reddish or almost black when dry. Stems 0.5–12 cm long, epidermal cells thin walled, usually collapsing, subtended by 1–3 layers of small thick-walled cells; cortical cells large, thin walled; central strand lacking. Leaves oblong to ligulate, sometimes spatulate, mostly 2–4 mm long (excluding the awn), canaliculate, broadly rounded to slightly narrowed toward the apex, obtuse to truncate or slightly emarginate, loosely appressed to imbricated, longitudinally infolded, often slightly plicate and slightly twisted when dry, typically strongly squarrose-recurved from a subclasping base when moist; margins revolute for 4/5 the length of the leaf or to the apex; costa stout, reddish, usually roughened on the back above the papillae, these varying from low convex forms to coarse, simple, bifurcate or stellately branched forms, rarely nearly smooth, abruptly excurrent as a long, hyaline, spinulose awn about ½–¾ the length of the leaf blade, occasionally shorter, frequently tinted at the base; upper cells densely chlorophyllose, often opaque, 12–16 μ, moderately thick walled, low-convex to low-conical and bearing 2–12 papillae which are typically coarse, simple, C- or O-shaped, but in some forms bifurcate or stellately branched, either solid, or, in extremely coarse forms, hollow; basal marginal cells small, usually green or reddish, forming a border; basal medial cells abruptly hyaline, larger, longer, and thin walled. Dioicous.

Plate 37.   Tortula ruralis. 1. Habit sketches, X.4. 2. Portion of shoot showing typical dry habit, X3.2. 3–4. Typical leaves, X8. 5. Three cross sections of costa at different levels. 6. Cross sections of upper lamina from three different leaves, showing variations in papillae. 7. Upper medial leaf cells from three different plants showing variations in shape, size, and papillation, X120. 8. Capsules. 9. Leaves of a small form frequent in deserts, X8.

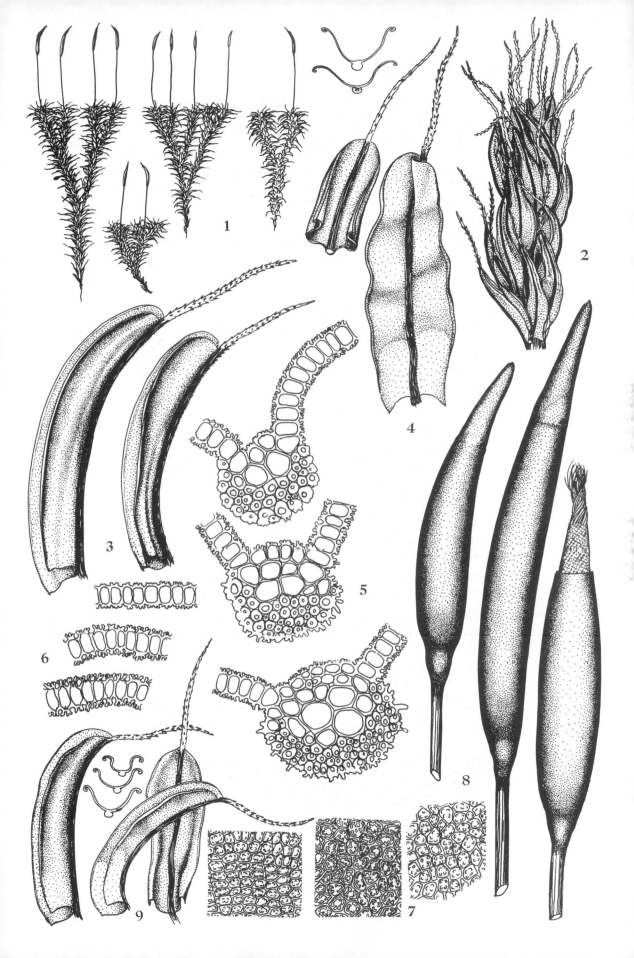

Seta 1–3 cm long, reddish; capsule oblong-cylindric to long cylindric, mostly 3–5 mm long without the lid, reddish to reddish brown, often dark brown when old; lid narrowly conic about half the length of the urn, cells disposed in spiral rows; annulus of 1–3 rows of smaller thick-walled cells, long persistent; peristome tube high and obliquely tessellated, frosty pink or peach colored; teeth about as long as the tube, twisted in 2 full turns, reddish and very densely papillose. Spores 10–14 μ, finely granular. Calyptra cucullate. Plate 37.

10.298   On soil, rocks, and bases of trees, in damp shady places to very dry exposed situations, from lowlands to the highest mountains.

10.299   Widely distributed throughout the United States and Canada, extending well into Mexico. Eurasia, North and South Africa, southern South America and Australia.

10.300   This is the most common moss in Utah. Westward, it is abundant in the Great Basin, except in western Nevada where it has not yet been reported. It is apparently replaced in California by *T. princeps*. To the northwest it extends to the east slopes of the Cascade Mountains of British Columbia. In Utah it ranges from the lowland to the highest mountain peaks.

10.301   **11. Tortula ruraliformis** (Besch.) Ingh. Plants in loose or dense tufts resembling *T. ruralis*, erect to ascending, yellowish to reddish brown below, green and often tinged with red above. Leaves appressed and usually ± infolded to spirally twisted when dry, squarrose-recurved when moist, ovate-lanceolate to oblong, canaliculate, apex usually tapering, acute to somewhat acuminate, gradually passing into the broad base of the hair point which may be hyaline throughout or reddish and strongly spinulose-dentate; upper cells 10–16 μ, each cell bearing 4–6 C-shaped or O-shaped papillae, these low and simple or tall and coarse, sometimes stellately branched; basal cells abruptly hyaline, smooth, more elongated. Dioicous. Sporophyte as in *T. ruralis*. Plate 36, figs. 8–9.

10.302   On dry or moist rock and soil, often in crevices or under exposed roots of trees, mostly in shaded places at middle elevation in the mountains.

10.303   Locally common. Montana and adjacent Canada southward to Colorado and westward to British Columbia and California. Southwest Asia and North Africa.

10.304   The general appearance of this plant is much like that of *T. ruralis* but it is less common. The most distinctive feature is the more narrowly tapered apex of the leaf, hyaline and toothed at the tip and merging with the broad base of the spinulose excurrent costa. Most forms are quite easily distinguished from *T. ruralis*, although forms are commonly

---

Plate 38. Tortula papillosissima. 1. Habit sketches, X.4. 2–3. Capsules. 4. Typical leaves, X8. 5. Upper medial leaf cells showing single large papillae branched at the apex, X120. 6. Cross sections of leaf at three levels, X24. 7–8. Cross sections of upper and lower leaf cells. 9. Cross section of portion of costa showing details of ventral cells, X120.

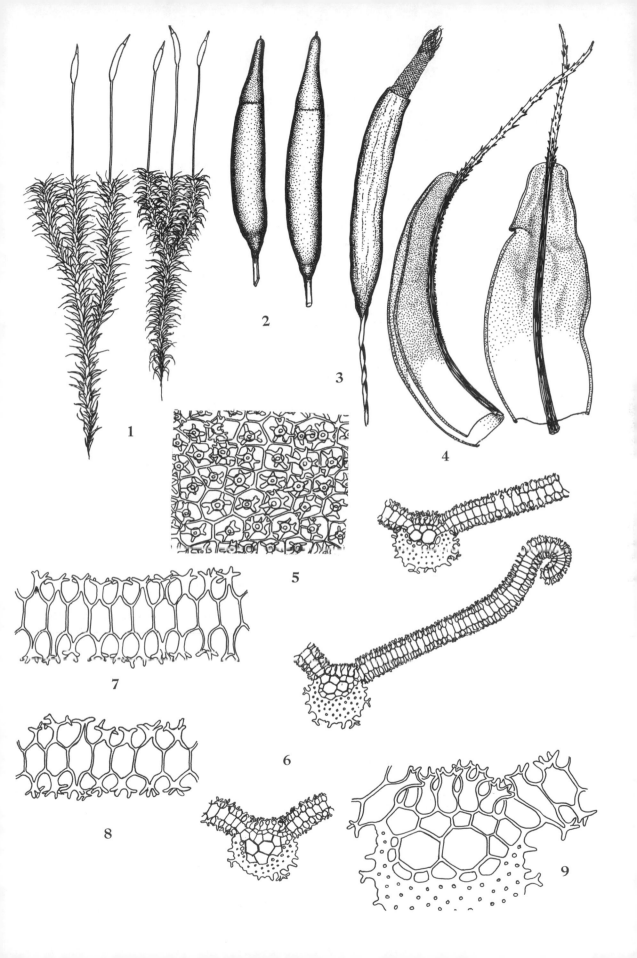

encountered where the apices of the leaves are broad, making an abrupt junction to the broad splayed-out base of the costa.

10.305   *Tortula norvegica* also has a form in which acute leaves gradually merge with the broad base of the costa. It is distinguished by plane leaves in the upper ½ or ⅔, often thinner walled and slightly larger leaf cells; red costa and lower portion of the shoots. It is more mesophytic, occurring mainly in shaded places in high mountains.

18. SCOPELOPHILA (Mitt.) Lindb.

10.306   Plants small to rather large, in tufts, mostly on wet rocks. Stems erect, branching monopodially or by subfloral innovations, central strand lacking; rhizoids mainly on the lower portion, few to dense, reddish and smooth, often bearing linear to globose multicellular brood bodies. Leaves variable, oblong to broadly ligulate or spatulate, mostly obtuse but varying to acute or shortly mucronate, ± flattish above, keeled below; margins entire, plane above, revolute below, usually bordered with thick-walled cells, these often yellowish or orange colored; costa ending shortly below the apex with a single stereid band; upper cells ± isodiametric to shortly rectangular, wider near the costa, fairly thick walled, smooth or finely papillose, becoming oblong, wider, thin walled to inflated and darker colored toward the base. Dioicous. Perigonium budlike, terminal, becoming lateral because of innovation. Perichaetium terminal, often becoming lateral because of innovation. Seta erect, less than 1 cm long; capsules erect and symmetric, shortly oblong to subcylindrical, urn 0.8–1.9 mm long, the neck short, sometimes not externally differentiated; peristome lacking, annulus double to multiple; lid conic with a short to long, inclined beak. Calyptra cucullate.

10.307   The name is derived from Greek and means rock loving.

10.308   **Scopelophila latifolia** (Kindb.) Ren. & Card. Plants variable in stature, medium sized to rather large, dark green, often tinged with red, reddish brown below. Stems 1.5–5 cm tall, the base often ragged with eroded leaves or naked with persistent costae; in cross section with a central area of large, thin-walled, angular cells with the outer 2–4 rows smaller, slightly or not at all thicker walled but usually darker colored. Occasionally bearing multicellular, globose to clavate gemmae on the rhizoids. Leaves crisped to curled or not much changed when dry, open to spreading when moist, the comal ones forming a rosette, the lower ones loosely erect, broadly spatulate to ligulate, a few obovate to oblong, 3–6 mm long, 1.5–3 mm wide, green, often with a conspicuous orange red border; apex broad, often rounded, terminating in an acute or bluntly acute tip, sometimes mucronate or shortly acuminate; lamina flattish to widely concave above, becoming narrowed and ± keeled toward the base; margins plane near the apex, becoming gradually recurved and finally strongly revolute toward the base on 1 or both sides; up to 170 μ wide at the base, prominent at back, smooth to finely papillose, percurrent or ending several cells below the tip, yellowish to reddish orange according to age; upper cells quadrate, rounded, shortly rectangular to hexagonal, 14–26 μ wide and up to 38 μ long, usually finely papillose above, up to 12 papillae per cell but often nearly smooth, walls thin, becoming thick and reddish with age; 3–7 marginal rows enlarged, especially dorsoventrally, with much thicker colored walls, sometimes bistratose here and there, the extreme marginal row very much smaller, 6–8 μ wide (lamina in cross section clavate at the margins); basal medial cells larger, oblong, 18–30 μ wide and up to 95 μ long, thin walled and often inflated; marginal ones narrower, linear, thick walled, and often colored. Fruit rare. Plate 39.

10.309 Mostly on damp or wet calcareous rocks, sometimes submerged in swift currents, occasionally on soil, brook banks, waterfalls, cement installations, and wooden water troughs.

10.310 British Columbia to Montana, southward to southern California, Black Hills of South Dakota, Colorado, Utah, and Arizona.

10.311 This rare moss is locally abundant. It varies widely in size, the larger forms generally having proportionately broader leaves. Plants growing on damp substrata where they are likely to dry out occasionally may be more highly tinted with orange or red than those growing in the spray of streams and waterfalls. Those submerged seldom show leaves with a colored margin, although most of them have a border of thicker-walled cells, and the lamina appears clavate in cross section. A few perichaetia with archegonia have been found among various specimens, both local and from other states, but I have not seen thus far perigonial plants. Schofield has found the moss with fruit in British Columbia, the capsules being cylindrical with a fragile peristome of 16 irregularly divided teeth, and he has in fact erected a new genus, *Crumia*, for this species, because of the presence of a peristome, among other reasons.

ENCALYPTACEAE

11.1 Plants tufted, 0.5–5 cm high. Stems branched, radiculose and reddish or brownish below; central strand mostly lacking. Brood bodies present in many plants, mostly oblong to filamentous, multiseptate, reddish brown, borne in the axils or on the bases of the leaves. Leaves crisped or not greatly changed when dry, patent to spreading when moist, ligulate to spatulate, the apex broadly rounded to subacuminate, obtuse, mucronate or hair-pointed, lamina ± concave, often cucullate; margins entire or erose-dentate because of projecting papillae, plane or revolute; costa extending to the apex or nearly so; upper cells ± isodiametric, quadrate, hexagonal or irregular, somewhat incrassate, 8–30 μ in diameter; papillae simple, forked or lunate, often full and hollow; basal cells becoming larger and oblong, up to 90 μ long, the longitudinal walls usually thin, the end walls often thickened, usually reddish, mostly smooth but frequently with projecting end walls, a few forms with strongly papillose basal cells; basal marginal cells linear, thick walled, paler in color. Perichaetial leaves not much differentiated. Setae 0.5–3 cm long, twisted when dry; capsules cylindric, 2.5–5 mm long, smooth or furrowed when dry, neck short, composed of enlarged cells, mouth

217

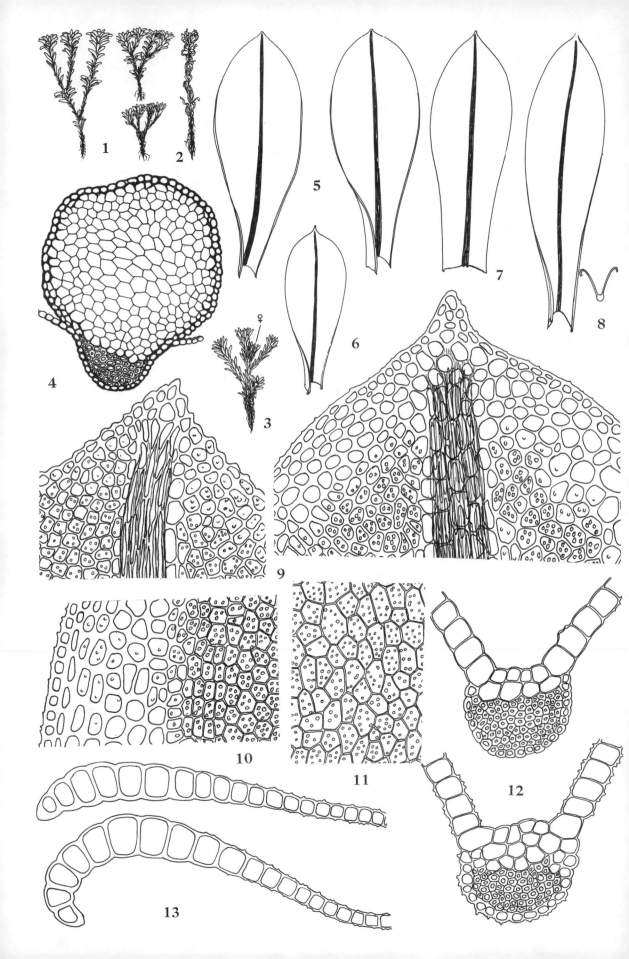

bordered by 2–many rows of colored, shorter and thick-walled cells; lid conic or convex, long beaked; annulus single, double, or triple; peristome lacking, simple, or double, teeth 16, lanceolate to linear; endostome, when present, forming a pale basal membrane adherent to the teeth; segments narrow, often split into linear divisions, adhering or free. Spores round or reniform, smooth, wrinkled, papillose, or warty. Calyptra completely covering the capsule, cylindric with a short or long beak, yellowish, smooth or scabrous, basal margin erose, lacerate, or fringed.

11.2   A small family forming a transition between the Haplolepideae and Diplolepideae. It is essentially northern and montane.

ENCALYPTA Hedw.

11.3   With characteristics of the family.

11.4   Plants on rock crevices and soil in both wet and very dry situations, mostly preferring an alkaline or lime-bearing substrate, and ranging from sea level to the highest mountain peaks. The habitat and varying climatic conditions influence the habit and stature of the plants. In dry situations the tufts are denser and shorter, the leaves more closely disposed and shorter with a tendency to become either very bluntly pointed or rounded or longer hair-pointed than usual; the setae are shorter, the capsule has a tendency to furrow more strongly and the calyptra becomes more strongly papillose or scabrous. Brood bodies have been observed in nearly every species, especially sterile plants of rather moist habitats.

11.5   The gametophyte shows a strong relationship to Pottiaceae and to a somewhat less degree to Orthotrichaceae. The broad leaves with strong costae and hair points, short cells, papillae, and general habit characteristics are much like those of the Tortulaceae.

11.6   The name, from the Greek, means to cover with a veil, alluding to the large calyptra.

11.7   1. Calyptra fringed at the base with conspicuous hyaline segments, the cells of which are large and oblong, abruptly differentiated and small and quadrate at the base; peristome present; spores smooth to irregularly wrinkled when mature .... 1. *E. ciliata*   11.9

11.8   1. Calyptra not fringed, at most erose or slightly incised at the base; spores coarsely papillose, reddish brown

2. Leaves obtuse to broadly rounded at the apex; peristome lacking; common in dry places .... 2b. *E. vulgaris* var. *mutica*   11.18

Plate 39.   Scopelophila latifolia. 1. Habit sketches, X.4. 2. Dry habit, X.8. 3. Archegonial plants, X.4. 4. Cross section of stem, X70. 5–8. Leaves from four different plants, X4.8. 9. Two leaf apices. 10. Leaf border and upper medial cells. 11. Lower medial cells. 12. Cross sections of costa. 13. Cross sections of leaf margins, X120.

2. Leaves mucronate to hair-pointed from a broadly rounded to narrowly tapered apex; less common in more mesic places

   3. Spores mostly 26-40 μ with coarse, distinct papillae 3–5 μ across; peristome lacking; calyptra usually papillose or scabrous to the base .... 2a. *E. vulgaris* var. *apiculata*   11.16

   3. Spores mostly 30–55 μ with large warty impinging papillae, 6–9 μ across; peristome present (often fragile or lacking in our plants); usually only the beak of the calyptra papillose .... 3. *E. rhabdocarpa*   11.23

11.9   **1. Encalypta ciliata** Hedw. Plants in dense tufts up to 4 cm high, brown and radiculose below, bright green above. Leaves oblong-ovate to ligulate, 2.5–5 mm long, apex abruptly contracted to a short point from a rather broad upper lamina or tapering to a longer point; margins plane or incurved, concave, often revolute at the base; costa stout, shortly excurrent or ending below the apex, reddish, prominent at the back, papillose; upper cells 10–17 μ in diameter, moderately papillose with simple, forked, or lunate papillae, 2–6 to a cell, chlorophyllose, sometimes clear; leaf base usually concave and subclasping, often abruptly narrowed below the upper portion of the lamina, cells hyaline or colored, 14–22 μ wide and up to 70 μ long, marginal cells linear, thicker walled and often paler, papillae lacking. Autoicous. Seta about 1 cm long; capsule yellowish or brown, 2–3 mm long, urn smooth or minutely rugulose when dry, base sometimes twisted; lid conic, long-beaked, 1–1.5 mm long; stomata large, on the lower half; peristome simple, teeth reddish, lanceolate, 0.32–0.42 mm long, arising deeply within the mouth, 6–9 jointed, finely longitudinally striate with coarser simple papillae here and there, occasionally densely and finely papillose; annulus single, large, mouth of capsule bordered by 2–5 rows of red, quadrate, thick-walled cells. Spores smooth but wrinkled-reticulate on the inner surface, 31–36 μ. Calyptra 4–6 mm long, yellowish, smooth or somewhat roughened above, base fringed and lacerated, the fringe somewhat spreading and composed of abruptly enlarged, oblong, hyaline cells bordering 1–7 rows of smaller quadrate cells forming the basal margin of the calyptra proper. Plate 40, figs. 1–5.

11.10   This is one of the most common species in the northern United States and Canada, Europe, and Asia. Rare in Utah. Summit County: Uinta Mountains near falls of the Upper Provo River, ca. 9,000 ft., Henry's Fork, ca. 9,200 ft.

11.11   It is not likely to be confused with anything else. The smooth capsule and single peristome aid in field identification.

Plate 40.   **1–5. Encalypta ciliata.** 1. Habit sketches, X.4. 2. Two typical leaves. 3. Capsules and calyptra, X8. Portion of peristome, X60. **Note:** Teeth range from smooth to fairly coarsely papillose. 5. Spores, X120.

6–10. Hyophila involuta. 6. Habit sketches. X.4. 7. Leaves, X8. 8. Two leaf apices showing upper cells. 9. Basal cells. 10. Cross sections of costa at two levels, X120. 11. Cross section of stem, X60.

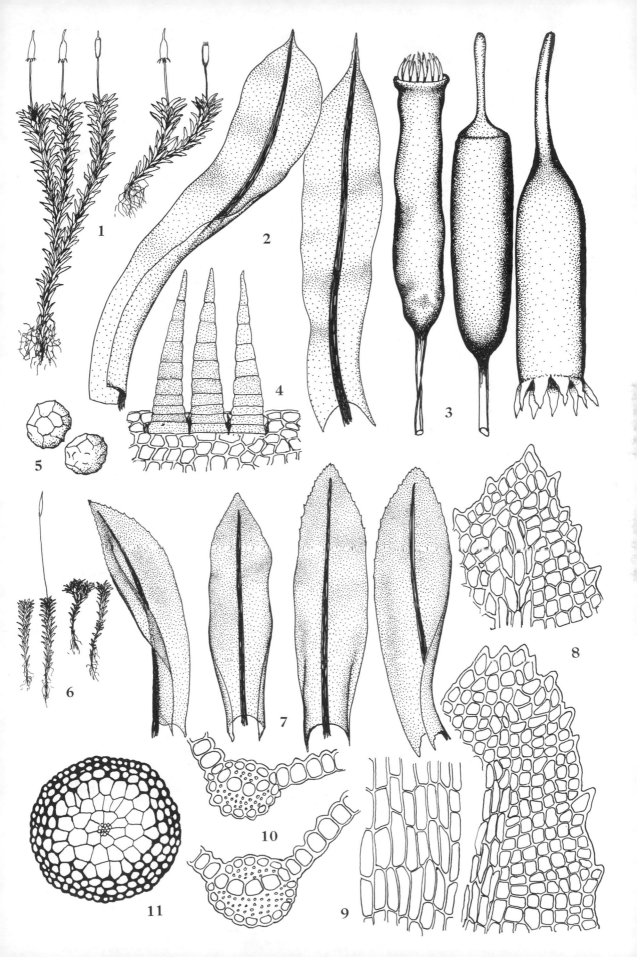

11.12   **2. Encalypta vulgaris** Hedw. var. **vulgaris.** Plants in dense tufts. Stems 0.5–2 cm high, branched, radiculose below, brownish or reddish in the lower portion, green at the tips. Leaves not or only slightly crisped when dry, open to recurved when moist, oblong-ligulate to spatulate, apex acute, mucronate or shortly piliferous, lamina flat, incurved or cucullate; costa stout, prominent at the back, mostly strongly papillose but often smooth, especially above, ending below the apex, percurrent or extending into a short hair point; margins plane or revolute from the middle downward, erose-dentate by the projecting papillae; upper cells isodiametric to irregularly hexagonal, 12–16 μ in diameter, papillae dense, simple, forked or lunate, C-shaped, 2–6 per cell; basal cells larger, oblong, 14–18 x 20–60 μ, reddish, the end walls usually thickened, basal marginal cells linear, thick walled, forming a paler border, smooth or slightly papillose. Autoicous. Setae 2.5–12 mm long, smooth or slightly twisted when dry, yellowish, becoming reddish with age; capsules cylindric, about 3 mm long and up to 1 mm wide, smooth or minutely wrinkled when dry, often striate and becoming strongly furrowed when old and empty; exothecial cells thin walled or with longitudinal striae of thicker-walled colored cells, mouth bordered by 2–3 rows of quadrate colored cells, neck short, cells larger; stomata uniformly distributed over the surface; lid conic, long beaked, 1–1.5 mm long; annulus single; peristome mostly lacking, when present short and fugacious. Spores reniform or globose, 24–35 μ, with rounded, distinct papillae, 3.2–4.8 μ in diameter. Calyptra cylindric, about 4.5 mm long, beak tapering and rather short or longer and clavate, base pale, slightly ragged, surface variously papillose, often only the beak papillose, smooth below, or the entire calyptra densely scabrous. Plate 41, figs. 1–4.

11.13   In crevices and on soil.

11.14   Europe and Asia. Throughout the Rocky Mountains and westward; less common in the eastern states.

11.15   This species is uncommon in North America. The greatest number of plants referred to this species represent the following easily distinguished varieties.

11.16   2a. Var. **apiculata** Wahlenb. Leaf apices hair-pointed, often very long; costa sometimes extending into the hair point; capsules more constantly ribbed or furrowed. Plate 41, fig. 5.

Plate 41.   1–4. Encalypta vulgaris. 1. Habit sketches, X.4. 2. Leaves. 3. Capsules, X8. 4. Spores, X120.

5. Var. **apiculata.** Leaves, X8.

6–12. Var. mutica. 6. Habit sketches, X.4. 7. Leaves, X8. 8. Upper medial leaf cells. 9. Basal cells (typical of the genus), X120. 10. Dry capsules. 11–12. Calyptrae, X8.

13–16. Encalypta rhabdocarpa. Note: Habit and leaves like **E. vulgaris.** 13. Capsules, X8. 14. Thin fragile peristome teeth of xerophytic plants. 15. Peristome teeth of mesophytic plants from British Columbia showing form of preperistome in dorsal side views, X60. 16. Spores, X120.

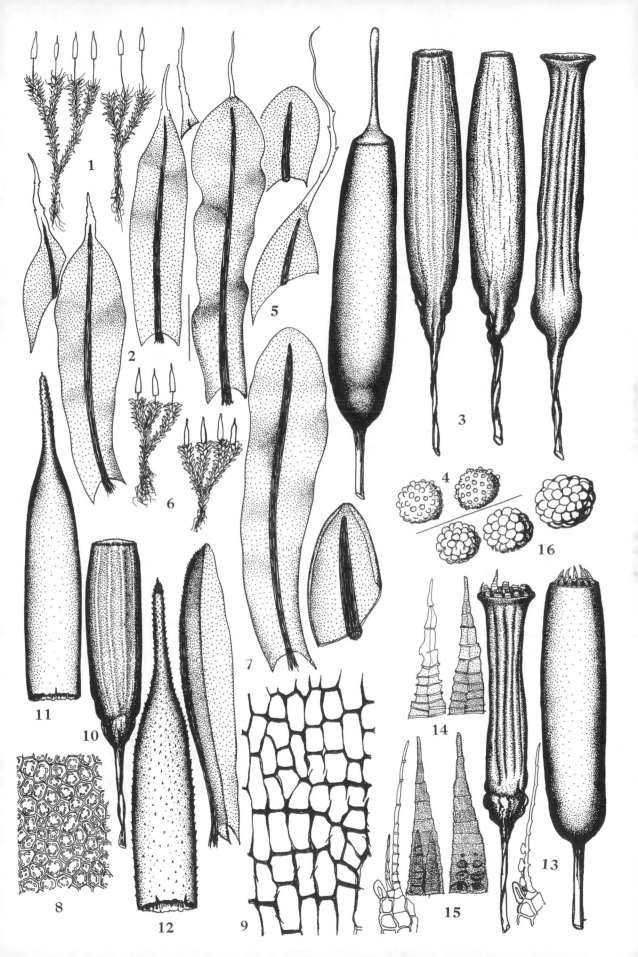

11.17   Throughout central and southern Utah.

11.18   2b. Var. **mutica** Brid. Our most common representative; tufts very dense and compact; leaves obtuse to very broadly rounded; costa ending well below the apex; capsules more constantly ribbed and furrowed when dry; calyptra often very scabrous to the base. Plate 41, figs. 6–12.

11.19   Throughout most of Utah.

11.20   This variety, predominantly a crevice plant, forms large tufts in moist canyons and even grows on the tops of barren windswept peaks above 13,000 ft. elevation. In the low basin ranges and even on the soil in the dry desert regions of the Great Basin it forms short and more compact tufts with the capsules emergent. There are many variations both in stature and structural details, some tending toward the species while several extreme forms are worthy of mention. Some forms from extremely dry desert situations show a very large and broad costa with a boat-shaped lamina. In regions of climatic extremes, the young leaves often show cells that are larger than typical. Where the plants are very limited in growth, all the leaves have the larger cells. This seems to be entirely a habitat effect.

11.21   *Encalypta vulgaris* has often been confused with *E. rhabdocarpa* because in North America these species vary strongly toward one another, and many of their characteristics are not as strongly contrasted as is apparent in European specimens. Most manuals separate the two on the basis of smooth capsules without a peristome in *E. vulgaris,* a furrowed capsule with a peristome in *E. rhabdocarpa.* Relatively few American plants of *E. vulgaris* have smooth or minutely wrinkled capsules, while the great majority have ribbed or furrowed capsules. In both species, plants show capsules that are smooth or nearly so, and parallel forms showing various degrees of furrowing may be traced. Usually the young or mature capsule has reddish or orange colored ribs, and with age it becomes more or less shrunken and strongly furrowed. *Encalypta vulgaris* var. *apiculata* and var. *mutica* nearly always have a ribbed capsule at maturity before the spores are shed. The former parallels *E. rhabdocarpa*, while *E. vulgaris* has a parallel form in *E. rhabdocarpa* var. *subspathulata*. A weak and fugacious peristome is sometimes formed in *E. vulgaris* but it is seldom seen. *E. rhabdocarpa* may be identified in the field if the peristome has not fallen, but in most specimens in various herbaria the peristome had already fallen when collected, and it was difficult to separate them from *E. vulgaris* and its varieties.

11.22   Plants with peristomate capsules, either smooth or furrowed, may be assigned to *E. rhabdocarpa,* and in the absence of the peristome the large warty spores will identify the plant in some cases. Plants may be referred to *E. vulgaris* if the peristome is absent and the spores have smaller distinct papillae. In cases where the capsules are furrowed and the spores and their papillae are of intermediate size, the species identification becomes questionable. Unfortunately a large number of North American plants fall into this uncertain group.

11.23   **3. Encalypta rhabdocarpa** Schwaegr. var. **rhabdocarpa.** Much like the last species, differing in the following respects: generally more mesophytic, dark green, the leaves crisped and often curled when dry, softer and more tender in texture, acute to rather suddenly acuminate, occasionally broadly rounded obtuse, abruptly to gradually mucronate to long hair-pointed. Seta generally longer, 8–10(14) mm long; capsules usually more narrowly cylindric, the urn 2.5–3 mm long, 0.5–1 mm thick, at maturity yellowish with reddish streaks when moist, ribbed, becoming reddish brown and deeply furrowed with age; peristome normally present and usually with an external preperistome free or adherent to the teeth and ranging from fragments 1–2 joints high to as much as half the length of the teeth. (In our plants the peristome is usually lacking or imperfect but occasionally fairly well developed although fragile.) Spores generally larger, when fully mature 34–55 μ in longest diameter, the basal face beset with large warty papillae 6–8 μ in diameter, brown. Calyptra entire or erose at the base, usually smooth with only the beak roughened, but occasionally lightly papillose a varying distance toward the base. Plate 41, figs. 13–16.

11.24   Mostly on rich humus soil, at bases of trees and rocks, or in crevices, usually in shady places.

11.25   In all states and provinces of the Pacific Northwest to California, Nevada, Utah, Colorado and South Dakota.

11.26   *Encalypta rhabdocarpa* and *E. vulgaris* var. *apiculata* intergrade so closely that it is often difficult to separate them, especially when the former has no peristome teeth. Both inhabit situations usually more mesophytic than in the case of *E. vulgaris* and its var. *mutica*. The latter have a wider range of tolerance toward xerophytism and persist in desert hills and upward to near the tops of Utah's highest mountains. In the present species occasional plants with smooth capsules are referred to the following:

11.27   3a. Var. **subspathulata** (C. Muell. & Kindb.) Flow. Plants smaller than the type; leaves piliferous; capsules usually proportionately more slender, mouth often small, smooth to finely longitudinally wrinkled when dry; peristome present, without preperistome, teeth lanceolate, somewhat irregular, finely papillose. Spores 28–40 μ in longest diameter, with large warty papillae 6–8 μ across. Occasional in the range and habitat of the species.

11.28   Salt Lake County: Dutchy Hollow, north of Salt Lake City, 5,100 ft.

GRIMMIACEAE

12.1   Plants dark green to blackish, frequently hoary on the surface, almost entirely confined to rocks, loose spreading to very compactly tufted. Stems erect, ascending or sometimes ± prostrate with erect branches; rhizoids usually confined to the base of the stem, often dense, smooth. Leaves in many rows, usually dense, frequently bearing white hair points; upper cells quadrate, rounded, oval or shortly oblong, 1- to 3-

225

stratose, smooth (or papillose in a few species), thick walled; basal cells undifferentiated to linear, walls smooth to sinuous or nodulose. Dioicous or autoicous. Seta terminal or on a very short lateral branch, straight and erect to variously curved or arcuate; capsules immersed, emergent or long exserted, globose to cylindrical, symmetric to asymmetric; operculum low convex to conic, mammillose to rostrate; peristome single (lacking in a few species), teeth 16, shortly triangular-lanceolate to long and hairlike, entire to variously cleft or divided, often perforated below, nearly smooth to papillose, mostly reddish and strongly barred.

12.2   1. Leaf cells smooth or slightly papillose above in a few species, the walls smooth to moderately sinuous-nodose in some species or in part of the leaf; capsules globose to oblong-cylindric; operculum obtuse to long rostrate; peristome teeth cuneate to lanceolate, entire, irregularly cleft and often cribrose or divided, divisions often slender but never hairlike, lacking in a few species

      2. Plants small to medium sized, on dry or wet rocks; leaves muticous to hyaline-tipped or hair-pointed, without rhizoids at back of the costa; capsules immersed to exserted; operculum free or attached to the columella and falling with it; urn thin walled, nearly smooth to wrinkled when dry, yellowish brown to dark reddish brown ⎯⎯⎯⎯⎯⎯⎯⎯⎯⎯⎯⎯⎯⎯⎯ 1. *Grimmia*   12.4

      2. Plants large and coarse, submerged or on frequently inundated rocks; leaves muticous, usually with a dense tuft of rhizoids on the dorsal side of the costa; capsules immersed, depressed-globose; operculum attached on the stout persistent columella; urn thick walled and fleshy, contracting proximally, smooth when dry, reddish brown, becoming black with age ⎯⎯⎯⎯ 3. *Scouleria*   12.112

12.3   1. Leaf cells strongly papillose throughout (in our species) or smooth, the walls strongly sinuous or nodulose throughout; capsules oblong to cylindric; operculum acicular; peristome teeth divided to the base into almost equal linear to hairlike divisions ⎯⎯⎯⎯⎯⎯
⎯⎯⎯⎯⎯⎯⎯⎯⎯⎯⎯⎯⎯⎯⎯⎯⎯⎯ 2. *Racomitrium*   12.104

GRIMMIA Hedw.

12.4   Plants small, in loose tufts or dense cushions, on rocks, mostly dark green to blackish, frequently white or grayish hoary because of hyaline hair points on the leaves. Stems erect or ascending, usually fastigiately branched, central strand usually present, often indistinct. Leaves strongly hygroscopic, mostly erect and closely imbricated but crisped or spirally twisted in a few species when dry, various when moist, broadly ovate to linear, muticous or ending in a short to long hyaline hair point formed mainly by the lamina; costa mostly strong, percurrent or nearly so, in cross section showing a homogeneous structure or variously developed subventral guides and/or stereids; lower leaves smaller, shorter, and muticous; upper cells rounded quadrate to shortly oval-rectangular, walls thick, sinuous in some species, 1- to 4-stratose, smooth to slightly papillose in some species; basal cells various, Autoicous or dioicous. Perichaetia terminal; archegonia usually few; perigonia small and bud-like, terminal but soon becoming lateral by innovation; inner perigonial leaves small and short, muticous, the base broad and clasping; antheridia and paraphyses relatively few. Perichaetial leaves larger and longer hair-pointed than the stem leaves, the basal cells commonly hyaline and often thin walled. Seta terminal on the main stems or branches, short, straight or curved, twisted to the left when dry; capsules globose-ovoid to cylindrical, mostly symmetric, neck not differentiated; peristome of 16 teeth (lacking in *G. anodon*), entire to variously perforated, cleft or divided.

12.5 The genus honors Johann Friedrich Karl Grimm, a physician and amateur botanist of Gotha.

Key to the Species Based Mainly on Fruiting Plants.

12.6 1. Columella attached to the lid and falling with it; capsules immersed, longer than the straight seta, symmetric; calyptra small, covering only the lid; autoicous (Schistidium)

   2. Leaves without white hair points, the comal and perichaetial ones occasionally hyaline-tipped with 1–several cells

      3. Leaves elongate-oblong to linear-lanceolate, flattish, margins plane; costa brown; growing in or near water in high mountains .... 1. *G. agassizii*   12.10

      3. Leaves ovate to ovate-lanceolate, keeled; costa the same color as the lamina

         4. Plants mostly less than 1 cm tall, growing on dry rocks; stem leaves up to 1.3 mm long, obtuse

            5. Stem leaves 0.5–0.7 mm long; seta 0.1–0.3 mm long; capsules ovoid-globose to shortly ovoid, 0.4–0.7 mm long ...... 2. *G. atricha*   12.14

            5. Stem leaves 1–1.3 mm long; seta 0.2–0.6 mm long; capsules ovoid to ovoid-oblong, 0.8–1.5 mm long .... 3. *G. dupretii*   12.18

         4. Plants larger; leaves 1.5–3(5) mm long

            6. Leaf apices not prolonged into a thickish brownish green hair point; leaf margins revolute

               7. Leaves ovate-lanceolate to oblong-lanceolate

                  8. Leaf margins entire; on dry rocks .... 4. *G. alpicola*   12.22

                  8. Leaf margins repand-dentate or irregularly notched above; submerged or on wet rocks .... 4a. var. *rivularis*   12.26

227

7. Leaves ovate to broadly ovate-lanceolate, margins entire; submerged or on wet rocks .... 4b. var. *latifolia* 12.29

6. Leaf apices commonly prolonged to a thickish, blunt, brownish green hair point of variable length up to 1.8 mm long; margins mostly plane, bistratose; leaves of sterile shoots ovate-lanceolate to linear-lanceolate, 2.5–5 mm long, incurved, recurved, or falcate .... 5. *G. cinclidodontea* 12.31

2. Leaves with hyaline hair points, at least on the comal and perichaetial ones, the lower leaves often muticous; bistratose on the margins; autoicous

9. Hair points mostly short, not exceeding ⅓ the length of the blade; lamina ± 2-stratose above; capsules shortly elliptical; calyptra mitrate

10. Upper stem leaves 1.5–2 mm long; upper cells 7–10 μ wide; plants dark green to blackish green; capsules mostly ellipsoid .... 6. *G. apocarpa* 12.35

10. Upper stem leaves 0.7–1 mm long; upper cells 5–7 μ wide; capsules subglobose to ovoid; plants usually grayish green .... 6a. var. *conferta* 12.39

9. Hair point reaching ½ the length of the blades; margins plane or slightly recurved; lamina mostly 1-stratose; capsules mostly oblong; teeth entire or only slightly cleft; calyptra cucullate or mitrate; plants grayish green to bright green .... 6b. var. *ambigua* 12.42

12.7 1. Columella free from the lid and persistent within the urn; leaves hair-pointed, at least in some of the plants

11. Calyptra campanulate, yellowish, plicate, covering ½ or more of the urn, cucullate or becoming mitrate; walls of the basal cells of the leaves not sinuous (Coscinodon)

12. Leaves ovate to obovate or shortly spatulate, rounded at the back, scarcely keeled, 1-stratose; margins plane throughout; capsules immersed, oblong, truncate at the base, longer than the seta; plants medium sized; autoicous .... 7. *G. rauii* 12.46

12. Leaves oblong-lanceolate to lanceolate, keeled above, 1- to 2-stratose above; margins plane or recurved on 1 side; capsules exserted, oblong-elliptic to subcylindric, shorter than the seta; plants rather large, often hoary; dioicous .... 8. *G. calyptrata* 12.52

11. Calyptra smaller, smooth, scarcely covering more than the lid or reaching nearly to the middle of the urn, tall conic to ± rostrate from a dilated base. (Eugrimmia)

13. Capsules asymmetric, ventricose at the base, immersed; seta very

short, curved or sigmoid; calyptra mitrate; leaf margins plane; walls of the basal cells not sinuous

14. Capsules subglobose, peristome lacking .... 9. *G. anodon*   12.56

14. Capsules mostly ovoid, peristome present .... 10. *G. plagiopodia*   12.61

13. Capsules symmetric, exserted, or emergent

15. Seta erect and straight when moist; leaves 2-stratose in the upper part

16. Walls of the basal cells not sinuous

17. Leaves rounded at the back; margins plane, erect to slightly incurved; costa flat, not prominent at the back; dioicous

18. Inner basal leaf cells quadrate to shortly oblong, mostly 1:1–1.5; leaves rather broad at the apices, patent to stiffly spreading, base not differentiated, 1–1.5 mm long; calyptra small, mitrate, barely reaching below the lid .... 11. *G. laevigata*   12.65

18. Inner basal cells oblong to linear; leaves narrower at the apices, gradually tapering into the hair point, ± squarrose from an ovate or oblong base, 2–2.5 mm long; calyptra rather large, cucullate, often extending to the middle of the urn .... 12. *G. ovalis*   12.71

17. Leaves ± strongly keeled, especially in the upper part, mostly lying folded in a slide; costa prominent at the back

19. Inner basal cells oblong to linear, 1:3–8(10); upper cells sinuous, 7–10 μ wide; leaves 2–3 mm long; calyptra small, mitrate; autoicous .... 13. *G. donniana*   12.75

19. Inner basal cells quadrate to shortly oblong, 1:1–3(4), the cross walls often thicker than the longitudinal walls, upper leaf cells not sinuous; leaves 2 mm or less long; calyptra medium sized, often reaching nearly to the middle of the urn, cucullate, dioicous

20. Plants in low, compact, velvety cushions, often glaucous; leaves up to 1.5 mm long; mainly 2-stratose above; upper cells 10–12 μ wide, rather clear; capsules shortly oblong-cylindric .. 15. *G. tenerrima*   12.83

20. Plants in looser tufts, not velvety, darker, without glaucous cast; leaves reaching 2 mm long, 1- to 2-stratose above; upper cells 7–10 μ wide, rather opaque; capsules elliptic-oblong .... 14. *G. montana*   12.79

16. Walls of inner basal cells ± sinuous or notably thick, oblong to linear; leaves 2–3 mm long

    21. Leaves rounded at the back; costa flat; margins plane, erect or slightly incurved, lamina 2-stratose above, smooth, mostly with long hair points .... 12. *G. ovalis* 12.71

    21. Leaves keeled, the costa prominent at the back; margins recurved on 1 or both sides, at least in the lower half of the blade

        22. Lamina 2- to 3-stratose above, smooth; costa crescent-shaped in section; hair points long; apices of the upper leaves without gemmae .... 16. *G. affinis* 12.87

        22. Lamina 1-stratose, margins 2- to 3-stratose, bearing longitudinal cuticular ridges resembling papillae in cross section; costa thick, terete, prominent; hair points short and slender; apices of the upper leaves often bearing globose, multicellular, brown gemmae .... 19. *G. hartmanii* var. *anomala* 12.100

15. Seta curved, capsules inclined to pendulous when moist; leaves 1-stratose above; margins recurved on 1 or both sides in the middle; cells ± sinuous

    23. Leaves oblong to oblong-lanceolate, up to 1.5 mm long, keeled; hair points long; capsules ribbed when dry; autoicous

        24. Leaf margins 2-stratose; inner basal cells quadrate to oblong, mostly 1:1–3; lid long beaked; calyptra mitrate .... --- 17. *G. pulvinata* 12.92

        24. Leaf margins 1-stratose; inner basal cells oblong to linear, 1:3–7(9); lid obtuse or mammillose; calyptra cucullate .... --- 18. *G. orbicularis* 12.96

    23. Leaves slenderly lanceolate from an ovate base, hair points short and slender, often lacking, the apices then narrowly acute to obtuse; upper lamina bearing longitudinal cuticular ridges; comal leaves of some plants bearing clusters of globose, multicellular, brown gemmae at the apices .... 19. *G. hartmanii* var. *anomala* 12.100

Key to the Species Based Mainly on Vegetative Characters

12.8 1. Upper leaves without hair points, occasionally hyaline-tipped; capsules immersed, subglobose to ovoid-oblong; autoicous

    2. Plants small, mostly less than 1 cm tall, growing on dry rocks; stem leaves 1.3 mm long or less, obtuse

        3. Stem leaves 0.5–0.7 mm long; seta 0.1–0.3 mm long; capsules

globose-ovoid to shortly ovoid, 0.4–0.7 mm long ....
.... 2. *G. atricha*   12.14

3. Stem leaves 1–1.3 mm long; seta 0.2–0.6 mm long; capsules ovoid
   to ovoid-oblong, 0.8–1.3 mm long .... 3. *G. dupretii*   12.18

2. Plants large for the genus; leaves 1.5–3(5) mm long

   4. Upper leaves of sterile shoots ovate-lanceolate to linear-lanceo-
      late, 2.5–5 mm long, incurved, recurved or falcate, the apices
      commonly prolonged into a thickish, blunt, brownish green hair
      point as much as 1.8 mm long; margins mostly plane, bistratose;
      in or near water .... 5. *G. cinclidodontea*   12.31

   4. Upper leaves without hair points

      5. Leaves elongate-oblong to linear-lanceolate, flattish, margins
         plane; costa brown; in or near water in high mountains ....
         .... 1. *G. agassizii*   12.10

      5. Leaves ovate to ovate-lanceolate, keeled; margins recurved to
         strongly revolute

         6. Leaves ovate-lanceolate to oblong-lanceolate

            7. Leaf margins entire; on dry rocks .... 4. *G. alpicola*   12.22

            7. Leaf margins repand-dentate to irregularly notched above;
               in or near water .... 4a. var. *rivularis*   12.26

         6. Leaves ovate to broadly ovate-lanceolate; margins entire; in
            or near water .... 4b. var. *latifolia*   12.29

12.9   1. Upper leaves with distinct hyaline points or long hairs, lower leaves
          often muticous

   8. Leaves keeled above, at least some lying folded on a slide; costa
      terete to semiterete

      9. Mature upper leaves 1–1.5 mm long

      10. Leaf margins plane, erect to incurved

          11. Leaves broadly oblong-lanceolate; hair points often very
              long and wide at the base; capsules immersed, subglobose,
              ventricose at base; peristome lacking; seta very short and
              curved; autoicous .... 9. *G. anodon*   12.56

          11. Leaves lanceolate to linear-lanceolate, mostly narrowly taper-
              ing to the hair points; seta long and straight; capsules ex-
              serted; peristome present; dioicous

              12. Plants in low, compact, velvety cushions, often glaucous;
                  leaves 2-stratose above; upper cells 10–12 μ wide, rather
                  clear; capsules shortly oblong-cylindric ....
                  .... 15. *G. tenerrima*   12.83

12. Plants taller and darker, less compact, not velvety or glaucous; leaves 1- to 2-stratose above; upper cells 7–10 μ wide, rather opaque; capsules elliptic-oblong; some leaves reaching 2 mm long .... 14. *G. montana* 12.79

10. Leaf margins mostly recurved to revolute, often only on 1 side; autoicous, usually fruiting

13. Upper leaves ovate-lanceolate to lanceolate, mostly 0.7–1 mm long; hyaline points less than ¼ the length of the blade; margins ± strongly revolute; cell walls smooth; capsules immersed, longer than the short straight seta ....
.... 6a. var. *conferta* 12.39

13. Upper leaves oblong to oblong-lanceolate, 1–1.5 mm long, some hair points reaching at least ¾ the length of the blade; cell walls ± sinuous, especially toward the base; capsules exserted and ± pendulous on a long curved seta, ribbed when dry

14. Leaf margins 2-stratose; inner basal cells quadrate to rectangular, mostly 1:1–3; lid long beaked; calyptra mitrate .... 17. *G. pulvinata* 12.92

14. Leaf margins 1-stratose; inner basal cells oblong to linear, 1:3–7(9); lid obtuse or mammillose; calyptra cucullate .... 18. *G. orbicularis* 12.96

9. Mature upper leaves 1.5–3 mm long

15. Comal leaves of some plants bearing clusters of globose gemmae; upper lamina bearing longitudinal cuticular ridges resembling papillae in cross section; inner basal cells quadrate to oblong, the walls sinuous; stem leaves lanceolate, some with short hyaline tips; seta long and curved; dioicous ....
.... 19. *G. hartmanii* var. *anomala* 12.100

15. Comal leaves not bearing gemmae, mostly with long hair points; upper lamina smooth

16. Leaf margins plane, erect; autoicous or monoicous

17. Leaves mostly lanceolate, narrowly and evenly tapering to a slender apex, 2- to 3-stratose above; inner basal cells oblong to linear, 1:4–9(10), walls smooth; capsules emergent .... 13. *G. donniana* 12.75

17. Leaves mostly ovate-lanceolate to oblong-lanceolate, less narrowly tapered, 1- to 2-stratose above; inner basal cells quadrate to oblong; capsules immersed ....
.... 6b. var. *ambigua* 12.42

16. Leaf margins recurved to revolute on 1 or both sides, at least in the lower half of the blade

18. Inner basal cells oblong to linear, ± thick walled and sinuous; alar cells quadrate to shortly oblong, clear; capsules emergent to exserted; calyptra mitrate .... 16. *G. affinis*   12.87

18. Inner basal cells quadrate to oblong, walls rather thin, smooth; alar cells much the same

    19. Tufts mostly moderately or not at all hoary on the surface when dry; in ± shaded places in mountains; hair points reaching about ⅓ the length of the blade; capsules immersed; calyptra small, mitrate, smooth; autoicous .... 6. *G. apocarpa*   12.35

    19. Tufts mostly very densely hoary, usually growing in exposed situations; hair points long, often equaling the length of the blade; capsules exserted; calyptra large, campanulate, yellowish, plicate, covering the capsule nearly to the base .... 8. *G. calyptrata*   12.52

8. Leaves rounded at the back, many of them lying flat on a slide; costa flat, not prominent at the back; margins plane, ± erect

  20. Leaves lanceolate to linear-lanceolate from an erect base, the upper part curving outward and then upward, 2–2.5 mm long; inner basal cells oblong to linear, the walls thick, smooth to moderately sinuous; lamina 2-stratose above; dioicous .... 12. *G. ovalis*   12.71

  20. Leaves broader, up to 1–1.5 mm long; base not differentiated; inner basal cells quadrate to oblong

    21. Leaves ovate to obovate or shortly spatulate, 1-stratose; capsules oblong, truncate at the base; calyptra large, yellowish, plicate .... 7. *G. rauii*   12.46

    21. Leaves ovate to oblong-lanceolate or lanceolate; calyptra small, smooth

      22. Leaves mostly imbricated, 1-stratose, thin and soft; upper cells 10–12 µ wide, quite clear; capsules immersed, on a very short curved seta, subglobose and ventricose at the base; autoicous, freely fruiting .... 10. *G. plagiopodia*   12.61

      22. Leaves patent to stiffly spreading, 2-stratose above or well toward the base, thickish and quite firm; upper cells 8–10 µ wide, rather opaque; capsules emergent, shorter than the straight seta, ovoid to oblong-ellipsoid, symmetrical; dioicous, fruit rare .... 11. *G. laevigata*   12.65

12.10 **1. Grimmia agassizii** (Sull. & Lesq.) Jaeg. Plants in loose or compact tufts, dark olivaceous to blackish above, light brown to blackish below. Stems erect or ascending, 1–3 cm high, usually freely branched; central strand lacking or vague, small and weakly developed in some older main stems; rhizoids mostly confined to the base of the stem where they are dense, reddish, and very stout. Leaves erect, ± appressed or imbricated when dry, erect-patent when moist, 1–3 mm long, rather flattish or widely channelled, apex mostly blunt or obtuse, less frequently narrowly acute, mostly muticous, occasionally with a single terminal hyaline cell; margins plane throughout or widely recurved near the base, entire in most young leaves, becoming crenulate, erose, and at length ragged and much eroded with age; costa stout, nearly uniform in width from base to apex, subpercurrent; upper leaf cells ± quadrate or rounded, moderately thick walled when young, becoming strongly incrassate and often colored with age, mostly 9–12 µ wide, smaller on the margins, smooth, mostly unistratose but occasionally bistratose in part; basal cells oblong, slightly wider and usually thinner walled, the marginal ones shorter. Autoicous. Perichaetial leaves variable from shorter to longer than the upper stem leaves in length. Seta very short and straight; capsules shortly ovoid to subglobose, the urn 1–1.3 mm long and nearly as wide, becoming hemispheric to funnel-form when dry and empty, mouth wide and flaring when old, dark red, smooth to minutely wrinkled when dry; teeth dark red, cuneate-lanceolate, nearly entire to 1–3 cleft as much as ⅓ above, ± perforated above, finely or rather coarsely papillose; lid conic-convex with a straight or slightly inclined short beak. Spores 12–17 µ in ours (Jones gives 15–25 µ, variable) smooth and yellowish. Calyptra small, cucullate. Plate 42, figs. 1–7.

12.11 On dry or wet rocks.

12.12 Europe, Quebec, Ontario, British Columbia, California, Utah. Duchesne County: Uinta Mountains, near Bald Mountain, 10,300 ft., Ottoson Basin, 10,900 ft.

12.13 Apparently rare. Superficially resembling forms of *G. alpicola.* The narrow, more erect and appressed leaves are distinctive.

12.14 **2. Grimmia atricha** C. Muell. & Kindb. in Macoun. Plants small, in low, loose or compact tufts, sometimes spreading or scattered among other mosses, dark green to blackish when dry, bright green when moist. Stems erect to ascending, 5–12 mm tall, branched, rhizoids few at the base. Leaves erect and appressed when dry, erect-patent when moist, the stem leaves ovate-ligulate to ovate-lanceolate, 0.5–0.7 mm long, obtuse, muticous, keeled, unistratose; margins plane or slightly recurved, occasionally bisatrose near the apex; costa stout and conspicuous above, sometimes papillose at the back, becoming weaker and narrower toward the base; comal leaves of mature shoot slightly larger. Autoicous.

Plate 42. 1–7. Grimmia agassizii. 1. Habit sketch, X.4. 2. Portion of shoot, X2. 3. Three stem leaves. 4. Perichaetial leaves, X8. 5. Three leaf apices and cross section of the lamina, X120. 6. Three capsules, X8. 7. Peristome teeth, X60, detail, X160.

8–13. Grimmia apocarpa. 8. Habit sketches, X.4. 9. Portion of shoot, X2. 10. Five stem leaves. 11. Three perichaetial leaves, X8. 12. Two capsules, X8. 13. Two portions of peristome showing variations, X60, detail, X160.

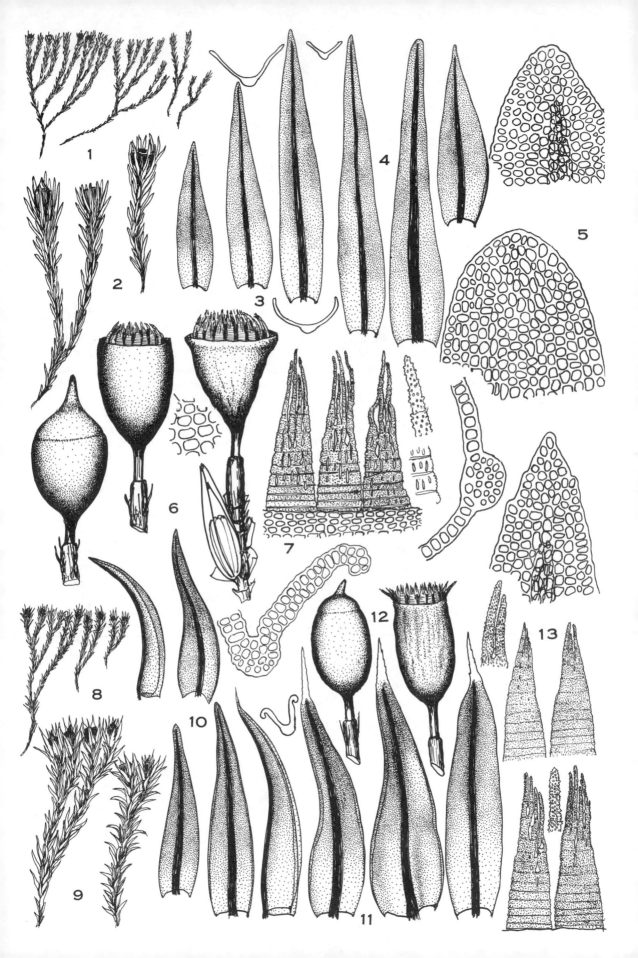

Perichaetial leaves abruptly larger and broader than stem leaves, up to 1.8 mm long, broadly ovate to oblong or ligulate, concave, obtuse or bluntly acute, muticous. Seta very short, 0.1–0.3 mm long; capsules immersed, globose-ovoid to shortly ellipsoid, urn 0.4–0.7 mm long, wide mouthed when dry, rounded at the base, reddish brown; lid convex with a short straight beak; annulus lacking; peristome teeth cuneate, yellowish brown to darker reddish, entire to slightly cleft or perforated, finely papillose with simple tall papillae or with very short ridges variously oriented. Spores light yellowish brown, mostly 8–11 μ, smooth. Calyptra cucullate. Plate 52, figs. 8–16.

12.15 Growing on dry rocks, usually in shady places.

12.16 British Columbia and Alberta, southward to California and Utah.

12.17 Our smallest species of *Grimmia* is locally abundant mainly on limestone in the Wasatch Mountains. The original description does not agree in all particulars with the type specimen. The description states, "the leaves being small and when dry appressed, muticous, short, ordinarily ovate-oblong, not recurved on the margins, the cells not incrassate. . . . Teeth of the peristome orange only below, yellow or hyaline above, entire, not rimose or papillose." A closer look at the type specimen reveals that some of the leaves are slightly recurved on one or both margins and, in addition, some leaves have cells bistratose at the upper margins and also occasionally in small patches here and there in the lamina. The upper cells vary from fairly thin walled to thick walled, according to age. The peristome teeth may be slightly cleft and occasionally perforated with a few thin spots; all the peristome teeth I examined were finely papillose and of more or less uniform color throughout—light yellowish brown. Jones, in Grout's *Moss Flora*, states that the spores are 6–9 μ, but in the type I find them to be mostly 9–11 μ.

12.18 **3. Grimmia dupretii** Thér. Plants small, in short rather loose to fairly compact tufts, often widely expanded, green when moist, becoming darker or olivaceous when dry, brown or blackish below. Stem slender, mostly 0.5–1 cm tall, sometimes becoming taller, branched. Stem leaves appressed when dry, erect-patent to somewhat squarrose-recurved when moist; mostly ovate-lanceolate to lanceolate, 1–1.3 mm long, obtuse and muticous, keeled; lamina unistratose or occasionally with small patches or rows of cells bistratose; margins usually revolute, but some leaves plane, the upper part sometimes bistratose and rarely toothed at the apex; costa rather narrow below, becoming broad and stout above, disappearing in the apex, occasionally toothed at the back above; upper

---

Plate 43. 1–4. **Grimmia apocarpa** var. **conferta.** 1. Six stem leaves. 2. Three perichaetial leaves. 3. Two capsules, X8. 4. Peristome teeth, X60, detail, X160.

5–8. **Grimmia apocarpa** var. **ambigua.** 5. Four stem leaves. 6. Two perichaetial leaves. 7. Three capsules, X8. 8. Peristome teeth, X60, detail, X160.

9–14. **Grimmia dupretii.** 9. Portion of shoot, X4. 10. Five stem leaves. 11. Two perichaetial leaves, X8. 12. Apical and basal cells, X120. 13. Four capsules, X8. 14. Peristome teeth, X60.

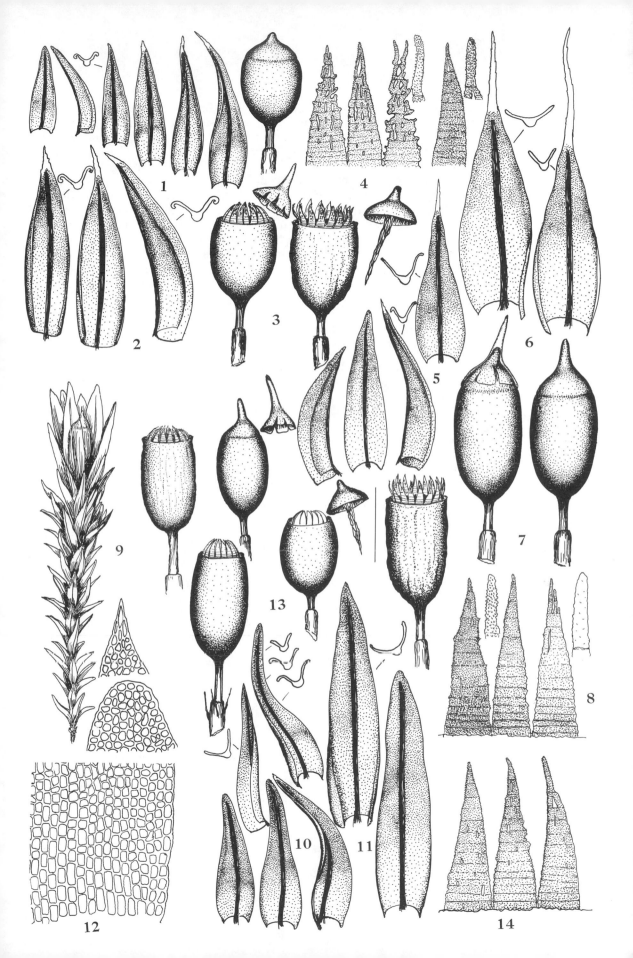

cells 6–9 μ wide, usually thick walled, quadrate to rounded, chlorophyllose, sometimes paler on the margins; basal cells quadrate to shortly oblong, slightly wider, those toward the margins usually shorter and paler. Perichaetial leaves conspicuously larger than stem leaves, 1.5–2.5 mm long, broadly ovate-lanceolate, oblong-lanceolate to ligulate, acute to broadly rounded, rarely white tipped with 1 to several hyaline cells, never a hair. Seta 0.3–0.6 mm long; capsules immersed, ovoid-oblong to oblong-ellipsoid, urn 0.8–1.3 mm long, reddish brown, smooth to finely striate and often wide mouthed when dry and empty; annulus lacking; lid convex with a short to longish beak usually inclined; peristome teeth cuneate, reddish, entire or sometimes with a few thin spots and occasionally cleft, smooth to very finely papillose. Spores 10–15 μ, smooth, yellowish brown. Calyptra small, mitrate. Plate 43, figs. 9–14.

12.19   On various kinds of rocks, usually in shade.

12.20   Quebec, Ontario, Massachusetts, Minnesota, Wyoming, Colorado, Utah, Arizona, Idaho, and British Columbia.

12.21   Locally abundant in the mountains of Utah. Much like *G. atricha* differing mainly in the larger leaves, usually with revolute margins, and the longer capsules. The spores are said to be much smaller in *G. atricha*, but in nearly all specimens from this region they are larger, 8–11 μ while in *G. dupretii* they range from 10–11(15) μ. The calyptra in the former is usually cucullate but may have 1–2 minor clefts, and the beak on the lid is usually straight. These traits are not too constant. Many plants are intermediate and one will have difficulty in deciding which name to apply to some specimens.

12.22   4. **Grimmia alpicola** Hedw. var. **apicola.** Plants dark green or olivaceous, darker below, the younger tips often yellowish green, growing in dense or rather loose tufts on dry rocks. Stems erect to ascending, 1–3 cm tall; central strand present, often vague; rhizoids dark reddish, confined to the base. Leaves loosely imbricated when dry, erect-patent when moist, ovate-lanceolate to lanceolate, 1–3 mm long, acute to narrowly obtuse, muticous, strongly concave-canaliculate, usually keeled above; margins plane or strongly revolute in the middle, bistratose above, entire or sometimes slightly dentate above; costa strong and prominent at the back, sometimes dentate on the back above, disappearing in the apex; lamina unistratose to bistratose above (often only in lines or patches); upper cells quadrate to irregular, 8–11 μ wide, thick walled, smooth or becoming sinuous; basal cells shortly rectangular, often quadrate on the margins. Perichaetial leaves larger, ovate to ligulate or linear-lanceolate, acute to broadly rounded, 2.2–3.5 mm long. Seta ¼–½ the length of the capsule; capsules immersed to slightly emergent, globose-ovoid to ovoid, 0.8–1 mm long, dark reddish when fully mature, wall of urn 4–6 layers of cells thick, becoming hemispheric to obovate-cupulate when empty, the mouth very wide when dry; lid low convex to hemispheric, mammillate to straight beaked; teeth dark red, usually with a purplish cast when dry, comparatively large, cuneate, $\pm$ cleft at the apex and perforated below, moderately to densely finely papillose. Spores yellowish to light reddish brown, 16–22 μ, finely punctate. Calyptra cucullate, entire to lobed at base. Plate 44, figs. 1–8.

12.23   Mostly on dry or wet siliceous and ferromagnesian rocks in our region; occasionally on limestone; essentially alpine but extending downward to 5,000 ft. in Utah, and to sea level in British Columbia and northward.

12.24   Europe, Asia, North Africa. Greenland to Newfoundland, Quebec, Pennsylvania, Michigan; Alaska to Oregon; Yukon to Arizona and Texas.

12.25   The dark reddish ovoid-globose capsules, with dark red teeth when fully mature and the large spores, 16–22 μ, are especially distinctive. When dry the capsules are very wide mouthed with the teeth spreading. Infrequent but locally abundant.

12.26   4a. Var. **rivularis** (Brid.) Wahlenb. Plants growing on wet rocks or in water, often floating, dark green to blackish, in loose or straggling tufts. Stems 2–10 cm long, freely branched. Leaves ovate-lanceolate, 0.5–2.5 mm long, mostly blunt or obtuse, muticous; margins ± repand-dentate above, 2- to 3-stratose; costa stout. Plate 44, figs. 9–10.

12.27   In alpine brooks in Utah, on wet rocks or submerged.

12.28   Greenland to Quebec, Pennsylvania, Wisconsin, Alaska to California, and in the Rocky Mountains to Utah and Colorado.

12.29   4b. Var. **latifolia** (Zett.) Moell. Plants in loose tufts on wet rocks or submerged. Stems up to 3 cm long; leaves ovate to oblong-ovate, mostly blunt or obtuse, 1.5–2.3 x 0.8–1.2 mm; margins entire. Plate 44, figs. 11–12.

12.30   Salt Lake County: Wasatch Mountains, Bells Canyon, 5,000 ft.

12.31   **5. Grimmia cinclidodontea** C. Muell. in Roell. Plants medium sized, forming rather dense tufts or widely spreading mats, usually in beds of intermittent streams, the young tips green, the lower parts dark green, olivaceous, or reddish brown, sometimes denuded and blackish at the base. Stems erect or becoming long and ascending or prostrate, 1–3.5(6) cm long, branched by short or elongated, slender, lateral or subfloral innovations, the sterile shoots often hooked at the tips; central strand lacking, rhizoids few at the extreme base. Leaves dense above, loosely appressed to erect-patent when dry, variable when moist, recurved, straight, incurved toward the stem or falcate, those of the sterile shoots often secund, lower leaves ovate-lanceolate to lanceolate, 2–2.5 mm long, the upper ones becoming linear-lanceolate, 2.5–5(6) mm, gradually narrowed to a thickish apex and often prolonged to a thickish, blunt, brownish green hair point, as much as 1.5 mm long, canaliculate, and rounded at the back; margins entire, mostly bistratose, plane throughout or slightly recurved in the lower ⅔; costa stout, commonly 85–100 μ wide at the base, terete or strongly convex, prominent at the back, percurrent or vaguely excurrent, gradually merging with the thickened margins of the lamina; lamina unistratose to variably bistratose above, often in lines; upper medial cells quadrate to shortly oblong or irregular,

239

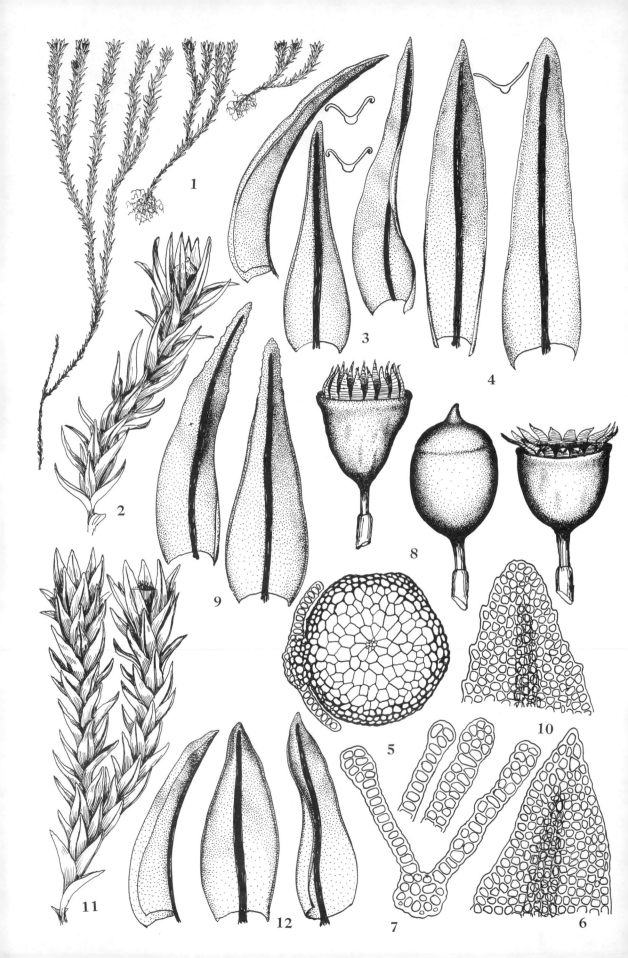

mostly 8–11 μ wide, rather thick walled, smooth or somewhat sinuous, usually clear and smooth, becoming $\pm$ elongate toward the base. Autoicous. Perichaetial leaves erect, straight, sheathing the immersed capsule, oblong or ligulate, the margins strongly incurved, gradually to suddenly narrowed to an acute, blunt, or broadly obtuse apex. Seta very short and thick, 0.2–0.5 mm long; capsules ovoid-globose to shortly oval-oblong, 1–15 mm long, rounded at the base, not much changed or minutely wrinkled when dry, wide mouthed, teeth erect or spreading, walls firm, 4–5 layers of cells thick, yellowish brown at maturity, becoming reddish with age; exothecial cells isodiametric to shortly elongated, irregular, thin walled at maturity, becoming very thick with age; stomata lacking; lid low conic or convex, abruptly narrowed to a tapering beak, straight or inclined; teeth intensely orange red, entire or variously 2–3 cleft or perforated, sometimes with cribrose, pale, thin places, papillose with moderately strong scattered papillae, these sometimes joined in lines or forming ridges. Spores light yellowish brown, smooth, 10–12 μ. Calyptra small, cucullate, but $\pm$ lobed at the base, scarcely covering the lid. Plate 45.

12.32   On wet or dry rocks, usually in intermittent stream beds. Rare or uncommon.

12.33   Washington to California; Utah, Colorado.

12.34   Related to G. *alpicola* but somewhat larger and often with long prostrate shoots forming mats, and as Dixon aptly stated, "The striking feature is the prolongation of the leaves into a long narrow proboscis, but this is not quite constant and I am inclined to believe it is rather in the nature of a sport." In nearly all specimens a considerable portion of the plants have the leaves with a thick coarse acumination joining the stout costa and sometimes only a few shoots here and there bear leaves with the long prolongation. This strongly suggests an ecological response. It should be pointed out further that these leaves are often secund and sometimes falcate, unistratose (except on the upper margins) or variously bistratose above, the capsules usually oval-oblong but sometimes ovoid-globose, like those of G. *alpicola*, but the spores are consistently smaller, mostly 9–11 μ as opposed to 16–22 μ. Specimens from Mariposa County, California, and Longs Peak, Colorado, as well as the seven cited above, were all collected on wet or dry rocks in the beds of intermittent streams.

12.35   **6. Grimmia apocarpa** Hedw. var. **apocarpa.** Plants in rather loose tufts, sometimes fairly compact but never in tight cushions, usually dark green, olivaceous or nearly blackish when dry. Stems slender and branched,

---

Plate 44. 1–8. Grimmia alpicola. 1. Habit sketches, X.4. 2. Portion of shoot, X2. 3. Three stem leaves. 4. Two perichaetial leaves, X8. 5. Cross section of stem, X60. 6. Apical cells. 7. Cross sections of leaves, X120. 8. Three capsules, X8.

9–10. Var. **rivularis.** 9. Two stem leaves, X8. 10. Apical cells, X120.

11–12. Var. **latifolia.** 11. Portion of shoot, X3.2. 12. Three stem leaves, X8.

1–2(3) cm long; central strand vague or lacking; rhizoids few, mostly confined to the base. Leaves imbricated when dry, erect-patent to open-recurved when moist, dark green, ovate-lanceolate to lanceolate, 1.5–2 mm long, ± strongly keeled above, concave to somewhat spoon-shaped at the base, acute to blunt, the comal leaves often bearing short, smooth, or somewhat dentate hyaline hair points, these often very short, often broad and channelled at the junction with the leaf apex up to ¼ the length of the blade, lower leaves muticous; margins recurved to revolute, entire; costa stout, usually channelled on the ventral side and prominent dorsally; upper lamina ± bistratose, often only on the margins, frequently in streaks, variable even in leaves of the same stem; upper leaf cells quadrate to rounded, thick walled and tending to become sinuous, about 10 μ wide; basal cells becoming shortly oblong to rectangular, usually ± chlorophyllose, slightly wider. Autoicous. Perichaetial leaves much larger and wider, ovate-lanceolate to somewhat ligulate, canaliculate, 2–2.5 mm long, the hair points stronger. Seta 0.4–0.6 mm long, ¼–½ as long as the capsule; capsules immersed, typically oval-oblong, 1 x 1.5, some shorter, some longer, base rounded to the seta, mouth rather wide when dry and empty, reddish brown, rather thick walled, composed of 4 layers of cells; lid conic with the columella persistent on it, beak short, straight or slightly bent, bright reddish; teeth triangular lanceolate, reddish, spreading to reflexed when dry, entire to slightly perforated above, sometimes slightly divided at the apex, densely and finely papillose; spores smooth, yellowish brown to light reddish brown, smooth, 9–12 μ. Calyptra mitrate but often more deeply divided at 1 point. Plate 42, figs. 8–13.

12.36 On various kinds of rocks, commonly in the shade and mainly in the mountains, in Utah.

12.37 Widely distributed throughout the United States, Canada, and the northern hemisphere in general.

12.38 In some specimens relatively few shoots have the upper and perichaetial leaves with white hair points while the majority have the leaves muticous or merely white tipped. Occasionally one encounters plants with long decurrent leaves.

12.39 6a. Var. **conferta** (Funck) Spreng. Differing from typical *G. apocarpa* in the following respects: tufts more compact and cushionlike, dull grayish green when dry, the leaves smaller, 0.7–1 mm long, on the whole more erect-patent when moist, the hair points proportionally shorter, less than ¼ the length of the blade, often only a white tip, in some plants muticous and obtuse; capsules shorter, more ovoid-globose, thinner walled; peristome somewhat more perforated but less cleft above. Calyptra mainly cucullate, often lobed at the base. Plate 43, figs. 1–4.

Plate 45. Grimmia cinclidodontea. 1. Habit sketches, X.4. 2. Two sterile shoots showing stance of the leaves, X2. 3. Portion of fertile shoot, X4. 4. Leaves of sterile shoots, X8. 5. Cross sections of leaf at different levels, X120. 6. Perichaetial leaves, outer to inner, X8. 7. Capsules. 8. Calyptra, X8. 9. Three teeth from different capsules showing sculpturing, X60.

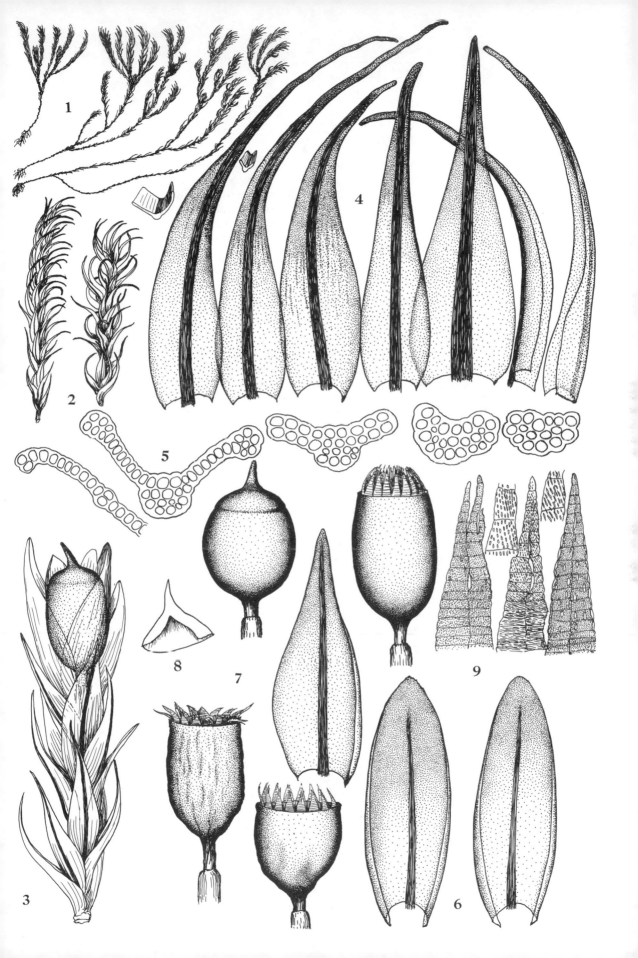

12.40   On dry rocks.

12.41   Europe. Yukon to California, eastward to Nova Scotia and Quebec, southward to North Carolina.

12.42   6b. Var. **ambigua** (Sull.) Jones in Grout. Differing in the typical form as follows: hyaline hair point of upper leaves longer, $\frac{1}{3}$–$\frac{1}{2}$ the length of the blade; leaf margins plane or nearly so; upper lamina mostly unistratose; upper cells 6–8 μ wide (in ours, 9–11 μ); capsules longer, shortly oblong-cylindric, 1–1.5 mm long, immersed. Spores 6–8 μ (in ours, 9–12 μ). Calyptra mainly cucullate, sometimes lobed at the base and partially mitrate. Plate 43, figs. 5–8.

12.43   On dry rocks.

12.44   Washington, Idaho, Colorado, Utah, Arizona, New Mexico, New Jersey, and Pennsylvania.

12.45   Intergrading with the species and with var. *conferta*. Thus far, none of the present plants show all of the traits attributed to this taxon, but at least some of the shoots show the somewhat longer hair points on the leaves, the plane margin, and the longer capsules. In local plants the length of the white hair points on the upper leaves seems to be of little use in distinguishing the species from the varieties.

12.46   **7. Grimmia rauii** Aust. Plants in low, compact, convex cushions or expanded sods, yellowish green to dark olivaceous, sometimes hoary on the surface. Stems erect, rather slender, 5–10(18) mm tall, sometimes shorter, branched. Leaves imbricated when dry, erect-patent to widely patent when moist, the lower ones small and often without hair points, the upper ones 0.5–1 mm long, broadly ovate to obovate, narrowed at the base, strongly concave, scarcely keeled, the apex usually tapering and ± acuminate, terminating in a short or long, hyaline, smooth or indistinctly dentate hair point, this ranging from slender throughout to broad and flat at the base, sometimes equalling or exceeding the length of the blade; margins plane, entire, or sometimes somewhat dentate at the apex, unistratose; costa stout, prominent at the back, channeled on the ventral side, extending into the hair point; lamina unistratose throughout; upper leaf cells quadrate, rounded, oval or irregular, 7–10 μ wide, chlorophyllose when young, becoming remarkably clear, walls fairly thick and smooth, becoming wider below, shortly rectangular to oblong, 12–16 μ wide, usually thin walled and clear, those in the alar region sometimes shorter, the transverse walls are said to be thicker than the longitudinal walls (a trait not consistently shown in our plants). Autoicous. Perichaetial leaves larger than stem leaves, 1–1.5 mm long, obovate to spatulate, gradually acute to more or less broadly rounded and abruptly piliferous; hair points longer, occasionally reaching 1.7 mm long. Seta shorter than the capsule, about 0.5 mm long, straight; capsules erect and symmetric, immersed, subglobose to ovoid when fresh and just mature, becoming ± oblong when fully mature and open, suddenly contracted and truncate at the base, 0.8–1 mm long, yellowish to yellowish brown, becoming light reddish brown with age, generally more or less longitudinally wrinkled when dry, the exothecial cells thin walled; lid conic with a straight beak; annulus strong and persistent, of 2–3 rows of cells; teeth slenderly triangular-lanceolate, often somewhat acuminate, light reddish brown, strongly perforated or cribrose nearly to the base and often ± cleft above into 2–4 slender divisions, very densely papillose with high papillae. Spores yellowish to light brown, about 10 μ, smooth. Calyptra large, about 1.3 mm long, campanulate, plicate, mitrate, straw colored with a reddish tip, covering about ¾ of the capsule. Plate 46, figs. 1–8.

12.47   On dry, often exposed rocks, especially abundant in sandstone in the Colorado-Green River basin.

12.48   South Dakota, Kansas, Oklahoma, Colorado, Utah, and Arizona. Minnesota.

12.49   The low more or less expanded sods of yellowish green to dark olivaceous are sometimes hoary all over the surface, or only at one side, the development of the hyaline hair points of the leaves being extremely variable. At times large tufts may have nearly all the plants with very short hairs, scarcely enough to change the prevailing color of the plant, with only isolated plants here and there with long hairs, these usually fertile.

12.50   I have repeatedly noted that large older tufts tend to exfoliate the sandstone upon which they grow, sometimes to the extent that that tuft lies free on a thin sheet of sandy rock, or falls from vertical rocks.

12.51   This is a distinctive moss not likely to be confused with any other species. Once the capsules are empty and dry, it is practically impossible to get them to return to their original shape, no matter how long they are soaked in water. The capsule wall, being composed of unusually thin-walled, yellowish exothecial cells, does not swell in water and usually remains quite wrinkled. The teeth stand erect when moist and are so strongly perforated as to have a somewhat lacy appearance.

12.52   8. **Grimmia calyptrata** Hook. in Drumm. Plants stout for the genus, in dense, usually strongly convex, compact cushions, rather light olivaceous to blackish green, typically densely hoary on the surface. Stems erect, moderately stout, branched, 1–2.5 cm tall; central strand vague. Leaves appressed and imbricated when dry, erect to patent when moist, the lower ones small and often muticous, the upper ones lanceolate to somewhat lanceolate-ligulate, gradually tapering or rather abruptly contracted to the apex, 1.5–2.5 mm long, concave-canaliculate, keeled above; hair points ½–⅔ the length of the blade, smooth to slightly dentate, broad and flat at the base; upper lamina unistratose to bistratose, usually in lines or patches; margins plane or recurved on 1 side, bistratose; upper leaf cells quadrate to rounded, usually quite clear; walls smooth, fairly thick, 6–8 μ wide, becoming wider downward and somewhat sinuous; basal cells oblong, some of them often shortly so or even quadrate in the same leaf, the walls usually smooth, often quite thick;

cells of the alar region usually not differentiated but sometimes shorter. Dioicous, but often well fruited. Perichaetial leaves larger than stem leaves, 2–2.5 mm long, the hair points very long, often exceeding the length of the blade, up to 3.2 mm long. Seta straight, 2–3 mm long; capsules exserted, oblong-elliptic to shortly cylindric, 1–1.7 mm long, reddish brown, smooth to minutely longitudinally ribbed and slightly contracted at the mouth when dry; lid conic with a rather long, straight beak; annulus and stomate lacking; teeth elongate-triangular, reddish, usually cleft into 2–3 slender divisions, finely papillose. Spores yellowish to brownish, finely granular, 12–14 μ. Calyptra large, covering the capsule to the base, campanulate, plicate, mitrate to cucullate, $\pm$ fringed at the base, straw colored, becoming light reddish brown with a darker beak, 2–2.5 mm long. Plate 46, figs. 9–14.

12.53   On dry exposed rocks of various kinds, mainly in foothills and mountains of our region.

12.54   British Columbia to Alberta and southward to California, Arizona, and New Mexico.

12.55   Common throughout the state. The large size, hoary surface of the cushions, large yellowish or straw colored calyptra, seta longer than the exserted capsule, lanceolate leaves, and dioicous habit make this plant easy to recognize.

12.56   **9. Grimmia anodon** B.S.G. Plants densely tufted, in small cushions to expanded sods, olivaceous or brownish to nearly black, often hoary when dry, brownish to reddish below. Stems erect to ascending, 0.5–2 cm tall, usually branched; central strand present; rhizoids mainly basal. Leaves appressed to loosely imbricated when dry, erect to erect-patent when moist, the lower ones short, ovate to oblong, obtuse to bluntly pointed, the upper ones oblong to oblong-lanceolate, (0.8–)1–1.7 mm long, obtuse or acute, mostly with a short to long flat hair point, concave below, keeled above; lamina unistratose to bistratose (often only in line); margins plane, entire; costa stout, percurrent above, weak below; upper cells quadrate to rounded, 8–10 μ wide, smooth, rather thick walled, chlorophyllose, often $\pm$ obscure; basal cells becoming noticeably wider and longer, oblong, thin walled and usually clear, the extreme basal ones hyaline; basal marginal cells usually narrower. Autoicous. Perichaetial leaves larger, 2–2.8 mm long, variable according to habitat, usually broadly ovate-lanceolate to oblong-lanceolate, sometimes broadly ovate or ovate-oblong, usually widest below the middle and tapering to a rather broad apex, very concave with the margins incurved, the costa often arched inward toward the apex giving the leaf a deep

---

Plate 46.   1–8. **Grimmia rauii.** 1. Habit sketches, X.4. 2. Portion of shoot, X2. 3. Capsule with calyptra, X4. 4. Stem leaves. 5. Perichaetial leaves, X8. 6. Leaf apices and upper cells, X80. 7. Capsules, X8. 8. Peristome teeth, X60, detail, X220.

9–13. **Grimmia calyptrata.** 9. Habit sketches, X.4. 10. Lower stem leaves. 11. Perichaetial leaves, X8. 12. Cross section of leaf at different levels, X120. 13. Capsule with calyptra, X4.8. 14. Capsules, X8, with a peristome tooth, X60.

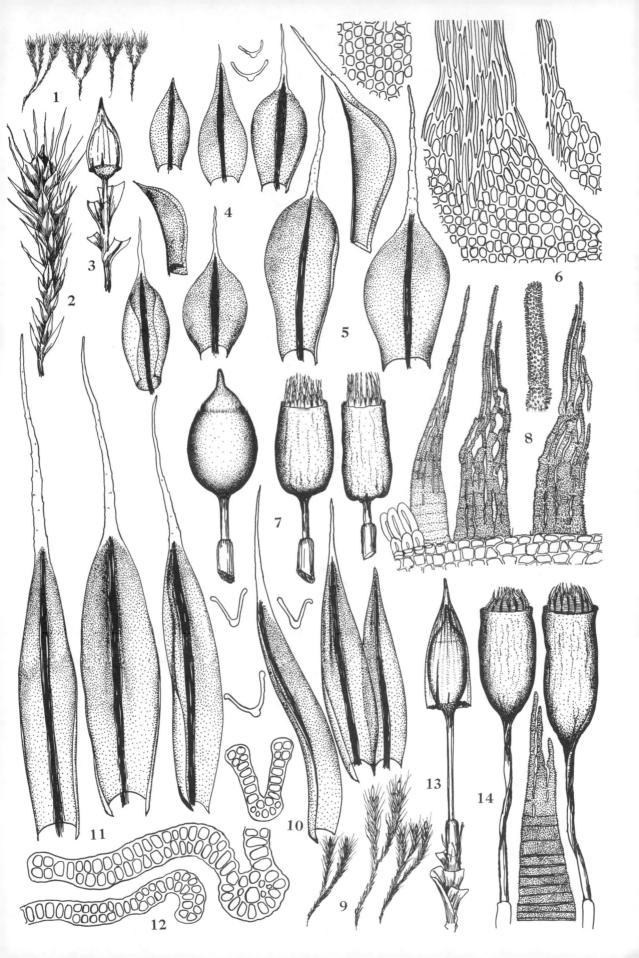

spoonlike form; hair point short to very long, often equal to the length of the blade, frequently ± decurrent at the base, smooth to dentate. Seta very short, curved, or sigmoid, about ¼ the length of the capsule; capsules immersed, subglobose to ovoid, urn 0.8–1 mm long, gibbous at the base on 1 side, asymmetric, wide mouthed, smooth to faintly striate when dry; annulus simple; lid low convex to conic-convex, mammillate, the tip sometimes nearly lacking; peristome absent. Spores light yellowish to reddish brown, smooth, 7–10 μ. Calyptra mitrate, smooth, scarcely covering the lid. Plate 47, figs. 1–7.

12.57   On dry rocks of various kinds.

12.58   Europe and Asia. New Brunswick, British Columbia to Saskatchewan, south through the Rocky Mountains and Great Basin to Arizona, California.

12.59   The most common lowland moss in Utah is *Grimmia*. It occurs most abundantly on deserts, mesas, and lower mountain slopes up to about 7,000 ft., usually in the more dry and exposed situations; less frequently it extends upward to 12,000 ft. It is especially common in the southern half of the state and particularly in the Colorado-Green River basin.

12.60   The most variable feature is the development of the hair points of the leaves. In some plants the points may be scarcely developed in non-fruited shoots and only moderately developed on a few fruited ones. Sometimes sterile specimens have the upper leaves barely white tipped, not enough to offset the predominantly blackish color of the tuft, but at the other extreme, the entire tuft may be densely hoary with long white hairs.

12.61   **10. Grimmia plagiopodia** Hedw. Plants densely to rather loosely tufted, commonly forming low thin cushions but sometimes deeper and more strongly convex, typically brownish to reddish green, varying to olivaceous above, brownish or reddish below. Stems erect to ascending, often curved upward or downward, branched, 0.5–2 cm tall; central strand usually evident; rhizoids basal. Lower leaves small, the upper larger, 1–2 mm long, concave-canaliculate but not keeled, oblong to ovate-lanceolate, obtuse and muticous or hair pointed; margins entire, plane and ± incurved; lamina unistratose throughout; costa slender above, weak below, semiterete to flattish, percurrent; upper cells quadrate to rounded or oval, thick walled, smooth and clear, 10–12 μ wide; basal cells becoming wider, shortly rectangular to oblong, usually hyaline at the extreme base. Autoicous. Perichaetial leaves reaching 2.7 mm long, broadly ovate-oblong to somewhat oblong-lanceolate, strongly concave

---

Plate 47. 1–7. Grimmia anodon. 1. Habit sketches, X.4. 2. Portions of three shoots, X2. 3. Stem leaves. 4. Perichaetial leaves, X8, with upper and basal cells, X80. 5. Cross sections of leaves, X80. 6. Dissected shoot tip with perigonium and capsule, X4. 7. Capsules, X8.

8–14. Grimmia plagiopodia. 8. Habit sketches, X.4. 9. Portion of shoot, X4. 10. Lower stem leaves. 11. Perichaetial leaves, X8. 12. Capsules, X4. 13. Capsules, X8. 14. Peristome teeth, X60.

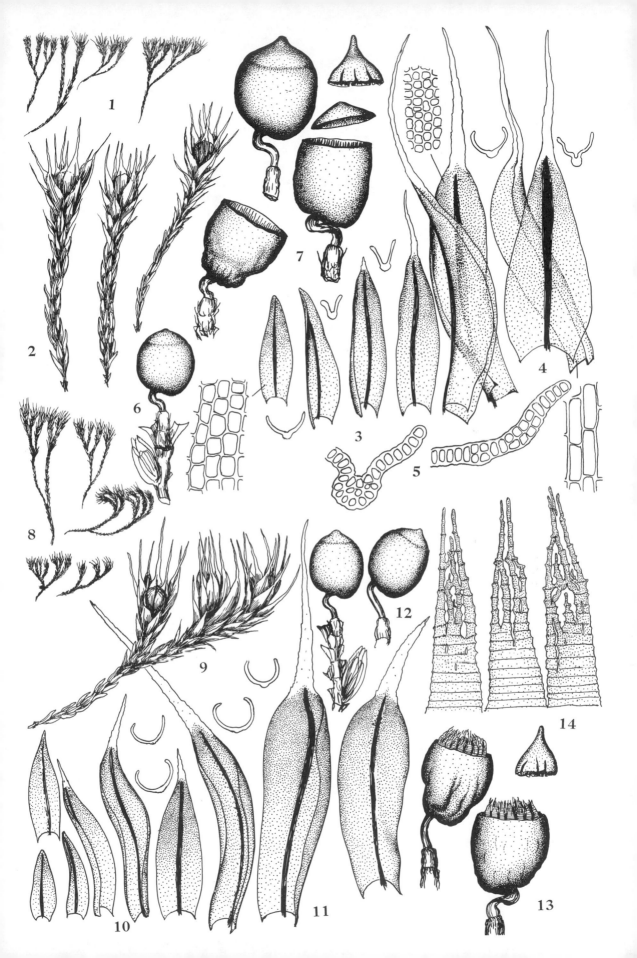

with margins incurved and frequently arched inward toward the apex, deeply spoon-shaped or boat-shaped, often curved to 1 side on ascending branches, from gradually to abruptly narrowed to long hair points. Seta much shorter than the capsule, curved to sigmoid, yellowish; capsules immersed, usually inclined to 1 side, subglobose to ovoid, gibbous at the base, smooth to faintly striate when dry, urn about 1 mm long; peristome teeth reddish, 2–5 cleft and perforated, cuneate or occasionally narrower and nearly entire, smooth to finely and densely papillose, spreading to reflexed when dry; annulus of 1–2 rows of cells; lid convex mammillate to conic with a short rostrum. Spores yellowish brown, smooth, 10–12 μ. Calyptra mitrate, scarcely covering the lid. Plate 47, figs. 8–14.

12.62   On various kinds of rocks.

12.63   Europe, British Columbia to Alberta, southward to Arizona and New Mexico, California, Nevada, Iowa, Missouri.

12.64   Rather common in the Colorado-Green River basin and the southern half of the state. The presence of the peristome and the larger, clear, unistratose upper leaf cells distinguish this from the last species.

12.65   **11. Grimmia laevigata** (Brid.) Brid. Plants loosely to fairly densely tufted, dull, dark green to yellowish or brownish green above, usually hoary on the surface, quite variable in appearance. Stems erect to ascending, quite stiff, 0.5–1.5 cm tall; central strand usually large and conspicuous. Leaves appressed to closely imbricated, the shoots often ± julaceous when dry, usually stiffly spreading at about 45° when moist, 1–1.5 mm long, ovate-lanceolate to somewhat triangular or oblong-lanceolate, evenly tapered upward from a broad base or suddenly narrowed at the rather wide apex and passing into the stout, hyaline, often strongly spinulose hair point which is frequently decurrent, equalling the length of the blade of the comal leaves, shorter or lacking in the lower ones, widely concave-canaliculate, rounded at back; margins erect to slightly incurved, plane; lamina bistratose to the margins and well toward the base; costa weak and flattish, often wide at the base, not at all prominent at the back, bistratose above and scarcely differentiated from the cells of the lamina except for the larger ventral cells, in the lower part with 1 to partially 2 rows of medial stereids; upper leaf cells quadrate to rounded, a few oblong, mostly 8–10 μ wide, smooth, clear to chlorophyllose and often somewhat opaque, quite uniform to the base, all rather thick walled; basal cells occupying a small area, rather abruptly wider, up to 22 μ wide, quadrate to transversely elongated, in some leaves those adjacent to the costa becoming oblong, all firm and ± thick walled, usually clearer but often ± chlorophyllose. Dioicous. Perichaetial leaves larger than stem leaves, commonly 2.5 mm long, the hair points sometimes exceedingly stout and spinulose. Seta straight and erect, 1–2.3 mm long, yellowish brown; capsules usually emergent, erect to very slightly inclined, ovoid to oblong-ellipsoid, the mouth narrow, reddish brown, quite smooth when dry; lid convex with a short to rather long, straight or slightly inclined beak;

annulus triple; peristome teeth reddish, nearly entire to 2–3 cleft into slender divisions about halfway down and cribrose below, joints quite strong, moderately papillose all over. Spores round, smooth, yellowish brown, 12–16 μ. Calyptra mitrate, usually covering about ⅓ of the urn. Plate 48, figs. 1–10.

12.66   On dry, often exposed rocks, usually sandstone and ferromagnesian rocks, mainly at low altitudes.

12.67   Europe, Asia, Africa, Australia, and New Zealand. New York to British Columbia, southward to Alabama, Oklahoma, Arizona, and California, Utah. Washington County: 10 mi. east of Hurricane, 3,800 ft.

12.68   This moss does not fruit freely in our region and is probably overlooked or passed up since some sterile specimens of *Grimmia* are not easily identified. Our single specimen is sterile but nevertheless clear-cut and in a state easily identified. In general it is a lowland species tending toward a southern distribution. Western plants appear to be stiffer in habit than eastern forms. The leaves may be erect-patent and somewhat curving upward or straight and diverging stiffly at about a 45° angle; they are often arranged in vertical or slightly spiral rows. The lamina is usually uniformly bistratose toward the base giving the leaf a firm, somewhat fleshy texture. The flat costa, scarcely changing the rounded contour of the back of the leaf, and the short basal cells are especially characteristic.

12.69   The development of the leaves varies widely with the conditions under which the plants grow. As in many species of *Grimmia,* the lower leaves of plants growing in dense tufts become progressively larger toward the tip of the stem. Occasionally the lowermost leaves are scalelike and tightly appressed to the stem. Some specimens from California are extreme in their stiff habit, the leaves often quite uniform in size well toward the base of the stem and disposed in vertical rows. As compared with eastern forms, they scarcely seem to belong to the same species. The single specimen from southern Utah is intermediate between the two extremes and differs from typical forms mainly in the much less spinulose hair points.

12.70   Other specimens with weak flat costae and rounded nonkeeled leaves include G. *plagiopodia,* which has leaves merely unistratose, and G. *ovalis,* which has conspicuously elongated basal leaf cells and a much narrower leaf apex.

12.71   **12. Grimmia ovalis** (Hedw.) Lindb. Plants densely tufted, olivaceous to blackish green or sometimes yellowish above, brownish below, ± hoary on the surface. Shoots generally slender and branched, 1.4 cm tall, in tall forms commonly leafless below, the naked portions often cohering; central strand rather large. Upper stem leaves 2–2.5 mm long, loosely appressed when dry, erect-patent to somewhat squarrose-spreading when moist, lanceolate to linear-lanceolate, the base ovate to oblong, erect with the upper portion curving outward and then arching upward and narrowly passing into the hair point, concave-canaliculate, rounded at the back; margins erect to somewhat incurved, plane, not at all recurved; costa rather wide and prominent but flattish and not conspicuous at the back; hair points stout and often decurrent, ± dentate but not strongly so; lower leaves becoming much shorter, the lowest ones muticous and arching outward; upper leaf cells quadrate to rounded or irregular, 6–9 μ wide, the walls rather thick, smooth or slightly sinuous, 2- to 3-stratose in the upper half, ± obscure; inner basal cells oblong to linear, thick walled, moderately sinuous to smooth; alar cells quadrate to oblong, clear with smooth walls. Dioicous. Perichaetial leaves larger than stem leaves, 2.5–3 mm, the bases long and ± clasping, the hair points reaching 1.5 mm long. Male plants smaller than the female; perigonia terminal soon becoming lateral by innovation, usually several on a stem, inconspicuous, small, erect, ovate-lanceolate in outline. Seta erect or sometimes slightly curved, 2.5–3(4) mm long; capsules exserted to emergent, elliptic-oblong, erect and symmetric, usually somewhat wrinkled when dry, 1.5–2 mm long, reddish brown, neck often somewhat differentiated, mouth small, lid conic-rostrate, the beak usually stout and bent; annulus of 3–4 rows of cells; peristome teeth fairly stout, triangular-lanceolate, dark reddish, usually closely barred, 1- to 3-cleft above and irregularly cribrose below, moderately papillose all over. Spores smooth, yellowish to yellowish brown, 8–10 μ. Calyptra rather large, 1.5–2 mm long, cucullate, becoming lacerate at the base, covering the upper half of the capsules and sometimes nearly to the base, smooth, becoming reddish brown with a darker beak. Plate 48, figs. 11–16.

12.72 On dry, often exposed rocks, mainly in western North America.

12.73 Europe, Asia, and North Africa. British Columbia through the Rocky Mountains to Arizona; Minnesota, Wisconsin, Quebec, Greenland.

12.74 This moss seems to fruit quite freely in southern Utah, but being dioicous and often sterile, it may be commonly overlooked in collecting. The slender leaves more or less squarrose from a broad erect base, rounded at the back with a flat costa, and plane at the margins are the distinctive characteristics. It closely resembles *G. affinis* and *G. donniana* in appearance and leaf shape but differs in the characteristics cited in the key.

12.75 **13. Grimmia donniana** Sm. Plants usually in small (or rarely extensive) tufts, loose to fairly compact, dark to blackish green, commonly densely hoary. Stems erect, often with several short branches, 1–2 cm tall; central strand small but fairly distinct. Leaves closely appressed to some-

---

Plate 48. 1–10. **Grimmia laevigata.** 1. Habit sketch of local, moderately thick form. 2. Same of unusually thick form from California, X.4. 3–4. Dry and moist shoots, X4. 5. Cross section of stem, X60. 6. Stem leaves. 7. Perichaetial leaves, X8. 8. Cross sections of leaf at different levels. 9. Basal leaf cells, X80. 10. Capsule, X8.

11–16. **Grimmia ovalis.** 11. Habit sketches, X.4. 12. Portion of shoot, X4. 13. Stem leaves. 14. Two perichaetial leaves, X8. 15. Basal leaf cells, X80. 16. Capsules with calyptra, X8, peristome teeth, X60.

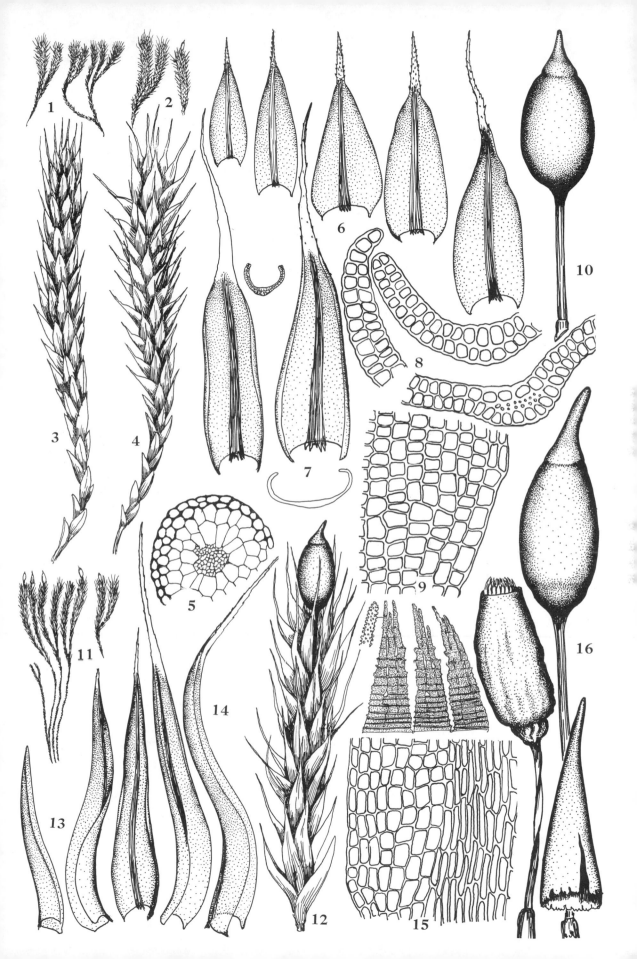

what loosely incurved and imbricated when dry, erect-patent to patent when moist, 2–3 mm long, lanceolate, often quite narrowly so, mostly tapering evenly upward and passing into the hair point, but the apex sometimes slightly broader and contracted to the base of the hair, strongly keeled above in younger leaves, tending to become flattened in older ones; margins plane and erect, commonly 2- to 3-stratose above; lamina ± bistratose in the upper half, often only in lines or patches; hair points variable, short in some plants and up to 3 mm long in others, smooth to distantly spinulose-toothed, often wide at the base; costa stout and conspicuous at back, terete; upper cells quadrate to rounded, 6–9 μ wide, walls thick and ± sinuous, chlorophyllose, opaque to fairly clear; basal cell adjacent to the costa, oblong to linear, wider and more pellucid, becoming shortly rectangular and often hyaline toward the margin. Autoicous or monoicous. Perichaetial leaves larger than stem leaves, with longer hair points. Perigonial buds terminal, becoming lateral by innovation, on separate branches or subtending the perichaetia; perigonial leaves ovate, broadly concave-clasping, acute to obtuse, the outer ones longer and usually with hair points. Seta erect and straight, 1.5–2.5 mm long; capsules emergent, erect and symmetric, ovoid- to oblong-ellipsoid, 1–1.5 mm long, light yellowish brown or slightly darker, walls fairly firm, nearly smooth to lightly striate-wrinkled when dry; neck not differentiated, lid conic-convex with a rather short, thick, blunt beak; annulus of 2–3 rows of cells (often pale and poorly developed); peristome teeth triangular-lanceolate, nearly entire to 1- to 2-cleft above and often perforated below, bright reddish, densely papillose, sometimes in indistinct vertical lines. Spores pale and yellowish or yellowish brown, smooth, 7–9 μ. Calyptra small, about 1 mm long, mostly mitrate but occasionally split only on 1 side. Plate 49, figs. 1–8.

12.76 On various kinds of dry rocks in mountains.

12.77 Europe and Asia. Greenland, Quebec, Vermont. Alberta through the Rocky Mountains to New Mexico and Utah.

12.78 Well-developed plants have almost the same appearance as G. *calyptrata* (though perhaps slightly smaller and darker). The leaves differ only slightly, but the capsules are only emergent with much smaller

---

Plate 49. 1–8. **Grimmia doniana.** 1. Habit sketch, X.4. 2. Dissected portion of shoot showing autoicous habit, X4. 3. Stem leaves. 4. A perichaetial leaf, X8. 5. Upper medial leaf cells. 6. Cross sections of lamina. 7. Inner basal leaf cells from two different plants; narrower form is more typical, X80. 8. Capsule with calyptra, X8.

9–17. **Grimmia alpestris.** 9. Habit sketches, X.4. 10. Portion of male shoot showing perigonial bud and dissection. 11. Portion of archegonial plant with capsule, X4. 12. Stem leaves. 13. Perichaetial leaf, X8. 14. Upper medial leaf cells. 15. Cross sections of leaf at different levels. 16. Basal leaf cells, X80. 17. Capsules and calyptrae, X8.

18–25. **Grimmia montana.** 18. Habit sketches, X.4. 19. Portion of antheridial plant, X4. 20. Stem leaves. 21. Perichaetial leaf, X8. 22. Upper medial leaf cells. 23. Basal cells. 24. Cross sections of a leaf, X80. 25. Capsules with calyptra, X8.

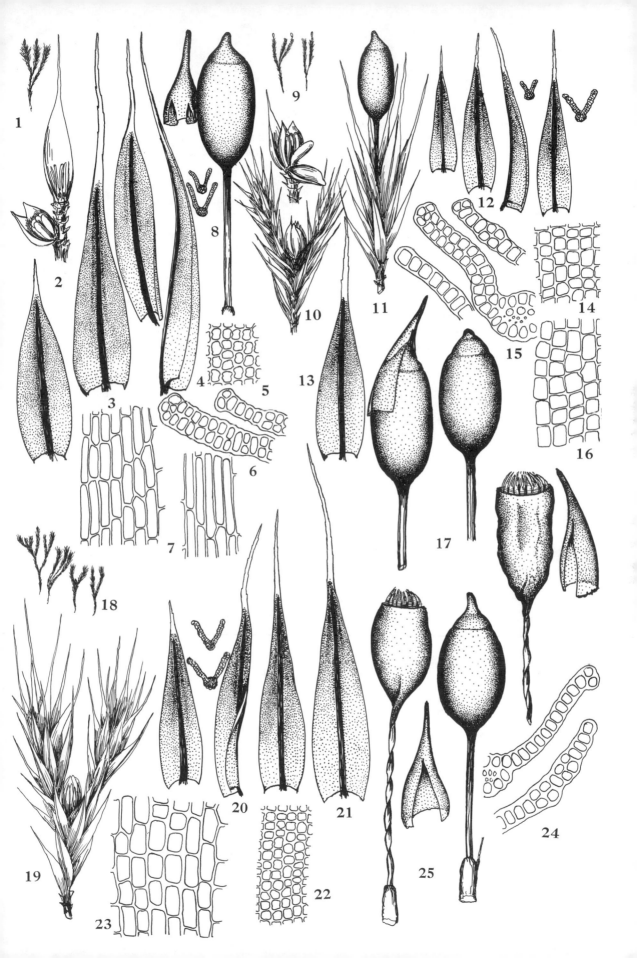

mitrate calyptrae scarcely covering the upper third of the urn, and the plants are autoicous. Sterile plants may be difficult to identify since about one half of the stems with perichaetia have no subtending perigonia and could easily be called dioicous. The species is not common in Utah.

12.79 **14. Grimmia montana** B.S.G. Plants in dense tufts, dark green, olivaceous to blackish, usually loosely hoary on the surface (but sometimes sparsely so). Stems erect and branched, ascending on the margins of the tufts, 1–2(3) cm tall, slender; central strand indistinct or lacking. Leaves erect and appressed when dry, erect-patent when moist, 1.5–2 mm long, lanceolate, the base ± oblong, the upper part mostly elongate triangular-lanceolate, evenly tapering and passing into the hair point or sometimes slightly contracted at the apex, strongly keeled above; margins erect and plane; lamina unistratose throughout, bistratose at the margins, or variably 2- to 3-stratose in the upper ½ or ⅔; hair point generally quite slender, entire to distantly dentate, often nearly as long as the blade in the upper leaves, becoming shorter or lacking in lower leaves; costa terete, prominent at the back; upper cells quadrate to rounded, 6–9 μ wide, walls quite smooth and fairly thick, chlorophyllose, clear to opaque; basal cells quadrate to shortly oblong, with smooth walls, those toward the margins generally shorter, sometimes with cross walls thicker, but variable in the same plant, the marginal cells sometimes narrower, thin walled, and hyaline. Dioicous. Perichaetial leaves larger than stem leaves, 2–3 mm long, broader at the base, with hair points longer and stouter. Male plants smaller than the female, the leaves smaller and the upper and comal ones not much differentiated; perigonia terminal, soon becoming lateral or, (in the axils of branches because of innovation), fairly conspicuous, outer leaves much like the stem leaves but with a shorter upper part and a proportionately longer base. Seta erect and straight, 2–3 mm long; capsules emergent to shortly exserted, ovoid to shortly elliptic, usually appearing oblong when dry, 1–1.5 mm long, usually pale yellowish to light yellowish brown, quite thin walled, smooth to wrinkled when dry; neck not differentiated; lid convex or conic, the beak short and obtuse to fairly long and inclined, up to 0.7 mm long; annulus none; peristome teeth rather short and fragile, triangular-lanceolate, entire to 1- to 2-cleft above, usually ± perforated below, erect, spreading or reflexed when dry, yellowish to yellowish brown, densely papillose. Spores pale yellowish to light yellowish brown, smooth, 10–14 μ. Calyptra cucullate, about 1.5 mm long, covering about the upper half of the urn, the beak usually somewhat curved. Plate 49, figs. 18–25.

12.80 On various kinds of dry rocks, in mountains.

12.81 British Columbia to California, Montana to Arizona; Greenland; Europe. Summit County: Uinta Mountains, Henry's Fork, 9,200 ft.

12.82 This plant is closely related to *G. alpestris* but in aspect it often resembles more closely an undersized *G. donniana* or *G. calyptrata*. As compared with *G. alpestris* it is usually not quite as compactly tufted, lacks the velvety surface with a glaucous or bluish cast, and has larger leaves and proportionately shorter capsules; also the upper leaf cells are smaller. Typically the lid has a long inclined beak, but in our single specimen the beak is short and straight or slightly inclined, much like that of *G. alpestris.*

12.83   **15. Grimmia tenerrima** Ren. & Card. Plants low, in very compact cushions or expanded sods, dark green, olivaceous or blackish, usually with a distinctive bluish or glaucous cast, often hoary with a velvety appearance. Stems very slender, erect and branched, 0.5–1.5 cm tall; central strand indistinct or lacking. Leaves erect and closely appressed when dry, erect-patent when moist, lanceolate to narrowly triangular-lanceolate, 1–1.5 mm long, the apex evenly tapering into the hair point, the lower ones shorter and muticous, strongly keeled; margins erect to slightly incurved, 1- to 3-stratose; lamina ± bistratose in the upper half, often only in lines; costa terete and prominent at the back, channelled on the ventral side, hair points smooth to distantly spinulose, varying up to ¾ the length of the blade; upper leaf cells mainly quadrate, some becoming rounded, 10–12(14) μ wide, comparatively thin walled but becoming thicker with age, chlorophyllose, clear to opaque, smooth; basal leaf cells not strongly differentiated, quadrate to shortly oblong, ± chlorophyllose but clear or sometimes hyaline, marginal cells usually quadrate and hyaline, often with thickened cross walls. Dioicous. Perichaetial leaves larger than stem leaves, mostly 1.5 mm long, a few reaching 1.8 mm long, the hair points longer. Male plants smaller than the female, the comal leaves not notably different from the upper leaves; perigonial buds terminal, becoming lateral by innovation, (often in the axils of branches); inner leaves ovate, strongly concave, obtuse to acute, the outer ones with hair points. Seta straight and erect, 1.5–3 mm long; capsules 1–1.5 mm long, mostly shortly oblong-cylindrical, usually light yellowish brown, thin walled and rather fragile, minutely wrinkled when dry, neck not differentiated; lid convex, mammillose or with a short blunt beak; annulus lacking; peristome teeth triangular-lanceolate, 1- to 3-cleft above into irregular slender divisions, nearly entire to perforated below, joints moderately conspicuous, finely papillose, typically reddish but often paler, especially in capsules which fail to mature fully. Spores yellowish to pale brownish, smooth, 8-14 μ. Calyptra rather large, 1.5–2 mm long, cucullate, smooth, light reddish brown below with a darker beak, covering about ½ of the urn on 1 side. Plate 49, figs. 9–17.

12.84   On various kinds of dry rocks (especially siliceous rocks) in mountains.

12.85   Europe and Asia. Quebec; Greenland. Mainly western in North America; British Columbia to California, Alberta to Colorado and Utah.

12.86   This, our most common species of *Grimmia* in the higher mountains of Utah, occurs in all counties of the state. The compact cushions, usually velvety and grayish or bluish, are easily recognized. When sterile, it is distinguished from other small species by the small, keeled, more or less bistratose, lanceolate leaves with terete, ventrally channelled costa and rather large upper leaf cells. It does not fruit freely. On dry south-

257

facing slopes of our lower and more open canyons it is often more blackish and less hoary on the surface, and if a few capsules form they commonly do not mature before the dry season sets in.

12.87   **16. Grimmia affinis** Hornsch. Plants in rather small, loose, dark green to olivaceous or blackish tufts, sometimes quite hoary on the surface. Stems erect to ascending, 1.5–2.5 cm tall, branched, often denuded below; central strand present. Leaves erect and appressed when dry, erect-patent to somewhat spreading from erect bases when moist, keeled, 1.5—2.5(3) mm long, lanceolate from an ovate or oblong base, the upper part commonly curving outward then arching upward, the apex abruptly contracted to or gradually merging with the hyaline, slightly dentate hair point, the latter up to as much as 1.3 cm long, the lower leaves muticous; upper lamina 2-stratose; margins plane above, usually recurved on 1 side below; costa rather narrow and thin but arched and appearing prominent at back; upper cells quadrate to round or irregular, thick walled and commonly slightly sinuous, mostly 7–9 μ wide; the inner basal cells becoming wider and longer, oblong to linear, the walls thick and $\pm$ sinuous, alar cells quadrate to shortly oblong, thick walled and clear. Lower leaves much shorter, ovate-lanceolate, the limb commonly recurved, muticous. Autoicous or dioicous. Perichaetial leaves larger than stem leaves, with longer hair points. Seta erect 1.3–2.5 mm long; capsules emergent to exserted, ovoid to ellipsoid or ellipsoid-oblong, occasionally subcylindric, urn 1–1.3(1.5) mm long, yellowish brown, becoming darker reddish brown with age, smooth or somewhat striate when dry; lid convex with a short to rather long beak, often quite thick; annulus of irregularly shaped thick-walled cells, 3–4 cells wide; peristome teeth bright red, irregularly cleft, densely and finely papillose. Spores 8–10 μ, yellowish brown, smooth. Calyptra mitrate or sometimes cucullate, with a long beak.

12.88   On dry rocks in mountains.

12.89   Alaska to Greenland and Labrador, southward in the Cascade and Rocky Mountains to Mexico, Central America and the northern Andes Mountains: Europe. Duchesne County: Uinta Mountains, near Moon Lake, 8,100 ft.

12.90   In appearance this moss resembles *G. donniana* which has the leaf margins plane throughout and oblong to linear inner basal leaves with smooth rather than sinuous walls. Also, the lid of the capsule is much shorter and often obtuse. *G. ovalis* differs mainly in the weak flattish costa, not prominent at the back, and the leaves rounded at the back rather than keeled while the lamina is somewhat incurved with margins plane throughout; also the calyptra is cucullate and rather large.

12.91   Uncommon in Utah but locally abundant in surrounding states. According to Elva Lawton, it is very common in the Black Hills of South Dakota.

12.92   **17. Grimmia pulvinata** (Hedw.) Sm. Plants in small dense cushions, dark green, grayish green to olivaceous, usually $\pm$ densely hoary.

258

Stems slender, branched, 0.5–2.5 cm high; central strand present, usually distinct. Upper stem leaves ± erect and imbricated, the comal ones incurved, erect or with the tips recurved when dry, erect to erect-patent when moist, somewhat oblong to oblong-lanceolate, the base not set off, the apex rather broad to fairly narrow, usually acute, 1–1.5 mm long, keeled, the hyaline hair points equaling the length of the blade or shorter, ± flexuous, moderately denticulate to nearly entire; margins commonly recurved below the middle, but often plane on 1 or both sides; costa moderately strong and convex at the back; lamina unistratose, the upper margins 2- to 3-stratose; upper leaf cells mostly quadrate to rounded, some shortly rectangular, 6–10 μ wide, the walls usually thick and ± sinuous; differentiated basal cells occupying a small area, short and fairly uniform, the inner ones quadrate to oblong, 1:1–2(3), walls mostly thin; alar cells similar or more often narrower, only occasionally hyaline and extending up the margins; in older leaves the walls of the basal cells thin to fairly thick, smooth or sometimes sinuous. Lower leaves smaller and often muticous. Autoicous. Perichaetial leaves larger than stem leaves, about 2 mm long, hair points longer and often broader at the base. Seta curved to arcuate when moist, frequently erect when dry; capsules exserted, shorter than the setae, horizontal to pendulous when moist, elliptic or elliptic-oblong, urn 1–1.4 mm long, reddish brown, typically 8-ribbed but often ± irregularly ribbed or wrinkled when dry; lid conic to convex with a short to moderately long beak, straight or inclined, sometimes obtuse to shortly beaked; annulus double or triple, ± revoluble but commonly persistent and spreading; peristome teeth erect to spreading when dry, reddish, 2- to 3-cleft above into irregular slender divisions, ± perforated below, finely and densely papillose, strongly jointed. Spores yellowish brown, smooth to finely punctate, 10–12 μ. Calyptra mitrate, about 1.3 mm long, usually dilated at the base. Plate 50, figs. 1–9.

12.93 On dry rocks at low elevations; abundant on dry sandstone across southern Utah below elevations of about 6,000 ft.

12.94 British Columbia to Alberta, southward to southern California, western Colorado and Arizona. Europe, Asia, Africa, and Australia.

12.95 Much like *G. orbicularis* and commonly growing with it at lower elevations across southern Utah where they are the most common lowland species. (See notes under the next species for further remarks.)

12.96 **18. Grimmia orbicularis** Bruch in Wils. Related to the last species and commonly growing with it. Plants in dense tufts, forming deep and often expanded cushions, dark green to blackish green, ± hoary. Stems rather slender, branched, mostly 1–3 cm tall, often uniformly leafy well toward the base; central strand well developed. Leaves mostly oblong-lanceolate, fairly broad at the apex and widely acute to nearly obtuse, but often lanceolate and narrowly tapering into the hair point, mostly about 1.3 mm long, hair point usually shorter than the blade, distantly and usually weakly dentate, strongly keeled; lamina 1–stratose; margins 1–stratose or occasionally 2-stratose at the extreme apex of a few leaves,

± widely recurved in the middle, but often plane on 1 or both sides; costa moderately stout, semiterete, upper cells quadrate to rounded or shortly oblong, the walls thick and ± sinuous, 8–12 μ wide; inner basal cells variable, mostly oblong, but frequently linear, the walls sometimes becoming strongly thickened and colored, smooth or sinuous; alar cells usually slightly narrower, the walls thinner and smoother, 1–4 rows usually hyaline and extending up to the margin. Lower leaves smaller, becoming muticous, acute to rounded obtuse. Autoicous. Perichaetial leaves larger than stem leaves, 1.5–2.2 mm long, the hair points longer, sometimes exceeding the length of the blade. Seta yellowish, twisted and nearly erect when dry, curved to arcuate when moist; capsules inclined to pendent when moist, shorter than the seta, irregularly wrinkled to ribbed when dry, typically ovoid-globose but in our region more commonly varying to shortly ovoid-ellipsoid, the mouth rather small, urn 1–1.3 mm long, reddish brown when fully matured; lid convex to conic, rounded, obtuse, or mammillate, dark reddish brown and usually shiny; annulus double or triple, rather large, ± revoluble or persistent and divergent from the mouth; teeth elongate-triangular, 2- to 3(4)-cleft above and often slightly perforated below, densely and finely papillose, light reddish brown to paler, occasionally reduced to a few imperfectly formed joints (which are sometimes pale and scarcely exceed the annulus). Spores yellowish, smooth, 9–13 μ. Calyptra tall conic, cucullate (when old, dilated and ragged at the base), covering about ½ the urn. Plate 50, figs. 10–18.

12.97   On dry rocks at low elevations. On dry sandstone and basalt across southern Utah.

12.98   Europe, Asia, and Africa. Utah, Arizona, New Mexico, and Mexico.

12.99   Although this moss is said to be a calciphile, all our plants grew on sandstone or basalt. The infiltrated sand and rock show some calcium reaction with hydrochloric acid, but often weakly so. In *G. pulvinata*, the cushions are smaller, lower, more grayish green, and of a finer texture. The leaves of typical forms are said to be narrower, especially at the apex, than those of *G. pulvinata*, but among our plants there is little to choose between the two species, both having mostly oblong-lanceolate, keeled leaves, with more or less recurved margins in the middle part. Occasionally plants of the present species have narrower leaves, the apices gradually tapering into the hair points. At the opposite extreme, some forms have oblong-ligulate leaves with apices broadly acute to widely rounded and all but the upper ones muticous. Some of these leaves have the costa curved upward at the apex like the prow of a

---

Plate 50.   1–9. Grimmia pulvinata. 1. Habit sketches, X.4. 2. Portion of shoot with capsules, X4. 3. Capsules with portion of annulus. 4. Calyptrae. 5. Stem leaves. 6. Perichaetial leaves, X8. 7. Upper medial leaf cells. 8. Basal leaf cells from two different plants. 9. Cross sections of the leaf margin, X80.

10–18. Grimmia orbicularis. 10. Habit sketches, X.4. 11. Portion of shoot. 12. Capsules. 13. Three lids showing variations. 14. Calyptra, X4. 15. Four stem leaves. 16. Three perichaetial leaves, X8. 17. Upper medial leaf cells. 18. Two areas of basal cells from different plants, X80.

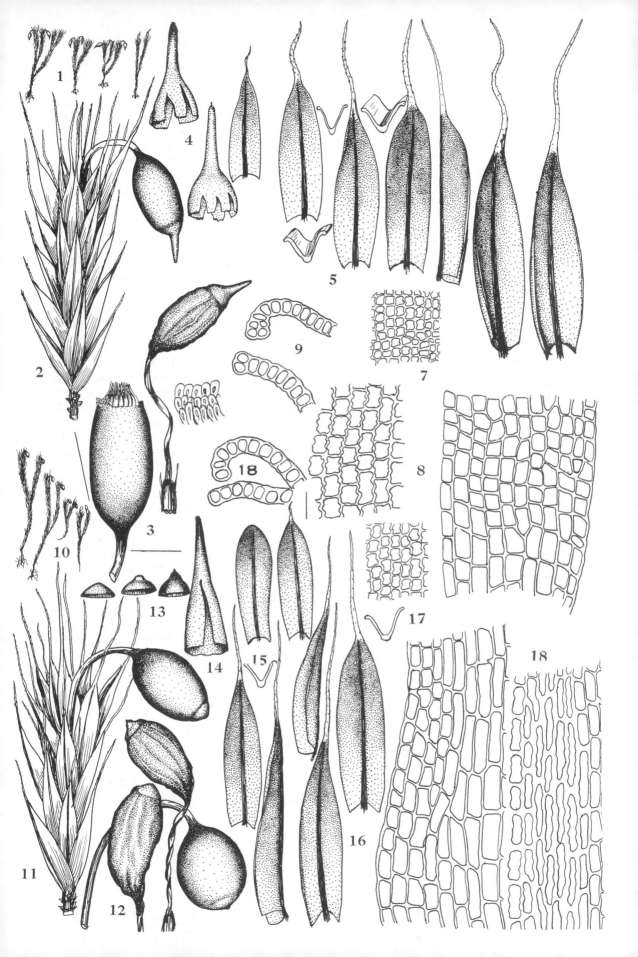

boat. The main differences between the two species are given in the key, and, as far as our collections are concerned, they are constant. Other traits frequently used in keys are less reliable among our plants. I find the average width of the upper leaf cells to be 1.83 μ wider in *G. orbicularis*. This difference can scarcely be appreciated in ordinary observations and measurements but shows up better in carefully made camera lucida drawings, (figs. 7, 16). The inner basal cells vary widely, in some leaves being so much like those of *G. pulvinata* as to be indistinguishable. But ordinarily some leaves from the same stem show more elongated inner cells. Only a few of the present specimens show the typical ovoid-globose capsule. The majority of the plants have them shortly ellipsoid. The latter may be so much like the shortly oblong-ellipsoid capsules of *G. pulvinata* as to appear practically identical, but in the field, when the capsules have reached maturity and have not had a chance to dry out, the difference is quite noticeable. (Incidentally, it is usually difficult to get dry empty capsules to return to their original shape even after prolonged soaking.)

12.100   **19. Grimmia hartmanii** Schimp., var. **anomala** (Hamp.) Moenk. Plants in rather loose tufts, bright or yellowish green at the tips, dark brown or blackish below. Stems $\pm$ prostrate-ascending, the tips often curved or hooked when dry, 2–4 cm long, slender, simple or branched, often naked at the base; central strand present, often indistinct; rhizoids basal. Leaves loosely erect, somewhat contorted and at the tips often secund when dry, when moist erect-patent to recurved, lanceolate from an ovate base, 2–3 mm long, keeled above, slenderly tapering to a narrowly acute or blunt apex, some of them terminating in a short, smooth or slightly spinulose, white hair point, the apices of the comal ones often bearing clusters of rather large, multicellular, greenish brown, $\pm$ globular gemmae on short stalks formed by the prolongation of the apical cells of the lamina, costa, or hair point, at length becoming brown, 50–110 μ across; lamina unistratose; margins entire, 2- to 3-stratose, revolute on 1 or both sides; costa stout, nearly terete, prominent and papillose at back above, in section showing fairly well-developed ventral guides, 2 toward the apex, 3–4 toward the base; upper cells rounded-quadrate, chlorophyllose, 7–10 μ wide, the walls fairly thick, smooth above, becoming $\pm$ sinuous at mid-leaf, bearing clear, transparent, longitudinal cuticular ridges extending over 4–10 or more cells in a row, the surface view appearing as pale streaks and in cross section as low to globose pearl-like papillae; basal cells wider, quadrate to oblong, smooth, the walls usually strongly sinuous, those toward the basal margins shorter; extreme inner basal cells with smooth walls. Dioicous. Seta 3–5 mm long, $\pm$ curved; capsules elliptic-oblong; annulus persistent; lid with a long straight beak; urn about 1 mm long, smooth when dry; teeth reddish, entire. Calyptra mitrate. (Sporophytes not seen.) Plate 51, figs. 1–10.

12.101   On dry or moist siliceous rocks, alpine in our region. Rare.

12.102   Europe, northern Michigan; Idaho and Utah: Summit-Duchesne County lines: Uinta Mountains, brooklet below Mirror Lake, 10,100 ft., Bald Mountain above Mirror Lake, 10,300 ft.

12.103 Local collection specimens are sterile, but the plant is readily identified by the dense clusters of gemmae on the tips of the comal leaves of some shoots. The more or less prostrate-ascending habit and the upper leaf cells with longitudinal cuticular ridges are distinctive.

2. RACOMITRIUM Brid.

12.104 Plants large, in dense to loose tufts or spreading mats, on wet or dry rocks, rarely on wood or soil, yellowish green to blackish. Stems erect to long prostrate and ascending, sympodially and monopodially branched, the branches few to numerous, elongated or short, tuftlike, crowded, basal, rather coarse, reddish brown. Leaves mostly imbricated when dry, erect-patent to strongly squarrose-recurved when moist, ovate-lanceolate to lanceolate, obtuse, slenderly acute to acuminate, often terminating in a hyaline point or hair; margins plane to recurved, entire or variously toothed at the extreme apex; costa percurrent or ending well below the apex, homogeneous in cross section; upper leaf cells mostly small, quadrate-rounded to oblong, the walls mostly thick and sinuous (sometimes nearly entire), smooth to papillose; basal cells oblong to linear, usually with ± thick sinuous walls, usually to the degree of being nodulose, rarely nearly smooth. Dioicous. Perigonia and perichaetia terminal on the main stems or branches, often becoming lateral by innovation. Seta long, straight or curved; capsules long exserted, erect and symmetric, ovoid to cylindric, smooth to somewhat sulcate when dry; annulus present; stomata usually in 2 rows in the basal part; lid conic with a long subulate beak; peristome teeth 16, cleft to divided into 2–3 slender, often hairlike divisions. Calyptra mitrate, usually dilated at the base and with a long beak.

12.105 Related to *Grimmia*, differing mainly in the slender, deeply divided peristome teeth, longer beak on the operculum, longer seta, basal leaf cells oblong to linear and cell walls strongly sinuous to nodulose. On the whole the plants occur in looser tufts or expanded mats, many with prostrate main stems with erect branches.

12.106 The name (Greek) means ragged cap, alluding to the calyptra.

12.107 **Racomitrium canescens** (Hedw.) Brid. Plants in loose or somewhat matted tufts, yellowish green to dark green, often appearing somewhat granular or mealy with a pale or whitish cast at the tips of the stems, dark brownish or blackish below. Stems erect to prostrate with ascending branches 1–10 cm long, branches short to moderately long, occasionally with a few very short tuftlike branches. Leaves loosely imbricated, very little wrinkled when dry, erect-patent to squarrose-recurved when moist, shortly ovate-lanceolate to oblong-lanceolate, 1.5–2.5(3) mm long, gradually and evenly tapering from the broad base to an acute apex or slenderly acuminate and usually terminating in a hyaline flat tip sometimes prolonged into a short hair, entire to coarsely toothed and strongly

263

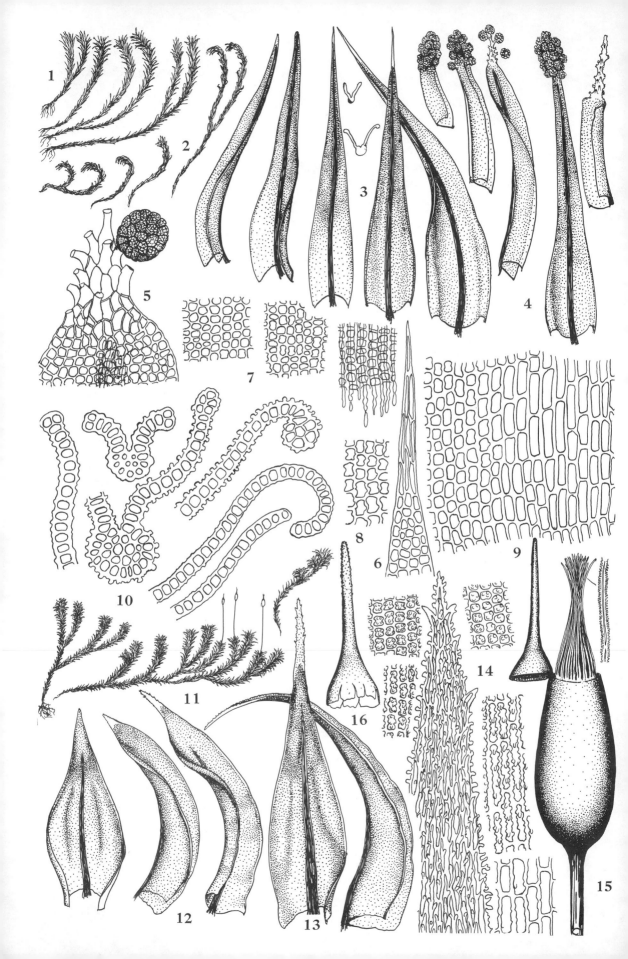

papillose all over, lamina concave to slightly keeled, unistratose; margins entire, widely recurved to the base, bistratose above; costa rather wide, flattish convex, extending to the middle of the leaf to percurrent, variable in different specimens; cells of the hyaline tip oblong to linear, coarsely papillose; upper leaf cells chlorophyllose, quadrate, rounded or oblong, the walls thick and usually sinuous but sometimes nearly entire, 8–12 μ wide, papillose on both sides; basal cells becoming longer, the inner ones oblong to linear, usually strongly sinuous or nodulose, those at the extreme base often wider and with nearly entire walls, those toward the margin becoming shorter, an alar group frequently thin walled and hyaline, sometimes forming small auricles. Seta elongated, 5–25 mm long, straight to slightly flexuous, twisted clockwise when dry; capsules ellipsoid to oblong-ellipsoid, urn about 2 mm long, gradually narrowed to the mouth, dark reddish brown, smooth to longitudinally sulcate when dry; annulus of 2 rows of darker reddish cells, revoluble; lid conic with a long, acicular beak; peristome teeth 16, united at the base as a low membrane and divided nearly to the base into 2 long hairlike divisions, 1–1.5 mm long, reddish brown and very densely and finely papillose, fragile. Spores smooth, globose, yellowish to yellowish brown, mostly 8–10 μ. Calyptra dilated and mitrate at the base, prolonged into a long slender beak, papillose at the apex. Plate 51, figs. 11–16.

12.108   On wet or dry rocks, from sea level at higher latitudes and extending to the subalpine zones in the mountains southward.

12.109   Europe, Asia, and Africa. Greenland, Labrador, New Hampshire, Michigan. Alaska to California, Montana, Utah.

12.110   Occasional to frequent in the Uinta Mountains which apparently marks its southern limit in this region. So variable that one must interpret the description with considerable latitude. The description and illustration of the sporophyte were taken from specimens collected in British Columbia. Our specimens are sterile and not quite typical. The leaves are shorter and on the whole broader, more rapidly tapering to the apex, shortly ovate-lanceolate to somewhat oblong-lanceolate and more or less squarrose-recurved. More typical plants have leaves lanceolate with longer and narrower apices, the costae percurrent or nearly so, and sometimes so strongly recurved as to be circinate. In our plants the costa of many leaves reaches only the middle of the leaf and only occasionally becomes subpercurrent. The upper leaf cells vary from leaf to leaf;

Plate 51.   1–10. Grimmia hartmanii var. **anomala.** 1. Moist habit. 2. Dry habit, X.4. 3. Five stem leaves. 4. Four comal leaves from the innermost juvenile state to outer mature form showing apical propagulae, X8. 5. Apex of propaguliferous leaf. 6. Apex of upper stem leaf. 7. Upper medial leaf cells of different leaves and a horizontal section to show the longitudinal cuticular ridges. 8. Sinuous leaf cells toward the base. 9. Basal leaf cells. 10. Cross sections of leaf at different levels, X80.

11–16. Racomitrium canescens. 11. Habit sketches, X.4. 12. Stem leaves. 13. Perichaetial leaves, X8. 14. Leaf apex, and cells from various levels, X80. 15. Capsule. 16. Calyptra, X8.

in some they are quadrate with entire walls, in others rounded quadrate to oblong with strongly sinuous walls. The inner basal cells also vary widely, typically oblong to linear and very strongly sinuous or nodulose; only the extreme basal ones are smooth walled and wider. In our plants the inner basal cells are mostly oblong, quite wide as compared with the cells above, while the walls are thinner and nearly smooth.

12.111   Variations of this species have been treated as separate species, varieties, or merely forms, as follows: fo. *ericoides* (Hedw.) Brid. with numerous short tuftlike branches and leaves with white hair points, and fo. *epilosum* (Mild.), with few or no tuftlike branches and the leaves mostly without white points. Traces of these characters often appear in otherwise typical plants.

3. SCOULERIA Hook. in Drumm.

12.112   Plants large in coarse loose tufts or long straggling masses on wet or inundated rocks of streams; black below, dark green above. Stems elongated, sympodially or sometimes monopodially branched; central strand lacking, outer cortical cells small and thick walled; rhizoids basal, coarse. Leaves usually crowded above, oblong-ovate, lanceolate or oblong-ligulate; costa stout and wide, ending below the apex, in cross section showing medial guides with dorsal and ventral stereid bands; upper leaf cells comparatively small, mostly isodiametric. Dioicous. Perichaetium terminal, leaves undifferentiated. Perigonia becoming lateral by innovation, budlike. Sporophyte terminal on a short section of the main axis, appearing as a lateral branch due to innovation; seta very short; capsule mostly oblate-globose, immersed to emergent, dark reddish brown to blackish, shiny; wall of the urn thick and fleshy, without air chambers, composed of 6–9 layers of cells, the outer ones thick walled; mouth small, annulus undifferentiated; lid mostly flattish with a central papillate protuberance; peristome, when present, of 16 short teeth, variously cleft to divided or sometimes nearly entire, inserted well within the mouth. Spores large, up to 60 μ in diameter. Calyptra cucullate. (When dry the urn shrinks proximally, remaining smooth and shiny, and resembles a small, thick rubber tire, the small lid persistent on the thick, longitudinally ribbed columella which projects high above the incurved mouth.)

12.113   Named for John Scouler, a physician and botanical collector prominent in the exploration of the Pacific Northwest, who collected the type species.

12.114   **Scouleria aquatica Hook.** Stems 1–15 cm long, densely leafy above, becoming strongly eroded below with only the costae of the leaves remaining. Leaves loosely appressed, ± incurved and the upper ones somewhat crisped when dry, patent to spreading-recurved when moist, ovate-lanceolate to oblong-ligulate, sometimes undulate, widely concave to slightly keeled, 2.5–3.5 mm long, the apex broadly rounded to widely acute in a few leaves, flat to cucullate; margins ranging from entire in the lower leaves to coarsely and often irregularly dentate in the upper ones, the dentations composed of 1 to many cells (usually thicker walled and of a dark smoky color), unistratose; lamina unistratose, in cross section often appearing clavate toward the margin; costa dorsally convex, often papillose above and bearing dense tufts of rhizoids on the back below; upper cells mostly rounded hexagonal, thick walled, especially toward the margins, 7–16 μ wide, smooth or occasionally low mammillose; basal cells variable, quadrate to rectangular, often with a longitudinal zone of oblong to linear, ± thick walled cells toward the basal margin, edged by several rows of ± quadrate marginal cells. Capsules 2–2.3 mm wide; peristome teeth mostly cleft or divided to the base, ± perforated, the divisions irregular, 32–46 or more, mostly triangular to oblong-lanceolate, the tips slender to bluntly truncate, reddish brown, rather closely jointed and smooth, incurved when moist, erect to reflexed against the mouth when dry. Spores globose, 30–60 μ, smooth to finely crenulate, greenish to brown. (Sporophytes described from material from British Columbia.) Plate 52, figs. 1–7.

12.115   On submerged or frequently inundated rocks of streams.

12.116   Alaska to California, eastward to Wyoming and Utah. Salt Lake County: Wasatch Mountains, Brighton, rocks in Lake Mary Creek, 8,800–9,000 ft.

12.117   All our specimens are sterile and antheridial.

ORTHOTRICHACEAE

13.1   Plants loosely to densely tufted, but sometimes creeping and often ± solitary, on rocks or trunks of trees, mostly dark green to olivaceous, sometimes yellowish. Stems without a central strand. Leaves usually dense, oblong-ligulate to narrowly lanceolate, usually keeled, slenderly acute to broadly obtuse, variously 1- to 2-stratose in upper part; margins mostly entire, plane to revolute; upper cells small, rarely exceeding 16 μ wide, isodiametric to rounded or shortly rectangular, mostly thick walled, papillose or smooth; basal cells oblong to linear, usually smooth, often colored; brood bodies often present on leaves or in leaf axils. Sporophytes terminal or becoming lateral by innovation; seta shorter than the capsule or much longer, erect; capsules globose to pyriform or cylindric, smooth to longitudinally 8-ribbed or furrowed when dry; lid convex to conic, ± rostrate; annulus present but not well developed, stomata present; peristome lacking in *Amphidium* and a few other species, mostly single or double, the teeth separate or in pairs, inner peristome composed of 8–16 cilia, lacking in some species. Calyptra mitrate, small to large, ± campanulate and hairy, sometimes plicate.

13.2   Dry capsules often require prolonged soaking, sometimes for several days, to restore their fully distended condition and reveal their exact shape. Even then, the neck may never become fully distended.

13.3   1. Leaves not conspicuously crisped when dry; perichaetial leaves not different from the stem leaves .... 1. *Orthotrichum*   13.5

13.4   1. Leaves strongly crisped when dry; perichaetial leaves much larger and broader than the stem leaves, strongly incurved and sheathing the seta .... 2. *Amphidium*   13.93

1. ORTHOTRICHUM Hedw.

13.5   Plants in loose or dense tufts, dark colored and occurring on rocks or trunks of trees. Stems erect, monopodially or sympodially branched; rhizoids usually confined to the base. Leaves appressed and imbricated to slightly crisped when dry, oblong-ligulate to slenderly lanceolate, keeled, obtuse to narrowly acute; margins mostly revolute, plane, entire to slightly toothed at the apex; costa stout, percurrent or nearly so, in cross section showing a ± homogeneous structure, usually of 2 rows of ventral cells and 1 row of dorsal cells (the latter sometimes smaller); upper cells quadrate, rounded or shortly rectangular, usually thick walled and papillose, the papillae simple or forked; basal cells mostly oblong, smooth, and often colored. Mostly autoicous (a few species dioicous). Perigonia small, on the main stem or 2–4 on a very small branch below the perichaetium. Perichaetial leaves usually larger and often narrower at the apices. Seta sheathed at base by an ochrea, vaginule sometimes hairy; capsules immersed to rather long exserted, subglobose to subcylindrical, obovate or pyriform; smooth or ribbed and ± contracted below the mouth when dry, often becoming strongly furrowed when old and empty, ±8-striate, the striae formed by several longitudinal rows of thick walled darker colored cells alternating with several rows of smaller or thinner-walled pale cells; stomata superficial or immersed below, thick-walled, ± projecting adjacent cells; annulus poorly defined; peristome teeth cuneate, separate or in pairs, erect and spreading or reflexed against the wall of the urn when dry; preperistome present in some species; cilia 8–16, often rudimentary or lacking. Calyptra conic to campanulate, ± plicate, smooth or with erect hairs.

13.6   The name, derived from Greek, means erect hair, alluding to the upright hairs on the calyptra.

13.7   1. Stomata superficial

2. On bark of trees; capsules emergent, oblong-cylindric when moist, ribbed to strongly furrowed when dry

3. Leaves acute .... 5. *O. affine*   13.32

3. Leaves mostly narrowly obtuse .... 5a. fo. *obtusum*   13.36

Plate 52.   1–7. Scouleria aquatica. 1–2. Moist and dry habit sketches, X.4. 3. Portion of stem with leaves removed to show terminal position of perichaetia and sympodial nature of axis, X4. 4. Upper leaves, X8. 5. Two upper leaf margins and medial cells. 6. Basal leaf cells (inner linear cells often lacking), X80. 7. Moist and dry capsules, X8, with cellular detail from a cross section of the urn, X80.

8–16. Grimmia atricha. 8. Habit sketches, X.4. 9. Shoot, X4. 10. Stem leaves. 11. Perichaetial leaves, X8. 12. Leaf apex. 13. Basal cell. 14. Cross sections of a leaf at different levels, X80. 15. Five capsules, X8. 16. Peristome teeth, X60, detail, X200.

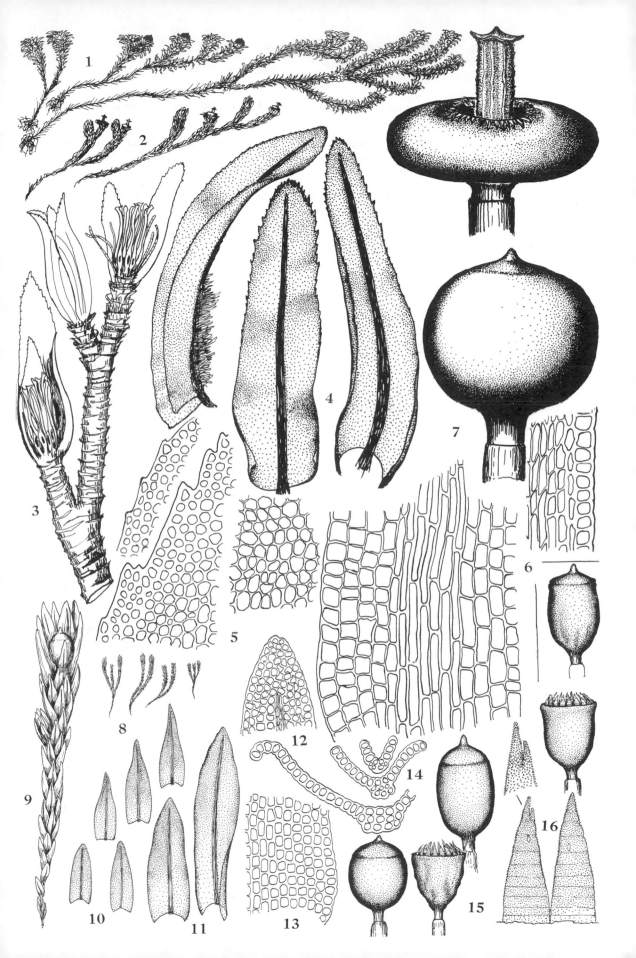

2. On rocks; capsules smooth to faintly ribbed only below the mouth when dry

    4. Capsules immersed to emergent, obovate to oblong when moist, usually appearing oblong when dry; leaves lanceolate, acute, or blunt

        5. Peristome teeth finely granular-papillose or striate, occasionally smooth .... 1. *O. rupestre* 13.9

        5. Peristome teeth coarsely papillose to warty, often irregularly so .... 2. *O. texanum* 13.13

    4. Capsules exserted, oblong to elongate-pyriform when moist, usually appearing cylindric when dry; peristome teeth finely to moderately papillose, the lower joints often finely striate (coarsely ridged throughout in 4a)

        6. Leaves mostly broadly lanceolate, ± broadly tapering upward and rather suddenly narrowed to a bluntly acute or obtuse tip .... 3. *O. laevigatum* 13.18

        6. Leaves ovate-lanceolate to narrowly lanceolate, gradually tapering upward to a narrowly acute tip

            7. Peristome teeth without straight or curved ridges, moderately papillose .... 4. *O. macounii* 13.23

            7. Peristome teeth with straight or curved ridges, interspersed with a few large and irregular papillae .... 4a. fo. *vermiculare* 13.30

13.8   1. Stomata immersed

    8. Plants growing on rocks

        9. Capsules emergent exserted, oblong; teeth ± finely ridged-striate .... 9. *O. anomalum* 13.54

        9. Capsules immersed to emergent

            10. Leaves oblong-lanceolate to ligulate, narrowly to broadly obtuse; capsules obovate to pyriform; teeth finely to coarsely ridged-striate .... 7. *O. jamesianum* 13.44

            10. Leaves ovate-lanceolate to lanceolate

                11. Upper leaves hyaline-apiculate and often denticulate at the tips; cells large and thin walled, 10–20 μ wide, clear, low; cilia 16, appendiculate .... 14. *O. garrettii* 13.88

                11. Upper leaves slenderly acute to blunt (only a few obtuse), never apiculate; cells usually thick walled, mostly 10–12 μ wide; cilia not appendiculate, often lacking

                    12. Teeth striate with continuous ridges, sometimes inter-

spersed with papillae (*O. strangulatum* may be sought here)

13. Leaves 1-stratose throughout or occasionally 2-stratose in small patches or in lines; capsules immersed to shortly emergent, subglobose, ovoid or shortly pyriform; cilia lacking or occasionally 8 and short .... 6. *O. cupulatum* 13.40

13. Leaves 2-stratose in the upper half; capsules emergent, shortly oblong to pyriform; cilia usually present but often broken .... 8. *O. hallii* 13.48

12. Teeth papillose throughout or upper joints vertically striate with rows of papillae sometimes fused in nodulose to smooth continuous ridges, usually interspersed with scattered papillae; capsules immersed to emergent

14. Plants mostly less than 1 cm tall, in compact, dull, dark green tufts; upper leaves 1- or occasionally 2-stratose above, papillae mostly low, simple, scarcely forked; capsules small, rarely exceeding 1.7 mm long; teeth 200–270 μ long, often separating early, variously papillose to ridged-striate; preperistome present or lacking; cilia 8, slender, or lacking .... 10. *O. strangulatum* 13.58

14. Plants larger and forming loose bright to yellowish green tufts; leaves 1-stratose throughout with tall simple or forked papillae; capsules 1.5–2.2 mm long; teeth 250–400 μ long, in pairs, finely papillose throughout or with the upper joints vertically ridged-striate or with papillae in lines; preperistome lacking; cilia 8, occasionally 16 .... 11. *O. alpestre* 13.61

8. Plants growing on trees; capsules ribbed when dry

15. Plants less than 1 cm tall, in small low tufts; upper leaf cells 12–16 μ wide or wider, mostly with small low papillae or smooth; capsules immersed to emergent; calyptra without hairs

16. Stomata mostly widely exposed; upper leaf cells 12–16 μ wide, thick walled and chlorophyllose

17. Leaves narrowly lanceolate to lanceolate from an ovate or oblong base; apex narrowly to broadly acute or narrowly obtuse, entire; cilia 8–16, the intermediate ones short or rudimentary .... 12. *O. pallens* 13.70

17. Leaves ovate-lanceolate to oblong-ligulate, narrowly obtuse to broadly rounded, often abruptly mucronate, rarely a few acute, apex often denticulate, cilia 8 .... 12a. var. *parvum* 13.74

16. Stomata deeply immersed and mostly obscured by the over-

hanging thickened walls of the adjacent exothecial cells, only occasionally exposed; leaf cells 14–17(20) µ wide, thin walled and clear

18. Capsules immersed to slightly emergent, oval to oval-oblong, rounded at the base; cilia 8

19. Leaves ovate-lanceolate to oblong-lanceolate, mostly slenderly acute .... 13. *O. pumilum* 13.79

19. Leaves mostly broadly oblong-ligulate, broadly rounded, some widely acute to blunt .. 13b. var. *ligulaefolium* 13.86

18. Capsules strongly emergent, often apparently exserted when dry; elliptic-oblong to subcylindric, the neck longer and broadly tapering to the seta; cilia 8–16, the intermediate ones short or rudimentary; leaves mostly narrowly lanceolate and slenderly acute .... 13a. var. *fallax* 13.83

15. Plants 1–3 cm tall, in looser or expanded tufts; calyptra with few to numerous hairs

20. Capsules exserted; oval-oblong to subcylindric; teeth ridged-striate .... 9. *O. anomalum* 13.54

20. Capsules immersed to emergent, seta short, oblong to pyriform

21. Leaves bistratose above, teeth strongly ridged-striate .... 8. *O. hallii* 13.48

21. Leaves unistratose throughout; teeth papillose throughout or vertically striate above .... 11. *O. alpestre* 13.61

13.9   **1. Orthotrichum rupestre** Schleich. ex Schwaegr. Plants in loose or dense tufts on rocks, dull, dark green to yellowish above, brownish to blackish below. Stems erect or ascending, 1–10 cm long, moderately branched, quite stiff when dry. Leaves lanceolate, gradually narrowed above to a narrowly obtuse or acute apex, 3–5 mm long, mostly erect and appressed when dry, patent to recurved when moist, strongly keeled; margins entire, revolute to the apex; costa stout, percurrent or disappearing shortly below the apex; upper cells rounded to irregularly quadrate or oval-oblong, thick walled, mostly 8–12 µ wide, unistratose or bistratose here and there in lines, moderately to strongly papillose; basal cells rectangular in mature leaves, smooth, usually thick walled, sometimes very thick and nodulose; alar cells often quadrate. Autoicous. Seta typically short, sometimes up to 0.5 mm long; capsules immersed to emergent, ovoid, oblong or elongate-pyriform, mouth usually small, especially when the urn is short; the neck typically gradually tapering to and imperceptibly merging with the seta, but in some forms shorter and more suddenly narrowed to the seta, yellowish to light brown, 0.7–2.5 mm long, when dry only slightly contracted under the mouth or not at all, smooth to rather prominently ribbed below the mouth (with age remaining smooth or becoming more strongly ribbed); stomata few, superficial, opposite the lower portion of the spore sac; annulus double; peristome teeth in 8 pairs, becoming separate, erect to spreading, entire to variously perforated along the medial line, joints usually short, smooth to finely granular-papillose, often finely sinuous-striate; cilia variable, lacking, rudimentary, or well developed and composed of 2 rows of cells, nearly as long as the teeth; lid convex-conic with a short to rather long beak. Spores globose, 12–16 μ, greenish brown to brown, coarsely low papillose. Calyptra broadly campanulate, plicate and densely hairy, yellowish. Plate 53, figs. 1–8.

13.10   On noncalcareous rocks, mostly in the mountains and favored by partial shade.

13.11   Europe. British Columbia to Montana and southward through the Rocky Mountains to western Texas; westward to the Pacific Coast.

13.12   The degree to which the capsule tapers to the seta varies so much that the length of the seta proper ranges from practically nil to as much as 0.7 mm. The neck is usually much shrunken and requires prolonged soaking to restore it to a fully distended state. Only then can the actual contours of neck and seta be determined. (Even with weeks of soaking some capsules fail to become distended.) Some forms with the peristome teeth rather coarsely papillose are difficult to distinguish from *O. texanum*. As a matter of fact, the two species intergrade, and there is evidence that some of our collections of *O. rupestre* may be *O. texanum* with imperfectly developed papillae on the teeth. On the other hand, some plants of *O. rupestre* found in mixture with *O. texanum* are as sharply set off as any species should be. The accompanying illustrations apply to local forms and not to some of the remarkable variants of the species in other parts of its range.

13.13   **2. Orthotrichum texanum** Sull. & Lesq. Gametophytes almost exactly like those of *O. rupestre* and showing about the same range of variation but without bistratose laminae. Capsules immersed to emergent, often appearing exserted when dry, shortly obovate, pyriform or shortly oblong-cylindric, urn 1–2.5 mm long, smooth or faintly ribbed under the mouth when dry, sometimes quite strongly furrowed in old empty capsules, yellowish to yellowish brown at maturity; neck often imperceptibly merging with the seta, the latter ranging from practically nil to 1.5 mm long, or more abruptly narrowed and the seta more distinctly set off, peristome teeth erect when dry, in pairs, yellowish to yellowish brown, often ± perforated down the middle, coarsely papillose to warty, sometimes with short thick ridges; cilia short or lacking. Plate 53, figs. 9–11.

13.14   Usually on dry, noncalcareous rocks in mountains, favored by shade.

13.15   British Columbia through the Rocky Mountains to Texas; westward to the Pacific Coast.

13.16   Quite common in Utah and intergrading with *O. rupestre*. Typically the capsules are oblong to oblong-cylindric and rather suddenly nar-

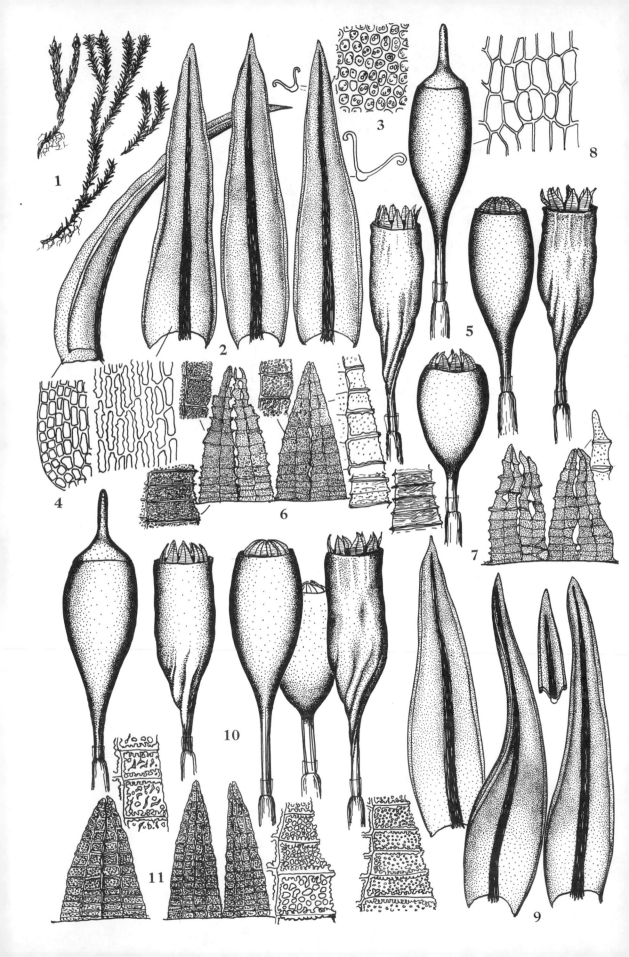

rowed to a seta about 0.5 mm long and thereby moderately emergent or seemingly exserted when dry. In several collections, the necks imperceptibly merge with the setae. Other plants have immersed, shortly obovate or pyriform capsules with the neck tapering into an almost obsolete seta. Some of the latter might be referred to var. *globosum* Lesq., which was transferred to *O. rupestre,* as var. *globosum* (Lesq.), Grout in the *Moss Flora of North America.* However, that variety has an almost naked calyptra, while in the present plants the calyptra is quite hairy.

13.17   Variations in the sculpturing of the teeth are a matter of some consequence. Typically the teeth are coarsely papillose or beset with large wartlike protuberances or ridges, especially on the lower joints. When growth of the sporophyte is slowed up or interrupted, a variety of immature states of the peristome may be observed. For example, I have seen pale yellowish teeth with smooth plates and thick joints which may be smooth or with unusually thick scallops, lobes, or branched ridges extending toward the middle of the plates, sometimes with one to a few isolated papillae or warts here and there. Sometimes the teeth are variously incised at the margins, strongly perforated down the middle, or incomplete at the apex. I visited a colony of several square meters over a period of several years. One year the capsules were mostly exserted on long setae, but two years later they were immersed or moderately emergent on short setae.

13.18   **3. Orthotrichum laevigatum** Zett. var. **laevigatum.** Plants mostly in short, dark green, olivaceous tufts. Stems 0.5–2(3) cm tall. Leaves 2–4 mm long, broadly lanceolate, broadly tapering and suddenly or gradually narrowed to a bluntly acute or obtuse apex, much like those of *O. rupestre* but often more strongly papillose, the upper and perichaetial and comal ones sometimes gradually and evenly tapering to a slenderly acute tip like the stem leaves of *O. macounii;* margins mostly widely recurved; upper cells 10–14 μ occasionally 17 μ wide; basal cells more commonly thick walled, nodulose and reddish. Autoicous. Seta 1–2.5(4) mm long; capsules exserted, oval-oblong to oblong or sometimes pyriform, appearing narrowly cylindric and smooth when dry, occasionally some of them lightly ribbed below the mouth, yellowish to yellowish brown, darker with age, the urn 1–1.5(2) mm long, the neck typically long, gradually tapering downward and imperceptibly merging with the seta, usually much wrinkled when dry, in some forms more suddenly narrowed and more clearly set off from the seta; peristome teeth erect when dry, at first in pairs, pale yellowish to yellowish brown, finely granulose to moderately papillose; cilia 8, well developed, of 1–2 rows of

---

Plate 53.   1–8. Orthotrichum rupestre. 1. Habit sketches, X.4. 2. **Typical leaves,** X8. 3. Upper medial leaf cells. 4. Basal cells, X120. 5. Capsules, X8. 6–7. Peristome teeth from different plants showing variations in sculpturing, X60, details, X200. 8. Exothecial cells, X120.

9–11. Orthotrichum texanum. 9. Typical leaves. 10. Capsules, X8. 11. Peristome teeth from different plants showing variations in sculpturing, X60, detail, X200.

smooth cells, about ⅔ the length of the teeth, varying to rudimentary or none. Calyptra subcylindric, lightly ribbed, yellowish to reddish brown, sparingly hairy. Plate 54, figs. 1–5.

13.19 Mostly on noncalcareous rocks, usually in shady places.

13.20 Europe. British Columbia southward to southern California and eastward to Idaho, Wyoming, and Utah.

13.21 Var. **kingianum** (Lesq.) Grout. Extreme form of the species having exserted capsules with an ovoid urn suddenly narrowed to a long tapering neck. When dry the urn is slenderly cylindrical and smooth, only the neck being wrinkled. The teeth are finely granular-papillose and the joints indistinct.

13.22 *Orthotrichum laevigatum* is fairly abundant locally in Utah, especially on noncalcareous rocks. The bluntly pointed or obtuse leaves and well-exserted smooth capsules with long tapering necks are its strong points. It may be mistaken for *O. macounii,* especially if the perichaetial and inner comal leaves are evenly tapered to slenderly acute tips. All or nearly all the stem leaves of *O. macounii* are of this kind.

13.23 **4. Orthotrichum macounii** Aust. Plants in rather large loose tufts or sometimes forming mats. Stems quite stout, erect or prostrate and ascending at the tips, 1–3(5) cm long or tall; branches few, often distant. Leaves closely to loosely imbricated when dry, erect to patent when moist, 2.5–4 mm long, ovate-lanceolate to lanceolate, mostly evenly tapering to a slenderly acute apex; margins recurved to narrowly revolute well toward the apex; costa ending 2–7 cells below the tip or vaguely percurrent; upper leaf cells rounded, oval or irregular, thick walled and usually with rather small, low papillae, 8–12 μ wide; basal cells oblong to linear, walls thick and smooth or becoming nodulose in older mature leaves, basal marginal cells shorter and narrower. Autoicous. Seta rather long, 1.5–2(4) mm long; capsules exserted, light yellowish to yellowish brown, ovoid-oblong to oblong when moist, becoming oblong-cylindric to cylindric when dry, the urn smooth or sometimes lightly ribbed below the mouth when dry; neck usually gradually tapering into the seta but sometimes rather abruptly contracted; stomata superficial, usually in 2 rows opposite the lower portion of the spore sac; peristome teeth erect when dry, yellowish, becoming tinged with brown in old capsules, in pairs at first, finely to moderately papillose, the basal joints often with narrow ridges or vague designs; cilia 8, about ⅔ the length of the teeth or shorter, usually of 2 rows of cells, smooth or sometimes strongly nodulose or sub-appendiculate; lid conic, shortly rostrate. Spores yellowish to light brownish, 12–17(23) μ, finely punctate. Calyptra yellowish, plicate and sparsely hairy. Plate 54, figs. 6–9.

Plate 54.   1–5. **Orthotrichum laevigatum.** 1. Habit sketches, X.4. 2. Leaves. 3–4. Capsules from two different plants showing variations, X8. 5. Peristome teeth, X60, detail, X200.

6–9. Orthotrichum macounii. 6. Habit sketches, X.4. 7. Leaves. 8. Capsules, X8. 9. Peristome teeth and cilia, X40, detail, X200.

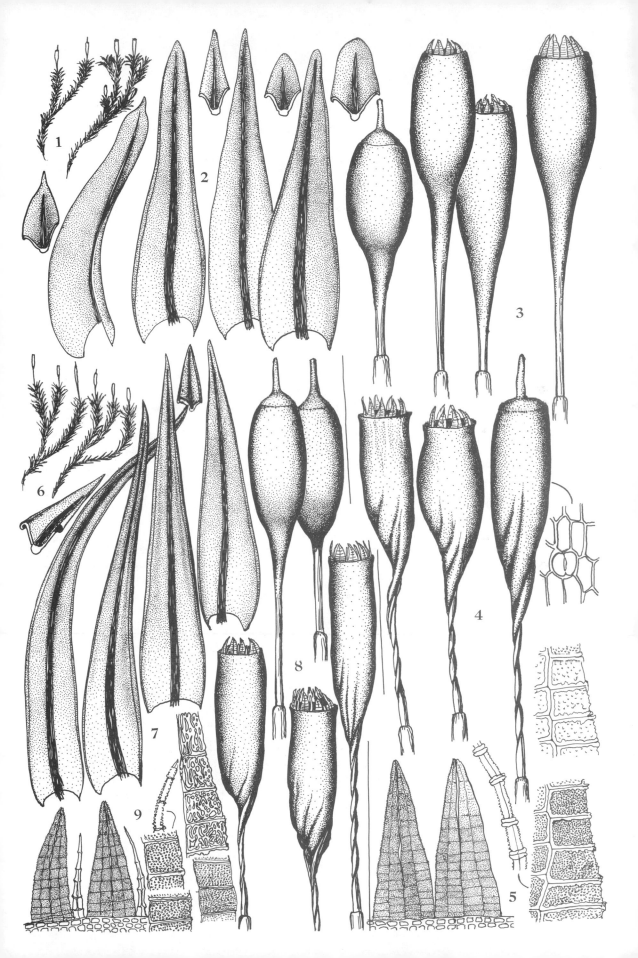

13.24 On dry rocks, mostly in shaded places.

13.25 Alaska, British Columbia, Washington, Idaho, Montana, Wyoming, Colorado, and Utah.

13.26 Frequent in the mountains of northern Utah. Typical plants are distinguished by their lanceolate leaves tapering gradually to very slender apices, well exserted capsules, and teeth with finely to moderately coarse papillae (these sometimes irregular and intergrading with straight or sinuous ridges on the lower joints). An extreme form with coarse vermicular ridges interspersed with a few large papillae is referred to the following variety. This plant is close to *O. roellii* Vent., which has finer, more elongated, sinuous ridges or striations throughout the teeth, but it has ovate-lanceolate leaves, much broader at the base and while mostly evenly tapered upward to acute points, some of them are blunt. Also, in the type, the capsules are emergent, although some appear exserted when dry.

13.27 *Orthotrichum macounii* intergrades with *O. laevigatum* through var. *lonchothecium* (C. Muell. & Kindb.) Grout, which has bluntly acute leaves like those of *O. rupestre* but not as broad in the upper part as those of *O. laevigatum*. I have a specimen from Grand Teton National Park in Wyoming in which some shoots have slender leaves on the former season's growth typical of *O. macounii*, while the leaves of the current season's growth are wide in the upper part and suddenly narrowed to a bluntly acute or even obtuse apex typical of *O. laevigatum*.

13.28 *O. schlotthaueri* Vent. differs only in having a shorter seta and capsules emergent and faintly ribbed below the mouth when dry.

13.29 The cilia of the peristome are usually present and in our specimens range from ½–¾ the length of the teeth, although I suspect that they may be rudimentary or lacking in some plants. They are usually composed of two rows of cells which are mostly smooth, but often become nodulose by the thickening of the joints and, in extreme instances, actually subappendiculate when the thickened joints extend laterally like elongated pegs. I regard all of these variations as developmental in nature and of no taxonomic significance.

13.30 4a. Fo. **vermiculare** Flow. Peristome teeth beset with coarse, straight, or curved ridges of varying length and interspersed with a few large irregular papillae.

13.31 Daggett County: Uinta Mountains, Carter Creek. 8,000 ft.

13.32 **5. Orthotrichum affine** Brid. Plants in low small tufts or sometimes widely expanded, dark or dull green, often tinged with brown above, brownish to blackish below. Stems erect, moderately to freely branched, 0.5–2(3) cm tall. Leaves straight and ± imbricated when dry, mostly ovate-lanceolate to oblong-lanceolate, the inner comal and perichaetial ones often ligulate, 2–3(4) mm long; apex variable even on the same shoot, gradually tapering to an acute or blunt tip or wider toward the upper part and then suddenly narrowed to an acute or obtuse tip;

margins widely to narrowly recurved well toward the apex; costa subpercurrent or ending below the apex; upper cells rounded-quadrate to oval or irregular, 12–17(21) μ wide, walls rather thin for the genus, becoming thicker with age, moderately papillose and quite clear; basal cells becoming wider and elongated, oblong to 5–6 sided, thin walled at first, often becoming thick walled, nodulose, and colored with age, the marginal ones shorter and narrower. Multicellular gemmae occasional on the leaves. Autoicous. Seta 0.5–1.5 mm long; capsule mostly emergent, sometimes nearly exserted, oblong-cylindrical when moist, strongly furrowed when dry; the neck long and gradually tapering into the seta and often extending nearly to its base; exothecial cells thick walled on the ridges and thin walled in the furrows; stomata superficial, mostly from the middle of the spore sac to its base; peristome teeth 16, in pairs, reflexed when dry and mature, finely to moderately papillose, the papillae $\pm$ scattered or in designs, simple, short-ridged or often fused in short lines or distinct striations, the latter frequently predominating; cilia 8, mostly of 2 rows of cells, papillose, about ¾ the length of the teeth, often shorter. Lid conic-rostrate, annulus of 2–4 rows of small thick-walled cells. Spores 14–18(20) μ, finely punctate, yellowish brown when fully mature. Calyptra $\pm$ campanulate, yellowish, slightly hairy. Plate 55, figs. 1–6.

13.33   On trunks and bases of trees, mostly in canyons and mountains, occasionally on rocks.

13.34   British Columbia to Montana, southward to Colorado and California.

13.35   Our most common tree-inhabiting species and our only tree inhabitant with superficial stomata. Locally abundant on the trunks and bases of narrow-leaf cottonwood, birch, bigtoothed maple, and boxelder. The shape and contour of the leaves varies widely, even in the same tuft, perhaps more so than in any other species. The leaves range from oblong-lanceolate to lanceolate, the average being ovate-lanceolate. At the extremes some of the leaves on a shoot may be oblong-ligulate or narrowly lanceolate. One of the most common outlines shows the blade widely tapering upward from an ovate base and suddenly narrowed at the apex. Some leaves taper more or less evenly from the base to a slender apex. The apices range from narrowly acute to narrowly obtuse or even broadly rounded. The latter types are mostly confined to the inner perichaetial leaves but frequently appear in well-developed stem leaves whence the plants are designated as the following:

13.36   5a. Fo. **obtusum** Roehl in Brid. Perichaetial leaves ligulate and broadly obtuse; upper stem leaves ovate-lanceolate or occasionally ligulate, mostly narrowly obtuse or a few broadly rounded. Plate 55, fig. 6.

13.37   Salt Lake County: City Creek Canyon, 6,000 ft., Mill Creek Canyon, 5,700 ft.

13.38   *Orthotrichum fastigiatum* Bruch. ex Brid. is included in the synonymy of this species. It is merely a smaller, shorter, more closely branched form with less emergent capsules in which the teeth are more striate than usual. The striations on the teeth have been used as a key character, but every degree of intergradation of these traits with those of typical *O. affine* occurs. The papillae may be small and round, more or less evenly scattered, composed of short, simple or branched ridges, or distinctly elongated ridges forming fine striations. Various mixtures of these markings may occur on teeth of the same capsules, or one may predominate. The accompanying illustrations show some of the common patterns. The cilia are always well developed, of one or two rows of cells and usually more or less papillose. I have yet to find this species without cilia or with rudimentary ones.

13.39 On two occasions in which *O. affine* and *O. alpestre* were growing together, I found some shoots of *O. affine* with capsules showing slightly sunken stomata. I would judge that these were hybrids. The reciprocal cross was not positively identified, although a few plants of *O. alpestre* with narrower, more strongly ribbed capsules and somewhat more widely exposed stomata resembling those of *O. pallens* var. *parvum* might well have been hybrid in origin.

13.40 **6. Orthotrichum cupulatum** Hoffm. ex Brid. Plants mostly in low, compact or loose tufts, occasionally becoming expanded, bright, dull or dark green to blackish, sometimes glaucous when growing in deep shade. Stems erect, rather closely branched, 1–2(3) cm tall. Leaves loosely to closely appressed when dry, erect-patent to slightly recurved when moist, broadly to narrowly ovate-lanceolate, rather broad in the upper part but ± gradually tapering to an acute or blunt tip, sometimes narrowly obtuse; margins widely recurved to revolute well toward the apex; costa stout, nearly percurrent; upper cells ± incrassate, 10–14 μ wide, beset with simple or forked papillae, these ranging from very low to very high, sometimes nearly as tall as the thickness of the cells, unistratose except sometimes in small scattered patches; basal cells wider, oblong to rectangular, thin walled, smooth and hyaline, the inner ones not or rarely thick walled and nodulose. Autoicous. Seta up to 1 mm long or less; capsules immersed to shortly emergent (rarely nearly exserted), longer than the seta subglobose, obovoid or shortly pyriform, mostly about 1.5 mm long, the neck usually not strongly differentiated externally, mostly quite abruptly narrowed to the seta, when dry appearing oblong to subcylindric, contracted under the mouth, strongly 8-ribbed, often with 8 shorter intermediate ribs, becoming strongly furrowed with age; exothecial cells thicker walled and darker along the ribs; stomata deeply sunken, in 1–2 rows opposite the spore sac; annulus of 2–3 rows of cells; lid low-conic, mammillate to shortly

---

Plate 55. 1–6. Orthotrichum affine. 1. Habit sketches, X.4. 2. Dry and moist fertile shoot tips, X3.2. 3. Typical leaves. 4. Capsules, X8, cellular details, X120. 5. Peristome teeth with variations of the cilia, X40, detail, X200. 6. Perichaetial leaves of var. **obtusum**, X8.

7–12. Orthotrichum cupulatum. 7. Habit sketches, X.4. 8. Dry and moist tips of fertile shoots, X3.2. 9. Typical leaves, X8. 10. Cross sections of leaves of two different plants, X120. 11. Capsules, X8. 12. Peristome teeth from different plants, with and without preperistome, X40, detail of sculpturing, X200.

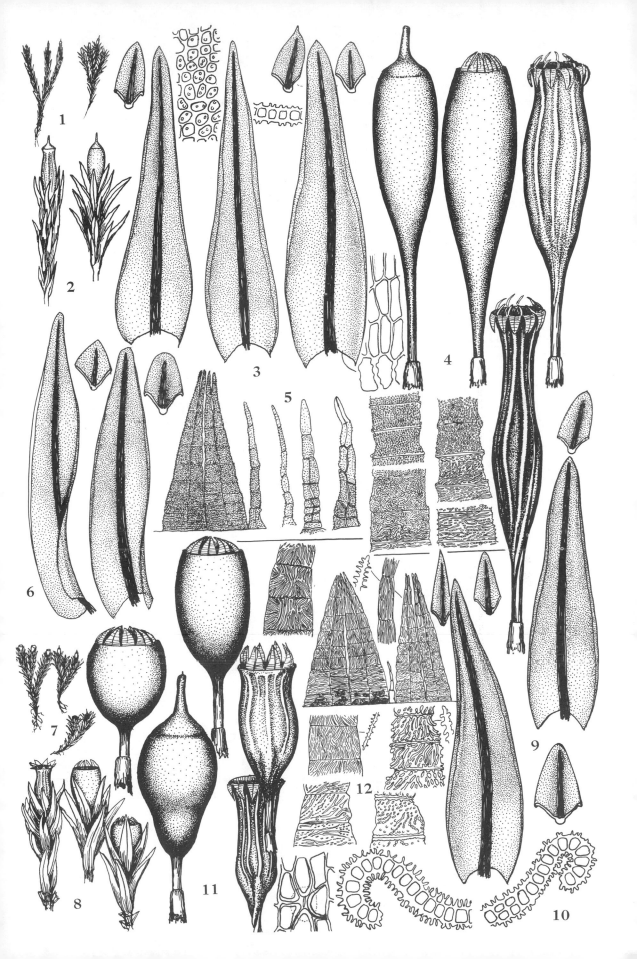

rostrate; peristome teeth in 8 pairs, erect to reflexed when dry, triangular-lanceolate, often narrowly so, entire to perforated or deeply parted down the middle, beset with fine to rather coarse, straight or flexuous ridges extending in various directions, with or without interspersed papillae, especially on the lower plates; cilia lacking or 8 of 1 row of cells, 2–3(5) joints high, smooth; preperistome often present, usually imperfect or irregular and fragmentary, sometimes pale and obscure but often appearing as darker blotches on the lower joints and plates of the teeth, sometimes much thickened and striate like the teeth. Spores 12–17 μ, beset with low, rounded, well spaced papillae. Calyptra campanulate, rather broad, sparingly to moderately hairy. Plate 55, figs. 7–12.

13.41   On dry rocks of various kinds, more abundant on limestone, mostly in mountains and canyons.

13.42   Europe. British Columbia and Alberta southward in the Cascade and Sierra Nevada Mountains to California and in the Rockies to Western Texas.

13.43   Common in Utah and Nevada, particularly on limestone rocks in shaded places. The color and texture varies from glaucous green in loose soft tufts in shaded rocky ravines to dense blackish tufts in drier, more exposed situations. Usually the species is quite distinct, but forms with broader, more obtuse leaves intergrade with *O. jamesianum,* while forms with smaller, but longer, shortly exserted capsules are much like *O. strangulatum.* In western norms of the latter the markings on the teeth range from finely papillose to ridged-striate as in *O. cupulatum.* Some forms also intergrade with *O. hallii* in having a considerable area of the upper lamina bistratose, in lines or patches or occasionally in the entire upper half. In the *O. hallii* the upper lamina is bistratose in most leaves; only in the younger leaves and sometimes those toward the bases of the innovations is the lamina unistratose throughout. In most leaves the areolation is clear, the papillae being small or very transparent, but in some instances the papillae are so dense as to render the lamina opaque and suggestive of bistratose condition. In *O. cupulatum* the apices of the leaves have a tendency to become eroded making them appear obtuse to broadly rounded. In most instances the erosion is quite evident, but occasionally the outer walls of the cells rendered marginal by erosion are so smooth as to give quite a naturally blunt appearance, and the unwary might place such plants in *O. jamesianum,* in which obtuse leaves are the rule.

13.44   **7. Orthotrichum jamesianum** Sull. in Jam. in Watson. Plants much like *O. cupulatum* in nearly all characters and variations, differing mainly in the predominance of somewhat shorter oblong-lanceolate to ligulate leaves with narrowly obtuse to broadly rounded apices and slightly thicker costae. Other traits include the smaller tufts, shorter sparingly branched stems, capsules obovate to shortly pyriform, mostly emergent but sometimes immersed, peristome teeth finely ridged-striate but more often with fine papillae scattered or disposed in straight or sinuous rows. Plate 56, figs. 1–3.

13.45 On dry limestone rocks in shade or partial shade.

13.46 British Columbia, Alberta, North Dakota, Utah, Nevada, and Arizona.

13.47 Usually this can be recognized when dry by blunt to rounded, often incurved leaf tips. Originally *O. jamesianum* was described as lacking cilia.

13.48 **8. Orthotrichum hallii** Sull. & Lesq. in Sull. Plants in rather low dense tufts, sometimes expanded over considerable areas of rocks, dark green to olivaceous, sometimes tinged with yellow. Stems 1–1.5 cm tall. Branched. Leaves mostly appressed or sometimes curved but not crisped when dry, erect-patent to patent when moist, lanceolate to oblong-lanceolate or sometimes ligulate, quite variable in different specimens, apices mostly narrowly obtuse but some of them broadly rounded, acute, or blunt; margins widely recurved in the lower ½–⅔; costa stout; upper lamina of many leaves bistratose, the younger ones and those toward the base of the stem often unistratose throughout; upper cells mostly rounded or hexagonal to oval, fairly thick walled, mostly 10–12 μ wide, each usually bearing 1–2 large simple papillae, some frequently forked; basal cells usually thin to moderately thick walled, the inner ones short to long rectangular, in some older leaves occasionally becoming very thick walled, nodulose, and colored. Autoicous. Seta 0.3–1 mm long; capsules immersed to shortly emergent, shortly obovate, pyriform or oblong, urn 1.5–2 mm long, sometimes appearing almost exserted when dry, typically abruptly narrowed to the seta but sometimes shortly tapering and the seta then appearing much shorter, 8-ribbed when dry, often with 8 shorter intermediate ribs, becoming deeply furrowed with age; stomata immersed; exothecial cells thick walled and darker colored along the ribs; peristome teeth finely to coarsely ridged-striate, sometimes interspersed with papillae, the striations straight to sinuous, simple, branched, or anastomosed, sometimes very short and thick, occasionally formed by rows of papillae; cilia 8, of 1 row of cells, variously developed, hyaline to colored, smooth or striate, in extreme forms 2 cells wide and nearly as long as the teeth; lid conic to convex, shortly rostrate. Spores 12–17 μ, with low rounded papillae well spaced. Calyptra moderately hairy. Plate 56, figs. 4–6.

13.49 Mostly on dry rocks, usually in shady places, occasionally on trees.

13.50 British Columbia to Nevada, Utah, Wyoming, and New Mexico.

13.51 Common in the mountains of Nevada, Utah, and Colorado. About a third of the plants collected intergrade with *O. cupulatum, O. strangulatum,* and *O. anomalum.* Except for the bistratose upper lamina, some specimens are so like those three species that it is difficult to know what to call them, especially when the leaves are bistratose in patches, or some of them unistratose throughout. Locally the species is more abundant in the mountains from 6,000 to 9,000 ft. and in shaded situations where the temperature is lower and the humidity higher. In such places the leaves tend to be narrower and lanceolate with narrowly obtuse or bluntly acute tips. At lower elevations, where it is warmer and less

283

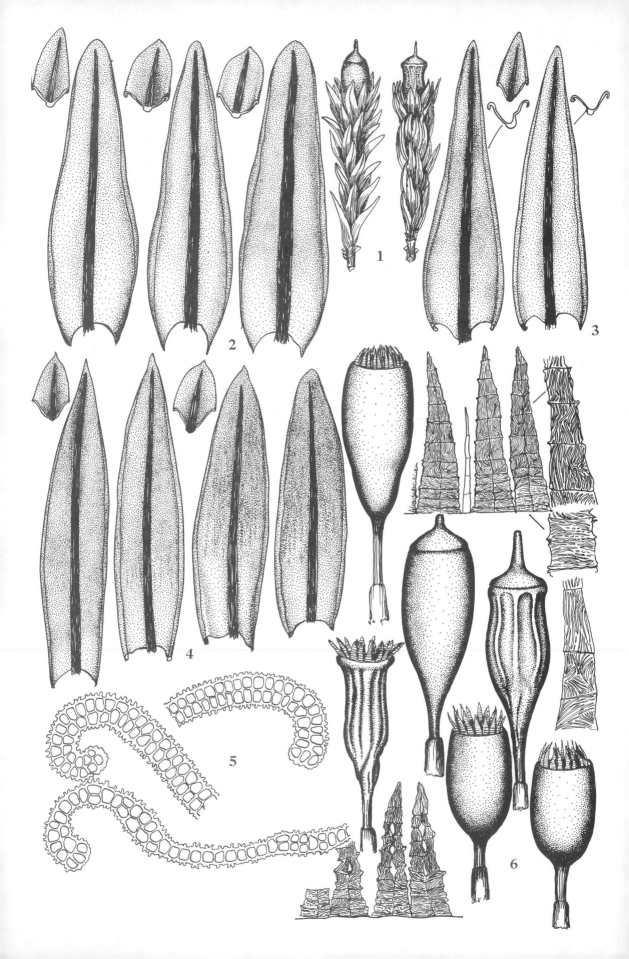

humid, the leaves tend to be ovate-lanceolate to oblong-lanceolate, wider in the upper part and often with the base abruptly wider and more or less ovate while the apex may be suddenly narrowed to a widely acute to broadly rounded tip. I have several specimens with some leaves as broadly rounded as in *O. jamesianum*. The bistratose upper half of the leaf is the most reliable trait and usually easily demonstrated. However, many specimens show only a few upper leaves bistratose, while the remainder are bistratose only in patches or lines and in some unistratose throughout. Some of these plants so resemble *O. cupulatum* or *O. jamesianum* that it becomes a matter of choice as to the name applied.

13.52   Forms with a rather long seta tend to make the capsules exserted, and the plants resemble *O. anomalum*. As a mater of fact, I found *O. anomalum* and *O. hallii* growing mixed together in the same tufts and while some plants seemed quite distinct, the majority showed traits of both species in various combinations. A. mixture of *O. strangulatum* and *O. hallii* also showed a variety of intermediate forms.

13.53   The sculpturing of the peristome teeth in most collections is quite typical, but a number of variations, mostly developmental in nature, are worth mentioning. Some such deviations are only occasional in a tuft of otherwise typical capsules, while others appear to be quite uniform throughout the specimen. The plates of the teeth may show unusually short, thick, more or less sinuous, simple or branched ridges sometimes interspersed with large papillae of various forms. These markings may be relatively few or numerous and crowded. In one peristome, coarse short striations were composed of large papillae in beadlike chains, some of them united in nubbly ridges with scattered papillae between them. In one specimen the ridges were so thick as to give the appearance of thick plates engraved with very narrow branched channels.

13.54   **9. Orthotrichum anomalum** Hedw. Plants in small to rather large tufts, sometimes matted. Stems erect to ascending, usually dark green, sometimes becoming dark olivaceous or even blackish, rather stiff, 1–2 cm tall, moderately to sparingly branched. Leaves appressed when dry, straight, erect-patent to patent when moist, ovate- to oblong-lanceolate, 1.5–2.5 mm long, usually rather wide in the upper part and ± suddenly narrowed to a widely acute, blunt, or narrowly obtuse tip (some leaves, even on the same shoot, may be evenly narrowed to blunt tips); margins widely recurved well toward the apex; costa stout, ending just below the apex, occasionally as much as 10–15 cells below the tip; upper cells rounded, oval or somewhat hexagonal, thick walled and clear, 10–

Plate 56. 1–3. Orthotrichum jamesianum. 1. Upper portions of shoots with capsules, moist and dry, X2. 2. Three leaves of typical form, X8. 3. Two leaves of the narrower form approaching those of **O. cupulatum,** X8.

4–6. O. hallii. 4. Four leaves showing variation of shape and apex, X8. 5. Cross sections of upper, middle, and lower portions of the lamina, X120. 6. Six capsules showing variations in shape and size with detail of the peristome teeth, X8, detail X40, and X120.

15 μ wide, unistratose, occasionally bistratose in patches, smooth or minutely verrucose with low simple papillae, 1–2 (or 4–5) per cell; basal cells rectangular, thin walled, hyaline and smooth, the inner ones rarely becoming thick walled and sinuous in older leaves. Autoicous. Seta 1.5–2.5(3) mm long; capsules emergent to well exserted when moist, appearing much more exserted when dry, ovoid-oblong to oblong-cylindric when moist; urn 2–2.8 mm long, the neck rather suddenly narrowed to the seta or gradually merging with the seta, when dry appearing cylindric, only slightly or not at all contracted under the mouth, 8-ribbed well toward the base, sometimes with small, shorter intermediate ribs, usually becoming strongly furrowed when old; stomata immersed, usually numerous, in 2–3 rows opposite the spore sac; exothecial cells thicker walled and more highly colored along the ribs; annulus of 2–3 rows of smaller cells; peristome teeth in 8 pairs, erect when dry, mostly narrowly triangular-lanceolate, in the upper part vertically to slightly obliquely striate with smooth narrow ridges, these straight or slightly flexuous, becoming more oblique and eventually horizontal on the basal plates, papillae few or none; cilia mostly lacking, but when present slender, of 1 row of cells, pale and fragile, up to ¾ the length of the teeth; preperistome often present, 1–4 joints high and free from the teeth or fragmentary and adhering to the lower joints, usually appearing as darker blotches. Spores 12–17 μ with low rounded papillae and short ridges. Calyptra sparingly to moderately hairy. Plate 57, figs. 1–8.

13.55   On dry rocks of various kinds and occasionally on the bases of trees or exposed roots, usually in shady places in canyons and on mountain sides.

13.56   Eurasia and Africa. Yukon across southern Canada and northern United States to Labrador, southward to Nevada and Arizona, and in the Rocky Mountains to Mexico.

13.57   Distinguished by the more or less exserted capsules with finely striated peristome teeth (occasionally with a preperistome), and by the rather broad leaves with blunt tips and low papillose cells. Several of our specimens approach var. *saxatile* (Schimp.) Mild., which has most leaves lanceolate and slenderly acute and longer cylindrical capsules well exserted on a seta two or three times its length. Our plants have such narrow leaves but have only emergent capsules. One also encounters

---

Plate 57.   1–8. Orthotrichum anomalum. 1. Three habit sketches, X.4. 2. Upper portions of three shoots showing dry and moist habit, X4. 3. Three typical leaves, X8. 4. Cross sections of the upper and middle part of the lamina, X120. 5. Two dry capsules, X8. 6. Pair of typical teeth, X40. **Note:** Cilia may be much more strongly developed or they may be lacking. 7. Side views of peristome teeth showing various degrees of development of the preperistome, X60. 8. Surface views of basal portion of teeth showing preperistome, X60.

9–12. Orthotrichum strangulatum. 9. Upper portions of two shoots showing dry and moist habit, X4. 10. Two typical leaves, X8. 11. Two capsules moist and dry, X8. 12. Typical peristome teeth showing fine papillae in sinuous lines, X40.

Note: Teeth quite variable, often broader, and papillae sometimes fewer and much coarser, occasionally united in nodulose to smooth ridges; preperistome sometimes present.

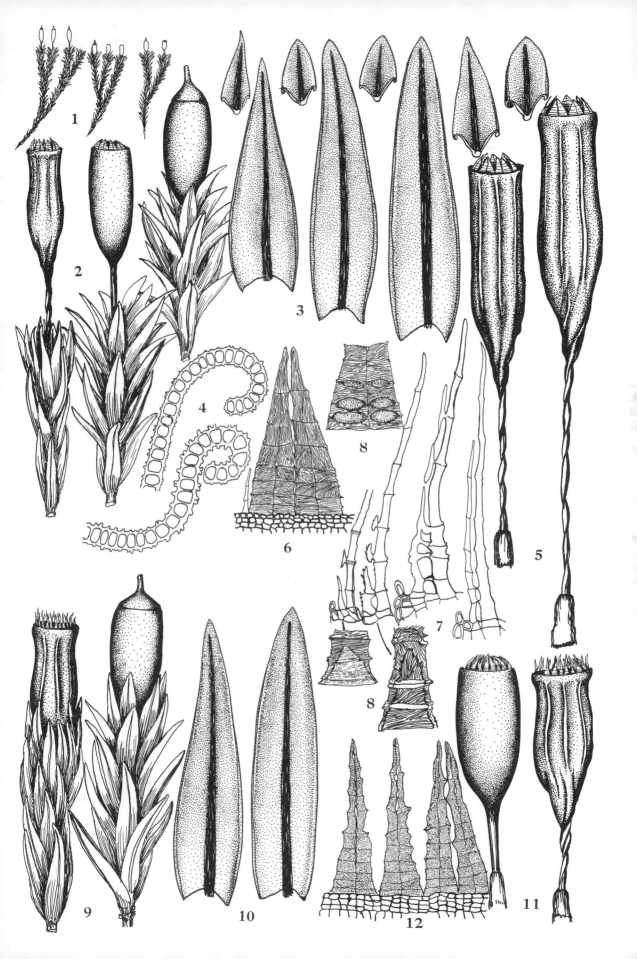

1

2

3

4

5

6

7

8

8

9

10

11

12

forms intermediate between *O. anomalum* and *O. strangulatum* or between *O. anomalum* and *O. hallii*. Among these plants the outlines of the leaves, length of the seta, shape of the capsules and the sculpturing of the teeth combine in a maze of forms difficult to associate with typical forms of the several species.

13.58 **10. Orthotrichum strangulatum** (P. Beauv.) Sulliv. Plants in low dense tufts, dark or dull green, only the tips brighter green. Stems about 1 cm tall. Stem leaves appressed and imbricated when dry, erect-patent to patent when moist, 1.5–2.5 mm long, ovate- to oblong-lanceolate, rather abruptly acute or blunt; margins revolute well toward the apex in the upper leaves, but in the lower leaves plane in the upper ½–⅔; lamina mostly 1-stratose or with 2-stratose margins or occasionally partially 2-stratose in patches or entirely so in the apex of a few leaves; upper medial cells 10–13 μ wide with low, simple or scarcely forked papillae; basal cells shorter than in related species. Autoicous. Seta about 0.5 mm long; capsules usually emergent, appearing more so when dry, mostly elongate-obovate to oblong-cylindric, urn about 1.7 mm long, not strongly constricted below the mouth, 8-ribbed when dry, the base gradually tapering to the seta but the urn well set off; stomata immersed, opposite the spore sac; teeth shorter than in related species, 0.2–0.3 mm long, frequently irregular on the margins and ± perforated along the middle line, ± uniformly finely papillose all over or with the papillae in straight or sinuous lines, often united in branched coralloid patterns; preperistome well developed, rudimentary, or lacking; cilia mostly lacking but when present 8, of a single row of cells and ranging from rudimentary to well developed. Plate 57, figs. 9–12.

13.59 On dry rocks, mostly on those containing lime.

13.60 Vermont to Alabama, westward to Minnesota, Tennessee, Missouri, Iowa and Utah.

13.61 **11. Orthotrichum alpestre** Hornsch. in B.S.G. Plants in dense to rather loose tufts, sometimes becoming matted, light to dark green, often yellowish green or dull olivaceous. Stems erect to ascending, branched, 1–2(3) cm high. Leaves straight and loosely appressed to slightly twisted when dry, typically lanceolate and slenderly acute, but locally more often ovate-lanceolate and slenderly to rather broadly acute, at times quite blunt or apiculate from a broader upper portion, 2.5–3.5 mm long, keeled; lamina unistratose throughout; margins strongly recurved to revolute well toward the apex, less so at the base; costa stout, subpercurrent; upper cells rounded hexagonal to oval, mostly 10–12 ± wide with low to very tall simple or forked papillae; basal cells wider and becoming more elongated, the inner ones rarely becoming very thick walled and nodulose. Multicellular gemmae often produced on leaves, stems, or densely branched rhizoids. Autoicous. Seta typically short, less than 0.5 mm long; capsules emergent, urn straw colored at maturity, darkening with age, 1.5–2.2 mm long, oblong- to elliptic-obovate or pyriform, the neck sometimes externally differentiated, gradually tapering to the seta which then appears quite short, and varying by degrees to

288

abruptly narrowed at the base and the seta appearing distinct and long-er, 8-ribbed when dry, the urn usually quite distended and not particu-larly contracted under the mouth when fully mature, but with age be-coming shrunken, deeply furrowed and contracted under the mouth; stomata immersed, few to numerous, opposite the spore sac; exothecial cells thicker walled and darker colored along the ribs; lid convex to high conic, shortly rostrate; teeth in 8 pairs, entire to ± perforated above, slenderly triangular-lanceolate when fully developed, often imperfectly formed, pale yellowish to yellowish brown at the base and paler above, erect or reflexed when dry, the basal plates with fine to moderately-sized, dense, ± evenly disposed papillae on the upper slender joints evenly disposed or in vertical rows of papillae, these sometimes fusing and forming ridges, both types frequently present, and often interspersed with scattered papillae; in some forms the basal papillae are lobed to shortly branched and often form irregular finely sinuous patterns; cilia usually well developed, 8 (rarely with 8 rudimentary to well developed intermediate cilia), of 2 rows of cells at the base and 1 above but often of 2 rows throughout, more rarely 1 throughout, mostly smooth, nearly as long as the teeth. Spores finely papillose, 12–16 μ. Calyptra with a few hairs. Plate 58.

13.62   On dry rocks and trunks of trees in canyons and mountains.

13.63   Europe. Yukon southward in the Rocky Mountains to Colorado, Utah, Arizona and Nevada. Mt. Whitney, California.

13.64   The habitat is generally stated as on rocks or occasionally on trees. To judge from local specimens, the plant is about equally distributed, 65 on rock and 74 on trees, mainly on the lower part of trunks and on exposed roots. It is especially abundant in canyons of the Wasatch and Uinta Mountains. Usually it is not easily confused with other species, although it varies widely. For example, abundant growth on a large rock or on trees may show considerable variation in 1 or more traits, such as larger size, more recurved and broader leaves, low, simple papillae, capsules immersed or shortly exserted, and different markings on the peristome teeth. These forms do not fit the description very well, but usually they cannot be placed in any other species. The description has been broad-ened liberally to embrace some of the variations since American forms of the plant vary more than the European. It is not uncommon to find the plants mixed with other species, mainly *O. hallu* and *O. anomalum* on rocks and *O. affine* on trees. Among these mixtures a few capsules show evidence of hybridization. In one outstanding instance, *O. alpestre, hallii, anomalum,* and *macounii* were growing more or less mixed to-gether on the same cliff and ledges in Sheep Creek Canyon, Uinta Mountains, and among them some capsules combined a maze of traits which certainly suggests hybrids of various crosses.

13.65   According to the illustration in *Bryologia Europaea* (plate 213), the typical form of the leaf is almost exactly lanceolate, not acuminate but tapering gradually and gently curving inward to a narrowly acute apex.

The base is not noticeably differentiated. Locally we have this form and a few specimens with even more narrowly lanceolate leaves, but in the majority of our plants the leaves tend to be more ovate-lanceolate, and extreme forms show a dilated base with the upper portion rather evenly tapering to a slender apex or broader well toward the apex, then suddenly narrowing to a widely acute or blunt tip. The *Bryologia Europaea* illustrations also show capsules elongate-obovate to pyriform and about 1:2–2.5 and 1.5–2.2 mm long with the neck tapered into a very short seta or more or less contracted and set off from a longer seta. The capsules of many of our plants are like that, while in others they are shorter. The seta is usually up to about 0.5 mm long or less, at times almost lacking, but at the other extreme there are forms with setae as long as 1.5 mm, making the capsules appear almost exserted, especially when dry. The lid varies from rather tall and conic-acuminate to convex with a short rostrum. The stomata are typically immersed and strongly overarched by thick-walled exothecial cells, but they are occasionally widely exposed, as in *O. pallens,* which is much smaller both in stature and in all its parts.

13.66   The variations in the sculpturing of well-developed peristome teeth are adequately described above, but it might be added that occasionally the vertical rows of papillae or ridges on the upper joints are branched to anastomosed. The illustrations in the *Bryologia Europaea* show the upper joints coarsely vertically striate and abruptly papillose below. In our plants the striations are finer and the transition to papillae more gradual. Blunt or imperfectly formed teeth are generally associated with unfavorable circumstances of the environment during development. Also, unusually pale or thin teeth that are smooth or with a scanty development of papillae, even when more or less perfect in shape, may be traceable to the same cause. Typically there are eight cilia dilated, two cells wide at the base, and one cell wide above the middle, smooth and nearly as long as the teeth. In some plants they are one cell wide throughout, sometimes stout and with thick nodulose joints; in other plants they may be two cells wide throughout, sometimes very widely dilated at the base and occasionally connected by a low basal membrane one or two cells high. Extreme forms have eight intermediate cilia ranging from rudimentary to nearly as long and as stout as the principal cilia. Occasionally the cilia are appendiculate in varying degrees. In an extreme

---

Plate 58.   Orthotrichum alpestra. 1. Three habit sketches, X.4. 2. Two portions of the upper part of the shoot showing dry habit, X4. 3. Two leaves of average shape. 4. Three leaves of narrow-leaved forms. 4. Two leaves of broad-leaved form, sometimes more widely recurved from the stem, X8. 6. Cross sections of lamina showing two types of cells and variations in the papillae, X120. **Note:** In some plants the papillae are much lower, and occasionally mostly simple. 7. Three capsules showing variations in shape and length of the seta, X8. 8. A portion of the peristome showing well-developed teeth and cilium, X60, details of papillae, X120. 9. Two capsules showing unusual variations in the longer seta, X8. 10. Portion of peristome showing uniform marking on the teeth, cilia of two rows of cells, and a shorter intermediate cilium, X60. Details of papillae, X120. 11. Details of papillae on lower joints of teeth, showing variation in pattern, X120.

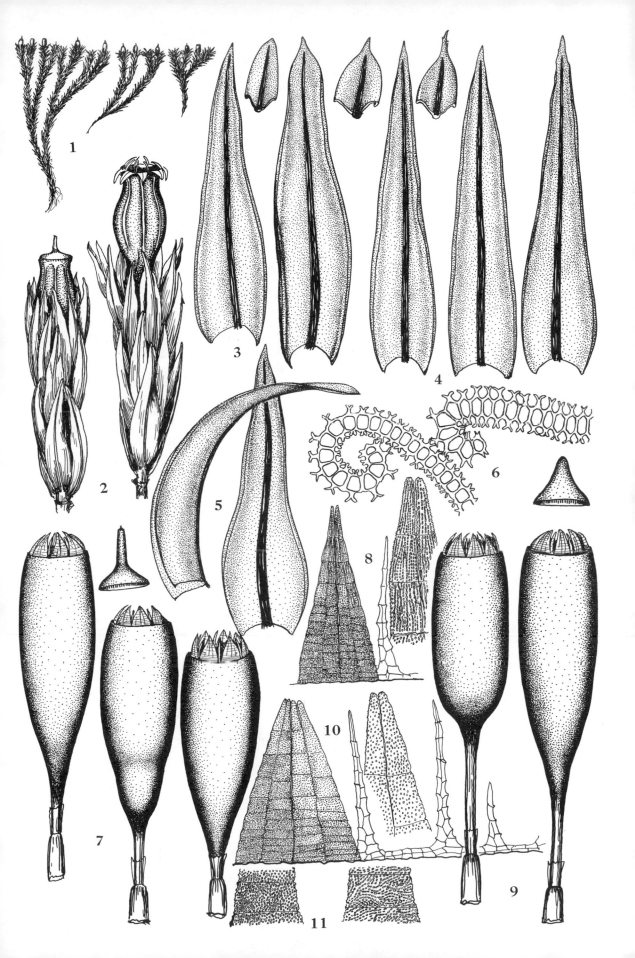

instance, one capsule with sixteen cilia showed a few trabeculae laterally connecting some of the principal cilia across the width of two teeth.

13.67 The species was described as having very tall simple or forked papillae, but I find that the papillae may be of any size down to relatively low and weak on otherwise typical plants. In cross sections of the leaves, the cells usually appear vertically short rectangular, the exposed surfaces flat to slightly convex, but vigorous plants may show hexagonal cells with conical or strongly convex surfaces crowned with unusually tall forked papillae.

13.68 I have 30 specimens which were determined routinely as they were collected over the years and assigned to variety *occidentale*. Five proved to be typical of the species while the remaining twenty-five are a complex of intergrading forms. The variety was described as more robust and glaucous green, with leaves broader and reflexed on the margins, papillae longer, simple or forked, and peristome teeth longer, entire, and minutely above. These were found in Utah in the Uinta Mountains and Provo Canyon, on rocks at 8,000 ft. About half of the specimens showing some varietal traits are rather small. Some plants have slightly larger leaves, especially broader at the base, and some are more recurved from the stem, but the size and habit intergrade with the species. The glaucous green color is not often encountered; most plants are yellowish green. The size and character of the papillae on the leaves vary among these plants to about the same degree and range from low to very tall. The longer peristome teeth seem to be a rather strong character, although not sharply set off, while the punctulate markings on the upper joints are not often encountered. I find little difference in the papillae on the teeth as they show the same general range of coarseness to fineness as in the species proper. The papillae on the upper joints often form vertical rows or ridges in this species as opposed to the even scattering in the variety, but again I find every degree of intergradation. As a matter of fact, both types of markings can be found in capsules of the same tuft and occasionally even on different teeth of the same capsule. A number of specimens which lean toward the variety have much longer setae than those shown in the Sullivant's *Icones muscorum*, (plate 49).

13.69 The exact locality in the Uinta Mountains and Provo River where the original specimens were collected is not clear, but I have collected throughout these regions and it seems that the variety represents only chance combinations of trait extremes in a continuous series of intergradations. It is my opinion that the concept of the species should be broadened to include the phantom var. *occidentale*.

13.70 **12. Orthotrichum pallens** Bruch ex Brid. var. **pallens.** Plants in small, low, dense tufts on the bark of trees, mostly dark to dull brownish green. Stems less than 1 cm tall, branched, frequently with dense reddish rhizoids at base. Leaves appressed and imbricated when dry, erect-patent to somewhat spreading or slightly recurved when moist, 1.5–3.2 mm long, lanceolate to narrowly lanceolate from a broadly ovate or oblong base, quite variable, the upper part slender to rather broad and rather suddenly narrowed to an acute or blunt apex, sometimes obtuse, occasionally ending in a clear pointed cell, strongly keeled above, often somewhat plicate in the middle; margins revolute to near the apex or in some leaves only in the middle and plane above and below; costa ending shortly below the tip; upper cells 12–16 μ wide, rounded angular, thick walled, chlorophyllose, each with 1–3 simple or double moderately high papillae but sometimes nearly smooth; basal cells rectangular, mostly thin walled and clear, shorter on the margins. Septate gemmae often abundant on the leaves. Autoicous. Perigonial buds single and axillary or 1–4 on small leafy branch below the perichaetium. Seta about 0.3 mm long, scarcely exceeding the ochrea, sometimes a little longer; capsules small, 1.3–2.2 mm long, immersed to slightly emergent, narrowly obovate to ellongate-elliptical, $\pm$ rounded at the base but sometimes tapering to the seta, 8-ribbed and slightly to moderately contracted under the mouth when dry, generally yellowish brown at maturity, becoming darker with age; neck short; stomata usually only slightly sunken and widely exposed or at times nearly superficial but ranging to deeply immersed and partially concealed by the strongly thickened walls of the overhanging adjacent exothecial cells, in 1–2 rows opposite the spore sac, sometimes few; peristome teeth reflexed when fully mature and dry, finely and densely papillose throughout or the upper joints with the papillae in $\pm$ vertical rows, varying to finely ridged-striate throughout; cilia 8 or sometimes 16, the intermediate ones shorter to rudimentary, the principal ones 2 cells wide throughout or only in the lower part, often as long as the teeth; lid conic, shortly beaked. Spores 13–17 μ, crenulate. Calyptra campanulate, light yellowish, smooth or with a few short hairs at the tip. Plate 59, figs. 1–9.

13.71   On bark of trees.

13.72   Europe. British Columbia and Utah.

13.73   Uncommon. Much like *O. pumilum* which differs in a slightly larger, thinner-walled, clear green leaf cell. Both species have widely exposed stomata, but this trait shows much more frequently in the present species, whereas more deeply immersed stomata are more common in *O. pumilum* (cilia only 8). The following variety is more frequently encountered.

13.74   12a. Var. **parvum** Vent. Tufts usually smaller and more compact; leaves loosely appressed, the tips often incurved when dry, open to somewhat recurved when moist, mostly oblong-ligulate to ligulate from an ovate or oblong base, broadly rounded to obtuse, sometimes ending in a single clear cell or mucronate, a few younger leaves sometimes acute; upper lamina deeply channeled or keeled, 1.5–2.5(3) mm long, variable in different plants; apex often irregularly dentate or crenulate by the projecting marginal cells; margins widely revolute nearly to the apex; areolation as in the species; gemmae often abundant. Capsule generally smaller, 1.4–2 mm long, immersed, obovate to oval-oblong, $\pm$ rounded at the base, abruptly set off from the short seta; stomata variable in

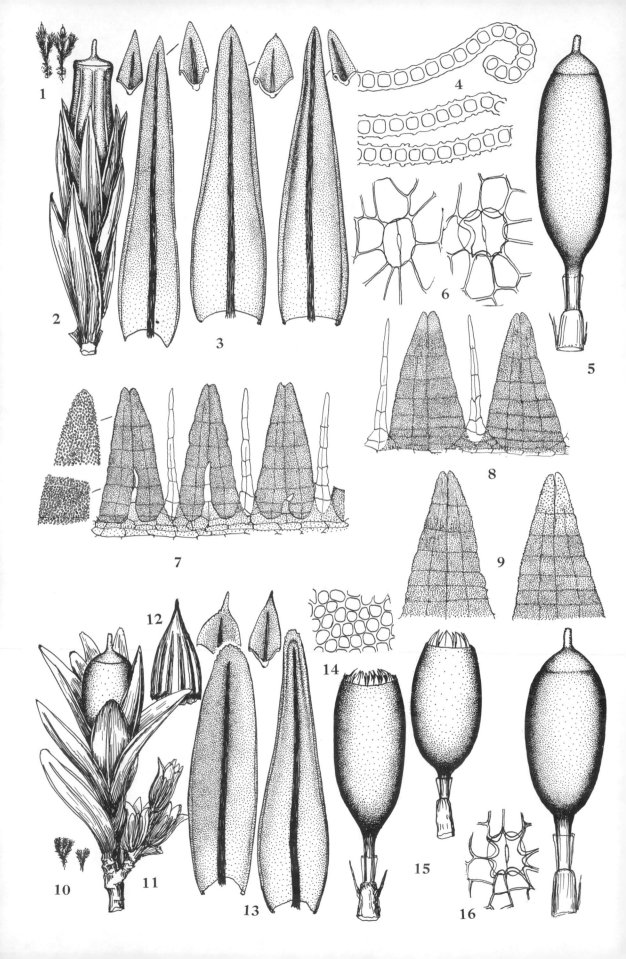

the same tuft or even in the same capsule, immersed, widely exposed to partially concealed by overhanging adjacent exothecial cells; cilia mostly 8, strong, sometimes as long as the teeth, smooth and pale, occasionally with 8 rudimentary intermediate cilia. Plate 59, figs. 10–16.

13.75   On the bark of trees.

13.76   Europe and northern Asia. Manitoba, Yellowstone National Park, and Utah.

13.77   After prolonged study of the literature concerning the O. *pallens-rogeri-microcarpum* complex, I have, in extremes, settled on Venturi's somewhat unsatisfactory varietal name for our plants. European bryologists have named and described nearly every combination of minute traits available either as species or varieties, and later authors have reduced some of them to synonymy or to varieties under various species, contributing little to the understanding of the bewildering whole.

13.78   Our plants occur most commonly in the bark of bigtooth maple (*Acer grandidentatum*), boxelder (*Acer negundo*), and the narrowleaf cottonwood (*Populus angustifolia*).

13.79   **13. Orthotrichum pumilum** Sw. var. **pumilum.** Plants in small, compact, dark green tufts, mainly in furrows on bark of trees. Stems erect and branched, mostly about 0.5 mm tall and rarely exceeding 1 cm. Leaves 1.5–2.3 mm long, the comal ones the largest, closely imbricated when dry, erect-patent to slightly spreading when moist, broadly ovate-lanceolate to narrowly lanceolate or oblong-lanceolate, tapering upward or rather wide in the upper part and more suddenly narrowed to an acute or blunt apex, at times narrowly obtuse, occasionally terminating in a simple, pale, apiculate cell, strongly keeled; margins revolute well toward the apex; costa stout, ending several cells below the apex; upper cells bright or pale green, clear, unistratose, 12–17(20) μ wide, usually thin walled, rounded to angular, mostly with 2–3 low simple papillae, at times almost smooth; basal cells oblong and clear, becoming quadrate on the margins. Septate gemmae often abundant on the lower half of the leaves. Autoicous. Antheridial buds single and axillary or more often 2–4 on small branches below the perichaetium. Seta very short, mostly about 0.3 mm long, scarcely exceeding the ochrea, occasionally slightly longer; capsules immersed to slightly emergent, light yellowish brown to straw colored, ovoid-oblong to oblong, 1.3–1.6 mm long, the base ± rounded and well set off from the seta, only occasionally having the neck somewhat differentiated externally, 8-ribbed and slightly con-

---

Plate 59.   1–9. Orthotrichum pallens. 1. Habit sketch, X.4. 2. Portion of shoot with dry capsule, X4. 3. Three leaves, X8. 4. Cross sections of leaves showing variation in the papillae, X120. 5. Typical capsule, X8. 6. Stomata, X120. 7–8. Portions of peristome showing cilia. 9. Teeth showing variations in papillae, X60.

10–16. Var. parvum. 10. Habit, X.4. 11. Portion of shoot showing capsule and clustered antheridia on a small lateral branch, X4. 12. Naked calyptra, X4. 13. Two leaves, X8. 14. Upper medial cells, X120. 15. Three capsules, X8. 16. Partially exposed stoma, X120.

tracted under the mouth when dry and mature, becoming strongly furrowed and darker colored with age, exothecial cells thicker walled and darker along the ribs; stomata rather widely exposed to nearly hidden by the adjacent exothecial cells, usually in 2 rows opposite the spore sac; peristome teeth in pairs, short, rarely perforated, reflexed when dry and fully mature, densely and finely papillose throughout; cilia 8, 2 cells wide at the base and usually uniseriate above, sometimes nearly as long as the teeth but often shorter, mostly smooth, occasionally with low rounded papillae. Spores 10–15 μ, reddish brown, with low, rounded papillae. Calyptra conic-campanulate, smooth or with a few short hairs at the apex.

13.80   On bark of trees.

13.81   Europe, Asia, and North Africa. Southeastern Canada southward to Tennessee, westward to Utah and Idaho.

13.82   The small size, large, clear, thin-walled leaf cells and small immersed capsules are outstanding traits of typical forms. However, some forms may have somewhat smaller cells, 12–14 μ wide and moderately chlorophyllose, although fairly clear. At the other extreme some plants have some of the leaves with cells as much as 22 μ wide and unusually clear and thin walled. The stomata in the walls of the capsules are occasionally widely exposed but usually more or less obscured by overhanging exothecial cells.

13.83   13a. Var. **fallax** (Bruch) Kickx. Similar to the typical variety but differing in the longer capsules, oblong to oblong-cylindric, more tapered at the base, lightly straw colored at maturity and strongly emergent, at times almost exserted and appearing so when dry; cilia 8, often as long as the teeth; septate gemmae common.

13.84   On bark of trees.

13.85   Europe and North Africa. Montana, Idaho, and Utah.

13.86   13b. Var. **ligulaefolium** Flow. Plants very short. Leaves appressed with tips $\pm$ incurved when dry, patent when moist, mostly oblong-ligulate, broadly rounded at the apex, lamina canaliculate-concave with upper part incurved like the bowl of a spoon, a few oblong-lanceolate, narrowly obtuse or widely acute; costa disappearing well below apex; upper cells 14–17 μ wide, thin walled and clear, becoming thicker walled with age. Gemmae often abundant. Seta very short; capsules shortly oval to oblong-oval; stomata mostly exposed. Calyptra without hairs.

13.87   Utah. Washington County: Zion Canyon, on *Acer negundo*, 4,450 ft.

13.88   14. **Orthotrichum garrettii** Grout & Flow. in Grout. Plants in short compact tufts, green to dark green. Stems 1 cm tall or less, sparingly branched. Leaves $\pm$ infolded and imbricated when dry, erect-patent to slightly recurved when moist, broadly lanceolate, 2–2.8 mm long, strongly keeled, tapering upward to a slenderly acute apex, in the upper and perichaetial leaves terminating in a very slender tip composed of elongated and often hyaline thick-walled cells, the marginal ones often projecting and forming teeth; margins widely revolute to near the apex but plane above in some leaves; costa stout, ending slightly below the apex; upper cells large and clear, 14–20(23) μ wide, angular to rounded, thin to thick walled, each with a single low papilla, sometimes nearly smooth; basal cells oblong, quadrate on the margins. Gemmae composed of uniseriate cells common on the bases of the leaves. Autoicous. Antheridial buds axillary or 1–3 on a small leafy branch. Seta short, about 0.5 mm long; capsules emergent, shortly oblong with a short, ± tapering neck, the urn 1.5–1.8 mm long, 8-ribbed and slightly contracted under the mouth when dry; stomata opposite the spore sac in 1–2 rows, immersed, widely exposed to ± obscured by the overhanging exothecial cells; peristome teeth at first in pairs, short, about 0.18 mm long, slightly perforated down the middle or entire, finely and densely papillose throughout; cilia 16, of 2 rows of cells, as long as the teeth, ± appendiculate, the processes often extending laterally and sometimes joining those of the adjacent cilia, beset all over with fine low papillae; lid conic with short beak. Spores 14–20 μ, yellowish brown, moderately papillose. Calyptra conic-campanulate, sparse short hairs above. Plate 60, figs. 1–9.

13.89   On rocks in shade.

13.90   Utah and disjunct in Ohio near Columbus. Carbon County: Emma Park, 7,800 ft. Garfield County: Henry Mountains, Sawmill Basin, Mt. Ellen, 9,700 ft.

13.91   This moss is apparently related to *O. pumilum* and *O. pallens* by the large leaf cells with thinner walls and lower simpler papillae and the immersed stomata which are sometimes widely exposed. The elongated, thick-walled, hyaline cells forming the narrowly acute apices of the upper and comal leaves serve adequately to identify even sterile specimens. Since only the type specimen shows details of the peristome, it may be that the strongly appendiculate cilia are less well developed in some plants. Occasionally appendiculate cilia are found in other species in instances where it appears that the plants developed under optimum environmental conditions.

13.92   A doubtful species, *Orthotrichum utahense* Sull. in Lesq., was briefly compared with *O. hallii*, which preceded it in a list, as follows: "Related to the last (species) but more robust; leaves broader, strongly papillose; capsules with immersed stomata. The specimens (too old) have not any capsule with peristome. Hab. Ogden Canyon on shaded perpendicular rocks. Lesquereux." In my opinion both the specimen and the description are worthless, and the name should be abandoned.

2. AMPHIDIUM Schimp.

13.93   Plants medium sized, densely tufted, sometimes deep and soft, dark green to yellowish green or brownish yellow, growing on damp or wet rocks. Stems mostly branched, central strand lacking. Leaves rather uniform, narrowly lanceolate to linear-lanceolate, papillose on both sides, twisted to strongly crisped when dry; costa nearly percurrent, with medial guides and small dorsal and ventral stereid bands; upper medial cells rounded to quadrate, often transversely elongated, usually strongly incrassate and densely beset with small papillae on both surfaces; basal cells longer and wider, smooth and usually clear. Autoicous or dioicous. Perichaetial leaves ovate-lanceolate to oblong, the inner ones incurved to subtubulose, loosely clasping the seta, gradually to abruptly narrowed above to a slender point; upper cells oblong to linear, often irregular, thick walled, and smooth. Seta short, erect or slightly curved; capsules immersed to almost exserted, elongate-pyriform, the neck longer than the spore sac, thick, with superficial stomata, abruptly or gradually narrowed at the base to the thick summit of the seta, when dry urn or goblet shaped, the neck strongly shrunken, 8-ribbed and often contracted below the mouth; exothecial cells below the mouth and on the ribs thick walled, dark reddish, shiny; annulus and peristome lacking. Calyptra cucullate, smooth.

13.94 The name is derived from Greek, amphora, a vase or urn, alluding to the shape of the capsule.

13.95 **Amphidium lapponicum** (Hedw.) Schimp. Plants densely tufted, forming cushions or deep, soft sods, mostly yellowish green, becoming brownish yellow below, green only at the tips. Stems 1–3 cm tall, sometimes quite short, elongating by subfloral innovations, sometimes branched; leaves crisped when dry, open to widely recurved when moist, oblong-lanceolate to linear-lanceolate, 1.5–2.5 mm long, apex gradually to rather abruptly acute, sometimes blunt; base not differentiated, or ovate in some upper leaves; margins entire, flat or sometimes narrowly recurved below; upper cells rounded-quadrate to transversely oval, 8–10(13) μ wide, thick walled, both surfaces of the lamina papillose with low rounded papillae over the cell lumina and the vertical cell walls; basal cells becoming longer but only slightly wider, oblong to linear, 1 x 3–7, clear and smooth. Autoicous. Male bud small, below the perichaetium. Perichaetial leaves large and sheathing, oblong, abruptly narrowed to a slender tip. Seta about 1.5 mm long; capsule reddish brown, immersed to scarcely exserted, pyriform, 1.3–2 mm long, urn- or goblet-shaped shrunken below the wide mouth and with 8 shiny reddish ribs when dry, the neck thick, longer than the spore sac, greatly shrunken and tapering into the seta, lid low conic-convex with a short curved beak. Spores more or less globose, 10–12 μ, smooth. Plate 61.

Plate 60. 1–9. Orthotrichum garrettii. 1. Habit sketches, X.4. 2. Moist and dry tip of shoots, X4. 3. Leaves, X8. 4. Two leaf apices showing hyaline denticulate tips. 5–6. Upper medial leaf cells. 7. Cross sections of the upper lamina, X120. 8. Capsules, X8. 9. Peristome teeth and cilia, X60.

10–16. Physcomitrium pygmaeum. 10. Habit sketches, X.4. 11. Shoot with capsule and calyptra, X3.2. 12. Upper leaf, X4.8. 13. Same, X8. 14. Leaf apex and cells, X120. 15. Capsule, X8. 16. Suboral exothecial cells, X60. (After Bull. Torr. Bot. Club 21: pl. 197.)

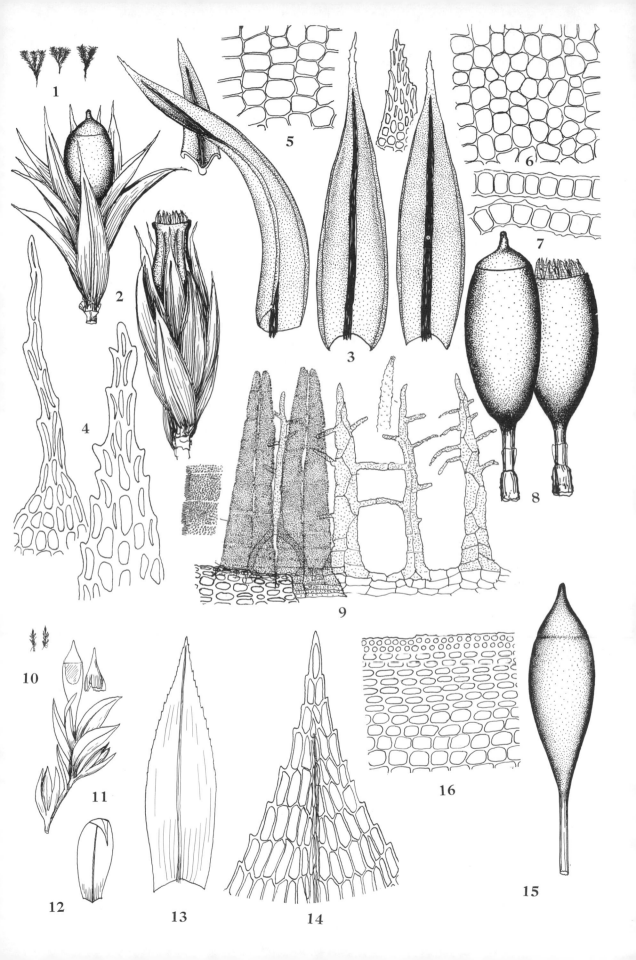

13.96 Growing on moist, wet or rather dry siliceous or ferromagnesian rocks, often in crevices, usually in shade in cool mountainous regions.

13.97 Eurasia and northern Africa. Northeast United States and adjacent Canada; Greenland. Alaska to California, Arizona, and Colorado.

FUNARIACEAE

14.1 Plants mostly small or minute annuals or biennials, usually light green. Stems mostly short and erect, simple or sparingly branched; rhizoids confined to the base, central strand present, sometimes small or indistinct. Upper leaves the largest and commonly clustered, obovate, oblong, oblanceolate or lanceolate ± concave and erect-patent, broadly acute to acuminate; margins plane or incurved; the lower leaves smaller and distant; costa strong, percurrent to shortly excurrent; upper leaf cells mostly large, oblong to rhomboidal or hexagonal, thin walled, and smooth, becoming longer in the base. Monoicous. Seta very short to long; capsules immersed to long exserted, globose to pyriform, erect and symmetric or inclined to pendulous, curved and asymmetric, variously shrunken or longitudinally furrowed when dry; stomata numerous in the neck region, consisting of a single guard cell with a central pore; lid low-convex to hemispherical, apiculate, peristome single, double, or lacking, when present the teeth 16, lanceolate, slightly curved to the right, strongly jointed, the segments, opposite the teeth, cilia lacking. Calyptra large, inflated at the base, with a long beak, mainly cucullate but often split in 2–3 places around the base.

14.2 1. Capsules asymmetric, ± curved, inclined or widely pendulous when moist; peristome double .... 1. *Funaria*   14.4

14.3 1. Capsules symmetric, erect

   2. Peristome single or with low rudimentary segments ....
   .... 2. *Entosthodon*   14.23

   2. Peristome lacking .... 3. *Physcomitrium*   14.36

1. FUNARIA Hedw.

14.4 Plants loosely tufted or scattered. Stems erect, mostly short and simple, sometimes with 1–2(3) branches from the base; comal and upper leaves the largest, sometimes forming an ovate or globose budlike cluster, especially in young plants, the lower leaves much smaller, ovate, obovate to oblong, acute to acuminate, margins flat, entire to serrate; costa usually slender, ending below the apex to shortly excurrent; upper cells thin walled and usually lax, oblong or oblong-hexagonal to short-rhomboidal; basal cells oblong, narrower on the margins. Autoicous. Perigonia terminal on a small branch; the perichaetium terminal on the

---

Plate 61.   Amphidium lapponicum. 1. Habit sketches, X.4. 2. Leaves, X8. 3. Dry habit, X4. 4. Three leaf apices. 5. Upper leaf cells. 6. Basal cells, X8. 7. Perichaetial leaves. 8. Upper medial cells of perichaetial leaf, X120. 9. Capsules, X8.

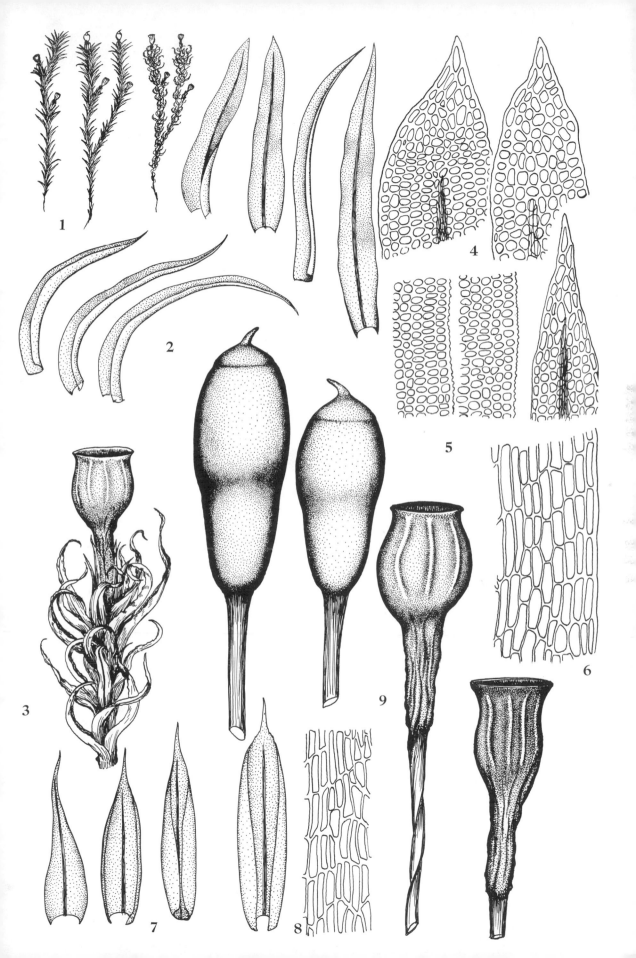

main stem. Seta short to long, strongly twisted when dry; capsules erect, inclined or pendulous when moist, pyriform with a distinct neck, erect and symmetric or curved and asymmetric, and the mouth ± oblique, longitudinally furrowed or irregularly wrinkled to smooth when dry; peristome usually double in our species, teeth lanceolate, slenderly tapering above, strongly jointed, slightly spiral to the right; segments linear from a broadly dilated base to lanceolate, sometimes rudimentary or lacking. Spores globose.

14.5 *Funaria* comes from the Latin *funis* meaning a cord which alludes to the seta which is twisted and cordlike when dry.

14.6 1. Seta 1.6–6 cm long; capsules 2–3 mm long, furrowed when dry; annulus large, red, revoluble

    2. Capsules mostly elongate pyriform, the mouth large, 0.7–1 mm across; spores 14–17 μ .... 1. *F. hygrometrica* 14.8

    2. Capsules shortly pyriform, mouth often small, 0.5–0.7 mm across; spores 18–24(34) μ .... 1a. var. *utahensis* 14.12

14.7 1. Seta 0.4–1.5 cm long; capsules 1.5–3 mm long, usually small, only the neck irregularly shrunken when dry; annulus lacking

    3. Teeth lanceolate, appendiculate by trabeculae projecting laterally; exothecial cells linear, thick walled; spores mostly 25–30 μ, coarsely papillose .... 2. *F. muehlenbergii* 14.16

    3. Teeth linear-lanceolate to nearly linear, not at all appendiculate, trabeculae less strong; exothecial cells oblong-hexagonal, thin walled; spores 20 μ or less, nearly smooth .... 2a. var. *lineata* 14.20

14.8 **1. Funaria hygrometrica** Hedw. var. **hygrometrica.** Stems usually short, 4–10 mm tall; comal and upper leaves bright green, often imbricated and forming a dense, ovate or subglobose, budlike cluster, at least when young, later becoming ± erect to spreading, wrinkled to somewhat twisted when dry, 2–4 mm long, obovate to oblong-ovate, very concave with margins widely incurved, entire to bluntly serrate at the apex, acute to briefly acuminate; costa ending shortly below the apex to shortly excurrent; upper cells oblong-hexagonal, a few rhomboidal or oblong, 26–36 μ wide, becoming elongated toward the base, the marginal ones narrower; lower leaves much smaller. Leaves in general ± tender and lax, often becoming flaccid with loss of green color toward the end of the season. Seta 1.6–6 cm long, yellowish to dark reddish, strongly twisted when dry; capsules 2.4–3.2 mm long, inclined to widely pendulous when moist, becoming ± erect when dry, typically elongate-pyriform, asymmetric, curved and gibbous above, the mouth oblique, becoming irregularly furrowed, often with the mouth arched downward and almost parallel with the wall of the urn when dry; lid low conic with a very short point, bright red on the margin, 0.7–1 mm across; annulus large and revoluble, red; teeth lanceolate, strongly jointed, the upper lamellae appendiculate, the tips of the appendages usually fimbriate, the lower joints dark reddish, vertically or obliquely striate with fine ridges, the upper ones pale, strongly and finely papillose, the tips united with a lacy central disc; segments pale, yellowish to yellowish brown, typically lanceolate but varying to linear from a dilated base, 2/3–4/5 the length of the teeth, finely papillose. Spores reddish brown, 12–17 μ, smooth but finely punctate. Plate 62, figs. 1–8.

14.9   A species of many habitats; on dry soil of plains and hillsides, often under rocks and bases of bushes and trees where water drains or drips during winter and spring, on wet soil and in crevices of dripping cliffs. One of our most common mosses, which grows in gardens, lawns, and in greenhouses.

14.10   Cosmopolitan.

14.11   It varies considerably in stature, length of the seta, and size of the capsule. More frequently represented in Utah by the following variety.

14.12   1a. Var. **utahensis** Grout. Capsules pendent to nearly erect when moist, shorter pyriform, the neck usually shorter, the urn therefore appearing thicker, the mouth often much smaller, 0.5 mm across, the teeth more strongly striate on the basal joints and more slenderly papillose above. Spores larger, 17–24(34) μ. Plate 62, figs. 9–10.

14.13   In many habitats from dry saline plains to wet places in the mountains.

14.14   Wyoming, Colorado, Arizona, New Mexico, Nevada. Probably general throughout the Western States.

14.15   The leaves are much the same as in the species, but the capsules are shorter and more often nearly erect when moist and the spores larger. I find some specimens with spores 17–20 μ, others 21–24 μ and a few 24–27 varying up to 34 μ. Otherwise there are no constant characters which might warrant nomenclatural notice. As in the species, the length of the seta ranges from 1.5–6 cm, and the color of the capsule may range from pale yellowish through yellowish brown to reddish brown. The capsules may be small to large, but the mouth is generally smaller than in the species. One may attempt to place small-mouthed forms in *F. microstoma,* but that species requires rudimentary peristome segments, a character seldom encountered in our local plants. A small-mouthed form with the segments reduced to stubs proved to be only a subnormal development as most of the capsules in the same tuft had well-developed segments.

14.16   2. **Funaria muehlenbergii** Hedw. f. ex Lam. & DC. var. **muehlenbergii.** Plants small, loosely tufted. Stems usually naked below, bearing a comal tuft of leaves, 1–5 mm high. Leaves 1.5–3 mm long, oblong-obovate to oblong-lanceolate, gradually to rather abruptly long and slenderly acuminate, the apex often hairlike; margins entire to serrate, plane; costa slender, ending well below the apex; upper leaf cells mostly oblong to oblong-hexagonal, 20–27 μ wide, thin walled and often lax; basal cells slightly longer and at the margins narrower. Seta 5–15 mm long, erect, reddish brown, twisted when dry; capsules 2–3 mm long, erect to inclined, elongate-pyriform, asymmetric, gibbous above, mouth

303

small, the spore sac quite smooth when dry, the neck as long as or longer than the spore sac and irregularly wrinkled when dry, making the capsule appear much smaller than it actually is; exothecial cells typically linear and thick walled, but varying to irregularly oblong or oblong-hexagonal and thin walled; lid low conic; annulus lacking; peristome teeth narrowly lanceolate to linear-lanceolate, reddish below, pale above, slightly spiral, strongly trabeculate, with or without projecting appendages; vertically to diagonally striate and finely papillose; segments typically lanceolate, about $\frac{2}{3}$ the length of the teeth, yellowish to yellowish brown, often linear from a $\pm$ dilated base, or sometimes poorly developed, short and irregular, finely papillose. Spores 20–30 μ (mostly 25–32 μ in our region), beset with numerous small wartlike papillae. Plate 62, figs. 11–15.

14.17 On dry soil, often in saline regions, around bases or shrubs, among grasses, at bases of rocks and cliffs.

14.18 Europe. Arizona, California, southern Utah, Yukon.

14.19 The spores of the present specimens vary widely in size, some of them smaller than the general range given by some descriptions.

14.20 2a. Var. **lineata** Grout. Exothecial cells of the capsules broader and thinner walled, irregularly oblong to oblong-hexagonal. Peristome much narrower, 30–45 μ wide at the base, usually strongly vertically striate but nearly lacking papillae above; trabeculae of teeth less well developed and not or slightly projecting laterally as appendages; the segments are shorter, often rudimentary. Spores usually smoother and less than 20 μ. Plate 63, figs. 1–3.

14.21 Same habitat as the species.

14.22 Southern Utah and Arizona.

2. ENTOSTHODON Schwaegr.

14.23 Mostly small plants intermediate between *Funaria* and *Physcomitrium* and having the same general gametophyte features, $\pm$ annual or perennial by innovations, the structure of the leaves similar with a strong slender costae and large thin-walled cells, usually tender and often lax. Monoicous. Setae short to fairly long, erect and straight to slightly curved; capsules pyriform, erect and symmetric or nearly so, the neck usually well defined and shrunken when dry, the mouth bordered by

---

Plate 62. **1–8. Funaria hygrometrica.** 1–2. Moist and dry habit sketches, X.4. 3. Dissected perigonial bud, X8. 4. Leaves, X8. 5. Upper medial leaf cells, X120. 6. Capsules, X8. 7. Peristome teeth and segments, X60, detail, X200. 8. Spores, X120.

9–10. Var. **utahensis.** 9. Capsules, X8. 10. Portion of annulus and spores, X120.

11–15. Funaria muehlenbergii. 11. Habit sketches, X.4. 12. Leaves. 13. Capsules, X8, detail of exothecial cells, X120. 14. Peristome teeth and segments, X60, detail, X160. 15. Spores, X120.

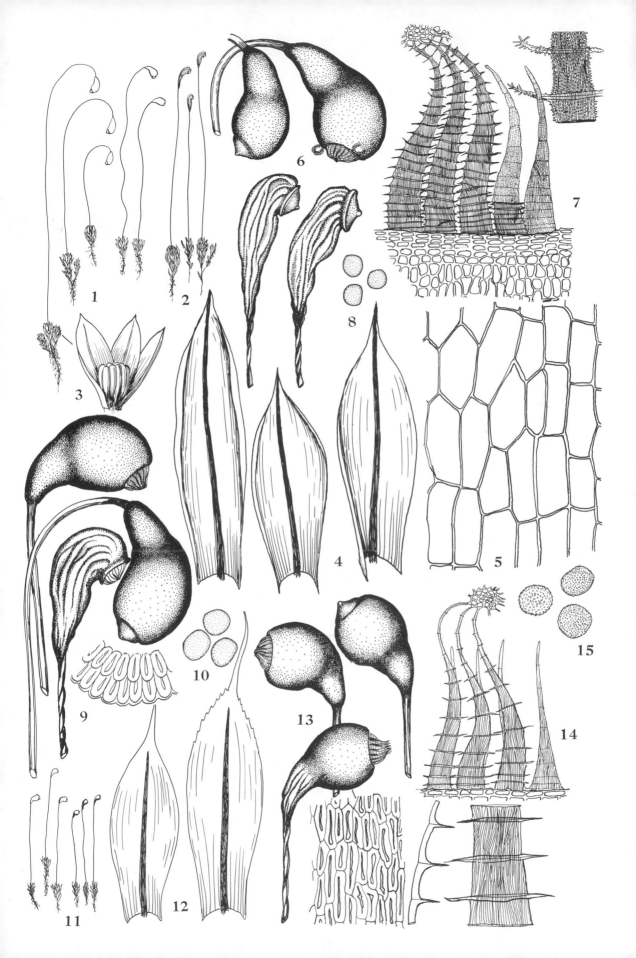

several rows of thick walled transversely elongated cells; lid flattish-convex to conic-apiculate; annulus lacking; peristome arising deeply within the mouth, lanceolate, with relatively few joints, usually striate with narrow ridges and sometimes papillose as well; endostome lacking or rudimentary, of 1–3 joints high, inconspicuous and difficult to demonstrate. Spores smooth to coarsely papillose. Calyptra large, inflated, deeply split on 1 side, long beaked.

14.24 The name means "within tooth," alluding to the teeth arising deeply within the mouth. Some authors include this genus in *Funaria*.

14.25 1. Leaves mostly abruptly short acuminate or apiculate, the point terminating in a single linear cell; capsules mostly 1.5–2 mm long; spores smooth or with few widely spaced papillae ....
.... 1. *E. planoconvexus* 14.27

14.26 1. Leaves acute to gradually short-acuminate, the terminal cells rhomboidal or fusiform; spores coarsely papillose on the outer face ....
.... 2. *E. wigginsii* 14.31

14.27 **1. Entosthodon planoconvexus** (Bartr.) Grout. Plants densely to loosely tufted, sometimes scattered, light to yellowish green. Stems short, 4–7 mm tall, branched from the base. Upper leaves crowded, usually forming a rosette, ± spreading, much shrivelled when dry, oblong-ovate to oblong-spatulate, 2–2.5 mm long, concave, apex rather broad, quite abruptly narrowed to a shortly acuminate or apiculate tip, often ending in a single linear cell; margins plane somewhat incurved, ± bluntly serrate in the upper part; costa ending well below the apex; upper leaf cells oblong to oblong-hexagonal, variable in width, 13–30 μ wide, the marginal ones longer and narrower; basal cells not much wider, more regularly oblong. Autoicous. Seta erect, straight or slightly curved, reddish at base, pale above, 6–10 mm long, capsules erect and symmetric or nearly so, pyriform, 1.5–2 mm long, the neck about as long as the spore sac, much wrinkled lengthwise when dry, urn rather firm, sometimes slightly contracted under the mouth when dry; exothecial cells oblong to sublinear-hexagonal, thin walled; annulus lacking; peristome single or with rudimentary segments 1–2 joints high, obscure and difficult to demonstrate; teeth lanceolate, slightly oblique, 155–230 μ long, trabeculae rather few and weak, not projecting laterally, joints vertically and obliquely striate with narrow ridges, reddish throughout when fully mature; lid plano-convex without a point. Spores about 20 μ,

---

Plate 63. 1–3. Funaria muehlenbergii var. lineata. 1. Exothecial cells, X120. 2. Peristome teeth and segments from two different capsules, X60. 3. Spores, X120.

4–10. Entosthodon planoconvexus. 4. Habit sketches, X.4. 5. Leaves, X8. 6. Leaf apex and upper cells, X120. 7. Capsules, X8. 8. Exothecial cells, X120. 9. Peristome teeth and segments viewed from the inside of two different capsules, X60. 10. Spores, X120.

11–17. Physcomitrium hookeri. 11. Habit sketches, X.4. 12. Leaves, X8. 13. Leaf apex and upper cells, X120. 14. Capsules, X8. 15. Suboral exothecial cells. 16. Portion of the annulus. 17. Spores, X120.

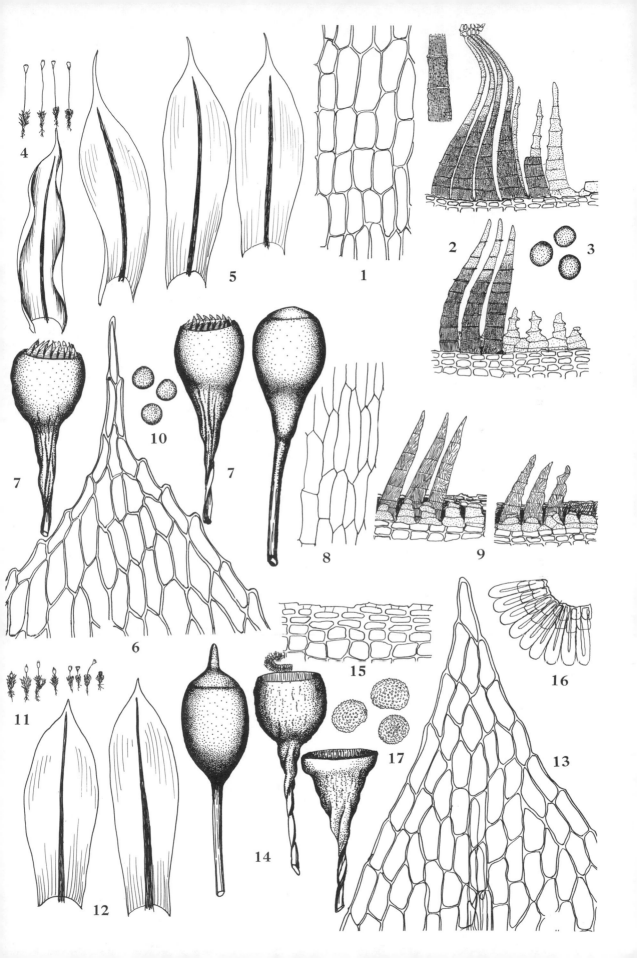

smooth to finely granulose, occasionally with a few widely spaced papillae. Plate 63, figs. 4–10.

14.28 On dry soil, usually at the bases of rocks and cliffs.

14.29 Arizona and southern Utah. Washington County: Santa Clara Creek, ca. 2,600 ft.

14.30 The above specimen has much shorter teeth than the original description indicates. It grew scattered among the thalli of the hepatic, *Targiona hyphophylla.* Growing with it were three shoots having much longer setae and larger capsules, the latter elongate-pyriform with longer more tapering necks and longer spore sacs containing spores ranging from 20–27 μ and roughened with rather dense coarse papillae. These plants look much like *E. wigginsii,* but since the lids and peristome were lacking, definite identification was not possible.

14.31 **2. Entosthodon wigginsii** Steere. Plants loosely to rather densely tufted, often scattered, bright or yellowish green. Stems 3–15 mm tall, sparingly branched or simple, rhizoids rather coarse, reddish and confined to the base. Upper and comal leaves erect-patent to spreading and forming a rosette when moist, lower leaves much smaller or the lower stem naked, obovate to shortly spatulate, 2–3 mm long, concave, often recurved from the shortly erect base, much shrivelled when dry, acute to shortly acuminate; margins ± incurved on 1 or both sides, bluntly dentate with rather swollen divergent upper ends of the marginal cells, becoming entire below; costa slender, extending 4/5–5/6 the length of the blade; upper cells around the end of the costa shortly oblong to hexagonal, variable in width, 15–35 μ wide, thin walled, becoming longer downward, marginal cells narrower and the basal cells more regularly oblong to sublinear. Autoicous or paroicous. Seta 6–12 mm long, reddish when mature; capsules 1.5–2.5 mm long, yellowish brown when young, becoming reddish with age, pyriform to elongate-pyriform, the mouth small, the neck rather thick, about as long as the spore sac, gradually narrowed to the seta, irregularly furrowed when dry; exothecial cells oblong to linear, thin walled, the end walls transverse to pointed; peristome teeth slenderly lanceolate from a wide base, tapering to a very slender tip, often irregular, slightly spiral, 0.24–0.3 mm long, lamellae few, 7–9, vertically and obliquely striate with fine ridges, the upper joints smooth to finely papillose; endostome lacking or very short and fragile, 2–3 joints high, difficult to demonstrate, inserted below the mouth; lid plano-convex, ca. 0.6 mm in diameter; annulus lacking. Spores dark brownish, mostly 20–23 μ, rather coarsely papillose, the papillae widely spaced to rather dense, often adhering in tetrads. Plate 149, figs. 1–6.

14.32 On damp or dry sandy soil, usually at the bases of rocks and cliffs or in crevices.

14.33 Arizona and southern Utah. Washington County near La Verkin, 3,250 ft.

14.34   The present specimen, consisting of six well-fruited shoots, differs from the original description in the taller stems (up to 9 mm as opposed to 2–4 mm), the longer seta (up to 11 mm as opposed to 2–4 mm), the slightly larger capsules (2.5 mm as opposed to 1.5–2 mm), and the spores which do not always remain in tetrads. In two of the capsules the spores were in tetrads when first pressed out. When mounted in glycerin jelly, most of them separated, some of them retained the three-angled inner face, while others became sunken on this face and assumed a more or less broadly reniform shape. The bases of some of the stems are swollen and bulbous with irregularly isodiametric cells from which slender innovations arise, and the bulbous base appears to have arisen as an innovation from a much disintegrated earlier stem. Slender innovations also arise from the base of the stem and from the old perigonium.

14.35   Much like *E. planoconvexus* but differing in the slightly larger size, leaf apices acute or very shortly acuminate rather than mostly apiculate with a single linear cell, longer basal cells, blunt serrations on the margins extending further toward the base, larger capsules with less narrowed neck, peristome teeth much more slenderly lanceolate, and smoother spores.

3. PHYSCOMITRIUM (Brid.) Fuernr.

14.36   Plants small, in loose tufts or scattered. Stems usually short, 2–6 mm tall, up to 25 mm in a few unusual forms. Leaves bright green, obovate, oblong to broadly oblanceolate or spatulate; upper cells oblong to oblong hexagonal, usually thin walled and clear; basal cells, usually larger. Monoicous. Perigonia terminal on a small branch. Capsules subglobose to pyriform, erect and symmetric, immersed on a very short seta to well exserted on a long seta; neck short and thick, becoming wrinkled when dry, the urn firm but variably contracted under the mouth when dry, sometimes not at all, at other times strongly so, even in the same tuft; lid rather large, convex to conic, apiculate to long rostrate; peristome lacking; annulus present. Spores large, papillose. Calyptra small to large, ± lobed at the base and with a long straight beak.

14.37   The name is from the Greek and means bladder cap, referring to the swollen calyptra.

14.38   1. Seta 1–3 mm long; capsules immersed to exserted; plants small, stems 1 5 mm tall

   2. Leaves acute, serrulate; capsules oblong-pyriform, neck thick, gradually merging with the urn and seta; suboral cells in 5–8 rows of transversely elongated cells; annulus of 2 rows of small persistent cells .... 1. *P. pygmaeum*   14.40

   2. Leaves shortly acuminate, entire; capsules ovoid with 2–4 rows of transversely elongated thick-walled cells below the mouth; annulus of 3 rows of vesicular cells, revoluble .... 2. *P. hookeri*   14.42

14.39   1. Seta 4–14(20) mm long; capsules exserted, pyriform with 7–12 rows

309

of thick-walled, transversely elongated cells below the mouth; annulus large

3. Leaf margins distinctly serrate above, not noticeably bordered above, but the lower marginal cells usually narrower, thin walled, and often with chloroplasts like the medial cells .... 3. *P. pyriforme* 14.46

3. Leaf margins entire or nearly so, bordered with 2–3 rows of thick-walled, clear, yellowish linear cells, becoming rhomboidal toward the apex .... 4. *P. californicum* 14.50

14.40 **1. Physcomitrium pygmaeum** Jam. "Plants small, 3–5 mm high, stems leafy, simple or sparingly branched; leaves longest at the apex, oblong-acuminate, serrulate, vein ending in or below the apex; seta short, almost immersed, twisted to the left, as long as the oblong-pyriform capsule; annulus of 2 rows of narrow cells, persistent; mouth bordered by 5–7 rows of oblong cells; neck tapering, with few stomata; lid large, conic-apiculate; calyptra lobed and beaked; spores rough, 28–31 μ, maturing in late spring." Type locality, Utah, S. Watson, "on ground above Parley's Park, in the Wasatch Mountains, Utah, at 6,500 ft. altitude." Plate 60, figs. 10–16.

14.41 I have seen only a single slide bearing the leaves of the type specimen which is only fragmentary and preserved in the Farlow Cryptogamic Herbarium at Harvard University. James also left a fairly good drawing of the specimen and its parts which is reproduced in Mrs. Britton's paper on the *Physcomitrium* [Bull. Torr. Bot. Club 21 (1894):189–208, and in Group's *Moss Flora of North America* 2 (1935):pl. 31]. It is here copied together with a leaf and details of the apex. A second specimen was collected by Baker (908) in western Nevada. These are the only known specimens. I have scoured Parley's Park, the area around U. S. Highway 40 in the vicinity of Kimball's Junction and Snyderville, Summit County, and the surrounding hills but have found no trace of the moss. Small specimens of *P. californicum* near the Mountain Dell Reservoir were reported by me as *P. pygmaeum*. Later, more abundant material was collected which revealed the wide variation of the former species so that the latter plant still remains to be collected a second time in Utah.

14.42 **2. Physcomitrium hookeri** Hamp. Plants small, bright green, densely to loosely tufted. Stems short, 1–2 mm long, simple or with 1–2 branches. Leaves broadly ovate to oblong-ovate, a few oblong-obovate, acute to slightly acuminate, 2–2.5 mm long, when moist widely spreading, much shrivelled when dry; margins plane, mostly entire, occasionally ± dentate near the apex; costa percurrent or nearly so; upper cells oblong to hexagonal, thin walled, 17–27 μ wide, 1–2 rows narrower at the margins but not forming a noticeable border; basal cells more regularly oblong, slightly wider, up to 31 μ, sometimes ± inflated, the marginal row often smaller and shorter, alar cells not differentiated. Seta short and thick, 2–3 mm long; capsules emergent to shortly exserted, ovoid to obovate, becoming obconic to globose-pyriform when dry, neck short, spore sac ± globose; exothecial cells irregularly 4- to 6-sided, isodia-metric to oblong or hexagonal, thin walled, 2–5 rows below the mouth transversely elongated and thick walled; annulus of 3 rows of vesicular cells, revoluble or often persistent; lid convex, beaked. Spores globose to slightly reniform, 23–28 μ, coarsely papillose, dark brown when ripe. Calyptra rather small, the base covering only the lid and mouth, 2- to 3(4)-lobed at the base, long beaked. Plate 63, figs. 11–17.

14.43   On damp or wet soil.

14.44   Saskatchewan to Ontario, southward to Ohio and Kansas; Utah. Box-elder County: Brigham City, 4,307 ft.

14.45   Distinguished by its small size, unbordered, entire leaves, large annulus, and fewer differentiated cells below the mouth of the capsule. Crum and Anderson [Bryologist 58(1955):10] found that *P. coloradense* Britt. is no more than a form of *P. hookeri* with a short seta which may cause the capsules to appear emergent in some plants. A. O. Garrett collected it on the saline plains west of Salt Lake City, but I have not seen the specimen.

14.46   **3. Physcomitrium pyriforme** (Hedw.) Hamp. Plants loosely to densely tufted, often scattered, bright green. Stems 2–15 mm high, usually branched from the base. Leaves shrivelled when dry, spreading when moist, the comal ones larger and forming a rosette, 3–5 mm long, the lower ones smaller, extremely variable in outline, usually ovate-lanceolate to oblong-spatulate, mostly shortly acuminate, moderately to strongly con-cave; margins plane, mostly serrate in the upper ½ to ⅔, occasionally some leaves entire; costa mostly percurrent, sometimes very shortly ex-current or ending below the apex; upper cells mostly oblong-hexagonal to rhomboidal, the marginal ones longer and narrower, sometimes slightly thicker walled but not forming a noticeable border; basal cells becoming larger and more regularly oblong, thinner walled, the alar cells enlarged and inflated. Seta 2–5 mm long, mostly erect, sometimes curved; capsules subglobose to shortly pyriform when moist and fresh, the mouth small, when dry usually becoming ± turbinate, the neck and lower part of the urn becoming shrunken, the mouth then appearing wide and flaring, varying to urceolate or well rounded with the neck shrunken; exothecial cells quadrate to hexagonal, some irregular, 7–12 rows below the mouth transversely elongated and thicker walled; an-nulus of 2 rows of cells, commonly persistent and bent inward in the mouth. Spores globose to shortly reniform, 27–52 μ, coarsely low papil-lose to nearly spinulose with tall papillae, extremely variable as to size and character of papillae in different collections, dark reddish brown when mature. Plate 64, figs. 1–7.

14.47   On damp or wet soil in a wide variety of places.

14.48   Europe, North Africa, Azores. Nova Scotia to Florida, westward to the Great Plains, from Manitoba to Utah and Texas. Utah County: Wasatch Mountains, Mt. Timpanogos, 6,500–8,000 ft.

14.49   Rare in Utah. Differs from *P. californicum* in the serrated leaf margins without a noticeable border of narrower cells. For many years American plants of this species were known as *P. turbinatum* (Michx.) Britt. In a recent revision of the genus, Crum and Anderson [Bryologist 58(1955): 1–15] found such wide variations in North American collections which seemed to embrace the less variable European form known as *P. pyriforme* that they referred our plants to the latter name. Formerly much had been made of the shape assumed by the capsules when dry, e.g., those having a strongly shrunken neck and spore sac, the mouth flaring (*P. turbinatum*) as opposed to those having the spore sac well rounded with only the neck shrunken or sometimes with the spore sac urceolate. There seems to be every degree of intergradation between the two extremes, even in the same tuft. Mrs. E. C. Britton defended the status of *P. turbinatum* in her revision of the genus [Bull. Torr. Bot. Club 21(1894):189–208, pls. 197–203].

14.50   **4. Physcomitrium californicum** Britt. Plants usually tufted, often in open sods, bright green. Stems erect, 2–8 mm high with 1 to several smaller branches arising from near the base. Leaves largest at the summit, forming a rosette, smaller and distant below, shrivelled and contorted when dry, patent to spreading when moist, broadly ovate-lanceolate to oblong-lanceolate or spatulate-obovate, 3–6.5 mm long, the lower ones smaller, the size and shape varying in different stands of plants according to age and degree of development, moderately to rather strongly concave, apex mostly acute, in some leaves ± short acuminate; margins plane, entire or nearly so, bordered by 2–3 rows of linear, thick-walled, yellowish, clear cells, these becoming shorter and more rhomboidal toward the apex; costa slender, percurrent or ending well below the apex; upper cells mostly oblong, a few sometimes oblong-hexagonal to rhomboidal, thin walled, 20–34 x 57–100 μ (smaller in less well developed plants), becoming larger and thinner walled in the base, 34–50 μ wide, the alar cells frequently inflated and sometimes extending nearly to the costa. Seta 4–13 mm long; capsules subglobose to shortly pyriform, mouth small, the neck short, the urn yellow brown becoming darker with age, when dry globose and only slightly shrunken to strongly contracted under the mouth and hence urceolate in shape, the neck always strongly shrunken and longitudinally wrinkled; exothecial cells irregularly quadrate to rectangular, 5–10 rows below the mouth transversely elongated, reddish and thicker walled; annulus of 2 rows of cells, usually persistent and arched inward; lid conic-apiculate or shortly rostrate. Spores shortly reniform to nearly globose, 30–34 μ in longest diameter, dark reddish brown when fully mature, densely and coarsely papillose, at times almost spinulose. Calyptra beaked, lobed at the base. Plate 64, figs. 8–13.

Plate 64. 1–7. Physcomitrium pyriforme. 1. Habit sketches, X.4. 2. Habit moist and dry, X4. 3. Leaves, X8. 4. Leaf apex and upper cells. 5. Upper and lower marginal leaf cells, X120. 6. Capsules, X8. 7. Spores, X120.

8–13. Physcomitrium californicum. 8. Habit sketches, X.4. 9. Habit, X4. 10. Leaves, X8. 11. Lower marginal leaf cells, X120. 12. Capsules, X8. 13. Spores, X120.

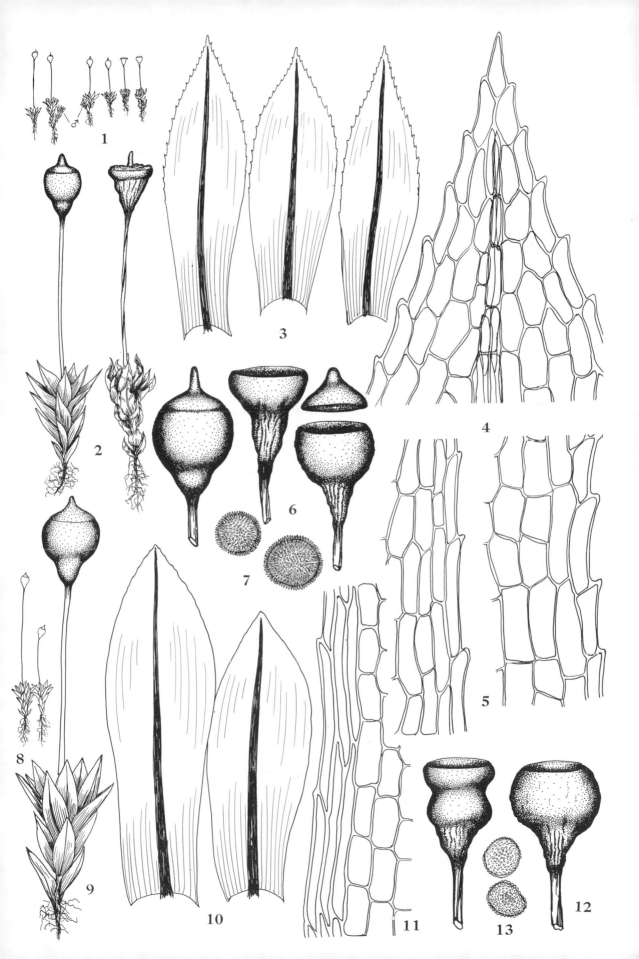

14.51   FUNARIACEAE

14.51   Lowlands and in the mountains, mostly on damp or wet soil.

14.52   California, Nevada, and Utah.

14.53   Locally abundant. Grout treated this plant as a variety of *P. megalo-carpum* Kindb. which ranges from northern California to British Columbia and eastward to Idaho. In a recent revision of the genus by Crum and Anderson [Bryologist 58(1955):1–15] it is returned to specific rank because of the following features. *P. megalocarpum*: leaf apices acuminate, margins recurved, entire to slightly toothed, bordered with yellowish linear cells below and rhomboidal above, upper cells laxly oblong-rhomboidal becoming greatly enlarged below, alar cells clearly differentiated. *P. californicum*: leaf apices broadly acute, margins plane, entire or nearly so, indistinctly bordered with narrower cells; upper cells uniformly rectangular, not greatly enlarged below, the alar cells not differentiated.

14.54   All the collections made in Utah have been studied and named by Dr. Crum. I agree with the return of *P. californicum* to specific rank, but all the traits contrasted by Crum and Anderson do not hold up in the present specimens. I find that the linear thick-walled marginal cells of the leaves form as strong a border as in *P. megalocarpum* and that the alar cells are equally differentiated in most of the fully developed upper leaves. Thus *P. megalocarpum* differs from our present specimens mainly in the acuminate leaf apices, which are often acute in some leaves, the recurved margins and predominantly oblong-hexagonal upper leaf cells becoming greatly enlarged in the lower part.

14.55   *Physcomitrium pyriforme* differs from the present species mainly in the serrated margins of most well-developed leaves, the marginal cells narrower than the medial cells, but not or rarely forming a noticeable border.

SPLACHNACEAE

15.1   Plants tufted to scattered, pale to light green. Stems mostly erect, occasionally ascending, soft and tender with reddish brown papillose rhizoids at the base; central strand large. Leaves usually lax and often flaccid, broadly obovate, oblong or spatulate, narrowed at the base, apex broadly rounded, obtuse or apiculate to briefly and slenderly acuminate; costa ending below the apex; upper medial cells thin walled, often lax, oblong, hexagonal, or rhomboidal. Dioicous, autoicous, or synoicous. Perigonia terminal, often becoming lateral or axillary by innovations, globose to subdiscoid; perigonial leaves erect-patent to squarrose from a ± clasping, often orange base. Seta 1–20 cm long, in most genera ± dilated at the junction with the urn, forming a hypophysis composed of green photosynthetic tissue with numerous stomata in the surface, originating from tissue of the seta rather than the capsule, ranging in size and form from narrowly clavate and resembling an unusually long narrow neck to a much distended bulbous structure as much as 10 times the width of the urn, at maturity yellowish or brownish like

314

the urn to bright red, varying to dark purple, when dry the larger ones become much wrinkled or inverted downward like an umbrella; capsules erect, subglobose to cylindric, yellowish brown to reddish, columella dilated at the apex and forming an expanded disc across the mouth, included or exserted when dry; peristome of 32 narrow divisions, sometimes very long, composed of 2–3 layers of cells, united in pairs or 4s (except in *Tayloria splachnoides*), erect to reflexed when dry.

15.2   Mostly rare mosses of northern latitudes or high altitudes in mountains southward. Confined to soil rich in organic matter, rotten wood, dung, and decaying carcasses of animals, usually in damp or wet places.

TAYLORIA Hook.

15.3   With traits of the family, differing from the other genera as follows: Seta 1–4 cm long, hypophysis narrower than the urn and of the same color, forming an unusually long neck which gradually tapers into the seta; capsules globose to ovoid or occasionally cylindrical, when dry not much changed or sometimes moderately contracted under the mouth, hypophysis much shrunken; teeth of 2 layers of cells, split to the base into 32 divisions deeply inserted in the mouth, erect or reflexed when dry; lid conic to conic-apiculate. Spores 15–45 μ, mature in summer. Calyptra short and constricted at the base.

15.4   The name commemorates Thomas Taylor, Irish botanist and physician.

15.5   **Tayloria acuminata** Hornsch. Shoots becoming 1–2.5 cm tall, branched, often with slender innovations, reddish with age. Leaves ± shrunken and erect-patent when dry, to spreading when moist, obovate, oblong-spatulate or ligulate, 1–3.5 mm long, mostly acute to short-acuminate, the tip often ending in a single row of 2–5 cells, some leaves broadly rounded and obtuse; margins sharply serrate in the upper part; costa rather weak, ending several cells below the tip; upper cells rhomboidal to oblong-hexagonal or some irregular, 30–45 μ wide, thin walled, often lax; marginal cells smaller and slightly thicker walled; cells in the lower ½–⅔ more elongated, slightly wider and extremely thin walled. Autoicous or synoicous. Seta 1.5–3 cm long, yellowish, becoming reddish with age; capsules ovoid to ovoid-cylindric, yellowish, 1–1.5(2) mm long; exothecial cells short, ± angular, hexagonal to very irregular, transversely elongated, the walls thick and firm, the horizontal one the thickest, the urn very firm and little changed on drying, moderately contracted under the mouth; hypophysis forming a long narrow neck, 1.5–3 mm long and tapering imperceptibly into the seta, strongly wrinkled when dry; peristome teeth divided into 32 very long ribbon-like divisions about 0.6 mm long, reddish and finely papillose, deeply inserted in the mouth, when dry arched outward at the base and helically coiled inward toward the mouth, usually much tangled and often broken off; lid convex or conic with a longish beak, blunt at the tip. Spores globose, pale yellowish or light yellowish brown, smooth, 12–17 μ. Plate 27, figs. 8–12.

15.6   On damp or wet humus, rotten wood, soil, or rocks.

15.7 Europe. British Columbia, Quebec. Alaska, Idaho, Utah. Salt Lake County, Wasatch Mountains, mouth of Bell's Canyon, 5,500 ft.

15.8 Extremely rare. Our single specimen was growing in a mat of *Eurhynchium pulchellum* with *Tortula mucronifolia, Bryum creberrimum,* and *Timmia bavarica.* There were about a dozen well-fruited plants and twice as many sterile ones.

AULACOMNIACEAE

16.1 Plants densely to loosely tufted, green to yellowish green above, brownish below. Stems simple or freely branched, erect to ascending, often with a dense ferruginous tomentum on the lower part; central strand present. Leaves shortly ligulate to narrowly lanceolate, broadly rounded, obtuse or acute; costa strong, ending below the apex to shortly excurrent; upper cells small, $\pm$ isodiametric to shortly oblong, angular to rounded, smooth to strongly papillose; stems prolonged into a more or less naked green pseudopodium bearing gemmae. Autoicous or dioicous. Capsules oblong to cylindric, erect to horizontal, commonly furrowed when dry; peristome double; annulus present.

AULACOMNIUM Schwaegr.

16.2 Stems ascending or erect, solitary and scattered to densely tufted. Leaves various; costa in cross section showing a single row of guides with 1–2 rows of ventral stereids and 3–6 rows of dorsal stereids, upper cells thin to thick walled, each bearing a single central papilla on each surface; basal cells shortly oblong, walls firm or thin and much swollen, sometimes in 2–3 layers. Dioicous (in our species). Perichaetium terminal, rather conspicuous and budlike, antheridia numerous, short stalked, among numerous paraphyses. Seta long, erect, twisted when dry; capsules nearly erect to strongly inclined when first mature and moist, symmetric to slightly curved, when dry more strongly inclined or horizontal, strongly longitudinally furrowed and $\pm$ contracted under the mouth; exothecial cells $\pm$ oblong in alternate bands of thin- and thick-walled cells, each band 3–5 cells wide, several rows of cells below the mouth small, rounded, and very thick walled; annulus of 2 rows of cells, revoluble; lid mammillose to conic, obtuse or apiculate; peristome teeth 16, lanceolate, hyaline above and finely papillose, yellowish and very finely papillose below; stomata present in the neck; inner peristome with a high basal membrane, about half the height of the teeth, segments thin and pale yellowish with 2–4 cilia between them. Calyptra narrow, cucullate, about as long as the capsule.

16.3 The name means furrowed moss, alluding to the furrowed capsule.

16.4 1. Plants mostly erect, green; pseudopodia bearing a globose cluster of fusiform gemmae at the summit, growing on moist or dry soil, rocks, bases of trees, stumps, or rotten logs .... 1. *A. androgynum* 16.6

16.5 1. Plants commonly ascending but frequently erect, yellowish green, pseudopodia bearing lanceolate gemmae widely spaced on the lower

316

part and clustered at the summit, growing in and around water, bogs, wet meadows, banks of alpine brooks and lakes .... 2. *A. palustre* 16.10

16.6   **1. Aulacomnium androgynum** (Hedw.) Schwaegr. Stems 1–4 (rarely to 7) cm tall, ± tomentose in the lower part. Leaves mostly green, somewhat imbricated and slightly crisped when dry, patent when moist, 1.5–5 mm long, ovate-lanceolate to narrowly lanceolate from a ± oblong base, apex acute to obtuse; margins crenulate-dentate to rather coarsely serrate near the apex, narrowly revolute in the lower part and sometimes nearly to the apex (plane in small-leaved forms); costa stout, mostly ending below the apex, occasionally percurrent; upper leaf cells rounded, oval, or somewhat irregular, thick walled, 6–12 μ wide, usually strongly papillose but occasionally smooth or nearly so; basal cells shortly oblong to sublinear, smooth and usually thick walled (scarcely different from the upper cells in short-leaved forms). Pseudopodium yellowish green, becoming reddish brown with age; gemmae fusiform, of 2–6 cells, in a dense globose cluster at the summit, ± persistent, tardily deciduous. Dioicous. Perigonia terminal, gemmiform. Seta 1–2 mm long, yellowish to reddish brown, shiny, twisted to the right; capsules 2–3 mm long, oblong-cylindric, erect to horizontal, strongly furrowed and slightly contracted under the mouth when dry, the ridges chestnut brown, the furrows yellowish brown; lid conic to mammillose, blunt to apiculate; peristome teeth lanceolate-acuminate, the apices hyaline filiform and papillose, becoming yellowish and very finely papillose below; segments narrow, cilia 2–3, pale, exceedingly slender, often slightly appendiculate. Spores 7–10 μ, globose, pale yellowish and smooth, maturing in June or July. Plate 65, figs. 1–11.

16.7   On rotten wood, stumps, bases of trees, soil, or rocks, usually in shady places.

16.8   Eurasia. British Columbia to Labrador, southward to New York, Michigan, and in the mountains of Utah, Nevada, and California.

16.9   Rare in Utah, becoming more frequent northward in Idaho and the Pacific Northwest where it is often very abundant.

16.10   **2. Aulacomnium palustre** (Hedw.) Schwaegr. Plants prostrate-ascending, often matted, to erect and densely tufted, often solitary and scattered, yellowish green with a tomentum of ferruginous rhizoids in the lower part. Stems simple to freely branched, 1.5–8 cm long. Leaves dense to widely spaced, mostly narrowly lanceolate, 2–4 mm long; bases appressed and the upper part flexuous to crisped when dry, erect-patent to widely spreading when moist, slenderly acute to obtuse or rounded; margins entire to denticulate at the apex, plane above, revolute below, often well toward the apex; costa stout, prominent at the back, whitish to pale yellowish and shiny when dry, mostly ending below the tip; upper leaf cells 6–15 μ wide, ± isodiametric to shortly elongated, angular to rounded, oval or irregular, usually thick walled, usually strongly papillose on both faces but sometimes nearly smooth; basal cells en-

317

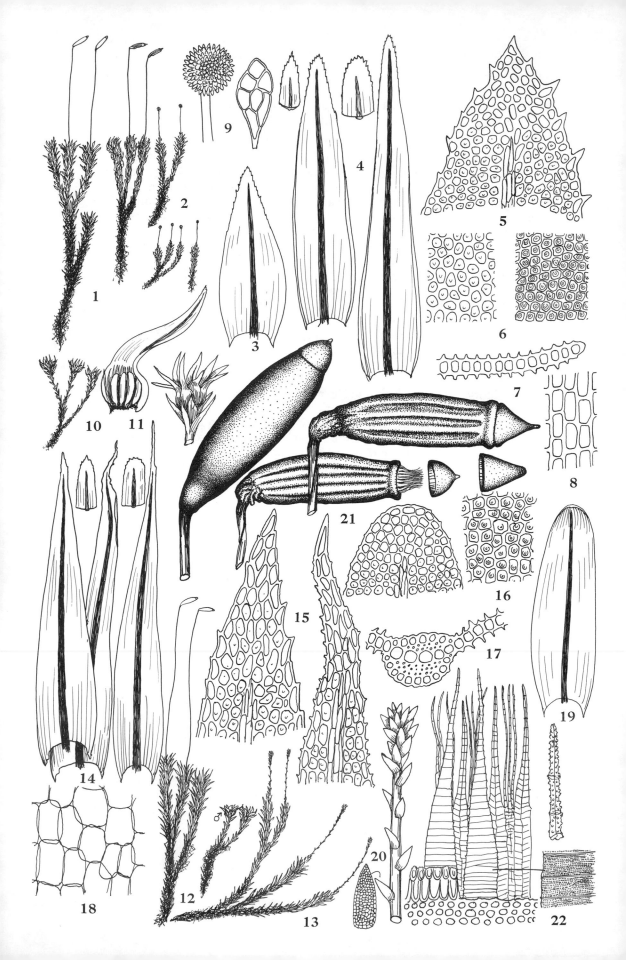

larged and swollen. Pseudopodia usually single, but in some plants 2 to several branching from below on the main axis; gemmae widely spaced below, densely clustered at the apex, lanceolate, 0.2–0.3 mm long, of numerous small cells, 2- to 3-stratose in the lower middle part. Dioicous. Perigonium large, discoid to budlike. Seta usually erect (occasionally ascending), 2–4.5 cm long, reddish brown; capsules suberect to inclined, oblong to subcylindric, usually slightly curved and asymmetric, 2–4 mm long, when dry becoming strongly inclined to horizontal, slightly contracted under the mouth and strongly 4- to 8-furrowed, yellowish brown at maturity, becoming a rich chestnut brown when dry and empty; lid mammillose to conic, obtuse to apiculate; peristome teeth slenderly lanceolate-acuminate, pale and papillose above, yellowish and very finely papillose below, segments narrow, cilia filiform. Spores yellowish brown, smooth, 10–12 μ. Plate 65, figs. 12–22.

16.11 Abundant in noncalcareous regions in and around bogs, banks of brooks and lakes and in wet meadows.

16.12 Europe and Asia. Alaska to Greenland and southward throughout the United States, except Arizona.

16.13 Locally abundant at high altitudes where siliceous and ferromagnesian rocks predominate. It is essentially an acid lover ecologically similar to *Sphagnum,* the two plants commonly growing together. There is considerable variation in leaf apex, the typical form being slenderly acute or acuminate, but nearly every stem may show some leaves with blunt or rounded tips, and some plants may have the latter type of leaf predominating. If collections are made early in the season when the new shoots have grown out ¼ to ½ their eventual length, the juvenile leaves are usually pale or whitish green, closely imbricated, oblong-ligulate, very broadly rounded and often cucullate at the apex. The leaves of last year's growth will usually be found to be normal with slenderly acute apices. Often the lower leaves on a given season's growth are shorter and blunter than the upper ones.

TIMMIACEAE

17.1 Plants usually densely tufted. Stems erect, simple or sparingly branched. Leaves mostly linear-lanceolate from an oblong sheathing base; costa strong; upper leaf cells rather small, ± isodiametric, those in the base

---

Plate 65. 1–11. **Aulacomnium androgynum.** 1. Fertile plants moist and dry, X.4. 2. Sterile plants with pseudopodia and propagulae, X.4. 3. Leaf of small-leaved form. 4. Typical leaves, X8. 5. Leaf apex. 6. Two areas of upper medial leaf cells. 7. Cross section of lamina. 8. Basal cells, X120. 9. Globose cluster of propagulae, X8, single propagulum, X120. 10. Male plant, X.4. 11. Perigonial bud, X2, X4.

12–22. **Aulacomnium palustre.** 12. Habit of fertile plants. 13. Sterile plants with pseudopodia and propagulae, X.4. 14. Leaves, X8. 15. Three leaf apices. 16. Upper medial leaf cells. 17. Cross section of the costa. 18. Basal cells, X120. 19. Juvenile leaf of young innovations, X8. 20. Portion of pseudopodium, X8, with propagulum, X30. 21. Capsules, X8. 22. Portion of the peristome, X60, detail, X200.

oblong to linear. Seta long, erect; capsules suberect, inclined or horizontal, occasionally pendent, subglobose to oblong-ovoid when first mature in the moist condition, becoming ovoid to oblong when dry and usually not returning to the original shorter dimensions when moistened again; annulus present; peristome double, of 16 teeth and an inner peristome consisting of a high basal membrane, ⅓–½ the length of the teeth, divided above into 64 slender partially united cilia. Calyptra rather large, cucullate, the base clasping the seta just below the capsule.

TIMMIA Hedw.

17.2 Plants green above, brown below. Stems with a large central strand. Leaves mostly linear-lanceolate, canaliculate, acute, blunt or broadly rounded at the apex, the base usually abruptly dilated and clasping the stem; margins coarsely serrate or dentate in the upper ⅓–½, the teeth composed of 1 to several cells, entire or serrulate below; costa strong and prominent at the back, percurrent or ending a few cells below the tip, in cross section showing a single row of guides and both dorsal and ventral stereid bands; upper cells 6–15 μ wide, mostly quadrate to hexagonal with some shortly oblong, angular to somewhat rounded, usually mammillose or convex on the ventral side and smooth or papillose on the dorsal side; basal cells abruptly elongated, thin walled, hyaline or colored. Antheridia large, borne on long basal stalks among slenderly clavate paraphyses; archegonia large. Capsules greenish to light brown at maturity, becoming yellowish to yellowish brown when dry and empty, often darker when old, wall with large stomata; lid mammillose to conic-apiculate; annulus of 2–3 rows of swollen cells; peristome teeth yellowish to yellowish brown, oblong-lanceolate to lanceolate, entire or perforated above, coarsely vertically striate and papillose above, becoming abruptly very finely transversely striate and papillose in the lower half; inner peristome slightly paler, the 64 cilia nearly as long as the teeth, ± united in 2s and 4s, nodulose at the joints, usually coarsely papillose on the outer side, but sometimes smooth. Spores brown, globose to ovoid, smooth to finely papillose.

17.3 Named in honor of Joachim Christian Timm, burgermeister of the town of Malchim in Mecklenberg, Germany, and an ardent botanist.

17.4 1. Cells of the clasping leaf base more or less hyaline throughout; costa not toothed at the back near the apex; cilia with conspicuous appendages at the joints; autoicous .... 1. *T. bavarica* 17.6

17.5 1. Cells of the clasping leaf base usually orange above or throughout; costa with coarse teeth on the back near the apex; cilia nodulose but without appendages; dioicous .... 2. *T. austriaca* 17.10

17.6 **1. Timmia bavarica** Hessl. Plants coarse, dark green above, brownish below, forming loose or dense tufts. Stems 1–4 cm tall, brownish orange. Leaves ± crisped when dry, widely spreading to squarrose when moist, 5–8 mm long, linear-lanceolate from a clasping base comprising 1/6–1/5 of the leaf length; apex gradually tapering to a narrowly acute or blunt tip; margins usually widely incurved, coarsely serrate in the upper ⅓, the teeth of 1–3(4) cells, entire to serrulate below; costa smooth on the back below, sometimes papillose near the apex but not toothed; upper cells small, 6–10 μ wide, more or less isodiametric, quadrate to irregularly hexagonal; cells of the sheath abruptly differentiated, oblong to linear, hyaline or yellowish throughout, 6–12 x 44–98 μ, shorter on the margins. Autoicous. Seta 12 mm long, yellowish brown, not much twisted when dry; capsules mostly inclined but often horizontal, ovoid, 2–2.5 mm long and about 1 mm thick, yellowish to yellowish brown, appearing narrower when dry, slightly contracted under the mouth, the urn faintly rugulose, rarely furrowed; cilia usually appendiculate. Spores 11–15 μ, ripe in July. Plate 66, figs. 1–5.

17.7   Mostly growing in dense shade on soil in crevices, under overhanging rocks, on roots of trees and similar places.

17.8   Europe and Asia. Yukon territory south in the Rocky Mountains to Nevada, Utah, Arizona, Colorado, North Dakota, Ontario.

17.9   A large moss somewhat resembling a *Polytrichum,* common in the mountains throughout the state. The cilia of the peristome are not always appendiculate, but merely nodulose. However, the colorless leaf base and the absence of coarse teeth on the back of the leaf at its apex serve in distinguishing it from the next species.

17.10   **2. Timmia austriaca** Hedw. Plants densely tufted. Stems erect to ascending, stout, reddish orange, 4–9 cm tall. Leaves typically 6–8 mm long, crisped to ± imbricated when dry, when moist abruptly spreading to squarrose from the erect clasping base which is orange colored in part or throughout, the upper part linear-lanceolate, acute to blunt or rounded; costa usually toothed on the back near the apex; the upper leaf cells 6–14 μ wide, quadrate, hexagonal or shortly oblong. Dioicous. Seta 3–4 cm long; capsules longer than the last species, 4–5 mm long and about 1 mm thick, contracted slightly below the mouth and somewhat furrowed when dry, neck more tapering and more furrowed; cilia of the inner peristome strongly nodulose at the joints but not appendiculate. Spores 12–18 μ, brown, smooth to finely papillose.

17.11   On soil in crevices, under overhanging rocks and on tree roots, on open banks in the shade or occasionally on wet brook banks exposed.

17.12   Greenland to Alaska, southward to Michigan, Nebraska, New Mexico, Arizona, and Nevada.

17.13   All our specimens are the short-leaved form: var. **brevifolia** Ren. & Card., Sayre. Stems 1–12 cm high, densely to loosely tufted, often scattered among other mosses; leaves 4–6 mm long, usually blunt to widely rounded at the apex; cells at the leaf tip usually thick walled and often orange colored. Seta shorter, 2.5–4 cm long; capsules shorter and thicker, subglobose to pyriform, 2.5–3 mm long, 1–2 mm thick when first mature and moist, when dry oblong, finely wrinkled to furrowed and slightly contracted under the mouth. Plate 66, figs. 6–11.

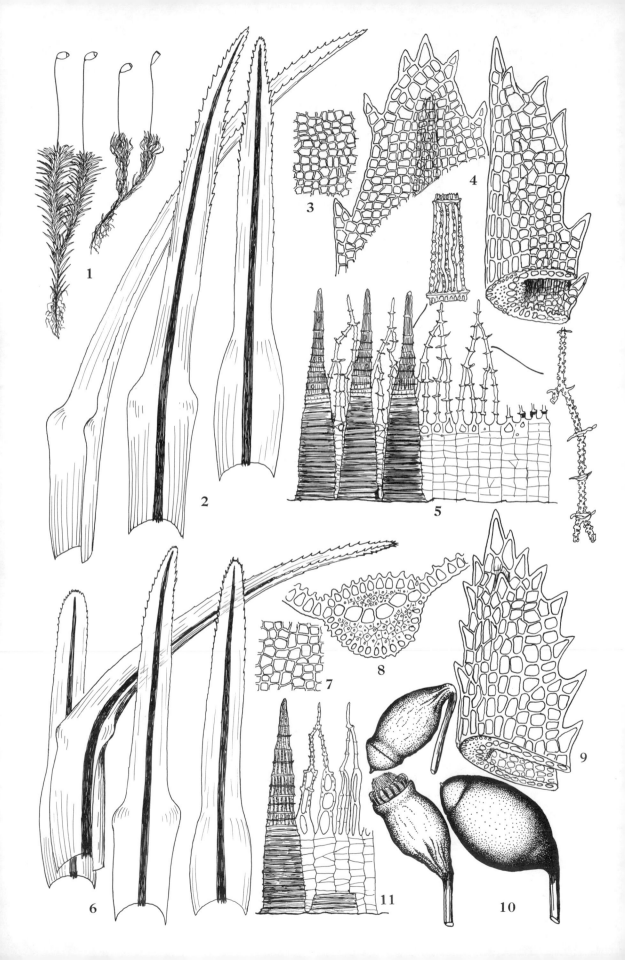

BARTRAMIACEAE

18.1 Plants mostly tufted, small to large, tall and robust. Stems variously branched, mostly fastigiate or whorled, often densely tomentose on the lower parts. Leaves broadly ovate-lanceolate to linear or subulate, plane or abruptly differentiated at the base and clasping the stem; costa mostly strong and broad, ending shortly below the apex to long excurrent; margins mostly serrate in the upper part, plane or revolute; upper leaf cells variable, mostly oblong to linear, usually papillose by projection of the end walls, less often with central papillae or smooth in some species; basal cells usually enlarged. Setae short to long; capsules mostly globose to ovoid, inclined to cernuous, and longitudinally furrowed when dry, or erect and smooth to rugulose in some genera; peristome double, single and rudimentary, or lacking; lid convex to conic. Spores globose to reniform, papillose or warty.

18.2   1. Leaves subulate to linear, ± abruptly divergent from an oblong clasping base; branching not whorled .... 2. *Bartramia* 18.10

18.3   1. Leaves broadly ovate to slenderly lanceolate, the base not strongly differentiated or clasping; ferruginous tomentum often conspicuous on the lower parts of the stems

      2. Leaves narrowly lanceolate to subulate from an ovate base, yellowish green, very closely appressed when dry; seta rather short; capsules erect and symmetric, mostly globose, thin walled, rugulose when dry; plants on damp or dry rocks and crevices .... 1. *Anacolia* 18.4

      2. Leaves various, imbricated to open when dry, usually green; capsules inclined to horizontal, thick walled, strongly furrowed when dry; branching often whorled; plants in wet places .... 3. *Philonotis* 18.16

1. ANACOLIA Schimp.

18.4 Plants densely to loosely tufted, yellowish green above and cohering below by dense feltlike reddish brown tomentum of rough or prickly rhizoids. Stems branched monopodially or sympodially by innovations, 3–10 cm long, 8-angled; central strand strong; epidermal cells papillose. Leaves 8-ranked, appressed and little changed when dry, straight and erect-patent to recurved-spreading when moist, the upper ones frequently slightly falcate or secund but the lower ones rarely so, mostly narrowly lanceolate from an ovate base with a strong fold on either side, deeply

---

Plate 66. 1–5. Timmia bavarica. 1. Habit sketches, moist and dry, X.4. 2. Three typical leaves, X8. 3. Upper medial leaf cells, X120. 4. Two leaf apices, smooth on the back, X120. 5. Portion of the peristome, X60, detail, X120. **Note:** Cilia not always appendiculate.

6–11. Timmia austriaca, fo. **brevifolia.** 6. Four typical leaves, X8. 7. Upper medial leaf cells, X120. 8. Cross section of leaf, X120. 9. Apex of leaf showing coarse teeth on back of costa, X120. 10. Three capsules, moist and dry, X6. 11. Portion of peristome, X60.

channelled above; margins revolute half the length of the leaf or more, 1- to 2-stratose and singly or doubly serrate in the upper $\frac{1}{3}$–$\frac{1}{2}$; costa stout, percurrent to long-excurrent, in cross section showing 1–2 rows of guides with a strong dorsal stereid band and with or without some ventral stereids; the upper lamina 1-stratose to variably 2-stratose; upper cells often variable in the same leaf, mostly oblong to linear, some often quadrate, strongly papillose to nearly smooth, thick walled, 3–8 μ wide; basal cells usually shorter and broader, sometimes linear near the costa, firm and thick walled. Dioicous. Perigonia terminal, budlike. Seta 2–15 mm long, straight or curved; capsule globose, ovoid or shortly oblong-cylindrical, 2–3 mm across, erect and symmetric, usually overtopped by the innovations, thin walled, rugulose when dry, neck lacking or very small, mouth small; peristome lacking in most species, only rarely present in *A. menziesii;* lid low convex and saucer-shaped to conic-obtuse. Spores globose to reniform, 17–23 μ with rather large blunt or warty papillae.

18.5   The name, Greek for a short base, refers to the short seta.

18.6   **Anacolia menziesii** (Turn.) Par. Stems erect to ascending, 3–5 cm high. Leaves mostly 2.5–3.5 mm long, narrowly lanceolate from an ovate base with a fold on each side, straight to slightly falcate; lamina mostly 1-stratose, 2-stratose on the upper margins and at isolated cells or in lines in the blade; upper cells rectangular to oblong, 7–10 μ wide, a few narrower, rhomboidal or flexuous, smooth to slightly papillose; basal cells shorter and slightly wider, quadrate to rectangular or transversely elongated. Seta usually lateral by innovation, 5–10 mm long; capsules globose to shortly ovoid, 2.2–2.8 mm in diameter, immersed below to slightly exceeding the current innovations, reddish brown, thin walled and fragile, rugulose when dry and often split around the small mouth; peristome usually lacking, when present variously developed, occasionally as a low thin membrane within the mouth, sometimes with a few joints but more often as short distinct lanceolate teeth varying up to 12 joints high, arising well within the mouth, pale yellowish to reddish brown, strongly jointed, smooth, very fragile and often broken; lid conic-obtuse. Spores 28–32 μ, with large low warts. Plate 67, figs. 1–7.

18.7   On rocks, in crevices, and on soil, usually in shade.

18.8   Alaska to southern California, eastward to Idaho and Montana, Wyoming, and southwestern Utah. Washington County: Zion Canyon, Lady Mountain, 5,600 ft.

18.9   Rare in Utah and probably restricted to deep canyons in the southwestern part of the state. My only specimen, small, scanty and sterile,

---

Plate 67.   1–7. Anacolia menziesii. 1. Habit sketches, X.4. 2. Dry and moist portion of shoots, X2. 3. Leaves, X8. 4. Upper and medial leaf cells. 5. Basal cells. 6. Cross section of leaf, X120. 7. Capsules, X8.

8–11. Bartramia ithyphylla. 8. Habit sketches, X.4. 9. Leaves, X8, cellular detail, X120. 10. Cross sections of leaf, X120. 11. Capsules, X8, and peristome teeth, X60.

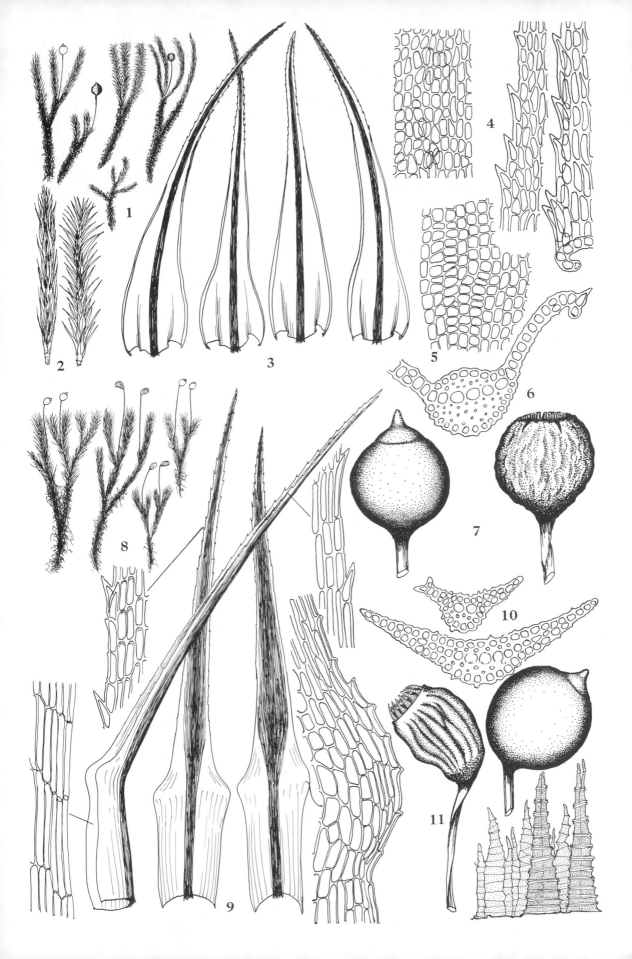

grew with *Selaginella utahensis* and *Bryum argenteum* on the edge of a sandstone ledge about halfway to the summit of Lady Mountain in Zion Canyon. Although the habitat was partially shaded by shrubs, it was very dry. The moss is locally abundant on the west side of the Cascade and Sierra Nevada mountains and ranges from sea level to about 6,000 ft. elevation. This is one of several species of plants widely distributed on the Pacific coast and extending into Utah only in Washington County.

2. BARTRAMIA Hedw.

18.10   Plants erect, in dense or loose tufts, 2–12 cm high. Stems branched but not whorled; central strand strong; epidermal cells small and thick walled; rhizoids fairly dense, sometimes forming a tomentum. Leaves linear to subulate from a moderately to strongly differentiated base; margins plane to revolute, serrate in the upper part; costa stout, often very broad, percurrent to excurrent; upper cells quadrate to linear, papillose at the upper ends; basal cells variously enlarged. Perigonia gemmiform. Seta very short to long; capsules globose to ovoid, erect to strongly inclined, often slightly asymmetric, becoming longitudinally furrowed when dry, 1–2.5 mm long, mouth usually small; peristome double, single or lacking, inner peristome often much reduced or lacking, cilia when present, poorly developed; lid small, convex, variously rounded to pointed. Spores globose to reniform, papillose. Calyptra small, cucullate.

18.11   Named in honor of John Bartram, a Pennsylvanian colonist and prominent naturalist who sent plants to European specialists.

18.12   **Bartramia ithyphylla** Brid. Plants rather small, in dense soft green or glaucous green tufts. Stems fastigiately branched, 1–4 cm high; rhizoids few to moderately dense, only occasionally forming a tomentum. Leaves dense, slightly appressed when dry, abruptly divergent and patent when moist, 3–5 mm long, lanceolate- to linear-subulate, abruptly narrowed and divergent from an erect, oblong, clasping base; costa wide in the base, spreading in the upper portion and apparently occupying the entire width of the lamina, indistinct, excurrent to a short sharp point, in cross section crescent-shaped, showing a single row of guides with dorsal and ventral stereids in 1–2 rows, the cells toward the margins 2- to 3-stratose; margins plane, finely serrate; upper cells of the narrow lamina oblong to linear, 4–6 μ wide, chlorophyllose, becoming shorter and broader at the shoulders, more distinct; basal cells clear and hyaline, linear to oblong, 7–10 μ wide, 60–100 μ long, thin walled, becoming abruptly shorter, colored or chlorophyllose at the shoulders. Synoicous. Perichaetial leaves 4.5–6 mm long, costa longer excurrent, the base more strongly clasping. Seta terminal, soon becoming lateral by innovation, 1.3–2 cm long; capsules globose to ovoid, slightly asymmetric, inclined to cernuous, 1.5–2.5 mm long, reddish brown, furrowed when dry, the mouth becoming distended; lid convex, obtuse or with a short blunt point which often turns upward; peristome double, teeth lanceolate, about 0.3 mm long, strongly barred, finely papillose above, coarser toward the base, reddish brown; segments from a basal membrane, shorter than the teeth, often irregular, yellowish; cilia short. Spores large, 27–36 μ, reniform, warty and brown. Plate 67, figs. 8–11.

18.13   On damp soil and in crevices of rocks, usually in shady places and in our region at high elevations.

18.14   Greenland, Europe, and Asia. Alaska to Labrador, New Hampshire and Pennsylvania. British Columbia to New Brunswick and following the mountains southward to California, Utah, Colorado.

18.15   Not uncommon in the Uinta Mountains mainly on wet or damp banks in and around seepage areas, and on banks above brooklets, usually in shady places. While I have collected it only in the Uinta Mountains, there is no apparent reason why it should not occur in other high mountains such as the La Sals, the Wasatch, and the Aquarius Plateau.

3. PHILONOTIS Brid.

18.16   Plants usually densely tufted, and $\pm$ interwoven with tomentum below. Stems erect to ascending, short and slender to tall and robust, branching various, monopodial, sympodial or falsely dichotomous and often with whorled subfloral innovations, in cross section showing a central strand surrounded by a broad zone of large thin-walled cells and an outer cortex of small, thick-walled reddish cells with an epidermis of large, thin-walled cells in 1 layer, the outer walls commonly collapsing; rhizoids reddish, smooth to finely punctate or papillose. Leaves variable, 0.5–3.5 mm long, 5- to many-ranked, broadly ovate to narrowly lanceolate, acute to acuminate, the lower ones sometimes obtuse, straight or falcate; costa mostly percurrent to excurrent, in cross section showing a single row of medial guides with a dorsal stereid band 2–4 cells thick and a ventral band 1 cell thick, the latter often reduced or lacking high up in the leaf and entirely lacking in leaves of some species of small size; margins denticulate to serrate; upper cells oblong to linear, papillose at the upper and lower ends; basal cells usually enlarged and thin walled. Small disarticulating brood branches occasional in axils of upper leaves. Dioicous or autoicous. Perigonia terminal, budlike, or discoid; bracts broadly ovate and sheathing at the base, abruptly narrowed above. Costa usually weak and disappearing upward. Seta long; capsules subglobose to ovoid, inclined to horizontal, longitudinally furrowed when dry; mouth small; peristome double, teeth 16, strongly barred, the upper joints with globose or ovoid thickenings on the inner face; segments from a high basal membrane, cilia 2, nearly as long as the segments, sometimes reduced to short stubs. Spores globose to reniform, papillose.

18.17   The name comes from the Greek and means loving moisture.

18.18   All our species belong to the subgenus *euphilonotis* (plants dioicous with discoid perigonia). Polymorphism is marked and intergradation endless. Normally the stems of sterile and female plants have larger broader leaves than those of male plants or whorled innovations and are to be considered typical. For diagnosis, leaves should ordinarily be taken between the middle and the upper fourth of the stems. The comal leaves are nearly always larger and longer pointed, and the basal leaves are often very much shorter and blunter pointed with the costa often ending below the apex.

18.19   Variation in the size, shape, and other traits of leaves is evident in nearly all plants, but in those of extreme aquatic, alpine, and arctic habitats this condition is often accentuated to such an extent as to give the plant an entirely different appearance from the typical form. On long stems showing three or more seasons' growth it is possible to find leaves typical of two or more "species" or "varieties." Typically the plants grow on wet soil or rocks, the upper parts being aerial, firm and rather strict, the leaves firm and the cells generally narrow well toward the base. When most of the lower portion of the stem is submerged, the submerged leaves are usually lax, closely appressed to the stem and the cells wide and thin walled. Stems growing in very cold water and surrounded by snow generally have the lower leaves broad, blunt to broadly rounded obtuse and often incurved or cucullate at the apex, while the cells are thin walled and lax. These lower leaves develop first when the conditions are cold and wet and possible under restricted light, while the apical leaves develop under more favorable conditions and have a more typical form. Plants submerged in water or growing in dense shade usually become long and slender, the stems weak, little or not at all branched, and bearing widely spaced lax leaves which are frequently crisped when dry. Many plants have falcate upper leaves and represent minor forms. Basically the leaves are spirally arranged; in most plants this is not particularly evident, but in some they may appear in very distinct vertical or spiral rows. Again, these are minor forms.

18.20   The papillae range from strong to weak or even lacking. In some plants the papillae on the leaf cells may be low and weak. Positive demonstrations can be made by folding the leaves longitudinally so as to show any papillae in profile. This is difficult as the leaves are too small to handle and one is obliged to hunt among leaves on the stems and those that have been removed to find leaves that have accidentally folded themselves lengthwise and show the profile of papillae. Another procedure is to boil the removed leaves in a drop or two of lactophenol which clears them and brings out the papillae better in surface view. (Lactophenol consists of equal parts of lactic acid, phenol, glycerin and distilled water.)

18.21   The term doubly serrate has two connotations: (1) when the adjacent ends of the marginal cells arch outward and form a pair of projecting points as shown in plate 72, fig. 2, and (2) when the recurved margin of the leaf has projecting points from only the upper ends of the marginal and submarginal rows of cells so that the cells lying side by side form a pair of teeth as shown in plate 72, fig. 3. The habit of recurved margins appears to induce the formation of teeth or papillae at the upper ends of the cells on the convex surface although the cells of the main portion of the lamina may be papillose at the lower ends. Sometimes this influence seems accentuated in cells of the narrowly acuminate portion of leaves where the papillae may be strongest at the upper ends. Some confusion may attend the identification of plants of this sort with part or all of the lower lamina appearing smooth because the papillae are so poorly developed. Whether the cells of the main part of the lamina are actually papillose at the upper or lower ends must be determined by profile views or by mounting leaves in lactophenol and carefully adjusting the light entering the microscope.

18.22   I find that in glycerin jelly slides twenty to thirty years old, the leaves have become so clear that papillae are shown distinctly where formerly they had not been evident.

18.23   Among some old slides of plants labelled *Philonotis marchica* and *P. muehlenbergii* by various bryologists, I find that the lower leaf cells are papillose at the lower ends and the plants are referable to *P. fontana* var. *caespitosa*. Experience has shown me that this error was not due to lack of thoroughness but to the fact that in all species of *Philonotis* the cells in the upper 1/6–1/4 of the leaf are papillose at the upper ends, and sometimes in 1–3 longitudinal rows of submarginal cells extending downward for as much as 2/3 the leaf length. According to most descriptions and keys to species, this would lead anyone to place a specimen, which apparently has the lower 2/3 of the leaf smooth, among the species with leaves typically papillose at the upper ends of the cells. Among plants of this sort I have found that those with triangular- to oblong-lanceolate leaves, broadest at the insertion, ultimately have shown some of the lower cells to be papillose at the upper ends and referable to *P. marchica*.

18.24   1. Leaf cells papillose at the upper ends only on the ventral surface; leaves typically narrowly triangular-lanceolate but often ovate-lanceolate, acute to slightly acuminate; costa percurrent to very shortly excurrent; plants small .... 1. *P. marchica*   18.26

18.25   1. Leaf cells papillose at the lower ends on both surfaces, occasionally at the upper ends or at both ends in the leaf apex; plants small to robust .... 2. *P. fontana*   18.30

18.26   **1. Philonotis marchica** (Hedw.) Brid. Plants rather small to medium sized, loosely to densely tufted, pale green, bright green or sometimes yellowish green, sometimes tomentose below, sometimes the rhizoids few. Stems 1–3(8) cm tall. Leaves erect-patent to patent when moist, ± imbricated when dry, typically triangular-lanceolate, only slightly narrowed at the base, but varying to ovate-lanceolate with the base fairly well narrowed, evenly tapered to a narrowly acute apex, sometimes slightly acuminate, usually appearing in no particular order but occasionally in distinct spiral rows, 1.5–2 mm long, slightly concave at the base, not plicate; costa slender, percurrent to shortly excurrent, ± toothed on the back in the upper part; margins plane to narrowly revolute, singly serrate, sometimes weakly so; upper leaf cells typically oblong-linear, parallel, toward the base larger and broader, sometimes thin-

ner walled, papillose at the upper ends on the ventral side only, sometimes scabrous, sometimes nearly smooth. Deciduous brood branches frequent. Dioicous. Perigonia large, terminal often subtended by whorled
branches. Seta 2–4 cm long; capsule ovoid to subglobose, 2–2.5 mm
long; teeth reddish, strongly barred, finely papillose below, coarser
above; inner peristome yellowish, shorter than the teeth, coarsely papillose, often in lines; cilia variable, 2–3, short and blunt to long and
slender, often equaling the segments, ± cohering in the lower part.
Spores reniform, 23–26 μ, reddish brown, bluntly papillose. Plate 68,
figs. 1–13.

18.27   On wet soil and rocks.

18.28   Europe. Quebec across southern Canada to British Columbia, southward to Georgia, Texas, Arizona, Utah.

18.29   This moss probably occurs throughout North America but has not yet
been reported from some areas. It is sporadic and perhaps often overlooked. Most specimens are sterile. Typical plants are recognized by
small size, triangular-lanceolate leaves broadest at the insertion with percurrent to very shortly excurrent costae and cells oblong to linear with
papillae at the upper ends on the ventral side only. Typical leaves are
also strongly papillose to the base. However, the plant varies considerably in that the leaves may be ovate-acute to ovate-lanceolate, being
broadest shortly above the base and narrowed at the insertion. In many
broad-leaved forms the upper cells are also much broader than in typical forms, being more or less shortly oblong to oblong-hexagonal with
thinner walls and usually with very weak papillae. Some leaves are
smooth. Concerning the papillae, I might emphasize that in some plants
they are so low and weak in the lower ¾ of the leaf that they may
escape detection, even after long and careful study.

18.30   **2. Philonotis fontana** (Hedw.) Brid. var. **fontana.** Plants exceedingly variable, typically in dense tufts with erect parallel stems but commonly
looser, 3–10 cm tall, bright green, often yellowish, pale or glaucous,
sometimes tinged with red. Leaves of sterile and female branches rather
crowded, patent to erect-patent, straight to ± falcate-secund at ends of
stems, typically ovate-lanceolate with a broad base and a slender acuminate apex, 1.5–2 mm long, 0.7–1.3 mm wide at the base; costa stout at
the base, tapering to the apex, percurrent to shortly excurrent, red and
prominent at the back; lamina concave with 1–2 plicae on either side

---

Plate 68.   **1–13. Philonotis marchica.** 1. Habit sketches, X.4. 2. Leaves of typical
form. 3. Leaves of small form. 4–5. Leaves of other forms, X8. 6. Upper medial
cells from three different plants showing variations in dimensions. 7. Basal cells.
8. Marginal cells of two forms, X120. 9. A typical inner perigonial leaf, X8. 10.
A deciduous brood branch occasionally occurring among the upper leaves, X30.
11. Capsules, X8. 12–13. Portions of peristomes of two different plants showing
variations in cilia, X60.

14–21. Philonotis fontana. 14. Habit sketches of typical forms, X.4. 15. Leaves
of typical form. 16–18. Leaves of three different larger forms. 19–20. Leaves of
two smaller forms, X8. 21. Inner perigonial leaves from different plants, X8.

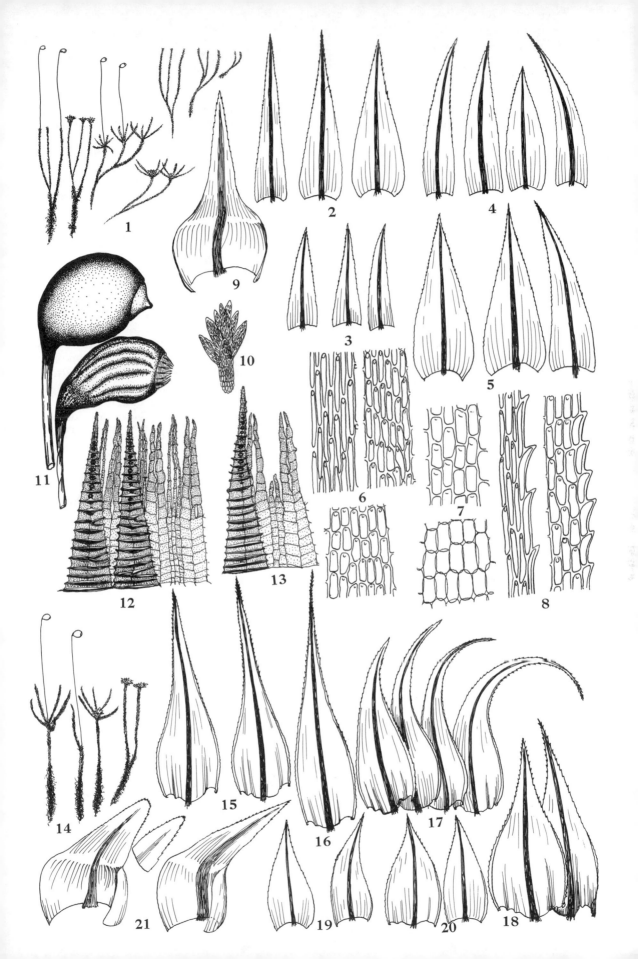

of the costa at the base; margins usually revolute halfway or more, typically doubly serrate, but often singly serrate, often merely dentate toward the base; in small forms the margins often plane on 1 or both sides and usually singly serrate; upper cells typically oblong-linear to linear, firm and thick walled, papillose at the lower ends on both sides, except in the upper 1/6–1/4 where they are usually papillose at the upper ends, sometimes at both ends or in the middle; basal cells larger and broader, oblong, firm to thin walled, the extreme basal row often lax and inflated. Stems of male plants usually red and prominent, the leaves more distant and closely appressed, extremely variable, often differing from those of the female and sterile stems in being either narrower or larger and broader, the apex usually less tapering; the upper cells tending to be shorter, laxer, and the papillae weaker. Dioicous. Perigonia large, discoid, terminal, becoming subtended by 1–7 whorled branches. Seta 2–4 cm long, reddish brown; capsules 2–3 mm long, ovoid to subglobose, inclined to horizontal, the mouth small and oblique, when dry oblong, slightly curved and deeply furrowed; lid conic; teeth reddish brown, strongly barred, 0.4–0.5 mm long, lanceolate, finely papillose below, coarsely papillose above; segments of inner peristome yellowish, keeled and perforated, nearly as long as the teeth, coarsely papillose above, basal membrane about ¼–⅓ the total length; cilia well developed, filiform and jointed. Spores ovoid to reniform, 24–28 μ, reddish brown to dark brown, bluntly papillose. Plate 68, figs. 14–21, and Plate 69, figs. 1–13.

18.31   On wet or damp soil, rocks and humus, sometimes in water, mostly in the mountains in Utah, but ranging from sea level to 14,000 ft.

18.32   Europe, Asia, and northern Africa. Throughout Canada and the United States, extending into Mexico.

18.33   Perhaps no other moss has so many variations in habit, size, form of the leaves, and character of the leaf cells. Variations in the habit of growth and numerous characters of the leaves of sterile, male, and female plants of the same specimen exhibit combinations of characters difficult to include in a description without numerous phrases of exceptions. Frequently each differs to such a degree that by itself it could pass for a separate variety or even a different species. Tall specimens several years old may show differences in leaves of each year's growth sufficient to make good species or varieties were they not on the same stem.

18.34   Male plants are nearly always more slender with more closely appressed leaves than female and sterile plants. Furthermore, the leaves are smaller, narrower, and less tapering or broader, more abruptly tapered, and often quite lax. The leaves of whorled innovations are smaller, narrower, and more slenderly pointed.

18.35   The comal and perichaetial leaves are nearly always the largest and have more gradually tapering apices and a longer excurrent costa; these traits become progressively less pronounced in leaves toward the base of the season's growth.

18.36   The leaves may be falcate in varying degrees, but this has little or no consequence since it may involve only the comal leaves, a few of the upper leaves or all of the leaves of the base of the stem.

18.37   Plants developing in very wet cold conditions frequently have leaves widely spaced, concave, and closely appressed to the stems, sometimes lax with the upper cells broad and thin walled and the area of enlarged thin-walled basal cells extending high up in the blade, the costa usually broad but flat, the apex broad, in the comal and upper leaves shortly acuminate while those below become progressively shorter and broader with the apices obtuse to broadly rounded and the costa ending below the tip. These forms have been called the var. *adpressa*. The extreme form shows nearly all the leaves, except the comal and a few of the upper-most ones, standing loosely appressed and parallel with the stem, broadly ovate to oblong-ovate, deeply concave, like the bowl of a spoon, rounded obtuse and sometimes cucullate at the tips, the margins plane and the broad flat costa ending below the apex. These have been called the var. *borealis*. It is not uncommon for plants of this sort to develop typi-cal leaves on the upper part of the stem later in the season when en-vironmental conditions are less rigorous. Such extreme variations due to abnormal conditions are not worthy of varietal names.

18.38   Submerged forms and those growing under greatly reduced light com-monly develop long, slender, simple or sparingly branched stems with widely spaced lax leaves (some of them the so-called var. *laxa*); such forms are not known to fruit. The leaves vary widely in size and form in different specimens. Lax leaves nearly always have broader, oblong, thin-walled upper cells and often have the much enlarged basal cells extending high up in the blade while the papillae are usually low and difficult to demonstrate.

18.39   The three varieties characterized here will have to be treated broadly, liberally allowing for variations. Typical forms will constitute a small minority of the specimens one collects at random. Most plants are inter-mediate in various combinations of characters and constitute a swarm of intergrading forms. Some bryologists have placed considerable faith in the blunt or obtuse tips of inner perigonial bracts of *P. fontana* as opposed to the pointed bracts of other species, but I find variation in this character in *P. fontana* and also occasional blunt bracts in the other species of the genus.

18.40   Numerous sterile varieties of *P. fontana*, such as var. *adpressa, laxa, gracilescens, heterophylla*, etc. should be relegated to synonomy and only the fertile varieties be given nomenclatural status. It is time to give up the pretense that certain segments of this array of plants represent discrete genetic groups. We are dealing instead with a highly involved situation where the interaction of heredity and environment produces a maze of populations stemming from essentially the same racial stock. To judge from field observations, less than twenty percent of the popu-lations of the major categories have a potential for sexual reproduction (that is, bear antheridia or archegonia). Among these, less than ten percent produce sporophytes. Even among active sexual plants there is so much variation that it is often difficult to assign them to species or variety with certainty. The great propensity of asexual reproduction among both fertile and sterile plants produces vast clones each of which assumes a particular form according to the environment in which it is obliged to grow. We find the greatest number of plants in the populations showing no evidence of having borne antheridia or archegonia, and it is among them that variations mount tenfold.

18.41   2a. Var. **americana** (Dism.) ex Crum. The stoutest of the *fontana* group, usually in deep tufts but often short; when dry, the leaves often having a characteristic appearance because of divergence from the stem at a very wide angle, with the tips curving upward and inward and often spirally twisted, sometimes in vertical rows, but not always showing these dry traits, since the leaves may be loosely to rather closely imbricated but always broadly ovate, short acuminate, straight or falcate, the costa percurrent to shortly excurrent (rarely long excurrent), the margin revolute well toward the apex, variously serrate, the lamina usually strongly plicate at base. Perigonial leaves vary, triangular to oblong-lanceolate, mostly acute, the inner often obtuse. Plate 69, figs. 14–16.

18.42   Alaska to Nova Scotia, across Canada and the adjacent northern United States, extending southward in the mountains to Vermont, New Mexico, Utah, Nevada and California.

18.43   2b. Var. **pumila** (Turn.) Brid. Plants slender, densely tufted and usually interwoven with dense tomentum in the lower $\frac{1}{2}$–$\frac{2}{3}$, short to tall. Leaves small, slender, typically lanceolate, long acuminate, mostly 1.5 mm long or less; costa short to long excurrent; margins revolute nearly to the apex, singly or doubly serrate; lamina not plicate at the base.

18.44   Range the same as the species but tending to occur at higher elevations. Plate 69, figs. 17–18.

Plate 69.   1–13. Philonotis fontana (continued). 1. Two areas of upper medial leaf cells from different plants. 2. Upper marginal cells showing double serration by projections from both ends of the cells. 3. Two recurved margins, left showing double serration by projections of both ends of the marginal cells, and right showing double serration by projections of the upper ends of the marginal and submarginal cells. 4. Basal cells, firm leaf, lax and inflated right. 5. Inflated basal cells in profile showing the broadly bulging papillae, often not visible in surface view, X120. 6. Capsules, X8. 7. Portion of the peristome, X60, detail, X200. 8. Spores, X120. 9. Portion of shoot showing typical stance of leaves. 10. Same of falcate form. 11. Same of adpressa form, X2. 12–13. Upper and basal leaves of adpressa form, X8.

14–16. Var. **americana.** 14. Habit sketches, X.4. 15. Dry and moist shoot showing stance of leaves, X2. 16. A typical leaf, X8, with upper marginal cells, X120.

17–18. Var. **pumila.** 17. Habit sketches, X.4. 18. Leaves, X8.

19–22. Var. **caespitosa.** 19. Leaves of typical form. 20. Leaves of falcate form. 21. Small-leaved form, X8. 22. Upper marginal cells, X120. **Note:** In many lax or small forms of these plants, the papillae are so weak that the leaves appear to be smooth, except in the apical cells that are nearly always papillose at the upper ends, a feature which may lead one to refer such specimens to **Ph. marchica.**

334

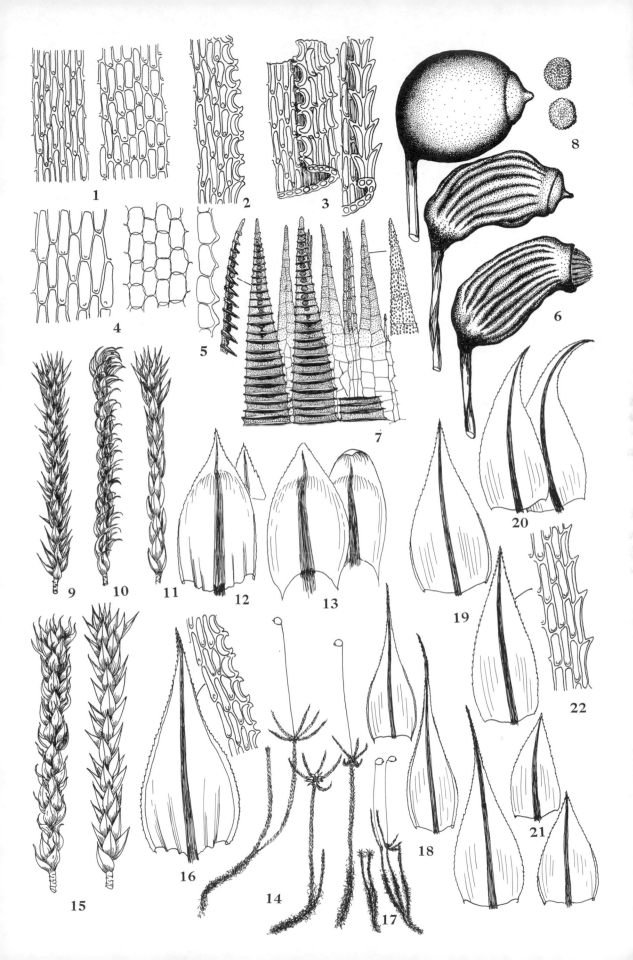

18.45   Scarcely more than a small slender form of *P. fontana,* and showing the same kinds of variations such as falcate broader leaves, often lax with wide thin-walled cells in the upper part, often plicate at the base, the costa wide and flat below, shortly excurrent, percurrent, or ending below the apex; the lower leaves often obtuse or rounded, the margins flat and singly dentate.

18.46   2c. Var. **caespitosa** (Jur.) Limpr. Usually densely tufted, short to rather tall. Leaves appressed and imbricated to rather open, moderately spaced to very dense, ovate-acuminate to ovate-lanceolate, usually shortly acuminate, mostly 1.5–2 mm long, straight or falcate; margins flat throughout or revolute in the lower third, typically singly serrate but often with some double teeth; lamina typically flattish, not plicate; costa percurrent to shortly excurrent, sometimes ending below the apex in the blunter lower leaves. Plate 69, figs. 19–22.

18.47   Range about the same as the species.

18.48   Typical forms are few, and numerous plants intergrade with the species proper. The lax and appressed-leaved forms are so much like those attributed to other species and varieties that only the most typical of these can be assigned to a definite variety. Many small plants with short plattish leaves and plane margins will key to the var. *caespitosa,* but many small specimens of the species proper may show leaves without plication at the base or with the margins fairly plane above and singly serrate. I have adopted the practice of referring all of these indefinite forms to the species proper, with no designation of variety or form.

BRYACEAE

19.1   Plants small to large, loosely to densely tufted, sometimes scattered, sometimes forming wide sods. Stems erect, simple or branched, short to tall, sometimes with long, prostrate, stoloniferous shoots, in cross section 5-angled, showing a central strand with a cortex of large colored cells; rhizoids reddish. Leaves of various shapes, the lower ones smaller and often distant, variously acute to acuminate, blunt to broadly rounded at apex; costa strong, ending below the apex to long excurrent; upper leaf cells various, smooth. Inflorescence various; in dioicous plants the terminal perigonium usually budlike or discoid. Seta long; capsules mostly inclined, horizontal or pendent, short to long pyriform, clavate, oblong, or cylindrical, neck mostly shorter than the urn but sometimes longer, sometimes not externally differentiated; stomata in the neck; peristome mostly double (the outer teeth lacking in *Mielichhoferia*); cilia well developed to rudimentary or lacking. Spores small, globose or nearly so. Calyptra cucullate.

19.2   1. Plants small to medium sized; upper leaf cells oblong-hexagonal to linear

    2. Upper leaf cells mostly linear; leaves not bordered

       3. Leaves linear-subulate or setaceous from a broader, ± oblong

or ovate base; costa wide, occupying almost the entire upper part of the blade; capsules horizontal, elongate-pyriform with a long slender neck .... 2. *Leptobryum* 19.10

3. Leaves mostly ovate to ovate-lanceolate, the comal ones sometimes linear; costa slender; capsules obovate to elongate pyriform

4. Peristome single, consisting of the endostome of 16 linear segments united at the base as a low membrane .... 1. *Mielichhoferia* 19.6

4. Peristome double, outer teeth present, endostome consisting of a conspicuous basal membrane with keeled segments and usually cilia, the latter sometimes rudimentary or lacking .... 3. *Pohlia* 19.16

2. Upper leaf cells mostly oblong-hexagonal to rhomboidal; leaves ± bordered with longer, narrower, thicker-walled cells .... 4. *Bryum* 19.63

19.3   1. Plants mostly large, some species with long procumbent sterile shoots with ± complanate leaves; upper leaf cells isodiametric or nearly so; capsules often without an externally differentiated neck, mostly oblong .... 5. *Mnium* 19.145

1. MIELICHHOFERIA Nees & Hornsch.

19.4   Plants in compact tufts; stems erect, branched, closely coherent with densely interwoven rhizoids. Leaves ovate to lanceolate, acute to short acuminate; margins entire to slightly denticulate, plane or slightly recurved; costa rather strong, percurrent or slightly excurrent; upper cells oblong- to linear-rhomboidal; basal cells wider, oblong. Dioicous. Perichaetia at apex of a short shoot much exceeded by a subfloral innovation, slender. Seta long, erect; capsules erect to horizontal, pyriform, thin walled, yellowish brown; lid low convex; annulus present; outer peristome teeth lacking; a rudimentary endostome of 16 linear segments, suddenly dilated below and united into a very low basal membrane. Spores globose, yellowish to yellowish brown.

19.5   The name honors Mathias Mielichhofer, who investigated the alpine mosses of Salzburg.

19.6   **Mielichhoferia macrocarpa** (Hook.) Bruch & Schimp. Plants in compact tufts or cushions, green above, often becoming yellowish green or brownish green with age, the lower parts yellowish brown to reddish brown, intricately interwoven with dense, reddish, papillose rhizoids extending high up the stems. Stems erect, branched because of subfloral innovations, 1–3 cm tall, tender and fragile. Leaves ovate, oblong-ovate to ovate-lanceolate, concave, acute or shortly acuminate, 1–1.5 mm long, lax to rather firm; margins entire, plane to narrowly recurved; costa rather strong, percurrent to very shortly excurrent, yellowish to reddish brown below; upper cells oblong- to linear-rhomboidal, 50–115 μ long; marginal cells narrower, linear, all thin walled; shorter and wider toward the base. Dioicous. Seta erect, yellowish to yellowish brown, about 5 mm long, appearing shorter due to the overtopping of the perichaetia by subfloral branches; capsules pyriform, inclined to horizontal, about 1.5 mm long, yellowish to yellowish brown, sometimes becoming light reddish brown with age, mouth usually bright reddish; neck thick, shorter than the spore sac; lid low convex, the apex widely rounded to slightly mammillose; annulus 1 row of thick-walled cells, reddish on the margins, ± revoluble; exothecial cells irregularly 4- to 6-sided, isodiametric to oblong, rather thick walled; stomata numerous, extending from the neck well up the base of the urn; peristome teeth lacking; endostome segments 16, linear to nearly filiform, pale yellowish to nearly hyaline, 165–270 μ long, with a midline, smooth, ± nodulose at the joints, the bases suddenly joined in a very low basal membrane attached within the mouth; cilia lacking. Spores 13–17 μ, very finely papillose. Plate 70, figs. 9–17.

19.7   Growing on or in the crevices of damp or wet rocks and cliffs.

19.8   Infrequent at widely separated stations across Arctic America from the Aleutian Islands to western Greenland, southward in the Rocky Mountains to Colorado and Utah. Utah County: Mt. Timpanogos, above Aspen Grove, 7,000–8,000 ft.

19.9   The tufts of this moss are generally so compact as to have a soft spongy texture. Sterile plants would likely be mistaken for a small, poorly developed *Bryum* or possibly a *Pohlia*. The leaves often become wholly or partially hyaline and transparent, soft and lax. The specimens cited above grew in crevices of dry limestone cliffs which had been dripping wet earlier in the season. The green color of the upper exposed leaves had largely faded, and the tufts were a dirty yellowish. All are well fruited with male and female plants present. The seasonal innovations are short as shown in the illustration.

2. LEPTOBRYUM (B.S.G.) Wils.

19.10   Plants loosely to densely tufted. Stems erect, simple and slender; in cross section ± triangular, showing a large central strand of small thin-walled cells, a cortex of large, ± angular, thick-walled cells 2–5 cells thick, and 1–2 layers of small thick-walled epidermal cells. Leaves setaceous or long linear; costa broad, occupying almost the entire width of the upper part, excurrent; upper cells of the lamina linear. Synoicous.

Plate 70. 1–8. Leptobryum pyriforme. 1. Habit sketches, X.4. 2. Cross section of the stem, X60. 3. Five stem leaves, X8. 4. Three perichaetial leaves, X8. 5. Upper leaf cells, X120. 6. Cross sections of leaf at four levels, X120. 7. Three capsules dry and moist, X8. 8. Portion of peristome, X60.

9–17. Mielichhoferia macrocarpa. 9. Habit sketches of male and female plants, X.4. 10. Male plant, X2. 11. Two perigonial leaves, X8. 12. Female plant, X2. 13. Five leaves, X8. 14. Leaf apex, X120. 15. Upper medial leaf cells, X120. 16. Capsules moist and dry, X8, with segments of the endostome. 17. Unusually slender segments, X60.

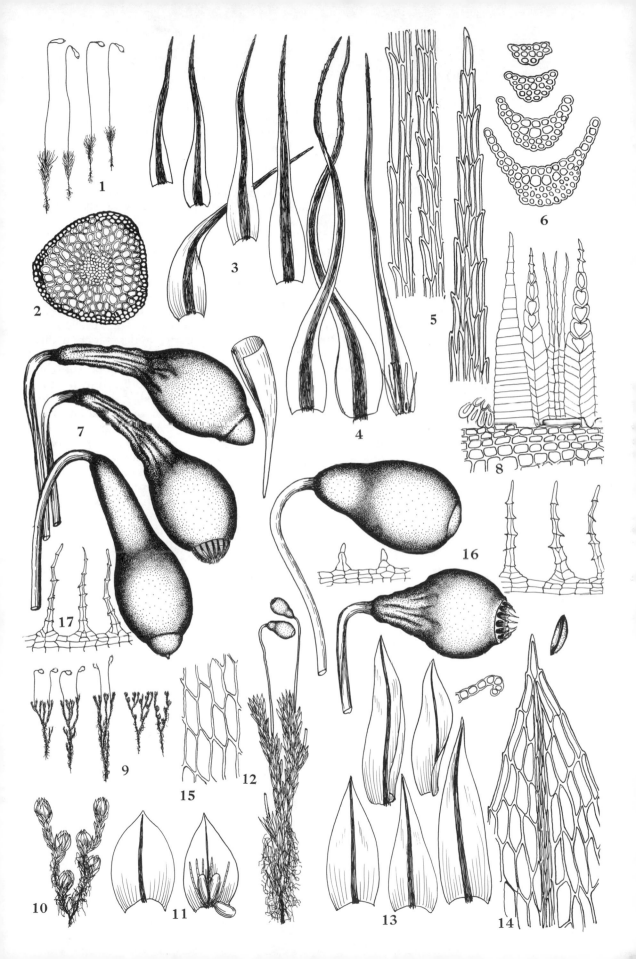

19.11 BRYACEAE

Perichaetial leaves much longer than the stem leaves, often hairlike. Seta erect, long; capsule elongate pyriform, horizontal to pendulous; neck as long as the spore sac, much shrunken when dry; peristome well developed, double, cilia apendiculate.

19.11   The name, from Greek, means slender moss.

19.12   **Leptobryum pyriforme** (Hedw.) Wils. Plants in loose or dense, green or yellowish green tufts of delicate texture. Stems slender, mostly less than 1 cm tall but occasionally as much as 3 cm, green above, reddish at the base; rhizoids few, reddish, the older ones papillose. Leaves setaceous to narrowly linear from a ± dilated, ovate to oblong base, the lower ones short and distant, 1.5–2 mm long, erect-patent to spreading, upper and perichaetial ones 2.5–4 mm long, ± flexuous-spreading, not much changed when dry; margins plane, denticulate above; costa broad in the base, occupying nearly the entire width of the blade above, long excurrent; lamina narrow and merging imperceptibly with the costa; upper cells linear, 50–100 μ long, becoming shorter and broader in the base. Purplish black, ovoid gemmae occasionally formed in the axils of the leaves and on rhizoids. Synoicous. Seta erect and slender, straight or flexuous, 1–3 cm long, yellowish brown becoming reddish brown with age; capsules slenderly pyriform, small, 1.5–2 mm long, horizontal to pendulous, thin walled, yellowish brown to reddish brown, shiny, the spore sac oval, often slightly gibbous above, not much changed when dry; neck equaling the spore sac or slightly shorter, strongly shrunken when dry accentuating the plump spore sac; mouth rather large, straight or slightly oblique; lid rather high convex, obtuse to mammillate; annulus present; exothecial cells irregularly oblong, mostly 5- to 6-sided, shorter in the neck, rather thin walled; stomata numerous in the neck region; peristome double; teeth yellowish to yellowish brown, lanceolate from a broader fundus, acuminate above, joints 20–26, lamellae strong, densely papillose; endostome paler, forming a high basal membrane, segments strongly perforated down the middle, connected at the joints; cilia 3, strongly appendiculate. Spores globose, yellowish to yellowish brown, 12–17 μ, finely papillose. Calyptra thin and yellowish, rather large, cucullate, long beaked, falling early. Plate 70, figs. 1–8.

19.13   Growing on wet or damp soil, humus, rotten logs, and rocks from the lowlands to the highest mountains, and as a weed in greenhouses.

19.14   Widely distributed throughout the world.

19.15   The narrow leaves, at times almost hairlike, give this pretty little moss a delicate texture, almost like soft silk. It is abundant in canyons and mountains throughout Utah and fruits freely. It also grows in flower pots and on damp walls of greenhouses where it is nearly always sterile but frequently forms rather large, purplish black, ovoid gemmae in the axils of the leaves and on rhizoids. I have seen it form extensive tufts or wide cushions as much as 40 cm across and 3 cm deep on the shaded banks of brooklets, and I have found it covering wet decaying branches of trees over 1 m long.

340

3. POHLIA Hedw.

19.16 Plants densely to loosely tufted, at times scattered among other mosses. Stems erect, mostly simple, occasionally with slender innovations, in cross section showing a small central strand; rhizoids usually few, reddish, and papillose. Upper and perichaetial leaves the largest, lanceolate to linear-lanceolate, the lower ones shorter and broader, mostly ovate to ovate-lanceolate, without a distinct border of narrower cells, margins ± denticulate in the upper part, plane or revolute; costa rather weak, and mostly ending below the apex, in cross section showing a single row of subventral guide cells with a row of ventral superficial cells and a dorsal band of stereids; upper cells elongate-rhomboidal or oblong hexagonal, fusiform or linear, becoming slightly broader and shorter toward the base. Propagula formed in the axils of the upper leaves in some species. Seta long, mostly ± curved or flexuous; capsules inclined, horizontal, or pendulous, pyriform to clavate; exothecial cells ± isodiametric to shortly oblong, the walls regular or sinuous; stomata in the neck, superficial or immersed; lid conic to mammillate; annulus usually present; peristome double, the segments of the endostome arising from a high basal membrane, cilia present or sometimes rudimentary or lacking, usually not appendiculate. Spores globose or nearly so, mostly finely papillose.

19.17 Named in honor of Johannes E. Pohl, a physician of Dresden.

19.18 A genus closely resembling *Bryum* from which it differs mainly in the longer cells of the leaves. The present treatment includes the genus *Mniobryum* of Limpricht which is based mainly on capsules broader than long or nearly so when dry and on ± immersed stomata. Several species of *Pohlia* proper have rather short capsules but with superficial stomata so that the distinction is not very strong.

19.19 Some species develop a characteristic glossy or tinsel-like lustrous quality of the leaves which may be general throughout the plant or more or less restricted to the upper and comal leaves. This trait shows best in the dry state. In some species the entire surface of the leaves glistens when light is reflected from it. In other species the leaves show only a slight degree of luster, especially where the light is reflected from the outermost convex surfaces of folds and undulations, but it is not particularly conspicuous.

19.20 Sterile specimens of some species of *Pohlia* (the Mniobryum group) have a remarkable resemblance to certain sterile forms of *Philonotis fontana*. The similarity is sometimes emphasized by the fact that some leaves of *Pohlia* may have the costa slightly toothed at back above, either bluntly or sharply so. Occasionally male plants of *Pohlia* have large bulbiform perigonia with squarrose-spreading bracts, and much resemble the male plant of some species of *Philonotis*.

19.21 1. Plants light green to pale whitish green; upper stem leaves 2–3 mm long
     2. Leaves glossy and firm, not much changed when dry; leaf cells

7–10 μ wide, 90–140 μ long, rather thick walled; capsules inclined to horizontal, elongate-pyriform, urn longer than wide when dry, neck $\frac{1}{3}$–$\frac{1}{2}$, not well set off; dioicous or sometimes paroicous .... 1. *P. cruda* 19.23

2. Leaves not glossy, lax, shrivelled when dry; leaf cells 15–22 μ wide, up to 100 μ long, thin walled; capsules pyriform, the urn nearly as long as wide when dry; dioicous .... 9. *P. wahlenbergii* 19.54

19.22   1.   Plants green to yellowish green; leaves of various sizes

3. Sterile shoots not bearing 3 to several propagula in axils of upper leaves (*P. drummondii* occasionally bearing single large budlike propagula).

4. Plants yellowish green; upper stem leaves 2–3 mm long, lustrous; upper cells 7–10 μ wide, 90–140 μ long; capsules clavate, inclined to horizontal, neck slender, $\frac{1}{3}$–$\frac{1}{2}$, paroicous .... 2. *P. longicolla* 19.27

4. Plants green to yellowish green, without noticeable lustre; leaf cells shorter than 90 μ

5. Plants large for the genus, upper stem leaves 3–4 mm long; cells 7–10 μ wide, 40–70 μ long; capsules 3–4 mm long, usually pendulous, the neck short, $\frac{1}{4}$–$\frac{1}{3}$, not strongly set off; paroicous .... 3. *P. nutans* 19.31

5. Plants small; upper stem leaves 1.5–2.5 mm long

6. Plants paroicous; capsules 2.5–3.5 mm long, elongate-pyriform, the neck not well set off; walls of exothecial cells regular; basal membrane of endostome rather low; cilia lacking; teeth narrowly lanceolate, papillose, and finely vertically striate above; leaf margins widely recurved; medial cells 5–7 μ wide .... 4. *P. elongata* 19.35

6. Plants dioicous; capsules 1–2.5 mm long, pyriform, the neck short and distinct; walls of exothecial cells sinuous; basal membrane of the endostome high, cilia 2–3, well developed (or sometimes rudimentary or lacking); teeth papillose but not striate; leaf margins plane or slightly recurved; medial cells 10–14 μ wide .... 5. *P. drummondii* 19.39

3. Sterile shoots, at least a few of them bearing 1 to several bulbils in the axils of the upper leaves; leaves lanceolate to oblong-lanceolate, 1–1.5 mm long; plants small

7. Propagula large, single in the leaf axils, subglobose or ovoid, red, with several erect, acute green leaf points, 1–3 per stem .... 6. *P. rothii* 19.43

7. Propagula smaller, various shapes, yellowish throughout, 2–5 in each leaf axil; numerous

8. Propagula subglobose to obovoid, borne on a **distinct stalk**, with 3–4 multicellular leaf points standing erect or arching over the apex .... 7. *P. bulbifera*   **19.48**

8. Propagula obovoid to linear, straight or spirally twisted, with an abscision layer, basal stalk lacking, pale green or yellowish, delicate

   9. Propagula with 1 or occasionally 2 leaf points, the tips often bent or hooked .... 8. *P. proligera*   **19.52**

   9. Propagula with 3–5 erect leaf points ....
   .... 10. *P. annotina*   **19.58**

19.23   **1. Pohlia cruda** (Hedw.) Lindb. Plants in loose or dense tufts, ± light to pale green, often with a whitish cast, nearly always with a high glistening lustre, reddish brown below. Stems red, erect, simple or occasionally branched, 1–2 cm tall. Upper leaves 2–3 mm long, typically ovate-lanceolate, acute to briefly acuminate, erect-patent, the comal and perichaetial ones becoming much longer and narrower, lanceolate to linear, up to 5 mm long, more spreading, all rather flattish, margins plane, denticulate in the upper part, when dry not greatly changed or somewhat imbricated and slightly twisted; costa green to yellowish, becoming reddish brown with age, mostly ending below the apex; cells mostly linear, 7–9 μ wide, 90–140 μ long, usually shorter in the lower leaves and in the leaves of sterile plants; basal cells slightly broader and shorter. Dioicous or occasionally paroicous. Seta erect, straight to somewhat flexuous, 1.5–2.5(3.5) cm long, yellowish brown, becoming reddish brown at the base, shiny; capsules inclined to horizontal, thick clavate to nearly cylindrical, 3–4(5) mm long without the lid, the neck region not or only slightly differentiated externally, slightly shorter than the urn, yellowish to yellow-brown, becoming red-brown with age; lid shortly conical to mammillate; annulus present; exothecial cells ± oblong, 4- to 6-sided, thin walled; stomata superficial; peristome teeth yellow, rather broadly oblong at base, acuminate, usually with a pale border, joints 25–32, close together, ventral lamellae strong, finely papillose below, somewhat coarse above; segments thin and pale, strongly keeled and cleft down the middle, from a rather low basal membrane, about ¼; cilia 2–3, ± nodulose. Spores 17–22 μ, finely papillose. Plate 71, figs. 1–7.

19.24   On damp or wet soil, crevices, or rocks, usually in shady places in the mountains of our region.

19.25   Common throughout Europe and Asia. Australia, New Zealand and Antarctica. Widely distributed across Canada to Alaska, extending southward to the mountains of California, Arizona and New Mexico, across eastern Colorado and eastward to Pennsylvania and New Jersey; sporadically southward in Mexico, Central and South America.

19.26   In its typical state this moss is pale or whitish green and set off by a strong glossy lustre, at least in upper and comal leaves. On some occasions it may be somewhat dull but usually some stems can be found which show the tinsel-like gloss characteristic of the species. It is much like *P. longicolla*, differing mainly in the paler color and thicker capsules in which the neck is often poorly set off from the urn. In the latter, the color is more yellowish green and the capsules much more slender with a narrower neck well set off from the urn.

19.27 **2. Pohlia longicolla** (Hedw.) Lindb. Plants similar to *P. cruda*. Plants green to yellowish green, glossy, at least in the upper and comal leaves. Paroicous. Capsules clavate to nearly cylindrical, 3–4 mm long, often contracted under the mouth; neck slender, slightly shorter than the urn, strongly shrunken when dry; basal membrane about ⅓–½ the height of the endostome, segments strongly keeled, ± perforated down the middle but not widely so. Plate 71, figs. 8–10.

19.28 On damp soil and rocks, in crevices, and on rotten wood; essentially montane and subalpine in our region. Mostly sporadic and nowhere common.

19.29 Circumboreal, extending southward in the Rocky Mountains to Utah and Colorado and in the Appalachian Mountains to North Carolina.

19.30 Since *P. cruda* is known to be both dioicous and paroicous, and *P. longicolla* differs only in a degree, one might consider the latter as a yellowish green phase with a predominance of longer capsules with a better-differentiated neck.

19.31 **3. Pohlia nutans** (Hedw.) Lindb. Plants loosely tufted or scattered, green to yellowish green without noticeable lustre. Stems rather slender, mostly less than 1 cm tall, occasionally taller, mostly simple, red. Lower leaves small and distant, upper ones crowded, ovate-lanceolate, 1.3–2.3 mm long, perichaetial leaves lanceolate to linear-lanceolate, 3–4 mm long, acute to slightly acuminate; margins plane above, narrowly revolute in the lower half, toothed in the upper part; costa ceasing just below the apex, or percurrent, reddish; upper cells oblong to linear-rhomboidal or fusiform-hexagonal, 7–9 μ wide, 40–70 μ long, narrower toward the margins, tending to be shorter in lower leaves and in sterile plants, longer in upper and perichaetial leaves. Paroicous. Seta 1.5–3(4) cm long, reddish at full maturity; capsules horizontal to pendent, elongate-pyriform, sometimes slightly curved, up to 3 mm long, neck rather short, not strongly differentiated externally; annulus present; exothecial cells irregularly rectangular, thin walled; stomata superficial in the neck;

Plate 71.   1–7. Pohlia cruda. 1. Habit sketches of fertile plants, X.4. 2. Habit sketches of male and sterile shoots, X.4. 3. Four stem leaves, X8. 4. Three perichaetial leaves, X8. 5. Medial leaf cells of leaves from sterile plants. **Note:** Shorter cells also often occur in lower leaves of fertile plants. 6. Upper medial and apical cells of fertile shoots, X120. 7. Three typical capsules, X8.

8–10. Pohlia longicolla. 8. Habit sketches, X.4. 9. Apex of stem dissected to show paroicous inflorescence, X4. 10. Four typical capsules, X8. **Note:** The leaves of **P. longicolla** are indistinguishable in form and areolation from those of **P. cruda.**

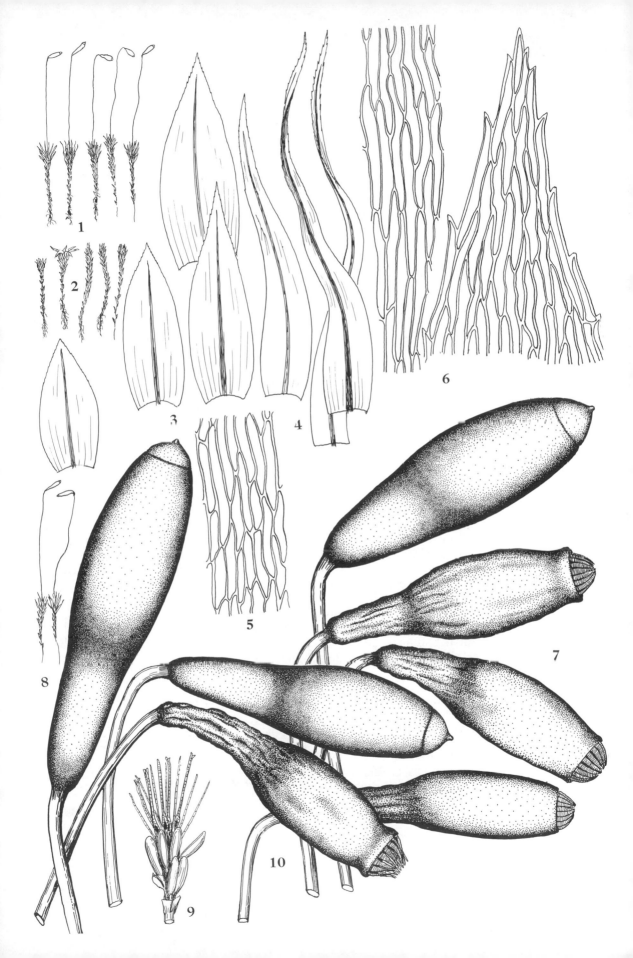

peristome teeth yellow, becoming reddish brown with age, finely papillose, lamellae numerous and close together; endostome pale, basal membrane about ½ the height, segments keeled and strongly perforated, cilia mostly 2, nodulose. Spores 17–22 μ. Plate 72, figs. 1–9.

19.32   On damp or wet soil, rocks, or rotten wood, often in shade, mostly in the mountains in our region.

19.33   Circumboreal, Alaska to Greenland, southward to North Carolina, Iowa, and the mountains to Arizona and California.

19.34   Next to *P. wahlenbergii*, our commonest species of the genus. Being paroicous, it fruits freely. Usually the shorter leaf cells and shorter neck of the capsule together with the lack of glossiness in the leaves can be relied on to distinguish it from *P. cruda* and *P. longicolla*.

19.35   **4. Pohlia elongata** Hedw. Plants usually short, densely tufted or scattered among other mosses. Stems slender, less than 1 cm high, simple or sparingly branched, reddish below; rhizoids usually numerous, red, and densely papillose. Leaves dull or yellowish green without lustre, the lower ones small and scale-like, the upper ones narrowly triangular-lanceolate to oblong-lanceolate, the base broad, only slightly narrowed at the insertion, not decurrent, mostly 1.5–2 mm long, the comal ones larger, linear-oblong and reaching 2.5(3) mm long; margins narrowly revolute nearly to the apex, bluntly dentate toward the tip; costa slender, green or yellowish, percurrent or sometimes ending below the apex; upper cells linear, rather thick walled and firm, 5–7 μ wide and as much as 70 μ long, often becoming shorter and broader in the leaf apex and towards the base, the basal ones oblong, usually about 12–14 μ wide, thinner walled. Paroicous or autoicous. Seta erect or curving upward, reddish at the base, 1–2 cm long; capsules variable, 2.5–3.5 mm long, yellowish brown with a red ring at the mouth, becoming darker reddish brown with age, mostly inclined to horizontal, sometimes nearly erect or again sometimes pendulous, typically elongate-pyriform or clavate, varying to short and thick, often slightly curved downward; neck sometimes not well set off, mostly shorter than the spore sac, but sometimes nearly equalling it; mouth rather small; lid conical, short beaked; exothecial cells mostly irregularly oblong, thin to moderately thick walled but not sinuous; stomata superficial; annulus of 2–3 rows of thick-walled cells, falling in pieces; peristome teeth narrowly lanceolate, ± joined at

---

Plate 72.   1–9. Pohlia nutans. 1. Habit sketch, X.4. 2. Apex of fertile stem showing paroicous nature of inflorescence, X60. 3. Three typical leaves, X8. 4. Two perichaetial leaves, X8. 5. Medial leaf cells of lower leaves and of leaves of sterile plants, X120. 6. Medial leaf cells of upper and perichaetial leaves, X8. 7. Average leaf apex, X120. 8. Axillary bud of rather rare occurrence, X120. 9. Four capsules showing variation in size and length of neck, X8.

10–17. Pohlia drummondii. 10. Habit sketches of female plants, X.4. 11. Habit sketches of male plants, X.4. 12. Upper part of male plant showing enlarged perigonium, X4. 13. Two typical stem leaves, X8. 14. Two perichaetial leaves, X8. 15. Medial leaf cells, X120. 16. Leaf apex, X120. 17. Three capsules, moist and dry, X8.

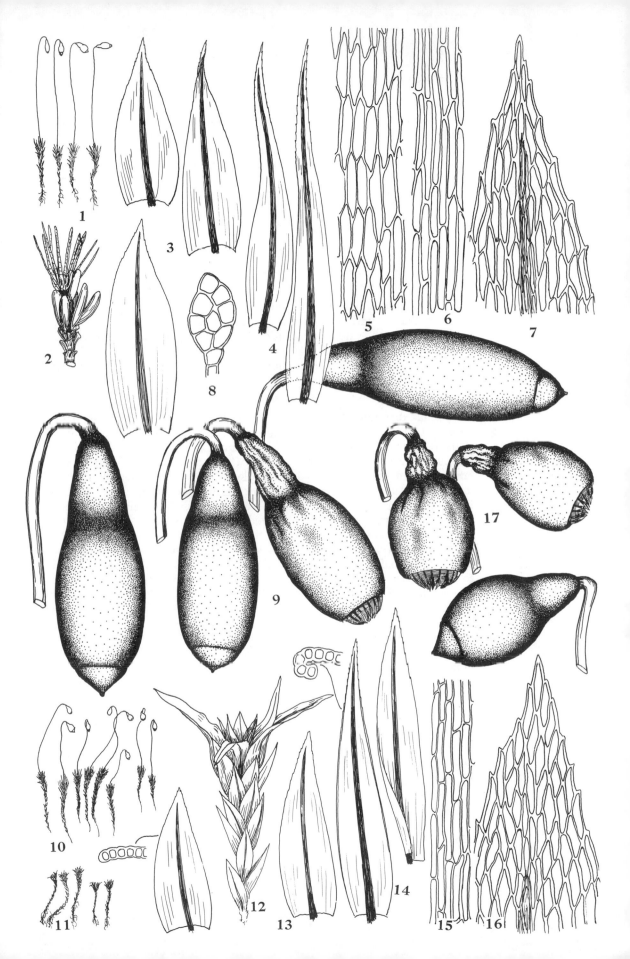

1   2   3   4   5   6   7   8   9   10   11   12   13   14   15   16   17

the base, gradually tapering upward, yellowish to yellowish brown, often slightly reddish at the base when old, joints close together, finely papillose and usually with fine vertical striations above; segments linear-lanceolate to linear, about as long as the teeth, narrowly perforated down the middle, arising from a low basal membrane, yellowish throughout, rather coarsely papillose above, but sometimes finely so, or even smooth; cilia lacking or rarely showing as blunt stubs. Spores yellowish to yellowish brown, mostly 15–20 μ, finely papillose. Plate 73.

19.36   On wet or damp soil, often in crevices, usually in shady places.

19.37   Circumboreal. Extending southward in the Adirondak Mountains of New York and through the Rockies to Arizona and in the Sierra Nevada to California.

19.38   Quite distinctive because of the dull yellowish green color, narrowly tapering leaves with margins revolute nearly to the apex, and narrow medial cells, rather slender capsules, the narrow peristome teeth vertically striate above, slender segments from an unusually low basal membrane, and absence of cilia. Sometimes leaves may be broader and shorter or the capsules shorter and thick necked, the teeth may be papillose as well as striate above.

19.39   **5. Pohlia drummondii** (C. Muell.) Andrews in Grout. Plants small, densely tufted or scattered among other mosses. Stems red, usually less than 1 cm tall, simple or sparingly branched; rhizoids few, red, and papillose. Leaves dull green to yellowish green without lustre, ovate-lanceolate to lanceolate, 1–1.5 mm long, the lower ones shorter and more widely spaced; margins plane or slightly recurved, entire to slightly toothed at the apex; comal leaves longer and narrower, more crowded, the margins often recurved and more sharply toothed above; costa fairly strong, ending below the apex or sometimes percurrent in the comal leaves, green to yellowish, becoming reddish at the base with age; upper leaf cells 10–14 μ wide, 40–100 μ long, oblong-rhomboidal to linear, with walls fairly thick or sometimes rather thin. Large budlike propagula occasionally produced singly in the axils of the upper leaves. Dioicous. Seta often flexuous and bent, up to 1 cm long, reddish brown below, yellowish brown above; capsules shortly pyriform, inclined to pendulous, 1–1.5(2) mm long, the neck about $\frac{1}{3}$, abruptly contracted to the seta, when dry much shrivelled, the urn then about as broad as long; annulus of 2–3 rows of thick-walled cells; exothecial cells ± isodiametric, quadrate to irregular, the walls irregularly thickened and

Plate 73.   1–9. **Pohlia elongata.** Dioicous form. 1. Female plants. 2. Male plant, X.4. 3. Perigonial bud, X4. 4. Lower leaves. 5. Upper leaves. 6. Capsules, X8. 7. Portion of peristome showing variations in teeth and very low basal membrane of endostome with slender segments without cilia or only rudimentary stubs, X60. 8. Exothecial cells. 9. Superficial stoma, X120.

10–15. **Pohlia elongata.** Paroicous form. 10. Habit sketches, X.4. 11. Leaves, X8. 12. Upper and apical cells, X120. 13. Perichaetial leaf with antheridia at the axil, X8. 14. Capsules, X8. 15. Portion of the peristome showing higher basal membrane with slender segments and without cilia, X60.

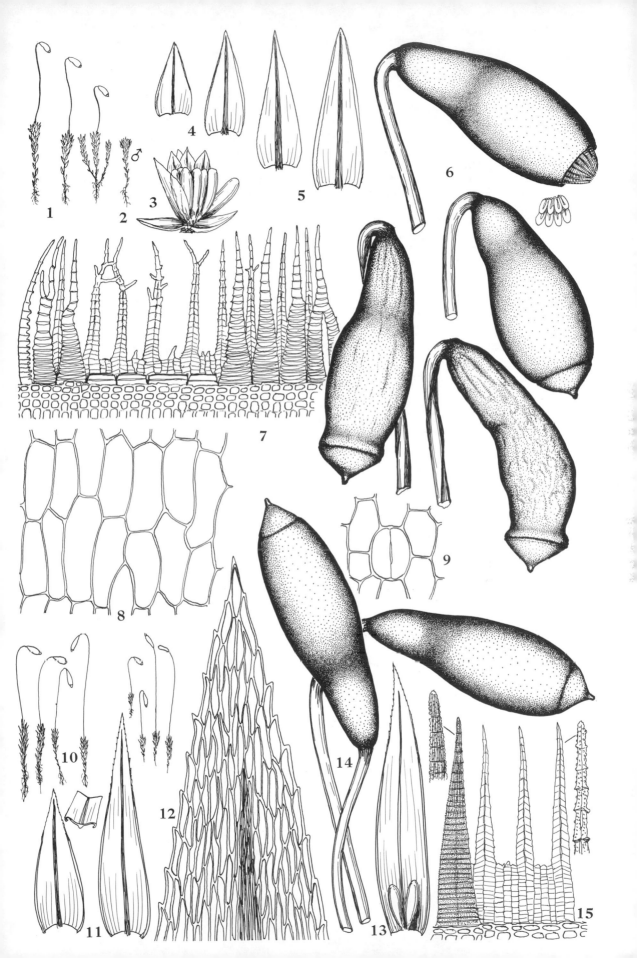

sinuous; stomata superficial; lid mammillate; peristome teeth narrowly lanceolate, slightly acuminate, closely set and sometimes connected at the base, joints mostly close and numerous (usually about 25 but as few as 18 in some small capsules), yellowish, becoming yellowish brown at the base with age, finely papillose below, somewhat more coarsely so above, without vertical striations; segments arising from a rather high basal membrane, pale yellowish, strongly keeled and perforated down the middle, slightly shorter than the teeth, smooth or papillose; cilia 2–3, well developed, filiform, scarcely nodulose, usually papillose, sometimes short, rudimentary or even entirely lacking. Spores 15–24 μ finely papillose. Plate 72, figs. 10–17.

19.40   On wet or damp soil, usually in shady places. In Utah it is confined to high mountains.

19.41   Greenland and northern Europe. Alaska, southward in the Cascade and Rocky mountains to California, Arizona, and Colorado.

19.42   The gametophyte resembles that of other small species, especially in leaf characters. However, at least some of the upper and comal leaves are revolute on the margins, and this trait together with the lack of numerous small gemmae among the leaves of sterile plants distinguish it from *P. annotina, P. proligera,* and *P. bulbifera. Pohlia drummondii* occasionally forms single large reddish propagula which are more in the nature of deciduous brood branches with prominent leaf primordia. From *P. elongata* it differs in the dioicous habit, nonstriate peristome teeth, higher basal membrane of the endostome, more regular presence of well-developed cilia and shorter capsules with sinuous exothecial cells. *Pohlia nudicaule* has been united with this species by several authorities. It is regarded as a form with shorter capsules and no cilia. Two specimens from the Uinta Mountains appear to be quite distinctive but the form is infrequent and there has been no opportunity to observe intergrading forms linking it more definitely with *P. elongata.*

19.43   **6. Pohlia rothii** (Corr.) Broth. Plants small, loosely to densely tufted or scattered among other mosses and liverworts, yellowish green to bright green, usually with lustre. Stems erect, red, usually about 1 cm tall, occasionally up to 2 cm, simple or sometimes with subfloral innovations; rhizoids confined to the base. Leaves rather distant, erect-patent or sometimes spreading, rather open when dry, 0.7–1.4 mm long, ovate-lanceolate, gradually tapering or briefly acuminate, acute; margins narrowly recurved, slightly toothed near the apex; costa rather stout, reddish at the base or green throughout, ending several cells below the tip or percurrent; upper cells linear-rhomboidal, 7–10 μ wide, rather thin walled, becoming broader in the base, 12–16 μ wide, often tinted. Sterile stems bearing subglobose to ovate propagula singly in axils of upper leaves, 1–3 per shoot, these usually bright red, clothed with very small, green, acute leaf tips (resembling very young branches but rounded at the base and easily dislodged). Dioicous. Seta 1–2 cm long, ± flexuous, yellowish red, becoming darker with age; capsules horizontal to pendulous, elongate pyriform, 2–3 mm long, neck shorter than the urn, strongly shrunken when dry; annulus present; lid low-conic with a short point; stomata superficial; peristome teeth yellowish; endostome pale yellowish, finely papillose; segments rising from a high basal membrane, keeled, with wide perforations; cilia 2, slender and nodulose. Spores reddish brown, finely roughened, 15–20 μ. Plate 75, figs. 10–18.

19.44   Growing on damp soil.

19.45   Europe. Apparently circumboreal; reported from the New England States and Alaska. Duchesne County.

19.46   Apparently overlooked because it is mostly scattered among other mosses and liverworts, and rarely fruits. It can be recognized in the field with a handlens, the reddish gemmae being rather conspicuous. It is frequently found in the high Uinta Mountains, and I suspect that it occurs elsewhere in Utah.

19.47   The plants are somewhat darker green than related species, and when dry the leaves have a characteristic loosely incurved stance with a slight glaze on the convex sides of the folds, but they are not glossy all over.

19.48   **7. Pohlia bulbifera** (Warnst.) Warnst. Plants small, tufted or scattered among other mosses, yellowish green and $\pm$ lustrous, in size and general character much like *P. annotina* but differing as follows: propagula yellowish, in clusters of 3 or more in the axils of leaves on short distinct stalks, subglobose to obovoid, 0.15–0.2 mm long, with 3–4 leaf points either standing erect or arching over the apex to give the propagula a rounded budlike appearance. Dioicous. Capsules short, pyriform, 2–2.5 mm long, nearly 1.5 mm thick; neck much shorter than the spore sac, much shrivelled when dry; stomata superficial; peristome teeth yellowish with numerous close joints, finely papillose; segments from a high basal membrane, keeled and perforated; cilia 2–3, slender and nodulose. Plate 74, figs. 16–19.

19.49   On wet or damp soil in high mountains of Utah.

19.50   Nova Scotia, White Mountains of New Hampshire, and Magnolia, Massachusetts. Duchesne County: near Mirror Lake, 10,500 ft.

19.51   The yellowish propagula are so densely crowded in the axils of leaves as to spread them wide open.

19.52   **8. Pohlia proligera** (Kindb.) Broth. Plants small, differing from *P. annotina* in the following respects: Leaves usually lustrous, on the whole broader, especially in the upper part, less tapering, the upper leaf cells larger, 10–14 μ wide and up to 100 μ long, thinner walled. Propagula ovate, obovate, cuneate, or elongate-vermicular, straight to somewhat spirally twisted, the tips sometimes bent or hooked, with 1 or at most 2 leaf points. Dioicous; fruit rare. Capsules 2–2.5 mm long, the neck shorter than the spore sac. Plate 74, figs. 10–15.

19.53   Yukon to Greenland, southward to Quebec, British Columbia, northern Michigan, Wisconsin, and Minnesota, and in the high mountains of

Utah and Colorado. Summit County: Uinta Mountains, Henry's Fork, 9,200 ft.

19.54 **9. Pohlia wahlenbergii** (Web. & Mohr) Andrews in Grout. Plants mostly loosely tufted, pale whitish green, sometimes with a bluish cast, without lustre, soft and tender. Stems usually long, simple or branched, green, becoming reddish with age, 1–3(5) cm tall; rhizoids confined to the base. Leaves rather distant, usually ± decurrent, ovate to ovate-lanceolate, 2–2.5(3) mm long, the lower ones shorter, patent to ± spreading, becoming strongly shrivelled when dry; margins flat, denticulate in the upper part; costa green, becoming reddish from the base upward with age, ending below the apex; upper cells rhomboidal to hexagonal or fusiform, thin walled and lax, large for the genus but varying widely in different plants, 15–26 μ wide, mostly 17–20, 60–120 μ long; marginal cells linear and much narrower. The upper $\frac{1}{4}$–$\frac{1}{3}$ of the shoots sometimes becoming deciduous by forming a swollen reddish abscission zone. Dioicous. Perigonia terminal, large and discoid. Seta 1–2(4) cm long, reddish brown, strongly twisted when dry; capsules pyriform to obovoid, dark reddish brown at maturity, horizontal to pendent, 1.5–2 mm long, neck shorter than the spore sac and strongly shrunken when dry, the urn then appearing as wide as long or nearly so; exothecial cells short, the walls thick and wavy, thickened in the angles; stomata immersed, narrowly elliptical; annulus lacking; lid convex mammillate; peristome teeth red brown throughout, closely jointed, finely papillose below, coarsely so above; segments keeled and ± perforated, sometimes widely so; cilia 2–3, nodulose to subappendiculate, papillose, arising from a high basal membrane. Spores 16–20 μ, very finely papillose. Plate 75, figs. 1–9.

19.55 On wet or damp soil banks of brooklets or around springs, seepage areas and similar places. Mostly in the mountains in our region.

19.56 Europe and Asia. More or less cosmopolitan and widely distributed throughout the United States and Canada.

19.57 This, our commonest species of *Pohlia*, rarely fruits. The loose tufts of elongated shoots of pale whitish green make it easily recognized in the field. It is very soft and tender and when dry the leaves strongly shrivel in a spreading position and often lose their whiteness and become a light green. The dry capsules have a characteristic twist at the summit of the seta. The large thin-walled leaf cells distinguish it from all other

---

Plate 74. 1–9. **Pohlia annotina** var. **decipiens.** 1. Habit sketches, X.4. 2. Two male plants, X.4. 3. Four typical stem leaves, X8. 4. Two perichaetial leaves, X8. 5–6. Leaf apex and upper medial cells, X120. 7. Two perigonial leaves, X8. 8. Two gemmae, X20. 9. Three capsules, X8.

10–15. **Pohlia proligera.** 10. Habit sketches, X.4. 11. Three typical stem leaves, X8. **Note:** The perichaetial and perigonial leaves are like those in figs. 4 and 7 above. 12–13. Leaf apex and upper medial cells, X120. 14. Six gemmae, X60. 15. Capsule, X8.

16–19. **Pohlia bulbifera.** 16. Two typical stem leaves, X8. 17. Leaf apex, X120. 18. Two capsules, X8. 19. Three gemmae, X60. **Note:** Habit of growth; perichaetial and perigonial leaves are like those of **P. annotina.**

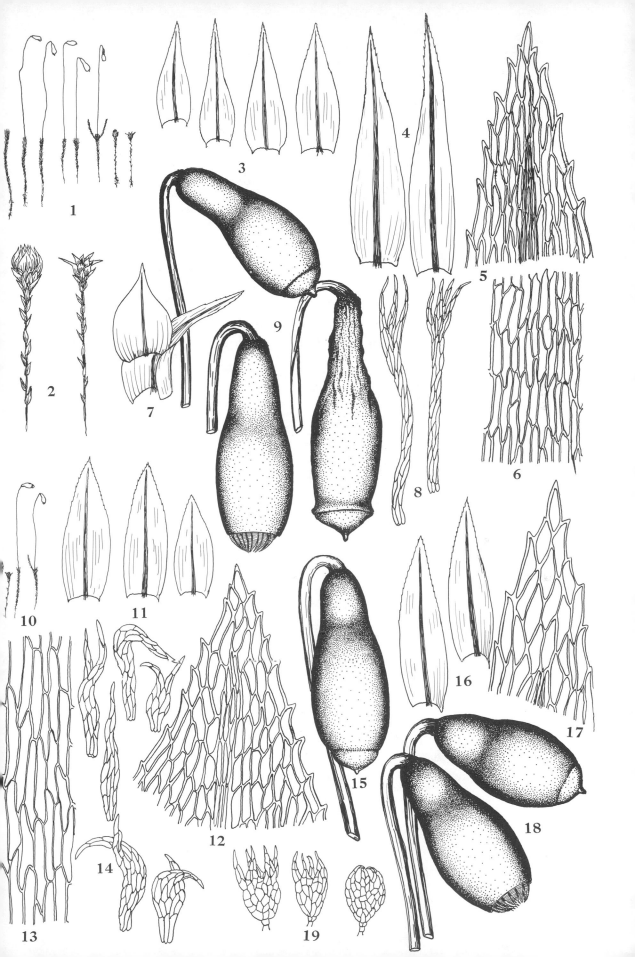

species in our region. Frequently the upper portions of the shoots break off due to the formation of an abscission zone of swollen reddish cells and continue growth on favorably moist substrata.

19.58   **10. Pohlia annotina** (Hedw.) Loesk. Plants small, less than 1 cm tall to as much as 2 cm, densely tufted or sometimes scattered. Stems red, erect, mostly simple but often producing 1 or more innovations near the summit; rhizoids usually few, dark reddish, smooth to coarsely papillose; leaves dull yellowish to darker green, usually without conspicuous lustre, erect-patent both dry and moist on the sterile shoots, more appressed on fertile ones, oblong-lanceolate to narrowly lanceolate, mostly 1–1.5 mm long, the comal ones up to 2.5 mm, slightly contracted at the broad base, usually narrowly decurrent; margins flat, sometimes narrowly recurved in the upper part on 1 side, ± bluntly toothed toward the apex; costa slender to fairly stout, green or yellowish, rarely reddish at the base, ending below the apex or nearly percurrent; upper cells typically linear and thick walled, 5–8 μ wide and up to 85 μ long but variable, especially in some sterile stems with shorter and broader leaves where the cells are up to 10 μ wide and shorter and thin walled; basal cells wider, oblong and thin walled. Yellowish or green propagula borne in axils of upper leaves, usually 2–5 per leaf; in the species proper small obovate to narrowly cuneate, in var. *loeskii* linear, straight to spirally twisted, in both kinds bearing 3–5 leaf points at the apex. Dioicous. Seta erect or curved, 1–2 cm long, reddish brown below; capsules strongly inclined, horizontal or pendulous, elongate-pyriform, 2–2.8 mm long, the neck as long as the urn or slightly shorter (sometimes quite short, the capsule then pyriform) variable in the same tuft, sometimes slightly decurved, yellow brown becoming darker red brown with age; lid convex mammillate; annulus of 2–3 rows of very thick-walled cells, fragmenting exothecial cells ± shortly oblong, firm but thinner walled than in related species; stomata superficial; peristome teeth narrowly linear-lanceolate, widely spaced at the base, joints numerous, yellowish, and finely papillose; endostome forming a high basal membrane; segments narrow and perforated, often poorly formed, the joints projecting like appendages and sometimes connected side by side, very pale to yellowish, smooth to finely papillose; cilia 2–3, very slender, separate or partly united, ± nodulose, sometimes subappendiculate, finely papillose, Spores 15–20 μ, yellow brown, globose and finely papillose. Plate 74, figs. 1–9.

19.59   On damp or wet soil in high mountains of Utah.

19.60   Circumboreal, extending southward in the Appalachian Mountains to

---

Plate 75. 1–9. Pohlia wahlenbergii. 1. Habit sketches, X.4. 2. Habit of sterile plants, X.4. 3. Typical leaves. 4–5. Perigonial leaves with antheridia, X8. 6. Upper medial leaf cells. 7. Leaf apex, X120. 8. Capsules, X8. 9. Immersed stoma in neck of capsule, X120.

10–18. Pohlia rothii. 10. Female plants. 11. Male plants. 12. Sterile plants with gemmae, X.4. 13. Portion of sterile shoot with gemmae, X4. 14. Leaves, X8. 15. Leaf apex and upper cells, X120. 16. Gemmae, X6. 17. Capsules, X8. 18. Portion of peristome, X60.

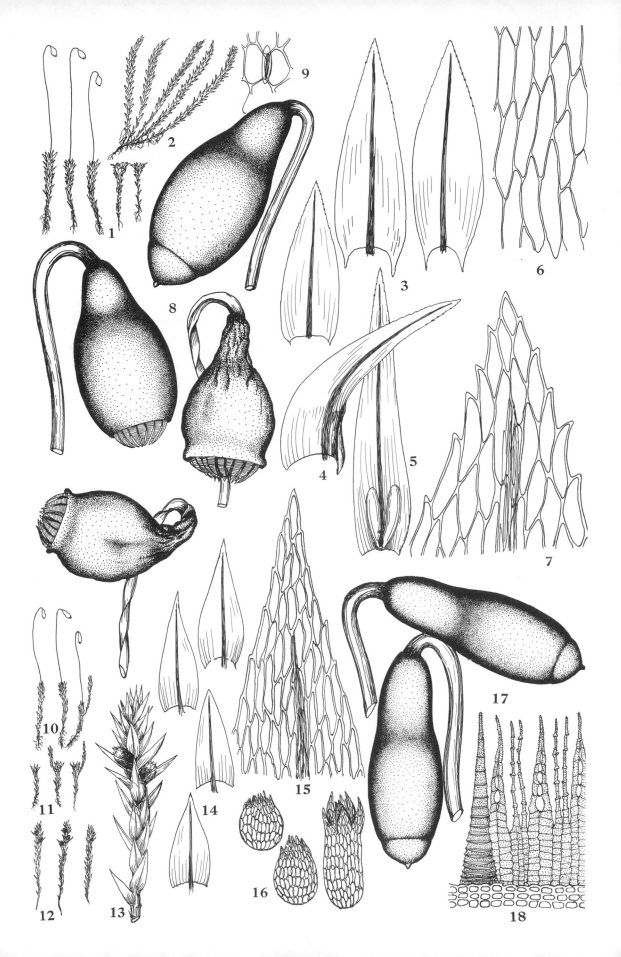

19.61   South Carolina, in the Rockies to Utah and in the Sierra Nevada of California and western Nevada.

19.61   All of our present specimens belong to the var. *loeskii* Crum, Steere & Anders., having elongated, straight or twisted propagula with 3–5 leaf points at the summit.

19.62   Being dioicous, this moss does not fruit very often, although most of the above specimens have abundant capsules. Sterile plants without gemmae are scarcely distinguishable from *P. proligera* and *P. bulbifera,* which are supposed to have lustrous leaves with the upper cells 10–14 μ wide, those of *P. proligera* longer, up to 100 μ long and those of *P. bulbifera* 70 μ or less.

4. BRYUM Hedw.

19.63   Plants loosely to densely tufted, usually green above and yellowish brown to reddish brown below. Stems erect, usually branched, in cross section $\pm$ 5-angled, showing a central strand with a cortex of large, thick-walled, $\pm$ colored cells, the epidermal ones small; rhizoids few to dense, mostly reddish. Leaves various, obovate, ovate to narrowly ovate-lanceolate, acute to acuminate or blunt or rounded in a few species; margins plane to revolute, with or without a distinct border of thick-walled linear cells; costa percurrent to long excurrent, sometimes ending below the apex; upper cells hexagonal or rhomboidal, usually narrower and longer at the margin; basal cells shorter and broader, quadrate to rectangular. Synoicous, autoicous, or dioicous. Seta long, essentially erect; capsules pyriform, turbinate, clavate or cylindrical, horizontal to pendulous, neck usually distinct, mostly less than ½ the length of the capsule; annulus present; lid mostly convex mammillate; stomata superficial in the neck; peristome double; endostome forming a high basal membrane, segments keeled, cilia present, rudimentary, or lacking. Spores globose. Calyptra cucullate.

19.64   *Bryum* is one of the oldest names used for a cryptogamic plant. It was used by Theophrastus in about the year 200 B.C. for the green alga, *Ulva lactucae,* also called sea lettuce and oyster green. Other early philosophers applied the name to fruticose lichens, particularly those of the genus *Usnea.* John Dillen (Dillenius) first used it in 1718 for a wide variety of mosses, including some *Brya* in our modern sense. Linnaeus established it as a more or less definite genus in 1735 and so did Hedwig, more precisely, in 1801.

19.65   It is a large genus in which numerous species have been proposed— many of which have recently been reduced to synonymy. Some of the commonest species vary widely in size and appearance, the leaves and capsules often being unusually small and not wholly typical when compared with those of well-developed plants. Species of *Bryum* growing under xerophytic conditions commonly have smaller parts. It is not uncommon to find a tuft having a wide range of sizes of the capsules, especially where there is evidence that the plants develop under short periods of alternately moist and dry conditions. For these reasons the measurements given in the descriptions may be somewhat misleading.

19.66   The disposition of sex organs is constant in most species. However, in some specimens it may be difficult to demonstrate the exact position of the antheridia and archegonia, especially if the material is old. The synoicous condition is usually easily demonstrated, but in many specimens the antheridia may be very elusive. Ordinarily one would call such plants dioicous, but in some specimens there will always be some doubt. Experience will generally convince the student of mosses that at least three demonstrations in each specimen will avoid embarrassing errors. Perhaps the most frustrating circumstance, and not an uncommon one at that, is when two closely related species occur in the same tuft.

19.67   1. Plants small, silvery white, the upper half of the leaves lacking chlorophyll; costa ending below the apex .... 18. *B. argenteum*   19.136

19.68   1. Plants small to large, green; leaves chlorophyllose throughout

2. Leaves bluntly acute to broadly rounded at the apex, margins not noticeably bordered with narrower cells; costa ending in or below the apex

3. Leaves ovate, oval or rounded from a narrow somewhat decurrent base, not noticeably concave, spreading when moist, crisped when dry .... 6. *B. tortifolium*   19.89

3. Leaves imbricated, not crisped when dry

4. Leaves ovate to oblong, broad at the apex, not narrowed or decurrent at base, strongly concave, spoon-shaped, erect-patent when moist .... 15. *B. miniatum*   19.124

4. Leaves ovate-lanceolate, bluntly acute to narrowly obtuse, canaliculate .... 17. *B. gemmiparum*   19.132

2. Leaves mostly acute to acuminate (some bluntly acute in some species), margins various

5. Plants large, usually light green; leaf blades 5–7 mm long, forming a rosette when moist, loosely imbricated and often slightly crisped when dry; cells lax, 100 μ or longer; lower leaves abruptly becoming shorter, scale-like, and distant; capsules clavate-cylindric, 5–7 mm long .... 19. *B. sandbergii*   19.140

5. Plants smaller, leaf blades mostly less than 4 mm long; cells much smaller; capsules shorter .... 4. *B. uliginosum*   19.81

6. Leaves strongly crisped and twisted when dry; cells thin walled; costa usually ending below the apex ....
.... 8. *turbinatum*   19.96

7. Leaves few, distant, rather small, ovate to ovate-lanceolate, acute to acuminate, conspicuously long decurrent, spreading, soft and tender .... 7. *B. weigelii*   19.92

7. Leaves dense, often forming a terminal rosette, obovate, gradually to abruptly cuspidate, the tip often twisted, often slightly decurrent; medial leaf cells broadly hexagonal; sterile shoots often bearing yellowish or reddish, jointed, linear propagula in axils of leaves .... 14. *B. capillare* 19.119

6. Leaves not crisped when dry, mostly imbricated and longitudinally folded, the apices sometimes ± spirally twisted; costa percurrent to excurrent

   8. Cilia rudimentary or lacking

      9. Peristome teeth with ventral lamellae connected by vertical or oblique cross thickenings and the lower half adhering to the endostome; mouth of capsule small, neck short .... 1. *B. angustirete* 19.69

      9. Peristome teeth without connections between the ventral lamellae, free from the endostome or nearly so

         10. Capsules symmetric, not incurved, neck short; leaf cells thick walled and firm; margins weakly bordered; synoicous .... 2. *B. stenotrichum* 19.73

         10. Capsules mostly slightly incurved and asymmetric when fully mature; leaf cells thin walled and lax; margins strongly bordered

            11. Capsules long clavate, 5–6 mm long, long necked; mouth small; teeth yellowish, autoicous .... 4. *B. uliginosum* 19.81

            11. Capsules elongate-pyriform, 3–4 mm long

               12. Segments linear; teeth slightly adhering to basal membrane, yellowish brown at the base, paler above; synoicous .... 5. *B. arcticum* 19.85

               12. Segments lanceolate, teeth free from the basal membrane, yellowish; dioicous .... 3. *B. pallens* 19.77

   8. Cilia present, mostly appendiculate

      13. Leaves not at all acuminate; bright green, acute, bluntly acute or narrowly obtuse, costa green to yellowish brown, percurrent or ending below the apex; plants growing on calcium-bearing rocks or soil .. 17. *B. gemmiparum* 19.132

      13. Leaves all acute to acuminate at the apex

         14. Outer peristome teeth yellowish to pale yellowish brown at the base; dioicous

            15. Leaves with strong border of narrow cells; capsules elongate-pyriform, usually slightly incurved .... 3. *B. pallens* 19.77

15. Leaves weakly bordered; capsules turbinate, symmetric .... 8. *B. turbinatum* 19.96

14. Outer peristome teeth conspicuously yellowish brown in the lower ⅔ or throughout, sometimes reddish at the base

16. Capsules short, 1.5–2.5 mm long, oval to shortly cylindrical, neck short, thick, and rounded to the seta. .... 16.   *B. bicolor* 19.128

16. Capsules elongate-pyriform, neck mostly narrower and more tapering to the seta

17. Costa ceasing below the apex to shortly excurrent; dioicous; leaves usually dark green, obovate, crisped when dry; cells broadly hexagonal, thin walled; margins strongly bordered and revolute; capsules clavate, slightly incurved; sterile shoots often bearing dark yellowish or reddish jointed propagula in clusters in the axils of leaves .... 14. *B. capillare* 19.119

17. Costa percurrent to long excurrent; leaf cells thick walled, firm in well-developed leaves

18. Leaves ± contorted when dry, decurrent*; costa percurrent to shortly excurrent; plants often tall and stout; dioicous or synoicous ....9. *B. pseudotriquetrum* 19.100

18. Leaves not contorted when dry, mostly longitudinally infolded or imbricated, the tips often yellowish and ± spirally twisted; costa shortly to longly excurrent

19. Stems typically with numerous short, erect branches and forming very dense cushions and sods; autoicous .... 11. *B. pallescens* 19.107

19. Stems sparingly branched, forming loose or dense tufts

20. Plants synoicous; leaves strongly bordered with narrow cells to the apex or nearly so

21. Costa shortly to moderately long excurrent; stems mostly less than 1 cm tall .... 10. *B. creberrimum* 19.104

21. Costa very long spinulose excurrent; stems reaching 2.5 cm tall but usually more slen-

---

*Usually the comal and perichaetial leaves are not decurrent in any of this group, and in short plants there may be few or no fully developed stem leaves with decurrent bases. Plants of this sort may be difficult to distinguish from the following two species.

der with smaller leaves ....
.... 12. *B. lonchocaulon*   19.111

20. Plants dioicous; leaves weakly bordered in
the upper part; costa long excurrent; upper
cells elongated .... 13. *B. caespiticium*   19.115

19.69   **1. Bryum angustirete** Kindb. Plants densely tufted, green to yellowish
green, sometimes brownish. Stems 5 mm tall or less, red, freely branched,
matted with reddish rhizoids at the base. Leaves generally small, the
blades up to 2 mm long, ovate to oblong-lanceolate, acuminate, often
narrowly so, usually dense to the base of the stem, ± patent, the comal
ones forming a rosette; when dry, erect and closely to somewhat loosely
appressed, frequently somewhat contorted, the tips often twisted but
not crisped, base reddish when older, not decurrent, apex gradually
tapering into the yellowish long-excurrent slightly toothed costa; margins strongly revolute to the apex or nearly so, entire; upper cells rhomboidal to irregularly hexagonal, mostly 10–15 μ wide, becoming linear
in the apex, thick walled with the ends often strongly thickened, toward
the margins becoming gradually narrower, longer, and thicker walled,
forming a broad indistinct border; basal cells becoming wider, oblong,
and thin walled. Synoicous. Seta 2–3 mm long, straight, and slender,
reddish brown; capsules pendulous to nearly horizontal, 2–3 mm long,
pyriform, often narrowly so, neck shorter than the urn or nearly equalling it in length, reddish brown to yellowish brown, mouth small, when
dry variable, the urn inflated or ± cylindric, often slightly contracted
under the mouth, the neck usually ± shrunken; lid small, ± persistent,
conic-convex with a broad or slightly elongated straight or oblique point;
exothecial cells oblong to irregular, thick walled; peristome teeth narrowly lanceolate, the base only slightly differentiated, gradually tapering
upward, 0.25–0.34 mm long, reddish brown in the lower ⅔, hyaline
above, densely and finely papillose below, more coarsely so above, joints
rather wide, ventral lamellae indistinct, joined by vertical or oblique
dark colored thickenings; endostome hyaline and finely papillose, basal
membrane ⅓–½, united with the corresponding part of the teeth;
segments narrow, narrowly to widely perforated; cilia rudimentary or
lacking. Spores large but variable in size, 20–31 μ. Plate 76, figs. 1–7.

19.70   On wet or dry soil.

19.71   Europe and Asia. Widely distributed in Canada and southward to a line
roughly extending from the District of Columbia to Colorado thence

---

Plate 76.   1–7. Bryum angustirete (B. pendulum). 1. Habit sketches, X.4. 2. Moist
and dry habits of the shoots, X2. 3. Three leaves, X8. 4. Upper medial leaf cells,
X120. 5. Linear apical cells, X120. 6. Five capsules, X8. 7. Portion of peristome
showing vertical and oblique cross connections between ventral lamellae of teeth
and rudimentary cilia, X70.

8–11. Bryum stenotrichum. 8. Habit sketches, X.4. 9. Three typical leaves, X8.
10. Three capsules, X8. 11. Two portions of peristomes showing the rudimentary
cilia and low basal membrane, X70.

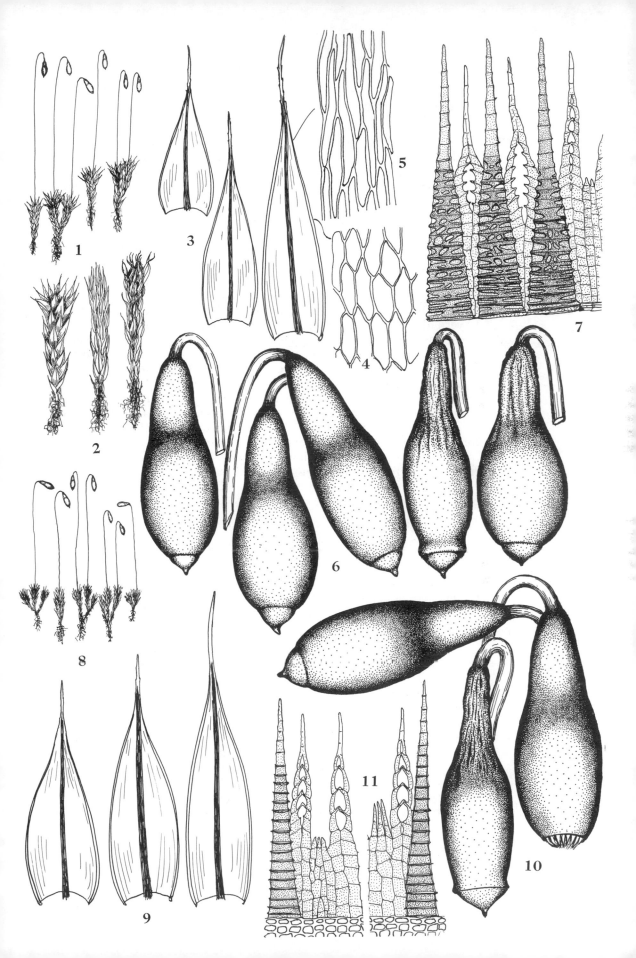

southward to Arizona and California. Frequent in Utah from the lowland to the high mountains.

19.72   The vertical and oblique thickenings connecting the ventral lamellae
of the teeth immediately distinguished this species. Also the absence of
cilia, firm union of the basal membrane of the endostome with the
teeth, the small mouth, darker capsules, and large spores are notable
traits.

19.73   **2. Bryum stenotrichum** C. Muell. Plants in low dense sods up to 1
cm tall, green to yellowish green. Stems branched, interwoven with
rhizoids at base. Leaves ovate- to oblong-lanceolate, narrowly acuminate,
costa long excurrent to a smooth or slightly toothed point, the blade 1–
2.5 mm long; margins revolute to near the apex, entire; medial cells oblong-hexagonal or rhomboidal, 12–17 μ wide, walls fairly thick, sometimes
slightly pitted here and there, becoming long linear and thick walled
toward the margin, forming a broad border, $\pm$ narrower toward the
apex; basal cells rectangular. Synoicous. Seta 1–3 cm long, yellowish to
reddish; capsules nearly horizontal to pendulous, elongate-pyriform,
2–2.8 mm long, straight, not bent, yellowish to reddish brown, neck
$\frac{1}{3}$–$\frac{1}{2}$ the length of the urn, fairly well set off, but sometimes quite
narrow, always gradually narrowed to the seta; lid and mouth medium
sized; peristome teeth narrowly triangulate-lanceolate, rather short, yellowish, sometimes yellowish brown to reddish at the extreme base, hyaline above, finely papillose below, more coarsely so above; endostome
hyaline to pale yellowish, finely papillose, basal membrane about $\frac{1}{3}$;
segments narrow, widely perforated down the middle; cilia lacking or
rudimentary, at most about $\frac{2}{3}$ the length of the segments, papillose.
Spores 17–22 μ. Plate 76, figs. 8–11.

19.74   On wet or rather dry soil and rocks in shade.

19.75   Circumboreal; widely distributed from Alaska to Greenland, extending
southward to Maine, Michigan, Colorado, and Utah.

19.76   The present specimens approach forms of *B. pallens* in the rather long,
though redimentary, cilia, but this is the only inconsistent trait, as the
fertile heads were consistently synoicous and the capsules straight.

19.77   **3. Bryum pallens** Sw. Plants usually densely tufted but sometimes
scattered among other mosses, green to yellowish green; stems branched,
up to 1 cm tall, red; rhizoids usually abundant at the base. Leaves
ovate- to oblong-lanceolate, sometimes rather broadly elliptical and narrowed at the base; the blade mostly 2–2.5 mm long, occasionally up to
3 mm, spreading when moist, erect and appressed to moderately contorted but not crisped when dry; apex mostly narrowly acuminate but
in broad-leaved forms rather abruptly so; costa stout, shortly to moderately long excurrent to an awl-shaped point; margins entire, usually revolute to near the apex; medial cells hexagonal to rhomboidal, variable,
12–25 μ wide, rather thin walled, toward the margins becoming narrower, linear, and thick walled, forming a distinct border, sometimes 2 cells
thick; basal cells rectangular. Dioicous. Seta 1–3 cm long; capsules pen-

dulous to subpendulous, occasionally strongly inclined, elongate-pyriform, curved inward at the neck, sometimes nearly straight, mostly 2–2.5 mm long but occasionally up to 5 mm; yellowish to yellowish brown; neck usually slender, shorter than the spore sac but sometimes nearly as long, gradually tapered to the seta; mouth rather large; lid large, conic to mammillate; peristome teeth yellowish to light yellowish brown at the base, hyaline above, narrowly lanceolate from a ± oblong base, gradually acuminate or narrowly triangular-lanceolate and evenly tapered upward, finely papillose below, ± coarsely so above, occasionally very coarsely; basal membrane of endostome high; segments narrow, split or widely perforated down the middle, finely papillose; cilia well developed and appendiculate to degenerate through all degrees, sometimes closely coherent, variously papillose. Spores mostly 18–20(25) μ. Plate 77, figs. 1–5.

19.78   On damp or wet soil.

19.79   Widely distributed in the Arctic and subarctic extending southward to the northern New England states, New York, Michigan, Montana, Washington and south in the mountains to Nevada, northern Arizona and Colorado.

19.80   Extremely variable. Usually the capsules are curved, but in some specimens they are short and pyriform and scarcely or not at all curved; on the other hand they may be clavate, up to 5 mm long. Many capsules show no curvature even when relaxed in water. Fresh capsules show curvature but once they are dried they may or may not return to their original contour, especially when the neck has been much shrunken. Some dried specimens that have degenerate cilia may closely resemble *B. stenotrichum*.

19.81   4. **Bryum uliginosum** (Brid.) B.S.G. Plants short, loosely tufted or scattered, green. Stems 1 cm or less tall, slender, erect, or flexuous, branched from the base, green above, reddish below; rhizoids rather few at the base. Leaves lax, few and rather widely spaced, spreading when moist, ± shrunken and contorted when dry, narrowly ovate- to oblong-lanceolate, acuminate, 4–5 mm long, not decurrent; margins plane, sometimes slightly toothed at the apex; costa percurrent to shortly excurrent to a smooth slender point; cells large, 20–25 μ wide, rhomboidal-hexagonal, thin walled and lax, rather abruptly narrowly linear on the margins forming a strong border; basal cells longer, rectangular. Autoicous. Seta erect, 5–7 cm long, reddish and shiny; capsules horizontal to somewhat pendent, elongate, clavate, curved downward at the neck, about 6 mm long, light brown, neck slender, usually longer than the spore sac, gradually tapering to the seta; mouth small, often slightly oblique; lid small, persistent, conic-mammillose; exothecial cells short and irregularly rectangular to rounded, thick walled; peristome teeth yellowish or sometimes reddish brown at the broad base, rather rapidly tapering to unusually slender, hyaline, incurved apices, finely papillose; endostome with a high basal membrane, segments wide at base, suddenly narrowed to slender filiform apices, keeled and perforated down the middle, finely papillose; cilia rudimentary or lacking. Spores 20–25 μ. Plate 77, figs. 6–9.

19.82 On wet or damp soil.

19.83 Europe and Asia. Circumboreal, extending southward to the New England states and Great Lakes region, Illinois, Ohio, Texas, New Mexico, Arizona, Nevada and California. Rare in Utah.

19.84 My single specimen is typical except that the peristome teeth are strongly reddish brown in the lower half. The large curved capsule and large lax leaves make this moss easily recognizable.

19.85 **5. Bryum arcticum** (R. Brown) B.S.G. Plants densely tufted, green to yellowish green. Stems short, up to 1 cm tall, red and branched. Leaves erect-patent to spreading when moist, imbricated to loosely contorted when dry, rather large, 2.5–3 mm long, elongate ovate to elliptical, broadest at about the middle or elliptic-obovate, broader in the upper part than in other species of this group, slightly gradually acuminate to nearly acute, narrowed toward the base, not decurrent; margins narrowly revolute well toward the apex or sometimes flat above, entire; costa yellowish, becoming reddish in older leaves, percurrent to rather long excurrent to a smooth or slightly serrulate point; upper cells rather long, 13–17(21) μ wide, regularly to quite irregularly oblong-rhomboidal, walls rather thin and sometimes slightly pitted, becoming rather abruptly linear and thick walled at the margins and forming a strong narrow border, sometimes bistratose, usually becoming indistinct toward the apex. Synoicous. Seta 3–6 cm tall, becoming reddish; capsules pendent, 3–4(5) mm long, yellowish when mature, elongate pyriform, typically slightly incurved in some capsules, neck well set off, about as long as the spore sac or shorter, $\pm$ tapering to the seta; mouth and lid typically small, sometimes slightly oblique; peristome teeth narrowly triangular-lanceolate, yellowish, often yellowish brown at the base, pale above; endostome pale yellowish to hyaline, basal membrane high, $\pm$ adhering to the teeth; segments narrowly linear-lanceolate, keeled, perforated with narrow slits down the middle; cilia short and rudimentary to nearly lacking. Spores 20–27 μ. Plate 78, figs. 1–7.

19.86 On wet or rather dry soil.

19.87 Yukon to Greenland, sporadically southward to Montana and Utah. Davis County: West Point, on a high bluff overloking Great Salt Lake, 4,240 ft.

19.88 The unusual habitat and southernmost extent of its range is notable. (Were it found in high mountains it would not be so unusual.) Except

---

Plate 77. 1–5. **Bryum pallens.** 1. Habit sketches, X.4. 2. Three typical leaves, X8. 3. Two portions of upper medial leaf cells from different leaves, X120. 4. Four capsules, X8. 5. Two portions of peristomes showing well-developed and rudimentary cilia, X70.

6–9. Bryum uliginosum (B. cernuum) 6. Habit sketches moist and dry, X4. 7. Two typical leaves, X8. 8. Upper medial leaf cells, X120. 9. Typical capsule, X8.

364

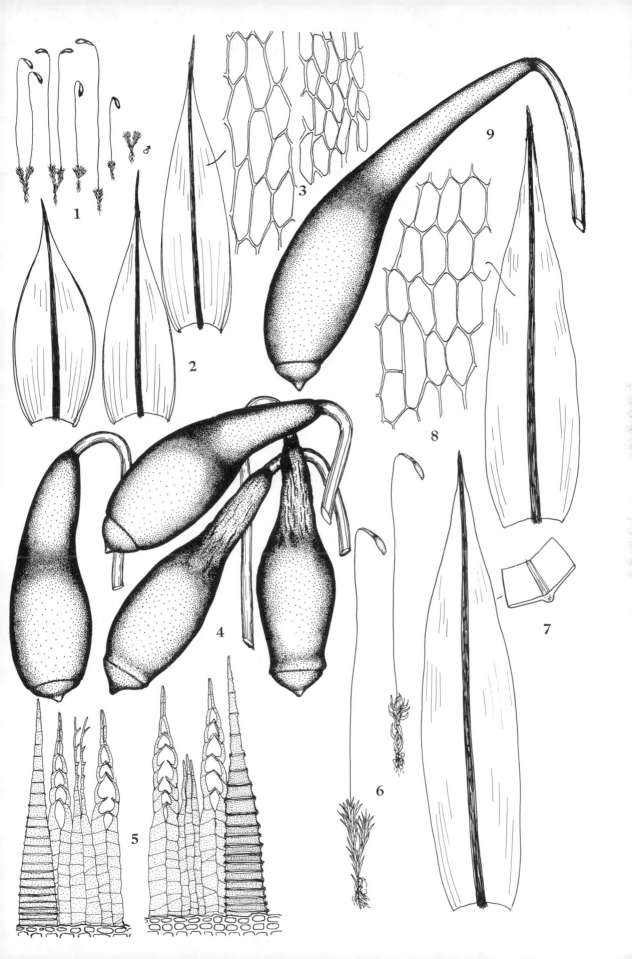

for the wider mouth and larger lid, the present specimens compare favorably with arctic material. Dr. A. L. Andrews identified the plants. The rather large shortly pointed leaves with wide cells and narrow border of linear cells more or less disappearing toward the apex are distinctive.

19.89 **6. Bryum tortifolium** Brid. Plants loosely to densely tufted, often scattered among other mosses, green to yellowish green. Stems mostly about 1 cm tall but known to become much taller, branching by slender innovations, green, becoming red with age. Leaves rather small and widely spaced, 1.5–2 mm long, oval to oblong, the lower ones smaller and nearly orbicular, broadly rounded to narrowly obtuse at the apex, a few widely acute or apiculate, markedly concave, sometimes cucullate; base narrowed and decurrent; margins entire, plane or revolute in the lower ⅓; costa slender, greenish, ending below the apex; upper leaf cells rhomboidal to hexagonal, becoming rectangular below, 17–23 μ wide, rather thin walled and often pitted; marginal cells oblong to linear not or slightly thick walled, usually green, but not forming a conspicuous border, disappearing toward the apex. Branched green or brownish propagula frequent in the axils of the leaves. Dioicous. Seta 2–3 cm long, reddish; capsules mostly pendent, elongate-pyriform, 3–4 mm long, yellowish brown, neck rather thick, shorter than the spore sac, when dry $\pm$ contracted under the medium sized mouth, neck shrunken; lid convex-mammillose; peristome teeth light yellow brown, lanceolate from a $\pm$ oblong base, slight-acuminate; basal membrane of endostome high; segments narrow, keeled, and widely perforated down the middle; cilia long, $\pm$ nodulose to subappendiculate, often in pairs. Spores 10–14 μ. Plate 78, figs. 8–14.

19.90 On wet or damp soil and humus.

19.91 Europe and Asia. Arctic America and Greenland, British Columbia. southward to New Jersey, Pennsylvania, Wisconsin, Utah.

19.92 **7. Bryum weigelii** Spreng. Plants in loose tufts, light green, often darker on drying. Stems green to yellowish green, mostly simple, branching by slender innovations, 1–3 cm tall; rhizoids few to fairly dense at the base. Leaves few and distant, erect-patent to patent when moist, strongly shrunken and contorted when dry, ovate to ovate-lanceolate, acute to shortly acuminate, 1–2.5 mm long, the lower ones smaller and obtuse; margins entire, flat or recurved in the lower ⅓: base narrowed and very longly and broadly decurrent; costa slender, yellowish green, ending just below the apex, percurrent or slightly excurrent; upper leaf

---

Plate 78. 1–7. Bryum arcticum. 1. Habit sketches, X.4. 2. A lower leaf. 3. Two typical upper leaves, X8. 4. Upper medial leaf cells, X120. 5. Upper marginal leaf cells, X124. 6. Capsules, X8. 7. Portion of peristome showing slender segments and rudimentary cilia, X70.

8–14. Bryum tortifolium. 8. Habit sketches, X.4. 9. Dry and moist habit sketches, X2. 10. Two basal stem leaves. 11. Three typical upper and comal leaves, X8. 12. Upper medial leaf cells, X120. 13. Upper marginal cells, X120. 14. A typical capsule, X8.

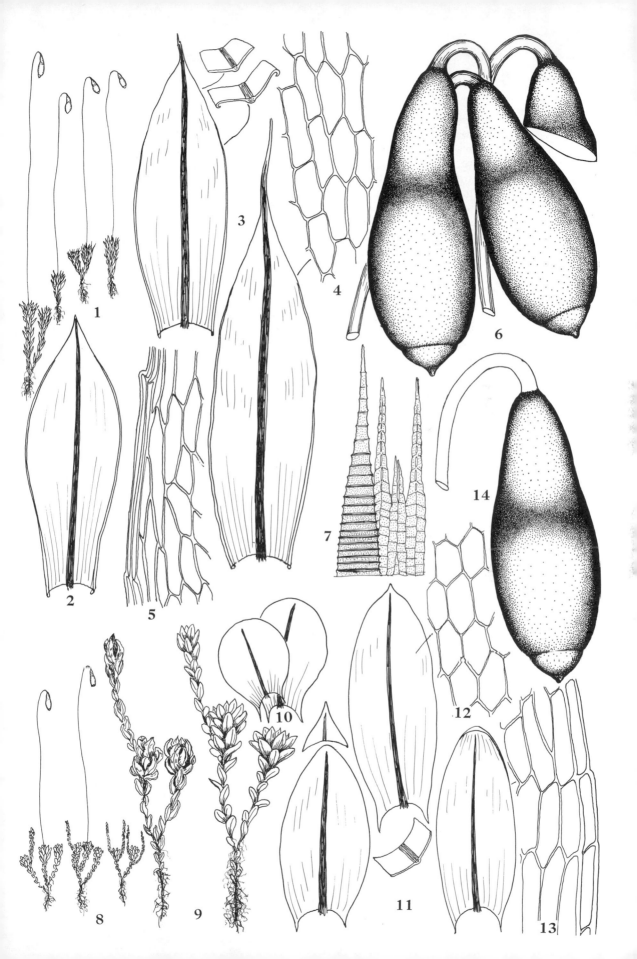

cells variable, shortly to longly rhomboidal, hexagonal, or somewhat rectangular, thin walled and sometimes slightly pitted, 17–22(27) μ wide; marginal cells narrower, linear at the extreme margin and rather thin walled and green, not forming a very conspicuous border; basal cells rectangular. Dioicous, rarely fruiting. Seta 1.5–3 cm long, reddish; capsules nodding to pendulous, 1.5–3 mm long, obovate-pyriform to elongate pyriform, straight, yellowish brown, the neck short and broad, mouth rather large; ± contracted under the mouth when dry, neck shrunken; lid convex-mammillose, annulus large; peristome teeth yellowish, narrowly lanceolate from a slightly oblong base; basal membrane of endostome high, segments slender, perforated down the middle; cilia filiform, appendiculate, finely papillose. Spores 10–12 μ.

19.93   On wet or damp soil, usually in shady places.

19.94   Europe and Asia. Across northern Canada, southward to the New England states, New York, the Great Lakes region, Colorado, Utah, California.

19.95   Frequent at high elevations but often overlooked because it tends to be scattered among other mosses and rarely fruits. It is distinctive because of leaves contorted when dry and long-decurrent leaves with flat weakly bordered margins. Tall sterile forms of *B. pseudotriquetrum* often have long decurrent leaves which are much stouter and show a strong border and revolute margins.

19.96   **8. Bryum turbinatum** (Hedw.) Turn. Plants variable, densely to loosely tufted, slender and lax to stout and firm, usually light green but varying to yellowish green or dark green, often pale and tinted with pink or red when growing in very wet sunny places. Stems erect to ascending, thick and fleshy to slender and weak, simple or branched from the base, green, often becoming reddish with age, 1–2 cm tall in fertile forms, often reaching 4–5 cm in some sterile forms; rhizoids often dense at the base. Leaves dense above, usually forming a terminal rosette in fertile plants, fewer and widely spaced in sterile ones, erect-patent to patent or sometimes spreading when moist, appressed to somewhat open and often slightly contorted when dry, broadly ovate to ovate-lanceolate, ± concave, acute to briefly acuminate, 1.5–2(2.5) mm long, the lower ones smaller and often obtuse, not or only slightly decurrent and then narrowly so; margins often slightly serrulate near the apex, plane throughout or revolute in the lower ½; costa stout, percurrent to shortly excurrent, often ending below the apex in the lower leaves; upper cells rhomboidal to hexagonal, thin walled, variable in size in different plants, mostly 17–22 μ wide, ranging upward to 34 μ wide in broad-leaved plants; marginal cells becoming linear, thick walled but not forming a conspicuous border, and less strongly differentiated toward the apex. Dioicous. Seta 2–4 cm long, reddish; capsules mostly pendulous, yellowish brown when mature, 2–3(3.5) mm long, obovate to pyriform, straight, the spore sac short and thick, the neck about as long, narrowing rapidly to the seta, when dry contracted under the rather large mouth; lid convex mammillose; annulus large; peristome teeth yellowish throughout or sometimes yellowish brown at the base, pale above narrowly triangular-lanceolate, the base slightly if at all differentiated; basal membrane of the endostome high, segments keeled, widely perforated below the very slender apex; cilia 2–3, slightly shorter than the segments, ± appendiculate, sometimes conspicuously so, sometimes only strongly nodulose and frequently united at the joints; spores small, 10–14 μ.

19.97   On wet soil and rocks, especially on banks, in seepage areas, dripping cliffs, frequently emergent in water, less frequently on damp soil away from water. In mountains of our region.

19.98   Europe and Asia. Alaska, across northern Canada, southward in the western states to New Mexico, Arizona, Nevada, and California.

19.99   Abundant locally. The weakly bordered flat leaf margins, shortly excurrent or percurrent costa and the light, yellow-brown, obovate to pyriform capsules with yellowish teeth are distinctive features. In some elongated sterile stems, the leaves may be long and narrowly decurrent because of a wing formed of linear cells 1–3 cells wide. In sterile plants the leaves are sometimes broadly ovate and concave with cells much shorter and wider than usual. In some plants all the leaves are entire at the apex, and in many the basal leaves are short, broad, very concave, or cucullate, obtuse, and apiculate. In a few plants most of the leaves are quite blunt. Plants growing in water in open sunny places may be pale green with pink or red tinges, usually soft and fleshy or slender and lax, strongly shrivelling when dried.

19.100   **9. Bryum pseudotriquetrum** (Hedw.) Schwaegr. Plants medium sized to robust, when well developed forming deep, dense, dark green tufts, often tinged with red, the lower parts reddish. Stems branched, short to much elongated, 1–6 cm tall or more, in sterile forms usually robust and tall, fertile plants usually shorter, red with densely interwoven rhizoids on the lower parts. Leaves variable, typically ovate-lanceolate, rather broad in the upper part, acute to briefly acuminate, varying to narrowly ovate-lanceolate or lanceolate and more narrowly tapering to a slender apex, or in some forms, broadly ovate, slightly to strongly decurrent, especially in tall sterile forms; patent when moist, ± open and irregularly contorted when dry; margins strongly revolute to the apex or nearly so, entirely to slightly serrulate at the apex; costa stout, yellowish brown, becoming reddish from the base upward with age, typically percurrent but sometimes shortly to longly excurrent, especially in the comal leaves; upper cells rhomboidal-hexagonal, 12–15 μ wide, fairly thick walled, ± pitted; marginal cells linear, thick walled, forming a strong border to the apex. Synoicous or dioicous. Seta straight or geniculate below, red to dark purplish, 2–5 cm long; capsules inclined to pendulous, symmetric, elongate-pyriform to subclavate or nearly cylindrical, 2.5–6 mm long, yellowish brown or tan when mature, becoming darker and often reddish with age, ± contracted under the mouth when dry; neck about as long as the spore sac or shorter, well differentiated to thickish and not well set off; mouth rather large; lid low to high convex, mammillose or shortly apiculate; peristome teeth strong, yellowish brown, often reddish at the base, lanceolate from a rather broadly oblong base, rapidly narrowed above to a slender yellowish or hyaline apex; basal membrane of endostome high, segments rather broad below, tapering to a very slender tip, widely perforated down the middle; cilia 2–3, appendiculate. Spores 10–14 μ. Plate 79, figs. 1–6.

19.101   On damp or wet soil, humus, rock, or rotten wood of many habitats.

19.102   Widely distributed throughout Europe and Asia, Canada and the United States.

19.103   Typical forms of fruiting specimens and large sterile forms are easily identified, but many short specimens are so much like *B. creberrimum* or *B. pallescens* that they produce difficulty in identification. Dixon, in *A Student's Handbook of British Mosses* 2d ed., treats the two latter plants as subspecies of *B. pseudotriquetrum*. Were it not for the fact that *B. creberrimum* is our commonest species of *Bryum*, I should be inclined to treat it as a synonym.

19.104   **10. Bryum creberrimum** Tayl. Plants in short tufts, green above, brownish or reddish brown below. Stems short, usually red, up to 1 cm tall, mostly with a few branches. Leaves ovate-lanceolate to triangular-lanceolate, 2–2.5 mm long, narrowly acute to slenderly acuminate, usually forming terminal rosettes, bright green, when dry appressed, the tips often yellowish and commonly spirally twisted; margins revolute to the apex or nearly so, entire to slightly toothed at the apex, base usually broad, slightly or not decurrent, often reddish; costa rather stout, shortly to rather longly excurrent, smooth or somewhat toothed, yellowish green becoming reddish from the base upward with age; upper leaf cells fairly thick walled but usually not at all pitted, rhomboidal to hexagonal, 10–15 μ wide, somewhat longer in the apex; marginal cells linear and thick walled, forming a distinct border to the apex. Synoicous, fruiting abundantly. Seta straight or geniculate below, 2–3(4) cm long, reddish brown; capsules nodding to pendulous, rich yellowish brown, becoming darker with age, 2–3.5 mm long, elongate-pyriform with the neck shorter than spore sac, usually well set off, when dry appearing quite slender, contracted below the mouth and shrunken at the neck; mouth rather large; lid convex-mammillose; peristome teeth yellow brown, often darker at the insertion, lanceolate from a ± oblong base, the apex acuminate and paler; basal membrane of endostome high; segments rather broad, keeled, and widely perforated down the middle; cilia 2–3, appendiculate. Spores 12–15 μ. Plate 79, figs. 7–12.

Plate 79. 1–6. Bryum pseudotriquetrum. 1. Habit sketches, X.4. 2. Portion of shoot showing contorted leaves, X2. 3. Portion of stem showing decurrent leaves in robust forms, X4. 4. Leaves from four different specimens showing variation in shape and extent of costa, X8. 5. Apex of leaf of typical robust form, X120. 6. Capsule, X8.

7–12. Bryum creberrimum. 7. Habit sketches, X.4. 8. Portion of shoot showing longitudinally folded and ± imbricated lower leaves and frequently spirally twisted comal leaves, X8. 9. Two typical leaves, X8. 10. Upper medial leaf cells, X120. 11. Apex of leaf, X120. 12. Capsules moist and dry, X8.

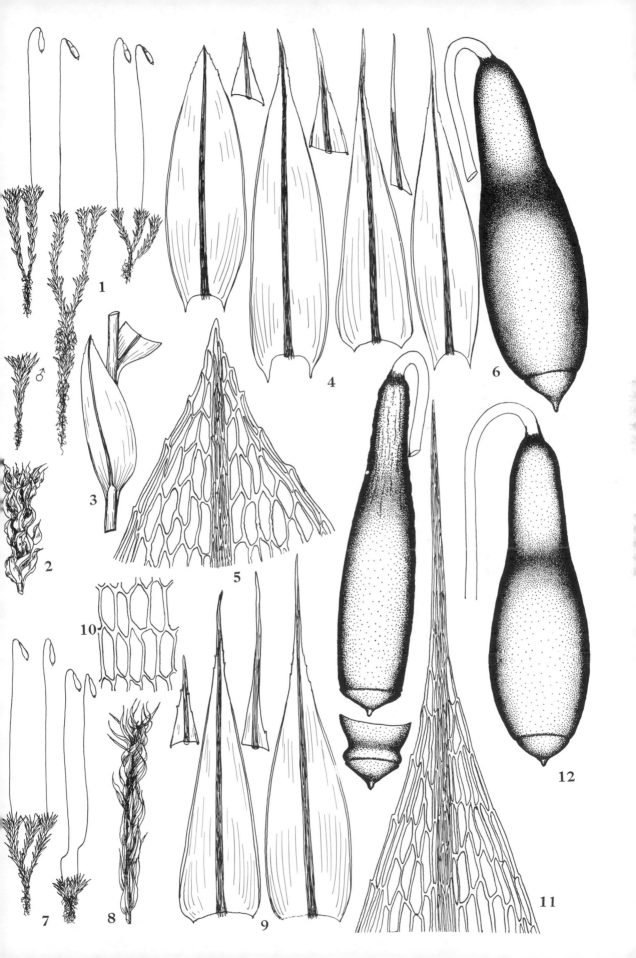

19.105   On damp or wet soil, rocks, humus, and rotten wood.

19.106   Widely distributed in Europe, Asia, Australia, and New Zealand, the United States, and far northward into Canada and Alaska.

19.107   **11. Bryum pallescens** Schleich. ex Schwaegr. Plants related to *B. creberrimum,* differing only in the following respects: plants in very compact sods and cushions, green to yellowish green. Stems abundantly branched with numerous short innovations, only the comal leaves of which are green, yellowish brown to reddish below and very densely interwoven with rhizoids, 1–3(5) cm tall; autoicous. Plate 80, figs. 6–7.

19.108   On wet and dry soil and rocks, in the mountains of our region.

19.109   Throughout the western United States and northward across Canada, in the East extending to the New England states and Ohio.

19.110   Common in our region. Short plants, especially if not densely branched, resemble *B. pseudotriquetrum* and *B. creberrimum* so closely that it may be difficult to distinguish them. Well-developed, much branched, typical specimens in very dense cushions are easily identified and it is usually easy to demonstrate the autoicous habit. Much care will need to be exercised in separating the shoots to make certain that some of the numerous branches are not broken off, or that closely adhering stems of a separate shoot are not taken to be part of only one plant.

19.111   **12. Bryum lonchocaulon** C. Muell. Plants mostly short and densely tufted, yellowish green. Stems less than 1 cm tall, erect, red with short branches, cohering because of copious brown rhizoids. Leaves rather small, the blades 1.3–2.5 mm long, ovate- to triangular-lanceolate, slenderly acuminate, not decurrent; costa yellowish or brownish, often red below, long excurrent, sometimes becoming half the length of the blade or longer, usually spinulose to the tip; margins strongly revolute to near the slightly toothed apex, strongly bordered with linear thick-walled cells; upper cells rhomboidal to hexagonal, 10–16 μ wide, often becoming sublinear in the apex. Synoicous. Fruit frequent; seta 1.5–4(6) cm long, straight or geniculate below, reddish; capsules 2–4(5) mm long, inclined to pendent, elongate-pyriform, yellowish brown, $\pm$ contracted below the mouth when dry, the neck rather thick, mostly less than half the length of the spore sac but sometimes equalling it and appearing quite long, shrunken when dry; lid conic to mammillate, rather large; peristome teeth oblong-lanceolate, abruptly narrowed above to slender apices, yellowish brown, darker at base, finely papillose; endostome pale yellowish, finely papillose, basal membrane high; segments broad and

---

Plate 80. **1–5. Bryum caespiticium.** 1. Habit sketches, X.4. 2. Three leaves, X8. 3. Upper medial and marginal cells, X120. 4. Leaf apex and apical cells, X120. 5. Capsules moist and dry, X8.

6–7. Bryum pallescens. 6. Habit sketches showing dense branching, X.4. 7. Portion of shoot dissected to show autoicous inflorescence, X4.

8–10 Bryum lonchocaulon. 8. Habit sketch, X.4. 9. Typical leaves, X8. 10. Upper medial leaf cells, X120.

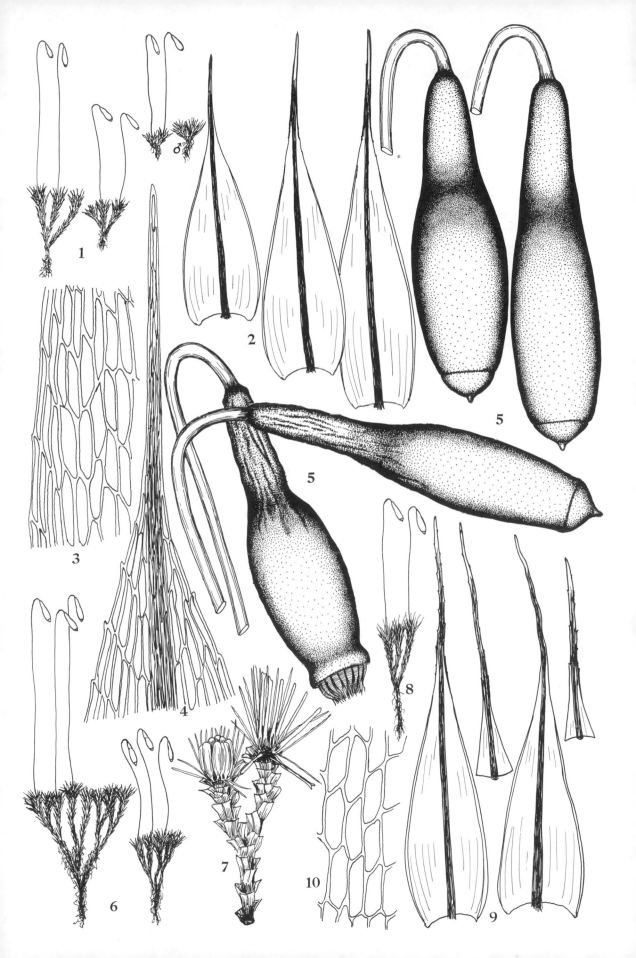

keeled, tapering to slender apices, widely perforated, cilia 2–3 strongly appendiculate. Spores 12–16 μ, brownish, finely papillose. Plate 80, figs. 8–10.

19.112 On damp soil or rocks, usually in shade, often on rather dry mountain sides.

19.113 Mostly western, in the mountains, southern Canada to New Mexico, westward to California.

19.114 Apparently not common in Utah. The very long excurrent costa (usually ⅓–½ the length of the blade), the small size of the plant, and the synoicous inflorescence make this plant easily identified. It resembles small forms of *B. caespiticium* and *B. creberrimum*.

19.115 **13. Bryum caespiticium** Hedw. Plants in short, dense tufts, usually less than 1 cm tall but sometimes becoming taller in wet places, green to yellowish green. Stems red, moderately branched, cohering below with interwoven brownish rhizoids. Leaves usually bright green, shortly to longly ovate-lanceolate, mostly slenderly acuminate, blades 2–3 mm long, the comal leaves patent in a dense rosette, the lower ones less crowded and smaller, ± imbricate when dry; costa long excurrent, to a smooth or slightly toothed yellowish awn; margins entire or slightly toothed at the apex, ± strongly revolute, often plane near the apex, not strongly bordered with linear thick-walled cells; upper cells elongate-rhomboidal to hexagonal, 9–12 μ wide, longer and narrower at the apex, shorter and broader at the base. Dioicous. Frequently fruiting; seta 1–3 cm long, straight or slightly flexuous, red below, yellowish brown above; capsules inclined to pendulous, variable in shape and size, mostly elongate-pyriform but ranging from shortly obovate-pyriform to long clavate, 1.5–3(4) mm long, ± contracted below the mouth when dry, neck shorter than the spore sac, yellowish to yellowish brown; lid conic to mammillate; peristome teeth rather abruptly narrowed from an oblong base to slender apices, yellowish brown, darker below, finely papillose; endostome pale yellowish or hyaline, basal membrane high, segments broad and tapering to slender tips, keeled and widely perforated, smooth to low papillose throughout; cilia 2–3, strongly appendiculate. Spores 7–11 μ, light yellowish, smooth or nearly so. Plate 80, figs. 1–5.

19.116 Mostly on damp or rather dry soil; sometimes in wet places where it often grows taller than usual.

19.117 Widely distributed in the United States and northward into Canada. Europe, Asia, North Africa, Argentina, Chile, Australia and New Zealand.

19.118 Common in Utah where it is found on dry hillsides, particularly around the edges of shrubby thickets and local open places, also on banks at the bases of rocks and trees. The traits stressed in the key together with the small spores and rather dry habitat are distinctive.

19.119 **14. Bryum capillare** Hedw. Plants densely tufted or scattered among other mosses, dark green above, brown to reddish brown below. Stems usually not over 1 cm tall, sparingly branched, often simple, green, becoming reddish with age; rhizoids reddish brown to purplish brown, often very dense. Leaves typically obovate to obovate-spatulate, broadest above the middle, acute to briefly acuminate, the tip often recurved or twisted, strongly crisped when dry, spreading to recurved when moist, the upper ones 2–3 mm long, usually forming a comal rosette, the lower ones progressively smaller and more widely spaced; costa ending below the apex to shortly excurrent; margins recurved below the middle or plane throughout, entire to slightly serrate at the apex; upper cells broadly hexagonal to rhomboidal, rather large, 17–30 x 40–60 μ, thin walled, becoming oblong at the base, narrower on the margins. Leaves varying to broadly ovate at one extreme and elliptic-lanceolate at the other extreme, the latter markedly narrowed to the base, when dry less crisped, $\pm$ shrunken and imbricated, when moist erect-patent; costa shortly to longly excurrent; margins revolute nearly to the apex. Sterile plants often bearing clusters of yellowish to reddish purple, filamentous, jointed and branched brood bodies in axils of leaves. Dioicous or sometimes synoicous. Seta $\pm$ flexuous or geniculate, 1–3 cm long, reddish and rather stout; capsules horizontal to inclined, clavate, usually incurved, mostly 3–4 mm long but variable, in some plants as little as 2 mm and in others as much as 5.5 mm, the neck usually shorter than the spore sac but sometimes longer, yellowish brown, when dry the neck wrinkled, the urn mostly shrunken throughout or sometimes contracted under the mouth; lid low conic to mammillate, bluntly tipped; peristome teeth light yellow brown below, paler above, papillose, narrowly lanceolate from an oblong base; segments from a high basal membrane, broad, strongly keeled and perforated, pale yellowish and papillose; cilia 2–3, appendiculate. Spores 8–12 μ, dark yellowish, finely roughened. Plate 81.

19.120 On moist shady soil, humus, bases of trees and rocks, mostly in our canyons and mountains.

19.121 Widely distributed throughout the world.

19.122 Typical specimens are distinctive, and even sterile material is easily recognized. In most of the present specimens the size of the upper leaf cells is near the lower range, being 16–22 μ wide, but all have the characteristic broadly hexagonal shape and thin walls.

19.123 Plants with elliptical, elliptical-lanceolate, or ovate-lanceolate leaves narrowing more or less gradually to the base have shortly to longly excurrent costae and margins plane-revolute well toward the apex; sometimes they have straight capsules. Plants with straight capsules and more or less imbricated dry leaves are sometimes referred to *B. obconicum*, while synoicous plants with straight leaves and curved capsules are sometimes referred to *B. torquescens*. The two latter variations resemble *B. pseudotriquetrum* but can be distinguished by narrower leaf bases and larger thin-walled leaf cells.

19.124 **15. Bryum miniatum** Lesq. Plants in dense, often deep tufts, green to dark green, often tinged with red or pink, brownish below. Stems erect and usually strict, rather thick and stout, reddish, simple or with erect branches; rhizoids usually few, not dense; shoots somewhat julaceous. Leaves erect and loosely imbricated to somewhat patent when moist, loosely imbricated when dry, ovate-oblong to oblong, the upper ones of sterile shoots often triangular-lanceolate, strongly concave, apex broadly rounded to bluntly acute; margins plane throughout, entire, not bordered; costa stout, yellowish green to brownish, ending abruptly shortly below the apex (the comal leaves of the previous season's growth are often very slenderly acute with the costa percurrent or very shortly excurrent); upper cells rhomboidal, 10–14 μ wide, the walls thick, without pits, 2–3 or as many as 6 rows of cells toward the margin becoming longer and narrower, linear on the extreme margin, but not thicker walled and not forming a distinct border. Then gradually becoming broader toward the base; only the extreme basal ones oblong. Dioicous. Fruit rare. Seta 2–2.5 cm long, flexuous, reddish, becoming darker with age, shiny; capsules inclined to pendent, yellowish brown sometimes becoming darker reddish brown, pyriform to clavate, 2.5–3(5) mm long with the neck shorter than the spore sac, tapering to the seta, when dry moderately shrunken, only slightly contracted under the mouth or not at all, the neck more strongly shrunken and wrinkled; lid conic-mammillate, darker reddish; annulus double to triple; peristome teeth well spaced at the base, yellowish brown except at the pale tips, suddenly narrowed from $\pm$ oblong base, or gradually narrowed from the base to the tips, joints close together, not very strong, but ventral lamellae strongly projecting, very finely papillose; endostome pale yellowish to hyaline, finely papillose, segments from a high basal membrane, quite narrow, keeled and strongly perforated; cilia 2, $\pm$ appendiculate. Spores 12–18 μ, yellowish brown, finely papillose. Plate 82, figs. 9–13.

19.125   On wet soil or rocks, usually along mountain brooks, frequently exposed to the sun.

19.126   British Columbia to California, inland to Montana and Utah. Davis County: Wasatch Mountains, Farmington Canyon at Halfway Canyon, 6,500 ft.

19.127   This is a distinctive species which may be identified in the sterile state by the leaves and somewhat julaceous shoots of soft yet firm texture. The tips of the shoots are usually tinted some shade of red, although plants growing in shaded places may show no added coloration. It is curious that specimens from California, Oregon, Washington, and Utah all show the previous season's stems with some or many of the upper leaves much narrower and more narrowly acute, and the costae percur-

---

Plate 81. Bryum capillare. 1. Habit sketches of typical broad-leaved form, X.4. 2. Portion of shoot showing dry state, X2. 3. Habit sketches of narrow-leaved forms, X.4. 4. Portion of shoot showing dry state of same. 5. Three typical leaves X8, 6. Three leaves of narrow-leaved form, X8. 7. Two leaves of unusually broad-leaved form, X8. 8–9. Two typical leaf apices and upper cells, X120. 10. Apex of leaf with excurrent costa, X120. 11. Three capsules, X8. 12. Portion of shoot dissected to show clusters of branched propagulae in axils of leaves, X4. 13. Detail of propagulae, X70.

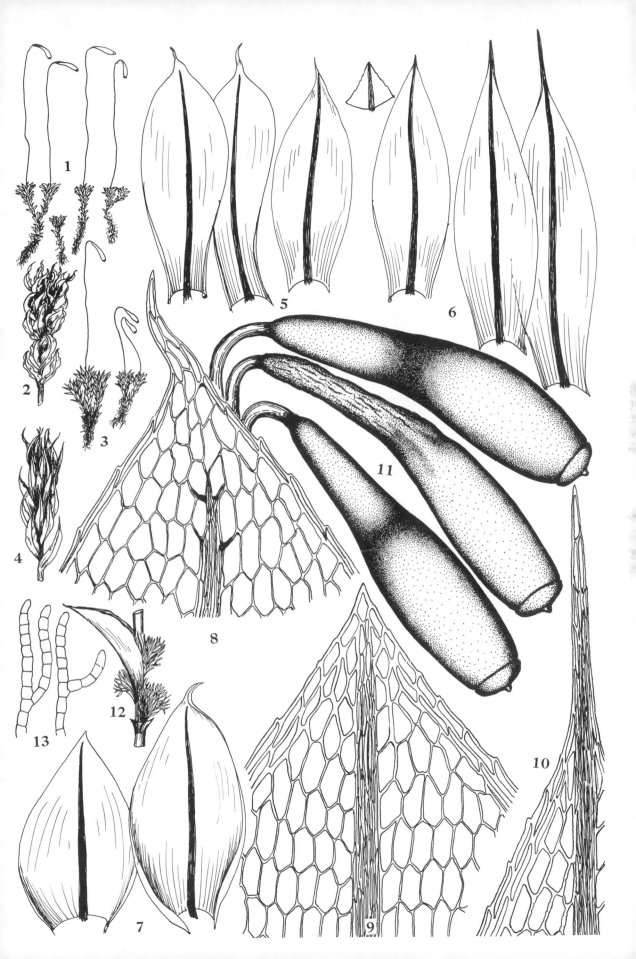

rent to very shortly excurrent. Thus, the general appearance of the previous season's growth may contrast quite strongly with the more or less julaceous habit of the current season's shoots.

19.128   **16. Bryum bicolor** Dicks. Plants in low compact tufts or ± scattered, green to brownish green above, brownish below. Stems short, mostly less than 5 mm tall, reddish, slender and branched; rhizoids reddish, few to abundant. Stem leaves erect-patent when moist, closely imbricated when dry, ovate-acuminate, blades 0.7–1 mm long, the lower ones smaller and often scale-like, comal leaves larger, ovate-acuminate to ovate-lanceolate, ranging up to 1.8 mm long; costa percurrent to rather longly excurrent, green to greenish brown, becoming reddish with age; margins plane throughout to ± revolute in the lower part, occasionally well toward the apex, entire, not distinctly bordered; upper leaf cells usually elongate-rhomboidal to hexagonal, 9–15 μ wide, the walls thick, unpitted, shorter and thin walled in plants infiltrated with fine soil, narrower and longer on the margins but not forming a conspicuous border, in the base becoming wider, rectangular. Dioicous. Seta straight to slightly flexuous, reddish, 1–1.5 cm long; capsules horizontal to pendulous, shortly oblong-ellipsoidal to obovate, rarely subglobose, small, 1–2 mm long with the neck short and broadly rounded to the seta, often not externally differentiated, not or slightly contracted below the mouth when dry but the neck usually strongly shrunken, yellowish brown, becoming dark reddish at maturity; lid conic to mammillate, darker red and shiny; annulus conspicuous, or 3–4 rows of cells; peristome teeth tapering rather abruptly from a ± oblong base, yellowish brown below, pale above, very finely papillose; endostome pale yellowish, finely papillose, basal membrane high; segments keeled and widely perforated; cilia 2, appendiculate. Spores 8–12 μ, yellowish, finely punctate. Plate 82, figs. 1–8.

19.129   On damp or moist soil. Not common.

19.130   Europe, Asia and North Africa. More or less throughout the United States and southern Canada. Salt Lake and Daggett Counties.

19.131   On mildly saline soils around the bases of greasewood and shadscale bushes west of Salt Lake City in Jordan Valley, mostly sterile but occasionally well fruited. Occurrence through a long span in elevation from the lowlands to Spirit Lake, Uinta Mountains, at 10,700 ft. does not seem to alter the main traits of this moss, although the upper and perichaetial leaves of plants from the highest locality are larger and longer. The short thick capsules with unusually short rounded necks are especially distinctive.

Plate 82.   1–8. Bryum bicolor. 1. Habit sketches, X.4. 2. Lower leaves of small plants. 3. Upper and perichaetial leaves of same, X8. 4–5. Lower and upper leaves of larger form, X8. 6. Leaf apex and upper leaf cells, X120. 7–8. Four capsules, X8.

9–13. Bryum miniatum. 9. Habit of fertile plants, X.4. 10. Tall sterile plant, X.4. 11. Five leaves showing variation in shape and apices, X8. 12. Two typical leaf apices and upper leaf cells, X120. 13. Two capsules, X8.

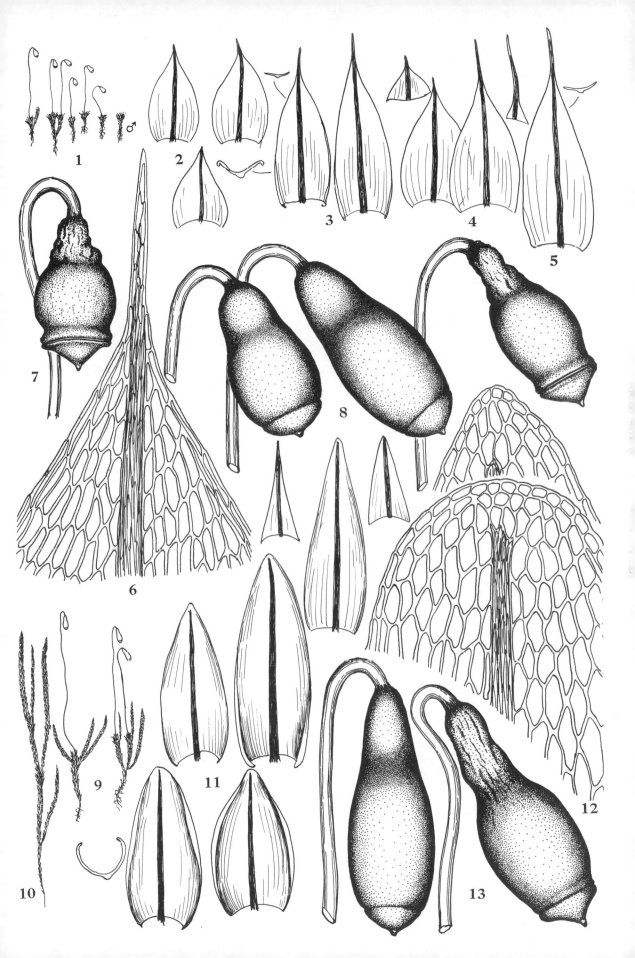

19.132 **17. Bryum gemmiparum** De Not., Cronac. Plants in loose or dense tufts, usually light green above, brownish to purplish brown below. Stems simple or branched from high up the main axis, mostly short, but often tall, 0.5–3 cm tall; rhizoids few to moderately dense. Leaves usually light green but varying to dark green, ovate, ovate-lanceolate, lanceolate, or oblong, concave-keeled, the margins ± evenly tapering upward from the base or arching inward from a broader upper part, narrowly to widely acute, blunt or sometimes narrowly obtuse at the apex, not at all acuminate, about 2 mm long, the lower ones shorter; costa strong, percurrent or ending shortly below the apex, green to yellowish green becoming brownish with age, rarely reddish except in leaves of the previous season's growth or in plants infiltrated with fine soil or calcium deposit; margins plane throughout or revolute in the lower half, erect, entire, or very vaguely dentate at the apex, inconspicuously to quite prominently bordered in the lower half; upper leaf cells rhomboidal to hexagonal, 12–20 μ wide, thin to thick walled, not pitted, 1 to several rows toward the margins becoming longer and narrower, usually thicker walled and often darker forming an indistinct to fairly distinct border below, fading toward the apex; basal cells slightly wider, usually rectangular but often not much differentiated. Dioicous. Seta variable, straight or flexuous, usually yellowish above, becoming reddish below; 1.5–4 cm long; capsules 2–4 mm long, elongate pyriform or subclavate straight or very slightly curved inward, yellowish to dark reddish brown according to age and habitat; neck longer or slightly shorter than the spore sac, tapering to the seta, when dry the urn smooth or lightly rugulose, rarely contracted under the mouth, neck usually strongly shrunken and wrinkled; annulus double; lid conic to mammillate, the tip sometimes very blunt and low; peristome teeth yellow brown, mostly narrowly triangular-lanceolate but more gradually tapered above, finely and densely papillose below; endostome pale yellowish with fine scattered papillae, basal membrane high; segments rather short, quite narrow, keeled, and moderately widely perforated; cilia mostly 2, rarely 3, sometimes united by their tips, usually appendiculate, sometimes merely nodulose. Spores 15–21 μ, yellowish, finely papillose. Plate 83, figs. 1–6.

19.133 On wet soil and rocks bearing calcium.

19.134 Mostly in eastern and southern Utah. Of scattered distribution, mainly western; Southern Europe, Newfoundland, New Jersey, British Columbia to California, Montana to Arizona, New Mexico, Colorado, Oklahoma.

19.135 A distinctive moss frequent and locally abundant along the Green and

---

Plate 83. **1–6. Bryum gemmiparum.** 1. Habit sketches, X.4. 2. Portion of shoot showing stance of leaves when moist, X4. 3. Five leaves showing various shapes, X8. 4. Four leaf apices, X120. 5. Upper and marginal leaf cells, X120. 6. Two capsules, X8.

7–11. Bryum argenteum. 7. Habit sketches, X.4. 8. Four leaves, X8. 9. Leaf apex, X120. 10. Upper chlorophyllose cells, X120. 11. Two capsules, X8.

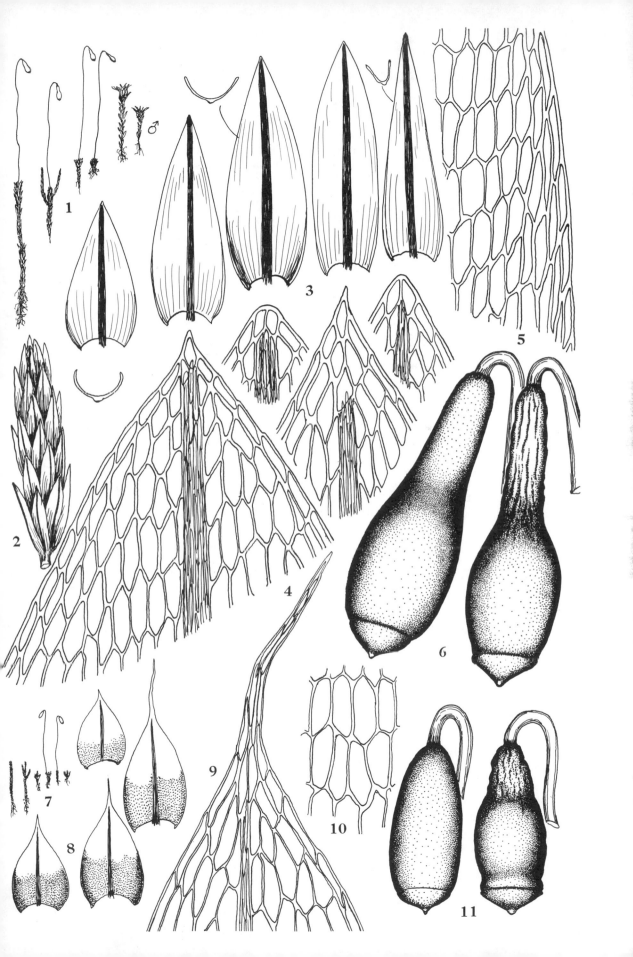

Colorado rivers and their tributaries and also across southern Utah. Although dioicous, it fruits quite freely in our region. It is favored by wet sandy soil or crevices of wet calcareous sandstone. It persists in mildly saline soil and is often encrusted with calcium sulphate which does not seem to have any injurious effect. Many plants of our region show considerable red in the stems and occasionally in the costa. The leaves of the previous season's growth commonly become ferruginous. The leaves are often described as obtuse, but this is usually true of some of them. In all of the local collections, all or most of the leaves are bluntly to sharply acute. This species intergrades with *B. alpinum,* which has a more northerly range and longer, narrower, more lanceolate leaves with red in the costa and leaf base, margins more strongly bordered and revolute higher up, and the upper cells longer, about 12 μ wide.

19.136 **18. Bryum argenteum** Hedw. Small plants densely to loosely tufted, sometimes scattered, whitish to light frosty green above, yellowish to brownish below. Stems erect, mostly less than 5 mm tall, rarely more than 1 cm, simple or bearing short, erect, deciduous branches, ± flexuous, reddish below, soft and tender; rhizoids usually few at the base. Leaves crowded, closely imbricated both wet and dry, the upper half hyaline, ovate-acuminate, shortly to longly tapering to a slender tip, sometimes cuspidate, very concave, the main portion of the blade 0.5–1 mm long; costa ending below the apex, or excurrent and forming a ± cuspidate point in some or most leaves of var. *lanatum;* margins entire, plane throughout or recurved near the base, not at all bordered; upper leaf cells colorless, elongate-rhomboidal to hexagonal, usually thin walled with thickened corners, 12–30 μ wide, lower cells chlorophyllose, similar in shape and size but the walls usually thicker, becoming rectangular at the base. Dioicous. Fruit rare; seta about 1 cm long, reddish; capsules yellowish brown, becoming dark reddish with age, small and pendulous, 1–1.5 mm long, oblong, when dry not much changed to variably wrinkled, the neck often shrunken and the urn sometimes rather strongly contracted under the mouth; the neck region not externally differentiated, broadly rounded to the seta; lid rather large, conic to mammillate, darker and shiny; annulus double; peristome teeth triangular-lanceolate, yellowish brown, darker at the base, finely papillose; endostome pale yellowish, finely papillose, the basal membrane rather short; segments broad and widely perforated; cilia appendiculate. Spores 14–18 μ, yellowish and smooth. Plate 83, figs. 7–11.

19.137 On dry or moist soil, rocks, walls, and cracks in cement.

19.138 Worldwide distribution.

19.139 The plants are usually very short but sometimes they are taller and form compact cushions or sods. They are nearly always white to pale frosty green on the surface. Other species may simulate the habit and color but they are larger and, in spite of paleness, have leaves chlorophyllose throughout. The var. *lanatum* (P. Beauv.) is not well delimited as the costa is not always excurrent in all leaves and is variable in different plants.

19.140   **19. Bryum sandbergii** Holz. Plants loosely tufted or scattered, light green. Stems 1–3 cm tall, erect, simple, quite strict, green above, reddish to purplish below; rhizoids confined to the base. Leaves 4–6 mm long, suddenly becoming smaller, scale-like and distant below the middle of the stem or sometimes below the comal rosette, mostly obovate to obovate-spatulate, sometimes ovate to elliptic-obovate, spreading, the comal ones in a rosette, when dry loosely open and undulate, not much contorted; apex narrowly to broadly acute, sometimes slightly acuminate or briefly mucronate, slightly to strongly decurrent at the base; lamina flattish above, rather strongly incurved at the base; costa slender, ending slightly below the apex, green or yellowish, with age becoming reddish brown from the base upward; margins plane, sometimes recurved at the base, ± strongly serrate in the upper half or nearly to the base, occasionally entire or nearly so, distinctly bordered with 2–3 rows of abruptly linear thick-walled cells; upper leaf cells large, 35–50 μ wide, 90–140 μ long, mostly elongate-hexagonal, thin walled without pits, becoming longer and rectangular in the base. Dioicous. Fruit rare. Seta stout, yellowish, becoming reddish brown and shiny from the base upwards with age, 3–5 cm long; capsules 5–7 mm long, inclined to horizontal, cylindrical, usually slightly curved, light yellowish brown, the neck much shorter than the long spore sac, when dry widely contracted below the mouth and finely wrinkled, the neck strongly longitudinally wrinkled or furrowed; mouth wide; annulus double; lid low conic-convex or mammillate, dull reddish; peristome teeth light yellowish brown throughout, gradually tapering upwards, often slightly acuminate, the lower joints very short and close together, finely papillose throughout; endostome pale yellowish, finely and very densely papillose throughout; basal membrane high; segments broad and keeled, shorter than the teeth, widely perforated; cilia 3–4, very slender, nodulose, appendages lacking. Spores 12–18 μ, yellowish brown, finely papillose. Plate 84.

19.141   On rather dry soil and humus in shady places in the mountains of Utah.

19.142   British Columbia to northern California, eastward to Montana, Wyoming and Utah.

19.143   At first sight this large moss may be mistaken for a *Mnium*, but the longer leaf cells will immediately identify it. Some bryologists segregate it as a separate monotypic genus under the name of *Roellia lucida* Kindb.

19.144   The male plants have practically all the lower portion of the stem naked with only the perigonium crowning the summit.

5. MNIUM Hedw.

19.145   Plants in loose tufts or loosely spreading mats, green above, brownish below. Stems mostly simple, the fertile ones erect, the sterile ones often becoming much elongated, prostrate, and stoloniform, in cross section showing a large central strand, a cortex of large thick-walled ± colored cells and an outer rind of small very thick-walled reddish cells; rhizoids reddish brown and papillose. Leaves variously obovate, oval, oval-oblong or oblong-lanceolate, broadly rounded, acute to briefly acuminate at the apex, 2–7 mm long, small and distant below, dense above, ± spreading or recurved and forming a comal rosette in erect stems, distant and often appearing to be ± in 2 rows, becoming smaller toward the ends of the prostrate stems; margins plane, entire to coarsely toothed, with or without a border of much narrower cells; costa ending below the apex, percurrent to shortly excurrent; upper cells rhomboidal, hexagonal, oval or rounded, sometimes thickened in the angles; basal cells variously elongated. Synoicous or dioicous. Male plants erect with a ± conspicuous, discoid, colored perigonium with a rosette of large spreading perigonial leaves. Sporophytes single or rarely several from the same perichaetium. Setae long; capsules horizontal to pendulous, oval to oblong, neck very short, often not differentiated, rather thin walled; stomata immersed in the neck; annulus present; lid convex or conic, mammillose to rostrate; peristome double, endostome from a high basal membrane, segments free, cilia present. Spores globose. Calyptra cucullate.

19.146 Mnium is an ancient Greek name believed to have been applied to a true moss but it is not recorded in any of the known Greek or Roman literature. It was first used for a bryophyte by Dillenium in 1718 and established as a genus of mosses by Linnaeus in 1753.

19.147   1. Leaves acute, acuminate, or apiculate from a rounded apex; margins bordered with narrow cells, mostly strong toothed, but sometimes nearly entire

    2. Leaf border not strongly differentiated, the teeth weak and blunt, sometimes lacking

      3. Leaf cells quadrate to shortly oblong, the angles rounded and thickened, ± in longitudinal rows, 17–36 μ wide, not uniform .... 1. *M. blyttii*   19.149

      3. Leaf cells rhomboidal, up to 20 x 50 μ, the long axis extending obliquely from the costa to margin, thick walled and pitted .... 2. *M. arizonicum*   19.153

    2. Leaf border strong, teeth usually strong but sometimes blunt or lacking

      4. Teeth (at least some) in pairs

        5. Plants dioicous

          6. Leaf cells large, up to 20 x 50 μ, rhomboidal, the long axis extending obliquely from the costa to margin, thick walled

---

Plate 84. Bryum sandbergii. 1. Habit sketches, X.4. 2. Perigonial head dissected to show numerous antheridia in axils of inner perigonial leaves, X4. 3. Three stem leaves, X8. 4. Leaf apex, X120. 5. Upper leaf cells showing narrow distinct border, X120. 6. Three capsules, X8.

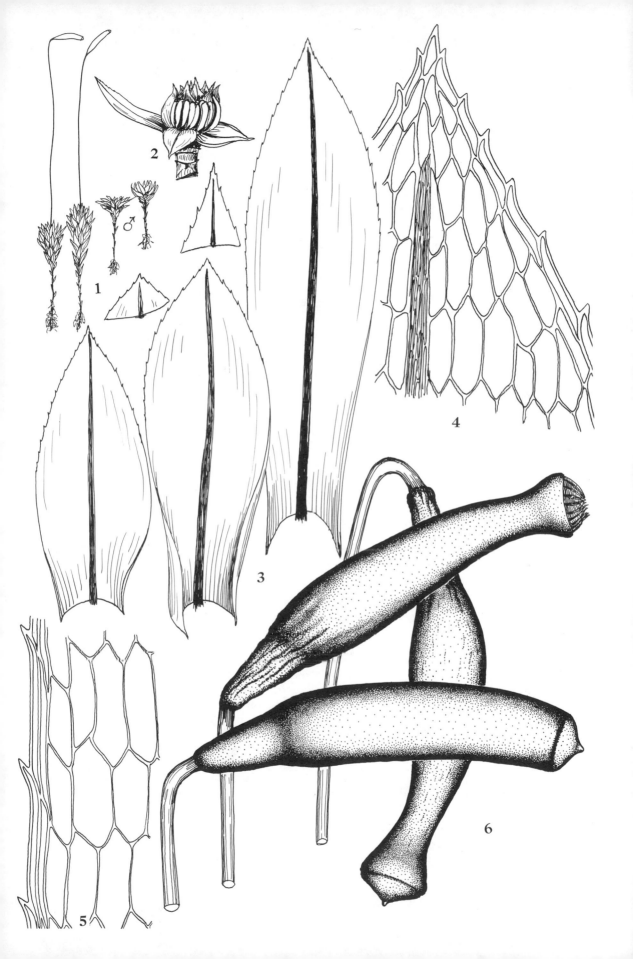

and pitted; marginal teeth both single and double ....
.... 2. *M. arizonicum* 19.153

6. Leaf cells smaller, ± isodiametric, angular, the angles **not**
thickened, 14–20 ±, not in rows ....
.... 4. *M. orthorhynchum* 19.161

5. Plants synoicous: leaf cell quite uniform, 25–35 μ in **longest**
diameter, quadrate-rounded to oval with thickened angles, ±
in longitudinal rows .... 3. *M. marginatum* 19.157

4. Teeth single throughout (sometimes lacking in *M. affine*)

7. Plants synoicous

8. Leaves acute to shortly acuminate; margins toothed only **in**
the upper ½–⅔; upper cells 15–25 μ in longest diameter,
rounded to oval hexagonal, quite variable in shape, not in
rows, thick walled, not pitted, angles thickened; capsules
single .... 5. *M. cuspidatum* 19.165

8. Leaves broadly rounded, abruptly short, cuspidate at the
apex; margins toothed to the base; upper cells widely variable, the medial ones 25–37 x 34–60 μ, rounded hexagonal,
not in vertical rows, walls rather thick, pitted, the angles
thickened considerably; capsules often 2–3 from same perichaetium .... 6. *M. medium* 19.169

7. Plants dioicous; leaf cells hexagonal to rounded hexagonal, **the**
medial 27–34 x 34–58 μ, walls thin or moderately thick, **pitted,**
rather angular, the angles slightly thickened; marginal teeth
of 1–3 cells, often short and blunt or entirely lacking ....
.... 7. *M. affine* 19.173

19.148 1. Leaves broadly rounded to emarginate, sometimes shortly apiculate;
margins entire, distinctly bordered; dioicous or synoicous but rarely
fruiting .... 8. *M. punctatum* 19.177

19.149 **1. Mnium blyttii** B.S.G. Plants loosely to densely tufted, erect, light
to dark green. Stems 1–4 cm tall, simple or branched, red; rhizoids usually dense, confined to the base. Leaves in a dense comal cluster, becoming more widely spaced toward the base of the stem, 2.5–3.5 mm long,
broadly ovate to elliptic-ovate, the apical ones often spatulate, mostly
broad at the apex, shortly mucronate, acute or broadly rounded, strongly
narrowed to the insertion, decurrent, patent to spreading when moist,
undulate to somewhat crisped when dry; costa slender but strong, ending below the apex or percurrent; margins plane, bordered with 1–2
rows of linear, thick-walled cells often becoming colored with age, not
as strongly developed and contrasted as in most species of *Mnium*,
entire to ± toothed in the upper part, the teeth occasionally in pairs; upper cells mostly quadrate, shortly rectangular or 5- to 6-sided, rather
thin walled with angles ± rounded and thickened, not pitted, often in
vague longitudinal rows, not in diagonal rows, 17–34 μ wide, often with

various shapes and sizes mixed in the same area of the leaf; basal cells gradually becoming more elongated, oblong, about the same width as the upper cells. Dioicous. Fruit extremely rare. Plate 85, figs. 1–4 and plate 87, figs. 1–2.

19.150   On wet soil usually along small shady brooklets in the high mountains of our region.

19.151   Northern Europe and Siberia, Alaska, Yukon, southward in the Rocky Mountains to New Mexico. Salt Lake County: Wasatch Mountains, Brighton, 8,700–9,500 ft. San Juan County: La Sal Mountains, near Geyser Pass, 9,900 ft.

19.152   While the narrow cells forming the leaf margin are abruptly differentiated, they do not stand out as prominently as those of other species of *Mnium*.

19.153   **2. Mnium arizonicum** Amann. Plants rather loosely tufted or scattered among other mosses, dark green, often tinged with red. Stems erect, simple or very sparingly branched, green above, becoming red from the base upward with age, 1–2 cm tall; rhizoids confined to the base. Leaves dense above, becoming smaller and more widely spaced below, patent to somewhat spreading when moist, moderately to strongly crisped or spirally twisted when dry, obovate to obovate-spatulate, 2.5–3.5(4.5) mm long, broadest above the middle, acute to very shortly acuminate, varying to spatulate and widely to narrowly acute, the base narrowed, not or only slightly decurrent; costa strong, mostly percurrent, occasionally ending below the apex; margins plane, weakly bordered with 1–2 rows of narrower cells, nearly entire to toothed in the upper ½ to ⅔, the teeth ranging from short, blunt, and single or a few in pairs to sharp, strong, and mostly in pairs; upper cells elongate-hexagonal, extending from the costa to the border in diagonal rows, 13–20 μ wide, 20–50 μ long, thick walled and pitted, the angles not particularly thickened; marginal cells oblong to linear, thick walled, often green, but not forming a conspicuous border; basal cells oblong, thick walled and pitted, sometimes thin walled in the younger leaves. Dioicous. Fruit rare. Seta 1–2 cm long, ± curved or flexuous, yellowish, becoming reddish from the base upward with age; capsules pendulous to subpendulous, straw colored, red at the mouth, oblong-elliptic to oblong; lid yellowish brown, high conic with a straight or inclined beak (strongly bent when dry); annulus large, reddish; urn 2–3 mm long, longitudinally rugulose when dry; neck short, sometimes externally differentiated; peristome teeth rather large and long, reddish brown, paler at the tips; endostome golden yellow to yellowish brown, finely papillose; basal membrane high; segments narrow with very slender tips, widely perforated; cilia 1–3, nodulose, without appendages, often irregular and short, sometimes coherent. Spores 17–24 μ, light yellowish, very finely punctate. Plate 85, figs. 5–8 and plate 87, fig. 3.

19.154   On damp or rather dry soil and humus, in crevices, and at the bases of rocks, fallen trees and shady banks at rather high altitudes.

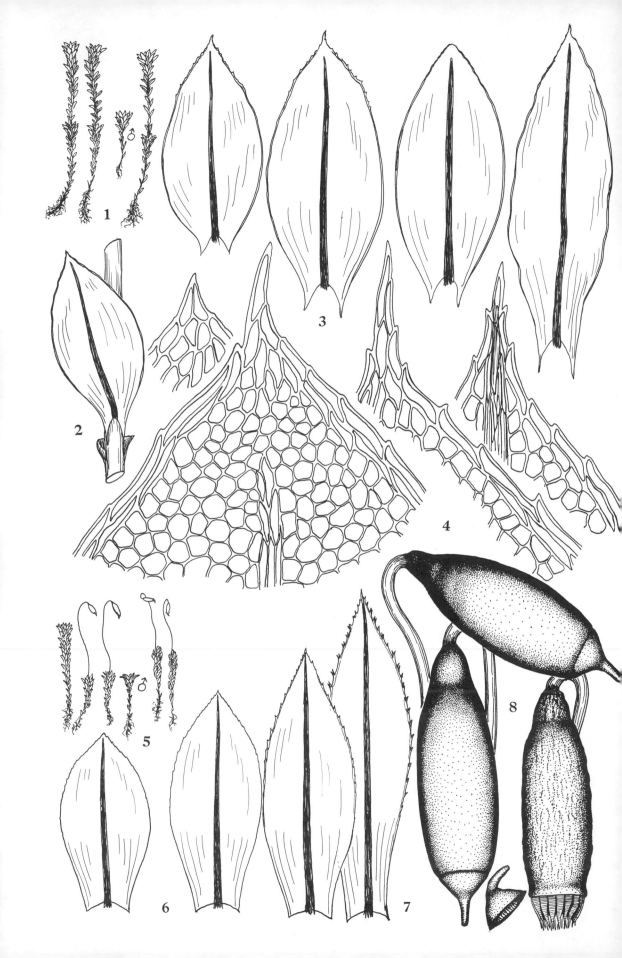

19.155   Idaho and Wyoming southward to New Mexico, Arizona, and Nevada.

19.156   Common in the higher mountains of Utah, usually above 7,500 ft. elevation. Unlike most species of the genus, this moss grows in drier places, usually not near water, but in damp shady places. The small size, the weakly bordered leaves, and rhomboid-hexagonal leaf cells in diagonal rows with thick pitted walls are distinctive features. I find considerably more variation in the marginal teeth than has been reported. It has been supposed that the teeth are mainly short, blunt, and mostly single, but in many plants some or most of the leaves are much more strongly toothed and the teeth mainly in pairs. It is common to find wide variation in the leaves of a single shoot, some entire or nearly so, some with blunt single teeth, and others strongly double toothed nearly to the base. I have a few specimens in which nearly all of the leaves are unusually narrow and mostly strongly toothed.

19.157   **3. Mnium marginatum** (With.) P. Beauv. Plants loosely tufted, often scattered among other mosses, bright to dark green, often becoming tinged with red. Stems mostly simple, erect, occasionally ascending, 2–4 cm tall, red from the base upward; rhizoids ± confined to the base. Leaves well spaced, erect-patent when moist, contorted or crisped when dry, mostly elliptic, varying to ovate or obovate, 2–4 mm long, the comal ones longer, ovate-lanceolate to oblong-lanceolate, 4–5 mm long, usually broad at the apex, acute to briefly acuminate, narrowed and ± long decurrent at the base; costa strong, percurrent to shortly excurrent to a short stout point, red, smooth on the back above, ending below the apex in the lower leaves; margins strongly bordered with linear thick-walled cells, often bistratose and usually colored, serrate with rather short teeth in pairs in the upper half or nearly to the base (sometimes rather weak or lacking and the leaves entire); upper leaf cells quadrate-rounded to oblong-rounded, 15–25 μ wide and up to 35 μ long, a few sometimes transversely elongated, thin walled with thickened angles, often in longitudinal rows; basal cells becoming oblong. Synoicous and paroicous. Seta erect or curved to flexuous, 1.5–2.5 cm long, yellowish, becoming reddish with age from the base upward; capsules horizontal to subpendulous, oblong to oblong-cylindrical, 3–5 mm long with a short, distinct neck rather gradually narrowed to the seta, yellowish to yellowish brown, becoming reddish with age, when dry finely longitudinally rugulose, slightly contracted below the mouth or not at all, the neck strongly shrunken; lid high conic with a straight or inclined beak which is bent at right angles when dry; annulus prominent; peristome teeth rusty to bright reddish, densely and finely papillose with tall sharp papillae throughout; endostome also similarly strongly papillose, yellowish to reddish brown, basal membrane high; segments broad, widely perfo-

---

Plate 85.   1–4. **Mnium blyttii.** 1. Habit sketches, X.4. 2. Portion of shoot showing decurrent leaf base, X6. 3. Four typical leaves, X8. 4. Four leaf apices, X120.

5–8. Mnium arizonicum. 5. Habit sketches, X.4. 6. Two lower leaves (often entire and without a distinct border). 7. Two upper leaves, X8. 8. Three capsules, X8.

rated; cilia nodulose. Spores 20–28 μ, yellowish, very finely punctate. Plate 86, figs. 1–8 and plate 87, figs. 4–5.

19.158   On wet or damp soil, humus, rotten logs, and similar substrata along brook banks and in seepage areas, usually in the shade.

19.159   Europe and Asia. Widely distributed throughout Canada and extending southward in the mountains of Tennessee, in the Great Lakes region and in the plains of Missouri, in the Rocky Mountains to New Mexico and Arizona and southward into Mexico, Nevada and California.

19.160   Frequent in Utah. Closely related to *M. orthorhynchum* but differing in the synoicous inflorescence and larger leaf cells which are quadrate-rounded to oblong-rounded with thickened angles and frequently in longitudinal rows. Our western forms of *M. serratum* have leaf cells smaller than usual, overlapping the range in size of *M. orthorhynchum*. Usually the synoicous inflorescence can be demonstrated easily so that many specimens can be verified on this basis. When the male shoots of *M. orthorhynchum* are present they can be picked out easily by the large budlike perigonium with more or less squarrose bracts. Quite a number of our plants have leaves weakly toothed or even entire.

19.161   **4. Mnium orthorhynchum** Brid. Plants closely resembling *Mnium marginatum* in size, color, and general appearance although tending to be smaller, differing mainly in the following respects: Leaves generally with costa $\pm$ toothed on the back above; upper cells distinctly angular, mostly hexagonal, the walls thin to moderately thick with little or no thickening at the corners, 12–20(24) μ wide or long, not in longitudinal rows. Dioicous. Plate 86, figs. 9–10 and plate 87, figs. 6–7.

19.162   On wet or damp soil, in shaded places.

19.163   Europe and Asia. Alaska across Canada, southward in the mountains to New Mexico and eastward to North Carolina.

19.164   Probably more common in Utah than the number of specimens indicates. It is usually sterile and overlooked. Our plants are small as compared with specimens from other regions, and only in a few older more strongly developed leaves are teeth shown at back of the costa.

19.165   **5. Mnium cuspidatum** Hedw. Plants in spreading mats, light green often becoming yellowish green. Shoots erect and 1–2 cm tall or prostrate and reaching 3–4 cm long, often developing numerous reddish rhizoids at the base or on the under side. Leaves strongly crisped and contorted

---

Plate 86.   1–8. Mnium marginatum. 1. Habit sketches, X.4. 2. Two lower leaves. 3. Three upper leaves, X8. 4. Upper leaf margin, X120. 5. Two leaf apices, X120. 6. Cross section of leaf margin showing 2- to 3-stratose border, X120. 7. Dissected perichaetium showing antheridia in axils of perichaetial leaves and also mixed with archegonia, X4. 8. Two capsules, X8.

9–10. Mnium orthorhynchum. 9. Habit sketches, X.4. 10. Upper part of male shoot showing conspicuous perigonium with squarrose leaves, X4. **Note:** Shape of leaves, costa, border, and serration are so much like **Mn. marginatum** that drawings show no difference.

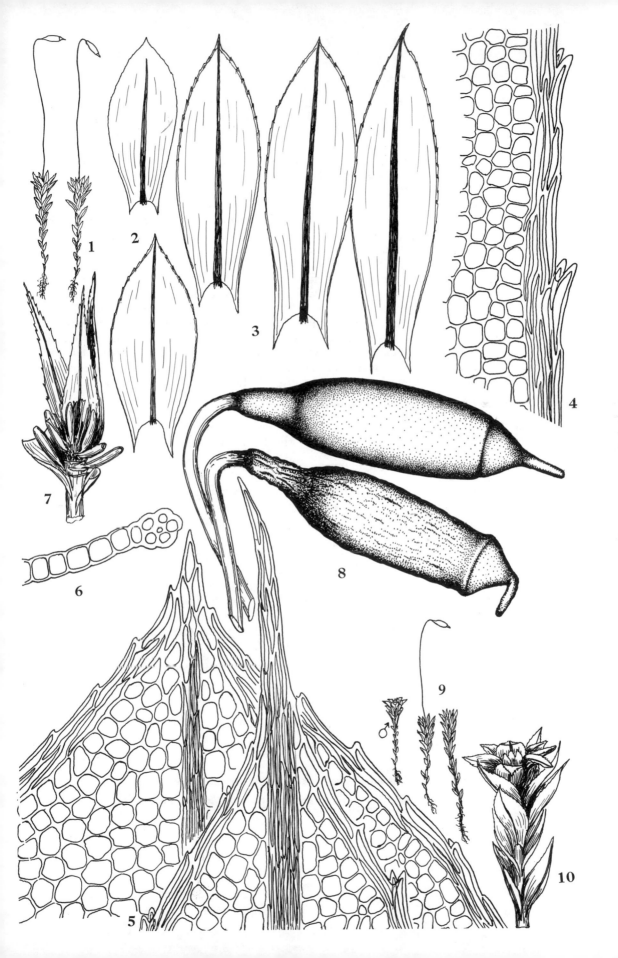

when dry, those of the erect stems largest at the summit, forming a rosette, 3–4 mm long, smaller and more distant below, often recurved; those of the prostrate stems becoming progressively smaller toward the end, ± complanate in 2 rows, obovate to spatulate, the base strongly narrowed and decurrent, acute to shortly acuminate; costa stout, percurrent or ending shortly below the apex; margins strongly bordered with 3–4 rows of linear thick-walled cells, toothed in the upper ½–⅔ with large, sharp, 1-celled, single teeth; upper cells rounded to oval-hexagonal, 15–25 μ long, variable in shape and arrangement, usually not in distinct rows, rather thick walled but not pitted, the angles considerably thickened; basal cell larger and more vertically elongated. Synoicous. Seta slender, yellowish, becoming reddish orange from the base upward, 2–3 cm long; capsules pendulous, mostly oblong, yellowish, becoming brownish with age, thin walled; urn 3–3.5 mm long, finely wrinkled when dry; neck usually not externally differentiated; annulus prominent; lid high conic, bluntly pointed; teeth greenish yellow, narrowly triangular-lanceolate, joints numerous and close; endostome light brownish, basal membrane high, ± strongly perforated; segment narrow, strongly perforated, the apices very slender, as long as the teeth; cilia 3–4, nodose. Spores yellowish, finely papillose 20–25 μ. Plate 89, figs. 1–4.

19.166 On damp or wet soil, humus, rotten logs, and rocks.

19.167 Circumboreal; very common in the eastern United States and across Canada, less common west of the Rocky Mountains, rare in Utah. Utah County: Wasatch Mountains, Mt. Timpanogos, North Fork Provo River, 5,800 ft.

19.168 Easily recognized by the acute to shortly acuminate leaves, toothed with single teeth only in the upper ½–⅔ of the margin and by the small cells.

19.169 **6. Mnium medium** B.S.G. Plants large, similar to *M. affine* but differing mainly as follows: leaf margins serrate to the base with single teeth composed of single cells, rarely much reduced or lacking; cells irregularly oval-hexagonal, less angular, the angles more heavily thickened, the walls pitted, tending to be thicker, the long axis often oblique and the cells sometimes in indistinct oblique rows but rarely in regular vertical rows, on the whole much larger, the medial ones mostly 30–38 x 40–70 μ. Synoicous. Fruiting more frequently, sporophytes usually 2–3 from the same perichaetium. Plate 88, figs. 10–12 and plate 87, figs. 9–10.

19.170 On damp or wet soil, humus, rotten logs, and rocks, mostly along small brooks, around springs and in seepage areas, mostly in shade.

19.171 Europe and Asia. Circumboreal, Alaska to Greenland, southward to Maryland and across the northern states to California.

19.172 Specimens without sex organs may be difficult to separate from *M. affine*.

Plate 87. Comparative sketches of the upper medial leaf cells, all X120.

1–2. **Mnium blyttii. 3. Mnium arizonicum. 4–5. Mnium marginatum. 6–7. Mnium orthorhynchum. 8. Mnium affine. 9–10. Mnium medium.**

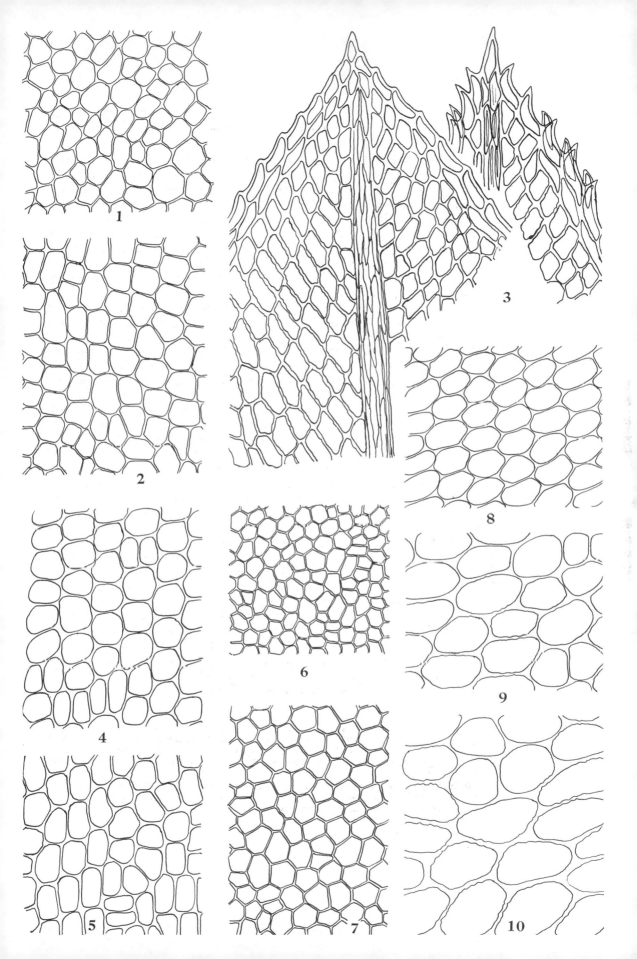

Usually the larger and more irregularly disposed leaf cells with strongly thickened angles will distinguish *M. medium*. The marginal teeth are more uniform, rarely reduced.

19.173 **7. Mnium affine** Bland. ex Funck. Plants large, in loose tufts or mats. Fertile stems erect, simple or branched from the base, 1–3 cm tall with dense reddish rhizoids at the base; sterile stems usually most abundant, simple or branched from the erect fertile ones, much longer, 2–6 cm long, procumbent and often stoloniferous, green, attenuated, with the leaves widely spaced in 2 ± opposite rows, the upper ones becoming gradually smaller toward the end and forming beautiful sprays; leaves of the erect stems forming a terminal spreading rosette, quickly becoming smaller below, variable in shape and size, obovate, oval, oblong-elliptic, or ligulate, the largest ones mostly 5–7 mm long and up to 10 mm in robust forms, 3–4 mm in smaller forms; base rounded or tapering to a very narrow insertion, ± strongly decurrent; apex mostly broadly rounded and apiculate, occasionally muticous; margins bordered with 2–4 rows of linear thick-walled cells in 1 layer, typically strongly and sharply toothed to the base, the teeth single and composed of 1–3 cells, the number variable in different plants, sometimes of blunt single cells and occasionally entire or nearly so; costa stout, mostly percurrent and joining the thick-walled marginal cells to form the apiculus; upper cells largest near the costa, up to 90 μ long, smallest next to the border, 17–27 x 20–42 μ; medial cells 27–34 x 34–58 μ, mostly hexagonal, ± usually disposed in oblique and vertical rows, the walls thin to rather thick and pitted, the angles thickened but not strongly so. Dioicous. Male plants with a large rosette of spreading to somewhat squarrose perigonial leaves. Fruit rather rare. Seta yellowish brown, becoming reddish from the base upward with age, 2–3 cm long; capsules mostly single from a perichaetium but occasionally 2–3, oblong, 3–5 mm long, neck very short and inconspicuous, yellowish, becoming yellowish brown and sometimes reddish with age, longitudinally rugulose when dry, rather thin walled; annulus prominent; lid mammillate to low conic with a short blunt point or shortly apiculate; peristome teeth yellowish to light yellowish brown, slenderly tapering above from a more or less oblong base, joints numerous below, finely papillose throughout; endostome orange, more coarsely but less densely papillose; basal membrane high, segments rather narrow but widely perforated down the middle, sometimes split apart and resembling strongly appendiculate cilia; cilia 2–3, stout, often short, nodose or slightly appendiculate. Spores yellowish, 21–27 μ. Plate 88, figs. 1–9 and plate 87, fig. 8.

Plate 88. 1–9. Mnium affine. 1–2. Habit sketches of male and female plants. 3. Erect shoot with prostate branch, average size. 4. Large form. 5. Dry habit, X.4. 6. Leaf of small form. 7. Leaves of average and larger size, X6. 8. Four sketches showing variation in upper marginal teeth of leaves of different plants, X80. 9. Capsules, X6.

10–12 Mnium medium. 10. Habit sketches of fertile plants, X.4. **Note:** Prostrate branches and shoots are like those of **Mn. affine.** 11. Perichaetial bud dissected to show synoicous inflorescence, X4. 12. Two sketches of marginal teeth of leaves, X80.

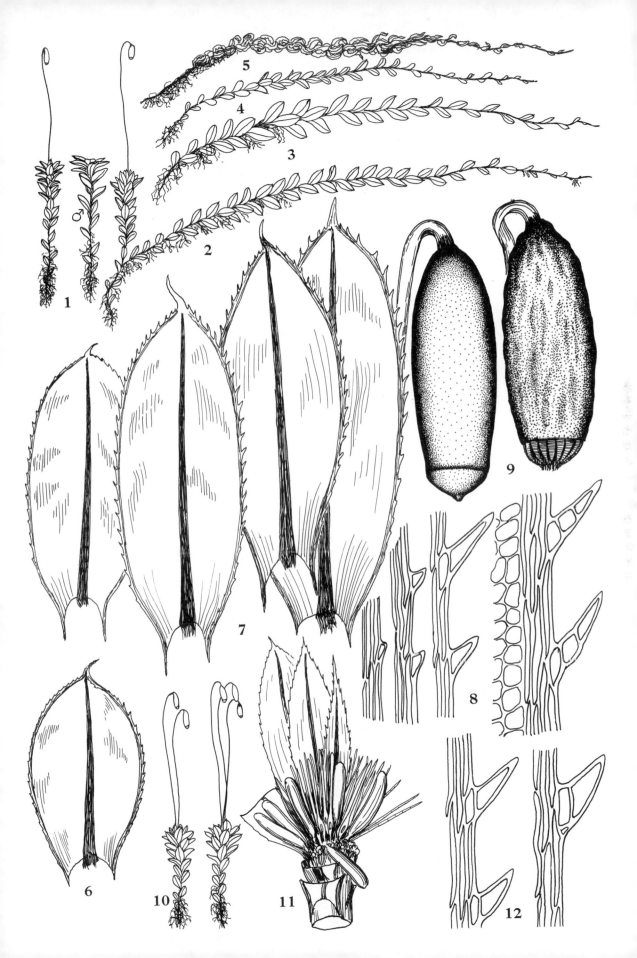

19.174 On wet or damp soil, humus, rocks, and rotten wood, usually in shady places along small brooks, seepage areas, and similar places.

19.175 South America, Europe and Asia. Mostly in the mountains of Utah. Throughout Canada and the United States.

19.176 Variable in size, especially of the leaves. Also the serration of the leaf margin varies from large sharp teeth composed of 2–3 cells, to forms with small blunt teeth of only 1 cell, while many plants have leaves practically entire. The latter have been treated as var. *rugicum* (Laur.) B.S.G. by some bryologists. Specimens without inflorescences may be difficult to distinguish from *M. medium*. Differences in the leaf cells are discussed in the notes under the latter species.

19.177 **8. Mnium punctatum** Schreb. ex Hedw. Plants large, bright or dark green, often with a pale whitish cast, sometimes tinged with red, forming loose tufts and mats, sometimes scattered. Stems ± erect 2–4(6) mm tall, mostly simple, green becoming red from the base upward; rhizoids dense at the base, ferruginous or dull brown. Leaves forming a terminal rosette, becoming smaller and more widely spaced below, mostly obovate to obovate-spatulate, varying to oval or orbicular, strongly narrowed at base, not decurrent, broadly rounded to slightly emarginate, sometimes shortly cuspidate at apex, varying widely in size, in small forms the largest leaves reaching 4 mm, in large forms as much as 10 mm long and 8 mm wide; lamina flattish, ± undulate when dry; costa wide at the base, tapering upward, ending below the apex or sometimes percurrent, in cross section appearing biconvex, without stereid bands, becoming reddish with age; margins entire, bordered with 1–4 rows of linear cells which may be 1–3 cells thick, varying in different plants; upper cells hexagonal to somewhat rhombic, regular to irregular, the long axis extending obliquely from the costa to the margin, in ± oblique rows, mostly thin walled and unpitted but sometimes becoming thick and pitted, the angles not thickened or only forming small triangular thickenings; marginal cells abruptly linear, thin walled without color to thick walled and often reddish. Dioicous or occasionally synoicous. Rarely fruiting. Seta 2–4 cm long, reddish; capsules single, nodding or pendulous, oblong-cylindrical to oval, neck not externally differentiated, urn 3–4(5) mm long, light yellowish, becoming brownish with age, finely wrinkled when dry; lid mostly conical and usually with a distinct beak; peristome teeth yellow or yellowish brown, finely papillose below, coarser above and often in vertical lines; endostome bright yellowish, papillose, basal membrane high; segments narrow, slender at the tips, moderately perforated below; cilia 2–3, nodulose, often united at the joints. Spores 35–40 μ, dull yellowish, finely papillose. Plate 89, figs. 5–6.

Plate 89. 1–4. Mnium cuspidatum. 1. Habit sketches, X.4. 2. Dissected perichaetial bud showing synoicous inflorescence, X4. 3. Typical leaves, X6. 4. Upper medial leaf cells from two different plants showing the usual variation, X120.

5–6. Mnium punctatum. 5. Three plants showing variation in size, X.4. 6. Leaves from different plants showing usual range in variation in shapes, X6.

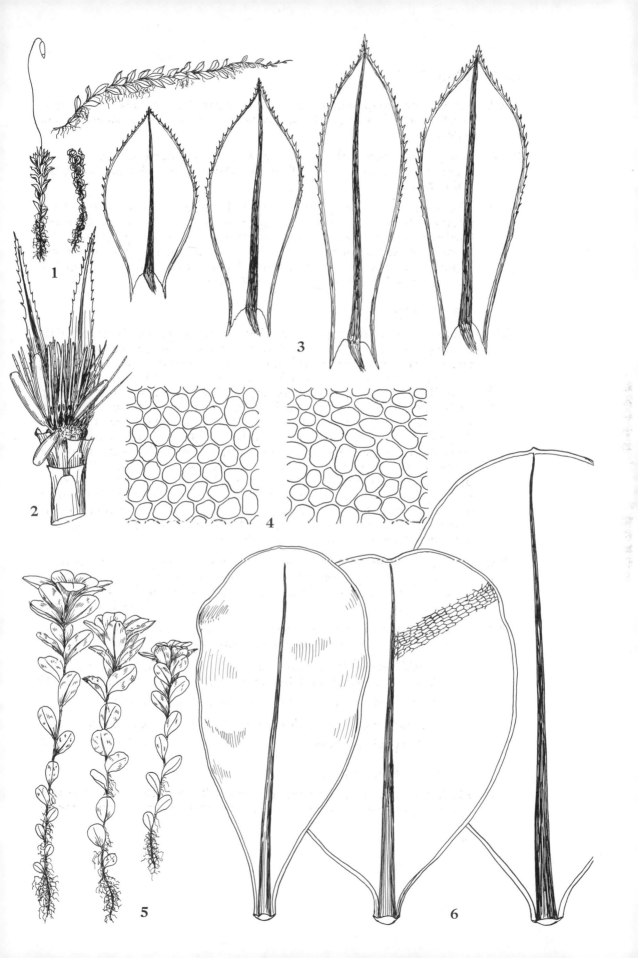

19.178 On wet or damp soil, rocks, humus, rotten logs, mainly along shady brooks, around springs and in seepage areas in the mountains of our region.

19.179 Europe and Asia. Alaska to Greenland, southward to Georgia and across the continent from Ohio and Indiana to Colorado and Utah. California.

19.180 The moss may be recognized by its obovate leaves, very narrow at the insertion, broadly rounded to emarginate at the apex and in its entire bordered margins. Locally abundant. Very large sterile plants referable to var. *elatum* Schimp. are not well set off. Synoicous plants with ovoid capsules are often referred to *M. pseudopunctatum* Bruch & Schimp. but are otherwise like the general run of *M. punctatum*.

LESKEACEAE

20.1 Plants small to medium sized, dark green to yellowish green, dull, growing in mats or erect and tufted when crowded; primary stems mostly creeping and often stoloniferous; secondary stems often ascending and sometimes erect, irregularly branched or sometimes regularly pinnate (in *Helodium* and *Thuidium*); ultimate branches short to long, central strand weak, vague, or lacking. Paraphyllia lacking to very numerous, sometimes branched. Stem and branch leaves usually of different shape and size, ovate to ovate-lanceolate, acute to slenderly acuminate; costa mostly strong but never excurrent; medial cells short, smooth or papillose, the papillae single and large or small and often 2 or more over each cell; basal cells usually longer than the upper one, smooth or less papillose. Seta long; capsules erect and symmetric to inclined or horizontal and ± curved and asymmetric, ovoid to oblong-cylindric; peristome perfect or with the cilia rudimentary or lacking; teeth usually with fine transverse striations on the lower joints.

20.2 1. Plants usually in deep, dense, erect tufts in wet places; shoots regularly pinnate; paraphyllia dense, filamentous and much branched; stem leaves with long, branched paraphyllia on the basal margins .... 1. *Helodium* 20.4

20.3 1. Plants forming mats and tufts on dry rocks or bases of trees, rarely on soil, paraphyllia numerous or entirely lacking, not on leaves

    2. Apical cells of the branch leaves papillose; paraphyllia very abundant, filamentous, and branched .... 2. *Thuidium* 20.10

    2. Apical cells of the branch leaves smooth or low papillose

        3. Paraphyllia short, multiform, not branched .... 3. *Lescuraea* 20.16

        3. Paraphyllia lacking .... 4. *Leskeella* 20.45

1. HELODIUM Warnst.

20.4 Plants medium sized, growing in deep tufts or masses in wet places, green to yellowish green above, light brownish below; rhizoids few at the base. Stems mostly erect, regularly to irregularly pinnate, the branches slender and attenuate; paraphyllia very dense, filamentous, and freely branched. Leaves broadly ovate, ovate-lanceolate or oblong, acuminate, concave and strongly keeled below, bearing paraphyllia like outgrowths from the basal margins; costa extending to the middle or into the acumen; medial cells oblong to sublinear, fusiform to rhomboidal, often irregular in width and shape, smooth to strongly papillose on 1 or both sides. Mostly autoicous. Seta usually very long; capsules oblong-cylindric, curved, inclined to horizontal; annulus present; lid conic, apiculate; peristome perfect; teeth finely transversely striate at the base; cilia 3.

20.5   The name is from Greek meaning marshy.

20.6   **Helodium blandowii** (Web. & Mohr) Warnst. Stems 4–11 cm long, quite stiff when dry, regularly pinnate with branches unequal, widely spaced, tapered. Stem leaves triangular-ovate, shortly and slenderly acuminate, concave, and somewhat plicate, abruptly narrowed to the somewhat clasping base; margins entire to irregularly serrulate or dentate, 1 or both sides widely revolute above and occasionally nearly to the base; costa extending half the length of the blade or into the acumen; leaf cells oblong to sublinear, fusiform to rhomboidal, 6–10 μ wide, often irregular in shape and width, each with a simple strong papilla on the upper end or upper half of the lumen on each side of the blade; basal cells wider, mostly oblong, smooth and clear, becoming orange red in older leaves. Branch leaves smaller, broadly ovate-acuminate to ovate-lanceolate. Autoicous. Seta 3–5 cm long, slender, reddish brown; capsules oblong-cylindric, curved, neck short, urn 3–4 mm long, yellowish brown becoming reddish brown with age, becoming strongly arcuate and incurved under the mouth when dry; lid conic, pointed; teeth reddish brown at the base, becoming pale and finely papillose above; basal membrane of the endostome rather high, yellowish-brown, segments keeled and narrowly perforated, finely papillose; cilia 3, slender and nodose. Spores mature in August. Plate 90, figs. 1–7.

20.7   In wet boggy situations, seepage areas and around alpine lakes in our region.

20.8   Europe and Asia. Across northern United States, New Jersey, Ohio, Colorado to Nevada and northwards.

20.9   Distinctive because of very abundant paraphyllia and wet habitat. Infrequent in Utah.

2. THUIDIUM B.S.G.

20.10   Plants mostly in loose tufts or masses, green to yellowish green, brown below. Stems regularly to irregularly pinnate or bipinnate, mostly brittle when dry; paraphyllia dense but not feltlike nor woolly, filamentous, simple or branched; rhizoids few at the base. Stem and branch leaves usually different in size and shape, somewhat appressed or patent at the base with the tips incurved when dry, erect-patent to spreading with tips erect when moist; stem leaves ovate to triangular-ovate or oblong, acuminate, ± cordate at base, concave and biplicate; costa strong, extending into the acumen; cells short, papillose on 1 or both sides; branch leaves smaller and narrower. Seta long; capsules suberect to curved, oblong-cylindric, asymmetric; annulus large; lid conic, pointed or long beaked; peristome perfect, cilia well developed, basal membrane about ⅓ the length of the endostome.

20.11 The name is a diminutive of *Thuja* or white cedar.

20.12 **Thuidium abietinum** (Hedw.) B.S.G. Plants medium sized, in dense tufts or loose masses, yellowish green or brown below. Stems ascending to nearly erect, 3–5 cm long or longer, regularly 1-pinnate; branches unequal, slenderly attenuate, stiff and brittle when dry; paraphyllia numerous, often branched, papillose; leaves closely appressed when dry, patent, often with the tips erect when moist. Stem leaves 1–1.5 mm long, broadly ovate, acuminate, ± cordate at base, with a deep fold on either side; margins widely recurved below, plane or ± revolute above, papillose-serrate above, occasionally with a few short paraphyllia attached to the basal angles; costa ending below the apex, strongly papillose or toothed at the back; medial cells thick walled, irregular in shape and size, mostly oval to oblong-rhomboidal, 8–12 μ wide, each with a single tall papilla on either side; basal cells longer and often slightly porose, extreme alar cells similar with those above smaller, quadrate-rounded or hexagonal. Branch leaves smaller, up to 1 mm long, ovate, shortly acuminate, not cordate; apical cells with 1–2(3) papillae besides the terminal one. Dioicous. Rarely fruiting. Plate 90, figs. 8–17.

20.13 On dry rocks and soil, usually in shaded places.

20.14 Europe. Alaska to British Columbia, Montana and Colorado, eastward to Greenland and southward to Virginia. Colorado: Moffat County, Dinosaur National Monument at Echo Park, Yampa River ¼ mi. east of junction with Green River, 4,740 ft.

20.15 This moss was gathered about 4 miles east of the Utah-Colorado state boundary. It was also gathered in Black Canyon of the Gunnison River in Gunnison County, Colorado.

3. LESCURAEA B.S.G.

20.16 Plants small to medium sized, dull green to yellowish green or brownish. Stems creeping, branched; paraphyllia mostly present, multiform but asymmetric, ovoid to oblong-ovoid, occasionally subcylindric, reddish brown; annulus lacking; lid conic with a short broad point; peristome

---

Plate 90. 1–7. Helodium blandowii. 1. Habit sketches, X.4. 2. Three stem leaves. 3. Three branch leaves, X8. 4–6. Basal, medial, and upper leaf cells. 7. Basal marginal cells with cilia, X120.

8–17. Thuidium abietinum. 8. Habit sketch, X.4. 9. Paraphyllia on stem, X60. 10. Same, X120. 11. Stem leaves. 12. Branch leaves, X8. 13. Leaf apices. 14–15. Medial and basal marginal cells of branch leaves. 16–17. Medial and basal marginal cells of stem leaves, X120.

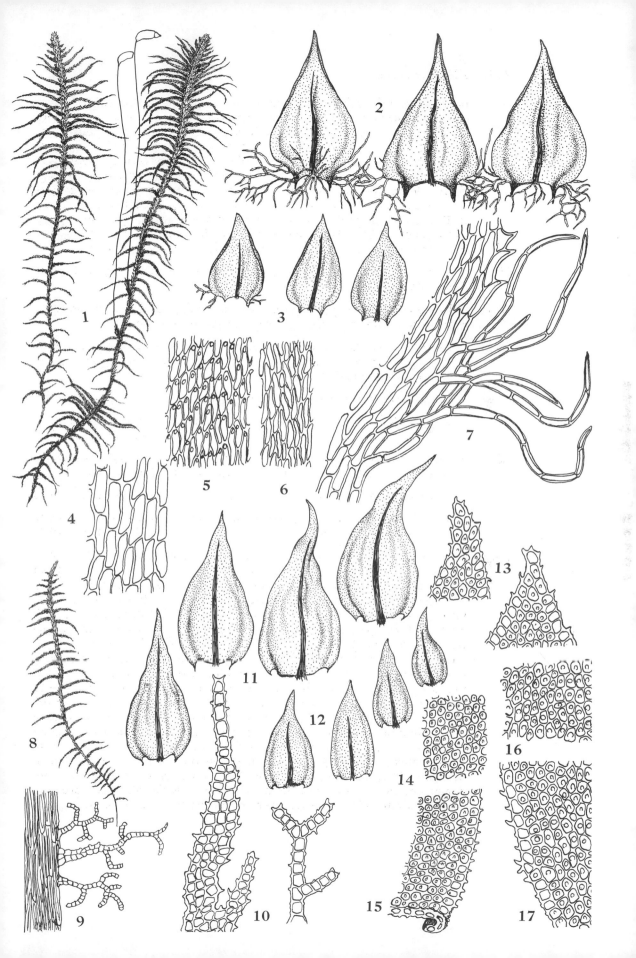

never branched, lacking in a few species. Stem leaves the largest, ovate to ovate-lanceolate, acute to acuminate, concave at the base with a fold on either side; costa ¾ the length of the blade or nearly percurrent; medial cells isodiametric to linear, often thick walled, round at the ends or sometimes angular, smooth or papillose; basal cells usually shorter and smoother; alar cells quadrate, transversely elongated or shortly oblong. Branch leaves smaller and narrower. Dioicous. Seta 5–20 mm long; capsules erect and symmetric or inclined to horizontal, often curved and teeth reddish, ± united at base in a low membrane, lower joints finely transversely striate; basal membrane of the endostome mostly rather high or sometimes very low; cilia 1–2, often rudimentary or lacking.

20.17 Named in honor of Leo Lesquereux, Swiss-American bryologist and paleobotanist.

20.18 When present, the papillae on the leaves are difficult to make out. They show best on the upper branch leaves or in cross sections.

20.19 1. Shoots ± swollen when dry with the leaves loosely disposed, widely divergent at the insertion but incurved above; areolation densely chlorophyllose and obscure

2. Leaf cells with a single central papilla .... 1. *L. patens* 20.21

2. Leaf cells smooth or with a single papilla from the upper ends .... 2. *L. incurvata* 20.25

20.20 1. Shoots slender when dry, the leaves closely imbricated their whole length; areolation clear; medial cells oval to linear-rhomboidal

3. Inner basal cells short .... 3. *L. radicosa* 20.32

3. Inner basal cells elongated; branch leaves concave above, usually serrulate and papillose .... 4. *L. saxicola* 20.41

20.21 **1. Lescuraea patens** (Lindb.) Arn. & Jens. Plants rather small, in thinnish or thicker mats, dark green to yellowish green, brown to reddish brown below, when dry slightly swollen, the leaves rather loose, widely divergent at the insertion, incurved above, the tips directed toward the stem. Stems slender, usually sparingly branched, 1.5–3(4) cm long, rhizoids in tufts; paraphyllia dense and multiform, the larger ones decurrent. Leaves loosely imbricated, somewhat infolded lengthwise and incurved at the tips but not much shrunken when dry, spreading when moist. Stem leaves ovate, acute to acuminate, straight or falcate, 0.7–1.2 mm long, concave at the base and often decurrent; margins serrulate to entire, revolute in the region of the acumen and at the base; costa extending well into the acumen, toothed on the back above; areolation chlorophyllose throughout, rather opaque, papillose to the base, medial cells isodiametric to shortly elongated, ± irregular, 7–10 μ wide, fairly thick walled, each with a single large central papilla over the lumen on both sides, not projecting from the upper ends; apical cells more elongated; inner basal cells broader, 10–14 μ wide; alar cells predominate-quadrate with some transversely elongated. Branch leaves smaller and narrower, more strongly serrulate and papillose. Seta 0.7–1.5 cm long; capsules obovoid to ovoid-oblong, mostly inclined and asymmetric but sometimes erect and nearly symmetric, urn 1–1.5 mm long, reddish brown, neck short but distinct; lid with a rather narrow point; cilia 1–2, usually poorly developed to rudimentary or lacking. Plate 91, figs. 1–8.

20.22 On dry shaded rocks, occasionally on soil, in mountains.

20.23 Europe. Manitoba, Michigan, New Hampshire, Nova Scotia and Newfoundland. Alaska to California, eastward to Montana, Wyoming and Utah.

20.24 This species resembles *L. incurvata* in the darker color, dry stance of the leaves and areolation but the papillae are central and not projecting from the upper ends of the cells. It is less frequent.

20.25 **2. Lescuraea incurvata** (Hedw.) Lawt. var. **incurvata.** Plants rather small, in loose or rather compact mats, commonly dark green but often yellowish green, sometimes strongly tinged with brown, the lower parts brown, when dry rather swollen, the leaves loose, widely divergent at the insertion and incurved above, the tips ± directed toward the stem, ± folded lengthwise but not much shrunken, when moist patent to widely spreading. Stems 1–3 cm long, irregularly branched, the branches usually rather long but sometimes short, the tips usually hooked; rhizoids few to dense. Paraphyllia few to dense and multiform, the larger ones sometimes dentate or somewhat lobed but not divided or branched. Stem leaves typically 1–1.5 mm long but shorter in small forms and larger in robust forms, ovate to ovate-lanceolate, short to rather long acuminate, often abruptly so, straight to falcate, chlorophyllose throughout, concave at the base with a strong fold on each side; margins entire to serrulate above, revolute near the base of the acumen and widely recurved at the base of the leaf, sometimes revolute throughout; costa stout, extending to the base of the acumen or well toward the tip, commonly papillose or toothed at the back above; medial cells predominantly short and rather opaque, oval, oval-oblong, rhomboidal or irregular, typically rounded at the ends but sometimes quite angular, thick walled, 6–10 μ wide, smooth or papillose from the upper ends on the ventral side; inner basal cells quadrate to shortly rectangular; alar cells quadrate to transversely elongated. Branch leaves smaller, narrower, usually more strongly serrulate and papillose. Seta 0.5–1.5 cm long, reddish brown; capsules mostly inclined to horizontal, ovoid to oblong-ovoid, slightly curved and asymmetric, occasionally erect and nearly symmetric, urn 0.7–2 mm long, reddish brown, the mouth sometimes slightly oblique; neck short, ± shrunken and contracted under the mouth when dry; lid with a short broad point; cilia 1–2, often poorly developed or lacking. Spores 14–20 μ. Plate 91, figs. 9–16 and plate 92, figs. 4–5.

20.26 Growing on dry or damp rocks, occasionally on soil, usually in shade in the mountains.

20.27 Europe and Asia. British Columbia, Oregon and Nevada, eastward to Alberta, Wyoming and Colorado.

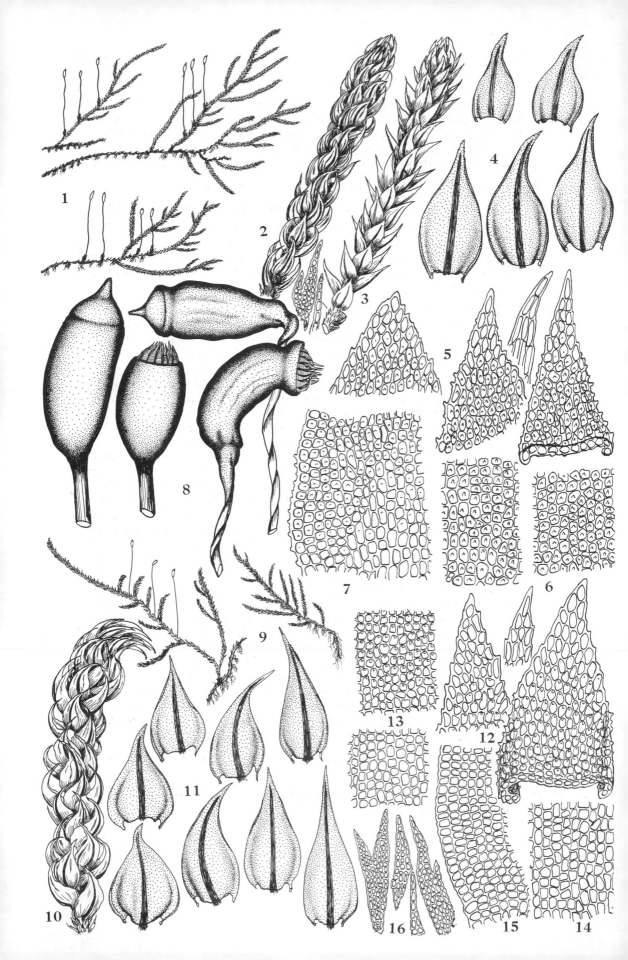

20.28   Locally abundant. This moss looks almost precisely like *L. patens* in the dry state.

20.29   2a. Var. **tenuiretis** (Culm.) Lawt. Somewhat smaller, more branched; leaves less falcate; medial cells shorter, mainly isodiametric and more angular; cells of branch leaves more strongly papillose with papillae on both sides of younger leaves. Plate 92, figs. 1–3.

20.30   Daggett, Salt Lake, and Utah counties.

20.31   In these specimens it is difficult to decide whether the papillae on very short cells lie over the middle of the lumen or at the upper end, both positions being evident on younger leaves. On older leaves they appear mainly central but often toward the forward end.

20.32   **3. Lescuraea radicosa** (Mitt.) Moenk. var. **radicosa.** Plants in thin or thick mats, yellowish green or sometimes dark green, often tinged with brown. Stems irregularly branched, 1–2(4) cm long; paraphyllia usually abundant. Leaves imbricated, the apices not noticeably incurved, when moist patent to spreading. Stem leaves quite variable, less than 1 mm to 1.7 mm long, ovate to ovate-lanceolate, abruptly to gradually short to long acuminate, the acumen sometimes as long as the base, straight to falcate, concave, mostly with a strong fold on either side at base, decurrent; margins entire to serrulate, recurved at the base and revolute at the base of the acumen, or plane in some leaves; costa stout, either little tapering in short leaves to more slenderly tapering in narrowly acuminate leaves, ending in the acumen or subpercurrent, usually toothed at the back above; areolation clear; medial cells oval to hexagonal or rhomboidal, 8–11 μ wide, usually thick walled, the ends $\pm$ rounded, smooth or papillose from the upper ends on the ventral side; apical cells oblong to sublinear, shorter in some leaves; basal cells slightly wider, mostly oblong, usually with a few shorter ones; alar cells quadrate to shortly oblong with a few transversely elongated. Branch leaves smaller, often more strongly papillose and serrate. Seta 0.5–1.5 cm long; capsules 1–2 mm long, obovate, ovoid or oblong-ovoid, erect and nearly symmetric to inclined, curved and asymmetric, urn 1–2 mm long, contracted below the mouth when dry, neck short; cilia well developed or sometimes rather short. Spores 14–18 μ. Plate 92, figs. 6–12.

20.33   On dry or damp rocks, usually in shady places in mountains.

20.34   Europe. Alaska to California, eastward to Alberta, Montana, Colorado and Arizona.

20.35   This is our most variable species both in stature and size and shape of the leaves. Its various forms are easily distinguished from the last two

---

Plate 91.   1–8. **Lescuraea patens.** 1. Habit sketches, X.4. 2. Portion of shoot, dry. 3. Same, moist, X4. 4. Branch and stem leaves, X8. 5. Leaf apices: medial leaf cells. 6. Apical cells, X120. 7. Basal and alar cells, X120. 8. Capsules, X8.

9–16. Lescuraea incurvata. 9. Habit sketch, X.4. 10. Portion of dry shoot, X4. 11. Stem leaves from three forms, X8. 12. Leaf apices. 13. Upper medial cells. 14. Basal cells, X120. 15. Alar cells, X120. 16. Paraphyllia, X40.

species by longer, clear, green leaf cells, not short and opaque. Some plants with unusually long leaf cells extending well toward the base resemble those of *L. saxicola*, but in the segments of the endostome they are broad and strong from a high basal membrane rather than very slender and weak or rudimentary from a very low basal membrane. In sterile state such plants might easily be referred to the *L. saxicola*.

20.36 3a. Var. **compacta** (Best) Lawt. Smaller than the species; leaves more shortly acuminate; medial cells shorter and apical cells markedly shorter. From the following variety it differs in the less concave branch leaves and the leaves in general slightly longer-acuminate with cells greener and not as clear. Plate 93, figs. 1–3.

20.37 Apparently alpine in our region, infrequent.

20.38 San Juan County: La Sal Mountains near Geyser Pass, 9,900 ft. Juab County: Deep Creek Mountains, Thomas Creek, 8,500 ft.

20.39 3b. Var. **pallida** (Best) Lawt. Smaller than the species; shoots straight or nearly so; stems often denuded below or clothed with old brown leaves; branches short and often numerous; stem leaves ovate, acute to broadly and shortly acuminate, straight or slightly falcate; medial cells much like those of the species but the apical much shorter, oval to rhomboidal; branch leaves shorter, deeply concave, the 2 lateral folds extending well toward the apex, the medial and apical cells even shorter; the leaves in general a clear, pale green. Plate 93, fig. 4.

20.40 Duchesne County: Uinta Mountains, east side of Mirror Lake, 10,300 ft. San Juan County: La Sal Mountains, near Geyser Pass, 9,900 ft.

20.41 **4. Lescuraea saxicola** (B.S.G.) Mol. in Lor. Plants dark green to light yellowish green, becoming brownish with age, in thin or thickish mats. Shoots slender, 2–4 cm long; paraphyllia usually dense. Leaves closely imbricated when dry, rather widely spreading when moist; stem leaves broadly ovate-acuminate to ovate-lanceolate, straight or falcate, 0.8–1.6 mm long, concave with a strong fold on either side extending well toward the apex, margins mostly widely recurved from the base nearly to the apex; costa strong, percurrent or merging into the apex, slightly papillose at back above; medial cells oblong-rhomboidal to linear, 6–8 μ wide, clear, smooth or slightly papillose from the upper ends on the ventral side; apical cells similar or slightly shorter; basal cells often slightly porose; alar cells ± quadrate. Branch leaves smaller and narrower, more gradually acuminate, serrulate at the apex, more frequently papillose on the upper surface. Seta 1 cm long or less; capsules

---

Plate 92. **1–3. Lescuraea incurvata** var. **tenuiretis.** 1. Portion of moist shoot. 2. Branch and stem leaves, X8. 3. Upper medial areolation, X120.

4–5. Lescuraea incurvata. 4. Capsules, X8. 5. Portion of peristome, X60.

6–12. Lescuraea radicosa. 6–7. Portion of shoot, moist and dry, X4. 8. Stem and branch leaves, X8. 9. Leaf apices. 10. Upper medial cells. 11. Basal and alar cells, X120. 12. Capsules, X8.

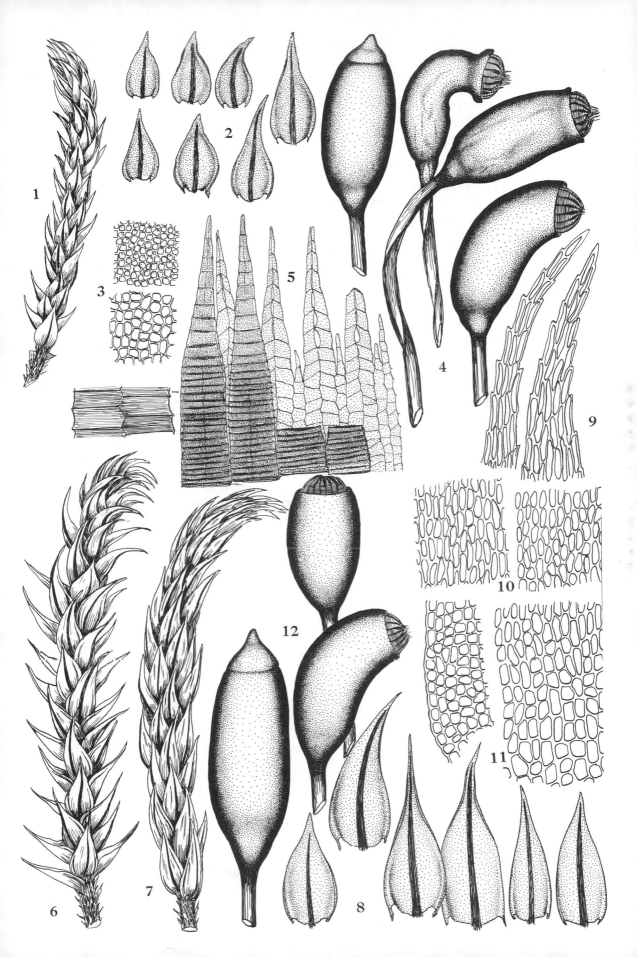

erect and symmetric, obovate to oblong-ovoid, 1–1.5 mm long, neck short, shrunken when dry; cilia lacking. Plate 93, figs. 5–12.

20.42 On noncalcareous rocks, alpine.

20.43 Europe. British Columbia, Alberta, Quebec, Labrador, Vermont, Utah.

20.44 The concave leaves with margins broadly recurved from the base nearly to the apex, clear areolation, and especially the elongated basal cells are distinctive features. When present the erect symmetric capsules with narrower teeth and segments—slender and imperfect from a very low membrane—are also distinctive. Infrequent.

4. LESKEELLA (Limpr.) Loesk.

20.45 Plants small and slender, dull green, often tinged with brown, in thin, spreading, closely adhering mats or low loose tufts. Main stems creeping, not stoloniferous, closely attached to the substrate by tufts of rhizoids, the older part leafy or denuded, somewhat regularly to irregularly pinnate; branches typically short but sometimes rather long, often becoming flagelliform; paraphyllia lacking or very few. Leaves crowded, appressed when dry, patent to loosely imbricated when moist, broadly ovate, abruptly slenderly acuminate to ovate-lanceolate and long acuminate, sometimes slightly falcate, 1 mm long or less; margins entire to serrulate above, ± recurved at base; costa broad and forked or single and extending into the acumen, occasionally thick, often lacking; medial cells oval to rhomboidal or oblong, the ends rounded; basal cells shorter; alar cells quadrate to transversely elongated. Dioicous. Fruit rare. Capsules cylindric, erect and slightly curved; annulus not well differentiated; lid conical with a thickish inclined beak; peristome teeth transversely striate below, obliquely above; lamellae numerous, 20–35, thickish; segments subulate and keeled, from a low basal membrane; cilia lacking.

20.46 The name is diminutive of *Leskea*, which was named in honor of Professor Gottfried Leske of Leipzig.

20.47 1. Costa short, often forked, extending ½ the length of the blade or less, often lacking; leaves recurved only at base, rarely vaguely serrulate at the apex .... 1. *L. tectorum* 20.49

20.48 1. Costa extending well into the acumen; many leaves revolute above,

---

Plate 93. 1–3. **Lescuraea radicosa** var. **compacta.** 1. Stem leaves, X8. 2. Leaf apices. 3. Medial leaf cells, X120.
4. Var. **pallida.** Stem leaves.
5–12. **Lescuraea saxicola.** 5. Habit sketches, X.4. 6. Portion of moist shoot, X4. 7–8. Stem and branch leaves, X8. 9. Leaf apices. 10. Upper medial cells. 11–12. Basal and alar cells, X120.
13–17. **Leskeella tectorum** fo. **cyrtophylla.** 13. Habit sketches, X.4. 14. Branch dry. 15. Two branches, moist, X2. 16. Stem and branch leaves, X8. 17. Medial and apical cells, X120.
18–22. **Leskeella tectorum** fo. **flagellifera.** 18. Habit sketches, X.4. 19. Branch dry. 20. Same moist, X2. 21. Stem and branch leaves, X8. 22. Apical and medial cells, X120.
23. **Leskeella arizonae.** Stem and branch leaves.

sometimes from base to apex, commonly serrulate ....
.... 2. *L. arizonae* 20.60

20.49 **1. Leskeella tectorum** (Brid.) Hag. Plants small, slender, in thin mats or rather loose masses, occasionally with dense erect branches forming tufts, usually dull dark green, yellowish green or olivaceous, often tinged with brown or red. Primary shoots prostrate and creeping, ± stoloniferous, sometimes ascending in looser mats, 1–5 cm long; branches few to numerous, irregularly to somewhat regularly pinnate, frequently 1-sided, central strand of 6–12, or as few as 24 small thin-walled cells; rhizoids in short dense tufts; paraphyllia none or occasionally very few, shortly filiform, lanceolate or ovate, entire or toothed. Flagelliform branchlets often clustered in leaf axils. Leaves of primary stems uniform and firm or bearing small and large leaves in alternating sections, these often of mixed forms and frequently decolorate, at length becoming eroded and the stems denuded. Well developed stem leaves broadly ovate, ± abruptly acuminate, 0.7–1(1.2) mm long, the acumen slender or rather broad, often recurved or sometimes falcate, concave at the base with a strong fold on either side; smaller stem leaves ovate-lanceolate, gradually acuminate, the acumen broad or slender and sometimes as long as the base, both kinds of leaves frequently on alternate portions of the same stem; margins plane or recurved toward the base on 1 or both sides, entire or occasionally serrulate at the apex; costa mostly short, thick at the base, occasionally forked, sometimes more slender and extending half the length of the blade or less, rarely toothed at the back above, occasionally lacking; medial cells clear, variable, oval to rhomboidal, ranging to oblong-oval or oblong-hexagonal, 6–8 μ or as much as 8–12 μ wide, sometimes in different leaves of the same plant, generally rounded at the ends and usually becoming shorter toward the margins and the base, smooth or rarely low-papillose above; alar cells quadrate to transversely elongated, often numerous and extending high up on the margins of larger leaves. Branch leaves dense, ± appressed and imbricated when dry, patent to spreading when moist, typically ovate, shortly acuminate to ovate-lanceolate and more slenderly acuminate, normally 0.5–0.7 mm long, becoming progressively smaller toward the tips of flagellate branches. Dioicous. Fruit rare. Seta about 1 cm long, reddish; capsules light reddish brown, oblong-cylindric, erect, slightly curved or nearly symmetric, urn 1.7–2.2 mm long, neck short, somewhat longitudinally ribbed or finely wrinkled and only slightly contracted under the mouth when dry; annulus lacking, consisting at most of 2 rows of very thick-walled cubic cells, not well set off; lid conic with a thickish beak, slightly longer than the base; teeth yellowish brown, linear-lanceolate, incurved when dry, very closely jointed, transversely striate below,

---

Plate 94. Leskeella tectorum. 1. Habit sketches, X.4. 2. Portion of dry shoot. 3. Same moist, X2. 4. Stem and branch leaves of broad-leaved form. 5. Same of narrow-leaved form, X8. 6. Two leaf apices. 7–10. Medial leaf cells showing variations in dimensions. 11–12. Two areas of alar cells, X120. 13. Cross section of stem with variation in central strand, X60. 14. Perigonia. 15. Two perichaetial leaves, X8. 16. Four capsules, X8. 17. Portion of peristome, X60.

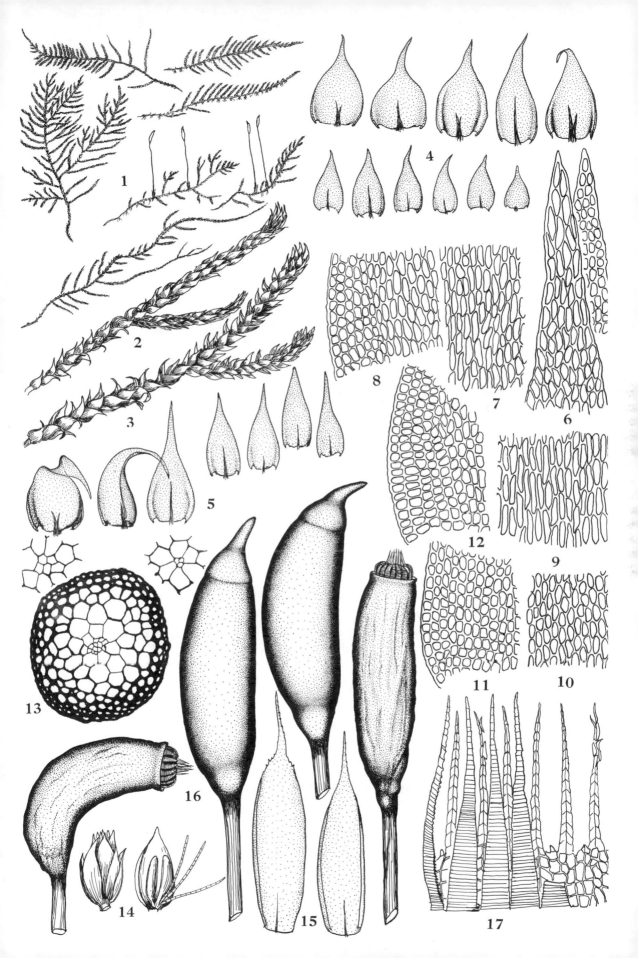

papillose above; basal membrane rather low, reddish brown, smooth and rather thick walled; segments nearly as long as the teeth, subulate, keeled, without medial perforations, often irregular at the tips, smooth or finely papillose; cilia lacking or mere stubs. Spores 10–12 μ, brown, smooth, ripe in July. Plate 94.

20.50 Growing on dry rocks, rotten wood, and bases of trees, usually in shade, lowland to alpine summits.

20.51 Europe and northern Asia. Common in Utah. Yukon, British Columbia, Nevada, east to Saskatchewan, North Dakota to New Mexico.

20.52 As originally described, *Leskea williamsii* differs from *L. tectorum* in being smaller and having smaller leaves more gradually and proportionately longer acuminate, the upper margins sometimes serrulate, the medial areolation with some cells about 6 μ wide, and the stem with a central strand. *L. tectorum* is supposed to have broader, more abruptly acuminate, entire leaves with shorter medial cells, 9–14 μ wide, and the stems without a central strand. We have many plants with the narrower type of leaves but none with serrulate margins. And, as far as was demonstrated, all of them have a central strand of small thin-walled cells which often become compressed by growth of the surrounding thicker-walled cortical cells. It is often difficult to determine if the vaguely denser spot in the center of the stem section is composed of several small crushed cells or a single large cell with a much infolded wall. Indeed, some stem sections show no evident central strand, but other supporting traits of *L. williamsii* are lacking. I find it impossible to separate the plants into two species.

20.53 1a. Fo. **cyrtophylla** (Kindb.) Grout. Plants usually with densely tufted, ascending to erect slender branches from prostrate, frequently denuded main stems. Plate 93, figs. 13–17.

20.54 Mostly in very dry habitats, sometimes exposed to the sun.

20.55 Cache, Sanpete, Carbon, Garfield, and San Juan counties.

20.56 1b. Var. **flagellifera** (Best) Grout. Plants loosely matted or somewhat tufted by the predominantly flagelliform branches, often appearing as a mass of green threads. Stems usually creeping, leafy or ± denuded. Plate 93, figs. 18–22.

20.57 Usually growing on dry rocks and bases of trees, and in crevices in cool shaded situations. Widely distributed in the range of the species.

20.58 Arizona, Daggett and San Juan counties.

20.59 Since the general run of *L. tectorum* specimens may show some stems with deciduous, flagellate branches which may range from a few slightly attenuated tips to long threadlike ends, I am limiting this form to those which are predominantly or entirely flagelliferous.

20.60 **2. Leskeella arizonae** (Williams) Flow. Plants small and slender, resembling typical *L. tectorum* and superficially indistinguishable. Stems irregularly to somewhat regularly pinnate, frequently becoming flagellate; paraphyllia lacking or very few. Stem leaves broadly ovate and abruptly acuminate to ovate-lanceolate, 0.5–1.2 mm long, concave with a deep fold on each side of the base; margins plane to revolute in part or from the base to apex on 1 or rarely both sides, entire to serrulate above; costa extending into the acumen, moderately slender and occasionally percurrent to very stout and thick, often ending bluntly and occasionally papillose or even toothed at back above; medial cells oval to oblong or rhomboidal, 6–8 μ wide; alar cells numerous, quadrate or often predominantly transversely elongated, extending high up on the margins. Branch leaves smaller, ovate-acute to ovate-lanceolate, $\pm$ serrulate at the tips, sometimes strongly so in young terminal leaves, occasionally low papillose at the apex and along the margins. Dioicous. Fruit rare. Capsules slightly inclined and slightly curved, about 1 mm long, ovoid, slightly contracted below the mouth and finely wrinkled when dry; lid conic with a short, straight beak; peristome teeth transversely striate below, papillose above; basal membrane of the endostome $\frac{1}{3}$–$\frac{1}{2}$ the length of the teeth; segments slender, keeled, scarcely perforated, finely papillose; cilia 1–2, nearly as long as the segments. (Description of sporophyte after Williams.) Plate 93, fig. 23.

20.61 On dry shaded rock and bases of trees.

20.62 Arizona, southern Utah, and probably adjacent states.

20.63 The present plants deviate from the original concept of *L. arizonae* in the larger size and serrulate apices of the leaves which also become papillose in some plants.

HYPNACEAE

21.1 Plants mostly prostrate, often forming interwoven mats. Stems usually regularly to irregularly pinnately branched but sometimes very sparingly branched, creeping and anchored by rhizoids on the lower side toward the base or stoloniferous and anchored throughout, sometimes becoming ascending or erect when crowded, especially when growing in shallow water, central strand lacking, weak or occasionally distinct. Leaves various, costa single, forked, short and double, or lacking; upper cells oblong, elongate-rhomboidal to linear, mostly smooth; basal cells mostly shorter and broader. Seta long, from a small budlike branch; capsules ovoid to cylindric, mostly curved and asymmetric; peristome perfect, double, the cilia often rudimentary or lacking in species with erect capsules; teeth strongly jointed, the lower joints with fine transverse lines, these sometimes lacking in species with erect capsules; segments mostly keeled.

21.2 A large family of diverse characteristics, often divided into subfamilies which are sometimes given the rank of families. In manuals covering small local areas, the limited number of genera and species are better accommodated in a more conservative treatment.

413

21.3   1. Costa mostly single, reaching the middle of the leaf or beyond (often forked in some leaves of *Hygrohypnum*)

    2. Plants large, treelike with erect secondary stems arising from horizontal underground stolons and bearing a dense cluster of branches at the summit .... 1. *Climacium* 21.5

    2. Plants medium sized to small, not treelike

      3. Leaves lanceolate with 1–2 strong plicae extending to the apex; plants glossy yellowish green when dry

        4. Plants growing on dry rocks and trees; branch tips curved when dry; capsules erect and symmetric, cilia rudimentary or lacking; montane .... 5. *Homalothecium* 21.114

        4. Plants of bogs at high elevations; branch tips straight; capsules curved, asymmetric, cilia well developed .... 6. *Tomenthypnum* 21.119

      3. Leaves plane, or if plicate the plications short, not continuous to the apex variously colored

        5. Branches strongly julaceous, usually hooked at the tips when dry; leaves subrotund to oblong, very concave, obtuse to apiculate .... 4. *Scleropodium* 21.102

        5. Branches not julaceous, or if so, small and slender; leaves various; medial cells shorter

          6. Leaves of the main stem and branches different in shape and size; capsules mostly short and thick, inclined and asymmetric, not or only moderately contracted under the mouth when dry

            7. Apices of the branch leaves acute to broadly obtuse, the apical cells much shorter than the linear medial cells, rhomboidal to rounded; lid long rostrate .... 2. *Eurhynchium* 21.10

            7. Apices of the branch leaves mostly acuminate; the apical cells not much different from the linear medial cells; lid usually pointed or shortly rostrate .... 3. *Brachythecium* 21.26

          6. Leaves of the main stem and branches not much different; capsules mostly cylindric, curved and usually strongly contracted under the mouth when dry

            8. Stems bearing abundant paraphyllia; leaves typically falcate-secund, except in forms of *C. filicinum*

            8. Stems without or very few inconspicuous paraphyllia

              9. Leaves mostly broad at the apex, blunt to broadly rounded, sometimes apiculate

10. Branches julaceous; alar cells much enlarged and in-
flated .... 10. *Calliergon*   21.213

10. Branches not julaceous, or if so the alar cells not or
only moderately enlarged; costa forked in some leaves
.... 11. *Hygrohypnum*   21.229

9. Leaves mostly acute to tapering or acuminate

11. Leaves typically falcate to circinate, usually secund,
shortly to very long and slenderly acuminate but
straight in some forms, mostly aquatic ....
.... 12. *Drepanocladus*   21.262

11. Leaves straight

12. Plants small; medial leaf cells short ....
.... 7. *Amblystegium*   21.124

12. Plants medium sized; medial cells longer

13. Leaves widely spreading to squarrose, in damp
or wet places .... 9. *Campylium*   21.190

13. Leaves patent to erect-patent

14. Leaves long acuminate; paraphyllia often present, at least on the stems; plants of damp to
wet places .... 13. *Cratoneuron*   21.292

14. Leaves not long acuminate; aquatic ....
.... 7. *Amblystegium*   21.124

21.4 1. Costa lacking or short and double or forking, 1 fork often reaching
the middle of the leaf

15. Leaves complanate, costa lacking or very faint ....
.... 15. *Plagiothecium*   21.351

15. Leaves not complanate

16. Plants aquatic; leaves broadly ovate, oblong or ovate-lanceolate,
falcate-secund, often only at the tips of branches or straight
throughout, acute, blunt or broadly rounded, often strongly concave and the branches julaceous   11. *Hygrohypnum*   21.229

16. Plants not aquatic

17. Leaves squarrose recurved .... 9. *Campylium*   21.190

17. Leaves not squarrose

18. Leaves mostly falcate to circinate, straight in *H. haldanianum;* capsules oblong to cylindric, mostly curved to arcuate .... 14. *Hypnum*   21.320

18. Leaves straight, ecostate; capsules erect and symmetric; peristome segments linear from a low basal membrane

19. Plants minute; leaves less than 0.5 mm long, in thin mats on bases of trees .... 8. *Platydictya* 21.183

19. Plants small to medium sized; leaves larger

   20. Branches commonly bearing numerous small deciduous brood branches with tiny leaves in the axils of the upper leaves; capsules cylindric; peristome cilia lacking .... 16. *Platygyrium* 21.369

   20. Branches without brood branches; capsules ovoid to oblong, occasionally inclined; peristome cilia single, well developed .... 17. *Orthothecium* 21.376

1. CLIMACIUM Web. & Mohr, Naturh.

21.5 Plants large, primary stems creeping, usually underground; secondary stems erect and treelike, naked below, densely branched above, branches ascending to widely spreading or drooping, both bearing branched filiform paraphyllia, triangular in cross section with a distinct central strand. Stem leaves large, thin and pale, clasping the stem; branch leaves smaller, firm and chlorophyllose, patent to erect-patent, of different shape; costa strong, extending nearly to the apex; upper medial cells oblong-rhomboidal to linear. Dioicous. Setae erect, long; capsules erect and symmetric or nearly so, cylindrical, neck short; lid tall conic and rostrate; annulus not differentiated; peristome teeth very narrowly linear-lanceolate, papillose, the joints numerous and close; segments from a low basal membrane, narrow and keeled, as long as the teeth, perforated between the joints; cilia lacking or rudimentary.

21.6 The name refers to a ladder or staircase, suggested by the perforated peristome segments, the halves of which are joined by transverse bars, like a ladder.

21.7 **Climacium dendroides** (Hedw.) Web. & Mohr. Stems erect, loosely tufted, dark to light green, 4–9 cm tall; main branches mostly ascending to erect-patent, sometimes drooping, 1–2 cm long, rebranched, all densely clothed with branched filiform paraphyllia, becoming reddish and sometimes feltlike on older parts. Leaves of the main stem mostly ovate, sharply acute or obtuse-apiculate, entire, 2–3 mm long. Leaves of branches green and firm, mostly 2–2.5 mm long, variable in shape and other traits, the upper ones oblong-lanceolate, acute to obtuse, coarsely serrate above; the lower leaves broader, ovate-lanceolate to oblong-ligulate, mostly acute, serrulate to nearly entire; lamina concave, plicate, often incurved at the apex, basal angles ± cordate-auriculate; costa extending nearly to the apex; upper cells rhomboidal to fusiform, sometimes linear-rhomboidal, mostly 10–12 μ wide; alar cells wider, shorter and irregular, sometimes inflated; basal cells broad and colored; large leaves with an oval area of large, thin-walled inflated cells between the costa and the margin on each side. Fruit extremely rare. Capsules shortly cylindric, the urn about 2 mm long, tapering to a short neck, the walls thick and firm, reddish brown at maturity; lid tall conic with a thick beak, straight or inclined. Spores 13–20 μ, light yellowish or yellowish brown. Plate 95, figs. 1–7.

21.8   On wet soil and humus along brook and pond banks, in seepage areas and bogs in high mountains of Utah.

21.9   Europe and Asia. Alaska, across Canada to New Brunswick, south to New Jersey and the Great Lakes states. In the mountains to New Mexico, Utah, and California. Locally abundant in the Uinta Mountains.

2. EURHYNCHIUM B.S.G.

21.10   Plants small to large, green to yellowish green; stems creeping or prostrate, ± stoloniferous, regularly to irregularly pinnately branched, forming interwoven mats or sometimes crowded into erect tufts. Branch leaves smaller and of different shape from the stem leaves, oval to ovate-lanceolate, acute to broadly obtuse, mostly serrulate to serrate; costa extending 1/2–4/5 the length of the blade, ending in a spine at back; medial cells linear; apical cells (in our species) shortly rhomboidal to rounded; alar cells usually differentiated, quadrate, rounded or shortly oblong, often irregular. Stem leaves larger, usually longer and with acute to acuminate apices, occasionally some of them narrowly obtuse, ± excavate at the base. Seta rather long; capsules ovoid to shortly oblong, asymmetric, inclined to horizontal, rather swollen above, often contracted under the mouth when dry; lid conic with a long inclined beak ¼–½ the length of the urn; peristome double.

21.11   The name refers to the long beak on the lid of the capsule.

21.12   1. Branch leaves 1–1.5 mm long; costa 7/8 the leaf length; stem leaves slightly larger, ovate-lanceolate, slightly acuminate or narrowly acute. .... 1. *E. substrigosum* 21.14

21.13   1. Branch leaves 0.5–0.9 mm long, about ½–¾; stem leaves deltoid, acute to strongly acuminate, 0.8–1.3 mm long; plant more slender .... 2. *E. pulchellum* 21.18

21.14   **1. Eurhynchium substrigosum** Besch. in Card. Plants in loose or dense mats, green to pale yellowish. Stems 2–4(10) cm long, usually with elongated, irregularly pinnate, secondary stems, 1–3 cm long; branches not julaceous, blunt or sometimes pointed. Branch leaves erect-patent to somewhat spreading, not imbricated when dry, 0.8–1.2 mm long, ovate to shortly lanceolate-ligulate, apex mostly obtuse to rounded, ± decurrent, costa 7/8 the leaf length, ending in a spine at back; margins ± serrate, often entire below; medial leaf cells linear, mostly 7–9 μ wide; apical cells shortly rhomboidal to rounded; alar cells rather numerous (7–10 marginal), irregularly quadrate or oblong rounded. Stem leaves larger, 1.2–1.5 mm long, ovate-lanceolate to elongate triangular-ovate, evenly tapering or slightly acuminate, margins serrate to nearly entire; costa usually not ending in a spine at the back; older leaves of primary stems usually longer acuminate. Monoicous. Seta smooth, erect about 1–1.5 cm long; capsules ovoid to oblong, inclined to horizontal,

417

urn 2–2.5 mm long, yellowish brown, becoming reddish brown with age, often contracted under the mouth when dry; lid conic, long rostrate; peristome reddish, cilia nodulose to somewhat appendiculate. Spores 10–12 μ, finely papillose. Plate 95, figs. 8–13.

21.15   On rather dry or damp soil, roots of trees, and rotten logs.

21.16   Alaska to British Columbia to Mt. Shasta, California, Idaho, Montana, Colorado, Utah and Arizona.

21.17   Several large specimens of *E. pulchellum* were referred to this species by routine determination, but comparative studies showed them to be different. The present specimens look more like a *Brachythecium* than a *Eurhynchium*. Some of the shoots are pale straw colored, and the stem leaves are much like those of several of the smaller *Brachythecia*. The spine terminating the tip of the costa at the back of the branch leaves together with the blunt or obtuse apex will distinguish it from that genus.

21.18   **2. Eurhynchium pulchellum** (Hedw.) Jenn. var. **pulchellum.** Plants mostly small, in loose or dense mats, green to yellowish green, often tinged with brown. Main stems 1–3(10) cm long, creeping, often stoloniferous, irregularly to somewhat regularly pinnately branched; branches 1–2(3) cm long, spreading to erect, slenderly attenuated, not julaceous but rather blunt at the tips. Branch leaves erect-patent to spreading dry or moist, not imbricated, those from the middle of the branch ovate-lanceolate, 0.6–0.9 mm long, acute to bluntly-acute, those toward the ends of branches progressively smaller and relatively broader, ovate to broadly ligulate, obtuse to broadly rounded, often $\pm$ imbricated at the tip of the branch, concave, not plicate; margins flat, serrate; costa slender, about 4/5 the length of the blade, ending in a spine and sometimes slightly toothed at back; apical cells shortly rhomboidal to rounded; medial cells linear; 7–10 μ wide; alar cells irregularly quadrate, oval, or oblong, 6–10 μ on the margin. Stem leaves larger, 0.8–1.3 mm long, more widely spreading, typically broadly deltoid but varying to triangular-ovate or ovate-lanceolate, acute to acuminate, the apex sometimes twisted; base excavate with a strong fold on either side, $\pm$ decurrent; margins usually serrate to the base but sometimes entire below the middle; costa slender; apical cells narrow, not strongly differentiated, alar cells numerous; leaves of older primary stems deltoid-ovate, long and slenderly acuminate, the costa often very short. Dioicous. Seta smooth, 1–2 cm long, reddish brown; capsules ovoid to oblong-cylindric, asymmetric, inclined to horizontal, reddish brown at maturity, urn 1.5–2 mm long, usually contracted below the mouth when dry; lid conic with a long inclined beak;

Plate 95. Climacium dendroides. 1. Two habit sketches, X.4. 2. Portion of branch showing filiform branched paraphyllia, X3.2, detail, X24. 3. Typical main stem leaf, X8. 4. Three branch leaves, upper, left; lower, right, X8. 5. Apical leaf cells, X120. 6. Upper medial cells, X120. 7. Capsule, X8.

8–13. Eurhynchium substrigosum. 8. Habit sketches, X.4. 9. Portion of a secondary stem and branch, X4. 10. Three branch leaves, X8. 11. Two typical stem leaves, X8. 12. Apex of branch leaf, X120. 13. Alar cells of the same, X120.

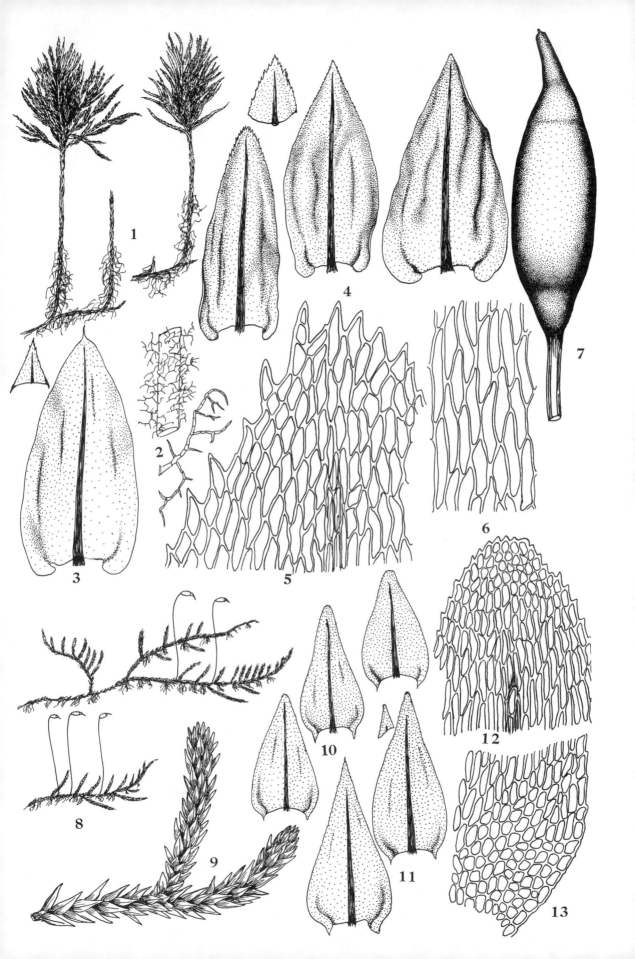

annulus double or triple; peristome teeth reddish at maturity, narrowly lanceolate from an oblong base, acuminate, joints rather close; basal membrane of the endostome rather high, segments rather broad, split down the middle, cilia 2–3, slender and nodulose, both yellowish and finely papillose. Spores 10–12 μ, smooth, maturing in summer or autumn. Plate 96, figs. 1–6.

21.19 On dry or damp soil, rocks, bases of trees, and fallen trunks, mostly on shaded hillsides and banks in our region.

21.20 Eurasia, northern Africa, and in the northern Andes to Bolivia. Alaska to Nevada and in the Rocky Mountains to Utah and Arizona, eastward across the northern United States to the New England states and adjacent Canada.

21.21 Several of the variations of this species have been treated as varieties or even species. *E. substrigosum*, given specific rank here, might be considered a variety or just a larger form with larger and proportionately narrower leaves. At the other extreme are smaller forms the most notable of which is the following.

21.22 2a. Var. **diversifolium** (B.S.G.) C. Jens. Plants smaller, in denser intricate mats. Stems more regularly and closely pinnately branched. Branches short, 0.5–1 cm long, often clustered, erect, julaceous and blunt or truncate at the tips. Stem leaves smaller, shorter, less acuminate and mostly acute, some blunt. Branch leaves smaller, 0.4–0.6 mm long. Plate 96, figs. 7–10.

21.23 Same habitat as the species but ranging higher in the mountains.

21.24 Northern Eurasia and northern Africa. Mostly western, British Columbia, Alberta, southward to Nevada and New Mexico.

21.25 Some specimens may contain a few plants of typical form, especially along the edges of the mat.

3. BRACHYTHECIUM B.S.G.

21.26 Plants small and slender to moderately robust, prostrate and creeping on various substrata, usually in shade, forming thin or dense mats. Stems irregularly branched or occasionally subpinnate; central strand present. Stem leaves deltoid to lanceolate, narrowly acute to long and slenderly acuminate, concave throughout or excavate at the base in most species, plane or plicate, costate to the middle or beyond; base often decurrent;

Plate 96. 1–6. Eurhynchium pulchellum. 1. Habit sketches, X.4. 2. Portion of secondary stem with branch, X6. 3. Five branch leaves from base upward, X8. 4. Seven stem leaves from different specimens showing the range of variation, X8. 5. Apex of branch leaf and alar cell with medial cells lower right, X120. 6. Four capsules, X8.

7–10. Fo. diversifolium. 7. Habit sketches, X.4. 8. Portion of secondary stem with branch, X6. 9. Seven branch leaves from base upward, X80. 10. Three typical stem leaves, X8.

420

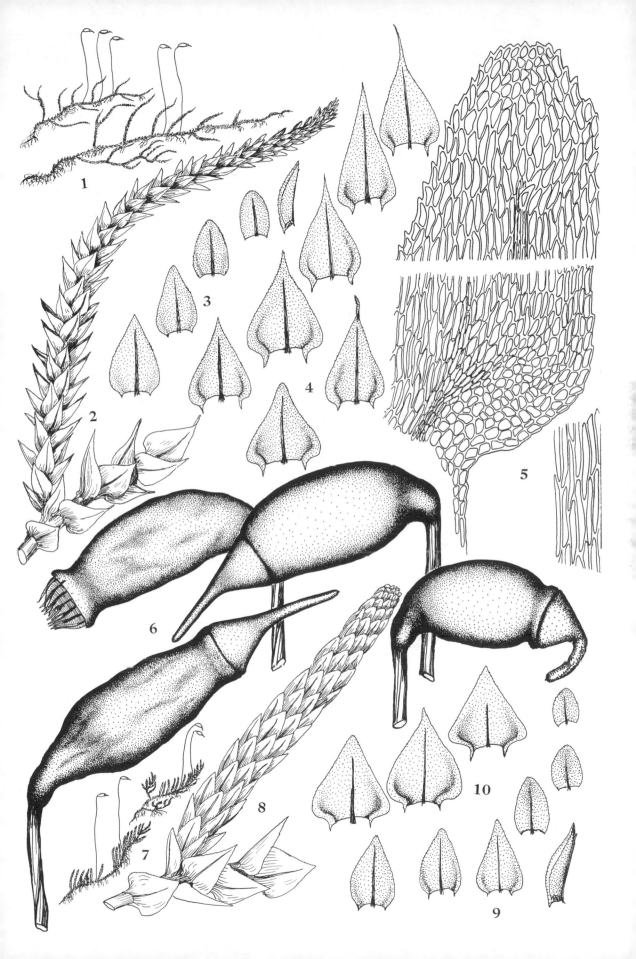

margins entire or serrate; upper leaf cells mostly linear-rhomboidal, often sinuous, mostly 7–10 μ wide; alar cells ± differentiated. Branch leaves smaller, shorter, and proportionately narrower, usually less narrowly acuminate; margins more strongly serrate; upper cells often shorter, alar cells fewer. Seta long, smooth or papillose, twisted to the right when dry; capsules short and thick, ovoid to shortly oblong, mostly curved and asymmetric, inclined to horizontal (subcylindric and nearly erect in *B. fendleri* and *oxycladum*); neck scarcely differentiated externally; annulus of 2–3 rows of cells, poorly differentiated, usually adhering to the mouth of the capsule; lid convex-conic, apiculate to rostrate; peristome typically hypnaceous, cilia well developed (or rudimentary in *B. fendleri*).

21.27 The name means short box, referring to the short capsule.

21.28 A large and difficult genus; our species may be divided into the following groups.

21.29 *B. collinum* group, including *fendleri, delicatulum, suberythrorrhizon,* and *erythrorrhizon,* characterized by the relatively small size, slender habit, and monoicous inflorescence (except in *B. erythrorrhizon* which is rather large and dioicous), the smooth seta (except in some forms of *B. collinum* and var. *idahense* in which it may be distantly low papillose), the capsules inclined to horizontal (suberect and subcylindric in *fendleri*) and by the drier habitat.

21.30 *B. salebrosum* group, including *flexicaule, albicans, campestre,* and *oxycladum,* characterized by the larger size, some forms robust, the stem leaves mostly ovate-lanceolate, monoicous inflorescence, short, inclined or horizontal capsules (except in *B. oxycladum* which is dioicous and often with erect subcylindric capsules), the quadrate or shortly oblong alar cells, often slightly enlarged but not sharply set off, never inflated, the smooth seta (except *B. campestre* in which it is weakly papillose above and smooth below), and by the damp or wet habitat.

21.31 *B. rivulare* group, including *lamprocrhyseum, asperrimum, nelsoni* and *starkei,* characterized by the larger size, often robust, the stem leaves broadly ovate-lanceolate to deltoid-ovate, dioicous (except in *B. starkei*), alar cells enlarged and often inflated at least in some leaves; seta papillose throughout and by the damp or wet habitat.

21.32 1. Plants relatively small and slender; branch leaves mostly up to 1 mm long

    2. Plants synoicous, branch leaves oblong-lanceolate to narrowly ovate-lanceolate; seta smooth; capsule nearly erect and symmetric, cilia rudimentary, basal membrane 1/5–1/4 .... 2. *B. fendleri* 21.39

    2. Plants monoicous; capsules slightly inclined to horizontal, cilia well developed, basal membrane 1/4–1/2

       3. Branch leaves ovate-lanceolate or shorter

422

4. Most leaves ± abruptly acuminate, straight, not plicate, sometimes a few falcate; branch leaves broadly ovate-lanceolate to suborbicular; stem leaves broadly ovate-lanceolate to deltoid; seta smooth or sometimes distantly low-papillose .... 1. *B. collinum* 21.34

4. Most leaves gradually acuminate, some of them falcate and/or plicate .... 4. *B. suberythrorrhizon*

3. Branch leaves narrowly oblong-lanceolate to lanceolate; stem leaves similar or slenderly ovate-lanceolate, usually long and slenderly acuminate, mostly straight with a fold on each side of the base; alar cells quadrate to oblong, 4–8 on the margins; capsules suberect to strongly inclined; seta smooth or distantly low-papillose .... 3. *B. delicatulum* 21.43

21.33 1. Plants medium sized to large; branch leaves mostly more than 1 mm long

5. Branch leaves entire; stem leaves ovate-lanceolate, very long and slenderly acuminate, lightly plicate; alar cells small, quadrate, and numerous; seta smooth .... 10. *B. albicans* 21.73

5. Branch leaves serrate to serrulate

6. Seta smooth throughout; leaves with a strong fold at the base on each side

7. Main shoots somewhat julaceous; stem leaves broadly ovate to deltoid, abruptly short acuminate, narrowly decurrent, strongly concave and spoon-shaped; alar cells rather large, quadrate, numerous .... 6. *B. digastrum* 21.55

7. Main shoot not julaceous; stem leaves ovate-lanceolate, mostly slenderly acuminate, only a few shortly so, excavate at the base, canaliculate above, not spoon-shaped

8. Stem leaves lightly plicate; basal cells becoming gradually shorter and broader; alar cells moderately enlarged, quadrate to shortly oblong, not sharply set off; monoicous; capsules asymmetric, curved, inclined to horizontal .... 8. *B. salebrosum* 21.63

8. Stem leaves strongly plicate; dioicous

9. Leaves mostly straight, only occasionally a few falcate; alar cells small, quadrate and usually numerous; capsules cylindric, suberect or curved .... 9. *B. oxycladum* 21.69

9. Leaves mostly falcate, often secund; alar cells few to rather numerous, rather small to moderately enlarged, mostly quadrate; capsules curved, inclined to horizontal .... 5. *B. erythrorrhizon* 21.51

6. Seta roughened with projecting papillae

423

10. Seta lightly papillose above, becoming smooth below; stem leaves broadly ovate-acuminate to ovate-lanceolate, plane or slightly plicate; margins narrowly revolute; alar cells quadrate to shortly oblong, few to rather numerous, slightly to moderately enlarged, not inflated; monoicous .... 7. *B. campestre* 21.59

10. Seta roughened throughout

11. Stem leaves mostly strongly plicate, broadly ovate, ovate-lanceolate or triangular, narrow at the apex, excavate at the base; alar cells variable, scarcely differentiated to much enlarged, thin walled, often inflated, few to numerous; dioicous; lid high conic, long rostrate; fruit rare in our region

12. Stem leaves gradually long and slenderly acuminate; leaves patent to erect-patent, the shoots appearing slender, gradually tapering to the ends, often stoloniform .... 14. *B. asperrimum* 21.93

12. Stem leaves rather abruptly short acuminate; leaves patent to spreading; the shoots appearing thicker and more robust, not much tapering, rather abruptly pointed, not stoloniform .... 15. *B. lamprochryseum* 21.97

11. Stem leaves not or only slightly plicate; lid conic with a short, often thick point

13. Alar cells numerous, moderately enlarged, ± quadrate, with walls firm, not inflated; stem leaves mostly triangular-ovate, much like *B. nelsonii*, but monoicous; seta less strongly roughened; usually on damp or dry substrata in shady places at high altitudes .... 11. *B. starkei* 21.79

13. Alar cells numerous, oval to oblong, usually thin walled and inflated, often forming auricles; dioicous, fruit infrequent

14. Stem leaves mostly triangular-ovate, narrowly acuminate, strongly excavate at the base, flattish above; alar cells numerous often extending more than ½ way toward the costa; in damp shady places at high altitudes .... 12. *B. nelsonii* 21.83

14. Stem leaves mostly ovate to broadly ovate-lanceolate, broad near the apex, shortly and broadly acute to acuminate, strongly concave like the bowl of a spoon, often strongly decurrent; alar cells rarely extending more than half way to the costa, sometimes forming large auricles; in wet places .... 13. *B. rivulare* 21.89

21.34 1. **Brachythecium collinum** (C. Muell.) B.S.G. Plants small, slender, in loose or dense mats, sometimes in compact cushions, variable in habit, green to yellowish green, sometimes straw colored, dull to glossy. Stems

424

1–5 cm long, short and closely branched to elongated with ± distant branches, sometimes becoming stoloniform and occasionally flagelliform; rhizoids usually abundant and tufted; branches usually short, 2–10 mm long, blunt to tapering at the ends, often upturned when closely and densely disposed, terete-foliolate, julaceous or with the leaves open; leaves widely variable according to habitat; when dry erectpatent, loosely appressed or tightly imbricated whence the shoots appear cordlike, when moist erect-patent to somewhat spreading or loosely appressed. Stem leaves broadly ovate to deltoid-ovate, rather abruptly short acuminate, 0.7–1(1.3) mm long; base ± rounded but sometimes with a broad insertion, slightly to rather strongly decurrent, very concave, not plicate; costa slender, extending to the middle or less; margins mostly strongly serrate to the middle or well toward the base, plane; upper cells fusiform to linear-oblong, 6–8 μ wide; alar cells quadrate to shortly oblong, 9–12 μ wide, ± chlorophyllose, numerous, 6–10 μ on the margins. Branch leaves typically 0.4–0.6(0.8) mm long, typically broadly ovate to ovate-lanceolate and more gradually acuminate, but in some forms subrotund to ovate, very concave and abruptly short acuminate, the tips frequently recurved when dry, strongly serrate to the base, costa extending ½–⅔ but often very short, occasionally ending in a tooth at the back and more rarely with 1–2 teeth lower down. Monoicous. Seta 5–12 mm long, yellowish brown becoming reddish with age, smooth or with low distant papillae; capsules asymmetric, inclined to nearly horizontal, typically ovoid, about 2 mm long, varying to ovoid-oblong and up to nearly 3 mm long, yellowish brown at maturity, becoming reddish brown with age, when dry contracted under the mouth; lid mammillate; cilia 1–2, nodulose to shortly appendiculate, sometimes rudimentary and half as long as the segments. Spores yellowish red, nearly smooth, 9–12 μ. Plate 97.

21.35 On dry or damp soil, humus, rocks, or decaying logs, mostly in shady places, foothills to high mountains.

21.36 Greenland and Europe. British Columbia to northern California, Nevada, Arizona, eastward from Alberta to western Texas and New Mexico.

21.37 This is one of the most common mosses in Utah. It grows on dry foothills under overhanging rocks and roots of trees or shrubs and ranges upward in rather dry or damp places to the highest mountains. It is variable in habit, appearance, and density of growth. In dry exposed situations it often forms compact mats: the stems short with closely crowded, julaceous, blunt branches, the leaves of which are usually only about 0.4–0.6 mm long, subrotund to broadly ovate, deeply concave, and abruptly short acuminate, the tip often divergent or recurved when dry. In this state it is usually straw colored although green around the margins where the branches and leaves are more like the typical form. At the other extreme, plants in damp shady places, often exceeding the typical form in size, with longer branches and leaves, are bright green.

21.38 There is considerable variation in the medial cells of the leaves. In typical plants they are relatively short, but often they are long, especially in the stem leaves. In a few plants the operculum is convex, without a terminal point. Other occasional variations include some leaves falcate and the tips of the stems slightly hooked; stem leaves predominantly deltoid, shortly acuminate, strongly decurrent, tips twisted; branch leaves somewhat complanate, the costa terminating in a tooth at the back; weakly papillose throughout or only in the lower part (especially in some large forms).

21.39 **2. Brachythecium fendleri** (Sull.) Jaeg. Plants in thin to rather dense mats, light green to yellowish green, usually glossy. Shoots slender, 2–3 cm long, irregularly pinnate; branches 0.5–1 cm long, usually tapering, sometimes slightly hooked. Stem leaves mostly ovate-lanceolate, acuminate, often slenderly so, moderately concave, not plicate; margins serrate above, serrulate or entire below the middle, usually plane, costa extending ½–⅓ the length of the blade; upper cells linear, 8–10 μ wide; alar cells quadrate to shortly oblong, 10–13 μ wide, usually clear but sometimes chlorophyllose, 5–10 μ on the margins; branch leaves smaller, ovate-lanceolate to oblong-lanceolate, serrate; alar cells fewer. Synoicous. Seta 0.5–1.5 cm long, reddish brown, smooth; capsules shortly oblong-cylindric, erect and symmetric, 1.5–2 mm long, yellowish brown at maturity, becoming reddish brown with age, slightly contracted under the mouth when dry; lid obtuse or with a short thick beak, usually inclined; cilia lacking or 1–2 rudimentary, up to ½ the length of the segments. Spores greenish yellow to yellowish brown, finely punctate, 10–15 μ. Plate 99, figs. 1–11.

21.40 Growing on dry or damp soil, often on open banks, under overhanging rocks or roots of trees, bases of shrubs, or ledges; foothills and mountains.

21.41 Utah and southern Wyoming to Arizona, New Mexico, and Texas.

21.42 This moss superficially resembles *B. collinum* but nearly always forms thinner more spreading mats and has narrower leaves, synoicous inflorescences, erect capsules, and an endostome with a low basal membrane and rudimentary cilia.

21.43 **3. Brachythecium delicatulum** Flow. Plants small, usually in thin, green or yellowish green, often somewhat silky mats. Shoots slender, ir-

---

Plate 97. **1–17. Brachythecium collinum.** 1. Habit sketches of the typical form, X.4. 2. Same, X2. 3. Three branch leaves, X8. 4. Four stem leaves, X8. 5. Typical leaf apex, X120. 6. Average upper medial leaf cells, X120. 7. Two areas of alar cells to show the range of variation, X120. **Note:** The righthand figure represents var. **idahense** better, although the extent of the area of the alar cells varies in leaves from the same stem and in different specimens. Intergradation is frequently encountered. 8. Five capsules, X8. 9. Two perichaetial buds showing the leaves and the smooth and distantly papillose setae, X8. 10. Habit sketch of a strongly julaceous form, X.4. 11. Same, X2. 12. Portion of branch showing the strongly and closely imbricated leaves when dry, X4. 13. Portion of branch of a form with closely imbricated leaves, tips recurved when dry, X4. 14. Three leaves of a small form, less acuminate. 15. Two stem leaves from same plant, X8. 16. Four branch leaves from a small julaceous form. 17. Three stem leaves from the same plant, X8.

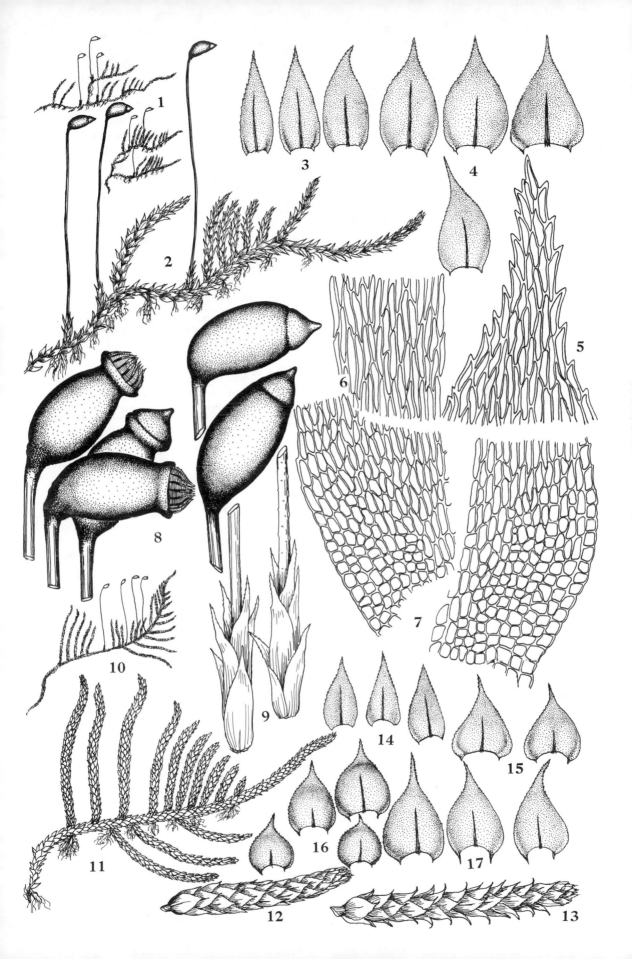

regularly branched to subpinnate, 1–5 cm long, often stoloniform with tufted rhizoids to the tips; branches up to 1.5 cm long, slender and often slightly hooked at the tips. Leaves appressed when dry, patent to widely spreading when moist. Stem leaves lanceolate to narrowly oblong-lanceolate, gradually slenderly acuminate, sometimes filiform, straight or slightly falcate, 1.5–2.5 mm long, 0.35–0.5 mm wide, excavate at base with a narrow fold on each side, flattish above; margins serrulate to the base or entire in the lower half, occasionally entire throughout; costa slender, extending ½–¾ the length of the blade; upper cells linear, 7–10 μ wide; alar cells quadrate to shortly oblong, 10–12 μ wide, usually clear, 5–10 μ on the margins. Branch leaves similar, smaller, narrower with alar cells fewer. Monoicous. Seta smooth to distantly low papillose, reddish, 1–1.5 cm long; capsules ovoid to ovoid-oblong, inclined and asymmetric to erect and nearly symmetric, 1.5–2 mm long, reddish brown; rounded or bluntly pointed; cilia 2, very slender and nodulose, nearly as long as the segments, but in erect capsules short to rudimentary. Spores yellowish brown, 10–15 μ, finely punctate. Plate 99, figs. 12–17.

21.44   Growing on damp or rather dry soil and rocks in shady places, often under overhanging rocks and exposed roots of trees.

21.45   Salt Lake County: Wasatch Mountains, City Creek Canyon, near the forks, 5,700 ft.

21.46   A small moss related to *B. fendleri* and *B. suberythrorrhizon,* differing mainly in the somewhat silky texture and the longer, narrower, lanceolate to oblong-lanceolate leaves with very long slenderly acuminate apices. On the whole the capsules are shorter, inclined and asymmetric or erect and nearly symmetric like those of *B. fendleri,* and with rudimentary cilia from a low basal membrane. The seta is usually distantly low-papillose, and the inner perichaetial leaves are filiform acuminate. The type was originally referred to *B. thedenii* and sanctioned by A. J. Grout, but I was never satisfied with this disposition since the plant does not fit Schimper's original description nor the illustration in *Bryologia Europaea,* plate 548. Over the years I searched the literature for a suitable name, especially among the varieties of small species, but those with narrow leaves are far off in other traits.

21.47   **4. Brachythecium suberythrorrhizon** Ren. & Card. Plants small to medium sized, green to yellowish green, somewhat glossy, in thin to fairly thick mats. Shoots slender, 2–3 cm long, irregularly pinnate, rather closely to distantly branched, often stoloniform; branches 5–12 mm long, straight or curved, slender to somewhat julaceous. Stem leaves 1.3–2.3 mm long, usually patent, ovate-lanceolate to oblong-lanceolate or some-

---

Plate 98. 1–4. **Brachythecium collinum** var. **idahense.** 1. Habit sketches, X.4. 2. Same, X2. 3. Five branch leaves, X8. 4. Five stem leaves, X8.

5–11. **Brachythecium suberythrorrhizon.** 5. Habit sketches, X.4. 6. Same, X2. 7. Four branch leaves, X8. 8. Four stem leaves, X8. 9. Apex of an average leaf, X120. 10. Area of alar cells, X120. 11. Four capsules, X8.

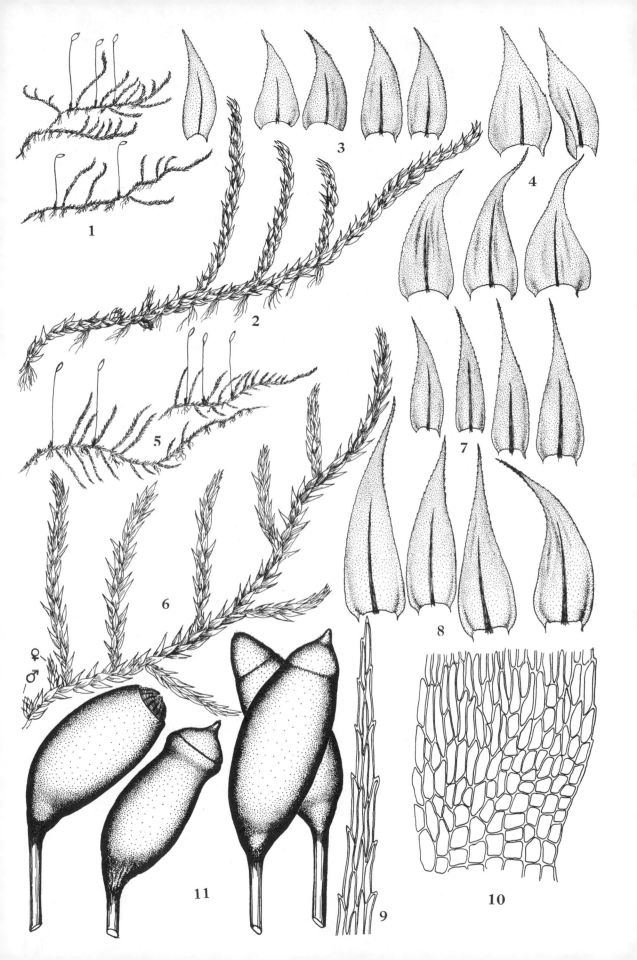

what triangular-lanceolate, gradually and narrowly acuminate, some-times very slenderly so, straight to slightly falcate, the lamina plane or moderately plicate; margins serrate to the base; costa extending about $\frac{2}{3}$ the length of the leaf; upper cells linear, 6–9 μ wide, variable in dif-ferent leaves and different plants; alar cells usually shortly oblong but sometimes quadrate, 10–14 μ wide, 4–9 μ on the margins. Branch leaves narrower, narrowly ovate-lanceolate to oblong-lanceolate, 1–1.5 mm long, more sharply serrate, alar cells fewer. Monoicous. Seta 0.8–1.5 cm long, reddish, smooth; capsules suberect to inclined, ovoid to ovoid-oblong, nearly symmetric to slightly curved, when dry slightly to rather strongly contracted below the mouth, more strongly inclined to horizontal, 1.5–2 mm long, yellowish brown at maturity, becoming reddish brown with age; lid sometimes shortly and broadly beaked; cilia 2–3, nodulose, near-ly as long as the teeth but sometimes only half as long. Spores 10–14 μ, finely punctate, yellowish brown. Plate 98, figs. 5–11.

21.48 On moist or rather dry soil, rocks, and bases of trees, frequently under overhanging rocks and roots, usually in shady places.

21.49 Eastern Oregon, Idaho, Wyoming, Utah, and Colorado.

21.50 Frequent in ravines and canyons, in the foothills up to about 6,000 ft. Close to *B. collinum* var. *idahense* (Ren. & Card.) Grout, differing in the narrower leaves with fewer differentiated alar cells, more of them ob-long rather than quadrate, the more erect capsules with the lid high conic-convex, obtuse, and the perichaetial leaves slenderly-long acumi-nate, often hairlike. In a few specimens I observed 1–2 antheridia in one or two of the perichaetia while abundant perigonia occurred on the same stem.

21.51 **5. Brachythecium erythrorrhizon** B.S.G. Plants medium sized, in spread-ing or interwoven mats, green to yellowish green or straw colored. Shoots moderately slender, irregularly pinnate, 2–5 cm long; usually not stoloniform; rhizoids abundant on older parts. Branches short, up to 1 cm long. Stem leaves patent, mostly ovate to broadly ovate-lanceolate, shortly to longly acuminate, ± falcate, 2–2.5 mm long, concave and usually strongly plicate, entire to slightly serrate above; margins ± re-curved to sharply reflexed; costa extending $\frac{2}{3}$–$\frac{3}{4}$ the leaf length; up-per cells linear, ± flexuous, 8–10 μ wide; alar cells quadrate, shortly oblong to rhomboidal, 10–15 μ wide, 4–8 on the margins, usually not sharply set off. Branch leaves ovate-lanceolate to lanceolate, 1–1.8 mm long, mostly falcate and plicate, serrate above, entire or nearly so below;

Plate 99. **1–11. Brachythecium fendleri.** 1. Habit sketches, X.4. 2. Same, X2. 3. Dissected synoicous bud, X8. 4–5. Branch and stem leaves of narrower form. 6. Branch and stem leaves of broader form, X8. 7. A perichaetial leaf, X8. 8. Leaf apex and upper cells. 9. Typical area of alar cells. 10. Capsules, X8. 11. Portion of peristome showing low basal membrane, narrow segments, and rudi-mentary cilia, X60.

12–17. Brachythecium delicatulum. 12. Habit sketches, X.4. 13. Portion of shoot, X2. 14. Three typical branch leaves. 15. Five stem leaves showing variations in different plants, X8. 16. Typical area of alar cells, X120. 17. Typical capsule, X8.

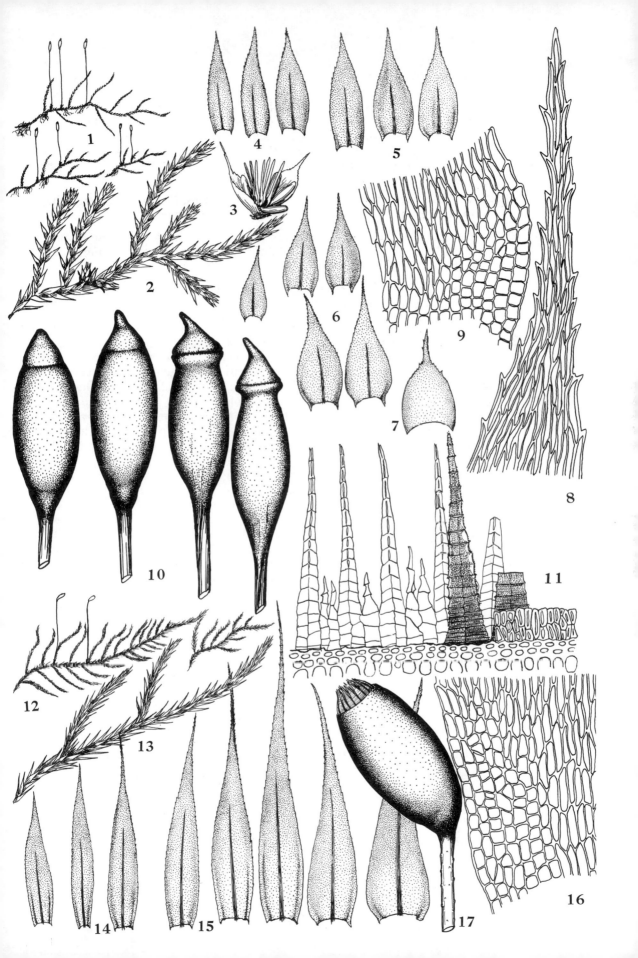

margins ± reflexed. Dioicous. Seta 1–1.7 cm long, smooth, reddish brown; capsules ovoid, asymmetric, strongly inclined to horizontal, about 2 mm long, reddish brown, becoming darker with age, contracted below the mouth when dry; lid with a thickish or narrow point; cilia 1–2, well developed, nodulose. Spores 14–20 μ, minutely papillose. Plate 100, figs. 1–6.

21.52   On damp or rather dry soil, humus, rotten logs, and rocks, mostly high in our canyons and mountains, usually in shaded places.

21.53   Europe and Asia, New Brunswick and Newfoundland, Whiteface Mountain, New York; White Mountains, New Hampshire. Washington to western Montana, south to Utah and Colorado.

21.54   Frequent and locally abundant at high elevations in Utah, mainly in dry or damp places but sometimes found on wet banks. The predominantly falcate and plicate leaves are especially distinctive.

21.55   **6. Brachythecium digastrum** C. Muell. & Kindb. in Macoun. Plants in closely adhering mats, usually bright yellowish green but often olivaceous, brownish below. Shoots irregularly branched to subpinnate, up to 7 cm long, usually densely foliolate and somewhat julaceous; branches up to 1 cm long, less densely foliolate, often loosely julaceous, the leaves open. Stem leaves broadly ovate to triangular-ovate, ± abruptly short-acuminate, sometimes very slenderly so, very deeply concave like the bowl of a spoon, some falcate, 1.3–2 mm long, 0.7–1 mm wide, ± plicate or wrinkled when dry, sulcate at the base on each side, otherwise plane or moderately plicate when moist, strongly so under pressure, short to long and narrowly decurrent; margins widely recurved at the base, plane above, sharply serrate to nearly entire; costa ⅔–¾ the leaf length; upper cells shortly linear-rhomboidal or fusiform, 6–7 μ wide; alar cells quadrate, shortly oblong or transversely elongated, 12–18 μ wide, rather firm, usually numerous and extending to the decurrent wings. Branch leaves smaller and narrower, mostly ovate-lanceolate, acute to gradually shortly acuminate, the tips often twisted, some of them falcate, concave, more strongly serrate, alar cells fewer. Monoicous. Seta 1.5–2 cm long, reddish brown, smooth; capsules oblong, curved, 2–2.5 mm long, strongly inclined to horizontal, yellowish brown at maturity; lid pointed. Plate 100, figs. 7–12.

21.56   On damp soil and rocks in shady places in mountains.

21.57   Canada and northeastern United States, North Carolina, Idaho, Utah, Arizona.

21.58   The present specimens are sterile. They are bright to yellowish green

---

Plate 100.   1–6. Brachythecium erythrorrhizon. 1. Habit sketches, X.4. 2. Same X2. 3. Four branch leaves. 4. Three stem leaves, X8. 5. Alar cells from different leaves showing variations in size and extent, X120. 6. Capsules, X8.

7–12. Brachythecium digastrum. 7. Habit sketch, X.4. 8. Portion of shoot, X1.6. 9. Three branch leaves. 10. Three stem leaves, X8. 11. Upper medial leaf cells. 12. Alar cells, X120.

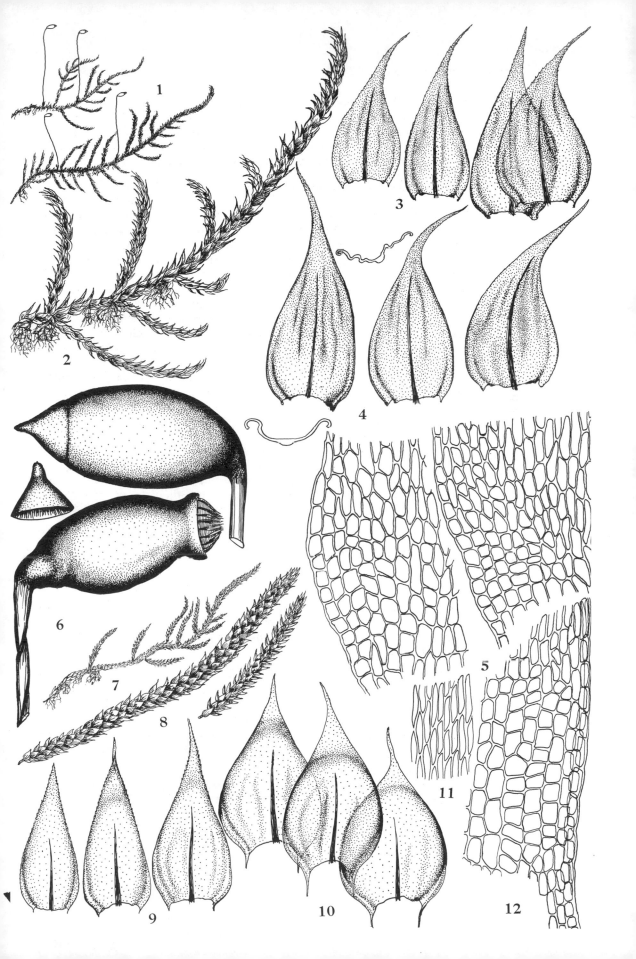

and not dull olivaceous as so many eastern specimens are. Our western forms are larger than those in the eastern states, and although the alar cells are clear, they compare favorably with eastern forms. In some plants many of the leaves are falcate and suggest a broad-leaved form of *B. erythrorrhizon,* but the latter has much longer leaf cells.

21.59   **7. Brachythecium campestre** (C. Muell.) B.S.G. Plants medium sized, yellowish green to dark green, dull to glossy, forming loose or compact interwoven mats. Shoots 3–6 cm long, often slender and stoloniform at the ends, irregularly branched, when dry appearing unusually slender because of closely appressed leaves; when moist the leaves patent to somewhat spreading; rhizoids rather numerous. Stem leaves mostly ovate-lanceolate, shortly to long and slenderly acuminate, 1.5–2.5(3) mm long, 0.6–1.2 mm wide, concave with a strong fold on each side extending high up in the blade, plicate, straight or slightly falcate, only slightly decurrent or not at all; margins serrulate to nearly entire, narrowly revolute; costa slender, extending ⅔–¾ the leaf length; upper cells mostly 7–9 μ wide, linear, often sinuous; alar cells quadrate to shortly oblong, moderately enlarged but not inflated, 10–20 μ wide, few to rather numerous, 4–10 on the margins and across the base, sometimes not well differentiated. Branch leaves lanceolate to ovate-lanceolate, shortly to longly acuminate, 1.5–2 mm long, narrower at the base, mostly serrate to the base or nearly so, not or only slightly plicate; alar cells few. Monoicous. Seta 1–2 cm long, reddish brown, distantly and weakly papillose, often becoming smooth below; capsules reddish brown, ovoid to oblong-cylindric, ± curved and asymmetric, 1.6–2 mm long, inclined to horizontal; lid with a short apiculus; cilia 1–2, slender, pale, strongly nodulose, occasionally slightly appendiculate at base, finely papillose. Spores 12–16 μ, yellowish brown, minutely papillose. Plate 101.

21.60   On damp or rather dry soil in meadows or on humus, rocks, bases of trees and downed logs, usually in shady places.

21.61   Europe, Asia and North Africa. Across Canada and adjacent United States, south to New Jersey, Ohio, Illinois, Utah.

21.62   This moss resembles a small *B. salebrosum* except for the plicate leaves, slightly roughened seta, and more variable alar cells. In our region it is neither common nor freely fruiting, although antheridia and archegonia are usually present.

21.63   **8. Brachythecium salebrosum** (Web. & Mohr) B.S.G. var. **salebrosum.** Plants medium sized to robust, yellowish green, glossy, creeping, in thin or dense mats, brown below. Stems irregularly to subpinnately branched, upward to 10–15 cm long, often much shorter, sometimes stoloniform; branches fairly thick and tapering, 1.5–3 cm long; rhizoids tufted. Stem leaves typically ovate-lanceolate, rounded at the base, usually not de-

Plate 101. Brachythecium campestre. 1. Habit sketches, X.4. 2. Portion of typical shoot, X2. 3. Branch leaves. 4. Stem leaves, X8. 5. Two leaf apices. 6. Two areas of alar cells, X120. 7. Capsules, X8.

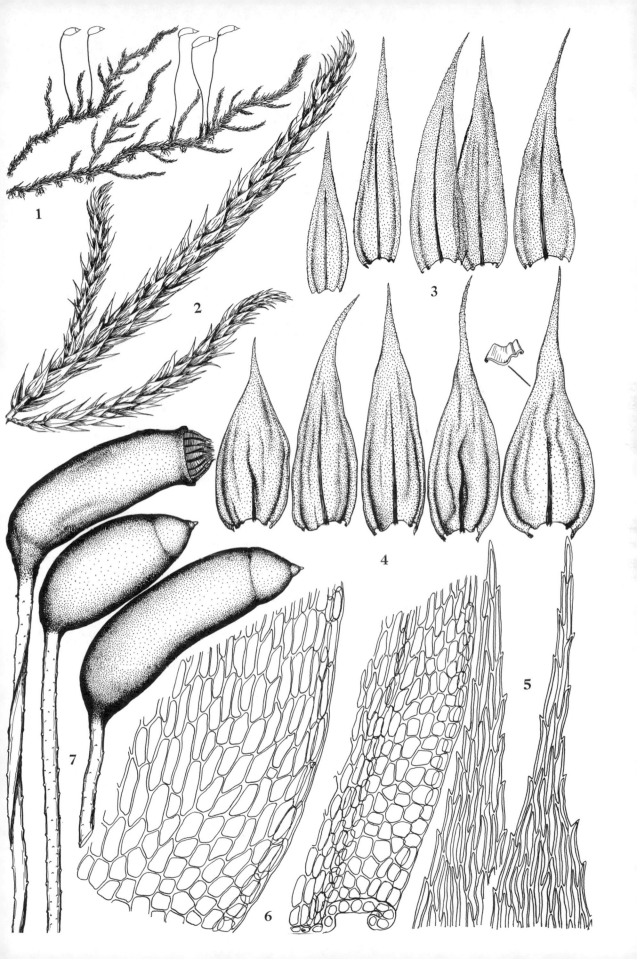

current but sometimes long and narrowly so, strongly acuminate, the apex rather short to long and slender, sometimes twisted, 2–2.5(3) mm long, 0.8–1.3 mm wide and strongly excavate at the base with a fold on each side, plane or slightly plicate above; margins narrowly recurved on 1 or both sides above, serrate above or entire throughout; costa extending ½–⅔ the length of the blade; upper cells linear, straight or vermicular, 7–10 µ wide, often shorter in the apex; basal cells becoming gradually broader and shorter; alar variable, few to fairly numerous, 3–10 µ on the margins, quadrate, oval or oblong, 2–3 times wider than the upper cells, usually not sharply set off, 18–24 µ wide. Branch leaves erect-patent or spreading, 1.3–2.5 mm long, narrowly ovate-lanceolate to lanceolate, usually long and slenderly acuminate, the upper margins typically strongly serrate but in some forms serrulate, less plicate, alar cells fewer. Monoicous. Seta 1–2 cm long, reddish brown, smooth; capsules ovoid to oblong-ovoid, curved and asymmetric, inclined to horizontal, 2–3 mm long; lid apiculate; cilia 2, nearly as long as the segments, nodulose or occasionally subappendiculate. Spores 15–20 µ, smooth or finely punctate. Plate 102.

21.64 On damp or wet soil, rotten logs, rocks, or bases of trees in shady places.

21.65 Eurasia, Africa, and Australia. Northeastern United States and Canada, south to North Carolina, westward to the Great Lakes states, less frequent further west and becoming much more variable, British Columbia to Texas.

21.66 Locally frequent in Utah but variable. We have some robust typical plants, but most of our specimens are small forms with leaves more widely spaced and sometimes slightly falcate.

21.67 8a. Var. **densum** B.S.G. Stem leaves triangular-lanceolate, ± evenly tapering from the base to a narrow apex, sometimes slightly acuminate, serrate above, concave and somewhat more plicate, the alar cells quadrate. Plate 103, figs. 7–8.

21.68 Sporadic across northern United States and Canada, Newfoundland, New Jersey, Indiana, Michigan, British Columbia, Utah.

21.69 **9. Brachythecium oxycladum** (Brid.) Jaeg. Plants in spreading or thick mats, yellowish green to golden yellow, glossy, dark brown below. Stems irregularly branched to subpinnate, 3–10 cm long, rhizoids relatively few, not stoloniform. Leaves erect-patent, appressed when dry, the shoots slender and tapering in the ends. Stem leaves ovate-lanceolate, slenderly acuminate, rounded at the excavate base, often narrowly decurrent, lamina mostly moderately plicate, 2–2.5(3) mm long, 0.8–1.2 mm wide; margins entire or serrulate above, narrowly recurved on 1 or both sides; costa ½–⅔; upper cells linear-fusiform, 7–10 µ wide, wider in the

---

Plate 102. Brachythecium salebrosum. 1. Habit sketch, X.4. 2. Portion of shoot, X1.6. 3. Three branch leaves. 4. Three stem leaves, X8. 5. Two leaf apices, X120. 6. Capsules, X8. 7–8. Alar cells from different plants showing variation in size and area, X120.

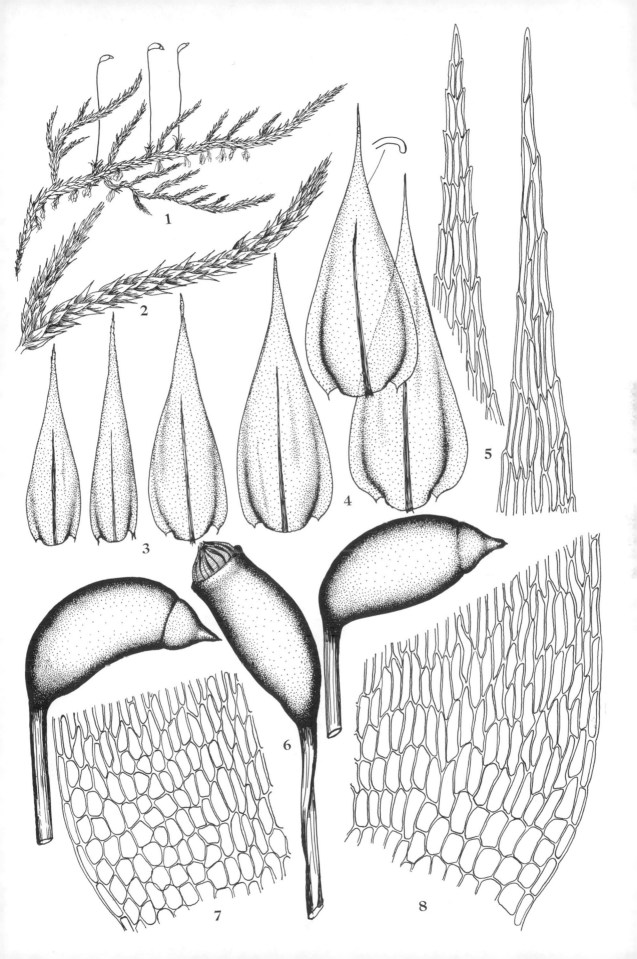

base; alar cells small, 2–2.5 times wider than the upper ones, quadrate, rather numerous, 5–10 μ on the margins, μ chlorophyllose, rather thick walled and firm, sometimes slightly pitted; branch leaves smaller and narrower, acute to slenderly acuminate, often slightly twisted at the tip, usually dentate or serrulate well toward the base and sharply so at the apex. Dioicous or partly monoicous. Capsules subcylindric, slightly curved and asymmetric, 2.5–3.5 mm long, suberect to inclined; lid often shortly beaked; cilia 2, strongly nodulose to appendiculate. Plate 103, figs. 1–6.

21.70 Growing on damp or rather dry soil, rocks, rotten logs, and bases of trees, usually in shady places.

21.71 Northeastern United States and adjacent Canada, southward to North Carolina, westward to Minnesota and Kansas, British Columbia to Texas.

21.72 Usually sterile in Utah, tending to occur at high elevations. The plant intergrades with *B. salebrosum* and *B. albicans*. A number of our western forms have some of the leaves falcate and in a few instances secund. One specimen from Shingle Creek, Summit County, with most of the leaves falcate, is referable to fo. *falcatum* Grout.

21.73 **10. Brachythecium albicans** (Hedw.) B.S.G. var. **albicans.** Plants medium sized to rather large, in thin or dense mats, pale green to yellowish green, glossy. Stems 3–10(15) cm long, irregularly to subpinnately branched, tapering but usually not stoloniform; branches usually short, 5–16 mm long. Stem leaves ovate-lanceolate, rather abruptly long and slenderly acuminate, sometimes filiform, 2.2–3 mm long, 0.7–1.2 mm wide, concave with a strong fold on either side of the rounded base, sometimes narrowly decurrent, ± plicate, sometimes slightly falcate; margins ± narrowly recurved above, entire to slightly denticulate at the apex; costa extending to or beyond the leaf middle; upper cells linear, straight or vermicular, 7–9 μ wide, the apical ones often very narrow; alar cells quadrate to shortly oblong, few to rather numerous, 5–11 μ on the margins, rather thick walled, 2–2.5 times wider than the upper cells, fairly well set off. Branch leaves smaller and narrower, reaching 2.2 mm long, shortly to long and slenderly acuminate, some often falcate, entire or slightly serrulate at the tips; upper cells usually shorter; alar cells fewer. Dioicous. Capsules much like those of *B. salebrosum* but with 2–3 cilia, these usually ± appendiculate. Plate 104, figs. 1–7.

21.74 Growing on damp or rather dry soil, rocks, and bases of trees.

21.75 Europe, north Africa and New Zealand. Alaska to Central California, eastward to Manitoba, Newfoundland. Uncommon in Utah, becoming

---

Plate 103. Brachythecium oxycladum. 1. Habit sketches, X.4. 2. Three branch leaves. 3. Three stem leaves, X8. 4. Leaf apex, X120. 5. Two areas of alar cells showing variation in size and extent, X120. 6. Capsules, X8.

7–8. Brachythecium salebrosum var. **densum.** 7. Typical branch leaves. 8. Stem leaves, X120.

438

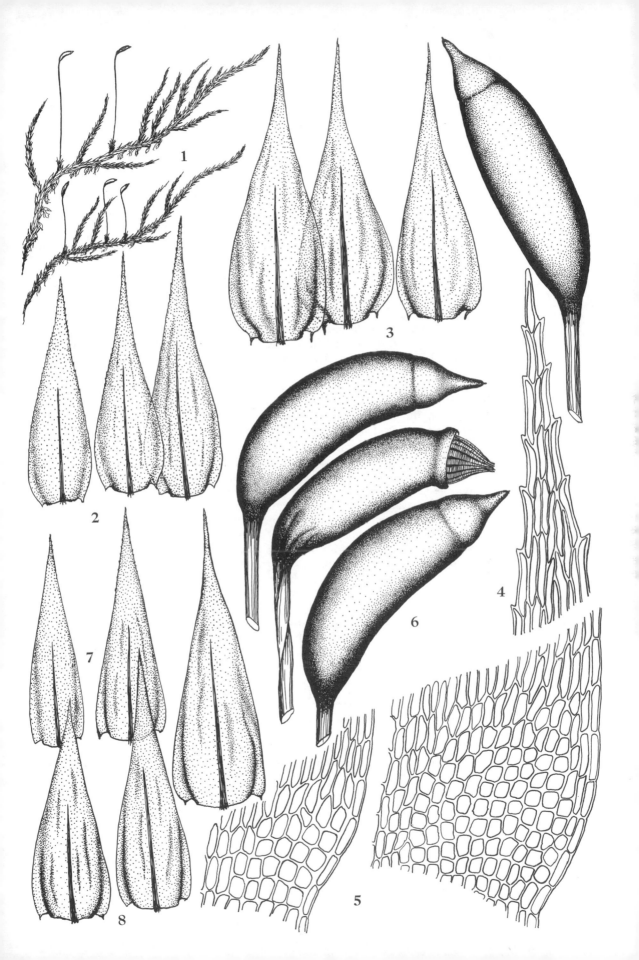

more frequent northward in the Rocky Mountains. Utah County: Mt. Timpanogos, cirque above Aspen Grove, 10,200 ft.

21.76 Closely related to *B. salebrosum*, differing in the dioicous habit, longer, acuminate and more strongly plicate leaves with entire margins and smaller alar cells.

21.77 10a. Var. **occidentale** Ren. & Card. Leaves shorter-acuminate with denticulate apices, slightly falcate and subsecund, and less crowded. Plate 104, figs. 8–9.

21.78 Limited to western North America, Uinta Mountains.

21.79 **11. Brachythecium starkei** (Brid.) B.S.G. Plants medium sized, green to yellowish green, mostly dull and stiffish, usually in loose or open mats, commonly straggling. Stems rather slender, 5(10) cm long, irregularly pinnate; branches 5–20 mm long, usually distant, the ends ± tapering, often somewhat stoloniform; leaves open or loosely appressed when dry, widely spreading or recurved when moist. Stem leaves moderately dense, 1.3–1.8 mm long, 0.5–1.2 mm wide, broadly ovate-deltoid to ovate-lanceolate, shortly acuminate, the tips often twisted, straight to slightly falcate, concave, strongly excavate at the base, not plicate, insertion broad, ± decurrent; margins serrate nearly to the base or only above, occasionally nearly entire, often recurved at base; costa rather slender, mostly $\frac{1}{3}$–$\frac{1}{4}$ the leaf length, occasionally reaching the base of the acumen; medial cells mostly shortly linear-rhomboidal to linear-hexagonal, 9–12 μ wide, usually quite firm; basal cells shorter and wider, often thick walled; alar cells usually numerous, 6–12 on the margin and across the base, mostly quadrate but often rectangular, rather large, 12–22 μ wide, the walls firm, rarely slightly inflated, clear or slightly chlorophyllose. Branch leaves smaller and narrower at the base, mostly ovate-lanceolate, rather broadly acuminate, less decurrent, serrate nearly to the base; alar cells fewer. Monoicous. Seta 1–1.5 cm long, reddish brown, becoming purplish brown with age, roughened with low papillae throughout or sometimes smooth at the base, less commonly with stronger and denser papillae; capsules strongly inclined to horizontal, mostly shortly ovoid, often thick and swollen, 1.5–2 mm long, yellowish brown to light reddish brown when mature, becoming much darker with age, slightly or not at all contracted below the mouth when dry; lid pointed; cilia 2–3, nearly as long as the segments, nodulose to slightly appendiculate. Spores nearly smooth, 12–16 μ. Plate 105, figs. 1–8.

21.80 On damp or rather dry soil, humus, rotten logs and rocks, usually in shady places. Frequent locally in mountains above 7,000 feet and especially in areas of siliceous or ferromagnesian rocks in Utah.

Plate 104. **1–7. Brachythecium albicans.** 1. Habit sketches, X.4. 2. Portion of shoot, X1.6. 3. Four branch leaves. 4. Three stem leaves, X8. 5. Leaf apex. 6. Two areas of alar cells showing variations in size of cells and extent, X120. 7. Capsules, X8.

8–9. Var. occidentale. 8. Stem leaves. 9. Branch leaves, X8.

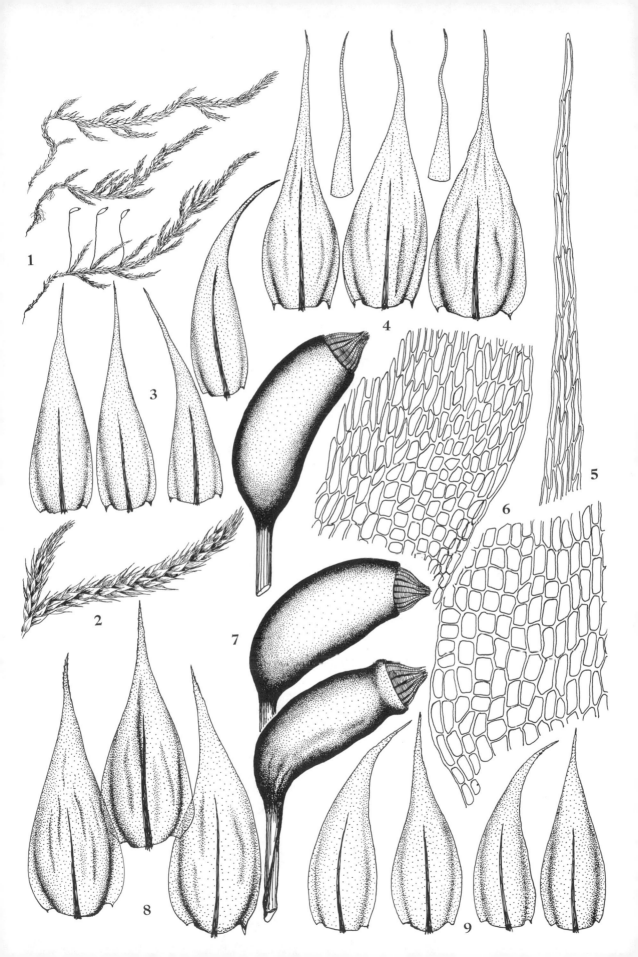

21.81 Europe and northern Asia. Across Canada and northern United States, south to Washington, Montana, Utah, Pennsylvania, and New Jersey.

21.82 When dry, this moss is dull in color and more or less straggling in habit of the slender shoots, but when moistened the appearance improves considerably, the broad, flattish, clear, decurrent stem leaves with a rather short slender costa and serrate margins are distinctive. The wider upper cells and somewhat enlarged quadrate to shortly oblong or rhomboidal alar cells, not inflated, and the monoicous habit distinguishes this from *B. nelsonii*. The leaves are much the same in shape and decurrent base, but the upper cells are linear, the alar cells much larger, often inflated and 18–30 μ wide, in a large area extending nearly to the costa, the seta is much rougher with tall dense papillae, and the plant is dioicous.

21.83 **12. Brachythecium nelsonii** Grout. var. **nelsonii**. Plants medium sized, in loose or dense mats, sometimes thin and straggling, mostly bright green, often becoming yellowish or straw colored. Stems reaching 5–8 cm long, irregularly to subpinnately branched, the branches becoming 1.5 cm long, the leaves sometimes ± complanate, especially in isolated creeping shoots and thin mats. Stem leaves typically deltoid varying to broadly ovate-lanceolate, 1.5–2 mm long, 0.9–1.2 mm wide, the apex usually rather shortly and abruptly acuminate but sometimes long and slender, the tips often twisted, excavate at the base, not plicate, insertion broad, slightly to strongly decurrent and ± auricled; costa rather wide at base, extending ½–¾ the length of the blade; margins entire to distantly serrulate above, usually revolute at base; upper cells linear, mostly 6–9 μ wide; basal cells shorter and wider, becoming 14–18 μ wide; alar cells numerous, suddenly enlarged and usually inflated, oblong to oval-oblong, 18–30 μ wide, often forming auricles and usually extending half way or more to the costa. Branch leaves narrower and smaller, ± elongate-triangular to ovate-lanceolate, the apex more slender, the margins more strongly serrate at the apex, denticulate to entire below. Dioicous. Seta 1.5–2 cm long, reddish brown, strongly and densely to moderately and rather distantly papillose, occasionally smooth at the base; capsules ovoid, strongly inclined to horizontal, asymmetric, 1.5–2 mm long, reddish brown, becoming darker with age, slightly or not at all contracted below the mouth when dry; lid pointed; cilia 2–3, nodulose or subappendiculate, papillose. Spores 9-12 μ, nearly smooth. Plate 106.

21.84 On wet, damp, or rather dry soil, humus, and rotten logs, usually in shady places at high elevations.

21.85 Montana, Idaho to Arizona, Nevada, and Colorado.

21.86 Readily recognized by the deltoid stem leaves with abruptly enlarged, oblong alar cells, often forming large auricles, the upper linear cells,

---

Plate 105. 1–8. Brachythecium starkei. 1. Habit sketches, X.4. 2. Same, X1.6. 3. Five branch leaves. 4. Three stem leaves, X8. 5. Leaf apex. 6. Upper medial leaf cells. 7. Alar cells, X120. 8. Capsules, X8.

9–11. Brachythecium nelsonii var. **intermedium.** 9. Stem leaf X8. 10. Leaves, X8. 11. Leaf cells, X120.

442

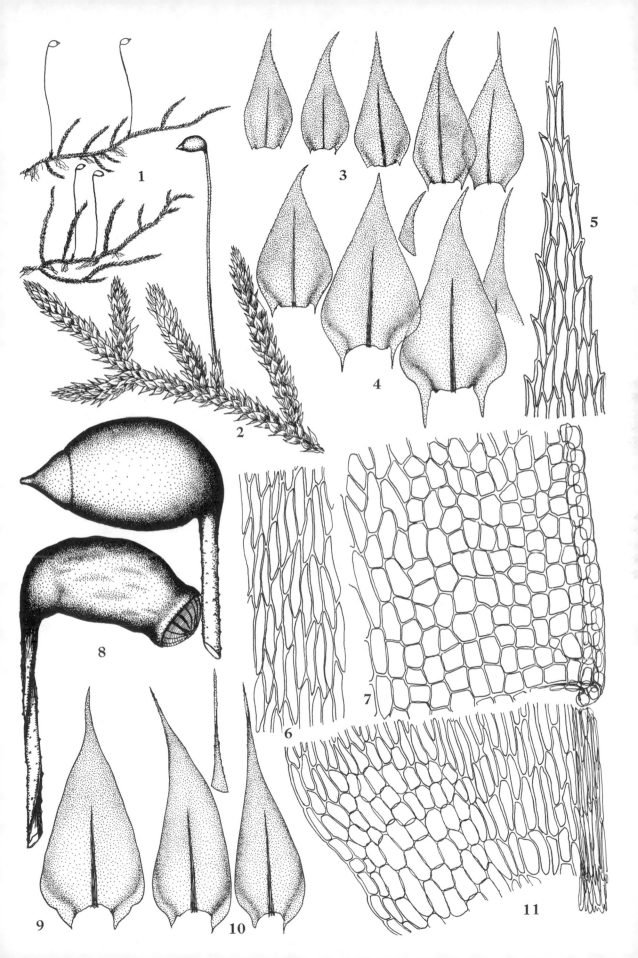

the margins entire or nearly so above, rough seta, and dioicous habit. (For contrasts with *B. starkei,* see notes under that species.) Most of our specimens were growing in regions of siliceous and ferromagnesian rocks, rarely fruiting.

21.87   12a. Var. **intermedium** Flow. Stem leaves longer, ovate-lanceolate to deltoid-lanceolate, rather abruptly long-acuminate. Branch leaves ending in much longer and narrower acumina, complanate, widely spreading when dry. Plate 105, figs. 9–11.

21.88   San Juan County: La Sal Mountains near Geyser Pass, 9,000 ft.

21.89   **13. Brachythecium rivulare** B.S.G. Plants medium sized to robust, variable in habit and color according to habitat, on wet soil and rocks, loosely to densely matted, dark green to yellowish green or straw colored, when submerged or emergent often forming long loose masses or when crowded often becoming erect in deep dense tufts. Shoots irregularly to subpinnately branched, mostly 3–6 cm long but sometimes reaching as much as 20 cm, commonly three times branched, the primary stems usually tough and woody, often becoming denuded or with shredded leaf bases; secondary stems stout, sometimes becoming dendroid with rather distant, open or loosely imbricated leaves, the ultimate branches usually more slender with smaller leaves. Leaves of the secondary stems the most typical, ovate to triangular, acute to shortly acuminate, 1.5–2.5 mm long, 0.8–1.3 mm wide, strongly concave excavate at base, ± decurrent (often strongly so), only slightly or not at all plicate; margins plane above, usually revolute at base, serrate with small distant teeth, denticulate toward the base, sometimes nearly entire throughout; costa ½–¾ the leaf length, occasionally forked; upper cells linear, 8–10 μ wide; alar cells numerous, abruptly enlarged, thin walled, and usually inflated, often forming large decurrent auricles. Branch leaves smaller and narrower, ovate-lanceolate to ovate-oblong, more strongly serrate, often lightly plicate; upper cells usually longer; alar cells fewer. Dioicous; rarely fruiting. Seta very rough with dense papillae, reddish brown, 1.5–2 cm long; capsules oblong-ovoid, asymmetric, slightly curved, 1.5–2.5 mm long, strongly inclined to horizontal, reddish brown, slightly or not at all contracted below the mouth when dry; lid shortly pointed. Plate 107.

21.90   Submerged in springs and slow-flowing brooks or growing on wet soil, rocks, humus, or rotten logs, on brook banks, in wet meadows and seepage areas from the valleys to the higher mountains.

21.91   Eurasia, South Africa, northern Africa, and Australia. Across northern United States and Canada south to Virginia, Missouri, Utah, and Nevada.

21.92   One of the most common mosses in Utah and one of the most variable.

Plate 106. Brachythecium nelsonii. 1. Habit sketches, X.4. 2. Same, X1.6. 3. Five branch leaves. 4. Four stem leaves, X8. 5. Upper medial leaf cells. 6. Alar cells, X120. 7. Capsule, X8.

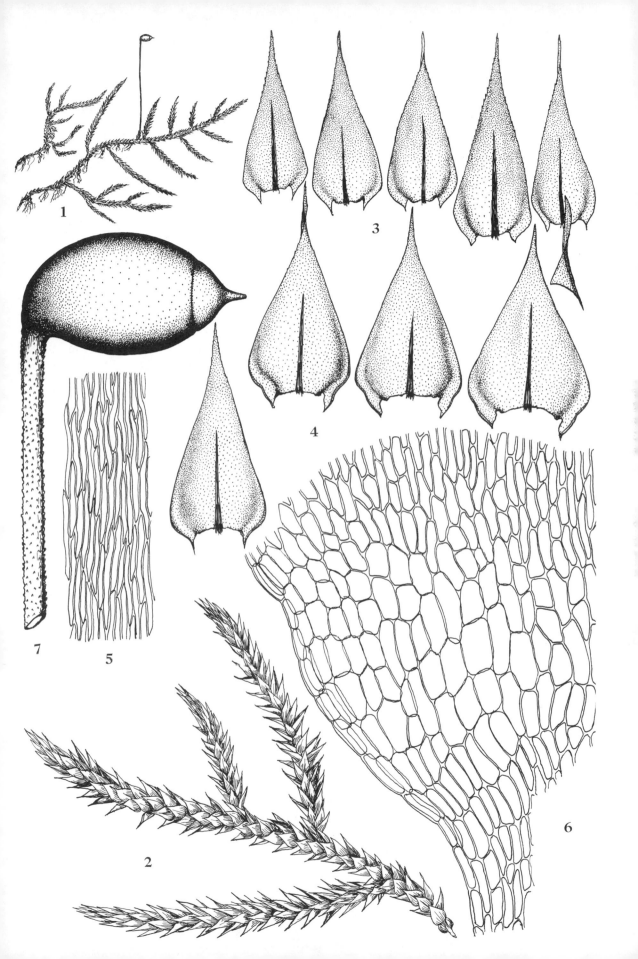

Typical forms on wet substrata in the air develop dense mats in which the shoots lie more or less parallel or radiate in a regular manner or form deep, loosely interwoven masses. Emergent aquatic forms may develop numerous, long parallel branches in loose or compact tufts, and submerged forms commonly grow in long, lax masses, sometimes with few or no branches. The leaves are commonly patent, moderately dense to well spaced but they are quite often more spreading and in some instances have upper parts of the blades curving inward giving the shoots a loosely julaceous appearance. Occasional forms growing submerged in still water grow into long lax shoots with distant, irregularly spreading leaves which may be more or less contorted when dry. Sex organs are uncommon and sporophytes rare.

21.93 **14. Brachythecium asperrimum** (Mitt.) Sull. Plants moderately stout, mostly in loose spreading mats, yellowish green to dark green. Shoots mostly gradually tapering. Stems 3–10 cm long, creeping and ± stoloniform or ascending; irregularly to somewhat regularly pinnately branched, the branches distant to dense and closely disposed, 1–3 cm long, mostly loosely foliolate; rhizoids few to numerous, often in dense tufts extending to the ends of the main stems. Stem leaves broadly ovate to ovate-lanceolate or elongate-triangular, gradually and slenderly acuminate, sometimes abruptly long and slenderly cuspidate, the tips often twisted, straight, or sometimes falcate, 1.5–2 mm long, 0.6–1 mm wide, erect-patent, the basal angles ± abruptly contracted to the insertion, concave below, flattish above, plane to strongly plicate, narrowly or not at all decurrent; margins entire or finely serrate, often narrowly revolute on one side above; costa slender, ½–¾ the length of the blade, often ending in a spine at the back; medial cells linear, 6–8 μ wide; basal cells wider and proportionately shorter; alar cells few to numerous, quadrate to shortly oblong and not greatly enlarged, or oblong and considerably enlarged, sometimes thin walled and inflated. Branch leaves smaller and narrower, less concave, plane or slightly plicate, usually not decurrent, more sharply serrate, alar cells scarcely differentiated. Dioicous. Fruit rare. Seta 1–4 cm long, reddish brown, coarsely papillose; capsules reddish brown, ovate to elongate-ovoid, asymmetric, mostly 2.5 mm long, inclined to horizontal, slightly contracted under the mouth when dry; lid slenderly rostrate with a blackish tip; cilia 2–3, nodulose, sometimes subappendiculate below. Spores 14–17 μ, finely roughened. Plate 108.

21.94 On decayed logs, bases of trees, and on damp soil or rocks, less commonly in wet places.

21.95 British Columbia to California, northern Idaho, western Montana, and Utah.

21.96 Uncommon in Utah. Differs from *B. lamprochryseum* in the more slen-

---

Plate 107. Brachythecium rivulare. 1. Habit sketches, X.4. 2. Four branch leaves. 3. Five leaves from secondary stems, X8. 4. Leaf apex. 5. Two areas of alar cells showing variations, X120.

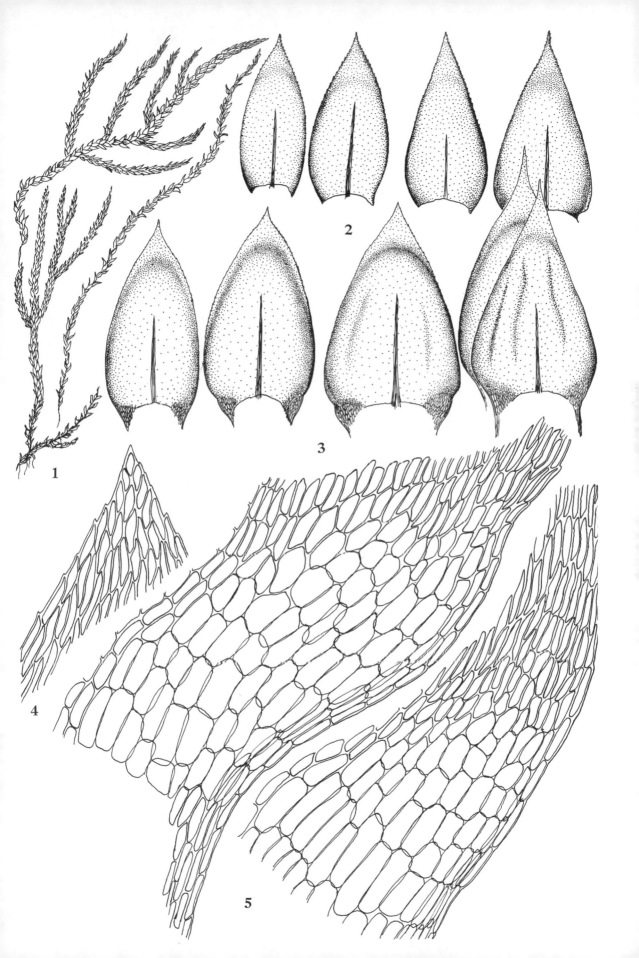

der habit with more gradually tapering branches, the leaves less open, the acumination longer and more gradually tapering to a slender apex, on the whole less plicate and the medial cells narrower. See comparative notes under *B. lamprochryseum.* As originally described, the leaves were supposed not to be decurrent and alar cells not conspicuously differentiated, but a study of a large series of plants discloses wide variations in these traits.

21.97 **15. Brachythecium lamprochryseum** C. Muell. & Kindb. in Macoun.[*] Plants stout and often robust, forming dense or loose tufts or spreading mats, mostly yellowish green, varying to bright golden yellow or sometimes darker green, ± glossy. Shoots thickish because of loosely patent leaves. Stems 5–12 cm long, coarse and thick, often denuded of leaves below or with shredded leaves, creeping or ascending but not stoloniform, sometimes in erect tufts when crowded, irregularly pinnate, the branches sometimes on 1 side. Secondary stems 3–4 cm long, sometimes nearly regularly pinnate, the ultimate branches stout and abruptly pointed to moderately tapering, straight or curved. Stem leaves 2–2.5(3) mm long, 0.8–1.3(1.6) mm wide, dense to rather distant, erect-patent to open, broadly ovate to ovate-lanceolate, mostly shortly acuminate, occasionally acute, the tips often twisted, straight, or occasionally falcate-secund; rather abruptly contracted to the insertion, sometimes auricled, not decurrent to markedly so, concave and excavate below, slightly to strongly plicate; costa extending 3/4–4/5 the length of the blade, often into the base of the acumen, often ending in a spine at back, occasionally with 1–3 dorsal teeth lower down; margins serrate in the upper half or well toward the base, plane above, sometimes ± revolute below; upper cells oblong-linear to linear, 6–8 μ wide, in the base becoming broader and shorter, sometimes with a row of larger cortical cells of the stem adhering across the base; alar cells gradually or suddenly enlarged, thin walled and often inflated, ranging from a small group of 4–5 cells to as many as 10 cells across the base and along the margin, sometimes extending into the decurrent wings. Branch leaves smaller and more narrowly ovate-lanceolate to elongate-triangular, usually more slenderly acuminate but less strongly plicate and less frequently decurrent; alar cells not particularly differentiated. Dioicous. Seta 1.5–3 cm long, reddish brown, densely papillose; capsules ovate to ovate-oblong, asymmetric, inclined to horizontal, 2–2.5 mm long, reddish brown at maturity, slightly or not at all constricted below the mouth when dry; lid with a rather long beak often very dark with age, cilia 2–3, nearly as long as the teeth, nodulose to subappendiculate, distantly papillose. Spores yellowish brown, 13–17 μ, smooth or very finely roughened. Plate 109.

[*]Treated as *B. frigidum* (C. Muell.) Besch. by E. Lawton.

Plate 108. Brachythecium asperrimum. 1. Male plants. 2–3. Female plants, X.4. 4. Four branch leaves. 5. Three stem leaves of Douglas's type, X8. 6. Typical leaf apex. 7. Alar cells of Douglas's type, X120. 8. Two stem leaves of Lyall's type. 9. Alar cells of same, X120. 10. Capsules of Douglas's type, X8. 11. Portion of inner peristome of same, X60.

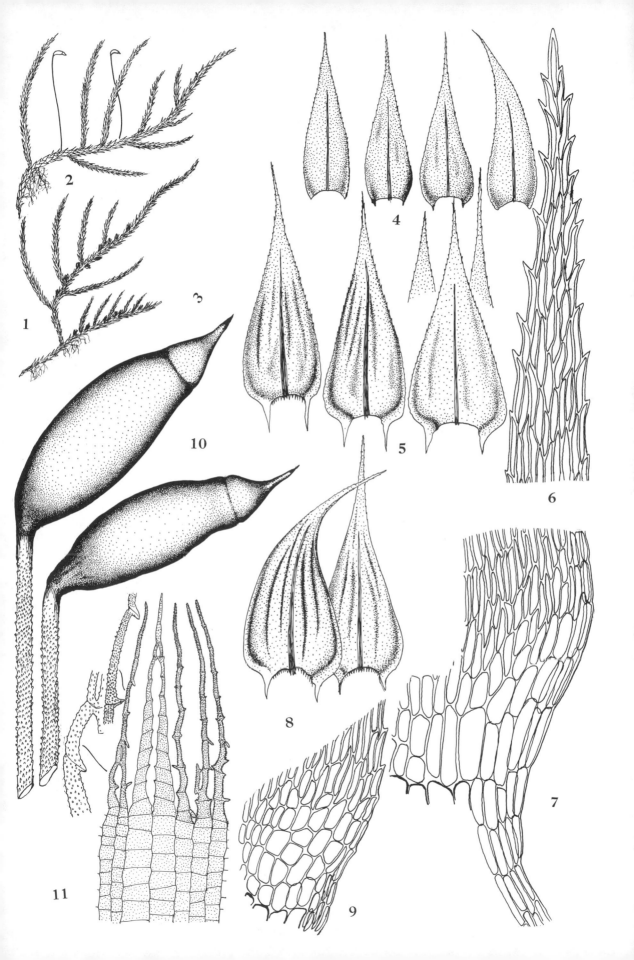

21.98   HYPNACEAE

21.98   Growing on wet or damp rock, soil, humus or rotten wood on brook
        banks, around springs, and in seepage areas, sometimes submerged.

21.99   Alaska, British Columbia to California and east to Utah and Wyoming.

21.100 Common in Utah but rarely fruiting. Some forms approach *B. rivulare*,
        which often has a similar habit and appearance, but the shoots are
        more slenderly tapering, the leaves more concave and wider in the up-
        per part, somewhat like the bowl of a spoon, abruptly narrowed to a
        short acute point and much less plicate. Also, it has a larger area of
        greatly enlarged, thin-walled, inflated alar cells often forming conspicu-
        ous auricles.

21.101 More robust than *B. asperrimum* which has more slenderly tapering
        shoots, often becoming stoloniform, the stem leaves gradually long
        slenderly acuminate, on the whole less plicate, medial leaf cells most-
        ly longer. I have spent considerable time studying these two plants in
        their type localities in British Columbia, especially at Goldstream, at
        the foot of Mt. Finlayson, and in the Fraser River Basin where both
        are common and frequently fruited. In these areas *B. lamprochryseum*
        nearly always occurs in wet places while *B. asperrimum* is largely con-
        fined to logs, bases of trees and lower branches, shrubs, and exposed
        roots. Only occasionally does it become established on soil, rocks, and
        humus, and rarely in very wet places.

        4. SCLEROPODIUM B.S.G.

21.102 Plants medium sized to rather large; primary stems irregularly divided
        into secondary shoots, these irregularly to subpinnately branched; the
        younger foliaceous parts julaceous and usually curved or hooked when
        dry. Leaves ovate to ovate-oblong to ovate-lanceolate, strongly concave,
        usually closely or loosely imbricated when dry, open to spreading when
        moist, usually not plicate, broadly rounded, obtuse or acuminate, ±
        abruptly narrowed at the base, usually not decurrent; costa single, ex-
        tending 2/3–5/6 the length of the blade, often ending in a spine at
        the back; upper leaf cells linear-vermicular, often becoming very short
        in the apex; alar cells various. Dioicous. Seta strongly papillose; cap-
        sules ovoid-oblong to subcylindric, ± curved and asymmetric, inclined
        to horizontal; annulus double, easily separable; lid tall conic, often long
        rostrate; peristome perfect.

21.103 The name, from the Greek, means rough foot and refers to the papillose
        seta.

21.104 1. Leaves ovate to ovate-oblong, suddenly narrowed above to an acute
           or acuminate apex; plants of rather dry or damp situations ....
           .... 1. *S. touretii*   21.106

Plate 109. **Brachythecium lamprochryseum.** 1. Habit sketch. 2. Robust aquatic
form, X.4. 3. Two branch leaves. 4. Two leaves of secondary stem. 5. Three leaves
of main stem, X8. 6. Typical leaf apex. 7–8. Two areas of alar cells showing
variations, X120. 9. Capsules, X8.

450

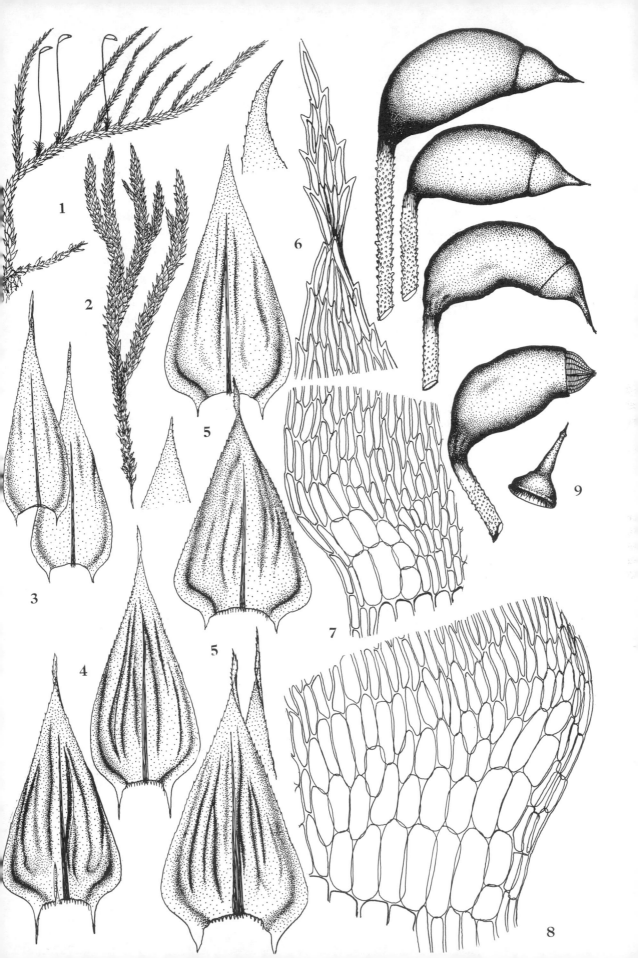

21.105   1. Leaves broadly ovate to ovate-oblong, the apices narrowly obtuse to broadly rounded, often apiculate; plants aquatic, in or along streams and waterfalls .... 2. *S. obtusifolium*   21.110

21.106   **1. Scleropodium touretii** (Brid.) L. Koch. Plants in thin or thick mats, dull green to glossy light yellowish green, brownish below. Primary stems prostrate, 2–8 cm long, often denuded; rhizoids rather few; secondary shoots irregularly to subpinnately branched, the branches usually julaceous and curved when dry. Leaves of secondary stems largest, intergrading in shape and size with larger leaves of ultimate branches, loosely imbricated when dry, open to spreading when moist, ovate to ovate-oblong, ± suddenly narrowed to an acute or acuminate apex, occasionally a few obtuse, 1.5–2(2.3) mm long, 0.7–0.8(1) mm wide, concave, abruptly narrowed and excavate at the base, usually not plicate or decurrent; margins variable, entire to sharply serrate above (often in leaves of the same plant); costa ⅔–¾ the leaf length, usually ending in a spine at back; upper cells narrowly linear-vermicular, 5–6 μ wide, rather thick walled, persisting nearly to the base, apical cells usually much shorter, oblong to rhomboidal, thicker walled; inner basal cells broader and shorter, mostly rhomboidal-oblong to subquadrate, often colored; alar cells usually few, shorter and wider, up to 16 μ wide, mostly oblong, sometimes irregular, firm or occasionally thin walled, rarely slightly inflated, sometimes not strongly differentiated (variable in leaves of the same plant). Seta 1–2 cm long, yellowish brown, becoming reddish with age, strongly papillose; capsules ovate-oblong to subcylindric, urn 1.7–2.5 mm long, neck short, ± contracted below the mouth when dry; lid high conic. Spores 10–13 μ, nearly smooth. Plate 110, figs. 8–9.

21.107   Growing on soil, rocks, bases of trees, and decaying wood, usually in damp or rather dry shady places, less frequently near water.

21.108   Europe, Asia Minor, and North Africa. British Columbia to Montana, California and Arizona. Juab County: Deep Creek Mountains, Birch Creek, 5,900 ft.

21.109   Our single specimen, collected on a wet rock by a stream, is darker green than usual, but the younger parts are light glossy green and curved-julaceous when dry.

21.110   **2. Scleropodium obtusifolium** (Jaeg.) Kindb. Plants submerged or on wet substrata, forming dense mats or ascending tufts, or hanging in waterfalls or dripping cliffs, dull dark green, the younger parts often brighter green and glossy. Primary stems irregularly branched, the lower

---

Plate 110.   1–7. Scleropodium obtusifolium. 1. Habit sketches, X.4. 2. Portion of main stem, dry and moist, X2. 3. Four leaves of typical plant. 4. Three leaves from different plants showing variations, X8. 5. Upper medial leaf cells. 6. Four leaf apices. 7. Two areas of alar cells, X120. **Note:** In some leaves the alar cells are scarcely differentiated.

8–9. Sceleropodium touretii. 8. Habit sketch, X.4. 9. Three typical stem leaves, X8.

parts often denuded or clothed with ragged leaf bases, 3–10 cm long; rhizoids few; ultimate branches short, up to 1.5 cm long, strongly julaceous, blunt at the tips, erect or ascending, sometimes curved or hooked when dry. Stem leaves broadly ovate to ovate-oblong or suborbicular, loosely to closely imbricated when dry, open when moist, deeply concave, occasionally cucullate, not plicate except under pressure, 1–2 mm long, 0.8–1.3 mm wide, obtuse to broadly rounded, sometimes bluntly apiculate; margins entire or bluntly dentate, occasionally extending halfway down the margin; base narrowed and $\pm$ half-clasping but not decurrent; costa strong, extending 5/6 the length of the blade, sometimes ending in a tooth at the back; upper cells linear-vermicular, 5–7 μ wide, the apical cells rhomboidal to subrotund; basal cells shortly oblong, sometimes thick walled and colored; alar cells typically abruptly enlarged and dilated, but in many plants not notably differentiated. Branch leaves much the same but smaller, alar cells less dilated. Fruit rare. Seta 1–1.5 cm long, very dark and rough; capsule ovoid, nearly or quite symmetric, cernuous, with operculum 3–3.5 mm long; operculum conic-rostellate; teeth dark red below, lighter and papillose above; cilia and segments about the same length as the teeth; cilia appendiculate, sometimes unequal; annulus apparently lacking. (Description of sporophyte taken from Grout.) Plate 110, figs. 1–7.

21.111   Submerged in brooks or on wet rocks and soil along the banks, often becoming dry at low water.

21.112   British Columbia to California, Montana, Colorado, and Arizona.

21.113   This plant resembles forms of *Hygrohypnum molle*, but the latter moss has a shorter, strongly forked costa. *Hygrohypnum palustre* var. *julaceum* has julaceous branches and leaves with a single costa, some of them occasionally forked. The blade is much narrower in the upper part and the margins are strongly incurved above, sometimes even subtubulose. According to some authors, *S. obtusifolium* has conspicuous auricles at the base of the leaves. I have gathered considerable material throughout the Pacific Northwest and find that this trait is only occasional, as most plants have no auricles or sometimes weak ones here and there. Occasionally a few leaves have the costae branched high up but not forked from the base as in some species of *Hygrohypnum*.

5. HOMALOTHECIUM B.S.G.

21.114   Plants straggling or in thin to very thick mats, bright glossy yellowish green, brown below. Stems closely and often regularly pinnate, often long; branches short, curved and hooked at the tips when dry. Leaves closely appressed-imbricated when dry, oblong-lanceolate to narrowly lanceolate, apices various, acute to long and slenderly acuminate with a strong fold on each side extending the length of the blade, often with smaller plicae between; costa stout, nearly reaching the apex; upper cells long linear-vermicular. Dioicous. Setae papillose to nearly smooth; capsules oblong-cylindric, nearly erect and symmetric; peristome teeth narrowly lanceolate; basal membrane of the endostome low, about ¼; segments narrow; cilia rudimentary or lacking.

21.115   The name, from the Greek, means straight capsule.

21.116   **Homalothecium nevadense** (Lesq.) Ren. & Card. Plants in thin or thick mats, often forming large cushions, glossy yellow green when dry, brown below, bright green when moist. Stems 5–15 cm long, closely pinnate, often ± 1-sided, commonly forming secondary branched stems; branches short, up to 1 cm long, curved or hooked when dry, straightening out when moist; outer cortical cells shortly oblong. Stem leaves dense, closely appressed and imbricated when dry, erect-patent to patent when moist, oblong-lanceolate to slenderly lanceolate, short to slenderly long acuminate, 1.5–2(2.5) mm long, strongly plicate, insertion quite broad; margins entire to slightly serrate or dentate in the upper part, rarely at the base, recurved below and often narrowly revolute on 1 side above; costa stout and extending well into the acumen; upper cells linear, 5–7 μ wide, extending nearly to the base; basal cells abruptly shorter and broader; alar cells quadrate, numerous. Branch leaves smaller, shorter and broader, less slenderly narrowed above, acute or acuminate, more strongly serrate or dentate; costa stout and spreading out in the apex, often ending in 1 to several teeth at the back; apical cells much shorter than those lower down in the blade; alar cells fewer. Leaves of the primary and secondary stems and branches gradually intergrading in shape and size. Seta 1–1.5 cm long, weakly to strongly papillose, often smooth below; capsules oblong-cylindric, occasionally slightly curved, urn 2.5–3 mm long, reddish brown when mature; annulus of 2 rows of cells; lid rather tall conic-rostrate, the tip straight or slightly bent; peristome teeth distantly jointed, reddish at the base, pale and papillose above, often standing erect when dry, very fragile; segments slender, strongly perforated, nearly as long as the teeth, pale yellowish and papillose. Spores 11–15 μ, nearly smooth. Plate 111, figs. 9–16.

21.117   Growing on dry soil, rocks, and trunks of trees, usually in shady places in canyon bottoms and ravines.

21.118   British Columbia to California, Montana, Colorado, and northern Arizona.

6. TOMENTHYPNUM Loesk.

21.119   Plants medium sized to rather large, in dense mats or tufts, glossy yellowish green, golden yellow or brown. Stems prostrate, ascending or crowded and erect, irregularly to regularly pinnate. Leaves dense, broadly to narrowly lanceolate, ± acuminate, strongly plicate; costa strong, extending beyond the middle, commonly bearing rhizoids on the back; upper cells linear; alar cells few to numerous, mostly quadrate, thick walled. Dioicous. Seta long, reddish; capsules oblong-cylindric, inclined to horizontal, ± curved, often becoming arcuate and strongly contracted below the mouth when dry; annulus present; peristome perfect, with well-developed cilia. Apparently monotypic.

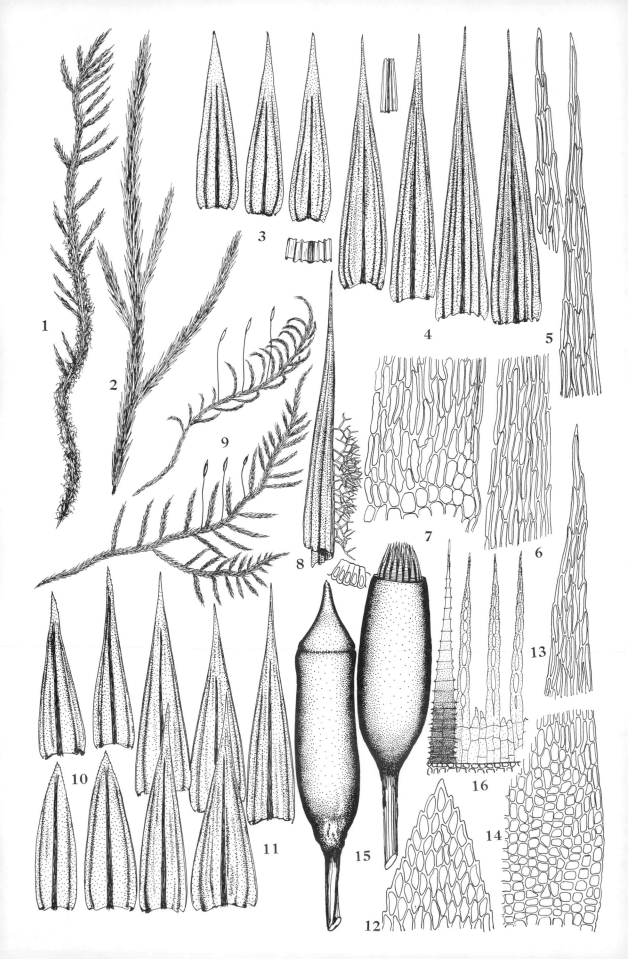

21.120 The name, from the Latin *tomentum,* stuffing of cushions (hair, wool, etc.), *Hypnum,* means woolly *Hypnum.*

21.121 **Tomenthypnum nitens** (Hedw.) Loesk. Stems 5–15 cm long, usually bearing dense tomentum of rhizoids high up; secondary stems frequent with ultimate branches about 1 cm long; stem leaves dense, narrowly lanceolate or triangular-lanceolate, most slenderly acuminate, appressed when dry, erect to erect-patent when moist, very strongly plicate, 3–4 mm long; margins narrowly revolute on 1 or both sides, entire or indistinctly dentate above; costa 3/4–5/6 the leaf length, often bearing branched rhizoids on the back; upper cells linear-vermicular, 3–5 μ wide; basal cells not much wider, those in 2–4 rows at the insertion 7–8 μ wide, often thicker walled and $\pm$ pitted; alar cells few, oblong to quadrate, usually wider, often colored, occasionally 2–3 slightly inflated. Branch leaves smaller, usually less slenderly acuminate. Fruit rare. Plate 111, figs. 1–8.

21.122 A handsome moss growing in swamps and bogs.

21.123 Eurasia and northern United States, extending to the Arctic and subalpine in the Uinta Mountains.

7. AMBLYSTEGIUM B.S.G.

21.124 Plants small and slender to large and stout, bright green to golden yellow or dark green to olivaceous, not glossy, prostrate and creeping in thin mats or ascending to erect and $\pm$ densely tufted, some species submerged in water. Stem mostly irregularly branched, central strand present, often vague with 1–2(3–4) rows of thick-walled outer cortical cells. Leaves erect to spreading wet or dry, broadly ovate to narrowly ovate-lanceolate, mostly rather flattish, acute to strongly acuminate; margins flat, entire to finely serrate or dentate; costa slender to very stout, extending half the length of the blade, percurrent or excurrent; medial cells oblong-rhomboidal or hexagonal, usually longest at the base of the acumen, shorter and broader below, smooth, mostly thin walled in aerial species, $\pm$ thick walled in submerged forms; basal cells shorter and wider, thicker walled, sometimes colored, never indistinct auricles; alar cells usually not particularly differentiated or strongly set off, occasionally a few inflated at the extreme angles, especially in submerged species. Monoicous. Fruit usually abundant except in submerged species. Seta long and smooth; capsules oblong to

---

Plate 111. 1–8. Tomenthypnum nitens. 1. Habit sketch, X.4. 2. Portion of a shoot, X2. 3. Branch leaves. 4. Stem leaves, X8. 5. Apices of branch and stem leaves respectively. 6. Upper medial cells. 7. Basal and alar cells, X120. 8. Leaf showing dorsal costal rhizoids, X8.

9–16. Homalothecium nevadense. 9. Habit sketches, dry and moist, X.4. **10.** Four branch leaves. 11. Five stem leaves, X8. 12. Broad top of branch leaf. 13. Apex of stem leaf. 14. Basal and alar cells, X120. **Note:** Alar cells are often not so numerous. 15. Capsules, X8. 16. Portion of peristome showing slender tooth and segments, rudimentary or absent cilia, X60. **Note:** Moist capsules are often slightly inclined and slightly unsymmetric.

subcylindric, curved and asymmetric, erect to cernuous, (nearly erect and symmetric in *A. compactum*), strongly constricted below the mouth when dry and empty, yellowish brown to reddish brown, often becoming darker reddish with age; lid conic to convex, acute to broadly pointed or mammillose; annulus of 2–3 rows of cells, usually adhering to the mouth for a short time; peristome typically hypnaceous. Spores small.

21.125 Name from the Greek for blunt, and cover, referring to the bluntly pointed lid of the capsules.

21.126 The genus is often divided into *Amblystegium,* small mosses with short leaf cells; *Leptodictyum,* intergrading forms said to have longer leaf cells, and *Hygroamblystegium,* aquatic species with very strongly percurrent or excurrent costa, coarser and dark or olivaceous green. *Leptodictyum trichopodium* and its variety *kochii* intergrade so closely with *Amblystegium juratzkanum,* it is often impossible to distinguish them as species, let alone genera. Some forms of *Hygroamblystegium* intergrade somewhat with forms of *Amblystegium varium,* but on the whole the former are distinguished by their darker color and stouter costa.

21.127 1. Plants bright green to yellowish; costa slender, pale, ending at midleaf or beyond (subpercurrent in *A. compactum* and *varium*)

    2. Medial leaf cells mostly longer; plants medium sized to large, submerged or in wet places, green to golden yellow .... 6. *A. riparium* 21.157

    2. Medial leaf cells shorter; plants small, not submerged but on damp or wet substrata

        3. Costa ending near midleaf or extending well into the acumen

            4. Leaves mostly patent and narrowly ovate-lanceolate, 1 mm long (0.4–0.7 mm in var. *tenue*) medial cells shortly rectangular; basal marginal cells mostly quadrate, sometimes transversely elongated .... 1. *A. serpens* 21.129

            4. Leaves mostly spreading wet or dry, especially the stem leaves; basal marginal cells shortly rectangular

                5. Stem leaves ovate-lanceolate, gradually acuminate; 0.8–1.3 mm long; base gradually narrowed ....2. *A. juratzkanum* 21.136

                5. Stem leaves broadly ovate to ovate-lanceolate, 1–1.5 mm long; long and slenderly acuminate, base ± cordate, costa sometimes extending to the base of the acumen ....4. *A. kochii* 21.147

        3. Costa subpercurrent, ending a few cells below the tip

            6. Leaves serrulate, narrowly decurrent; costa thin, often bear-

ing rhizoids on the back; plants in dense compact cushions or mats .... 5. *A. compactum*   21.152

    6. Leaves entire, not decurrent; costa strong, usually without rhizoids; plants mostly in loose or thin spreading mats .... 3. *A. varium*   21.143

21.128   1. Plants dull dark green or olivaceous, green only at the tips; submerged, emergent or on very wet substrata; costa thick and stout, green to dark yellowish, subpercurrent to excurrent

    7. Stem leaves ovate-lanceolate to triangular, $\pm$ long acuminate .... 7. *A. tenax*   21.167

    7. Stem leaves ovate to oblong-lanceolate, broader above, shortly or not at all acuminate, mostly narrowly obtuse .... 8. *A. fluviatile*   21.174

21.129   **1. Amblystegium serpens** (Hedw.) B.S.G. var. **serpens**. Plants small, in loosely to closely adhering mats, mostly bright green but not glossy; stems $\pm$ prostrate, 1–3 cm long, slender, irregularly pinnate, often becoming interwoven; branches prostrate, ascending, or erect. Leaves appressed to patent when dry, patent to somewhat spreading when moist, rather close to distant; stem leaves narrowly ovate-lanceolate to ovate and abruptly long-acuminate, up to 1 mm long, occasionally as much as 1.2 mm, narrowed at the base, sometimes slightly decurrent; margins entire to slightly denticulate; costa slender, extending about half the length of the blade, sometimes less; upper cells oblong-hexagonal or rhomboidal, 7–10 μ wide, basal cells wider, hexagonal, rhomboidal, or rectangular; basal marginal cells typically quadrate to transversely elongate but sometimes shortly rectangular. Monoicous. Usually freely fruiting; seta 1.5–3 cm long, reddish; capsules cylindric, curved and $\pm$ cernuous, 1.5–2 mm long, yellowish to reddish brown, becoming darker with age, strongly contracted under the mouth and arcuate when dry; lid conic to convex with a short blunt point; annulus of 2–3 rows of cells; peristome typically hypnaceous. Plate 112, figs. 1–8.

21.130   On damp or wet soil, rocks, and rotten logs; in seepage areas, small brooks, on moist soil in crevices; under overhanging rocks and roots of trees.

21.131   Worldwide in distribution.

21.132   Abundant from the lowlands to the mountains in Utah. Often intergrading with *A. juratzkanum* since the basal marginal cells are not exclusively quadrate in all leaves. Many of the leaves have shortly rectangular marginal cells on 1 or both sides. In addition there are many other variations with all sorts of intergrading characters, and it is doubtful if any 1 is sufficiently constant to warrant a name. Variability includes shorter broader leaves, shorter or longer leaf cells, more compact mats with more closely branched stems. More than forty varieties, mostly European, have been named.

21.133 Var. **tenue** (Brid.) B.S.G. is much smaller, exceedingly slender, the leaves about the same shape or somewhat broader, those of the stem up to about 0.5 mm long, the cells slightly shorter. When dry the leaves are usually quite closely appressed giving the shoots an unusually slender appearance, but when moist they become somewhat spreading. They resemble the larger leaves of *Amblystegiella subtilis,* but the costa is much stronger and more distinct, extending about half the length of the blade or slightly more with the margins sometimes serrulate. Contrary to the tendency in this family for erect capsules and rudimentary cilia to be correlated, and although the capsules are often nearly erect and symmetric, the cilia are well developed. Plate 112, fig. 9.

21.134 On wet, damp, or rather dry soil, rocks, and bases of trees, usually in shade.

21.135 Europe. Across northern United States and adjacent Canada.

21.136 **2. Amblystegium juratzkanum** Schimp. var. **juratzkanum.** Plants usually in thin, loose, bright green mats, varying to yellowish green or dark green, sometimes rather dense; stems slender, becoming 2–3 cm long, irregularly branched, ± stoloniform; branches spreading or ascending. Stem leaves 0.8–1.3 mm long, patent to widely spreading (often giving them a widely spaced appearance) both wet and dry, ovate to ovate-lanceolate, long and narrowly acuminate, rather gradually narrowed at the base; margins usually denticulate to the base; costa extending beyond the middle, sometimes into the acumen; medial cells typically oblong-rhomboidal to sublinear-rhomboidal, 7–10 μ wide; basal cells shorter and broader; basal marginal cells shortly rectangular. Branch leaves smaller, often not so widely spreading when dry. Monoicous. Freely fruiting; sporophyte as in *A. serpens.* Plate 112, figs. 18–20.

21.137 On damp or wet soil, rocks, and rotten logs, usually in shade. Frequent from lowlands to mountains.

21.138 Europe and Asia. Canada and northern United States, extending southward into the Rocky Mountains and Pacific Coast mountains to Arizona and Southern California.

21.139 This plant has been treated both as a subspecies and variety of *A. serpens.* Nearly every author has emphasized intergradations between *A.*

Plate 112. 1–8. Amblystegium serpens. 1. Three habit sketches, X.4. 2. Habit sketch, X2. 3. Three typical stem leaves. 4. Four branch leaves, X8. 5. Two areas of basal marginal and alar cells. 6. Upper medial cells. 7. Typical leaf apex, X120. 8. Four capsules, dry and moist, X8.

9. Var. tenue. Two stem and three branch leaves, X8.

10–17. Amblystegium kochii. 10. Two habit sketches, X.4. 11. Same, X2. 12. Four typical stem leaves. 13. Three branch leaves, X8. 14. Basal marginal cells. 15–16. Upper medial cells from two different leaves showing range of variation. 17. Typical leaf apex, X120.

18–20. Amblystegium juratzkanum. 18–19. Typical stem and branch leaves. 20. Stem leaves of a large form, X8.

juratzkanum and *A. serpens,* on the one hand, and *A. kochii* on the other. From the present collections they form an unbroken range of variations so that each species is merely a segment of a highly variable population. I have noted that the widely spreading leaves of many specimens, especially the branch leaves when collected moist, do not maintain the same degree of spreading when dried nor do they return to the original widely spreading stance when remoistened. Most of our specimens lack the spreading stance of branch leaves, but have the longer medial cells and rectangular basal marginal cells of *A. juratzkanum.*

21.140 2a. Var. **giganteum** (Grout) Grout. Plants much larger. Leaves rather broadly ovate-lanceolate, slenderly acuminate, rather gradually rounded to the base, 1.5–2.1 mm long; medial cells short; 2–3 rows of basal cells usually large and extending across the insertion.

21.141 Salt Lake County: Fairmont Park, Salt Lake City, 4,500 ft.

21.142 This specimen could also pass for a large *A. kochii.* There is actually no name suitable to it, but I am reluctant to base a new name on a single specimen, in such a genus as this.

21.143 3. **Amblystegium varium** (Hedw.) Lindb. Plants small to medium sized in thin or dense, often compact mats, light to dark green, sometimes becoming yellowish green; stems irregularly branched, 1–4 cm long, rhizoids few or in tufts, smooth. Stem leaves erect-spreading to ± spreading, usually broadly ovate-lanceolate but sometimes rather narrowly so, slenderly long acuminate, the base ± rounded but not decurrent, variable in size in different plants 0.9–1.2(15) mm long in larger plants; margins entire or nearly so; costa strong at the base, slenderly tapering and disappearing in the tip and appearing ± subpercurrent; upper cells short, oblong-hexagonal, often narrower in the apex, becoming shorter toward the base, rectangular; basal marginal cells subquadrate to rectangular. Branch leaves smaller and narrower, less acuminate and less rounded at the base. Monoicous. Capsules much like those of *A. serpens.* Plate 113, figs. 14–19.

21.144 On damp or wet soil, rocks, bases of trees, and on rotten wood, usually in shady places.

21.145 Widely distributed in Canada and United States, not reported from Arizona, Nevada, or California. Rare in Utah.

21.146 This moss covers a wide range of variation. The subpercurrent costa

---

Plate 113. 1–13. Amblystegium compactum. 1. Three habit sketches, X.4. 2. Same, X2. 3. Three typical stem leaves. 4. Stem leaves showing insertion and rhizoids from the back of the costa which frequently occur. 5. Three branch leaves. 6–8. Stem leaves from different large forms, X8. 9. Basal marginal cells from three different leaves, showing variations. 10. Upper medial cells. 11. Typical leaf apex. 12. Two propagulae which frequently occur on the back of the costa and occasionally on the lamina, X120. 13. Five capsules, moist and dry, X8.

14–19. Amblystegium varium. 14. Three stem leaves. 15. Two branch leaves, X8. 16. Upper medial cells. 17. Two leaf apices. 18. Two areas of basal and alar cells, X120. 19. Two leaves of a larger form, more slender, X8.

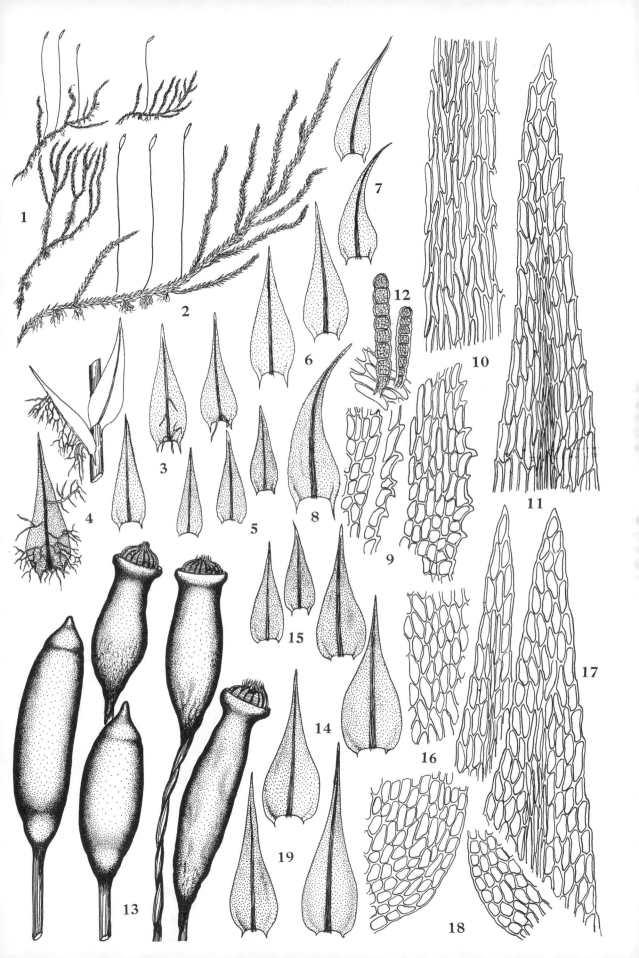

and nearly entire leaves are its strong points. Some specimens seem to intergrade with *A. kochii* in the somewhat shorter costa, and others with *A. juratzkanum* in the narrower stem leaves.

21.147   **4. Amblystegium kochii** B.S.G. Plants bright or dark green. in thin spreading mats; stems becoming 1–2(4) cm long, irregularly branched, sometimes stoloniform. Stem leaves widely spreading when moist and often so when dry, 1–1.5 mm long, ovate to broadly ovate-lanceolate, ± abruptly long-acuminate, ± cordate at the base; margins entire to slightly denticulate; costa usually extending about ⅔ the length of the blade, sometimes into the base of the acumen; upper cells oblong-hexagonal or rhomboidal, basal cells gradually becoming wider, mostly rectangular, the alar cells sometimes considerably enlarged, oblong and rather thick walled, occasionally reddish in old leaves. Branch leaves smaller, patent to spreading, narrower, not at all or less cordate at the base. Monoicous. Freely fruiting; sporophyte as in *A. serpens* and *juratzkanum*. Plate 112, figs. 10–17.

21.148   Growing on damp or wet soil, humus, decaying wood, and rocks, usually in shade, lowlands to mountains.

21.149   Europe and Asia. Widely distributed in the United States, and Canada, less common in Mexico and Central America; southern South America.

21.150   Typically slightly larger than the last two species with broader, more cordate stem leaves, but intergrading forms are common. The branch leaves are often nearly identical to the stem leaves of *A. juratzkanum* in size and shape. Long, straggling, aquatic forms are occasionally encountered with the stem leaves maybe very widely spaced, at about right angles with the stem and narrower than typical, like those of *A. juratzkanum*. Only leaves from the emergent portions of the same stems show the typical broad shape. Larger forms merge with *A. trichopodium*, which typically has more gradually acuminate leaves, broader in the upper part and not so abruptly cordate at the base. Both *A. kochii* and *trichopodium* are supposed to have longer leaf cells than *A. serpens* and *juratzkanum* but among the former, short-celled forms are common, and long-celled forms are infrequent.

21.151   I have not detected a clear-cut example of *Leptodictyum trichopodium*, which is supposed to have larger leaves than *A. kochii* with broader leaf cells and a longer costa, often extending well into the acumen.

21.152   **5. Amblystegium compactum** (C. Muell.) Aust. Plants small and slender in dense mats or ± erect tufts or expanded sods, bright to dark green, often dull, sometimes becoming yellowish green, yellowish below; stems becoming 2–3 cm long, irregularly branched, sometimes densely so; rhizoids usually dense, becoming dark reddish and finely papillose. Stem leaves patent to spreading, ovate-lanceolate to lanceolate, typically about 1 mm long but in many western forms up to 1.5 mm, frequently falcate, slightly to strongly acuminate, sometimes elongate-triangular, narrowly decurrent; margins serrulate to the base, the basal teeth frequently recurved or double, or some leaves serrulate only in the

464

lower half and in some plants nearly entire throughout; costa slender but strong, extending nearly to the tip, subpercurrent, usually bearing few to numerous rhizoids on the back and occasionally on the lamina; also occasionally bearing linear, jointed brood bodies; upper cells typically sublinear, in which instance the leaves resemble those of a *Brachythecium;* variable in width in different plants and often in leaves of the same plant, 7–11(13) μ; basal cells becoming gradually shorter and wider, mostly oblong or rhomboidal; alar cells not particularly differentiated or a few quadrate; apical cells usually becoming shorter. Branch leaves smaller, usually less acuminate. Monoicous. Seta 1.5–3 cm long, reddish; capsules nearly erect, oblong to subcylindric with an evident neck, often slightly curved, contracted under the mouth when dry, but never arcuate, dark red; annulus of 2–3 rows of cells; lid high conic-convex, bluntly pointed; teeth reddish; cilia usually short or rudimentary. Plate 113, figs. 1–13.

21.153   Growing on rather dry, damp or wet substrata, soil or rocks of calcareous areas, bases of trees, and decaying wood, usually in shade.

21.154   Europe. Across Canada and northern United States, except the New England states, south in the mountains of Colorado, Arizona, Nevada, and California.

21.155   Easily recognized by the decurrent leaves with a subpercurrent costa often bearing rhizoids on the back and by the more or less strongly serrulate margins, especially at the leaf base (although some leaves may be nearly entire). The capsules are shorter, nearly erect and symmetrical, and the cilia are short.

21.156   Many of our local plants are larger than normal, the leaves reaching 1.5 mm long with longer leaf cells. These large forms are much like *A. americanum* Grout, which is similar but distinguished by numerous paraphyllia on the stems.

21.157   **6. Amblystegium riparium** (Hedw.) B.S.G. Plants variable with habitat, when growing on damp or wet soil and rocks usually medium sized, creeping in loose mats, green to yellowish green, with stems 3–10 cm long, branches short, irregular, often few, rhizoids few to moderate; when growing in water longer, usually less branched, and often lax. Stem leaves moderately dense to distant, usually spreading wet or dry, broadly ovate-lanceolate, oblong lanceolate to lanceolate, shortly to long and narrowly acuminate, somewhat rounded to a narrow insertion, not decurrent or auricled, mostly 2–2.5 mm long, entire, costa to the middle or beyond; upper cells linear-rhomboidal to linear, 8–11 μ wide; becoming broader and shorter toward the base; alar cells oblong, rhomboidal or hexagonal, larger but not sharply set off, not inflated or forming auricles. Branch leaves smaller and narrower. Monoicous. Fruit rare; capsules similar to those of *A. serpens.* Plate 114, figs. 1–6.

21.158   Occurring mainly along larger clear rivers, lake shores, ditches, and wet meadows.

465

21.159 HYPNACEAE

21.159 Europe, Asia, Africa and Australia. Throughout Canada and United States.

21.160 Abundant locally but on the whole rather uncommon in Utah for lack of adequate wet habitats. Quite variable. Some forms having broadly ovate-lanceolate leaves with short cells suggest a form of *Drepanocladus aduncas* var. *kneiffii* lacking auricles and inflated alar cells. Some larger forms with narrower leaves intergrade with the next two forms.

21.161 Var. **longifolium** (Schultz) Schimp. A large form usually floating in slow-flowing streams or in ponds, yellowish green, stems becoming 6–10 cm long, often sparingly branched, sometimes denuded at the base; leaves distant, 3.5–5 mm long, slenderly lanceolate with a long tapering acumination, sometimes filiform. Intergrading with the next form. Plate 114, figs. 7–8.

21.162 Salt Lake and Wasatch counties.

21.163 Var. **fluitans** (Lesq. & Jam.) A large submerged form, at times long and stringy, often denuded below, green to dirty yellowish. Stems up to 20 cm long, moderately to very sparingly branched. Leaves usually rather dense, erect-patent to somewhat imbricated or widely spaced and ± spreading, often somewhat complanate, firm to flaccid, 3–4 mm long, 0.5–1.5 wide, lanceolate, short- to long-acuminate, rounded to a narrow insertion; alar cells gradually enlarged but firm, only occasionally with 2–3 at the extreme angles inflated, not in auricles or reaching the costa. Plate 114, figs. 9–10.

21.164 Rich, Utah, Wasatch, and Duchesne counties.

21.165 Some forms of this plant are much like forms of *Drepanocladus aduncus* var. *kneiffii,* which has alar cells abruptly enlarged and inflated in triangular areas from the margins to the costa and typically in distinct auricles. Among our plants are stems with some leaves typical of *Amblystegium riparium* var. *fluitans* and others with enlarged alar cells.

21.166 Extremely slender lax plants with leaves smaller, distant and widely spreading, ovate to lanceolate and shortly acuminate with leaf cells unusually short may be called fo. *flaccidum* (Lesq. & Jam.). This form grows mostly along canal banks, often in puddles or on wet mud.

Plate 114. 1–6. Amblystegium riparium. 1. Habit sketch, X.4. 2. Three typical stem leaves. 3. Same from a different plant, X8. 4. Upper medial leaf cells. 5. Two leaf apices. 6. Three areas of basal, marginal, and alar cells showing variations, X120.

7–8. Var. longifolium. 7. Aquatic state with few or no branches, X.4. 8. Two stem leaves, X8.

9–10. Var. fluitans. 9. Robust aquatic form, X.4. 10. Three stem leaves, X8. **Note:** Intergradations among the species and the two forms are numerous and often perplexing. Some forms intergrade with **Drepanocladus aduncus** var. **kneiffii** which has enlarged and inflated alar cells in more or less distinct auricles. It is not uncommon to find on the same stem some leaves typical of **A. riparium** and others, usually the lower ones, typical of **D. aduncus kneiffii.**

466

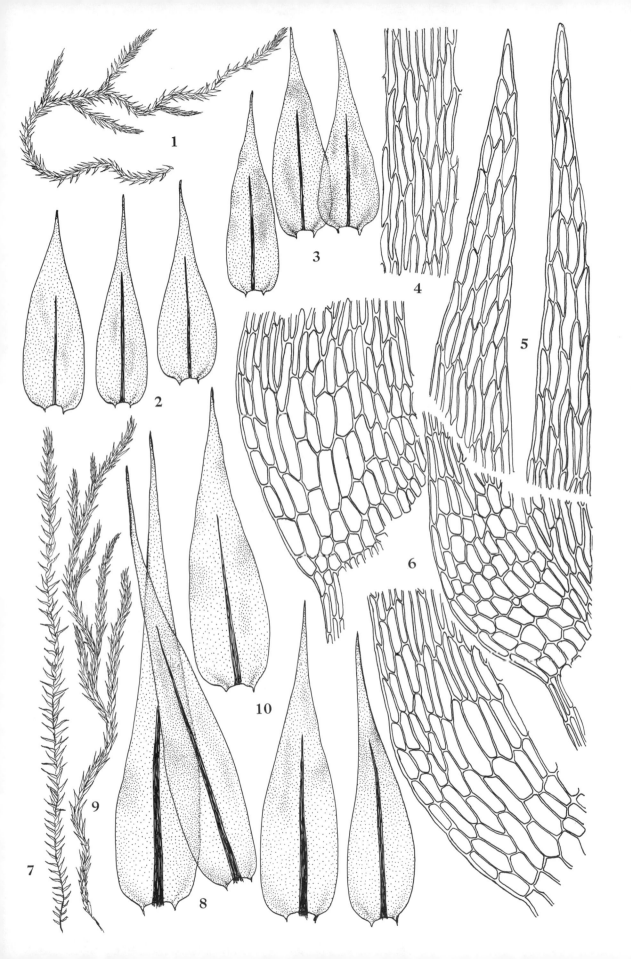

21.167   **7. Amblystegium tenax** (Hedw.) C. Jens. Plants medium sized, growing in loose tufts or mats, typically submerged, dull dark green or olivaceous, only the tips in brighter green. Stems up to 10 cm long, irregularly branched, the older portions in cross section showing a row of small, thick-walled, outer cortical cells; rhizoids few, in tufts. Stem leaves the largest, about 1 mm long, typically distant, firm, erect-patent to patent, ovate-lanceolate to triangular-lanceolate, long-acuminate with the tips narrowly acute to blunt, the base gradually narrowed or somewhat rounded, sometimes slightly decurrent; margins entire to slightly dentate, often only in part; costa stout, only slightly tapered, dark green, ending indistinctly near the apex or occasionally 6–7 cells below it; upper cells rhomboidal, 8–11 μ wide, often shorter at the tip; basal cells usually shorter and slightly wider, often not much different, in older leaves becoming thicker walled and sometimes colored; alar cells quadrate-round to oblong, thick walled and usually opaque, occasionally slightly inflated at extreme angles. Branch leaves smaller and usually narrower, ovate-lanceolate to oblong-lanceolate. Monoicous. Rarely fruiting. Seta up to 3 cm long; capsules oblong-cylindric, 2–3 mm long without the lid, curved, becoming strongly arcuate and contracted under the mouth when dry; lid conic-convex, bluntly pointed. Plate 115, figs. 1–8.

21.168   Usually growing attached to rocks submerged in brooks, ditches, springs or ponds, occasionally hanging in and around waterfalls, mostly in calcareous regions.

21.169   Europe, Asia, northwestern Africa, northwestern South America. Common throughout southern Canada and United States.

21.170   The aquatic habit, dull green color, tough stems, and long-acuminate leaves with stout subpercurrent costa are outstanding features of typical forms, but plants intergrade with the following varieties and with *A. fluviatile.* Not very common in Utah but sometimes locally abundant.

21.171   7a. Fo. **spinifolium** (Schimp.) Demar. Plants larger than the typical form, usually submerged and forming long stringy masses of darker green, often blackish below; stems thick and stiff, 5–15 cm long, the older parts in cross sections showing 1–3 rows of very thick-walled, colored outer cortical cells; rhizoids usually confined to the base. Branches irregular, widely spaced, often long and ± parallel. Stem leaves rather distant, erect to erect-patent when moist, erect and often imbricated when dry, 1.3–1.6 mm long, ovate-lanceolate to triangular-lanceolate, lamina acuminate above; costa very stout, percurrent or excurrent to a stiff thick point; basal cells adjacent to the costa unistra-

---

Plate 115.   1–8. Amblystegium tenax. 1. Habit sketch of typical form. 2. Same of a slender, stiff, wiry form with most lower leaves much eroded, X.4. 3. Three leaves of a typical form. 4–6. Leaves of three other forms, X8. 7. Upper medial cells. 8. Two leaf apices, X120.

9–17. Fo. spinifolium. 9. Habit sketch, X.4. 10. Three leaves, X8. 11. Upper medial cells. 12. Leaf apex. 13. Alar cells, X120. 14. Two leaves of a small slender form growing with above but exposed to the air, X8. 15–16. Upper medial and alar cells of latter, X120. 17. Capsules of latter, X8.

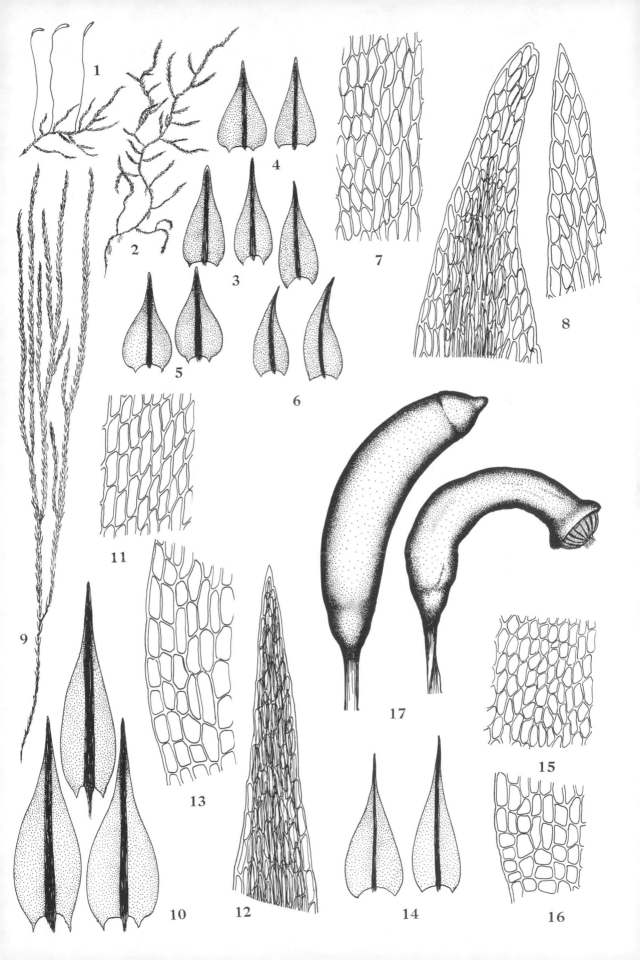

21.172 tose; older leaves toward the base of the stem often much eroded leaving the subulate costa standing erect with the remaining basal cells thick walled and colored. Sterile. Plate 115, figs. 9–17.

21.172 Rich County: Bear Lake near Lakota, 5,990 ft. Millard County: Deep Creek Mountains at Gandy, 4,500 ft.

21.173 Plants grow exposed to the air, but adjacent to submerged tufts, they usually have less strongly excurrent costa and are paler and shorter. Near Gandy, at the south end of the Deep Creek Mountains, there is a large spring with numerous vents from which slightly warm water highly charged with calcium carbonate is discharged over an area of perhaps an acre. Great masses of this moss grow both submerged and on the wet tufts. Some plants exposed to the air are bright green and fruiting, with leaves broadly ovate and long acuminate with a costa much more slender than usual, but long excurrent. These forms also have very short leaf cells and on the whole look very much like *A. varium*, except for the long-excurrent costa. In the same tuft are stems with more typical leaves and submerged plants of the typical *spinifolium* kind. There are all sorts of variations other than these, but any attempt to describe them would lead to confusion.

21.174 **8. Amblystegium fluviatile** (Hedw.) B.S.G. var. **fluviatile.** Plants small to medium sized, when submerged dark, dull green, in long, loose tufts. Stems up to 15 cm long; branches irregular, often lying parallel. Stem leaves oblong-ovate to oblong-lanceolate, 0.8–1.3 mm long, ± evenly narrowed to the apex, the tips blunt or narrowly obtuse, not or very slightly acuminate, broad at the base, only slightly narrowed; margins entire or slightly dentate; costa stout, dark green, little narrowed upward, ending vaguely in the opaque apex, subpercurrent. Plants on damp or wet substrata; in air often lighter dull green or yellowish green. Monoicous. Rarely fruiting. Seta long; capsules oblong-cylindric, curved, 1.5–2 mm long without lid; arcuate and contracted under the mouth when dry and empty; lid convex-conic, obtuse or bluntly pointed. Plate 116, figs. 1–9.

21.175 In and around streams, ponds and lakes.

21.176 Europe, Asia, Africa, South America, Mexico. More or less throughout the United States and southern Canada.

21.177 More or less sporadic in Utah but sometimes locally abundant. After comparing a series of eastern forms of this moss I find that it is practically impossible to draw a line between this species and what has been called *A. orthocladon* (P. Beauv.) Macoun. The only differences in the

---

Plate 116. **1–9. Amblystegium fluviatile.** 1. Habit sketch, X.4. 2. Three typical leaves. 3–4. Leaves of two other forms, X8. 5. Robust form, X.4. 6. Leaves of same, X8. 7–8. Apical and basal cells, X120. 9. Capsules, X8.

10–15. Var. noterophilum. 10. Habit, X.4. 11. Same, X2. 12. Two typical leaves. 13. Eroded basal leaf, X8. 14. Cross section, base of well-developed leaf. 15. Cross section of lower stem, X120.

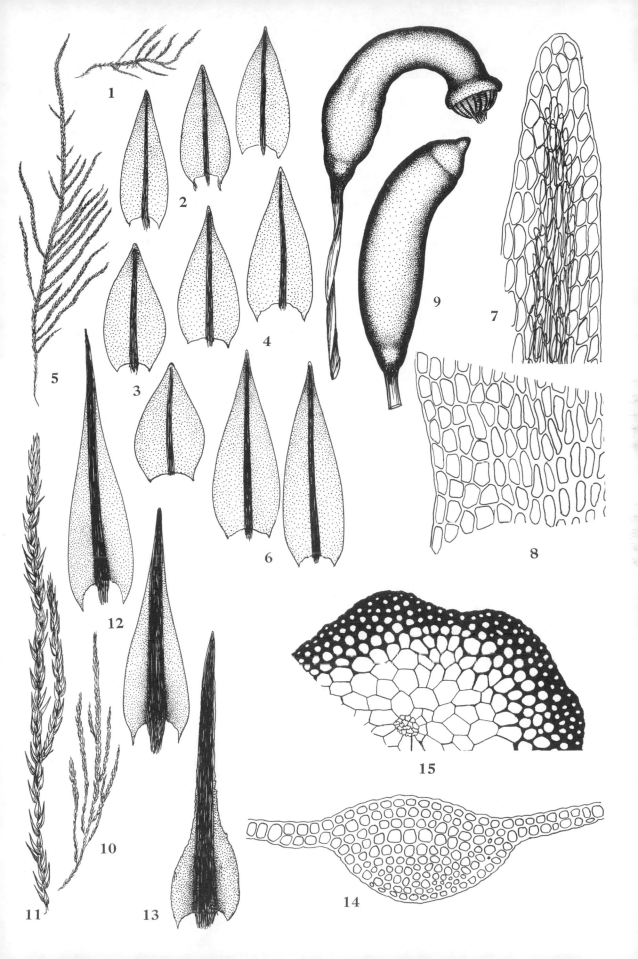

latter are the ovate leaves with a thinner costa and, in some plants, a brighter green color. It strikes me that it is nothing more than a short-leaved form of the species which is brighter green when growing exposed to the air. It is also generally small and superficially resembles *A. varium*, but the leaves are not at all or only shortly acuminate and blunter, and the costa is usually thicker. I have included two such specimens here, the ones from Bear Lake and Johnson Creek. *Hygroamblystegium fluviatile* var. *ovatum* Grout, Moss Fl. N. Am. 3:74, 1931 is a similar form with obtuse leaf apices and a scarcely percurrent costa.

21.178   8a. Var. **noterophilum** (Sull. & Lesq.) Flow. Plants the largest of this group, coarse and stiff, submerged in loose or dense dark green tufts, when dry acquiring a vitreous, metallic color. Stem becoming 10 cm long or more, the older parts in cross section showing 3–4 rows of small, very thick-walled, colored outer cells; branches irregular, long and often parallel, rather numerous, blackish and often denuded below. Stem leaves erect-patent to patent, 1.5–2.5 mm long, ovate-lanceolate to lanceolate, lamina only slightly or not at all acuminate; costa exceedingly stout, occupying up to ⅓ of the width of the leaf base, strongly convex on both sides, excurrent to a thick rigid tip; lamina adjacent, the costa in the lower part bistratose; older basal leaves usually much eroded leaving only the stout subulate costae standing, the remaining basal cells thick walled and colored. Sterile. Plate 116, figs. 10–15.

21.179   In springs and brooks in Utah, usually in lowlands.

21.180   Across northern United States to Montana. Tooele County: Johnson Spring, Clover Creek, south end of Stansbury Mountains, 6,000 ft.

21.181   A large population grows at Johnson Spring, forming the source of Clover Creek in the dry foothills. Collections taken there over a period of 15 years show some variation in size of plants and in shapes of leaves. Plants growing on wet banks exposed to the air are often more broadly ovate than those growing in water. Several collections taken elsewhere in the state seem to be forms intermediate between this and the species, the leaves having a much narrower costa, less strongly excurrent or only percurrent. Another specimen from Gorgorza, Summit County, has much smaller green leaves with narrower costae, percurrent or shortly excurrent, quite blunt, and I have referred them to the species proper.

21.182   Cheney (*Bot Gaz.* 24:236-291, 1897) states that the cross sections of older stems show a large central strand of 12–21 layers of cells. I have several duplicates of Cheney's specimens, and in none can I find a central strand of more than 4–6 cells across (as in my specimens from Johnson Spring).

8. PLATYDICTYA Berk.

21.183   Plants very small and fine, forming thin mats, green to yellowish green. Stems exceedingly slender, often filiform and stoloniform, 1–2.5(3) cm long, irregularly branched, central strand lacking. Leaves usually erect-patent, often distant, ovate-lanceolate to slenderly lanceolate, up to 0.6

mm long; margins plane, entire or slightly serrulate; costa lacking or in-distinctly short and double, often broad and sometimes extending to the middle of the blade; medial cells short, rhomboidal to hexagonal or oval, alar cells quadrate or oblong. Seta up to 1 cm long; capsules most-ly erect and symmetric, often inclined and curved, sometimes becoming horizontal, shortly obovoid to subcylindric, less than 1.6 mm long; lid convex or conic with a short or longish point; peristome teeth with fine transverse striations on the lower joints; cilia 1–2, rudimentary or lack-ing.

21.184   The name, which is from the Greek, means a flat net.

21.185   **Platydictya jungermannioides** (Brid.) Crum. Plants in fine mats on soil and rocks, bright green to yellowish green, sometimes scattered among other mosses. Stems very slender, often filiform, sometimes stoloniform, often quite straight, 1–2 cm long, irregularly and sparingly branched. Leaves distant, loosely appressed when dry, erect-patent to spreading when moist; stem leaves ovate-lanceolate to lanceolate, shortly to rather longly acuminate, ± curved to the insertion, 0.25–0.4 mm long, 0.1–0.13 mm wide, concave; margins plane, entire to serrulate; costa lacking or very short, broad and indistinct, sometimes vaguely extending about half the length of the blade; cells rhomboidal-hexagonal, often irregular, 7–10 μ wide, walls rather thickish; alar cells not particularly differen-tiated or 2–3 quadrate in the margins. Dioicous. Fruit rare. Seta less than 1 cm long; capsules obovate to obovate-oblong, erect and sym-metric or nearly so, urn 0.8–1.5 mm long, the neck rather long, the mouth flaring when dry; annulus quite large; lid convex-mammillate to convex-conic with a short to rather long point; peristome teeth trans-versely striate; segments from a high basal membrane, narrowly lanceo-late; cilia lacking or very rudimentary. Plate 117, figs. 10–17.

21.186   On damp or rather dry rocks and on soil in crevices or on ledges in shady places.

21.187   Across southern Canada and adjacent United States, south in the Rocky Mountains to Utah and New Mexico.

21.188   **Amblystegium serpens** var. **tenue** may be sought here because of its very small size and slender habit, but the stem has a small central strand, the leaves are slightly larger with a stronger costa and the cap-sules are larger, usually curved. The peristome always has cilia. Plate 117, figs. 1–9.

21.189   Var. **minutissima** (Sull. & Lesq.) Differs chiefly in the triangular-lanceo-late leaves, not narrowed to the insertion; medial cells slightly longer; alar cells shortly oblong but otherwise scarcely differentiated. Monoicous. Capsules ovoid, erect and symmetric or slightly curved, inclined to nearly pendulous; peristome with single cilia. Plate 117, figs. 18–19.

9.   CAMPYLIUM (Sull.) Mitt.

21.190   Plants small to medium sized, bright or dark green to golden yellowish, in thin or dense mats or tufts, often scattered among other mosses.

Stems irregularly pinnate, central strand small or lacking; rhizoids few to numerous. Stem leaves broadly to narrowly ovate-lanceolate, ± squarrose to widely spreading, short- to long-acuminate, ± channeled above, usually broadly rounded and ± cordate at base; margins entire to slightly serrulate; costa lacking, very short and weak, or single and extending to the middle or slightly beyond, upper cells oblong-linear to linear, 5–9 μ wide, becoming wider in the base; alar cells few and quadrate or much enlarged and inflated, sometimes colored. Branch leaves smaller and narrower. Seta long; capsules oblong to cylindric, curved and cernuous, becoming ± strongly arcuate and contracted under the mouth when dry; annulus present; lid conic or convex, obtuse to broadly pointed; peristome perfect.

21.191   The name means bent or curved, alluding to the capsule.

21.192   1. Costa lacking or very short and weak; leaves squarrose-spreading

2. Plants small and slender; stem leaves mostly less than 1 mm long; alar cells subquadrate, firm .... 1. *C. hispidulum* 21.194

2. Plants medium sized, rather robust; stem leaves, 1.5–2.5 mm long .... 3. *C. stellatum* 21.202

21.193   1. Costa present, narrow but distinct, extending to the middle of the blade or beyond

3. Leaves squarrose-spreading; alar cells few, subquadrate, firm; plants small to medium sized .... 2. *C. chrysophyllum* 21.198

3. Leaves not squarrose, erect-patent to widely spreading, narrowly to rather broadly acuminate; alar cells abruptly enlarged and inflated; plants medium sized .... 4. *C. polygamum* 21.209

21.194   **1. Campylium hispidulum** (Brid.) Mitt. Plants small, in intricate mats, bright green to yellowish green. Shoots slender, creeping with ascending tips, 1–2 cm long or longer, irregularly branched; rhizoids often numerous. Stem leaves ± squarrose-spreading, 0.6–0.8 mm long, broadly ovate-cordate, rather abruptly narrowed to a long slender acumination, channelled above, in some leaves as long as or longer than the base, insertion narrow, slightly decurrent; margins entire to slightly serrulate; costa lacking; upper cells linear-rhomboidal, 5–7 μ wide, wider in the base and irregularly oblong to hexagonal; alar cells quadrate to shortly oblong, firm. Branch leaves smaller and narrower, not so abruptly acuminate. Monoicous. Seta 1–2.5 cm long; capsules short, urn 1.5–2 mm long, curved. Plate 118, figs. 1–6.

Plate 117. 1–9. **Amblystegium serpens** var. **tenue.** 1. Habit sketches, X.4. 2. Portion of shoot, X4. 3–5. Stem leaves from three different plants, X8. 6. Cross section of stem, X60. 7. Basal and alar cells, X120. 8. Typical leaf apex, X120. 9. Capsules, X8.

10–17. **Platydictya jungermannioides.** 10. Habit sketches, X.4. 11–12. Portions of shoots, X2. 13. Cross section of stem, X60. 14. Stem leaves, X8. 15. Stem leaf, X120. 16. Capsules, X8. 17. Portion of peristome, X60.

18–19. Var. **minutissima.** 18. Leaves, X8. 19. Leaf, X120.

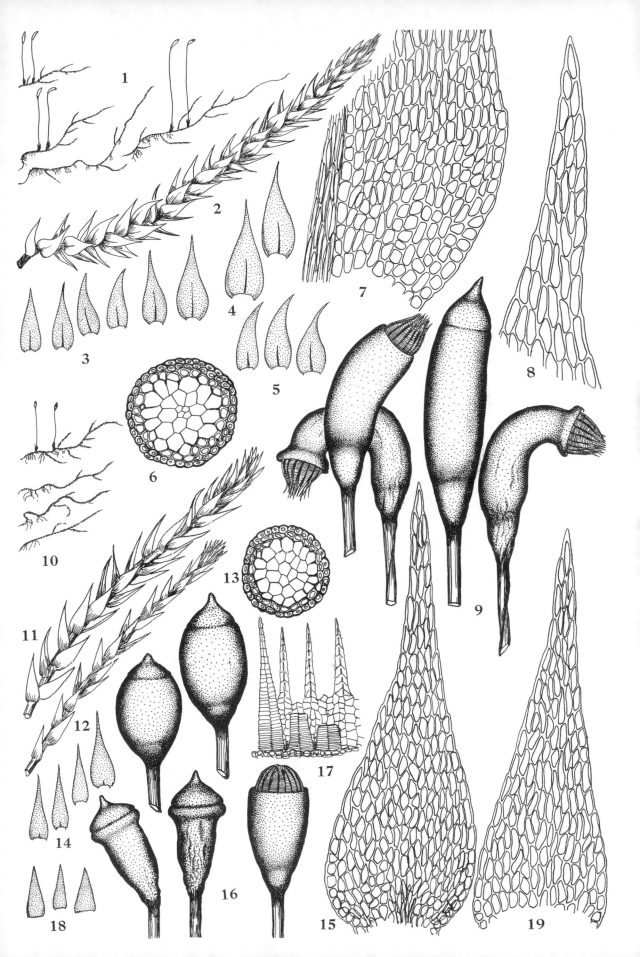

21.195 On damp or wet soil, rocks and rotten wood in cool shady places.

21.196 Eurasia, Andes Mountains of northern South America. Across southern Canada and northern United States. Utah County: Mt. Timpanogos at Aspen Grove, 6,700 ft.

21.197 Rare in Utah and the West in general. Our single specimen has stem leaves with narrower bases than the typical form with only a few differentiated alar cells and entire margins. It approaches var. *sommerfeltii* (Myr.) Lindb. but lacks extremely long acumination of that plant (where it becomes twice the length of the base).

21.198 **2. Campylium chrysophyllum** (Brid.) J. Lange. Plants variable, small to medium sized, forming interwoven mats, bright green, becoming yellowish green to golden yellow. Stems reaching 3 cm long or longer but usually shorter, freely branched; rhizoids often numerous. Stem leaves widely squarrose spreading to widely patent, some of them often falcate, mostly about 1.5 mm long but reaching 2.5 mm in large forms, rather abruptly narrowed to a long slender, ± channelled acumen from a broadly ovate, slightly clasping base, insertion narrow and slightly decurrent; margins entire to vaguely serrulate; costa slender, reaching the middle or beyond; upper cells oblong-linear, 5–7(9) μ wide; basal cells wider; alar cells few, subquadrate. Branch leaves smaller, the base ovate but not as broad, less abruptly acuminate. Dioicous. Frequently fruiting. Seta 1.5–3 cm long; capsules oblong-cylindric, curved, urn 2.5–3.5 mm long. Plate 118, figs. 7–13.

21.199 On damp or wet substrata, usually in shady places, often scattered among other mosses.

21.200 Antilles, Europe, Asia and northern Africa. Throughout Canada and United States. Daggett County: Uinta Mountains, near Spirit Lake, 10,700 ft.

21.201 Both of our specimens were growing in mixture with other mosses. Easily recognized by the spreading squarrose leaves with slender channelled acuminations, weak slender costa and excavate and slightly clasping bases. On a slide they do not lie flat owing to the slightly recurved base and channelled upper part. Small forms may be mistaken for *Amblystegium juratzkanum, A. kochii,* or *A. compactum.*

21.202 **3. Campylium stellatum** (Hedw.) C. Jens. var. **stellatum.** Plants medium sized to rather stout, forming dense mats or rather deep tufts, bright or yellowish green, often becoming golden yellow. Stem prostrate to ascending, 2–10 cm long, irregularly branched, thick and densely leaved,

---

Plate 118. **1–6. Campylium hispidulum.** 1. Habit sketch, X.4. 2. Portion of shoot, X2. 3. Five stem leaves, X8. 4. Upper medial and apical cells. 5. Basal and alar cells, X120. 6. Three capsules, X8.

7–13. Campylium chrysophyllum. 7. Two habit sketches, X.4. 8. Two portions of main stem showing variation in stance of leaves, X6. 9. Three stem leaves, X8. 10. Two areas of upper medial leaf cells showing variation in dimensions. 11. Typical leaf apex. 12. Alar cells, X120. 13. Three capsules, X8.

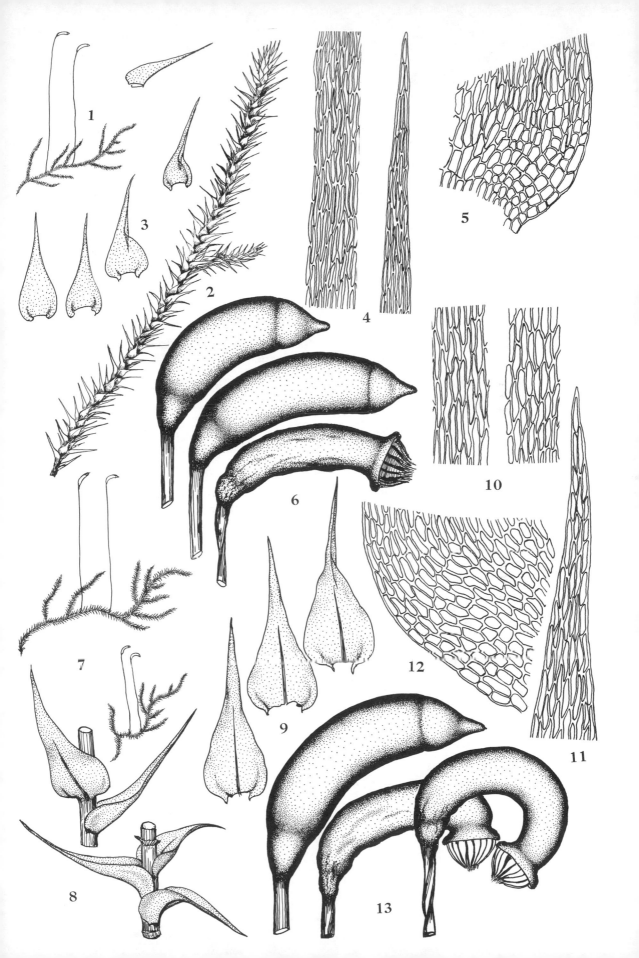

rhizoids usually few at the base. Stem leaves 1.5–3 mm long, patent to widely spreading, ± squarrose, triangular-lanceolate and very gradually acuminate or ovate-lanceolate and more abruptly acuminate, channelled above, the tips ± twisted when dry; base rounded-cordate, excavate and slightly clasping but not decurrent; margins entire; costa lacking or sometimes very thin and short, occasionally double; upper cells linear, 4–7 μ wide, shorter at the margins and the tips, becoming wider in the base; basal cells often thick walled and colored, becoming pitted in some older leaves; alar cells abruptly enlarged, sometimes inflated, becoming thick walled in older leaves. Dioicous. Fruit sparse and infrequent. Seta up to 3 cm long; capsules oblong to oblong-cylindric, urn 1.5–2.5 mm long, curved and cernuous, usually contracted under the mouth when dry. Plate 119, figs. 1–7.

21.203   On damp or wet soil and humus, often scattered among other mosses, at high elevations in Utah.

21.204   Mexico, Eurasia, and northern Africa. Across Canada and northern United States, south to Pennsylvania, Ohio, Iowa, Colorado, and Utah.

21.205   Our specimens are very typical and apparently favored by noncalcareous habitats.

21.206   3a. Var. **protensum** (Brid.) Bryhn. More prostrate, the stem leaves very broadly ovate or triangular at the base, more abruptly narrowed to a longer narrower upper part, slenderly acuminate. Plate 119, fig. 8.

21.207   Summit County: near Kimball's Junction, Parley's Park, 6,000 ft.

21.208   This plant is not noticeably smaller or more regularly branched than the species (as described by Dixon and other authors).

21.209   4. **Campylium polygamum** (B.S.G.) C. Jens. Plants medium sized, growing in loose or dense mats, green to yellowish green often becoming golden yellow. Stems prostrate with ascending tips and branches, 2–6 cm long, irregularly branched, rhizoids few to numerous. Stem leaves erect-patent to spreading but not squarrose, ovate-lanceolate, gradually and evenly tapering to a long, slender, channelled acumination, varying to more broadly ovate-lanceolate with a shorter, less channelled acumination, varying to more broadly ovate-lanceolate with a shorter, less channelled apex, 2–2.5 mm long, rounded-cordate and excavate at the base; entire; costa slender, distinct but rather weak, extending about ½ the length of the blade or slightly more; upper cells linear, often flexuous, 5–8 μ wide; basal cells much broader; alar cells enlarged and inflated. Branch

---

Plate 119. 1–7. **Campylium stellatum.** 1. Two habit sketches, X.4. 2. Portion of main shoot showing stance of leaves, X2. 3. Three stem leaves, X4. 4. Upper medial leaf cells. 5. Leaf apex. 6. Two areas of alar cells showing variation, X120. 7. Two capsules, X8.

8. Var. **protensum.** Two typical stem leaves, X8.

9–11. **Campylium polygamum.** 9. Habit sketch, X.4. 10. Portion of main stem, X2. 11. Four stem leaves showing variations, X8.

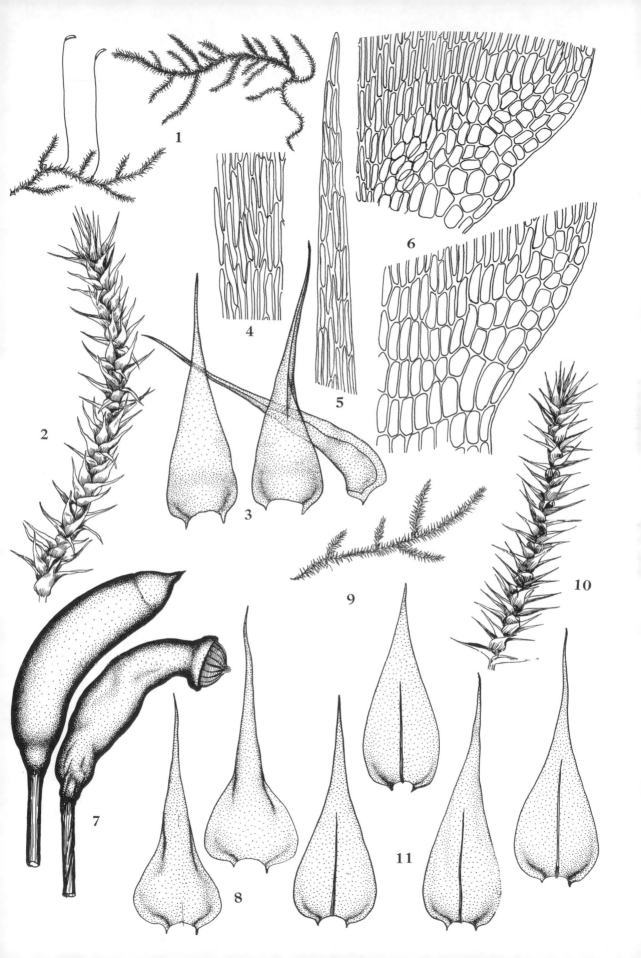

leaves smaller and narrower. Monoicous or polygamous. Seta 2–3 cm long; capsules oblong-cylindric, curved, urn 2–2.5 mm long. Plate 119, figs. 9–11.

21.210   Growing on damp or wet substrata, especially in and around springs and wet meadows.

21.211   Europe, Asia, North Africa, Andes Mountains of South America, Australia and New Zealand. Across Canada and northern United States, south to Virginia and westward. Rich County: Bear Lake, 6,000 ft. Summit County: Uinta Mountains, Black's Fork, 9,200 ft.

21.212   The Bear Lake specimen is typical, but the one from Black's Fork has broader leaves, shortly acuminate and less channelled, and might be mistaken for a form of *Drepanocladus aduncus* because of the broad leaves with inflated alar cells, but most of them show a clasping base, channelled acumen, firmer, spreading stance, and weaker costa.

10. CALLIERGON (Sull.) Kindb.

21.213   Plants medium sized to large, light green to yellowish green or golden brown, ascending to erect in dense mats or tufts, sometimes creeping and, in some species, floating in water. Stems simple to pinnately branched with a central strand; rhizoids usually few at the base. Leaves broadly ovate to ovate-lanceolate or oblong, usually concave, not plicate, acute to broadly obtuse, often cucullate and sometimes apiculate; margins plane, entire; costa single and nearly percurrent or short and weak or double; upper cells linear-rhomboidal to linear, shorter in the apex; basal cells shorter and broader, hyaline, often inflated and forming decurrent auricles. Seta long, smooth; capsules ovoid-oblong to subcylindric, curved and asymmetric, suberect to cernuous, often contracted below the mouth when dry; peristome perfect.

21.214   The name (from Greek) means beautifully wrought.

21.215   1. Alar cells enlarged, thin walled, hyaline and forming decurrent auricles; plants slender, green or yellowish green

    2. Costa percurrent or nearly so; leaves ovate to ovate-oblong, green to yellowish green .... 1. *C. cordifolium*   21.217

    2. Costa extending 1/2–5/6 the length of the blade; leaves ovate-oblong to ligulate; yellowish green to straw colored .... 2. *C. stramineum*   21.221

21.216   1. Alar cells small, mostly oblong, thick walled; basal cells elongated, very thick walled and porose, usually reddish brown; costa short and double or single and extending ⅓ the length of the blade; plants stout and tumid, olivaceous to golden brown .... 3. *C. turgescens*   21.225

21.217   **1. Calliergon cordifolium** (Hedw.) Kindb. Plants slender to rather robust, in mats or tufts, often scattered among other mosses, mostly light

480

green to yellowish green, brownish below. Stems reaching as much as 20 cm long but usually much shorter, simple or sparingly branched, the branches usually short. Stem leaves varying in size in different colonies, 2–5 mm long, loosely erect-patent to spreading, closely imbricated and forming a slender pointed bud at the stem tips, soft and tender, ± shrunken when dry, ovate to ovate-oblong, concave, apex obtuse to broadly rounded, often cucullate, base cordate and decurrent; margins plane and entire; costa strong, percurrent or nearly so; upper medial cells linear, 8–12 μ wide, the ends ± pointed; shorter in the apex; becoming shorter and broader in the base, rarely colored; alar cells much enlarged, thin walled and hyaline, often inflated, usually forming decurrent auricles, not sharply set off. Autoicous. Seta 2–5 cm long, capsules large for the size of the leafy shoots, urn 3–3.5 mm long, oblong, curved, inclined to cernuous, rich brown; lid conic, shortly apiculate; annulus lacking; spores 12–14 μ, smooth, reddish brown. Plate 120.

21.218   Growing in wet meadows, seepage areas, and boggy situations at high elevations in our region.

21.219   Across Canada and northern United States, south to New Jersey, Pennsylvania, Ohio, and westward to Colorado and Utah. Duchesne County: Uinta Mountains, Bald Mountain at Fehr Lake, 10,500 ft.; Ottoson Basin, 11,110 ft.

21.220   Uncommon in Utah. Distinctive by the light green, soft, tender mats or tufts and the spreading to loosely erect-patent leaves with a strong percurrent costa and conspicuous inflated alar cells.

21.221   **2. Calliergon stramineum** (Brid.) Kindb. Plants slender, in soft mats or tufts, often scattered among other mosses, yellowish green to straw colored. Stems slender, simple or with a few short branches, 2–4 cm long or longer; rhizoids few on the older parts. Stem leaves loosely erect-patent to spreading, imbricated and convolute at the stem tip, forming a slender bud, ovate-oblong to oblong-ligulate, 1.5–2 mm long, concave, obtuse to broadly rounded, sometimes cucullate, some older ones bearing a tuft of rhizoids from the back at the apex, the base gradually narrowed and decurrent, loosely imbricated and slightly plicate when dry; costa single, extending 1/2–5/6 the length of the blade, not percurrent; medial cells oblong to linear, 6–8 μ wide with the ends tapered, shorter in the apex, becoming shorter and wider toward the base; alar cells abruptly enlarged, thin walled and inflated, hyaline and forming decurrent auricles. Dioicous. Fruit rare. Seta 3–6 cm long. Capsules oblong-cylindric, curved, inclined to cernuous, urn 2.5–3 mm long; lid conic and bluntly pointed; annulus lacking. Plate 121, figs. 1–5.

21.222   Growing in wet meadows and boggy areas at high elevations in our region.

21.223   Europe, Asia, and the Andes Mountains of South America. Across Canada and northern United States, Massachusetts, Michigan, Colorado, New Mexico, and Utah's Uinta Mountains.

21.224 HYPNACEAE

21.224 The pale yellowish or straw color and the oblong to ligulate leaves with a rather short costa distinguish this plant from *C. cordifolium.*

21.225 **3. Calliergon turgescens** (T. Jens.) Kindb. Plants stout, growing in thick mats or deep tufts, golden yellowish at the tips, olivaceous to yellowish brown below. Shoots 3–10 cm long, swollen and turgid because of the dense spreading leaves, sparingly branched; rhizoids few at the base. Stem leaves 2–2.7 mm long, loosely imbricated to spreading, broadly oblong-elliptic to elliptic-lanceolate, strongly concave, the margins often incurved and overlapping at the apex, obtuse and usually apiculate; base rounded or more gradually narrowed, ± clasping the stem, not decurrent; margins entire; costa very thin, single and extending ⅓ (½) the length of the blade or short and double; upper cells linear with tapering ends, 6–8 μ wide, shorter and thicker walled in the apex, shorter, broader, and more highly colored in the base, thick walled and porose; alar cells smaller and narrower with thinner walls, mostly oblong but some of them quadrate. Dioicous. Fruit not seen. Plate 121, figs. 6–10.

21.226 Growing in bogs or on wet banks at high elevations in our region.

21.227 Rare and of scattered distribution. Europe and Asia. Greenland, Ontario, British Columbia, Rocky Mountains to Utah. Summit County: Uinta Mountains, Black's Fork, 9,200 ft.

21.228 The generic relationships of this plant remain in doubt. Various authors have placed it in *Drepanocladus,* but later changed to *Calliergon* or *Scorpidium.* It bears a strong resemblance to *S. scorpioides* in size, color, and nearly every other trait, except that the latter has falcate-secund leaves with the costa even weaker or none at all. It resembles some species of *Hygrohypnum* but can be distinguished by the entire leaf tips and the golden to yellowish brown color.

11. HYGROHYPNUM Lindb.

21.229 Plants medium sized to rather large, dull green, yellowish green or brownish, in loose or dense mats or ascending tufts, submerged in water or on very wet soil, rocks, and rotten wood. Stems irregularly branched, often denuded below; rhizoids few or lacking, central strand present but often vague; pseudoparaphyllia sometimes present in axils of branches. Leaves straight to falcate secund, nearly orbicular to oval or ovate- to oblong-lanceolate, ± concave; apex broadly rounded, obtuse, or bluntly pointed, sometimes mucronate or widely acute; costa usually stout but variable, short and double, forked or single and extending 1/2–4/5 the length of the blade; upper cells linear; basal cells broader and shorter, alar cells ± enlarged, sometimes inflated or colored and occasionally decurrent. Monoicous or dioicous. Seta long; capsules ovoid to subcylindric, inclined to horizontal, asymmetric or

Plate 120. Calliergon cordifolium. 1. Habit sketches, X.4. 2. Portion of shoot, X2. 3. Three stem leaves. 4. Two branch leaves, X8. 5. Leaf apex and upper cells. 6. Basal and alar cells, X80. 7. Capsules, X8.

482

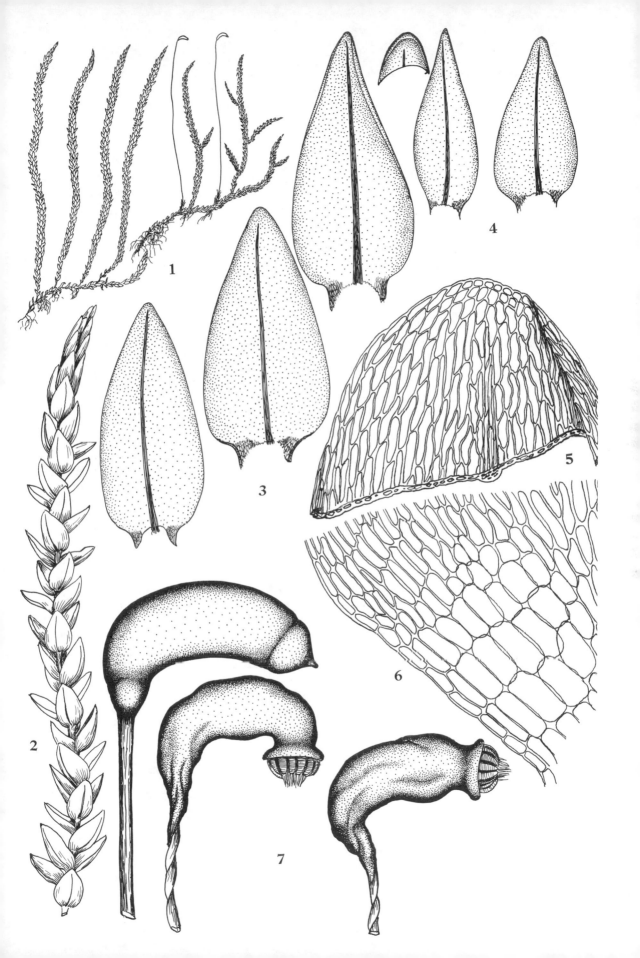

curved; annulus present; conic-convex, sometimes mammillate; peristome perfect.

21.230 The name means aquatic moss.

21.231   1. Epidermal cells of the stem abruptly enlarged, thin walled and hyaline; alar cells of the leaves, large, thin walled, often forming auricles .... 1. *H. ochraceum*   21.233

21.232   1. Epidermal cells of the stem not enlarged, small and thick walled; alar cell mostly only moderately enlarged, more or less chlorophyllose, rarely inflated

      2. Leaves ovate-lanceolate, oblong or oblong-lanceolate ....
.... 2. *H. luridum*   21.241

      2. Leaves broadly ovate to nearly orbicular, mostly obtuse, not falcate or secund

         3. Leaves slightly to deeply concave; costa mostly forked

            4. Leaves reaching 1.5 mm long, widely spreading, soft when dry .... 3. *H. molle*   21.251

            4. Leaves reaching 3 mm long, loosely spreading to erect-patent and julaceous, often harsh when dry .... 4. *H. bestii*   21.255

         3. Leaves dense, deeply concave, widely spreading to erect-patent, the shoots swollen, cordlike .... 5. *H. smithii*   21.259

21.233   **1. Hygrohypnum ochraceum** (Wils.) Loesk. var. **ochraceum.** Plants medium sized, submerged or in wet places, forming large loose soft mats or tufts, dull green or yellowish green, often becoming brown or nearly black. Stems rather slender, 2–4(10) cm long, simple or sparingly branched; central strand of a few small cells; epidermis of abruptly enlarged, thin-walled, hyaline cells 10–15 μ wide. Leaves 1–1.8 mm long, concave, oblong-ovate to oblong-lanceolate, narrowed to a short or long, broad, blunt or obtuse apex, straight to strongly falcate-secund; the base slightly rounded and ± decurrent; margins plane, usually bluntly dentate at the apex, entire below; costa forked or single and extending 1/2–4/5 the length of the blade; cells linear, 5–8 μ wide; apical cells short, rhomboidal-hexagonal; basal cells shorter and broader, often thicker walled; alar cells ± abruptly enlarged, oblong, thin walled, sometimes becoming inflated and forming small or large decurrent auricles. Dioicous. Capsules infrequent, ovoid-oblong, inclined to horizontal, asymmetric, 2–2.5 mm long without the lid, yellowish brown, becoming darker with age, contracted under the mouth when dry; annulus of 2–4 rows of reddish cells; lid conic-convex and apiculate. Plate 122, figs. 1–7.

Plate 121.   1–5. **Calliergon stramineum.** 1. Habit sketches, X.4. 2. Portion of shoot, X2. 3. Leaves, X8. 4. Leaf apex and upper medial cells. 5. Basal and alar cells, X80.

6–10. **Calliergon turgescens.** 6. Habit, X.4. 7. Portion of shoot, X2. 8. Leaves, X8. 9. Upper medial cells, X80. 10. Basal and alar cells, X80.

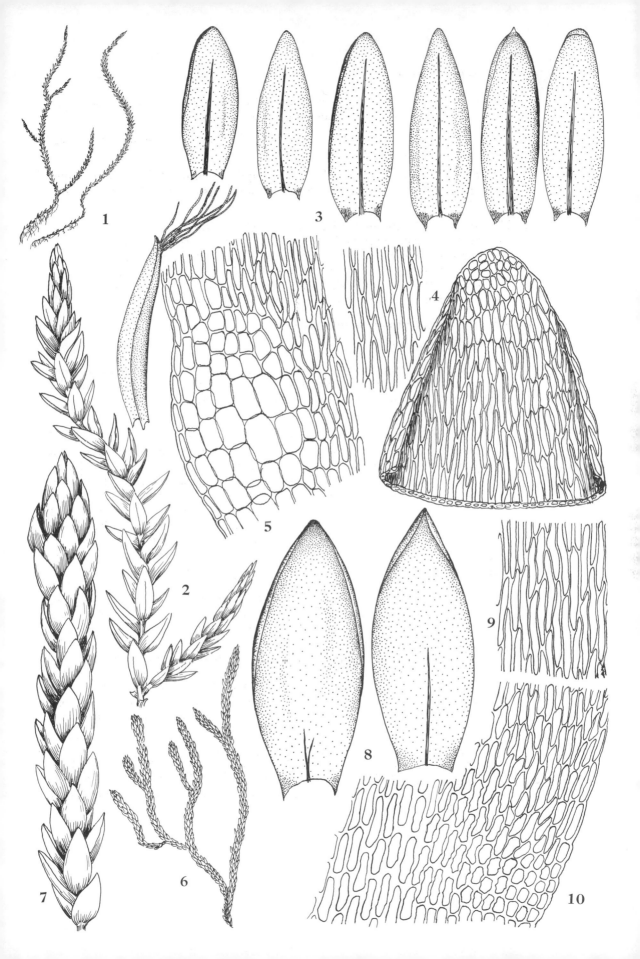

21.234   Submerged or on wet rocks, soil, and rotten wood, in and around mountain brooks, springs, seepage areas, and waterfalls.

21.235   Europe, Asia. Across Canada and the United States, southward to Virginia, Texas, Arizona, and California.

21.236   Abundant locally in Utah. The abruptly enlarged hyaline, thin-walled epidermal cells of the stems immediately distinguish this species from the others.

21.237   1a. Var. **flaccidum** (Mild.) Amann. Plants larger than the type; stems long and lax, dull yellowish green, purplish brown or almost black; branches few but often long; leaves distant, straight to slightly falcate, somewhat complanate, oval-oblong to oblong-lanceolate, 2–2.5 mm long, apex obtuse and bluntly dentate; margins often strongly incurved, entire; costa single or forked, strong. Plate 122, figs. 8–9.

21.238   Submerged in mountain brooks.

21.239   Uinta Mountains.

21.240   The large, more loosely disposed and darker colored leaves are distinctive. The habit of growth and stance of the leaves differ markedly from the species but the large, thin walled epidermal cells of the stem are typical.

21.241   **2. Hygrohypnum luridum** (Hedw.) Jenn. Plants variable in habit and appearance, slender to fairly robust, bright green to dull yellowish or brownish green, in loose or dense mats submerged and often filled with sediment, in brooks or wet places. Stems irregularly branched, the tips often hooked, 2–8 cm long; rhizoids mostly confined to the base. Leaves variable in stance and shape, open and rather distant to close set and dense, sometimes loosely to closely imbricated rendering the shoots julaceous, straight to secund, sometimes falcate-secund, both forms occasionally occurring on the same shoot, typically oblong ovate but varying to ovate or ovate-lanceolate, sometimes briefly acuminate, concave, the upper margins strongly incurved and often subtubulose; apex acute to obtuse or rather broadly rounded, occasionally abruptly cuspidate; margins plane, entire, rarely slightly dentate at the extreme apex in a few leaves; costa variable, even in leaves of the same stem, very short and double to strong and forked or single and extending $1/2$–$3/4$ the length of the blade; upper medial cells linear-rhomboidal to linear flexuous, 5–7 μ, in the apex shorter, oval to rhomboidal, becoming shorter and broader in the base, the walls usually becoming thicker with age; alar cells either scarcely differentiated or becoming quadrate to oblong, 12–16 μ wide, rather thick walled and often opaque with dense

Plate 122.   **1–7. Hygrohypnum ochraceum.** 1. Three habit sketches, X.4. 2. Portions of two different stems, X2. 3. Cross section of the stem, X60. 4. Four typical leaves, X8. 5. Leaf apex and upper areolation, X120. 6. Two areas of alar cells, X120. 7. Four capsules, X8.
8–9. Var. flaccidum. 8. Portion of stem, X2. 9. Three leaves showing usual range of shape and size, X8.

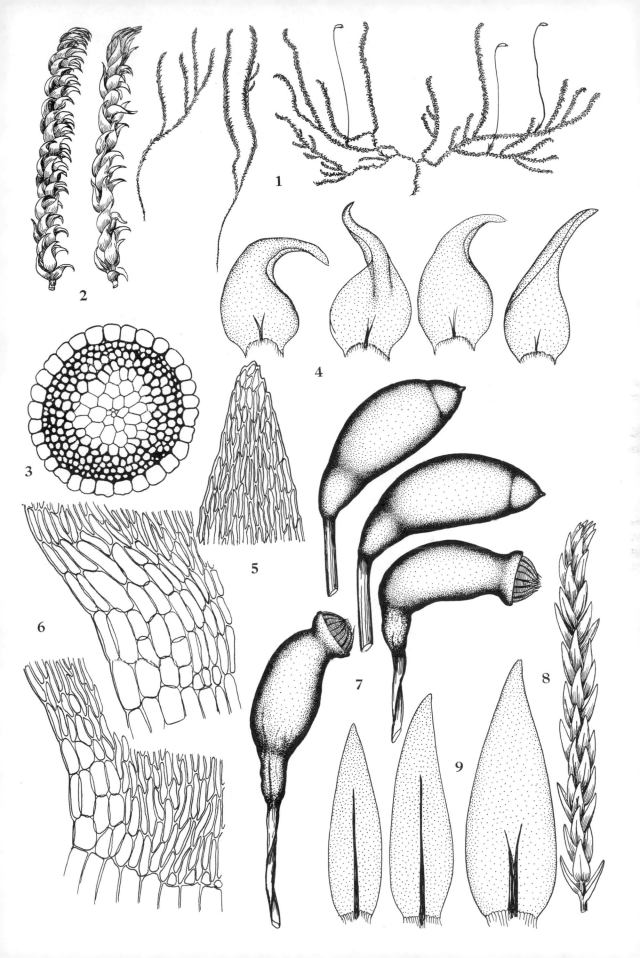

1

2

3

4

5

6

7

8

9

contents, as many as 2–5 on the margin and across the base, occasionally with 2–3 thin-walled inflated cells at the extreme angles. Monoicous, frequently fruiting. Seta 1.5–2 cm long; capsules asymmetric, ovoid-oblong to shortly oblong, 2–2.5 mm long, inclined to horizontal, when dry and empty ± shrunken and contracted under the mouth; annulus lacking, lid convex with a short blunt point. Plate 123, figs. 1–10.

21.242   Submerged or on wet rocks, soil, or rotten logs mostly in and along mountain brooks, waterfalls, and dripping cliffs.

21.243   Europe, Asia, Mexico. British Columbia eastward across Canada, south to California, Arizona, and Colorado, northern United States southward to New Jersey and Pennsylvania.

21.244   Locally abundant in mountain streams and extremely variable. Most of our plants have ovate to oval-oblong leaves, and the tips of the branches are usually straight and often secund, but in some plants they are broadly ovate and falcate. The form may vary considerably, even on the same stem. The alar cells also vary considerably, in some plants scarcely differentiated, in others gradually enlarged and quadrate to oblong, sometimes with thick walls, and in still others quite abruptly enlarged and 14–17 μ wide. Some of the latter plants approach *H. eugyrium,* but in that plant the alar cells are much larger and generally become highly colored, the inner ones being especially thick walled.

21.245   2a. Fo. **julaceum** (B.S.G.) C. Jens. Shoots julaceous. Leaves loosely imbricated, straight, broadly ovate to oblong-ovate; narrowly obtuse to broadly rounded, usually mucronate, concave; the margins erect, entire or indistinctly denticulate at the apex; costa single or forked. Same habitat and range as the species, and occasionally growing with it. Plate 123, figs. 11–13.

21.246   Salt Lake County: Mill Creek Canyon, 7,600 ft.

21.247   2b. Fo. **serratum** Flow. Plants light green above, brownish below. Shoots slender with few branches, often denuded below. Leaves approximate, loosely imbricated to spreading or somewhat complanate, ovate to oval-oblong, mostly 1.5 mm long, broadly obtuse to rounded, a few broadly acute, concave; margins erect, rather closely serrate above and serrulate well toward the base; alar cells gradually wider, mostly oblong, hyaline and firm but in some leaves thin walled and inflated.

21.248   Washington County: Berry Spring, about 2 miles west of Hurricane, 2,365 ft. Plate 124, figs. 1–5.

21.249   2c. Fo. **tenue** Flow. Plants dull, dark green. Shoots very slender, loose and flaccid with few, distant branches, stiff and brittle when dry. Leaves

---

Plate 123.   1–10. Hygrohypnum luridum. 1–3. Typical form with falcate leaves. 4. Two leaf apices. 5. Three areas of alar cells showing variations X120. 6. Capsules X8. 7–10. Form with straight leaves, sometimes secund toward summit of sex stems.

11–13. Fo. julaceum. 11. Habit sketch, X.4. 12. Stem, X60. 13. Leaves, X8.

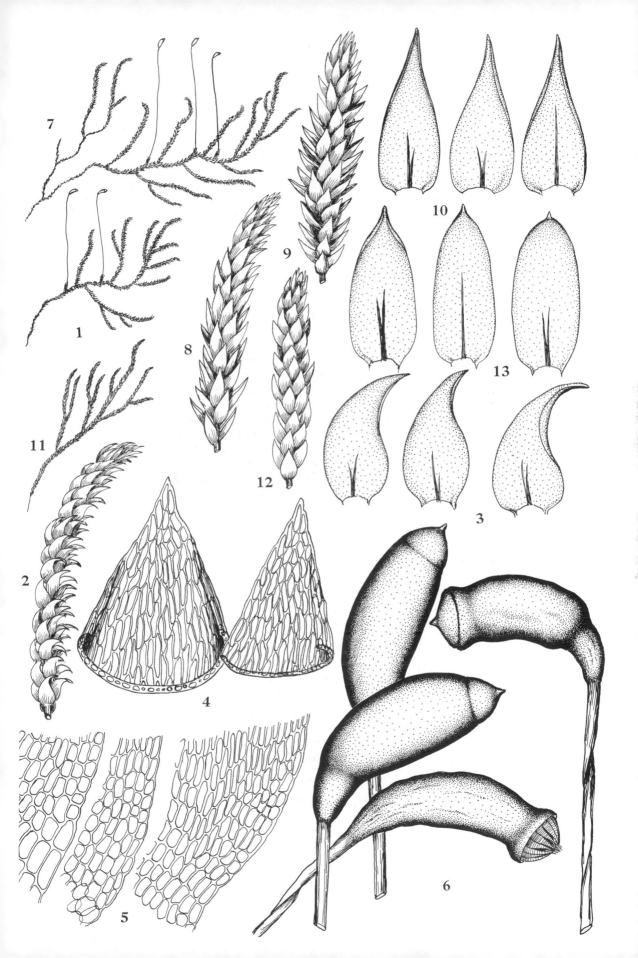

distant and rather lax, loosely erect-patent to patent when moist, ir-regularly spreading, shrunken, and twisted when dry, ovate- to oblong-lanceolate, straight or slightly curved and symmetric, up to 1.6 mm long, not acuminate, rather suddenly narrowing to an acute or blunt apex with a few teeth, concave; margins moderately incurved; costa short and forked, often indistinct; upper linear cells extending nearly to the base with only 1–3 rows of basal cells shorter and broader; alar cells not well set off, mostly oblong, chlorophyllose. Plate 124, figs. 6–10.

21.250   Salt Lake County: Holladay, submerged and attached to cement installa-tions of a fish hatchery, 4,560 ft.

21.251   **3. Hygrohypnum molle** (Hedw.) Loesk. Plants dark to light green above, yellowish to brown below, usually soft and lax but occasionally rather stiff and harsh, growing in loose tufts or mats on wet rocks, often sub-merged. Stems about 2–4 cm or sometimes as much as 10 cm long, ir-regularly branched, often denuded below, and sometimes stiff and wiry when old. Stem leaves broadly ovate, 1.2–1.7 mm long, 0.7–1.3 mm wide, obtuse to broadly rounded at the slightly dentate apex, base usually broadly rounded to fairly narrow insertion, not decurrent, concave, erect-patent to loosely imbricated rendering the shoots julaceous, the lower ones often less concave, distant and open to slightly spreading; costa strong, forked to trifid, 1 branch usually longer and extending ⅓–½ the length of the blade, occasionally single and longer in some leaves; upper cells variable according to habitat conditions, linear, firm to rather lax, 4–6 μ or as much as 7–9 μ wide; cells in the apex shorter and wider, often thick walled, $\pm$ rhomboidal; basal cells wider, often becoming very thick walled and highly colored at the insertion; differen-tiated alar cells lacking or few, oblong to quadrate, not sharply set off. Monoicous. Fruit infrequent. Seta 1–1.5 cm long; capsules shortly ovoid-oblong, asymmetric, strongly inclined to horizontal, 1.7–2.3 mm long, neck shorter than in other species; annulus of 2–3 rows of cells; lid con-vex with a short point. Plate 125, figs. 1–6.

21.252   Mostly on wet rocks in and around mountain brooks and rivers.

21.253   Europe and Asia. British Columbia to California, Nevada, Utah, and Colorado, across southern Canada to Quebec, Nova Scotia and the New England States where it is rare.

21.254   Infrequent in Utah and more variable than the original description suggests. It intergrades with *H. bestii* which differs mainly in being larger and with wider medial leaf cells and is said to be rough and harsh to the touch. It also intergrades with *H. dilatatum*, which has broader, often suborbicular leaves, and likewise is reputed to be harsh

---

Plate 124.   1–5. **Hygrohypnum luridum** fo. **serratum.** 1. Shoots showing the loosely imbricated and somewhat complanate stance of the leaves, X4. 2. Leaves, X8. 3. Two leaf apices. 4. Lower leaf margin. 5. Two areas of alar cells, X120.

6–10. **Hygrohypnum luridum** fo. **tenue.** 6. Habit sketch, X.4. 7. Portion of shoots showing moist and dry habits, X4. 8. Leaves, X8. 9. Two leaf apices. 10. Area of alar cell, X120.

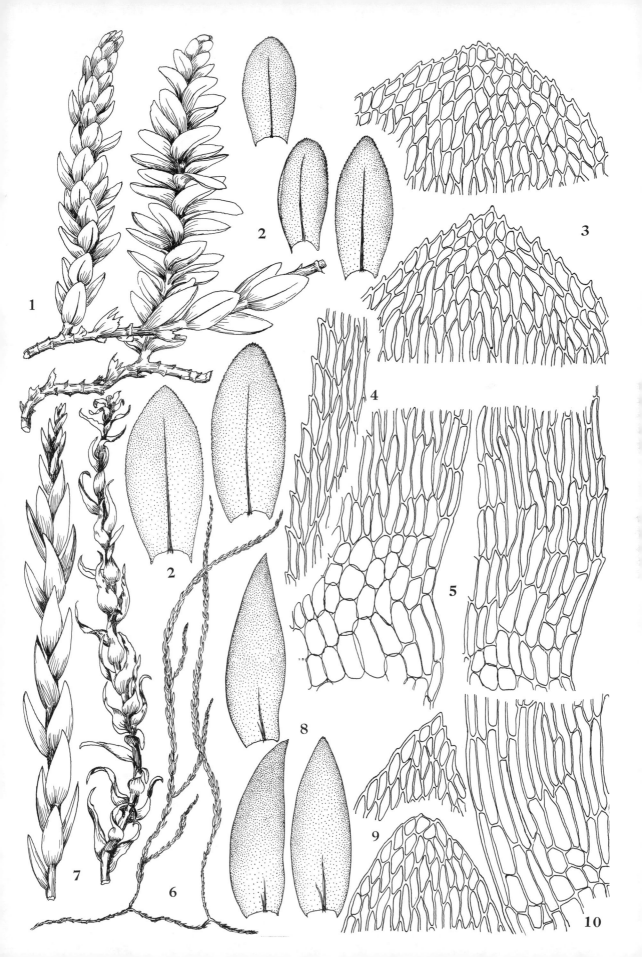

to the touch. The specimens listed above compare favorably with supposedly authentic specimens of *H. dilatatum,* some of which are not at all harsh. I have little faith in the texture of the mosses of this group as it varies too much in each species and appears to be a result of conditions of the habitat.

21.255 **4. Hygrohypnum bestii** (Ren. & Bryhn) Broth. Plants large, in deep loose tufts, green or olivaceous above, brown below, stiff and rough when dry. Stems stiff, often denuded below, rather sparingly branched, 7–8 cm long, divided into several secondary branches, these often slenderly attenuated. Leaves 2–3 mm long, 1–2 mm wide, smaller toward the ends of the branches, distant and ± widely spreading when dry, erect-patent to spreading when moist, broadly ovate, narrowing above the middle to a bluntly acute or narrowly obtuse apex, slightly to strongly concave, not plicate, the base rounded to a narrow insertion; margins entire or slightly denticulate at the apex, not incurved; costa very stout, forked from just above the base, 1 fork longer and usually extending to the middle of the blade or slightly beyond; upper cells linear-fusiform, 10–12 μ wide, becoming longer and narrower toward the base, 8–10 μ wide, usually thicker walled; apical cells much shorter, rhomboidal to quadrate; basal cells much shorter, very thick walled, some of them pitted, often bright orange; alar cells few, mostly oblong, 20–34 μ wide, usually thick walled and firm but occasionally thinner and inflated. Dioicous. Fruit unknown. Plate 125, figs. 7–9.

21.256 Submerged to emergent in mountain brooks or on wet soil, rocks, or wood, sometimes hanging in dripping water or in waterfalls.

21.257 Alaska to California, Montana, and Utah.

21.258 This is the largest species of the genus. The large, widely spaced leaves with forked costa and wide upper medial cells are especially characteristic. It may be harsh and rough to the touch, but this trait is quite variable. It intergrades with *H. molle,* which ranges smaller and tends to have leaves with broader apices and narrower cells.

21.259 **5. Hygrohypnum smithii** (Sw.) Broth. var. **smithii.** Plants typically slender, brownish green or darker with green tips, in dense tufts or mats on wet rocks in alpine brooks. Stems slender, irregularly branched, denuded below, stiff and wiry, especially when dry, 2–4 cm long. Stem leaves up to 1 mm long, broadly ovate to suborbicular, obtuse to broadly rounded, base rounded to a fairly narrow insertion, not decurrent, ± concave, spreading to patent or loosely imbricated rendering the shoots julaceous; margins entire, often indistinctly toothed at the apex; costa mostly single, extending 1/3–4/5 the length of the blade, in a few leaves shorter and forked; medial cells linear-flexuous, thick walled,

---

Plate 125. **1–6. Hygrohypnum molle.** 1. Three habit sketches, X.4. 2–3. Leaves, X8. 4. Leaf apices. 5. Upper medial cells. 6. Area of alar cells, X120.

7–9. Hygrohypnum bestii. 7. Habit sketch, X.4. 8. Leaves, X8. 9. Leaf apex and upper medial cells, X120.

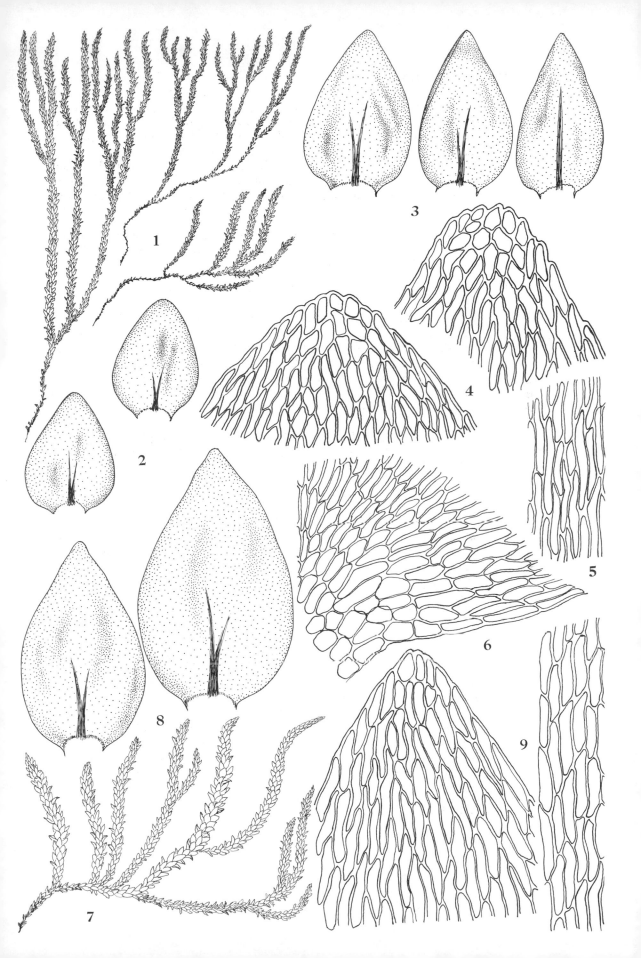

usually rather short, 6–9 μ wide, becoming rhomboidal toward the margins and upper portion and $\pm$ quadrate-rounded at the apex, thicker walled, occasionally colored; cells toward the base longer but near the insertion shorter and wider, often very thick walled and orange brown; alar cells mostly oblong, not sharply set off. Monoicous. Seta 1 cm long or less; capsules small, 1–1.5 mm long, shortly ovoid-oblong, asymmetric, inclined to horizontal, slightly or not at all contracted below the mouth when dry; annulus of 2 rows of cells; lid convex with a short point.

21.260 Europe, Cape Breton Island, Greenland. British Columbia east to Montana, south to California and Utah. Duchesne County: Uinta Mountains near Mirror Lake, 10,300 ft.

21.261 Var. **goulardii** (Schimp.) Wijk & Marg. Plants smaller and more slender, soft and sometimes flaccid but often denuded and rigid at the base, young shoots dark, dull green, often tinged with red or brown, especially in the older parts, $\pm$ julaceous. Leaves 0.6–0.8 mm long, very broadly ovate to suborbicular, a few broader than long, exceedingly concave (some almost hemispherical), rather distant, loosely imbricated, apex broadly rounded; base rounded to a narrow insertion; margins entire; costa short and forked or single and longer in leaves of the same shoot, sometimes indistinct and nearly lacking; cells much as in *H. smithii* but the alar cells fewer, often not strongly differentiated, mostly oblong and firm, occasionally with 2–3 abruptly enlarged and inflated cells at the extreme angles. Capsules not known. Rare. Known only on dripping cliffs and around waterfalls from two or three localities in Utah.

12. DREPANOCLADUS (C. Muell.) Roth.

21.262 Plants prostrate, often ascending in mats or $\pm$ erect in tufts, some forms in loose masses submerged in water, light green, yellowish, golden brown or purplish brown. Stems vary from slender to stout, usually irregularly branched but sometimes $\pm$ regularly pinnate; central strand mostly present but often small; paraphyllia lacking or rare. Leaves ovate to very long and slenderly lanceolate, acute to long acuminate, sometimes filiform in floating forms, typically falcate-secund to circinate with the stems hooked at the tips; costa single and extending well into the acumen, excurrent in some forms; upper cells typically narrowly linear but often shortly linear to oblong-hexagonal in short-leaved forms; basal cells shorter and wider, thicker walled, sometimes colored and porose; alar cells enlarged, thin walled, hyaline and inflated in most species, often forming decurrent auricles, but in some species few or not strongly differentiated. Seta long; capsules subcylindric and curved, inclined to cernuous, $\pm$ contracted below the mouth when dry, mostly light yellowish brown at maturity; annulus present or absent; lid conic or convex, mostly with a short point, sometimes blunt; peristome perfect.

21.263 The name means sickle, branch, alluding to the hooked tips of the branches.

494

21.264   Most of the species are exceedingly variable, and the genus is one of the most taxonomically difficult of all mosses. Nearly every species has several varieties and forms attached to it. That many of these variations are due largely to habitat conditions has been reiterated by many authors. Since a given clone may give rise to several "varieties" or "forms," the very plasticity of the plants mocks the wisdom of giving separate names to them. Some bryologists of long experience recognize only the basic species and a few of the stronger varieties and refer to the numerous variations around them simply as forms, without using a Latin name.

21.265   1. Leaves plicate; margins serrulate; alar cells usually few, quadrate to shortly oblong, firm, not forming auricles, occasionally 2–3 at the extreme angles enlarged and inflated; epidermal cells of the stem abruptly larger and thin walled .... 1. *D. uncinatus*   21.267

21.266   1. Leaves not plicate; epidermal cells of the stem small, thick walled and usually colored

2. Alar cells quadrate to shortly oblong and rather few or gradually enlarged but not inflated or forming decurrent auricles, not extending more than ½ way toward the costa; leaves serrulate at the base or the apex or both .... 3. *D. fluitans*   21.282

2. Alar cells mostly abruptly enlarged, thin walled, and often inflated, sometimes extending to the costa

3. Leaves entire, some or most with decurrent auricles ....
.... 2. *D. aduncus*   21.271

3. Leaves serrate at the apex or base or both; 2–3 rows of abruptly enlarged oblong cells extending across the base, slightly or not at all decurrent .... 4. *D. exannulatus*   21.287

21.267   1. **Drepanocladus uncinatus** (Hedw.) Warnst. Plants prostrate in thin or thick mats or ascending to erect in dense tufts, usually bright green to yellowish green to golden yellow, somewhat glossy, brownish below. Stem 2–8 cm long, mostly irregularly but occasionally regularly branched; epidermal cells abruptly enlarged and thin walled. Small ovate to lanceolate, leaflike pseudoparaphyllia present in the axils of the branches. Stem leaves 2.5–4(5) mm long, narrowly lanceolate, long and slenderly acuminate, strongly plicate both wet and dry, falcate to circinate, gradually to rather abruptly rounded to the insertion, slightly or not at all decurrent; margins serrulate to serrate above and occasionally well toward the base; costa fairly stout, extending halfway up the leaf or well into the acumen; upper cells narrowly linear and flexuous, 1:10–20, 4–6 μ wide, becoming short, slightly wider and thicker walled in the base; alar cells scarcely differentiated or forming a small group of quadrate to shortly oblong hyaline cells with firm walls or sometimes thin walled and occasionally inflated, rarely slightly decurrent but never forming auricles. Autoicous. Seta 2–3 cm long; capsules light yellowish brown, 2–3 mm long, cylindric, curved to arcuate, strongly contracted under

495

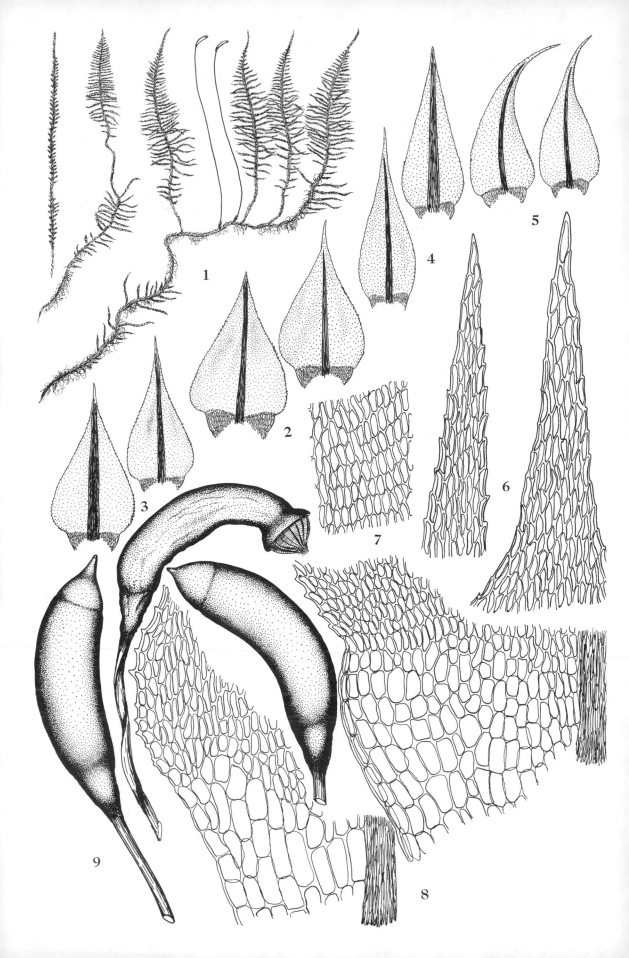

the mouth when dry; annulus of 3 rows of cells; lid shortly conic-convex with a sharp tip. Plate 126.

21.268   On damp or rather dry soil, rocks, and bases of trees, or frequently on very moist or wet substrata in seepage areas, along brooks and ponds, mostly in mountains. Frequent and locally abundant in our mountains.

21.269   Very widely distributed and present on all the major continents.

21.270   Distinctive in the strongly hooked tips of the stems and branches, the long, slenderly tapering, falcate to circinate, and plicate leaves, all or most of which are serrulate to serrate on the upper margins. The alar cells are quadrate to shortly oblong and occupy only a small area. Sometimes a few enlarged and inflated hyaline cells are attached to the basal angle of the leaves below the alar cells proper. Occasionally stems are found without the enlarged hyaline epidermal cells present in most specimens.

21.271   **2. Drepanocladus aduncus** (Hedw.) Warnst. var. **aduncus.** Plants soft, yellowish green, green, or golden brown, mostly prostrate in loose mats but often in erect tufts and sometimes submerged in water in very loose masses. Stems slender, mostly 2–5 cm long but becoming upward to 40 cm in aquatic forms, irregularly branched to regularly pinnate; branches various, few and short to long and slender, hooked at the tips; cells of the epidermis and outer cortex small, thick walled, and colored. Stem leaves ovate-lanceolate to oblong-lanceolate, slenderly acuminate, or in short-leaved forms broadly ovate to ovate-deltoid, acute to shortly acuminate and in some aquatic forms narrowly lanceolate and long-acuminate to filiform, ± falcate-secund but straight or nearly so in var. *kneiffii*, mostly 2–3.5 mm long, but as small as 1 mm or as large as 5 mm long in various forms, ± clasping the stem and decurrent, sometimes auricled, concave at the base, channelled above; margins plane and entire; costa typically strong, extending to the middle or well into the acumen but sometimes shorter; upper basal cells linear in long-leaved forms but oblong-rhomboidal in short-leaved forms; alar cells much enlarged and often inflated, hyaline, thin walled, sometimes forming decurrent auricles, often extending to the costa. Dioicous. Fruit rare. Seta long; capsules oblong-cylindric, urn 2–2.5 mm long, curved and cernuous, light yellowish brown at maturity; lid conic-convex, pointed; annulus of 3 rows of cells, persistent. Plate 127, figs. 1–7.

21.272   Growing in swamps, wet meadows, seepage areas, often among grasses and sedges, sometimes around flowing wells, on brook banks and around ponds and waterfalls.

21.273   Europe, Asia, North Africa, Andes or Peru, New Zealand. Across Canada and United States but lacking in the southeastern states.

Plate 126.   Drepanocladus uncinatus. 1. Habit sketches, X.4. 2. Portion of shoot, X4. 3. Cross section of stem, X60. 4. Leaves, X8. 5. Leaf apex and upper marginal cells, X120. 6. Two areas of alar cells, X120. 7. Capsules, X8.

21.274 Exceedingly variable in length of the stems, the manner of branching, the density of the leaves, their shapes, and the dimensions of the lower cells. A frequent form not adequately included in the above description is unusually long, weak, and flaccid with very slender branches widely spaced, lax leaves becoming much shrivelled when dry. The short leaved short celled forms are called var. *polycarpus* (Voit) Roth. by many authors. Besides intergrading with the species, it has seven or more forms attached to it, too many to mention.

21.275 Plate 127, figs. 6–7 shows a long slender form with extremely long and slenderly acuminate leaves that resembles var. *capillifolius* except that the costa ends far below the apex.

21.276 2a. Var. **kneiffii** (B.S.G.) Moenk. Leaves straight or nearly so, only those at the tips of the stems and branches falcate-secund, ovate-lanceolate to oblong-lanceolate, shortly to long and slenderly acuminate, flat above, not channelled; cells and areolation the same as in the species. Plate 127, figs. 8–9.

21.277 Habitat and distribution the same as the species.

21.278 One may find typical *D. aduncus* and var. *kneiffii* together in the same mat. Long slender forms with widely spaced leaves are not uncommon. Many plants are much like *Amblystegium riparium,* but the presence of enlarged, thin-walled, inflated alar cells forming auricles in at least some leaves will distinguish the var. *kneiffii.*

21.279 2b. Var. **capillifolius** (Warnst.) Riehm. Plants yellowish green at the tips, brownish green to brown below, erect and loosely tufted on damp or wet substrata. Stems 2–6 cm tall. Leaves mostly ovate-lanceolate, slenderly acuminate and falcate, 2–3 mm long, the lower medial cells oblong-rhomboidal to shortly linear. Stems of submerged, emergent, or stranded plants, long and slender, up to 20 cm long, often regularly pinnately branched, the branches usually distant, up to 2.5 cm long; leaves not crowded, lanceolate to narrowly lanceolate, long and slenderly acuminate, 3.5–5.5 mm long, upwards to 1 mm wide at the base, falcate-secund; lower medial cells linear, straight or flexuous, 4–6 μ wide (wider in some forms); alar cells as in the species. Costa in all forms rather stout, shortly to long filiform excurrent, often twisted. Plate 128, figs. 1–3.

21.280 Mostly submerged in ponds and slow flowing brooks, often stranded, occasionally erect and ± tufted on damp borders. Distribution the same as the species but less frequent.

21.281 Immediately identified by the distinctly excurrent costa. Uncommon in

---

Plate 127. **1–7. Drepanocladus aduncus.** 1–5. Typical form. 1. Habit sketches, X.4. 2. Five leaves showing variations in shape. 3. Leaf of a large form, X8. 4. Two areas of basal and alar cells with upper medial cells. 5. Average leaf apex, X120. 6. A large form with long slender leaves, X.4. 7. Leaves of same, X8.

8–9. Var. **kneiffii.** 8. Habit, X.4. 9. Seven leaves of various forms, X8.

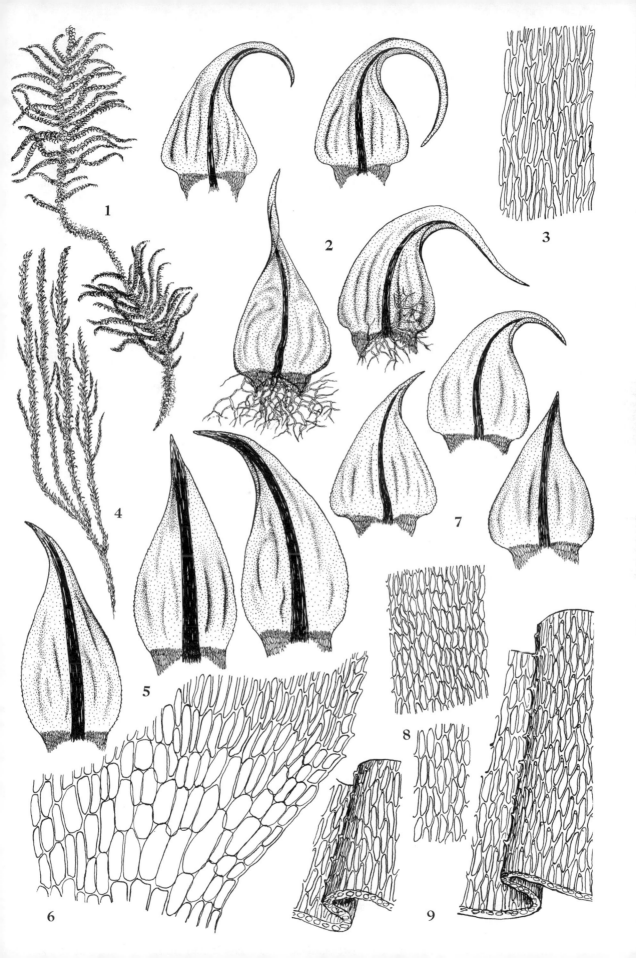

Utah but locally abundant in ponds and slow-flowing water, brooks or ditches.

21.282   **3. Drepanocladus fluitans** (Hedw.) Warnst. Plants extremely variable according to habitat, green, yellowish green to yellowish brown or darker, growing in loose or dense mats on damp or wet substrata or in loose stringy masses when submerged. Stems 3–20 cm long, nearly simple or irregularly to regularly branched with a small central strand of 2–3 small cells, the cortex of large, thin-walled, angular or rounded cells and 2–3 rows of much smaller, very thick-walled colored cells forming an outer rind. Stem leaves oblong-lanceolate to narrowly lanceolate, 2.5–3.5 mm long, 0.4–0.7 mm wide, usually long and slenderly acuminate, slightly to strongly falcate, gradually narrowed to somewhat rounded at the base, often slightly decurrent, not plicate; margins serrulate at the apex or base or both (entire or nearly so in some forms); costa rather slender, extending to the middle or well into the acumen; medial cells long-linear; extreme basal cells slightly wider and shorter, 2–3 rows at the insertion thick walled, colored, sometimes slightly porose; alar cells scarcely differentiated except for a small area of quadrate to shortly oblong cells or a few enlarged, thin- or thick-walled cells, only occasionally inflated but usually not extending more than halfway to the costa. Autoicous. Seta and capsules as described for the genus. Plate 128, figs. 4–9.

21.283   On wet soil, mostly in swamps, seepage areas or bogs, stream and lake sides, often submerged.

21.284   Northern Europe, Asia, New Zealand, Tasmania. Across Canada and northern United States.

21.285   Common in the eastern United States but uncommon in the West. Most of our specimens are forms with entire leaves, with alar cells small quadrate to oval or sometimes enlarged, with thin or thick walls, but not sharply set off, some of them merging with the other basal cells. Typically the linear upper cells extend nearly to the insertion; in most of the present specimens 1–3 rows across the insertion are shorter and wider, thick walled, yellowish brown or orange, and occasionally porose. Compared with *D. aduncus*, the alar cells are not as numerous and do not form decurrent auricles. In other respects the plants are dark colored, the leaves normally serrate. Both species have small, thick-walled, colored outer cortical cells. In *D. aduncus* these cells show a gradual transition with those of the leaf base, but in *D. fluitans* the transition is abrupt.

21.286   I have specimens with leaves so much like those of *Amblystegium ri-*

Plate 128.   **1–3. Drepanocladus aduncus** var. **capillifolius.** 1. Habit sketches, X.4. 2. Leaves, X8. 3. Upper medial leaf cells, X120.

4–9. Drepanocladus fluitans. 4. Habit of typical form, X.4. 5. Leaves, X8. 6. Three areas of basal and alar cells, X120. 7–9. Straight-leaved form. 7. Habit, X.4. 8. Leaf, X8. 9. Leaf apex, X120.

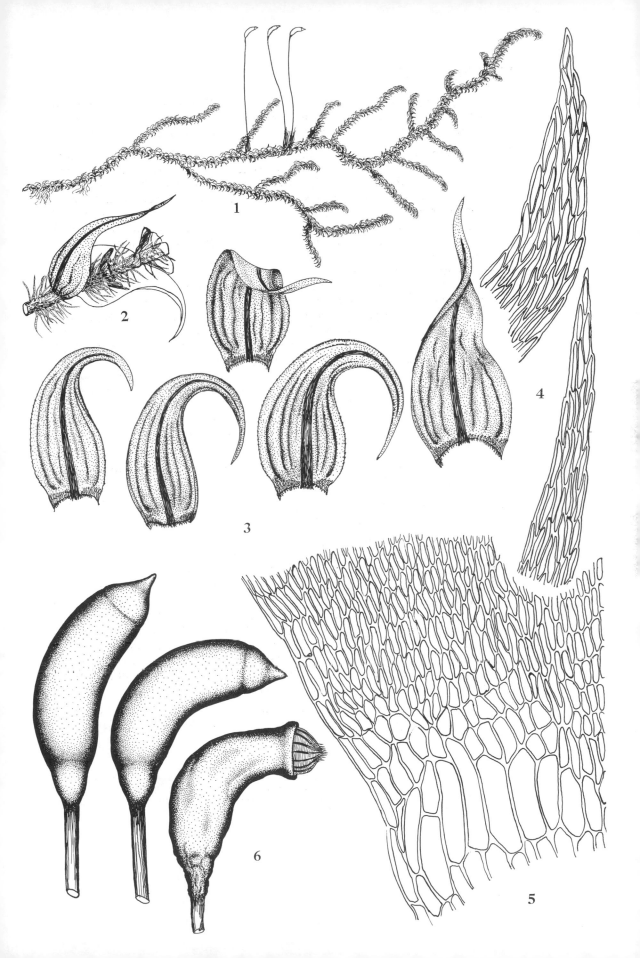

parium that I cannot be sure which species they represent. The slightly falcate leaves and slightly hooked tips of the stem favor *D. fluitans,* while the upper areolation and basal cells are like those of *A. riparium.*

21.287   **4. Drepanocladus exannulatus** (B.S.G.) Warnst. Plants mostly aquatic, submerged or emergent in loose masses, predominantly purplish brown varying to reddish brown, less frequently thinly to thickly matted or in erect tufts on damp or wet soil and rocks, green to yellowish green or golden brown. Stems 3–20 cm long, usually sparingly branched but sometimes simple or ± regularly pinnate, in section showing a small central strand of 2–3 small, thin-walled cells and an outer cortex of small, thick-walled colored cells. Stem leaves typically oblong-lanceolate to slenderly lanceolate, 3–6 mm long, ± long-acuminate to filiform with a twisted tip, strongly falcate-secund (the lower ones often weakly so or straight in fo. *orthophyllus*), gradually narrowed to the base or slightly rounded; margins serrate to serrulate at apex or base or both; costa usually purplish or brownish, extending well into the acumen (excurrent in var. *rotae*); medial cells linear, much shorter in some forms; basal and alar cells abruptly enlarged, mostly oblong, thin walled, and extending in 1–2 rows across the base to the costa, often becoming colored and occasionally thick walled in older leaves. Dioicous or rarely autoicous. Rarely fruiting. Seta long; capsules oblong-cylindric, curved, urn 1.5–2.3 mm long, light yellowish brown at maturity, becoming darker with age; annulus lacking; lid conic-convex with a longish point. Plate 129, figs. 1–8.

21.288   Mostly submerged or emergent in slow brooks or high mountain lakes, also on soil and rocks in wet meadows, bogs and swamps.

21.289   Eurasia. Across Canada and northern United States, south to New Jersey, the Great Lakes region, Colorado, Nevada, and California.

21.290   Frequent and locally abundant in high mountain lakes in Utah. Easily identified by the predominantly purplish brown color, the serrate or serrulate leaf margins and large oblong basal and alar cells extending in 1–2 rows across the base of the leaf to the costa. Darker submerged plants are the most common, but green to golden brown plants are not uncommon on damp or wet soil and rocks where they usually form mats. Dense erect tufts are occasionally found in *Sphagnum* bogs or seepage areas. Like other species of the genus, there are numerous intergrading variations. Forma *orthophyllus* (Mild.) Warnst. has the lower leaves straight. There are short-leaved short-celled forms and sometimes the marginal serrations are weak or even lacking.

21.291   4a. Var. **rotae** (De Not.) Loesk. Leaves more widely spaced and costa shortly to long filiform excurrent. Same habitat and range as the species. Plate 129, fig. 9.

Plate 129.   Drepanocladus exannulatus. 1–3. Habit sketches of submerged forms, X.4. 4. Habit of short form on damp substratum, X.4. 5–6. Six leaves of various forms, X8. 7. Leaf apex and upper medial cells. 8. Basal and alar cells, X120. 9. Single leaf of var. **rotae** with excurrent costa, X8.

502

13. CRATONEURON (Sull.) Spruc.

21.292   Plants medium sized to rather large, ± aquatic, green to yellowish green, prostrate in thick mats or erect in deep tufts. Stems regularly pinnate or irregularly branched, sometimes nearly simple; central strand lacking, paraphyllia abundant, often few or lacking in *C. filicinum*. Leaves usually dense, deltoid to ovate-lanceolate, shortly to longly acuminate, straight to falcate or strongly circinate, often plicate; margins entire to serrate; costa stout, ending well below the apex or percurrent to excurrent; upper cells oblong-rhomboidal to linear, alar cells usually much enlarged and frequently forming auricles. Dioicous. Seta long; capsules cylindrical, curved, inclined to cernuous, contracted under the mouth when dry and empty; annulus of 2–3 rows of cells; lid conic, apiculate; peristome perfect.

21.293   The name, from the Greek, means strong costa.

21.294   1. Leaves not plicate, straight to slightly falcate; stems often regularly and closely pinnate .... 1. *C. filicinum*   21.296

21.295   1. Leaves strongly plicate, falcate to circinate (some of them straight or nearly so in var. *fluctuans*)

  2. Stem leaves deltoid, cordate, ± decurrent and auricled

    3. Stems typically regularly pinnate; rhizoids numerous; stem leaves long acuminate, strongly falcate to circinate; medial cells linear; basal cells smooth .... 2. *C. commutatum*   21.300

    3. Stems irregularly pinnate; rhizoids often few; stem leaves shortly acuminate, ± falcate; medial cells shorter, elliptic-rhomboidal to sublinear; basal cells papillose from the upper ends at the back .... 3. *C. decipiens*   21.307

  2. Stem leaves ± ovate-lanceolate, not cordate, decurrent or auricled; plants stout, irregularly branched; rhizoids few or lacking

    4. Stem leaves broadly ovate-lanceolate, shortly acuminate, weakly falcate to straight; costa exceedingly stout, scarcely tapering upward, spreading out and disappearing in the broad apex; enlarged alar cells not abruptly set off .... 2a var. *fluctuans*   21.303

    4. Stem leaves ovate- to oblong-lanceolate, long and slenderly acuminate, strongly falcate to circinate; costa stout, tapering; enlarged alar cells abruptly set off .... 4. *C. falcatum*   21.312

21.296   **1. Cratoneuron filicinum** (Hedw.) Spruc. Plants variable according to the habitat, when growing on damp or wet substrata forming thin or thick green mats of prostrate to ascending shoots, when submerged or emergent in water forming loose or compact masses or erect tufts, bright to dark green above, pale yellowish to brownish below. Stems rather thick and stiff, 1–4 cm long, typically regularly pinnately branched with the branches closely disposed in 2 opposite rows, sometimes irregular or nearly simple but usually with numerous buds in opposite rows;

504

paraphyllia ovate, divided into slender segments, often few or lacking; rhizoids usually scarce in aquatic forms. Stem leaves patent, broadly to narrowly triangular or ovate-lanceolate, $\pm$ cordate at the base, narrowly acuminate, straight or slightly falcate, 1–1.5 mm long; margins plane, typically closely serrate to the base but often nearly entire; costa strong, ending at the base of the acumen to percurrent to shortly excurrent; upper cells rhomboidal to oblong-linear, variable in width, 6–9 μ wide; basal cells becoming wider and often proportionately much shorter; alar cells $\pm$ abruptly enlarged and usually forming conspicuous auricles, often colored and extending to the costa. Branch leaves smaller and narrower, more frequently falcate. Mostly sterile but occasionally fruiting. Sporophyte as in the genus. Plate 130.

21.297   On damp or wet rocks, soil, and logs, or submerged in springs, brooks, ponds or swamps.

21.298   Europe, southern Asia, northern Africa, Brazil, New Zealand. Throughout Canada and the United States.

21.299   Locally common in calcareous regions. Forms range from slender openly branched plants with ovate-lanceolate leaves in which the alar cells may be scarcely differentiated to stout stiff plants with thick stems bearing comparatively short, broadly deltoid leaves with large auricles of greatly enlarged alar cells (these sometimes thick walled and colored). Some aquatic forms may be nearly simple but usually have numerous buds in two opposite rows. The costa may be comparatively slender in some forms and range to forms with a broad costa spreading out in the tip of the acumination. I have one aquatic form with the stems reaching 17 cm long, unbranched below and openly pinnate with short branches above. Another specimen nearly as long is very lax with very long, slender, erect branches, and with leaves lax and flaccid.

21.300   **2. Cratoneuron commutatum** (Hedw.) Roth. var. **commutatum.** Plants stout, usually forming thick green, yellowish green, or yellowish brown mats, or when submerged, in $\pm$ erect deep tufts. Stems thick, 4–10 cm long, rather regularly pinnate with branches of variable length, paraphyllia dense, linear to lanceolate; rhizoids numerous, reddish brown. Stem leaves deltoid from a cordate decurrent base, tapering to a long canaliculate acumination, strongly falcate-secund to circinate, $\pm$ plicate; margins plane, denticulate in the lower half and sometimes above; costa stout, extending into the acumen, frequently with rhizoids on the base at the back; upper cells oblong-linear to linear, often flexuous, narrow, 5–7 μ wide; basal cells usually much enlarged, oblong to hexagonal, thick walled and becoming colored in older leaves, often forming decurrent auricles. Branch leaves smaller and narrower, the cells shorter. Fruit uncommon. Seta up to 5 cm long; capsules yellowish, becoming yellowish brown with age, 3–4 mm long without the lid. Plate 131, figs. 1–3.

21.301   Europe, Asia Minor, and northern Africa; sporadic across Canada and northern United States. Occasional in Utah. Salt Lake County: Holladay, 4,600 ft.; Big Cottonwood Canyon, Brighton, 9,200 ft. Utah County: Mt. Timpanogos, Stewart's Creek, 6,400 ft.

21.302 The stems are typically regularly pinnate but sometimes irregularly branched, depending largely on the habitat and the amount of water in which the plants grow. Sometimes the rhizoids are not very dense, especially high up on the stems.

21.303 2a. Var. **fluctuans** (B.S.G.) Wijk & Marg. Plants very stout, usually submerged in loose or dense erect tufts or masses; stems up to 10–20 cm long. Branches few and irregular, often short; rhizoids lacking except a few at the base; paraphyllia numerous. Stem leaves ovate-lanceolate, straight to falcate, plicate, broad at the base, up to 1.2 mm wide, not concave nor decurrent; costa very stout, prominent at the back, only slightly tapering upward, broadly disappearing in or below the apex, percurrent or even slightly excurrent. Alar cells fewer and not as greatly enlarged as in the species, not forming auricles and usually not sharply set off. Sporophyte not seen. Plate 131, figs. 4–6.

21.304 Usually submerged or on very wet substrata.

21.305 Europe, Asia Minor, Utah County: Mt. Timpanogos, Stewart's Fork, 6,100 ft.

21.306 This collection is the first and only recorded for North America.

21.307 **3. Cratoneuron decipiens** (De Not.) Loesk. Plants resembling a small form of *C. commutatum* but more slender and less regularly pinnate; rhizoids often dense. Stem leaves broadly deltoid, rather abruptly acuminate to a short or rather long upper portion, slightly to strongly falcate, 1.3–1.7 mm long, slightly decurrent and auricled at the base, plicate; costa stout; margins ± denticulate in the lower half; upper cells 7–8 μ wide, elliptic-rhomboidal to linear; basal cells ± papillose from the upper ends of some cells, the papillae low to sharp; alar cells rather abruptly enlarged, thin walled and often colored. Capsules not seen. Plate 131, figs. 7–9.

21.308 On soil and rocks in wet places.

21.309 Europe, Asia, and northern Africa. Salt Lake County: Wasatch Mountains, Lamb's Canyon, 8,600 ft.; Big Cottonwood Canyon at Brighton, 8,900 ft.

21.310 The above specimens are referred to this species with reservation since none are clear-cut. All of them have leaves with papillose basal cells, although in some leaves they are difficult or impossible to demonstrate.

21.311 Concerning *C. decipiens*, Dixon (*Student's Handbook of British Mosses*) states that the upper leaf cells are linear to elliptic-rhomboidal, the basal cells usually papillose from the upper ends of the cells, the branch

---

Plate 130. Cratoneuron filicinum. 1. Habit sketches, X.4. 2. Two typical leaves 3–5. Leaves of three different plants, X8. 6. Leaf apices. 7. Upper medial leaf cells. 8. Basal and alar cells showing variations, X120. 9. Capsules, X8.

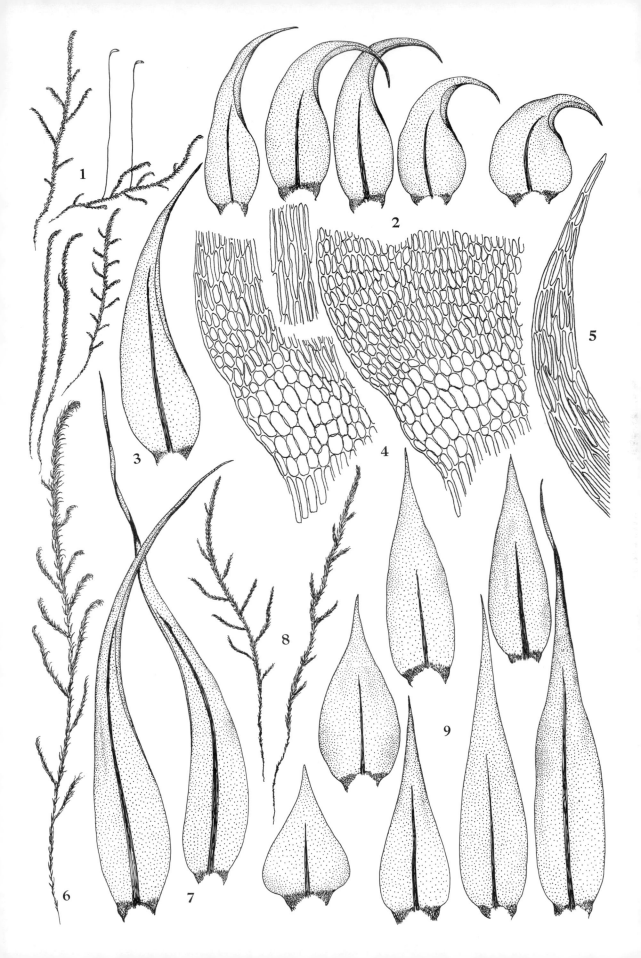

leaves sparsely but sharply papillose. This sounds much like the situation in our plants, where some leaves show short cells and some show
papillae, but none of our plants show these traits with any consistency
which would clearly mark them as a distinct species. It seems to me that
it puts a strain on the species concept when so few leaves show the
basic traits. I find the same condition in the papillae of *C. williamsii.*

21.312   **4. Cratoneuron falcatum** (Brid.) Roth. var. **falcatum.** Plants rather stout,
growing in thick mats and deep tufts, green to yellowish green above,
yellowish to brownish below, 6–10 cm long, irregularly branched to subpinnate, rhizoids few to rather numerous; paraphyllia numerous, ±
filiform, the larger ones serrate. Stem leaves slenderly triangular-lanceolate to ovate-lanceolate, with a long channelled acumination, falcate
to circinate, 1.5–2.6 mm long, mostly strongly plicate, not cordate nor
decurrent; margins mostly serrulate in the lower half and usually recurved at the base; costa stout and prominent at the back, extending
well into the acumen; upper cells oblong-linear to linear, 5–7 μ wide,
2–3 rows at the extreme base shorter and much wider; alar cells ±
abruptly enlarged, thin walled and sometimes inflated, often extending
to the costa, sometimes not sharply set off, not forming auricles, becoming thick walled and colored in older leaves, sometimes slightly
porose. Capsules ovoid-oblong, curved and asymmetric, 1.8–2.3 mm
long, yellowish brown at maturity, becoming reddish brown with age,
slightly contracted below the mouth when dry but not much shrunken;
lid convex-conic, apiculate. Plate 132.

21.313   On wet soil or rock, often submerged in springs, seepage areas, or
brooks.

21.314   Europe, Asia, and northern Africa. Across Canada and northern United
States. Frequent in mountains of Utah.

21.315   Various authors have treated this moss as a variety of *C. commutatum.*
I am wholly in sympathy with this view, but since this expression is so
much more common in Utah than *C. commutatum,* it seems easier to
treat it separately. Besides, *C. williamsii* is scarcely more than a papillose variety of *C. falcatum* forming a parallel with *C. decipiens* as a
variety of *C. commutatum.* It is often difficult to be consistent in ar-
ranging plants according to the relative taxonomic value of their traits,
but then nature is not very consistent either!

21.316   4a. Var. **williamsii** (Grout) Flow. Differing from the species in the
± papillose basal cells with the papillae projecting from the upper ends
on both sides or only on the dorsal side and the margins sometimes

Plate 131.   1–3. Cratoneuron commutatum. 1. Habit sketch, X.4. 2. Leaves, X8.
3. Leaf cells, X120.

4–6. Var. **fluctuans.** 4. Habit sketch, X.4. 5. Leaves, X8. 6. Basal and alar cells,
X120.

7–9. Cratoneuron decipiens. 7. Stem leaves, X8. 8. Two areas of upper medial
leaf cells. 9. Two areas of basal cells showing papillae, X120.

508

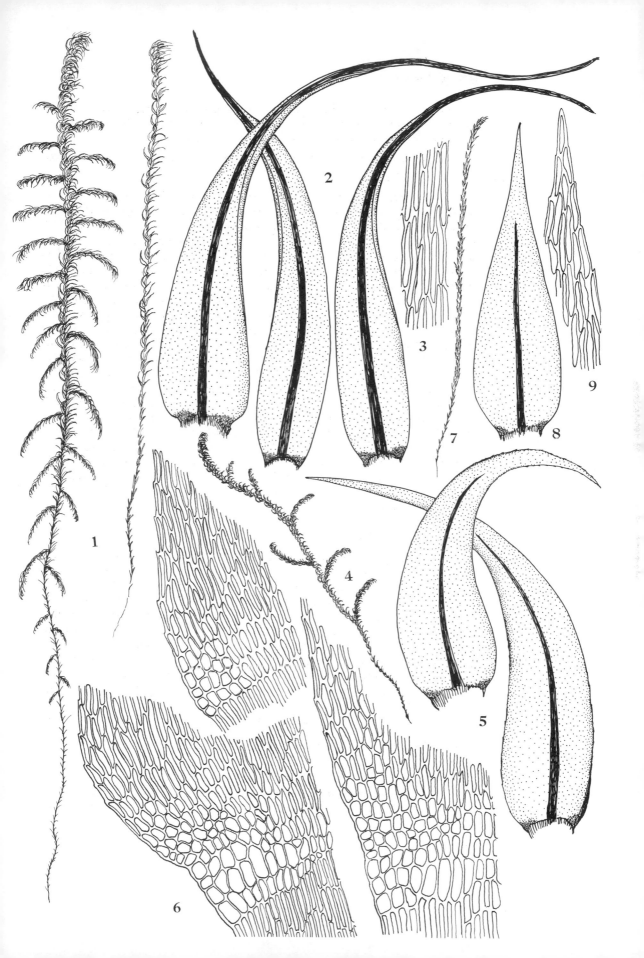

serrulate well toward the apex. No illustrations are provided since the plant so closely resembles *C. falcatum*. The papillose basal cells are the same as those shown for *C. decipiens* in Plate 131.

21.317 Submerged in brooks and springs or on wet soil, rocks, and rotten logs.

21.318 Montana to Utah.

21.319 Locally abundant in the Wasatch Mountains and the Wasatch Plateau, often forming extensive sods in springs or seepage areas and around waterfalls. In size, habit, and appearance it is almost exactly like *C. falcatum*, differing only in the basal leaf cells being papillose from the upper ends. The papillae range from a very low convex form, often difficult to demonstrate, to high, pointed ones easily seen. In some plants they can be seen clearly in surface view, but in others a profile view is necessary. The latter view is usually conveniently provided by the strong basal plications of the leaves. In some plants the area of papillose cells is restricted to a small zone between the basal margin and the first plication toward the costa. Sometimes they are quite strong here but absent elsewhere. Often the papillae develop only on the convex side of the plications and on the ventral side of the recurved basal margin. At the other extreme the papillose area may embrace the entire broad base of the leaf. It has been my practice to strip all leaves from a well-developed stem and examine as many as possible, frequently rearranging them on the slide so as to bring badly oriented leaves into a better position for observation. Many times, after long and tedious study, I have found a few leaves, or even only 1 out of 20 or 30 with papillae, while the remainder are without them. It becomes a problem what to call specimens of this sort for it is evident that the occurrence of papillae on the basal cells is not a consistent trait.

14. HYPNUM Hedw.

21.320 Plants creeping or ascending, forming thin or densely interwoven mats, sometimes erect in dense tufts, mostly green to yellowish green, often glossy, brownish below. Stems irregularly to regularly pinnately branched, often hooked at the tips; central strand present but small. Paraphyllia usually few and leaflike at the insertion of the branches. Leaves falcate and ± secund, often with the tips turned downwards, or straight in some species; costa short and double or lacking; upper cells, linear-oblong to long linear; alar cells few to scarcely differentiated or numerous and small and quadrate or abruptly enlarged, thin walled, hyaline and often inflated. Seta long; capsules oblong to cylindric, erect and symmetric to erect or inclined, curved and cernuous; lid conic-convex, pointed or shortly rostrate; peristome perfect; cilia well developed.

21.321 The name comes from the Greek *Hypnon,* applied to mosses and other cryptogamic plants.

Plate 132. Cratoneuron falcatum. 1. Habit sketch, X.4. 2. Portion of dissected stem showing paraphyllia, X4. 3. Stem leaves, X8. 4. Two leaf apices. 5. Basal and alar cells, X120. 6. Capsules, X8.

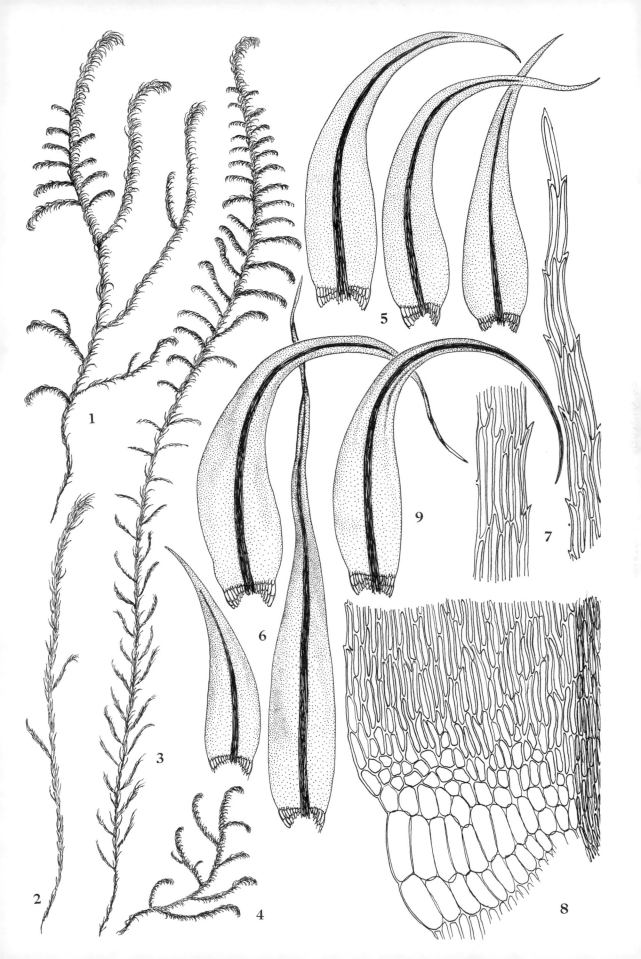

21.322 1. Leaves straight, not falcate, ovate to ovate-oblong, acute or shortly acuminate; alar cells abruptly enlarged, thin walled and hyaline, often inflated; paraphyllia large, few to numerous, multiform .... 6. *H. haldanianum* 21.347

21.323 1. Leaves falcate-secund, or if straight, the alar cells small and quadrate; paraphyllia small and inconspicuous, near the insertion of the branches

    2. Leaves 1.5–2.5 mm long; medial cells long and narrow. All leaves falcate, not complanate; alar cells abruptly enlarged, thin walled, hyaline, often inflated

        3. Leaves not rounded to the insertion .... 4. *H. lindbergii* 21.339

        3. Leaves rounded to the insertion .... 5. *H. pratense* 21.343

    2. Leaves less than 1.5 mm long, occasionally up to 2 mm; medial cells shorter; alar cells small and quadrate

        4. Alar cells very numerous, 12–14(20) on the margins; leaves falcate or straight, not appearing plaited, not striate when dry; margins plane throughout .... 3. *H. vaucheri* 21.335

        4. Alar cells fewer; leaves all falcate to circinate, ± plaited in 2 rows, the tips turned downwards

            5. Plants small to medium sized; stem leaves 1–1.5(2) mm long, striate when dry; 1 or both margins revolute ½ way up the leaf or more; alar cells few to numerous, 4–10(16) on the margins .... 1. *H. revolutum* 21.324

            5. Plants small; stem leaves 0.5–0.8 mm long, not striate when dry; margins plane; alar cells not differentiated or only 2–3 quadrate on the margins .... 2. *H. hamulosum* 21.330

21.324 **1. Hypnum revolutum** (Mitt.) Lindb. Plants in thin or thick mats, green to yellowish green, often becoming brownish green, dull or sometimes glossy. Stems creeping to ascending, 1–3(5) cm long, irregularly to regularly pinnately branched; central strand small, 2–3 rows of outer cortical cells very small and thick walled, the epidermal cells large with the outer wall thin and usually sagging inward. Leaves appearing plaited and ± in 2 rows with the tips turned downwards, 0.8-1.5 mm long or as much as 2.5 mm in larger plants, ovate and abruptly acuminate or ovate-lanceolate to oblong-lanceolate and more gradually acuminate, frequently very slenderly so, slightly to strongly falcate, concave below and canaliculate above, often longitudinally striate when dry; margins entire to slightly serrulate in the acumen, but in large forms finely and sharply serrate at the tips, especially in the apical leaves, variably revolute, in larger forms strongly and broadly revolute from the base to high up in the acumen, in most medium sized and small forms narrowly revolute on 1 or both sides, often very closely reflexed and difficult to observe, in some plants most of the leaf margins

512

are flat; costa faint, short and double or lacking; upper cells mostly oblong-linear with a few longer, 5–7 μ wide, becoming slightly shorter and wider in the base, often with 1–3 basal rows quadrate to oblong and with the wide thin outer walls of the epidermal cells of the stem attached; alar cells quadrate to shortly oblong, as few as 3–5 on the margins of small leaves, and as many as 10–16 in large leaves, the walls firm and sometimes rather thick, occasionally with 2–3 larger, hyaline, thin-walled cells at the extreme angles. Adherent hyaline epidermal cells of the stem 10–17 μ wide. Dioicous. Fruit rare. Seta 1–3 cm long; capsules cylindric, 2–3 mm long without the lid, usually curved but occasionally erect and nearly symmetric, yellowish brown, when dry contracted under the slightly oblique mouth and with the urn finely striate; annulus double; lid conic with a short point; peristome perfect. Plate 133.

21.325   Very common in the mountains of Utah but rarely fruiting. On damp or dry rocks, soil, often on ledges and in crevices, sometimes on rotten logs, usually in shade, from foothills to high mountain summits.

21.326   Eurasia, Greenland. British Columbia through the Rocky Mountains to Nevada, Arizona, New Mexico, and western Texas. Black Hills of South Dakota.

21.327   An exceedingly variable species but usually easily identified by size, color, habit, and by leaves plaited and crowded in more or less 2 rows with the tips all turned downward. The leaves vary in size and shape and in the length and slenderness of the acumen. While typical plants have the leaf margins strongly and widely revolute from the base well up into the acumen, most of our plants have some leaves with margins revolute on 1 or both sides, sometimes only in the lower half, while many leaves are plane margined. Since the leaves tend to be strongly channelled, it is often difficult to observe whether the margin is actually revolute. I have often had to prove the point with cross sections of the leaves.

21.328   The upper cells of most plants are oblong to sublinear. Most of the cells have rounded ends and are either slightly or not at all tapered. The alar cells are small and quadrate to shortly oblong, not particularly clear, the walls firm or sometimes thickened. The extent of the area they occupy varies in different plants and sometimes in leaves of the same shoot. Sometimes the group is small and not particularly set off from the other basal cells, especially in medium sized or small leaves, but in many larger forms the group is large and usually stands out in stronger contrast. The thin outer walls of the epidermal cells of the stem often remain attached to the bases of the leaves when they are stripped off. Some authors describe the epidermal cells as small and thick walled, but in every instance I have found them much larger than the underlying small thick-walled outer cortical cells. Sections of the stem show the outer epidermal walls much thinner than the radial and internal walls, and they usually sag inward so strongly that the outline of the section appears nubbly.

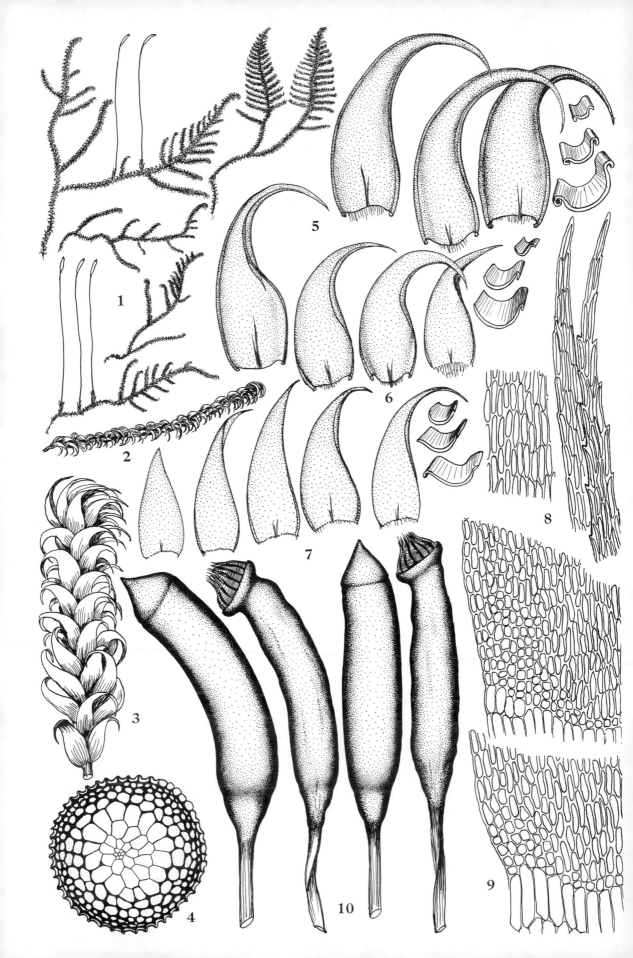

21.329   Small forms resemble *Hypnum hamulosum,* but in that species the plants are smaller, darker green, and less regularly branched, with leaves less than 1 mm long, plane on the margins, and with alar cells scarcely or not at all differentiated.

21.330   **2. Hypnum hamulosum** B.S.G. Plants small and slender, growing prostrate in thin or thickish mats or sometimes ascending and forming tufts, green to yellowish green, usually yellowish below. Stems 1–5 cm long, irregularly branched or in thin creeping mats often regularly pinnate; epidermis of enlarged, thin-walled, hyaline cells, usually clinging to the bases of the leaves when they are stripped off. Stem leaves ovate to ovate-lanceolate, long and slenderly acuminate, strongly falcate-secund, usually with the tips turned downwards, 0.4–1 mm long, concave at base, channelled above; margins entire or serrulate above, plane or slightly recurved at the base, not decurrent; costa lacking or short and double; upper cells linear, 4–5 μ wide; basal cells shorter and slightly wider; alar cells variable, either oblong and not clearly differentiated, or quadrate and forming a small group, 3–4 on the margin, but not sharply set off from the adjacent basal cells. Branch leaves smaller. Monoicous. Locally not freely fruiting. Seta 1–2 cm long, capsules shortly cylindric, curved, 1.5–2.5 mm long; lid conic, shortly pointed, yellowish brown. Plate 134, figs. 8–11.

21.331   Occasional or locally frequent at high elevations on damp or dry soil, rocks or rotten logs, usually in shade.

21.332   Europe. Utah, Rocky Mountains, northward to Alaska.

21.333   This little moss resembles small forms of *H. revolutum,* and a positive determination is often almost impossible. For this reason I have only a few specimens close enough to the typical form to be of reasonably certain identity. None of our specimens is fruited, and only a few stems have been found with sex organs, none with both perigonia and perichaetia on the same stem. However, this is not conclusive proof that the plants are not fundamentally monoicous, as a number of monoicous mosses are known which, for some reason, do not often form sex organs.

21.334   Among the troublesome intermediate forms are those with leaves the size of *H. revolutum* but without revolute margins and without particularly differentiated alar cells. A few of these were proven to be dioicous and referable to *H. revolutum.* Some specimens approach *H. fastigiatum* Brid., which differs mainly in having small, thick-walled epidermal cells of the stem and more slenderly acuminate leaves. Some of the larger forms answer well for *H. dolomiticum* Mild., a European species not

Plate 133.   Hypnum revolutum. 1. Five habit sketches, X.4. 2. Portion of shoot, side view, X2. 3. Portion of shoot from above showing plaited arrangement of the leaves, X4. 4. Cross section of stem, X60. 5. Four leaves of typical form with margins revolute nearly to the apex. 6. Three leaves of the most common form, broadly to very narrowly revolute on one or both sides. 7. Four leaves of the small form with leaf margins flat or revolute only at the base, X8. 8. Upper medial leaf cells and two leaf apices. 9. Two areas of alar cells with epidermal cells of stem attached at the bases, X80. 10. Capsules, X8.

cited for North America. Any attempt to segregate our plants further becomes a matter of splitting hairs and leads only to confusion for the reader.

21.335   **3. Hypnum vaucheri** Lesq. Plants in thick dense mats, sometimes ascending, dull green to yellowish green, often becoming brownish green in the lower parts. Stems regularly to irregularly pinnate, 1–3 cm long, branches often few but sometimes becoming quite long, occasionally hooked at the tips, central strand small, outer cortical cells small and very thick walled; epidermal layer with thick inner and radial walls and thin outer walls which sag inward strongly, like those illustrated for *H. revolutum.* Stem leaves ovate to broadly ovate-lanceolate, gradually or rather abruptly acuminate, 1.3–2 mm long, straight to rather strongly falcate with the tips ± turned downward but not appearing plaited, rounded-concave, smooth and not plicate when dry, sometimes rather glossy; margins entire, sometimes serrulate at the tips of the apical leaves, plane, often widely incurved below the acumen and sometimes incurved-clasping at base, not decurrent; costa short and double, 1 fork sometimes nearly reaching the middle of the leaf; upper cells rather short, mostly oblong-hexagonal to oblong-linear with rounded ends, walls rather thick, a few longer or shorter, 8–11 μ wide, often shorter in the acumen; basal cells slightly wider and thicker walled, sometimes slightly porose; alar cells usually very numerous, quadrate, clear or somewhat chlorophyllose, extending half way toward the costa, mostly 12–14(20) on the margin, occasionally with 2–4 larger thin-walled cells at the extreme angles; thin-walled epidermal cells of the stem, 10–14 μ wide, cling to the bases of the leaves when the latter are stripped off. Dioicous. Fruit exceedingly rare, not seen. Plate 134, figs. 1–7.

21.336   On damp or dry soil, rocks, and ledges, mostly in partial or total shade.

21.337   Europe. British Columbia, Alberta, Saskatchewan, Quebec, Newfoundland, Minnesota, Montana to New Mexico, Arizona, and Nevada.

21.338   Distinctive because of the dense mats, the backs of the leaves rounded and not striate when dry, the older leaves often brownish green and somewhat glossy when dry, the tips usually turned downward but not appearing plaited, plane margins, and large area of quadrate alar cells. It is one of the dominant mosses in localized parts of the Colorado-Green River Basin, where it grows on dry rocks and ledges, often on sandy soil sheltered by overhanging rocks, bases of trees, shrubs, and bunchgrasses. Elsewhere in the state it is less frequent.

21.339   **4. Hypnum lindbergii** Mitt. Plants rather large, in thick or rather thin spreading mats, green to yellowish green, usually glossy above, red-

---

Plate 134.   1–7. **Hypnum vaucheri.** 1. Three habit sketches, X.4. 2. Portions of shoots of straight-leaved and falcate forms, X4. 3. Five leaves of falcate forms. 4. Three leaves of predominantly straight-leaved form, X8. 5. Upper medial leaf cells. 6. Two leaf apices. 7. Two areas of alar cells, X80.

8–11. **Hypnum hamulosum.** 8. Three habit sketches, X.4. 9. Seven leaves, X8. 10. Upper medial leaf cells and 2 apices. 11. Two areas of alar cells, X80.

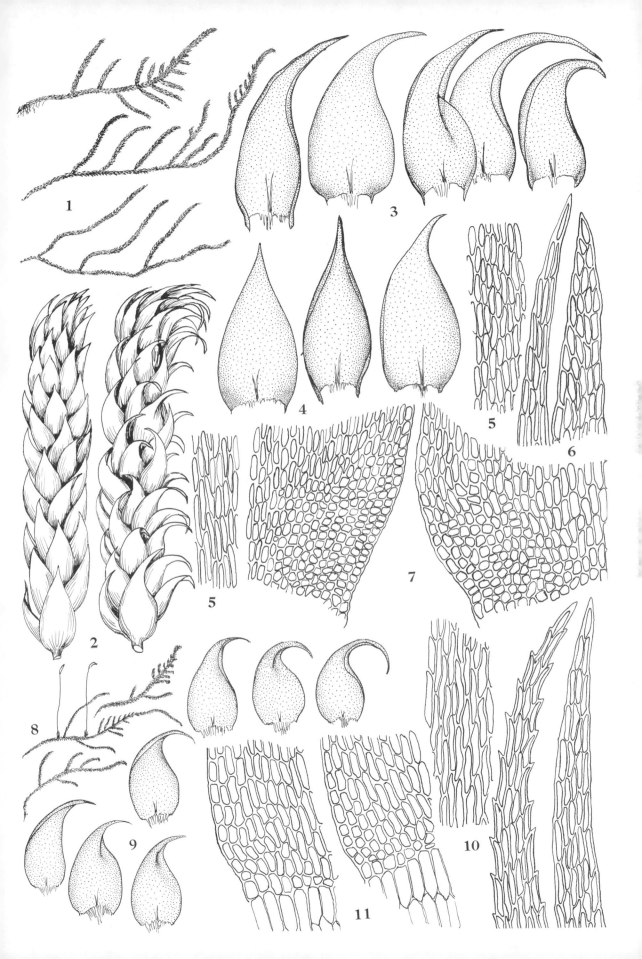

dish brown below. Stems 1–8(11) cm long, mostly irregularly branched, epidermal cells thin walled and hyaline, often sunken inward, usually remaining attached to leaf bases when leaves are stripped off the stems. Leaves ovate- to oblong-lanceolate, broadly to narrowly acuminate, strongly falcate and often secund, hooked at the tips of the stems, concave and channelled, 1.5–2.5 mm long; base slightly rounded to the insertion, ± decurrent, smooth or somewhat plicate; margins plane, entire or ± serrulate at the apex; costa short and double, often with 1 fork extending about ⅓ the length of the blade, or lacking; upper cells linear, 5–7 μ wide; the apical cells much shorter; basal cells wider and shorter, thick walled and often porose, in older leaves becoming orange red; alar cells abruptly enlarged, thin walled, hyaline and inflated. Dioicous. Fruit rare. Seta 2–3 cm long; capsules oblong-cylindric, 1–3 mm long without the lid, curved from the erect or inclined base, reddish brown when mature, slightly contracted below the mouth and usually furrowed when dry; annulus rather large; lid conic-convex, pointed. Plate 135, figs. 1–5.

21.340   On wet or very moist soil and humus, often in grassy places, meadows, brook banks, seepage springs, boggy areas, and lake shores, in mountains.

21.341   Europe, Asia, Japan. Across Canada, northeastern United States and south to Florida, Rocky Mountains to Colorado and Utah, Washington.

21.342   Our largest *Hypnum*, recognized by size, enlarged hyaline alar cells, large cortical cells, and wet habitat. Occasional to frequent. Some of the above specimens are referable to var. *elatum* (Schimp.), which is a robust form with more narrowly acuminate and more strongly falcate, or even circinate leaves. Plate 135, figs. 6–7. The present specimens intergrade in such a way that a sharp distinction cannot be made.

21.343   **5. Hypnum pratense** (Rabenh.) Koch. Plants in thick mats, light green yellowish green or straw colored, brown below, the leaves lax and complanate, falcate only towards the tips of stems and branches, usually curved downward, straight elsewhere. Stems 3–6 cm long, irregularly branched, branches often few, epidermal cells thin walled and enlarged. Leaves ovate-lanceolate to oblong-lanceolate, 1.5–2.5 mm long, acute to shortly acuminate, broadly rounded at the base, not decurrent, concave, curving forward on the stem; margins plane, serrulate in the upper part or entire throughout; costa lacking or very short and double; upper linear-flexuous, 4–6 μ wide, the apical ones shorter; basal cells shorter and broader, thicker walled; alar cells slightly or not at all differentiated, gradually enlarged, at most oblong and wider, occasionally with a few thin-walled turgid cells at the extreme angles. Plate 136, figs. 1–7.

Plate 135.   1–5. Hypnum lindbergii. 1. Three habit sketches, X.4. 2. Three stem leaves, X8. 3. Two leaf apices. 4. Upper medial cells. 5. Basal and alar cells, X80.

6–7. Var. **elatum.** 6. Habit sketch, X.4. 7. Two leaves, X8.

8–13. Hypnum haldanianum. 8. Habit sketch, X.4. 9. Portion of shoot, X.4. 10. Three paraphyllia, X60. 11. Four leaves, X8. 12. Area of alar cells, X80. 13. Capsule, X8.

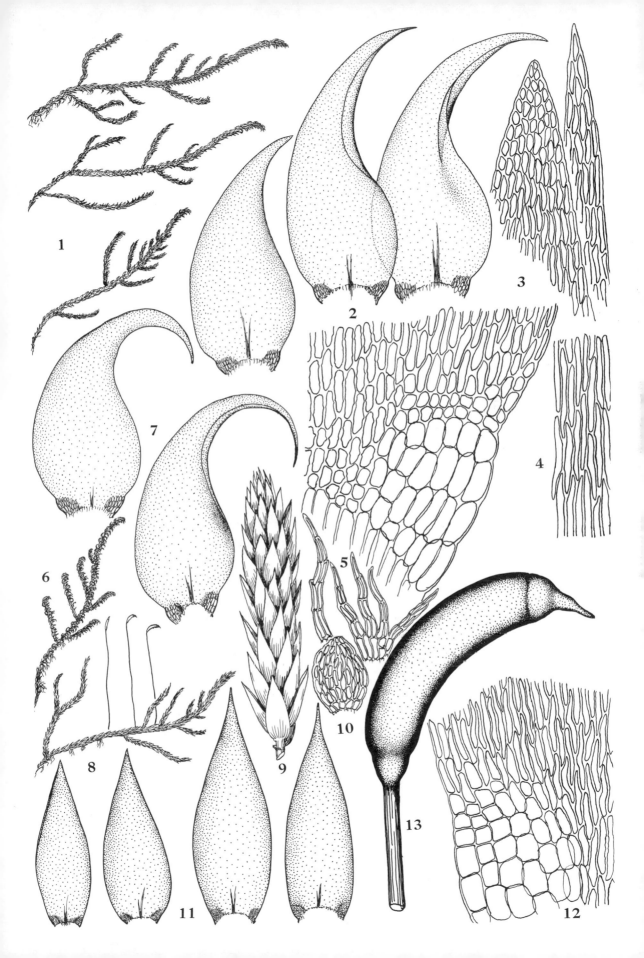

21.344 HYPNACEAE

21.344 In wet alpine meadows, swampy places, banks of brooks and lakes.

21.345 Europe. Rare but widely distributed across Canada and northern United States. Duchesne County: Uinta Mountains, Baldy Mountain, near Fehr Lake, 10,500 ft.

21.346 Resembling a *Plagiothecium* in the complanate habit, but the uppermost leaves are falcate. It also resembles *Hypnum lindbergii* in appearance and in the large thin-walled epidermal cells of the stem, but most of the leaves are straight and not decurrent, and the alar cells are not abruptly enlarged or inflated.

21.347 **6. Hypnum haldanianum** Grev. Plants in rather thin mats, dark green to light or yellowish green. Stems irregularly branched, becoming 3–5(8) cm long; epidermal cells not different from the underlying cortical cells, all thick walled. Shoots slender when dry due to the appressed leaves. Paraphyllia rather large, various, linear, lanceolate or ovate, sometimes palmately cleft or parted, few to numerous. Stem leaves 1.5–2 mm long, ovate to ovate-oblong, sometimes ovate-lanceolate, shortly acuminate, straight, not at all falcate, loosely imbricated, concave, with margins widely incurved, plane and entire, gradually narrowed to a rather wide base, not decurrent; costa short and double or lacking; upper leaf cells linear-flexuous, 5–7 μ wide, firm and rather thick walled; basal cells wider and proportionately shorter, thicker walled and often slightly porose; alar cells abruptly enlarged, thin walled and hyaline, sometimes becoming inflated, usually forming conspicuous auricles. Monoicous. Usually fruiting. Seta 1–2 cm long, reddish; capsules oblong to cylindric, slightly curved and asymmetric, erect to inclined, sometimes erect and symmetric, 2–3 mm long without the lid; mouth sometimes oblique; annulus present; lid conic with a rather long beak, straight or inclined; cilia single, slender. Plate 135, figs. 8–13.

21.348 Mostly on rotten logs but also on soil and humus in shaded places.

21.349 Europe and northern Asia. Across eastern Canada and United States to Montana and Utah, south to the Gulf States. Salt Lake County: Wasatch Mountains, Bell's Canyon, 5,600 ft.

21.350 The paraphyllia may be palmately divided into linear or lanceolate segments or simple and both linear and lanceolate, none broadly ovate as in eastern specimens; they are not numerous but fairly large.

15. PLAGIOTHECIUM B.S.G.

21.351 Plants small to fairly large, forming rather thin or loose glossy mats on damp soil, rocks or rotten logs, often scattered among other mosses.

Plate 136. 1–7. Hypnum pratense. 1. Two habit sketches, X.4. 2. Portion of shoot, X4. 3. Portion of cross section of stem, X60. 4. Six leaves, X8. 5. Two leaf apices. 6. Two areas of medial leaf cells. 7. Basal and alar cells, X80.

8–14. Plagiothecium pulchellum. 8. Habit sketch, X.4. 9. Portion of shoot, X8. 10. Portion of cross section of stem, X60. 11. Five leaves, X8. 12. Leaf apex. 13. Two areas of basal and alar cells, X80. 14. Five capsules, X8.

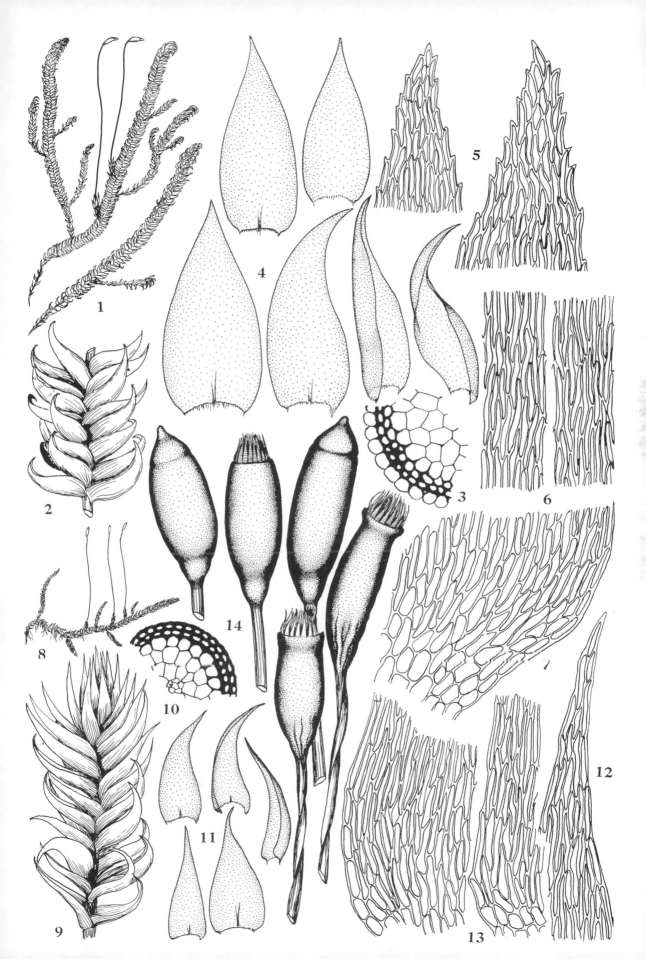

Stems usually creeping, irregularly branched, sometimes stoloniferous; central strand lacking, weak, or vague; the shoots usually flattened by the complanate stance of the leaves spreading in 2 opposite rows, but in some species terete-foliate. Leaves ovate, ovate-lanceolate or oblong-lanceolate, more or less acuminate, occasionally blunt, often somewhat asymmetric at the base, one side being narrower than the other due to twisting to one side, flat or concave; margins plane, entire or serrate; costa lacking, short and double or occasionally longer and forked; medial leaf cells mostly linear, flexuous; basal cells not strongly different, those at the insertion shorter and wider; alar cells either not particularly differentiated or strongly so. Paraphyllia present in some species. Seta long; capsules ovoid-oblong to cylindric, erect and symmetric to curved, cernuous and unsymmetric; peristome perfect or the cilia lacking in some species.

21.352   The name means inclined box, referring to the capsule.

21.353   1. Plants small and slender; leaves less than 1.5 mm long, not decurrent

2. Epidermal cells of the stem small and thick walled; branches terete- or ± complanate-foliate; monoicous .... 1. *P. pulchellum* 21.355

2. Epidermal cells of the stem enlarged, thin walled and hyaline; leaves complanate; dioicous .... 2. *P. muellerianum* 21.359

21.354   1. Plants medium sized; leaves long decurrent, up to 3 mm long .... 3. *P. denticulatum* 21.363

21.355   **1. Plagiothecium pulchellum** (Hedw.) B.S.G. Plants small and slender, prostrate in thin mats or with branches erect to ascending and ± tufted, bright green, sometimes scattered among other mosses, shoots 1–2 cm long, flattish or terete, the leaves sometimes spreading and complanate, often with the tips curved forward and upward, folded lengthwise and appearing very slender when dry, narrowly ovate-lanceolate, gradually and rather slenderly acuminate, ± rounded to the base, 0.7–1.2 mm long, broadly concave-canaliculate, often slightly falcate or incurved toward the apex; margins plane, entire or ± serrulate at the apex; costa lacking or short and double; medial cells linear, often flexuous with pointed ends, 4–6 μ; basal cells wider and proportionately shorter, the walls thicker; alar cells not particularly differentiated, the extreme angular ones merely shorter. Monoicous. Seta 1–2 cm long; capsules small, ovate to oblong, urn 1–1.8 mm long without the lid, erect and nearly symmetric to inclined and slightly curved, only the neck region shrunken when dry, often slightly contracted under the mouth; annulus present; lid conic with a short point; peristome perfect. Plate 136, figs. 8–14.

21.356   Mostly growing on decayed logs, bases of trees, or on rocks in densely shaded places.

21.357   Europe. Across Canada to Alaska, northern United States. Summit County: Uinta Mountains, Stillwater Fork at Christmas Meadows, 8,900 ft.

21.358   Our specimen differs from the typical form in that the leaves are very plainly complanate, and the plants in thin flattish mats. If it were larger and the leaves more slenderly acuminate, it would answer well for var. *nitidulum* (Wahlenb.) Ren. & Card.

21.359   **2. Plagiothecium muellerianum** Schimp. Plants small and slender, in thin yellowish green mats, often scattered among other mosses. Shoots prostrate and creeping, sometimes stoloniform with rhizoids well toward the ends of the stems. 1–1.5 cm long, flat with complanate leaves, irregularly branched, the branches often ascending; epidermal cells of the stems large and thin walled. Leaves approximate to rather dense, 1–1.7 mm long, narrowly ovate-lanceolate, gradually narrowed to an acute or acuminate apex, slightly narrowed to the base, not rounded or decurrent, slightly asymmetric, 1 side narrower at the base; margins plane, entire; costa short and double or lacking; medial cells linear, 6–8(10) μ wide, the apical ones shorter; basal cells shorter and wider, thicker walled; alar cells not differentiated, at most oblong; branch leaves smaller. Dioicous. Fruit rare. Seta 1.5–2 cm long; capsules oblong-obovate or ovate-oblong, erect and nearly symmetric, sometimes slightly inclined, urn 1–1.5 mm long, neck typically narrowed and when dry shrunken and furrowed; annulus present; lid rather high conic and somewhat beaked; peristome perfect. Plate 137, figs. 7–12.

21.360   On damp or wet soil and rocks, often in crevices.

21.361   Europe and China. Nova Scotia to North Carolina, west to Minnesota and Illinois, Utah. San Juan County: La Sal Mountains, at Oowah Lake, 8,800 ft.

21.362   The above specimen is typical in gametophyte characters, but the 4 good capsules seen do not have a markedly differentiated neck nor are they particularly shrunken in the dry state.

21.363   **3. Plagiothecium denticulatum** (Hedw.) B.S.G. var. **denticulatum.** Plants prostrate, in thin or thickish mats, often scattered among other mosses, bright green, yellowish green, sometimes becoming straw colored, glossy. Shoots strongly complanate-foliate, 2–5 cm long or more, irregularly branched. Leaves closely disposed or widely spaced, spreading in 2 rows, some of them often slightly arched backward, oblong-ovate, 1.4–3 mm long, asymmetric, the anterior side broadly curved, the posterior side narrower and less curved towards the base, acute to briefly acuminate, occasionally blunt, slightly undulate when dry, concave at the base with the posterior margin $\pm$ overlapping the anterior half and often clasping the leaf above; base gradually narrowed, long decurrent; margins plane or narrowly revolute at the base, entire or slightly serrulate at the apex; costa lacking to short and double, sometimes with 1 fork about ⅓ the leaf length; medial cells linear or sometimes linear-rhomboidal, 10–15 μ wide, those at the apex shorter; basal cells shorter, wider, the alar cells mostly oblong, forming decurrent wings of loose, thin-walled, swollen cells. Monoicous. Seta 1.5–2.5(4) cm long; capsules ovoid-oblong to shortly cylindrical, inclined to nearly horizontal, slightly curved and asymmetric, 1.5–2.8 mm long without the lid, slightly furrowed and contracted under the mouth when dry; lid conic, usually with a short thick beak, often slightly bent; annulus of 2 rows of cells; peristome perfect. Plate 137, figs. 1–6.

21.364   On moist or wet soil, humus, rotten logs, and rocks, usually in shade, occasionally in water. In high mountains of Utah.

21.365   Eurasia, western and central Africa; Peru, Australia, and Tasmania. Widely distributed in the northern hemisphere, Canada to Georgia, Mexico.

21.366   Locally frequent and often well fruited. Distinctive because of the flat habit and the long decurrent leaf bases.

21.367   3a. Var. **obtusifolium** (Turn.) Moore. Leaves ovate, soft and lax, concave, apex broad, obtuse to rounded, often apiculate, the tips frequently incurved. About the same habitat and range as the species.

21.368   Duchesne County: Uinta Mountains near Mirror Lake, 10,300 ft.

16. PLATYGYRIUM B.S.G.

21.369   Plants small to medium sized; stems creeping, irregularly branched; leaves ovate to oblong-lanceolate, acute or acuminate, straight but sometimes slightly secund, costa short and double or lacking; upper medial cells broadly to narrowly linear; alar cells quadrate, numerous. Dioicous. Capsule erect and symmetric or nearly so; annulus present; lid short- to long-rostrate; teeth deeply inserted, narrowly lanceolate; segments linear or slenderly linear-lanceolate, free to the base or sometimes dilated and somewhat united into a very low basal membrane; cilia lacking.

21.370   Name from the Greek, for flat or broad ring, referring to the annulus.

21.371   **Platygyrium repens** (Brid.) B.S.G. Plants small, slender, in loose or interwoven mats on bases of trees and fallen trunks, dark green to yellowish green; stems creeping, irregularly branched, up to 5–6 cm long, mostly shorter, branches sometimes erect; sterile stems often bearing numerous very small brood branches in the axils of the leaves and more rarely multicellular, reddish brown gemmae at the summits of some stems. Leaves ovate-oblong to oblong-lanceolate, acute to acuminate, 0.6–1.3 mm long, concave with spreading or widely recurved borders, entire, erect-patent to patent when moist, closely imbricated when dry; costa lacking or short and double; medial cells shortly to moderately long linear, the apical ones becoming rhomboidal and shorter; basal cells slightly shorter; alar cells quadrate, in 2–4 vertical rows, 10–18 on the

Plate 137.   **1–6. Plagiothecium denticulatum.** 1. Two habit sketches, X.4. 2. Three leaves, X8. 3. Two leaf apices. 4. Upper medial cells. 5. Alar cells and portions of the decurrent wing, X80. 6. Three capsules, X8.

7–12. Plagiothecium muellerianum. 7. Habit sketch, X.4. 8. Four leaves, X8. 9. Leaf apex and medial leaf cells. 10. Alar cells, X80. 11. Cross section of stem, X60. 12. Three capsules, X60.

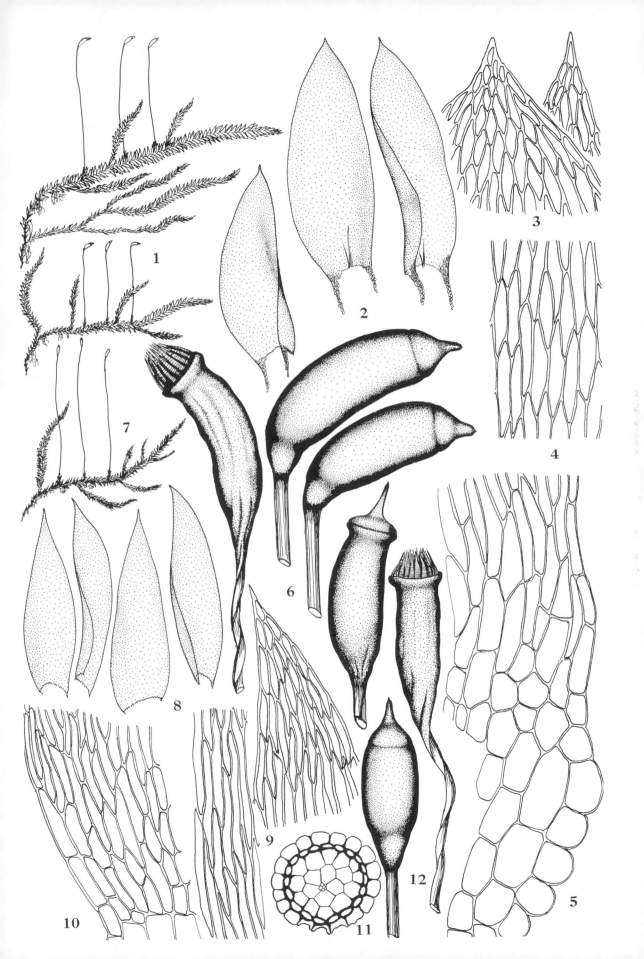

margin, often extending upwards ⅓ the length of the blade. Seta reddish brown, 1–2 cm long; capsules elliptic-oblong to subcylindric, neck very short, often not differentiated, 1.5–2.5 mm long; annulus of 2–3 rows of small dark cells; lid high conic, shortly to long rostrate; peristome teeth linear-lanceolate, finely papillose in sinuose lines, fine transverse striations on the basal joints lacking, hyaline bordered when immature; segments linear, nearly as long as the teeth, separate to the base, perforated or split down the middle, arising from a very low basal membrane within the mouth of the capsule. Spores globose, 12–16 μ, very finely punctate. Plate 138, figs. 1–9.

21.372   On lower trunks of trees and fallen logs, usually in shady places.

21.373   Europe. Eastern North America, common east of the Rocky Mountains. Rich County: Bear Lake at Lakota, 6,000 ft.

21.374   Exceedingly rare in Utah, the above collection being the westernmost record thus far in the United States. The very small brood-branches in the axils of leaves are especially characteristic. The long-rostrate lid, finely sinuose-papillose teeth, lacking transverse striations of the basal joints, and the linear, perforated or split segments separate nearly to the base distinguish this plant.

21.375   A small genus closely related to *Pylaisia* which has at least some of the leaves falcate-secund. The segments of the endostome are slender but strongly keeled and arise from a high basal membrane. *Pylaisia* has not yet been collected in Utah, but I feel certain that it occurs in the southeastern and southern part of the state since I have gathered it close by in Colorado and New Mexico where it is frequent on bases of trees.

17. ORTHOTHECIUM B.S.G.

21.376   Plants small to medium sized, forming spreading mats or scattered among other mosses, bright to yellowish green, often glossy. Shoots sparingly branched. Paraphyllia lacking. Leaves erect to erect-patent, ovate-lanceolate to slenderly lanceolate, acute to acuminate, usually concave; margins plane, entire, or serrulate above, not decurrent; costa short and double or lacking; upper cells linear; basal cells shorter and wider; alar cells not particularly differentiated. Seta long; capsules erect and symmetric or nearly so, ovoid-oblong to cylindrical; lid conic-convex, blunt to beaked, annulus large; peristome teeth slenderly lanceolate, the lower joints transversely striate; segments slender, evenly tapering, keeled, from a low or high basal membrane; cilia single or rudimentary or lacking, sometimes very pale and fragile.

Plate 138. **1–9. Platygyrium repens.** 1. Habit sketches, X.4. 2. Portion of shoot, X4. 3. Shoot bearing brood branches, and brood branches enlarged. 4. Five leaves, X8. 5. Two leaf apices. 6. Upper medial cells. 7. Alar cells, X80. 8. Capsules, X8. 9. Portion of peristome, X60.

10–16. Orthothecium diminutivum. 10. Habit X.4. 11. Portion of a shoot, X4. 12. Leaves, X8. 13. Two leaf apices. 14. Upper medial cell. 15. Alar cells, X80. 16. Capsules, X8.

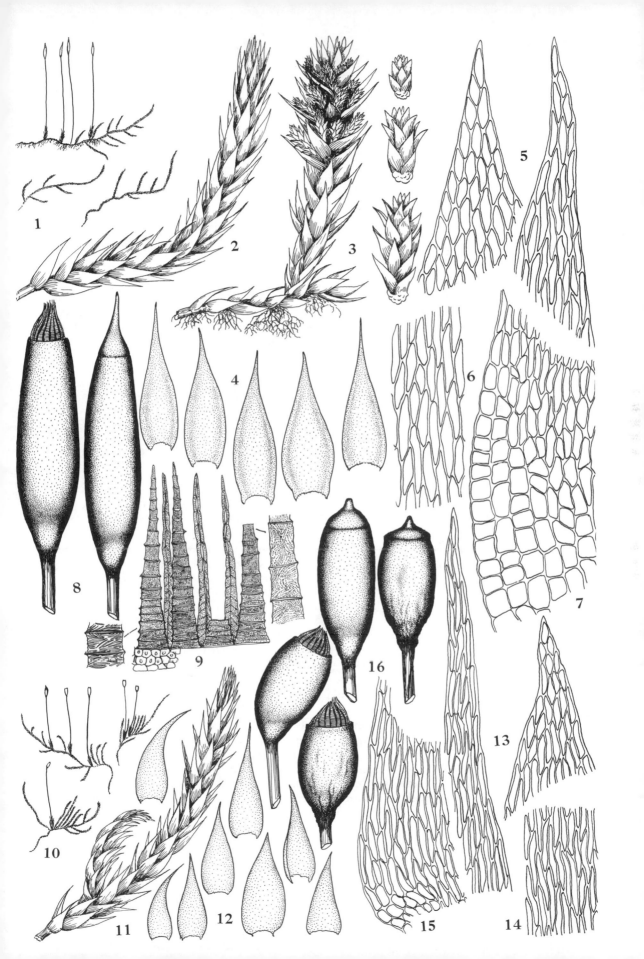

21.377 HYPNACEAE

21.377 The name means erect or straight little box, in reference to the erect capsule.

21.378 **Orthothecium diminutivum** (Grout) Crum, Steere & Anders. Plants small and slender, creeping or ± ascending, forming thin yellowish green mats or more often scattered among other bryophytes. Shoots 1–2 cm long, branches few. Leaves concave, erect-patent, ovate-lanceolate, and triangular-lanceolate, 0.5–0.7(1) mm long, shortly to moderately slenderly acuminate, sometimes slightly falcate, rounded or abruptly contracted to the base; margins plane, entire; medial cells linear-flexuous, 4–7 μ wide; a few alar cells often quadrate or shortly oblong, not set off. Monoicous. Seta 1–1.5 cm long, light reddish brown; capsules ovoid-oblong to oblong-cylindric, erect and symmetric to slightly inclined and asymmetric, 1–1.5 mm long, ± tapering to the seta, usually contracted below the mouth and at the neck when dry; annulus of 2 rows of large thick-walled cells; lid conic-convex, blunt or shortly pointed; cilia of endostome single, very slender and nearly as long as the segments, or rudimentary to lacking. Spores 9–12 μ. Plate 138, figs. 10–16.

21.379 Rare. On damp or moist soil, rocks, and humus, usually in shade at high elevations.

21.380 Colorado and Utah. Duchesne County: Uinta Mountains, near Mirror Lake, on bank of brooklet among *Pohlia, Drepanocladus* and *Lophozia*, 10,100 ft. Colorado. Boulder County: Mt. Alice, on a siliceous rock ledge, 13,000 ft.

21.381 Both of the above specimens are monoicous, a feature new to this genus which is generally cited as dioicous, and the capsules are ample. Those of the Colorado specimen show long, very slender cilia, while the Utah specimen mostly lacks cilia, although two ghostlike cilia were observed. In size the plant approaches species of *Platydictya*, but the much longer leaf cells immediately distinguish it.

NECKERACEAE

22.1 Primary stems naked and creeping with prostrate, spreading, ascending, erect or pendent branches, these regularly or irregularly pinnately branched again; central strand very small or lacking. Leaves mostly large, ovate-lanceolate, oblong, ligulate or culiform, acute to broadly obtuse and often apiculate; costa lacking, short and slender or reaching beyond the middle of the blade; medial leaf cells mostly short, rhomboidal to linear, smooth, the apical ones shorter. Perigonial and perichaetial buds lateral on secondary stems. Seta mostly shorter than the perichaetial leaves; capsules immersed to emergent, rarely long exserted, ovoid to cylindric, erect and symmetric; lid shortly to longly beaked; annulus lacking; peristome single or double, basal joints of the teeth usually without fine transverse lines; cilia lacking or very rudimentary. Calyptra smooth or hairy.

528

NECKERA Hedw.

22.2   With characters of the family.

22.3   Named in honor of N. J. Necker, a German bryologist of the eighteenth century.

22.4   1.   Costa extending 1/2–4/5 the length of the blade; paraphyllia present .... 1. *N. menziesii*   22.6

22.5   1.   Costa lacking, short and double, 1 fork sometimes about 1/3 the length of the leaf; paraphyllia lacking ....
.... 2. *N. pennata* var. *tenera*   22.13

22.6   **1. Neckera menziesii** Hook. in Drumm. var. **menziesii.** Plants large for the genus, in loose tufts or mats, dark green to yellowish green. Primary stems mostly naked, creeping and stoloniform, in our region 2–4 cm long; secondary shoots pinnately branched, prostrate, ascending or sometimes pendulous, occasionally becoming slenderly flagellate; branches very flat. Paraphyllia numerous, filamentous, simple or branched, the cells mostly 1- to 3-seriate. Leaves strongly complanate, spreading, 2–3.5 mm long, oblong-ligulate, apex broadly rounded, mostly apiculate, concave and transversely undulate; margins plane above, narrowly revolute towards the base on 1 or both sides, serrulate above, entire or nearly so below; costa slender, extending 1/2–4/5 the length of the blade; medial cells linear-flexuous, 6–9 μ wide, thick walled and porose, the apical ones shorter and broader, mostly rhomboidal to oval; basal cells thicker walled and more porose; alar cells irregularly oblong to quadrate, often wider than the other basal cells, but not well set off. Leaves of the slender or flagellate branches narrower, ovate to oblong-lanceolate, slenderly acute or acuminate, not complanate, becoming very small toward the ends of the stems. Dioicous. Perichaetial leaves long and slenderly lanceolate, exceeding the immersed capsules. Seta shorter than the capsule; capsules ovoid-oblong, 1.5–2.7 mm long; lid conic with a long beak. Plate 139, figs. 1–5.

22.7   On shaded rocks and trunks of trees.

22.8   Alaska to California, eastward to western Montana and Utah. Salt Lake County: Wasatch Mountains, City Creek Canyon above the forks, 5,800–6,400 ft.

22.9   The specimens from City Creek Canyon were growing on shaded limestone, one of them hanging from the underside of a large overhanging ledge. All are typical in leaf characters, but the plants are poor in size as compared with those of the Pacific Northwest. In the rain forest on the western side of the Olympic Mountains this moss forms great masses 2–4 inches thick on rocks and trunks and branches of deciduous trees, and often hangs in festoons.

22.10   Var. **limnobioides** Ren. & Card.* Plants smaller, dull dark green, usually in thin mats; shoots 1–2 cm long, often spindly with numerous naked

*Reduced to synonym by E. Lawton.

529

stems. Paraphyllia smaller. Leaves small, 1–1.5 mm long, most of them narrower near the apex, not broadly rounded or apiculate, but acute; medial cells shorter.

22.11 Oregon, Washington and Utah. Utah County: Wasatch Mountains, American Fork Canyon, trail of Timpanogos Cave National Monument, under overhanging limestone ledge, 6,000 ft.

22.12 This variety strikes me as nothing more than a depauperate form of the species. Acute leaves are found on the branches of typical forms.

22.13 **2. Neckera pennata** var. **tenera** C. Muell. Plants medium sized, the secondary shoots up to 3 cm long in our region, forming loose mats mainly on rocks. Leaves mostly oblong-ligulate, strongly complanate and usually culliform and asymmetric, 1.3–2.3 mm long, the upper part rounded or rather quickly narrowed to a short broadly acuminate tip, at times nearly apiculate (in younger leaves, especially of the ultimate branches, gradually narrowed to an acute tip), undulate, concave at the base, usually with 1 side folded over the other; margins plane, serrate above, entire below; costa thin, short and double, occasionally forked with 1 branch reaching as much as ⅓ the length of the blade; medial cells oblong-linear to linear, 6–8 μ wide, shorter and wider in the apex, rhomboidal to oval, thicker walled; basal cells shorter and wider, not porose; alar cells not particularly differentiated, at most oblong to subquadrate. Monoicous. Capsules ovoid-oblong, urn 1.3–2 mm long; lid beaked. Plate 139, figs. 6–10.

22.14 On shaded rocks.

22.15 Alberta and British Columbia southward in the Rocky Mountains to New Mexico and Arizona; eastward to the Atlantic states.

22.16 About the only difference between the species and the variety is the broader upper part of the leaves of secondary shoots. However, some leaves, especially those of the ultimate branches, are more or less tapered to acute apices, exactly like those of the species. As a matter of fact, poorly developed plants of the variety in our region resemble the species too closely to be distinguished with certainty.

FONTINALACEAE

23.1 Plants large, dark green to yellowish green, becoming olivaceous or blackish with age, submerged or floating in streams and ponds, attached at the base by a tuft of rhizoids, frequently becoming denuded and stringy below. Stems irregularly to regularly pinnately branched,

---

Plate 139. 1–5. Neckera menziesii. 1. Two habit sketches, X.4. 2. Portion of shoot with paraphyllia enlarged, X4 and X80. 3. Portion of flagellate branch, X4, with leaves enlarged. 4. Three leaves, X8. 5. Leaf apex and upper medial cells, X80.

6–10. Neckera pennata var. **tenera.** 6. Habit sketch, X4. 7. Portion of shoot, X4. 8. Four leaves, X8. 9. Two areas of medial leaf cells and two leaf apices, X80. 10. Two capsules, X8.

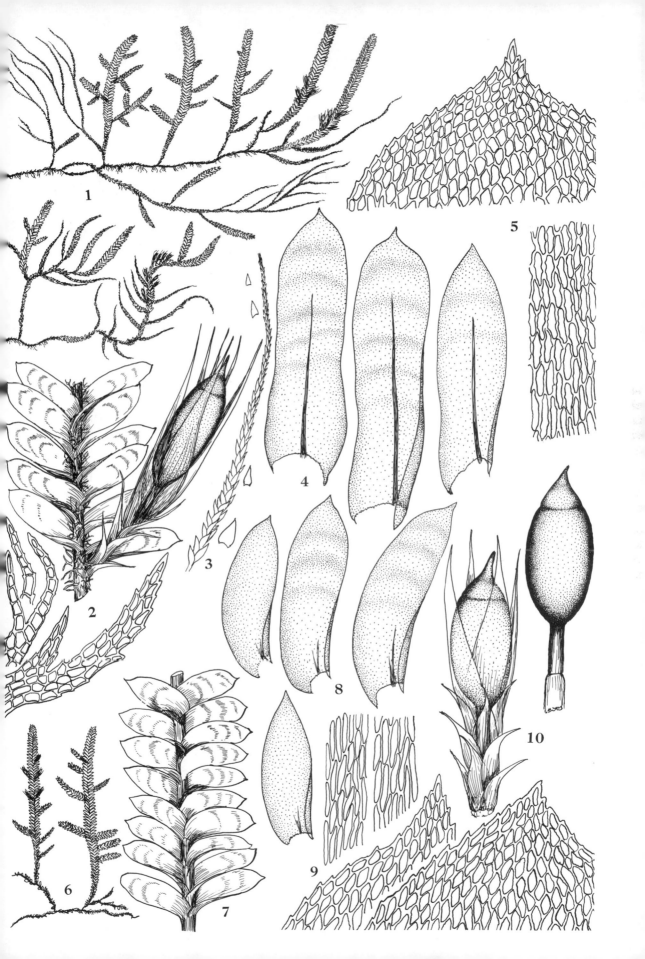

the branches mostly elongated, distant to fascicled, in cross section rounded 3- to 5-angled, central strand lacking. Leaves in three rows (in ours), distant below, becoming imbricated above, nearly orbicular to linear-lanceolate, keeled or flat, ± decurrent; costa present or entirely lacking; medial cells rhomboidal or linear-fusiform; alar cells usually larger, sometimes forming distinct auricles. Dioicous. Seta short to very short; capsules immersed to emergent or shortly exserted, closely invested by the imbricated perichaetial leaves, ovoid to oblong-cylindric, neck not differentiated, stomata and annulus lacking; lid conic, sometimes beaked, peristome teeth 16, very slender; endostome of 16 cilia, often or ± united by transverse appendages forming a conical trellis.

23.2   1. Leaves lanceolate or broader; costa lacking; plants robust .... 1. *Fontinalis* 23.4

23.3   1. Leaves slenderly lanceolate to linear-lanceolate, falcate to circinate, costa single, percurrent or excurrent; plants slender to moderately robust .... 2. *Dichelyma* 23.26

1. FONTINALIS Hedw.

23.4   Plants aquatic, slender to robust, usually in dense or loose tufts or masses; stem tough, commonly denuded and stringy at the base, green to yellowish green above, becoming olivaceous or blackish below; branches few to numerous, usually distant. Leaves in 3 rows, flat, concave or keeled-conduplicate, various shapes, lanceolate or broader, acute to obtuse; costa lacking; medial cells linear-rhomboidal to linear, the apical ones shorter; alar cells mostly enlarged, quadrate to oblong or hexagonal, sometimes forming auricles. Fruit very rare. Perichaetial leaves closely imbricated, orbicular to oval-oblong, rounded or apiculate at the apex, usually becoming lacerated with age. Seta very short; capsules practically sessile, oval to oval-oblong, immersed to ½ emergent; peristome teeth orange or brownish, linear-lanceolate to linear; cilia slender, united by transverse appendages forming a conical trellis. Spores greenish, smooth to finely punctate.

23.5   The name means inhabiting or belonging to springs.

23.6   1. Leaves keeled-conduplicate or markedly concave.

    2. Stem leaves oblong-lanceolate, 1–3x2.5–5 mm, acute to blunt; medial cells 1:10–25 .... 1. *F. neo-mexicana* 23.8

    2. Stem leaves ovate to oval-lanceolate, 2–4x5–8 mm mostly blunt or obtuse, a few acute; medial cells 1:6–15 .... 2. *F. antipyretica* 23.11

23.7   1. Leaves not keeled-conduplicate, flat or slightly concave, usually flaccid, mostly 2.5–5.5 mm, gradually acuminate

---

Plate 140. Fontinalis antipyretica. 1. Habit sketch, X.4. 2. Branch leaves. 3. Stem leaves, X4. 4. Two leaf apices. 5. Upper medial leaf cells. 6. Basal and alar cells, X120. 7–9. After B.S.G., Bryol. Eur. plate 429, capsules and peristome.

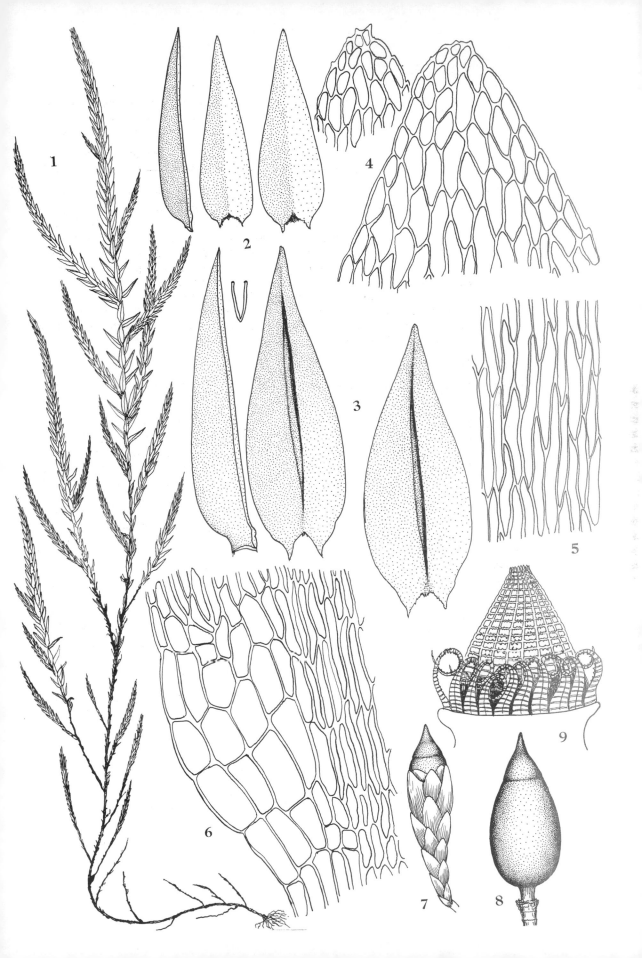

3. Leaf apices mostly long and narrow; leaves ovate-lanceolate, oblong-lanceolate or narrowly lanceolate; alar cells indistinct .... 3. *F. hypnoides* 23.18

3. Leaf apices mostly short and broad; leaves broadly ovate-lanceolate to oblong-lanceolate; alar cells distinct .... 4. *F. duriaei* 23.22

23.8   **1. Fontinalis neo-mexicana** Sull. & Lesq. Plants slender, in loose masses, bright or dull green to yellowish green to golden brown, often becoming blackish below. Stems tough and rigid below, commonly 10–30(50) cm long; branches distant and flaccid. Stem leaves 1–3x2.5–5 mm, distant and spreading below, becoming dense, erect-patent and imbricated above, mostly oblong-lanceolate, keeled-conduplicate, the keel slightly curved, the apices mostly acute, a few blunt or narrowly obtuse, entire or denticulate; medial cells linear, 5–15 μ wide, shorter in the apex; alar cells much enlarged, quadrate to oblong, thin walled and often inflated, becoming yellowish brown or rusty red with age. Fruit rare. Plate 142, figs. 1–4.

23.9   In brooks.

23.10   Rocky Mountain states and westward. Summit County: Uinta Mountains, Stillwater Fork of Bear River, 8,000 ft.

23.11   **2. Fontinalis antipyretica** Hedw. Plants large, slender to fairly robust, in rather dense clusters, often becoming long and stringy, dark green to olivaceous or yellowish green, often becoming golden brown or brown, the lower portions blackish. Stem commonly 20–30 cm long, sometimes reaching 70 cm, rigid and tough, becoming denuded below, distantly pinnate, the branches leafy and flaccid. Lower stem leaves distant and spreading, the upper ones becoming denser and imbricated, ovate to ovate-lanceolate, 2–4x5–8 mm, keeled-conduplicate, the keel curved throughout, narrowly obtuse, a few acute, entire or slightly denticulate at the tip; margin flat or recurved on 1 or both sides at the base; medial cells linear-rhomboidal to hexagonal, 10–15 μ wide, shorter in the apex; alar cells $\pm$ gradually enlarged, quadrate to oblong, thin walled and often inflated, becoming yellowish brown or orange with age, commonly forming $\pm$ distinct auricles. Branch leaves smaller, the younger ones narrower. Fruit rare. Perichaetial leaves oval or suborbicular, obtuse, entire, usually becoming lacerate with age. Capsules immersed or rarely ½ emergent, $\pm$ oval, 2–3 mm long; operculum short conic, about 1 mm long; peristome orange brownish, teeth linear, approximately 1 mm long, often united in pairs at their apices, papillose; inner peristome papillose, transverse bars $\pm$ appendiculate; spores olive green or yellowish green, slightly muricate, 15–18 μ in diameter. Plate 140.

Plate 141. 1–2. **Fontinalis antipyretica** var. **mollis.** 1. Branch leaves. 2. Stem leaves, X8.

3–7. Fontinalis duriaei. 3. Habit sketch, X.4. 4. Branch leaves. 5. Stem leaves, X4. 6. Two leaf apices. 7. Upper medial leaf cells (right) and alar cells (left), X120.

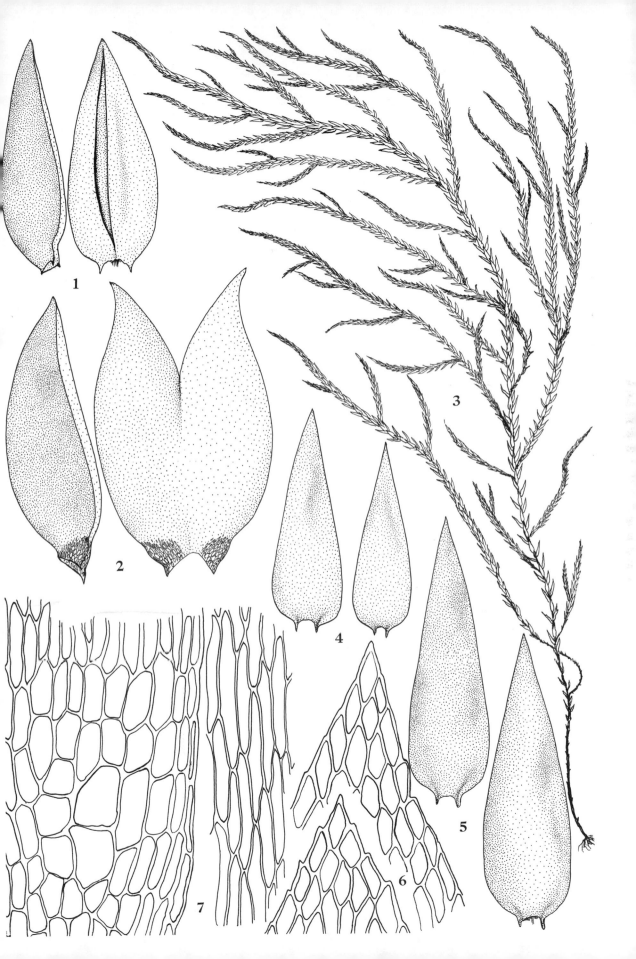

23.12 FONTINALACEAE

23.12 In ponds and streams.

23.13 Europe, Asia and Africa. Throughout Canada and the United States. Uinta Mountains in Utah.

23.14 2a. Var. **oregonensis** Ren. & Card. Keels of the leaves nearly straight above the basal curve, the leaf tips sometimes shortly and abruptly incurved. Plate 142, fig. 11.

23.15 Rocky Mountain states and westward, Alaska. Duchesne County: Uinta Mountains, about ½ mi. east of Mirror Lake, 10,000 ft.

23.16 2b. Var. **mollis** (C. Muell.) Welch. Plants appearing more leafy and somewhat more robust. Stem leaves broadly ovate to nearly orbicular, the keel strongly curved throughout, narrowly to broadly obtuse, sometimes cucullate. Branch leaves smaller, broadly ovate, the keel less strongly curved. Plate 141, figs. 1–2.

23.17 Washington County: Pine Valley Mountains, Santa Clara Creek, 7,200 ft.

23.18 **3. Fontinalis hypnoides** Hartm. Plants slender and flaccid, pale or bright green to yellowish green, becoming brownish below but rarely very dark. Stems slender, commonly 10–30 cm long, distantly pinnate, the branches irregular in length, denuded below, leafy above. Stem leaves lax and flaccid, distant and spreading below, erect and ± imbricated above, 0.7–1.75x3–6 mm, ovate-lanceolate, oblong-lanceolate to narrowly lanceolate, the apex narrowly acute or blunt, mostly entire, a few indistinctly denticulate; medial cells linear or linear-rhomboidal, 8–15 μ wide, shorter in the apex; alar cells ± enlarged, not well set off, quadrate to hexagonal, hyaline, becoming yellowish brown with age, usually not forming auricles. Plate 142, figs. 5–10.

23.19 In rivers, brooks, and ponds.

23.20 Europe and Asia. Throughout Canada and the United States. Uncommon in Utah. Duchesne County: Uinta Mountains, in side ponds along streams near Mirror Lake, 10,100 ft.

23.21 Much like the next species, differing in the narrower leaves with more slenderly acute apices which give the plant a more slender appearance. *F. duriaei* has been treated as a variety and a subspecies, but our plants, few though they be, seem distinctive.

23.22 **4. Fontinalis duriaei** Schimp. Plants slender and soft, usually in dense, lax and flaccid masses, pale green to yellowish green, becoming olivaceous to brownish and blackish in the older parts. Stems slender, 10–30 cm long, tough but not very rigid, pinnate, the branches distant and unequal. Stem leaves distant, erect or spreading below, loosely imbricated above, broadly ovate-lanceolate to oblong-lanceolate, flat or

Plate 142. **1–4. Fontinalis neo-mexicana.** 1. Branch leaves. 2. Stem leaves, X4. 3. Two leaf apices. 4. Upper medial cells, X120.

5–10. Fontinalis hypnoides. 5. Habit sketch, X4. 6. Branch leaves. 7. Stem leaves, X4. 8. Leaf apices. 9. Upper medial cells. 10. Alar cells, X120.

11. Fontinalis antipyretica var. **oregonensis.** Stem and branch leaves, X4.

536

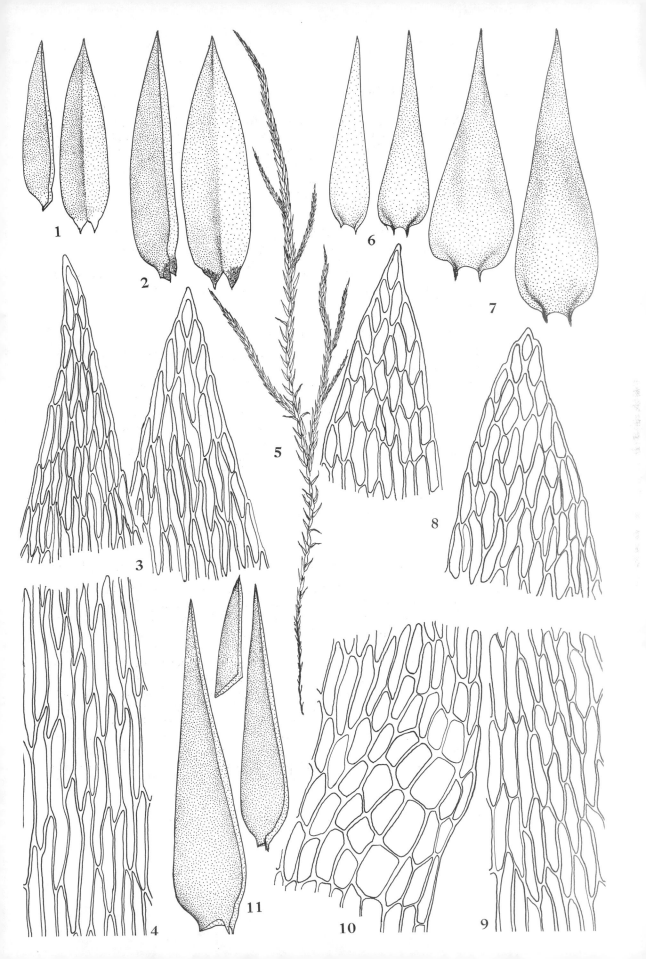

slightly concave, 3–5(6) mm long, 1–2.5 mm wide, the apices rather broad, acute, blunt or narrowly obtuse, entire or denticulate; margins plane, medial cells linear or somewhat linear-rhomboidal, 9–16 μ wide, shorter in the apex; alar cells slightly to moderately enlarged, not well set off, quadrate to rectangular or somewhat hexagonal, not forming auricles. Branch leaves smaller and narrower. Fruit rare. Plate 141, figs. 3–7.

23.23   In brooks and ponds, frequent in Utah from lowlands to high mountains.

23.24   Europe. Africa. Throughout Canada and the United States.

23.25   Much like the last species but more robust, the leaves on the whole larger and broader in proportion, wider toward the apex and not so narrowly pointed.

2. DICHELYMA Myr., K. Svensk.

23.26   Plants rather slender, attached, submerged or periodically inundated, green to yellowish brown at the tips, purplish brown or blackish below. Stem elongated, distantly and irregularly branched, hooked at the tips; leaves in 3 fairly distinct rows, narrowly lanceolate to linear-lanceolate, falcate-secund, keeled; margins plane, ± denticulate above; costa nearly percurrent to long excurrent; medial cells linear with tapering ends, basal cells scarcely different, a little wider; alar cells not differentiated or a few wider and shorter. Dioicous. Fruit very rare. Seta exceeding the perichaetial leaves and the capsule exserted, ovate, erect; lid conical with a long beak, straight or curved; teeth linear-lanceolate, often perforated down the middle; cilia 16, slightly longer than the teeth, often irregular in length, regularly or irregularly joined by transverse connections forming a conical trellis. Calyptra cucullate, covering the entire capsule.

23.27   The name means divided and a sail, alluding to split, sail-like calyptra.

23.28   **Dichelyma falcatum** (Hedw.) Myr. Plants medium sized to fairly large, bright green to yellowish green at the tips, becoming brownish green or reddish green below and often purplish black when old, dull to glossy. Stems commonly 5–18 cm long, often longer, irregularly branched, the branches unequal, sometimes slightly pinnate, hooked at the tips. Stem leaves in 3 rows, oblong-lanceolate to linear-lanceolate, keeled, falcate-secund, slenderly tapering to a narrowly acute to somewhat blunt tip, 3–5 mm long; margins plane or slightly recurved below, denticulate toward the apex; costa subpercurrent to slightly excurrent; medial cells linear, 5–7 μ wide; basal cells shorter and wider, becoming thick-walled, ± porose and yellowish to golden yellow with age; alar cells scarcely different or sometimes a few oblong. Fruit not seen. Perichaetium very long, narrowly cylindric; inner perichaetial leaves ecostate, strap-shaped, long acuminate, entire or slightly denticulate toward the apex, clasping

---

Plate 143.   **Dichelyma falcatum.** 1. Habit sketches, X.4. 2. Leaves, X8. 3. Two leaf apices. 4. Upper medial leaf cells. 5. Alar cells, X120.

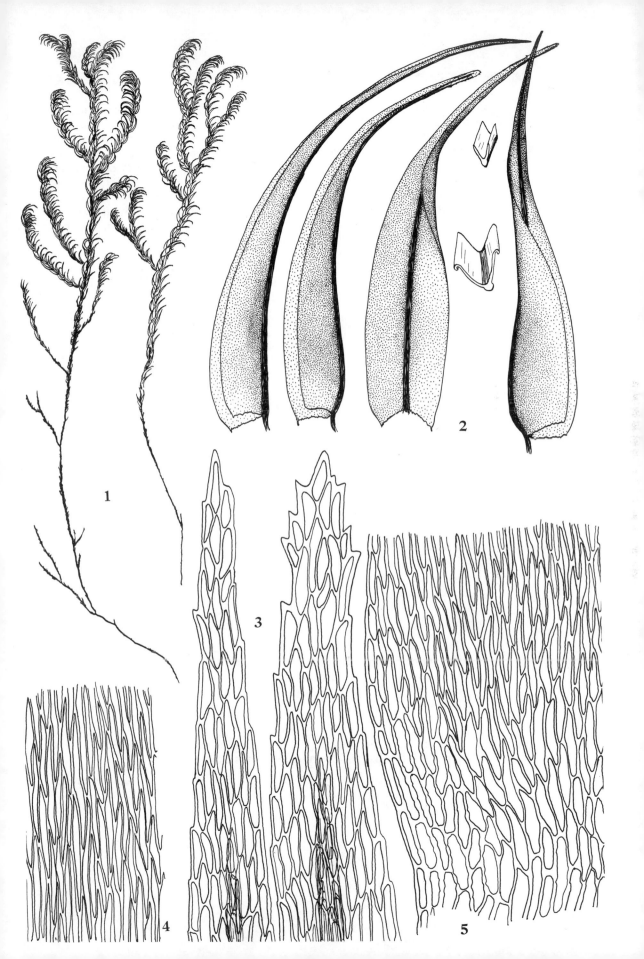

at the base, spirally twisted around the seta. Seta erect, reddish, usually extending a considerable length beyond the perichaetial leaves, 5–15 mm long; capsules erect, oval, oval-oblong or cylindric, occasionally contracted beneath the mouth when dry, yellowish to rust brown, sometimes darkening with age, 1.25–2 mm long; operculum conical-acuminate, commonly as long as the urn, obliquely beaked; peristome teeth reddish, teeth linear, about 0.5 mm long, strongly papillose; trellis perfect, rust brown, muricate, cilia longer than the teeth, about 0.6 mm. Spores smooth or minutely papillose, 10–14 μ, ripe in summer. Calyptra longer than the capsule, base closely clasping the seta. Plate 143.

23.29   In subalpine ponds and brooks in our region.

23.30   Northern Europe and Asia, northern United States and Canada. Uinta Mountains in Utah.

23.31   This moss closely resembles *Drepanocladus exannulatus* and commonly grows in the same habitats. Both have long, slender, falcate-secund leaves, but the leaves of *D. exannulatus* are in many rows, not keeled, and have large conspicuous alar cells across the base.

POLYTRICHALES

POLYTRICHACEAE

24.1   Plants mostly large, coarse and stiff, forming loose or dense tufts, often scattered, dark green when young, becoming reddish or brownish with age. Stems erect, usually arising from underground branched rhizomes, central strand large, of 2 kinds of cells; rhizoids few to very dense. Leaves ligulate to linear, ± sheathing at the base, erect and infolded to strongly crisped when dry, mostly spreading to recurved when moist; costa stout, often occurring nearly the entire width of the leaf, bearing longitudinal lamellae on the ventral surface in the upper part, in a few genera also on the dorsal surface; upper leaf cells ± isodiametric, often transversely elongated, or oblong; basal cells oblong to linear. Seta long, usually stiff and straight; capsules angular or terete, erect, inclined or horizontal, peristome composed of 32 or upward to 64 short, ligulate, unjointed teeth. Calyptra large, cucullate, usually densely hairy.

24.2   1. Leaf base narrowed; costa relatively narrow, occupying less than 1/5 the width of the blade and bearing 1–15 longitudinal lamellae on the ventral surface; lamina 1–stratose and more than 8 cells wide on each side; capsules cylindric and terete, not longitudinally ridged; hypophysis lacking .... 1. *Atrichum*   24.4

24.3   1. Leaf base strongly dilated; costa occupying nearly the entire width of the limb and bearing 25–70 longitudinal ventral lamellae; the lamina 1–8 cells wide at mid-leaf; capsules various

2. Capsules ovoid to cylindric, terete; peristome teeth 32 or more ....
.... 2. *Pogonatum*   24.9

2. Capsules longitudinally angular or ridged; peristome teeth 64

3. Capsules elongated, widest toward base, about half as wide at the mouth; 4-ridged, the 2 upper ridges close together .... 3. *Polytrichadelphus* 24.21

3. Capsules short, nearly cuboidal, to rectangular, mouth wide, 4–6 angled, the angles about equidistant .... 4. *Polytrichum* 24.27

1. ATRICHUM P. Beauv.

24.4 Leaves ligulate, ovate to lanceolate, mostly crisped when dry, erect to recurved when moist; base not strongly differentiated, apex acute to obtuse, margins bordered with narrow cells, often toothed, flat to undulate, often toothed on the back; costa percurrent or nearly so, narrow, bearing 2–6 ventral lamellae. Seta long, 1–6 from the same perichaetium; capsules ovoid to cylindric, smooth, inclined or slightly curved, neck usually evident, hypophysis lacking; lid long rostrate, teeth 32. Calyptra naked.

24.5 The name is from the Greek and means without hair.

24.6 **Atrichum selwynii** Aust. Plants dark green, becoming yellowish brown with age, solitary to loosely tufted; stems simple or rarely branched, 2–8 cm tall; central strand large; rhizoids usually few. Leaves much crisped and contorted when dry, widely spreading when moist, 5–9 mm long, oblong to oblong-lanceolate, ligulate, scarcely sheathing or dilated at the base, acute or obtuse, undulate with coarse teeth on the backs of the undulations; margins flat; bordered with small, thick walled, bistratose, oblong to linear cells and coarsely toothed, the teeth often in pairs; upper cells of the lamina 4- to 6-angled, usually ± rounded, isodiametric to transversely elongated, 18–40 μ in longest diameter, smooth; basal cells mostly oblong, hyaline; costa occupying 1/10–1/8 the width of the leaf and bearing 2–6 lamellae on the upper 1/2–3–4, these 6–13 cells high, smooth and flat; cells 4- to 6-sided, the marginal ones even and in cross section smoothly rounded, the walls ± uniformly thin. Polyoicous. Seta single, erect, reddish and smooth, becoming hollow, 2–4 cm high; capsules cylindric, terete, inclined, or curved, gradually narrowed at the base, neck region short, stomata lacking; peristome teeth 32. Lid convex, long and slenderly rostrate, often nearly equalling the length of the urn. Plate 144.

24.7 On soil, often on slopes or disturbed banks in shady places, usually on the edges or in open places in woods.

24.8 British Columbia to Alberta; Oregon, Montana, Utah, Colorado.

2. POGONATUM P. Beauv.

24.9 Stems erect and stiff, scaly below. Leaves ± erect, incurved or slightly outcurved, stiff when dry, spreading to recurved when moist, oblong to linear-lanceolate from a dilated clasping base, obtuse, acute or acuminate; margins entire to coarsely toothed; costa occupying nearly the entire width of the leaf and bearing numerous longitudinal lamellae on

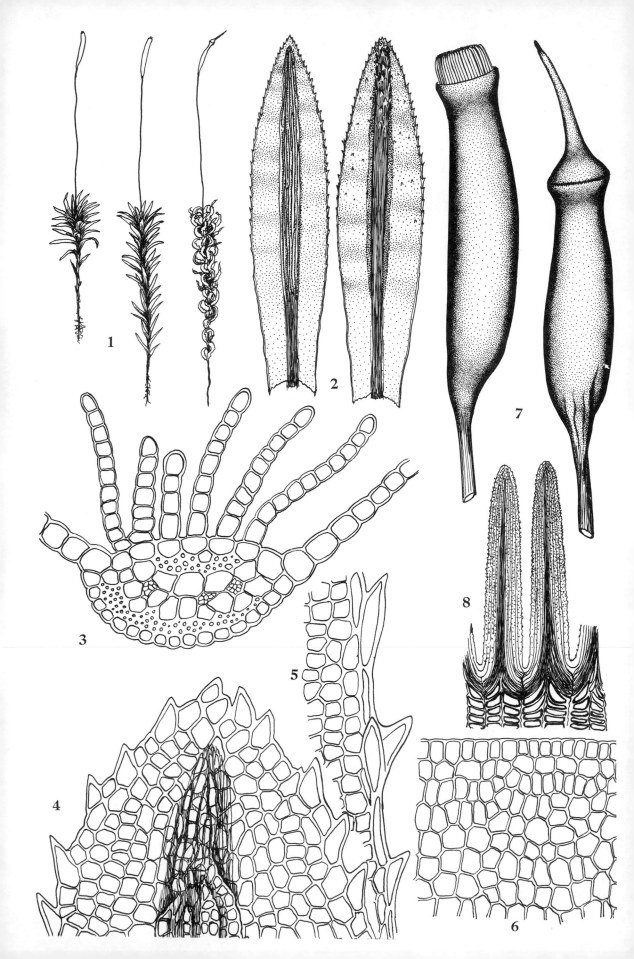

the ventral side above the base; base unistratose. Dioicous. Perigonia budlike to cup-shaped. Seta long; capsules terete, ovate to cylindric, erect, inclined or curved; neck region differentiated, with or without stomata; exothecial cells often mammillose; lid convex, rostrate; peristome teeth 32–64, often imperfect. Calyptra hairy.

24.10   The name means bearded, referring to the hairs of the calyptra.

24.11   **Pogonatum alpinum** (Hedw.) Roehl. Plants in loose tufts or scattered, green to glaucous green, becoming brownish with age. Stems simple or branched, 1–10 cm tall, angular in cross section; rhizoids confined to the base. Leaves ± erect and incurved when dry, the upper ones spreading to recurved when moist, 4–7 mm long, downward abruptly becoming shorter and reduced to erect scales, oblong-lanceolate to lanceolate from a broad sheathing base, apex acute to acuminate; margins serrate to the shoulders or nearly so, flat or erect; costa excurrent to a short point, toothed at back above; lamellae 40–50, 4–6 cells high, the margins entire, in cross section the marginal cells slightly thicker than the lower ones, oval to obovate, the walls very thick, finely and densely papillose, the lumen rounded or oval; cells of the sheath oblong to linear, hyaline to reddish, toward the shoulders becoming shorter and thicker walled, oblong to quadrate, rhomboidal and transversely elongated. Dioicous. Seta 1–5 cm long, reddish at the base; urn ovate to subcylindric, erect to slightly inclined, terete, yellowish brown to red-·dish brown, 2.5–3.4 mm long, the neck short, the mouth rather wide; exothecial cells mammillose, rounded to oval, thick walled, without a thin spot; lid convex with a straight or curved beak; teeth mostly 40–64 (rarely only 32), reddish. Spores 18–21 μ, smooth but finely punctate, light yellowish brown.

24.12   On soil, in Utah restricted to high mountains.

24.13   Europe, Asia, Pacific Islands, Antarctica. Greenland to Alaska, southward to California, and eastward to Colorado, New York and New Hampshire.

24.14   Sterile plants are so much like those of *Polytrichum gracile*, *P. commune* and *Polytrichadelphus lyallii* that careful note is required as to the nature of the marginal cells of the lamellae. Our representatives of this species can be referred to the 2 varieties:

24.15   2a. Var. **arcticum** (Schrad.) Brid. Leaves 7–8 mm long; capsule narrower, 4–5 mm long, 3–5 times longer than wide. Plate 145.

24.16   Greenland to Alaska, Nova Scotia, Minnesota, southward to Washington.

24.17   2b. Var. **brevifolium** (R. Brown) Brid. Plants small, 1–4 cm tall; leaves

---

Plate 144.   Atrichum selwynii. 1. Moist and dry habit sketches, X.4. 2. Ventral and dorsal views of leaves, X4. 3. Cross section of leaf. 4. Apical cells. 5. Marginal cells, X120. 6. Surface view of lamella, X120. 7. Capsules, X4. 8. Two peristome teeth, X60.

5–8 mm long, capsules shorter and thicker, 1.8–3 mm long. Plate 145, fig. 3.

24.18   On wet or damp soil and rocks, usually in shade.

24.19   Iceland; Europe and Asia. Greenland to Alaska, southward to California, across the continent through Colorado to Massachusetts.

24.20   Most of our present plants are referable to this variety although some approach var. *arcticum*. It is fairly common in the Uinta Mountains. Sterile plants can be distinguished by the thick-walled papillose marginal cells of the lamellae.

3. POLYTRICHADELPHUS (C. Muell.) Mitt.

24.21   Plants having the habit and appearance of *Polytrichum*. Dioicous; seta long; capsules erect to horizontal, ± oblong, usually narrowed from the middle to the mouth, 4-angled, the 2 upper angles close together, often somewhat asymmetric; hypophysis distinct; stomata present; teeth 64. Calyptra smooth to slightly hairy.

24.22   The name suggests a brotherhood with *Polytrichum*.

24.23   **1. Polytrichadelphus lyallii** Mitt. Plants in loose tufts or sometimes forming dense sods, frequently scattered, coarse and stiff, 0.5–5 cm tall. Stems mostly simple, the taller ones sometimes with 1 or 2 branches from the base. Leaves erect and appressed or sometimes slightly spirally twisted when dry, widely spreading to recurved when moist, lanceolate from a sheathing oblong base, the upper ones the largest, 6–12 mm long, the lower ones shorter, at length becoming scale-like toward the base of the stem and consisting mostly of the sheathing base, acute or shortly mucronate; margins plane, often incurved or erect above, mostly coarsely serrate or dentate; costa excurrent to a short red awn; costal lamellae mostly 40–50, 4–6 cells high, entire with the marginal cells slightly larger than those below, oblong to ovate, the outer wall ± evenly thickened and roughened by longitudinally elongated shallow pits. Setae solitary, erect and flexuous, yellowish to brownish, becoming reddish with age, 4–6 cm long; capsules oblong, 5–6 mm long, slightly inclined when young, becoming ± horizontal after dehiscence, faintly to strongly longitudinally 4-ridged, the 2 upper ridges close together, rather asymmetric, at times the ridges weak and the urn then nearly terete; when dry the urn thick at the base and narrowed to the mouth; hypophysis short but well constricted; stomata present; teeth 64, narrowly oblong-ligulate, acute to narrowly obtuse, finely papillose, from a distinct basal membrane; lid low conic with a subulate, inclined or curved beak. Spores 9–12 μ, smooth. Calyptra cucullate, not covering the capsule very well, usually bearing a few hairs, yellowish to brownish, darker at the tip.

Plate 145. Pogonatum alpinum var. **arcticum.** 1. Habit sketches, X.4. 2. Two typical leaves. 3. One leaf of var. **brevifolium,** X6. 4. Apical and marginal cells. 5. Cross section, upper part of leaf. 6. Surface view of lamella, X120. 7. Capsules, X6. 8. Peristome teeth, X60.

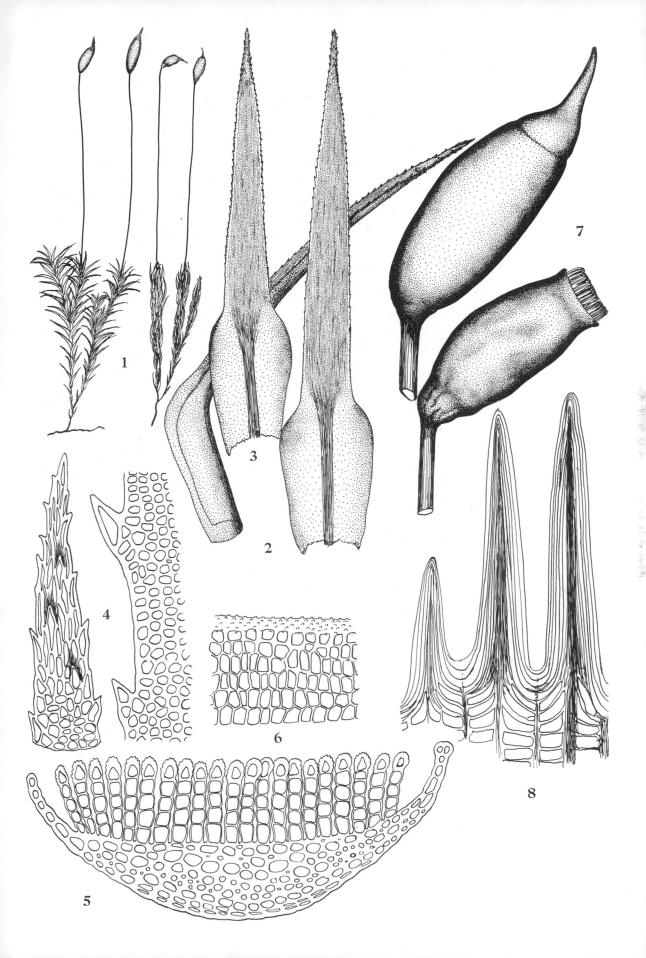

24.24 Mostly on damp soil or humus, occasionally in crevices of rocks in high mountains of Utah, usually in open places in the woods or in meadows.

24.25 British Columbia, Idaho and Montana southward to California, Utah, Arizona, and Colorado.

24.26 Sterile plants resemble *Polytrichum gracile*, *P. commune*, and *Pogonatum alpinum* but can be distinguished by observing the marginal cells of the lamellae which show the characteristic longitudinally elongated shallow pits on the moderately thickened walls. In cross section the marginal cells are oblong to ovate and appear only undulate on the outer surface and not papillose as in some species of *Pogonatum*.

4. POLYTRICHUM Hedw.

24.27 Plants rather small to large, in loose to dense tufts or scattered, green, becoming brownish or reddish with age. Stems stiff, often decumbent; central strand large, composed of large central cells surrounded by smaller thin-walled cells, inner cortical cells large with 2 to several rows of small, thick-walled, reddish outer cells. Upper leaves dense to well spaced, becoming scaly below, ± erect, stiff and wiry when dry, spreading to recurved when moist, shortly oblong-lanceolate to linear from a broad sheathing base, unistratose marginal portion of the limb 2–5 cells wide; costa occupying most of the width of the limb and bearing 30–70 ventral lamellae and mostly excurrent to an awn. Dioicous. Setae long and stiff; capsules single, 4–6 angled, the angles equidistant, nearly cuboidal to oblong, the neck region short and bearing stomata, hypophysis usually evident; mouth large; peristome teeth 64, ligulate, incurved; columella dilated as thin epiphragm across the mouth and attached to the tips of the teeth, lid flat to conical, rostrate. Calyptra densely or sparingly hairy.

24.28 The name refers to the many hairs of the calyptra.

24.29 1. Margins of the leaves ± toothed, flat or erect, not infolded

    2. Marginal cells of the lamellae in cross section about equal to those below, and free end rounded

        3. Marginal cells of the lamellae in cross section thin walled and smooth .... 1. *P. gracile* 24.31

        3. Marginal cells of the lamellae in cross section thick walled, crenulate because of shallow longitudinal pits ....
.... *Polytrichadelphus* 24.21

    2. Marginal cells of the lamellae in cross section broader than those below, thick walled and notched .... 2. *P. commune* 24.34

24.30 1. Margins of the leaves entire, thin and hyaline, sharply infolded and lying over the lamellae

---

Plate 146. Polytrichum gracile. 1. Habit sketches, X.4. 2. Leaves, X4. 3. Upper marginal cells of leaf, X120. 4. Outline of leaf apex, X30. 5. Cross section of leaf. 6. Surface view of lamella, X120. 7. Capsules, X4.

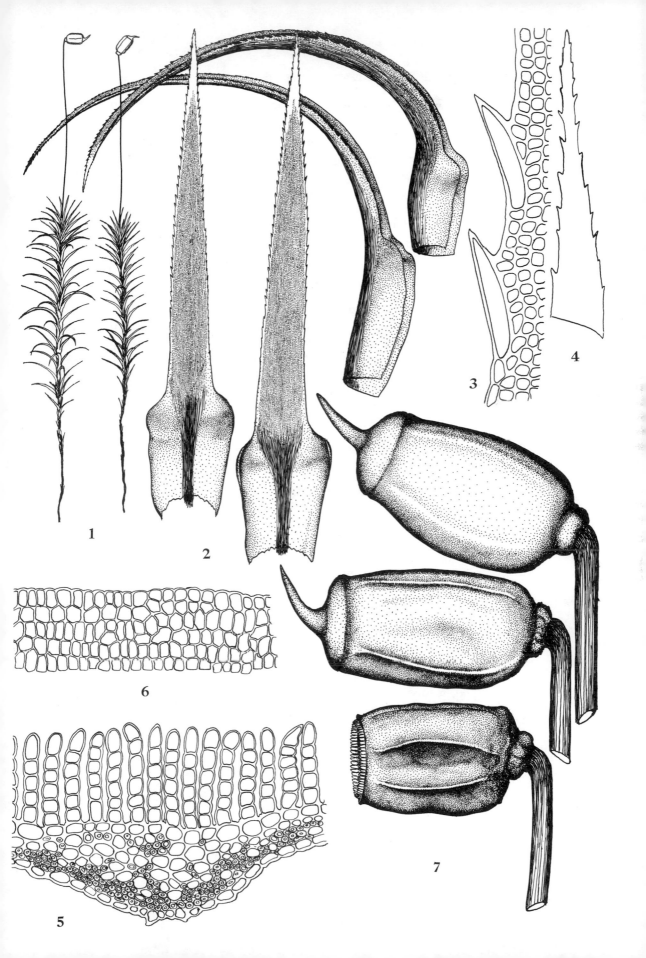

4. Awns of the leaves stout and reddish throughout, mostly short; plants 1–4 cm tall, short and stout to tall .... 3. *P. juniperinum* 24.28

4. Awns of the leaves slender and hyaline, mostly long; plants small and low in our region .... 4. *P. piliferum* 24.42

24.31   **1. Polytrichum gracile** Dicks. ex Menz. Plants usually in fairly **dense** tufts. Stems 3–10 cm tall, usually simple; rhizoids dense at the base, whitish. Leaves ± loosely erect to somewhat curled when dry, erect-patent to widely squarrose recurved when moist, dense to widely spaced, lanceolate to sublinear from a broad sheathing base, 8–10 mm long, gradually tapering above to a red strongly serrate mucro; margins serrate to the shoulders; costa excurrent, smooth or with a few teeth at the apex; lamellae 30–45, 4–6 cells high, the margins entire, the marginal cells in cross section not wider than those below, rounded, the walls thin and smooth. Capsules erect to horizontal, shortly rectangular or ovate, the urn mostly 4 mm long, 5- to 6-angled, the angles ± rounded, sometimes not strong, somewhat narrowed to the red mouth, yellowish green when young, becoming brown with age; hypophysis not strongly constricted; teeth 64, or fewer because of coalescence, often imperfect; exothecial cells smooth, without a central thin spot; lid conic, long rostrate. Spores olivaceous, finely crenulate, 17–20 μ. Plate 146.

24.32   On damp soil.

24.33   Eurasia and New Zealand. Alaska to Greenland, southward to California, Utah and Colorado, and eastward across the continent to Connecticut and Florida. Salt Lake County: Wasatch Mountains, Little Cottonwood Canyon at Alta, Mt. Baldy, 9,000–10,000 ft. (collected by M. E. Jones).

24.34   **2. Polytrichum commune** Hedw. Plants in dense, often deep tufts, **dark** olivaceous above, reddish or brownish below. Stems mostly simple, rarely forked, 10–40 cm tall from a 3-angled rhizome; rhizoids basal. Leaves erect or with spreading tips when dry, spreading to widely squarrose recurved when moist, densely to widely spaced, becoming scale-like below, lanceolate to sublinear from a broadly sheathing base, 8–12 mm long, gradually tapering to a slender, spinulose red mucro; margins serrate to the shoulders of the clasping base; costa excurrent, toothed at the back above; lamellae 40–70, 4–9 cells high, margins entire to crenate, in cross section the terminal cells wider than the ones below, thick walled and notched. Seta 6–12 cm long; capsules usually 4-angled, rarely 5- to 6-angled, reddish brown, the urn shortly rectangular to nearly cuboidal, 3–6 mm long; hypophysis very distinct and usually constricted; exothecial cells each with a conical papilla and a small elliptical thin spot in the center; lid low conic, rostrate. Spores small, 8–10 μ, yellowish and smooth. Plate 147.

Plate 147.   **Polytrichum commune.** 1. Habit sketches, X.4. 2. Leaves, X4. 3. Outline of leaf apex, X30. 4. Upper marginal leaf cells. 5. Cross section of leaf. 6. Surface view of lamella, X120. 7. Capsules, X4.

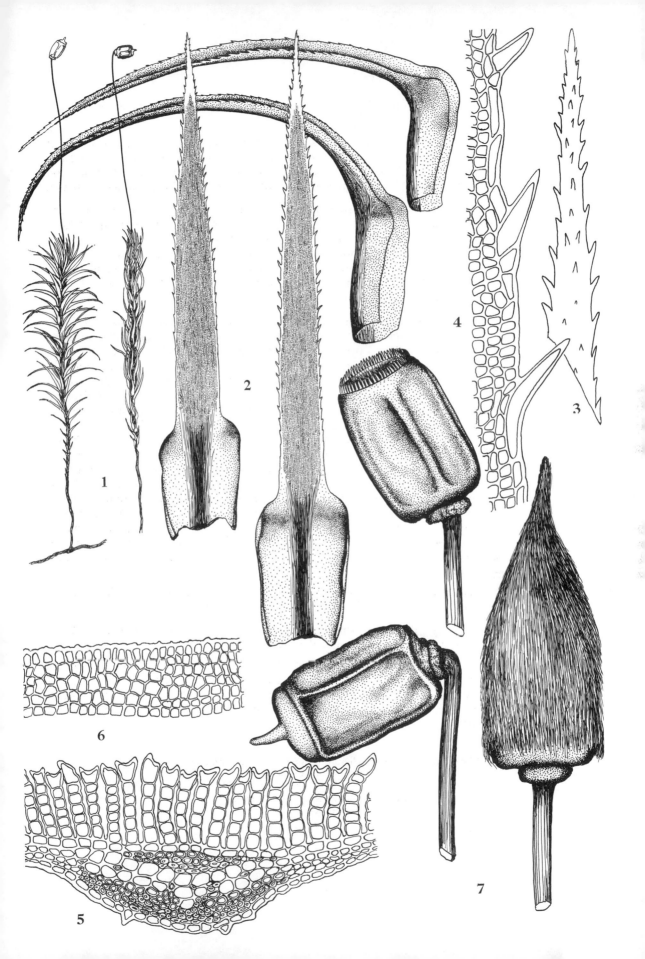

1

2

3

4

5

6

7

24.35 On damp soil, edges of woods, bogs, and banks of brooks and ponds.

24.36 South America, Eurasia, Africa and oceanic islands. Alaska to Greenland, southward to California and Arizona, eastward across the continent in favorable situations to Louisiana and Florida. Rare in Utah. Salt Lake County: Wasatch Mountains, Brighton, 8,700 ft; Little Cottonwood Canyon at Alta, about 8,500 ft (all collected by M. E. Jones in 1889).

24.37 From the abundant specimens collected by Jones in 1889, it would appear that this moss was plentiful at that time, but repeated explorations of the Brighton and Alta basins have not revealed the moss in more recent times. The disappearance of certain ferns in the same areas suggests that a decline in average annual precipitation may be the main factor. Since 1924 I have noted a marked decrease in the abundance and vigor of the vegetation as a whole.

24.38 **3. Polytrichum juniperinum** Hedw. Plants in low scanty sods or loose tufts, often scattered, mostly low in our region, 1–4 cm tall but occasionally becoming upward to 10 cm; rhizoids usually few at the base. Stems mostly simple, rarely forked. Leaves dense above, usually suddenly reduced and becoming scale-like below, erect and stiff when dry, patent to recurved spreading when moist, 6–10 mm long, lanceolate from a broad sheathing base, tapering to a short, stout, red, serrate mucro or arista; margins entire, thin and infolded over the lamellae, usually hyaline; costa wide, excurrent, toothed on the back above; lamellae 30–48, 4–8 cells high, the margins crenulate, in cross section the marginal cells about the same width as those below, ovate to pyriform, the outer wall very thick, smooth. Seta variable, 2–10 cm long, bright reddish and hollow when mature; capsules short, oblong, erect to horizontal, greenish brown when young, becoming reddish brown with age, sharply 4-angled, the hypophysis well set off by constriction; lid low conic and shortly rostrate; exothecial cells rather thick walled with a vertically oval thin spot in the center, quite smooth. Spores 8–12 μ, yellowish, smooth. Plate 148, figs. 1–7.

24.39 On moist to rather dry soil, often in open rock fields and on high mountain slopes, also in shade where it becomes taller.

24.40 Throughout North America, Eurasia, Africa, South America, West Indies and southern oceanic islands.

24.41 This is our most common species. It occurs freely in all our higher mountains and is more xerophytic than the other species. It has been gathered as low as 6,000 ft. and up to 12,500 ft. The smooth infolded leaf margins and sharp red arista make it easy to recognize with a hand lens.

Plate 148. **1–7. Polytrichum juniperinum.** 1. Habit sketches. 2. Male plant, X.4. 3. Leaves, X4, with outline of tip, X30. 4. Cross section of leaf, X30. 5. Same, showing details, X120. 6. Cells of inflexed margin, X120. 7. Capsule, X4.

8–10. Polytrichum piliferum. 8. Habit sketches, X.4. 9. Leaves, X4, with hyaline hair point, X30. 10. Capsules, X4.

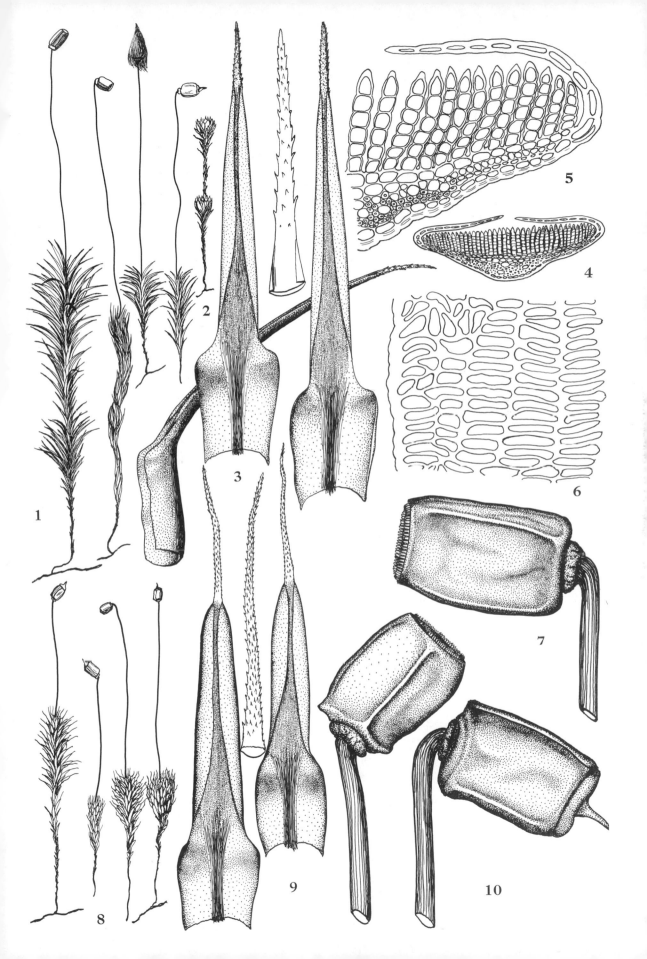

24.42 **4. Polytrichum piliferum** Hedw. Plants small for the genus, loosely tufted or scattered, dark green, the young parts glaucous, becoming reddish or brown with age. Stems simple, 1–10 cm tall (usually short in our region). Leaves ± erect when dry, spreading when moist, 4–6 mm long, shorter in dry situations, lanceolate from a rather short clasping base; margins entire, abruptly infolded over the lamellae, the edges meeting or nearly so; costa smooth at the back, excurrent to a long, smooth or spinulose, hyaline point which may be reddish at the base; lamallae 20–40, 4–7 cells high, in cross section the marginal cells ovate to pyriform, the walls very thick and smooth on the outer edge; cells of the inflexed portion of the limb unistratose, transversely elongated, hyaline, often in rows. Seta 2–3.5 cm long; capsules small, the urn nearly cuboidal or shortly oblong, 2–2.5 mm long, sharply 4-angled; hypophysis distinctly constricted; exothecial cells shortly oblong to transversely elongated and conic-papillose with a rather large thin spot in the middle; lid low conic, shortly to longly rostrate. Spores 9–12 μ, yellowish green and smooth. Plate 148, figs. 8–10.

24.43 On dry rocky soil in more or less open places.

24.44 Eurasia, South America, and Australia. Alaska to Greenland, southward to California, eastward to Colorado, Ohio and New Jersey. Uinta Mountains in Utah.

Plate 149. **1–6. Entosthodon wigginsii.** 1. Habit sketches, X.4. 2. Portion of fertile shoot, X2. 3. Calyptra, X4. 4. Five leaves, X8. 5. Two leaf apices, X120. 6. Capsules, X8.

7–8. Fissidens obtusifolius var. **marginatus.** 7. Habit, X8. 8. Basal marginal cells of vaginant laminae, X120.

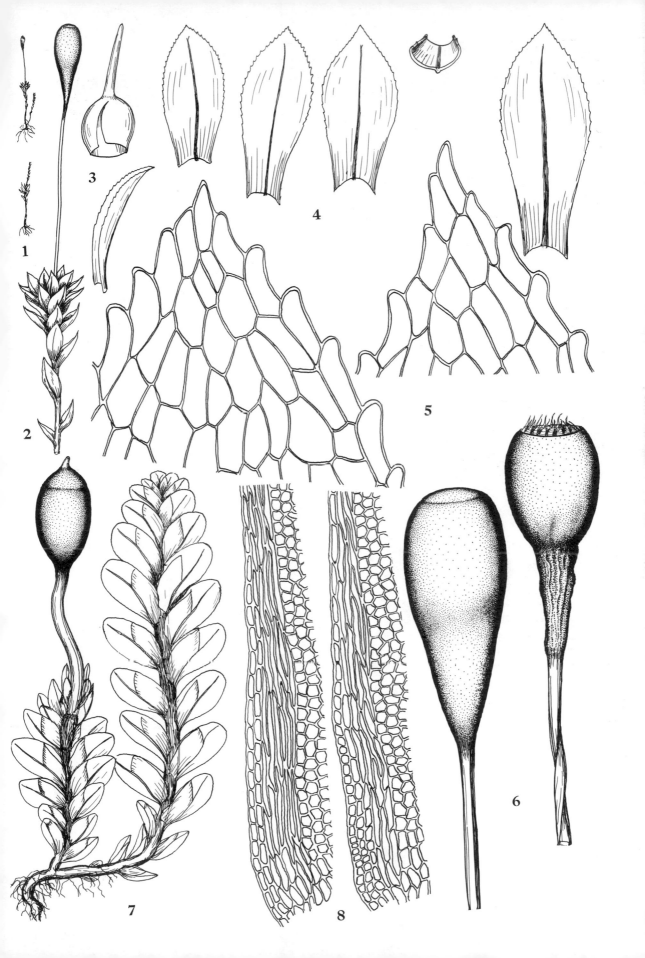

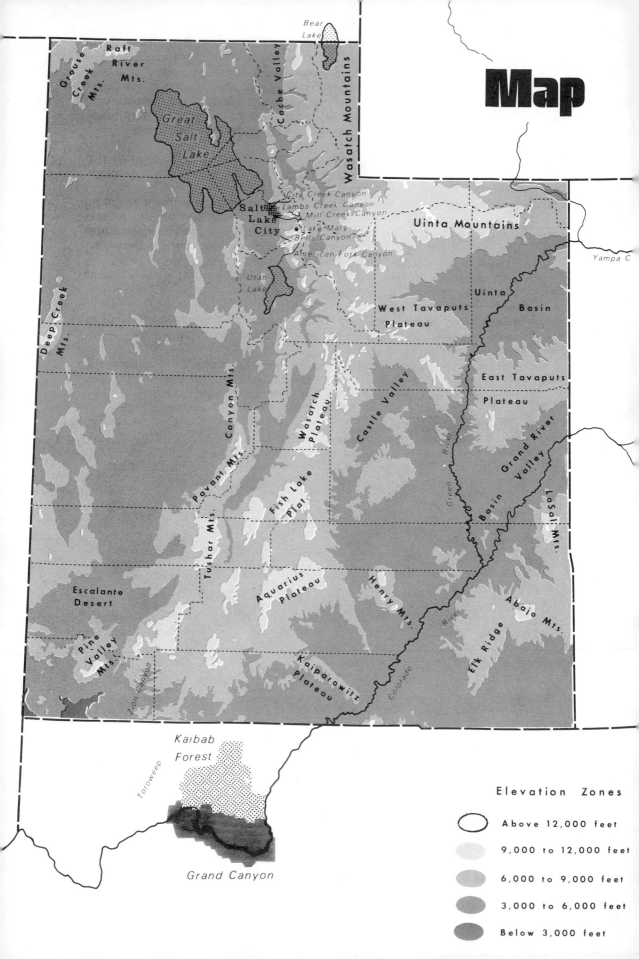

Map

Bear
Lake

Grouse
Creek
Mts.

Raft
River
Mts.

Great
Salt
Lake

Cache Valley

Wasatch Mountains

Uinta Mountains

Yampa C

City Creek Canyon
Lambs Creek Canyon
Mill Creek Canyon
Salt
Lake
City
Lake Mary
Bells Canyon
American Fork Canyon

Utah
Lake

Uinta Basin

West Tavaputs
Plateau

Deep Creek Mts.

East Tavaputs
Plateau

Canyon Mts.

Wasatch Plateau

Castle Valley

Green River

Grand River
Valley

Pavant Mts.

Fish Lake
Plat.

Basin

LaSal Mts.

Escalante
Desert

Tushar Mts.

Aquarius
Plateau

Henry Mts.

Colorado River

Abajo Mts.

Elk Ridge

Pine
Valley
Mts.

Zion Canyon

Kaiparowitz
Plateau

Kaibab
Forest

Toroweep

Grand Canyon

Elevation Zones

Above 12,000 feet

9,000 to 12,000 feet

6,000 to 9,000 feet

3,000 to 6,000 feet

Below 3,000 feet

Glossary

Acicular. Needle-shaped or long and slenderly pointed.

Acuminate. Tapering to a slender apex, at first curving inward and then reversing direction and narrowing more gradually to a slender tip. Figs. 68, 75, 81.

Acute. Ending in a sharp point, less than 90°. Figs. 59, 67, 69.

Acrocarpous. Having the sporophyte at the apex of the main stem or of a well developed branch.

Alar cells. Those at the basal angles of the leaves.

Amphithecium. The external layer of cells surrounding the sporogenous tissue in the sporangium of a moss.

Annulus. A ring of 1–3 or more rows of cells with differentially thickened walls between the lid and the urn of capsules. As the capsule matures the ring develops tension and dries out, causing the capsule to tear away from the adjacent cells. This brings about the separation of the lid from the urn. Figs. 188–89.

Antheridium. The male sex organ; in mosses a globose to shortly cylindrical sac 1 cell layer thick in which sperms are developed. Figs. 151, 152, 155m.

Apiculus, apiculate. An abrupt slender tip on leaves. Fig. 64.

Apophysis. A swelling of the seta at the base of the capsule, with many stomata, and functioning as chief assimilative part of the sporogonium.

Appressed. Usually applied to leaves when closely pressed to the stem; also applied to hairs lying close to another part. Fig. 43.

Archegonium. The female sex organ; in mosses a plus or minus cylindrical or tubular structure in which the egg develops in the slightly swollen base. Fig. 150.

Archesporium. The cell or group of cells from which spore mother cells develop.

Areolation. The network formed by cell walls, especially of leaves.

Arcuate. Strongly curved in an arc.

Aristate, arista. Ending in a slender, stiff, bristlelike point. Fig. 85.

Articulate. Jointed; in mosses applied to the peristome teeth which have ± strong transverse thickening, suggestive of joints.

Ascending. Curving upward from an inclined or horizontal base.

Auricle. Dilated earlike lobe at the basal angles of leaves. Fig. 80.

Autoicous. Having the antheridia and archegonia in separate buds on the same stem.

Awn, awned. Ending in a long hairlike point. Figs. 85–86.

Axil, axillary. The angle between the stem and leaf. Fig. 145.

Beak, beaked. Having a slender point on the operculum or lid; rostrate.

Bistratose. Having the cells in 2 layers, as in some leaves.

Blade. The leaf.

Border, bordered. Applied to leaves having 1 or more rows of cells of different shape, size, or color along the margins, and to the capsules when the mouth is bordered with smaller cells, in either instance often with a thicker and more highly colored wall. Fig. 90.

Bracts. The perigonial and perichaetial leaves surrounding the sex organs. Figs. 151–53.

Buds. Small propagative bodies having incipient stem and leaves borne on the protonemata of all mosses, and sometimes in the axils of the leaves of certain species. Figs. 145–49.

Bulbil. A minute bulb, same as the bud or propagula.

Caespitose. Densely clustered or tufted mosses.

Calyptra. A thin hood covering the lid of the capsule, usually falling early. Plate 46, fig. 12.

Campanulate. Bell-shaped, applied to the calyptra of some species of moss. Plate 46, fig. 12.

Canaliculate. Applied to leaves which are channelled from base to apex and rounded at the back. Fig. 76.

Capillary. Hairlike, filamentous.

Central strand. A group of small cells in the center of stems or setae. Figs. 36–37.

Cernuous. Having the capsule inclined or curved at or near right angles with the seta. Plate 31, fig. 14.

Chlorophyllose. Cells containing chloroplasts. Usually applied to leaves as lightly or densely chlorophyllose.

Cilia. Hairlike processes between the segments of the endostome, Fig. 163; or by themselves forming the endostome, Fig. 164.

Circinate. Applied to leaves curved to 1 side in a semicircle or nearly a circle. Fig. 73.

Clavate. Club-shaped; applied to gemmae, propagulae, paraphyses, antheridia, capsules, etc.

Cleistocarpus. Mosses having capsules without a separable lid but opening irregularly at maturity.

Columella. A central column of tissue in the capsule around which the spores develop. In some mosses it remains attached to the lid and falls with it. Figs. 158A and 160.

Comal leaves. The cluster of leaves at the apices of stems and branches.

Complanate. Having the leaves or branches flattened in 2 opposite rows so that the shoots appear flattened or spraylike. Fig. 53.

Conduplicate. Folded together. Fig. 79.

Convolute. Leaves sheathing or rolled one within the other.

Cordate. Heart-shaped. Fig. 81.

Costa. The midrib or nerve in moss leaves.

Costate. Having a costa.

Cribrose. Having the peristome teeth perforated with holes or thin spots.

Crisped. Strongly curled and twisted. Figs. 54–57.

Cucullate. Applied to the apices of leaves when they arch inward like a hood. Fig. 74. Also applied to the calyptra when it is split on 1 side only.

Cultiform. Leaves shaped like a short wide scimitar.

Cuneate. Wedge-shaped, as in some peristome teeth. Fig. 161.

Cuspidate. Ending in a rather long toothlike point. Fig. 84.

Cuticle. The outer wall substance of cells.

Cuticular. Of or belonging to the cuticle, such as irregular thickening.

Deciduous. Falling off early, not persistent.

Decurrent. Applied to leaves when the basal angles extend down the stem on each side in winglike fashion. Figs. 80–84.

Dehisce, dehiscent, dehiscence. Splitting open at maturity, as of capsules.

Deltoid. As of leaves shaped like an equilateral triangle or Greek letter delta.

Dendroid. Treelike in habit of growth. Fig. 32.

Dentate. Toothed, especially when the teeth are blunt and directed more or less outward from the leaves and other structures.

Denticulate. Finely toothed.

Denuded. Naked or nearly so, usually by having the leaves worn away from the lower part of the stem.

Dichotomous. More or less equally forked, as in the branching of some stems. Fig. 29.

Dimorphic. Having structures of 2 forms, as in leaves of some species.

Dioicous. Having the antheridia and archegonia on separate plants (i.e., male and female plants).

Discoid. Applied to broad antheridial buds as opposed to narrow buds. Fig. 153.

Divisural line. The medial line along which the peristome teeth split.

Dorsal. The back of the leaf away from the stem, the underside.

Ecostate. Leaves without a costa or midrib.

Emarginate. Having a notch at the apex of a leaf or other structure.

Emergent. Aquatic mosses partially extending out of the water. Of capsules projecting partially above the perichaetial leaves.

Endostome. Inner part of the peristome.

Endothecium. The central mass of cells within the young sporophyte that develops into sporogenous tissue.

Entire. Peristome teeth not lobed or divided; leaves with margins smooth, not toothed or notched.

Epiphragm. A taut membrane attached to the tips of the peristome teeth and closing the aperture of the capsule.

Erect. Perpendicular or nearly so; of leaves nearly parallel with the stem. Fig. 43.

Erect-patent. Leaves standing between erect and patent, at about 20-35°; also leaves briefly patent at the base and abruptly curving erect. Figs. 46–47.

Erose, eroded. Ragged or irregularly notched on the margins as if torn or gnawed.

Excavate. Applied to the base of a leaf when markedly concave or hollowed out. Figs. 69–70.

Excurrent. Applied to a costa which extends out beyond the lamina of the leaf. Fig. 84.

Exine. Outer of the 2 layers, forming a wall of spores.

Exostome. Outer part of peristome.

Exothecial cells. The outer layer of cells or epidermis of the capsule.

Exserted. Extending beyond; of capsules when the perichaetial leaves do not reach as high as the base.

Falcate. Curved like a sickle. Fig. 52.

Falcate-secund. Falcate and all turned to 1 side of the stem. Fig. 52.

Fascicled. In bunches or clusters, as to branches or leaves.

Fastigiate. Having the branches ± erect and reaching to about the same height. Fig. 25.

Ferruginous. Of rusty red color; iron rust.

Filiform, filamentous. Very slender or threadlike; applied to divisions of peristome teeth. Fig. 165.

Flagella, flagellate, flagelliform. Very slender shoots or branches, often tapering from thicker parts. Fig. 22.

Flexuous. Alternately bent forward and backward or from side to side, wavy; applied to the seta, some very slender stems; long slender leaf apices and leaf cells. Fig. 100.

Fuscous. Dull brown.

Fusiform. Oval to sublinear with narrowly tapering ends. Fig. 96.

Gemma, gemmae. A very small, globose to cylindric brood body. Figs. 145–49.

Gemmiform. Budlike.

Geniculate. Suddenly bent, like a knee, as in the setae of some mosses.

Gibbous. Applied to the capsule when swollen on one side. Plate 62.

Granulose. Roughened with fine granules.

Guides. Enlarged elongated cells in the leaf costa in the same plane with the lamina. Figs. 118–25.

Gymnostomous. Capsules lacking peristome teeth; naked mouth.

Homomallous leaves. All pointing in the same direction, either straight or falcate, secund.

Hyaline. Glassy, colorless, ± transparent, especially in cells lacking chloroplasts.

Hygroscopic. Rapidly absorbing water, thus changing form or position.

Imbricated. Closely overlapping. Figs. 44–45.

Immersed. Plants submerged in water; of capsules when the seta is very short and the tips of the perichaetial leaves extend beyond the lid. Plate 45, fig. 3.

Incrassate. Thick-walled.

Innovation. A new branch arising from an old stem. Figs. 29, 31.

Insertion, inserted. The point of juncture of the leaf with the stem or teeth in the mouth of the capsule.

Involute. Rolled inwards, as in the margins of some leaves. Plate 10, fig. 6.

Isodiametric. Having equal diameters in all directions.

Julaceous. Shoots rendered smoothly cylindrical by the closely and evenly imbricated leaves. Fig. 44.

Lamellae. Thin sheets of cells, mostly 1 cell thick, attached along 1 edge to the surface of the costa in certain mosses. Figs. 113, 114, 123. Also applied to the projecting horizontally thickened plates or joints on the inner face of peristome teeth. Fig. 168, i.

Lamina. The blade of the leaf as distinguished from the costa.

Lanceolate. Shaped like the head of a lance, broadest at the base and narrowed to the apex. Figs. 67–68.

Ligulate. Strap-shaped, narrow with margins ± parallel. Figs. 63–64.

Limb. The upper part of a leaf as distinguished from the base, especially when the latter is abruptly dilated and clasping the stem. Fig. 82.

Linear. Long and narrow with the margins ± parallel. Figs. 66, 99, 100.

Lingulate. Tongue-shaped, shorter and broader than ligulate.

Lumen (lumina, plural). The cell cavity.

Mammillate. Convex or hemispherical with a short point, as in the operculum of some species.

Mammillose. As applied to cells, bulging and nipple-like.

Mitrate, mitriform. As applied to the calyptra, cleft at two or more points around the base.

Monoicous. Bisexual, both antheridia and archegonia on the same plants.

Mucro. An abrupt, rather stout, short point.

Mucronate. Having a mucro. Fig. 62.

Muticous. Without a point, blunt or rounded at the apex.

Neck. The sterile basal portion of the capsule between the spore sac and summit of the seta, often narrowed, also the long upper portion of the archegonium.

Nodes. Thickenings or knots.

Nodose (nodulose, diminutive). Beset with nodes or knots. Applied to the swollen joints of peristome cilia, to the walls of some cells and to the male shoots of *Polytrichaceae.*

Oblanceolate. Lanceolate reversed with the narrow end lowermost.

Oblong. Proportioned about 1:3–6 with the margins ± parallel. Rectangular but ends not necessarily squared off. Fig. 62.

Obovate. Ovate reversed, with the narrow end lowermost. Fig. 60.

Ocrea. A short, thin, collarlike sheath around the base of the seta in *Orthotrichum.* Plate 59, fig. 5.

Operculum. The lid of the capsule.

Orbicular. Nearly round or circular. Fig. 58.

Oval. Proportioned 1:1.5–3, broadest in the middle and rounded at each end. Fig. 61.

Ovate. Broadest at the base. Fig. 59.

Ovoid. Usually of solid objects, like capsules, ovate or oval in outline.

Papilla. Minute nipple or protuberance on the surface of cells, usually formed by uneven deposition of cuticular substance as in figs. 103–8 or by the projecting end walls. Fig. 109.

Papillose. Beset with papillae.

Paraphyllia. Minute leaflike or filamentous structures borne on the stems or branches among the leaves. Figs. 134–38.

Paraphyses. Hairs borne among the sex organs. Figs. 150, 152.

Paroicous. Having the antheridia borne in the axils of the perichaetial leaves, just below the cluster of archegonia. Plate 71, fig. 9.

Patent. Open, spreading, diverging at angles of 30–60°. Fig. 48.

Percurrent. Of the costa when it reaches the apex but does not extend beyond. Fig. 83.

Perichaetium. A group of ± specialized leaves surrounding the archegonia; the female bud or flower.

Perigonium. A cluster of ± specialized leaves surrounding the antheridia; male bud or flower. Figs. 151–53.

Peristome. The fringe of processes surrounding the mouth of the capsule, becoming exposed after the lid falls. Figs. 161–65.

Persistent. Not falling off.

Piliferous. Bearing a long hyaline hair point. Fig. 85.

Pinnate. Featherlike; having numerous spreading branches on each side. Figs. 33, 34.

Pitted. Of walls of cells, having pits or thin places. Fig. 98.

Pleurocarpous. Bearing the archegonia and later the sporophyte on a very short branch apparently coming from the side of the stem. Mostly creeping or prostrate mosses. Fig. 33.

Plicae. Folds.

Plicate. Of leaves and capsules when they are folded longitudinally in pleats, or with ridges and furrows. Fig. 73; Plate 55, fig. 4.

Plumose. Featherlike; closely and regularly pinnate.

Polymorphic. Species of mosses occurring in many forms; leaves of many forms.

Porose. Of walls of cells indented or perforated with pores. Fig. 98.

Primordium. Rudiment of the growing elements.

Propagula. Deciduous brood bodies of various reductional forms (buds, branches, leaves). Figs. 139–44.

Protonema. The green branched thread produced on germination of spores bearing buds which grow into leafy moss plants. Figs. 1–14.

Punctate. Pointed; marked with minute round dots, sometimes minute depressions, sometimes minute papillae.

Pyriform. Pear-shaped, as applied to capsules. Plate 75, fig. 8.

Quadrate. Square or nearly so. Fig. 93.

Radicles. Rhizoids.

Radiculose. Having rhizoids

Recurved. Curving backward. Fig. 51.

560

Reflexed. Abruptly bent backward or downward.

Revolute. Rolled backward. Fig. 78.

Rhizoids. Filamentous branched outgrowths from the stems serving to attach the moss to the substratum; sometimes called radicles.

Rhizome. An underground horizontal stem. Figs. 21, 32.

Rhomboidal. Of cells with proportions 1:1.5–6 and ± parallel sides and end walls oblique in the same direction. Fig. 97.

Rosette. Of the comal or perichaetial leaves spreading in roselike fashion.

Rostrate. With a long slender point, beaked. Mostly applied to the long point on the operculum of some capsules.

Rugose. Wrinkled or finely wrinkled. Plate 67, fig. 7.

Saxicolous. Living or growing among rocks.

Secund. Of leaves directed or twisted toward 1 side of the stem. Fig. 52.

Serrate. Saw-toothed, having sharp teeth directed forward. Figs. 87–88, 90–92.

Serrulate. Finely or weakly serrate.

Sessile. Without a stalk or apparently so.

Seta, setae. The stalk of the sporophyte.

Sheathing. Having the leaves or bases of leaves ± surrounding or clasping the stem or base of the seta. Fig. 82.

Sinuous. Wavy, bending from side to side. Fig. 100.

Spatulate. Narrow at the base and broadened to a rounded apex, like a spatula. Fig. 65.

Spinulose. Beset with small spines or sharp points.

Sporangium. The spore sac within the capsule. Fig. 160.

Sporophyte. The asexual generation of the moss typically consisting of foot, seta, and capsule, the diploid generation.

Spreading. Diverging at wide angles. Fig. 49.

Squarrose. Spreading at right angles. Figs. 50, 51.

Stereid. Plant cell or cell derivative whose function is primarily mechanical support.

Striae. Very fine streaks or furrows.

Striate. Having streaks or furrows, by longitudinal furrowing, by rows or lines of small papillae or by thickened ridges of cuticular substance. Figs. 110, 164; Plate 63, figs. 2, 8.

Strict. Straight and rigid, stiff.

Struma. A goiterlike swelling.

Strumose. Having a struma. Plate 6, fig. 13.

Sub. A prefix meaning somewhat less than, almost.

Subula. An evenly tapering stiff point, usually stout, awl-shaped.

Subulate. Applied to stiffly pointed leaves. Fig. 82.

Sulcate. Deeply furrowed. Fig. 73; Plate 55, fig. 6.

Sympodium. Main axis not of terminal bud but of secondary axes.

Synoicous. Having the antheridia and archegonia mixed together in a common cluster in the same bud.

Terete. Cylindrical and smooth.

Tomentose. Covered with densely matted hairs. Fig. 31.

Trabeculae. Little bars; trabeculate, having thickened transverse bars on peristome teeth or the endostome. Plate 60, fig. 9.

Tubulose. Applied to leaves having the margins incurved and nearly touching. Fig. 77.

Tumid. Swollen. Fig. 45.

Turbinate. Top-shaped.

Turgid. Swollen.

Undulate. Wavy. Figs. 54, 75.

Unistratose, 1-stratose. Having cells in 1 layer.

Urn. A deoperculate capsule.

Vaginate laminae. The sheathing base of the leaves of *Fissidens*. Fig. 115.

Vaginula. A short cylindrical sheath surrounding the foot of the sporophyte or seta. Fig. 157.

Ventral. The upper side of the leaf facing the stem.

Ventricose. Swollen on 1 side. Plate 47, fig. 7.

Vermicular. Wormlike. Fig. 100; Plate 57, fig. 12.

Verrucose. Beset with wartlike papillae or protuberances. Plate 53, fig. 8.

Verticillate. Having 3 or more branches arising at the same point around the circumference of the stem. Figs. 26, 31.

Whorled. Verticillate.

Index

Aloina, 10.197
  pilifera, 10.199
Amblystegium, 21.124
  compactum, 21.152
  fluviatile
    fluviatile, 21.174
    noterophilum, 21.178
  juratzkanum
    giganteum, 21.136
    juratzkanum, 21.136
  kochii, 21.147
  riparium, 21.157
    fluitans, 21.163
    longifolium, 21.161
  serpens
    serpens, 21.129
    tenue, 21.133
  tenax, 21.167
    spinifolium, 21.171
  varium, 21.143
Amphidium, 13.93
  lapponicum, 13.95
Anacolia, 18.4
  menziesii, 18.6
Astomum, 10.6
  occidentale, 10.9
Atrichum, 24.4
  selwynii, 24.6
Aulacomniaceae, 16.1
Aulacomnium, 16.2
  androgynum, 16.6
  palustre, 16.10

Barbula, 10.110
  acuta, 10.134
  bescherellei, 10.138
  cruegeri, 10.114
  cylindrica, 10.147
  ehrenbergii, 10.126
  eustegia, 10.118
  fallax, 10.130
  unguiculata, 10.122
  vinealis, 10.142
Bartramia, 18.10

  ithyphylla, 18.12
Bartramiaceae, 18.1
Brachythecium, 21.26
  albicans
    albicans, 21.73
    occidentale, 21.77
  asperrimum, 21.93
  campestre, 21.59
  collinum, 21.34
  delicatulum, 21.43
  digastrum, 21.55
  erythrorrhizon, 21.51
  fendleri, 21.39
  lamprochryseum, 21.97
  nelsonii
    intermedium, 21.87
    nelsonii, 21.83
  oxycladum, 21.69
  rivulare, 21.89
  salebrosum
    densum, 21.67
    salebrosum, 21.63
  starkei, 21.79
  suberythrorrhizon, 21.47
Bryaceae, 19.1
Bryales, 8.1
Bryoerythrophyllum, 10.101
  recurvirostre
    dentatum, 10.107
    recurvirostrum, 10.103
Bryum, 19.63
  angustirete, 19.69
  argenteum, 19.136
  arcticum, 19.85
  bicolor, 19.128
  caespiticium, 19.115
  capillare, 19.119
  creberrimum, 19.104
  gemmiparum, 19.132
  lonchocaulon, 19.111
  miniatum, 19.124
  pallens, 19.77
  pallescens, 19.107
  pseudotriquetrum, 19.100

sandbergii, 19.140
stenotrichum, 19.73
tortifolium, 19.89
turbinatum, 19.96
uliginosum, 19.81
weigelii, 19.92

Calliergon, 21.213
cordifolium, 21.217
stramineum, 21.221
turgescens, 21.225
Campylium
chrysophyllum, 21.198
hispidulum, 21.194
polygamum, 21.209
stellatum
protensum, 21.206
stellatum, 21.202
Ceratodon, 9.17
conicus, 9.24
purpureus, 9.21
Climacium, 21.5
dendroides, 21.7
Cratoneuron
commutatum
commutatum, 21.300
fluctuans, 21.303
decipiens, 21.307
falcatum
falcatum, 21.312
williamsii, 21.316
filicinum, 21.296
Crossidium, 10.203
aberrans, 10.210
desertorum, 10.217
griseum, 10.207

Desmatodon, 10.221
cernuus, 10.244
convolutus, 10.248
latifolius
latifolius, 10.225
muticus, 10.228
laureri, 10.240
obtusifolius, 10.236
plinthobius, 10.232
Dichelyma, 23.26
falcatum, 23.28
Dichodontium, 9.33
pellucidum, 9.35
Dicranaceae, 9.1
Dicranella, 9.52
schreberiana, 9.54
Dicranoweisia, 9.44
crispula, 9.46
Dicranum, 9.57
scoparium, 9.69
spadiceum, 9.65
tauricum, 9.61
Didymodon, 10.82

rigidulus, 10.86
tophaceus, 10.91
trifarius, 10.97
Distichium, 9.5
capillaceum
capillaceum, 9.9
curvatum, 9.12
inclinatum, 9.14
Drepanocladus, 21.262
aduncus
aduncus, 21.271
capillifolius, 21.279
kneiffii, 21.276
exannulatus, 21.287
rotae, 21.291
fluitans, 21.282
uncinatus, 21.267

Encalypta, 11.3
ciliata, 11.9
rhabdocarpa
rhabdocarpa, 11.23
subspathulata, 11.26
vulgaris
apiculata, 11.16
mutica, 11.18
vulgaris, 11.12
Encalyptaceae, 11.1
Entosthodon, 14.23
planoconvexus, 14.27
wigginsii, 14.31
Eucladium, 10.48
verticillatum, 10.50
Eurhynchium, 21.10
pulchellum
pulchellum, 21.18
substrigosum, 21.14

Fissidens, 8.3
limbatus, 8.7
obtusifolius
kansanus, 8.16
marginatus, 8.18
obtusifolius, 8.13
Fissidentaceae, 8.1
Fontinalaceae, 23.1
Fontinalis, 23.4
antipyretica, 23.11
mollis, 23.16
oregonensis, 23.14
duriaei, 23.22
hypnoides, 23.18
neo-mexicana, 23.8
Funaria, 14.4
hygrometrica
hygrometrica, 14.8
utahensis, 14.12
muehlenbergii
muehlenbergii, 14.16
Funariaceae, 14.1

Grimmia, 12.4
    affinis, 12.87
    agassizii, 12.10
    alpicola
        apicola, 12.22
        latifolia, 12.29
        rivularis, 12.26
    anodon, 12.56
    apocarpa
        ambigua, 12.42
        apocarpa, 12.35
        conferta, 12.39
    atricha, 12.14
    calyptrata, 12.52
    cinclidodontea, 12.31
    donniana, 12.75
    dupretii, 12.18
    hartmanii
        anomala, 12.100
    laevigata, 12.65
    montana, 12.79
    orbicularis, 12.96
    ovalis, 12.71
    plagiopodia, 12.61
    pulvinata, 12.92
    rauii, 12.46
    tenerrima, 12.83
Grimmiaceae, 12.1
Gymnostomum, 10.33
    aeruginosum, 10.37
    recurvirostrum
        recurvirostrum, 10.41

Helodium, 20.4
    blandowii, 20.6
Homalothecium, 21.114
    nevadense, 21.116
Hygrohypnum, 21.229
    bestii, 21.255
    luridum, 21.241
        julaceum, 21.245
        serratum, 21.247
        tenue, 21.249
    molle, 21.251
    ochraceum
        flaccidum, 21.237
        ochraceum, 21.233
    smithii
        goulardii, 21.261
        smithii, 21.259
Hyophila, 10.60
    involuta, 10.62
Hypnaceae, 21.1
Hypnum, 21.320
    haldanianum, 21.347
    hamulosum, 21.330
    lindbergii, 21.339
    pratense, 21.343
    revolutum, 21.324
    vaucheri, 21.335

Leptobryum, 19.10
    pyriforme, 19.12
Lescuraea, 20.16
    incurvata
        incurvata, 20.25
        tenuiretis, 20.29
    patens, 20.12
    radicosa
        compacta, 20.36
        pallida, 20.39
        radicosa, 20.32
    saxicola, 20.14
Leskeaceae, 20.1
Leskeella, 20.45
    arizonae, 20.60
    tectorum, 20.49
        cyrtophylla, 20.49
        flagellifera, 20.56

Mielichhoferia, 19.4
    macrocarpa, 19.6
Mnium, 19.145
    affine, 19.173
    arizonicum, 19.153
    blyttii, 19.149
    cuspidatum, 19.165
    marginatum, 19.157
    medium, 19.169
    orthorhynchum, 19.161
    punctatum, 19.177

Neckera, 22.2
    menziesii
        limnobioides, 22.10
        menziesii, 22.6
    pennata
        tenera, 22.13
Neckeraceae, 22.1

Oncophorus, 9.39
    virens, 9.41
Orthothecium, 21.376
    diminutivum, 21.378
Orthotrichaceae, 13.1
Orthotrichum, 13.5
    affine, 13.32
        obtusum, 13.36
    alpestre, 13.61
    anomalum, 13.54
    cupulatum, 13.40
    garrettii, 13.88
    hallii, 13.48
    jamesianum, 13.44
    laevigatum
        kingianum, 13.21
        laevigatum, 13.18
    macounii, 13.23
        vermiculare, 13.30
    pallens
        pallens, 13.70

parvum, 13.74
pumilum
  fallax, 13.83
  ligulaefolium, 13.86
  pumilum, 13.79
rupestre, 13.9
strangulatum, 13.58
texanum, 13.13

Paraleucobryum, 9.73
  enerve, 9.75
Phascum, 10.152
  cuspidatum
    cuspidatum, 10.154
    henrici, 10.157
    schreberianum, 10.159
Philonotis, 18.16
  fontana
    americana, 18.41
    caespitosa, 18.46
    fontana, 18.30
    pumila, 18.43
  marchica, 18.26
Physcomitrium, 14.36
  californicum, 14.50
  hookeri, 14.42
  pygmaeum, 14.40
  pyriforme, 14.46
Plagiothecium, 21.351
  denticulatum
    denticulatum, 21.363
    obtusifolium, 21.367
  muellerianum, 21.359
  pulchellum, 21.355
Platydictya, 21.183
  jungermannioides, 21.185
  minutissima, 21.189
Platygyrium, 21.369
  repens, 21.371
Pogonatum, 24.9
  alpinum, 24.11
    arcticum, 24.15
    brevifolium, 24.17
Pohlia, 19.16
  annotina, 19.58
  bulbifera, 19.48
  cruda, 19.23
  drummondii, 19.39
  elongata, 19.35
  longicolla, 19.27
  nutans 19.31
  proligera, 19.52
  rothii, 19.43
  wahlenbergii, 19.54
Polytrichaceae, 24.1
Polytrichadelphus, 24.21
  lyallii, 24.23
Polytrichum, 24.27
  commune, 24.34
  gracile, 24.31

juniperinum, 24.38
piliferum, 24.42
Pottia, 10.162
  arizonica
    arizonica, 10.174
    mucronulata, 10.175
  heimii, 10.166
  latifolia
    latifolia, 10.177
    pilifera, 10.178
  nevadensis, 10.170
Pottiaceae, 10.1
Pterygoneurum, 10.181
  lamellatum, 10.193
  ovatum, 10.189
  subsessile, 10.185

Racomitrium, 12.104
  canescens, 12.107

Scleropodium, 21.102
  obtusifolium, 21.110
  touretii, 21.106
Scopelophila, 10.306
  latifolia, 10.308
Scouleria, 12.112
  aquatica, 12.114
Seligeria, 9.28
  campylopoda, 9.29
Sphagnaceae, 7.1
Sphagnales, 7.1
Sphagnum, 7.2
  capillaceum, 7.14
  fuscum, 7.19
  recurvum
    tenue, 7.11
  squarrosum, 7.9
  warnstorfii, 7.17
Splachnaceae, 15.1

Tayloria, 15.3
  acuminata, 15.5
Thuidium, 20.10
  abietinum, 20.12
Timmia, 17.2
  austriaca, 17.10
    brevifolia, 17.13
  bavarica, 17.6
Timmiaceae, 17.1
Tomenthypnum, 21.119
  nitens, 21.121
Tortella, 10.66
  nitida, 10.74
  tortuosa, 10.70
Tortula, 10.252
  bistratosa, 10.281
  intermedia, 10.273
  norvegica, 10.285
  papillosissima, 10.293
  princeps, 10.277

ruraliformis, 10.301
ruralis, 10.297
Trichostomum, 10.54
tenuirostre, 10.56

Weissia, 10.12
controversa, 10.17
ligulaefolia, 10.21
perligulata, 10.29
tortilis, 10.25